To my son Julian
on christmas 2013
I offer you the
world!

All my love, Dad.

THE ENCYCLOPEDIA OF
ANIMALS

THE ENCYCLOPEDIA OF
ANIMALS

David Alderton

CHARTWELL
BOOKS, INC.

This edition published in 2013 by

CHARTWELL BOOKS, INC.
A division of
BOOK SALES, INC.
276 Fifth Avenue Suite 206
New York, New York 10001
USA

ISBN: 978-0-7858-3080-1

Project Editor: Sarah Uttridge
Editorial Assistant: Kieron Connolly
Design: Andrew Easton
Picture Research: Terry Forshaw and Natascha Spargo

Printed in China

How this book works

The format for all the entries that follow is similar, enabling comparisons to be made easily. The
animals are not grouped on the basis of their common names, however, because this is unreliable; in
many cases, a species may be known under a variety of different common names. Furthermore,
different subspecies may also be accorded separate common names, adding to the confusion. This was
another reason why it was so important to develop a universal system of nomenclature, allowing for a
single species to be identified without confusion, creating what is effectively an international zoological
language. This approach also avoids the inevitable linguistic problems in cases where the same species
is known under different common names in neighbouring countries. The entries here are actually
grouped by order, on an A-Z basis, which has the advantage of ensuring that closely related species,
linked as members of the same order, can be found together.

CONTENTS

Introduction   8

AFROSORICIDA–ARTIODACTYLA

Common Tenrec   14
Common Eel   15
Mediterranean Moray Eel   16
Mallard   17
Griswold's Marsupial Frog   18
Pebas Stubfoot Toad   19
European Toad   20
Natterjack Toad   21
Small Strawberry Dart Frog   22
Common Midwife Toad   23
European Treefrog   24
Common Spadefoot Toad   25
Moor Frog   26
American Bullfrog   27
Water Spider   28
European Garden Spider   29
Curved Spiny Spider   30
Trapdoor Spider   31
Mexican Red-kneed Tarantula   32
Southern Black Widow   33
Crab Spider   34
Pronghorn Antelope   35
Impala   36
Barbary Sheep   37
Springbok Antelope   38
American Bison   39
European Bison   40
Gaur   41
Water Buffalo   42
Bezoar Ibex   43
Alpine Ibex   44
Southern Serow   45
Blue Wildebeest   46
Topi Antelope   47
Thomson's Gazelle   48
Dorcas Gazelle   49
Himalayan Tahr   50
Sable Antelope   51
Kirk's Dik-Dik   52
Rocky Mountain Goat   53
Arabian Oryx   54
Oribi Gazelle   55
Musk Ox   56
Argali (Mountain Sheep)   57
Bighorn Sheep   58
Mouflon   59
Yak   60
Mountain Reedbuck   61
Chamois (Gemse)   62
Saiga   63

Yellow-Backed Duiker   64
African Buffalo   65
Eland   66
Four-Horned Antelope   67
Greater Kudu   68
Bactrian Camel   69
Dromedary Camel   70
Llama   71
Vicuña   72
Roe Deer   73
Chital Deer   74
Elk   75
Red Deer   76
Sika Deer   77
Fallow Deer   78
Père David's Deer   79
Indian Muntjac   80
White-Tailed Deer   81
Southern Pudu   82
Caribou   83
Giraffe   84
Hippopotamus   85
Siberian Musk Deer   86
Babirusa   87
Giant Forest Hog   88
Red River Hog   89
European Wild Boar   90
Collared Peccary   91

CARCHARHINIFORMES–
CYPRINIFORMES

Common Whelk   92
Triton   93
Great Hammerhead Shark   94
Red Panda   95
Golden Jackal   96
German Shepherd Dog   97
Coyote   98

Grey Wolf   99
Dingo   100
Black-Backed Jackal   101
Maned Wolf   102
Dhole   103
African Hunting Dog   104
Raccoon Dog   105
Bat-Eared Fox   106
Grey Fox   107
Bush Dog   108
Arctic Fox   109
Red Fox   110
Fennec Fox   111
Siberian Husky   112
Cheetah   113
Caracal (Persian Lynx)   114
Domestic Cat   115
Eurasian Lynx   116
Sand Cat   117
European Wildcat   118
Ocelot   119
Serval   120
Bobcat   121
Clouded Leopard   122
Lion   123
Jaguar   124
Leopard   125
Siberian Tiger   126
Bengal Tiger   127
Puma   128
Jaguarundi   129
Snow Leopard   130

LEOPARD

Indian Grey Mongoose	131	Herring Gull	191	Common Kestrel	245
Meerkat	132	Ruff	192	Secretary Bird	246
Spotted Hyena	133	Common Vampire Bat	193		
Aardwolf	134	Indian Flying Fox	194	**GASTEROSTEIFORMES–**	
Striped Skunk	135	Lesser Horseshoe Bat	195	**GRUIFORMES**	
Sea Otter	136	Daubenton's Bat	196	Three-Spined Stickleback	247
American Mink	137	Noctule Bat	197	Sun Bittern	248
Wolverine	138	Nine-Banded Armadillo	198		
Otter	139	Brazilian three-banded Armadillo	199	**HAPLOTAXIDA–ISOPTERA**	
Pine Marten	140	Bombardier Beetle	200	Common European Earthworm	249
Beech Marten	141	Green Tiger Beetle	201	Shield-Backed Bug	250
Sable	142	Musk Beetle	202	Honeybee	251
Eurasian Badger	143	Seven-Spot Ladybird	203	Buff-Tailed Bumblebee	252
Honey Badger	144	Great Diving Beetle	204	Foraging Ant	253
Polecat	145	Stag Beetle	205	Red Wood Ant	254
Ermine	146	Common Cockchafer	206	European Hornet	255
Giant Otter	147	European Rhinoceros Beetle	207	Common Wasp	256
American Badger	148	Dung Beetle	208	Cape Hyrax	257
Walrus	149	Rose Chafer	209	Termite	258
Northern Fur Seal	150	Gravedigger Beetle	210		
Californian Sea Lion	151	Kingfisher	211	**LAGOMORPHA–LEPIDOPTERA**	
Hooded Seal	152	American Alligator	212	Snowshoe Hare	259
Bearded Seal	153	Nile Crocodile	213	Black-Tailed Jackrabbit	260
Leopard Seal	154	Gharial	214	Hare	261
Southern Elephant Seal	155	Hoatzin	215	European Rabbit	262
Mediterranean Monk Seal	156	Common Carp	216	Plateau Pika	263
Harp Seal	157			Great White Shark	264
Common Seal	158	**DASYUROMORPHA –DIPTERA**		Common Blue Butterfly	265
Northern American Ringtail	159	Tasmanian Devil	217	Purple Emperor	266
White-nosed Coati	160	Cleaner Shrimp	218	Monarch Butterfly	267
Kinkajou	161	Lobster	219	Morpho Butterfly	268
Raccoon	162	Fiddler Crab	220	Red Admiral Butterfly	269
Giant Panda	163	Hermit Crab	221	Queen Alexandra's Birdwing	270
Sun Bear	164	Common Earwig	222	Western Tiger Swallowtail Butterfly	271
Spectacled Bear	165	Colugo	223	Apollo Butterfly	272
North American Black Bear	166	Virginia Opossum	224	Death's Head Hawkmoth	273
Brown Bear	167	Common Mouse Opossum	225	Emperor Moth	274
Grizzly Bear	168	Matschie's Tree Kangaroo	226		
Kodiak Bear	169	Pretty-Faced Wallaby	227	**MACROSCELIDEA–**	
Polar Bear	170	Red Kangaroo	228	**MONOTREMATA**	
Asian Black Bear	171	Yellow-Footed Rock Wallaby	229	Giant Elephant Shrew	275
Binturong	172	Common Spotted Cuscus	230	Praying Mantis	276
Common Genet	173	Common Brushtail Possum	231	Duck-Billed Platypus	277
Common Mudpuppy	174	Koala	232	Short-Beaked Echidna	278
Alpine Salamander	175	Brush-Tailed Bettong	233		
Fire Salamander	176	Long-Footed Potoroo	234	**NUEROPTERA–ORTHOPTERA**	
Alpine Newt	177	Honey Possum	235	Common Antlion	279
Northern Right Whale	178	Common Wombat	236	Common Octopus	280
Blue Whale	179	Common House Fly	237	Emperor Dragonfly	281
Humpback Whale	180			Broad-Bodied Chaser	282
Commerson's Dolphin	181	**ECHINODERMATA–ESOCIFORMES**		Whale Shark	283
Common Dolphin	182	Sea Urchin	238	Blue-winged Grasshopper	284
Long-Finned Pilot Whale	183	Hedgehog	239	Great Green Bush Cricket	285
Killer Whale	184	Northern Pike	240	Field Cricket	286
Grey Whale	185			Oyster	287
Amazon River Dolphin	186	**FALCONIFORMES**			
Beluga	187	Golden Eagle	241	**PASSERIFORMES–PULMONATA**	
Narwhal	188	Black Kite	242	Chaffinch	288
Harbour Porpoise	189	Andean Condor	243	Raggi's Bird of Paradise	289
Sperm Whale	190	Peregrine Falcon	244	European Nuthatch	290

European Robin 291
Nightingale 292
Cormorant 293
Greater Bilby 294
Jewel Fish 295
Mudskipper 296
Siamese Fighting Fish 297
Yellow-Masked Angelfish 298
Common Clownfish 299
Queen Parrotfish 300
Yellow-Fin Tuna 301
African Wild Ass 302
Mustang 303
Domestic Horse 304
Kiang Tibetan Ass 305
Burchell's Zebra 306
White Rhinoceros 307
Indian Rhinoceros 308
Malayan Tapir 309
Leaf Insect 310
Greater Flamingo 311
Pangolin 312
Pygmy Anteater 313
Hoffman's Two-Toed Sloth 314
Giant Anteater 315
Southern Tamandua 316
Nancy Ma's Night Monkey 317
Red-Faced Black Spider Monkey 318
Brown Howler Monkey 319
Brown Woolly Monkey 320
Pygmy Marmoset 321
Golden Lion Tamarin 322
Emperor Tamarin 323
Cottontop Tamarin 324
Common Squirrel Monkey 325
White-Faced Capuchin Monkey 326
Vervet Monkey 327
Mantled Guereza 328
Pigtail Macaque 329
Rhesus Macaque 330
Barbary Ape 331
Mandrill 332
Proboscis Monkey 333
Hamadryas Baboon 334
Red-Shanked Douc 335
Hanuman Langur 336
Gelada Baboon 337
Aye-Aye 338
Bushbaby 339
Gorilla 340
Bonobo 341
Chimpanzee 342
Bornean Orangutan 343
Lar Gibbon 344
Siamang Gibbon 345
Indri Lemur 346
Ring-Tailed Lemur 347
Uakari Monkey 348
Dusky Titi 349
Spectral Tarsier 350

Asian Elephant 351
African Elephant 352
Edible Snail 353
Slug 354

RAJIFORMES–RODENTIA
Devil Ray 355
Naked Mole Rat 356
North American Beaver 357
Guinea Pig 358
Mara 359
Capybara 360
Mountain Viscacha 361
European Water Vole 362
European Hamster 363
Norwegian Lemming 364
Meadow Vole 365
Bank Vole 366
Muskrat 367
Gundi 368
Lesser Egyptian Jerboa 369
North American Porcupine 370
Botta's Pocket Gopher 371
Edible Dormouse 372
Common Dormouse 373
South African Porcupine 374
Libyan Jird 375
Harvest Mouse 376
House Mouse 377
Brown Rat 378
Coypu 379
Springhare 380
Black-Tailed Prairie Dog 381
Southern Flying Squirrel 382
Alpine Marmot 383
Red Squirrel 384
European Ground Squirrel 385
Siberian Chipmunk 386
Eastern Chipmunk 387

**SALMONIFORMES–
SYNGNATHIFORMES**
Rainbow Trout 388
Atlantic Salmon 389
Devil Lionfish 390
Mediterranean Scorpion 391
Common Cuttlefish 392
Wels Catfish 393
Portuguese Man o'War 394
Dugong 395
Manatee 396
Eurasian Water Shrew 397
Eurasian Shrew 398
European Mole 399
Emperor Penguin 400
Frilled Lizard 401
Thorny Devil 402
Slow Worm 403
Boa Constrictor 404
Green Anaconda 405

RED FOX

European Chameleon 406
Plumed Basilisk 407
Grass Snake 408
Black Mamba 409
Eastern Coral Snake 410
King Cobra 411
Tokay Gecko 412
Gila Monster 413
Marine Iguana 414
Green Iguana 415
Balkan Green Lizard 416
Common Wall Lizard 417
India Python 418
Shingleback Skink 419
Komodo Dragon 420
Texan Rattlesnake 421
European Adder 422
Tawny Owl 423
North Island Kiwi 424
Seahorses 425

TESTUDINES–TUBULIDENTATA
Green Turtle 426
Common Snapping Turtle 427
Leatherback Turtle 428
Red-Eared Terrapin 429
Galápagos Tortoise 430
Gopher Tortoise 431
Spiny Porcupinefish 432
Longfin Inshore Squid 433
Aardvark 434

VALVATIDA–VENEROIDA
Red-knobbed Starfish 435
Giant Clam 436

Glossary 437
Climate Map 438
Index 440

Introduction

I t is impossible to be certain how many species have existed on earth, simply because the majority have died out without leaving any evidence of their existence. What is clear is that only a tiny percentage of the total figure – perhaps just 1 per cent according to some estimates – are alive on the planet today.

Ignoring plants and microbes, the greatest number of these life forms are invertebrates. About 1.8 million living species have been identified by zoologists and given scientific names, and out of these, about two-thirds are invertebrates, with large animals therefore being very much in the minority.

Even today, there are literally millions of species still to be discovered and officially described. Many are doomed to become extinct even before they are documented. There are certain areas of the world, such as the canopy of the rainforest and the depths of the oceans, where we have only a vague appreciation and understanding of the numerous life forms that exist in these environments.

New discoveries

The scale of new discoveries in such habitats can be amazing. Following expeditions to the seas south of Tasmania, scientists were able to confirm the discovery of some 274 new species of marine creatures in October 2008. On the island of Borneo, more than 310 animals and invertebrates species previously unknown to science were recorded between 1994 and 2004. They included a fish that is the world's second smallest vertebrate, measuring less than 1cm (0.39in) in length.

Not all species remain in the same habitat throughout the year. Monarch butterflies are amongst those which undertake regular migrations.

Estimates suggest there could be as many as 15 million species sharing the planet with us, which means that barely 10 per cent of this total have been documented as yet. This does not apply just to invertebrates either. Every year brings confirmation of the existence of new vertebrate species, of which nearly 60,000 have already been documented. Fish are the most numerous group, accounting for approximately half of this total figure. Nevertheless, since the turn of the century, more than 25 species of primate have been documented for the first time, including the goldenpalace.com monkey which was discovered in western Bolivia. Its unusual name comes from the decision of those involved in its discovery to sell off the right to name the species to the highest bidder. This auction attracted some 25 interested parties, and ultimately raised US$650,000 for conservation work. The

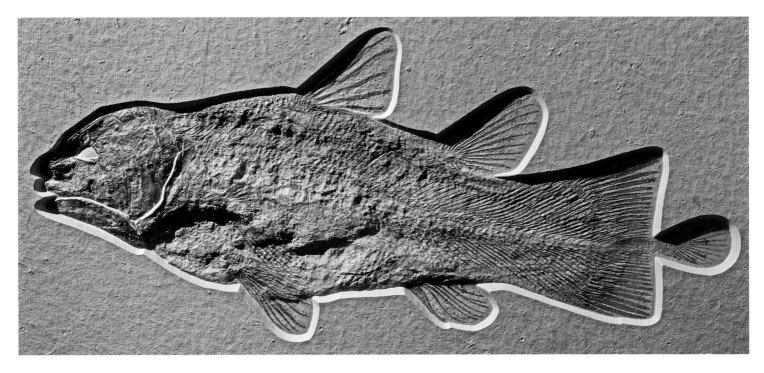

Ancestors of today's coelacanths were known as fossils long before their living descendants were discovered in the Indian Ocean.

monkey's scientific name, *Calliicebus aureipalatii*, also reflects the winning bid, meaning 'Callicebus of the Golden Palace'.

Even bigger species have been discovered in the oceans, although some remain mysterious and elusive, none more so than the spade-toothed whale (*Mesoplodon traversii*), named after the New Zealand naturalist Henry Travers. It was described originally on the basis of a jaw washed up in 1872 on a beach at Pitt Island, near New Zealand, but was subsequently considered to be simply a Layard's beaked whale (*M. layardii*). Another finding of a whale's skull from White Island in the same area during the 1950s seemed insignificant at the time, being attributed to a ginkgo-toothed beaked whale (*M. ginkgodens*). A further skull washed up on Robinson Crusoe island in 1986, off the Chilean coast, was then thought to come from a new species, christened Bahamonde's beaked whale (*M. bahamondi*).

In 2002, however, a review of these specimens involved DNA analysis to reveal that they were all from the same species. As a result of the rules surrounding scientific nomenclature, where the first name takes precedence, the name of the spade-toothed whale was reinstated. Even today however, no-one has seen a living example of this species, and it remains not only one of the most mysterious cetaceans, but also one of the least-known mammals on the planet.

When is a species extinct?

In the worst case scenario, there is no risk that this rare whale could yet be described as extinct. Convention dictates that a species can be described as extinct only if there have been no sightings of it for 50 years. Yet there have been remarkable cases of species seemingly coming back from the dead after a much longer interval. This may be a reflection of the species's habitat, combined with identification difficulties. As an example, the Bermuda petrel (*Pterodroma cahow*) was believed to have become extinct in 1620s, in spite of being officially protected – one of the earliest examples of a conservation plan. It was then miraculously rediscovered breeding on rocky islets some 330 years later, during 1951, having managed to remain hidden for so long thanks to its nocturnal nature and underground nesting habits.

The case of the coelacanth (*Latimeria chalumnae*) was even more remarkable, because here was a species straight out of the fossil record, whose ancestors were assumed to have died out around 65 million years ago, at the same time as the dinosaurs. A living example was caught in deep water off the southeast coast of Africa in 1938, and others followed. A second species of coelacanth, now known scientifically as *Latimeria menadoensis*, was then discovered off the coast

There are two distinctive races of the grey parrot, as reflected by their scientific names. This is the sub-species known as *Psittacus erithacus erithacus.*

of the Indonesian island of Sulawesi during 1999. One thing is certain – there are other species existing today, some of which will be large, still awaiting discovery.

What's in a name?

The way in which species are described follows a set convention. Early attempts to classify plants and animals were made by ancient Greeks, but modern taxonomy, as this science has become known, started to develop only about 300 years ago. In fact, the system in use today is still very similar in many respects to that originally devised by a Swedish doctor born in 1707, who was known variously as both Carl Linnaeus and Carl von Linné.

During 1735, Linnaeus produced his first publication on the subject, which was a pamphlet called *Systema Naturae*, based largely on botanical studies. This was subsequently expanded to become a multi-volume work, whose importance grew as overseas voyages of discovery from Europe to other parts of the globe returned with an ever-increasing range of specimens that needed to be named and classified.

One of the main legacies of Linnaeus's contribution in this field is the concept of a hierarchical ranking system. He recognized the fact that certain group of plants and animals were more closely related than others, providing the potential for a means of division. The Linnean system uses this as its starting point, operating through a series of levels, known as 'ranks'.

As you progress through these ranks, so the relationships become closer until, ultimately, it is possible to identify a specific population. The first basic division is between plants and animals, which is at a level known as the kingdom. Working through the system with the grey parrot as an example, the ranking system is as follows, with the accompanying explanations in parenthesis:-

Kingdom Animalia (the animal grouping)
Phylum Chordata (animals with backbones)
Class Aves (indicating a bird, rather than a reptile, mammal etc.)
Order Psittaciformes (a category containing all parrots)
Family Psittacidae (the smaller division within the order to which this parrot belongs)
Genus *Psittacus* (the group name for closely related species)
Species *Psittacus erithracus* (the name accorded to the individual parrot itself)
Sub-species *Psittacus erithacus erithacus; Psittacus erithacus timneh* (separate, distinct and recognizable populations of this parrot)

The basic classificatory rules apply just as much to invertebrates such as this southern black widow spider as to vertebrates.

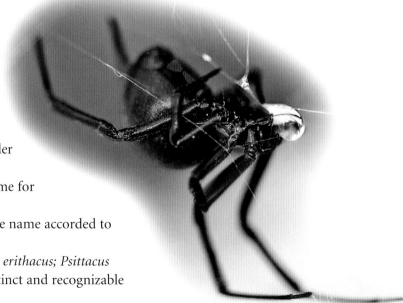

There can sometimes be confusion over the identity of a species based on its common name, such as the whale shark seen here, but its exact biological relationships will be made clear through the classificatory tree. This confirms it is a fish, not a mammal.

Certain key common endings will help to identify exactly where you are in this taxonomic tree. A description that finishes in '-formes' serve to indicate an Order, while '-idae' signifies a family. There is another clue too, in the way that names are written, because from genus downwards, these are always italicized. So when a word such as *Psittacus* appears, it has to be a generic description relating to one or more species.

The Binomial Method

In the 10th edition of *Systema Naturae,* which appeared in 1758, Linnaeus introduced the so-called binomial method, which enables subspecies to be distinguished at the bottom of the taxonomic tree. By this stage, he had classified some 4400 species. There can be a large number of such subspecies, which are also called races, but each one can all distinguished by an incontrovertible individual name. The species name may appear simply as an initial when writing out subspecies, as with *Psittacus e. erithacus.* The subspecies where the species' epithet is repeated is not in any way distinctive, other than it was the first to be described, in a historical sense.

It may appear that scientific names are chosen randomly, but they usually highlight specific features of the animal in question. In the case of the grey parrot above, *erithacus* refers to its distinctive red tail feathers. There may often be an interesting background behind the choice of names for individual species, as mentioned earlier in the case of *Calliicebus aureipalatii*. In order to be accepted as a valid species, however, a specimen has to be formally lodged with a museum somewhere in the world. This becomes known as the type specimen, and is used as the basis from which the description of the species is written up for a recognized scientific publication, leading to its ultimate recognition.

If new information becomes available, it is possible to move a species to another genus, for example, and it will then assume the new generic name, while keeping its old species epithet. Right through from Linnaeus's time up until very recently, taxonomy relied on detecting similarities in anatomy, when it came to grouping species. DNA analysis is now being applied increasingly in this area, however, and changing the science. The taxonomic tree is likely to be altered significantly in the future because genetic evidence allows close relationship between groups of animals to be determined, and can even provide insights as to when a particular lineage may have split off from its nearest relatives.

The categories

There are six different major divisions or classes, into which all animals are divided.

Invertebrates

The most numerous group of creatures on the planet, invertebrates are all distinguished by the lack of a vertebral column or backbone. The description of 'invertebrate' is often used

interchangeably with 'insect', but this is incorrect because a number of invertebrates such as spiders are not insects but members of other classes. They are, however, all arthropods, meaning that they have segmented bodies.

Invertebrates are often typified by their high rate of reproduction. However, some such as scorpions, practise a high degree of parental care, with correspondingly fewer offspring being produced. Although preyed on by many species, being at the bottom of the vertebrate food chain, some invertebrates are able to defend themselves by means of venom.

Fish
It is believed that the first fish developed in the oceans, and that they then started to invade fresh water by swimming up streams and rivers. Early fish had a skeleton of cartilage rather than bone. Examples of these primitive groups which still survive today are the sharks and rays. Fish are able to extract oxygen from the water by means of their gills, located just behind the eyes on each side of the head. They often reproduce by means of eggs that are scattered at random and which are fertilized externally, but in other cases, fish may display considerable devotion to their eggs and/or offspring.

Some amphibians such as the European tree frog have developed the ability to climb well, although most are terrestrial in their habits.

Amphibians
Believed to be descended from fishlike ancestors, these vertebrates took the first steps on to land, and developed lungs to help them breathe atmospheric air, although they may also breathe through the skin as well. Even today, amphibians require moist or damp surroundings, which means that they are not found in deserts but tend to inhabit wooded, shady areas. The life cycles vary, but amphibians must generally return to water to breed. The eggs laid here will hatch into tadpoles, and these will ultimately leave the water, losing their feathery gills on the sides of the head as their lungs become functional.

Reptiles
Covered in scales, but dependent on the environmental temperature to maintain their level of activity, reptiles tend to be concentrated in warmer areas of the world. Some lay soft-shelled, leathery eggs whereas those of others are characterized by their hard shell. It is now known that, in many cases, the incubation temperature will have a direct influence on the sex of the young.

The ostrich is one of the few birds that cannot fly, relying instead on its long legs to run away from danger.

The red squirrel is one of about 1500 different rodents alive today, out of a total of some 4000 mammalian species.

This is known as TSD, standing for temperature-dependent sex determination. The impact of this varies, however, according to individual species. In some cases, male offspring may be produced at higher temperatures, whereas it may be females in other species. This understanding can have important consequences for conservation programmes, when increasing the number of female offspring can be very significant.

Birds

The ability to fly is not unique to birds, as this is an ability possessed by bats and even insects. Instead, it is the covering of feathers that sets them apart. Plumage is important for flying and courtship display, as well as for insulation against the cold, as reflected by the different types of feathers that cover a bird's body. Birds are warm-blooded, so they can raise their body temperature above that of their environment. This trait has allowed them to colonize the entire globe, although a few species have actually lost their ability to fly. In some cases, as with the ostrich (*Struthio camelus*), this is a reflection of the size of the bird, which has resulted in it becoming too heavy to fly.

Mammals

They too have the ability to generate heat within their bodies to keep warm, and like birds, they are described as endotherms, although they have hair on their bodies rather than feathers. Mammals, with a very few Antipodean exceptions, all reproduce by giving birth to live young, rather than laying eggs. There is an intimate connection, called the placenta, through which the female nourishes her offspring during the gestation period, up until they are born. The young are then suckled for a variable period afterwards. Rodents are by far the most numerous order within the class Mammalia, with many species having a very high reproductive rate. By contrast, long-lived, bigger mammals have few offspring.

How this book works

The format for all the entries that follow is similar, enabling comparisons to be made easily. The animals are not grouped on the basis of their common names, however, because this is unreliable; in many cases, a species may be known under a variety of different common names. Furthermore, different subspecies may also be accorded separate common names, adding to the confusion. This was another reason why it was so important to develop a universal system of nomenclature, allowing for a single species to be identified without confusion, creating what is effectively an international zoological language. This approach also avoids the inevitable linguistic problems in cases where the same species is known under different common names in neighbouring countries. The entries here are actually grouped by order, on an A-Z basis, which has the advantage of ensuring that closely related species, linked as members of the same order, can be found together.

Common Tenrec

• ORDER • Afrosoricida • FAMILY • Tenrecidae • SPECIES • *Tenrec ecaudatus*

VITAL STATISTICS

WEIGHT	1.5–2.5kg (3.25–5.5lb)
LENGTH	26–39cm (10–15.5in); although called the tailless tenrec, this species has a short tail, measuring just 1cm (0.3in)
SEXUAL MATURITY	1 year
GESTATION PERIOD	50–60 days
NUMBER OF OFFSPRING	Litters usually comprise 10–12 young
DIET	Hunts invertebrates on the forest floor, as well as frogs and small rodents such as mice
LIFESPAN	3–6 years

ANIMAL FACTS

This species is the largest member of this family of primitive mammals, which are often described as insectivores, because of their diet. Common tenrecs can be found in a wide range of habitats, and are largely nocturnal by nature. They build a nest of grass and other vegetation hidden under rocks or logs. If challenged they erect their spiny hairs, which become particularly noticeable around the neck. Tenrecs will jump, bite and scream to defend themselves.

Tenrecs look rather like a combination of a shrew, thanks to their pointed faces, and a hedgehog, because of their long, spiny fur.

WHERE IN THE WORLD?

Occurs on the various groups of islands off the southwestern coast of Africa. These include Madagascar, Réunion, the Seychelles, Mauritius and the Comoros.

EYES
The eyes are relatively small, indicating the tenrec's nocturnal nature.

EARS
Small and rounded at their tips, the ears are quite mobile.

FUR
The fur is coarse, shortest on the head and varying from grey to reddish-grey, mixed with spiny hairs that offer protection against predators.

NOSE
Mobile and highly sensitive, the tenrec's nose allows it to locate its prey, even when hidden by leaves on the ground.

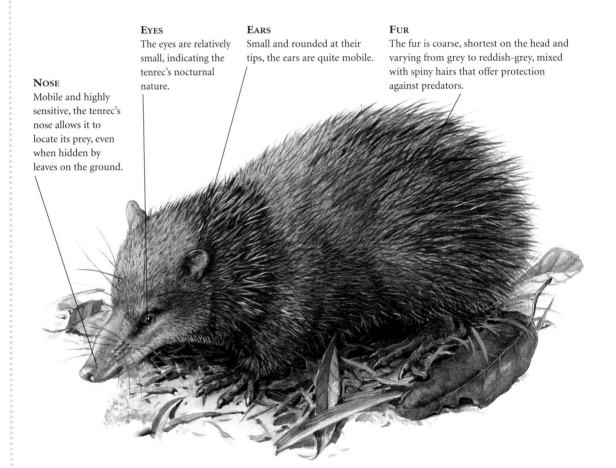

An aggressive posture

HOW BIG IS IT?

MOTHER AND YOUNG

Baby common tenrecs differ in appearance from adults because their fur is striped, being black and white in colour.

Common Eel

• **ORDER** • Anguilliformes • **FAMILY** • Anguillidae • **SPECIES** • *Anguilla anguilla*

VITAL STATISTICS

WEIGHT	4.5–13kg (10–29lb)
LENGTH	Can reach 100cm (39in)
SEXUAL MATURITY	9–23 years
HATCHING PERIOD	Unknown
NUMBER OF EGGS	Unknown
DIET	Invertebrates and small vertebrate prey
LIFESPAN	15–25 years; females live longer

ANIMAL FACTS

Much about this eel's breeding habits is still a mystery. Young of this species are known as glass eels (or leptocephali), and then change into young eels, called elvers, just before they enter freshwater. Their journey to Europe across the Atlantic Ocean may take three years. Eels used to be a staple food in some areas, such as the East End of London, where they were caught in special eel traps. Unfortunately their population has declined dramatically over recent years, for reasons that are not entirely clear.

These snake-like fish have a remarkable life history and can be found in both saltwater and freshwater. They can even travel across damp ground out of water.

WHERE IN THE WORLD?

Occurs widely in the waterways of western Europe, down to the Mediterranean. Also present in the Atlantic Ocean at certain stages in their lifecycle.

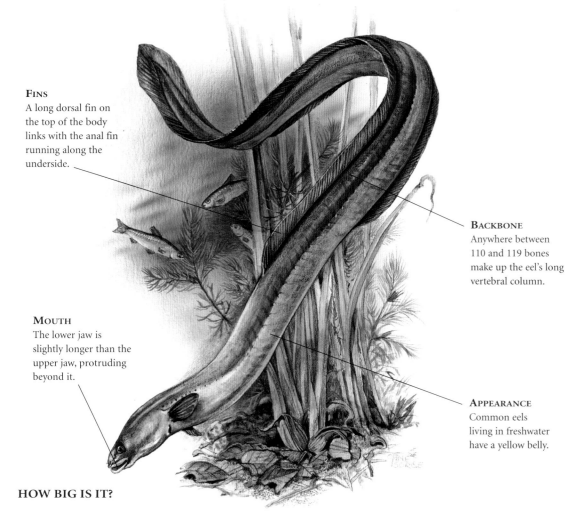

FINS
A long dorsal fin on the top of the body links with the anal fin running along the underside.

MOUTH
The lower jaw is slightly longer than the upper jaw, protruding beyond it.

BACKBONE
Anywhere between 110 and 119 bones make up the eel's long vertebral column.

APPEARANCE
Common eels living in freshwater have a yellow belly.

Eels become more streamlined when heading back to sea

HOW BIG IS IT?

ON THE MOVE

Adult eels will ultimately swim back to their spawning grounds in the Sargasso Sea, where they die. Their young are swept along by the current to Europe.

Mediterranean Moray Eel

• ORDER • Anguilliformes **• FAMILY •** Muraenidae **• SPECIES •** *Muraena helena*

These large, fearsome eels can lunge out of their rocky lair as a diver passes, in the same way that they ambush their prey.

VITAL STATISTICS

WEIGHT	Typically around 15kg (33lb)
LENGTH	Up to about 150cm (59in)
SEXUAL MATURITY	Probably around 5 years
HATCHING PERIOD	A few days, depending on water temperature
NUMBER OF EGGS	60,000, laid in open water, fertilized externally, from which larvae called leptocephali hatch
DIET	Crustaceans, cephalopods and fish; may also scavenge
LIFESPAN	Up to 20 years

ANIMAL FACTS

There are over 200 different species of moray eels, all of which are predatory in their feeding habits. They hunt largely by their sense of smell because their eyesight is poor – as reflected by their small eyes. They generally tend to seek their prey under cover of darkness. Moray eels are unique in having a set of secondary, so-called pharyngeal jaws at the back of the mouth, equipped with teeth that spring forward and help them to overpower and swallow prey.

WHERE IN THE WORLD?

Members of this family are confined to the world's tropical and sub-tropical waters, typically occurring around coral reefs, where they can hide.

TEETH
Strong, backward-pointing teeth allow these eels to rip flesh.

MOUTH
Wide jaws help to seize prey, with the gills located well back on the flanks.

APPEARANCE
The sleek, scaleless skin is covered by a thick layer of protective mucus.

FINS
The dorsal fin starts just behind the head and runs down the middle of the back.

The moray's patterning helps to disguise its presence

HOW BIG IS IT?

SMALL AND BRIGHT
These ribbon eels (*Rhinomuraena quaesita*), found in Asian waters, are black at first, but change colour as they grow. Males become blue and females yellow.

Mallard

• ORDER • Anseriformes **• FAMILY •** Anatidae **• SPECIES •** *Anas platyrhynchos*

VITAL STATISTICS

WEIGHT	1–1.5kg (2.25–3.25lb)
LENGTH	50–65cm (20–26in)
SEXUAL MATURITY	Unlikely to breed until they are two years old
HATCHING PERIOD	28 days
NUMBER OF EGGS	7–16, buff to greyish-green in colour
DIET	Feeds on plants and invertebrates, both in water and on land; also scavenges on human leftovers, especially bread
LIFESPAN	Averages 7–10 years

ANIMAL FACTS

Mallards are very adaptable waterfowl, but it is only possible to tell the sexes apart during the breeding season. For the remainder of the year the males, called drakes, resemble the female ducks, being mainly brownish in colour. They can still be sexed, however, because the bill of the drake is yellow, rather than orange. There is a shortage of females in many mallard populations, and in these circumstances drakes may interbreed with other species of duck, resulting in hybrid ducklings.

A domesticated white relative of the mallard

The mallard is a common sight in city parks and waterways, and will even breed in these surroundings. It is also an ancestor of today's domesticated ducks.

WHERE IN THE WORLD?

Naturally resident throughout most of western Europe, and a summer visitor further east. Present in much of North America to Mexico, and east to Greenland.

WING SPECULUM
This brightly coloured barring across the wings is most evident in flight.

PLUMAGE
The iridescent green plumage on the head distinguishes adult drakes in breeding plumage.

FEET
Webbing is present between the toes to help the ducks swim more easily. There are claws at the end of the toes.

TAIL
Mallard drakes have curled tail feathers.

HOW BIG IS IT?

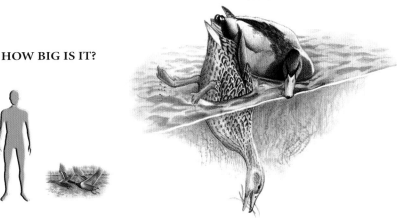

UP TAILS ALL
Mallards are dabbling ducks, upending their bodies in the water to reach aquatic plants, although they also seek food on land.

Griswold's Marsupial Frog

• ORDER • Anura • FAMILY • Amphignathodontidae • SPECIES • *Gastrotheca griswoldi*

VITAL STATISTICS

LENGTH	5–7cm (2–2.75in)
SEXUAL MATURITY	7 months
DEVELOPMENTAL PERIOD	Time spent in the pouch can vary from 2–4 months; the tadpoles are released into water at night
NUMBER OF EGGS	Usually 100–130 in total, with the male placing the eggs directly into the female's pouch
HABITAT	Humid mountain forest and cleared areas
DIET	Various invertebrates
LIFESPAN	2–3 years

ANIMAL FACTS

Breeding in the dry puna grasslands of South America would present a challenge for a typical amphibian, because there is no certainty that there will be areas of standing water for spawning for long. Marsupial frogs largely overcome this problem by being able to hatch their own eggs. Although they occur in a relatively restricted area of some 20,000km (7700 miles), these frogs are quite common within that relatively remote region, and they are not under any threat.

Tadpoles exit the pouch

The description of marsupial frog comes from the unusual breeding habits of these particular amphibians, as females carry their offspring with them in a pouch.

WHERE IN THE WORLD?

Found in the central area of the Peruvian Andes, in a region called Nudo de Pasco, occurring at an altitude between 3000–4000m (9800–13,120ft).

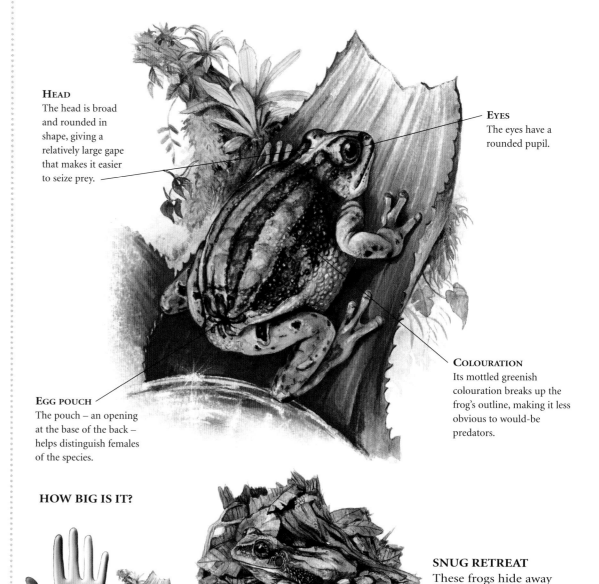

HEAD
The head is broad and rounded in shape, giving a relatively large gape that makes it easier to seize prey.

EYES
The eyes have a rounded pupil.

EGG POUCH
The pouch – an opening at the base of the back – helps distinguish females of the species.

COLOURATION
Its mottled greenish colouration breaks up the frog's outline, making it less obvious to would-be predators.

HOW BIG IS IT?

SNUG RETREAT
These frogs hide away under logs and leaves when conditions are very dry, and also seek protection here against the winter cold.

Pebas Stubfoot Toad

VITAL STATISTICS

LENGTH	2.6–3.9cm (1–1.5in); males are smaller, less than 3cm (1.2in)
SEXUAL MATURITY	About 1 year
HATCHING PERIOD	Tadpoles may hatch quickly, possibly just a day after the eggs are laid
NUMBER OF EGGS	May lay strings of about 350 eggs
HABITAT	Tropical rainforest
DIET	Feeds on a variety of invertebrates
LIFESPAN	Likely to be 3–4 years

ANIMAL FACTS

The toad's normal colouring helps it to blend into the background, but these amphibians have a particular way of disconcerting a would-be predator – by arching their backs in an aggressive posture, and revealing the bright-orange areas on the undersides of their feet. This is suggestive of danger. Their tadpoles develop in quite fast-flowing water, and so they have a large sucker close to their mouths, which helps to prevent them being swept away by the current.

These small, brightly coloured toads are terrestrial by nature and are active during the day. They live in the leaf litter, hiding under logs.

WHERE IN THE WORLD?

Northern South America, found in the Amazonian basin of Ecuador, Peru and Brazil, extending to Guyana, French Guiana and Surinam, occurring near water.

TOES
The toes of these toads are short with rounded tips, which explains their common name.

EYES
The iris is a golden shade.

FRONT LEGS
Males may use their strong front legs to hold on to females for several days before spawning occurs.

COLOURATION
The patterning on the back and sides of the body is quite distinctive, enabling individuals to be distinguished. The underparts are whitish.

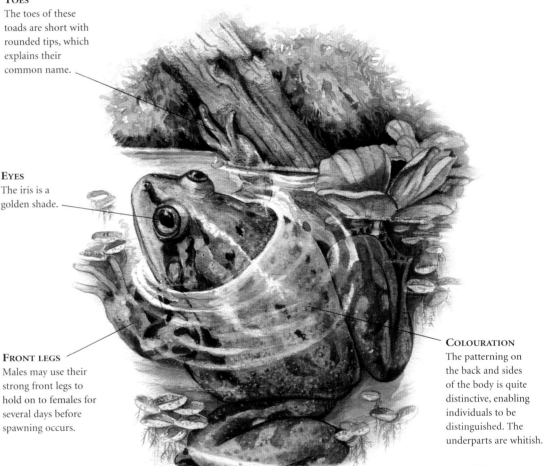

Males wait near water to mate

HOW BIG IS IT?

SPAWNING
Living in a warm and humid part of the world, these small toads may spawn at any stage during the year.

European Toad

• ORDER • Anura • FAMILY • Bufonidae • SPECIES • *Bufo bufo*

VITAL STATISTICS

WEIGHT	Variable, ranging from 5–55g (0.17–1.94oz); spawning females can weigh up to 120g (4.23oz)
LENGTH	Up to 18cm (7in)
SEXUAL MATURITY	4 years
HATCHING PERIOD	Tadpoles hatch after 8–10 days; metamorphosis takes 2–3 months
NUMBER OF EGGS	600–4000
DIET	Invertebrates and small vertebrates, including mice and small grass snakes
LIFESPAN:	Typically 15–20 years, but potentially up to 40 years

ANIMAL FACTS

Sadly, many common toads are killed on roads every year, trying to return to their traditional spawning grounds. In some areas, special toad crossings – tunnels under the road – have been constructed to reduce this death toll. Female toads lay their eggs in long triple strands. After spawning, toads revert to their solitary lifestyles. They are more active towards dusk, especially on rainy nights, seeking slugs and worms drawn out by the damp weather.

Bright orange iris

Traditionally linked with witchcraft because of its warty appearance, the European toad is an imposing amphibian, growing to a relatively large size.

WHERE IN THE WORLD?

Ranges widely through western Europe (although absent from Ireland), extending eastwards as far as central Asia. Also present in northwestern parts of Africa.

PAROTID GLAND
This gland produces toxic secretions that protect the toad from most predators.

COLOURATION
Body colour varies, ranging from shades of grey through sandy tones to dark brown, depending partly on the locality.

FACE
The snout is rounded in shape and the jaws can accommodate large prey.

LEGS
Females tend to have longer forelegs than males, which develop toe swellings called nuptial pads in the breeding season.

CATCHING PREY
Common toads have a long, sticky tongue, which they wrap around their prey before pulling it back into their mouths.

HOW BIG IS IT?

Natterjack Toad

• ORDER • Anura **• FAMILY •** Bufonidae **• SPECIES •** *Epidalea calamita*

These toads have a very loud call, heard during the mating period. Males are able to inflate a vocal sac under their chin for this purpose.

VITAL STATISTICS

WEIGHT	Averages about 20g (0.7oz)
LENGTH	6–7cm (2–2.5in)
SEXUAL MATURITY	2–3 years
HATCHING PERIOD	7–12 days; hatching takes longer when the weather is cold
NUMBER OF EGGS	Up to 2,600; Metamorphosis can take 10 weeks
DIET	Hunts various invertebrates, including slugs and earthworms; these toads only eat during the warmer months, hibernating over the winter
LIFESPAN	Up to 12 years

ANIMAL FACTS

Spawning occurs in the late spring and early summer, and females lay several times during this period. They often choose temporary pools, and if the water evaporates in hot weather, the tadpoles die before they can metamorphose into adult toads. The female produces strands of eggs that the male fertilizes, clinging on to her back as they are laid. These toads will hunt at night.

WHERE IN THE WORLD?

Found in suitable habitats throughout northern Europe, typically in heathland and sandy areas.

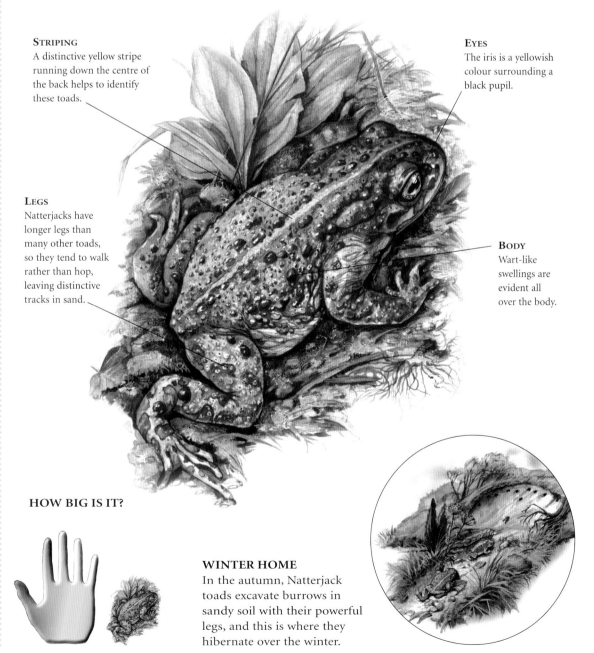

STRIPING
A distinctive yellow stripe running down the centre of the back helps to identify these toads.

LEGS
Natterjacks have longer legs than many other toads, so they tend to walk rather than hop, leaving distinctive tracks in sand.

EYES
The iris is a yellowish colour surrounding a black pupil.

BODY
Wart-like swellings are evident all over the body.

HOW BIG IS IT?

WINTER HOME
In the autumn, Natterjack toads excavate burrows in sandy soil with their powerful legs, and this is where they hibernate over the winter.

Male natterjack toad calling

21

Small Strawberry Dart Frog

• ORDER • Anura • FAMILY • Dendrobatidae • SPECIES • *Oophaga pumilio*

VITAL STATISTICS

LENGTH	1.7–2.4cm (0.66–0.95in)
SEXUAL MATURITY	9 months
HATCHING PERIOD	Tadpoles hatch after 5–15 days; metamorphosis takes 6–8 weeks
NUMBER OF EGGS	Between 3 and 17, laid on the forest floor in a damp location; the tadpoles are carried to a small reservoir of water by the female
HABITAT	Tropical rainforest
DIET	Small invertebrates of various types, especially ants
LIFESPAN	3–5 years

ANIMAL FACTS

The appearance of these small frogs varies greatly, to the extent that more than 30 different colour variants, or 'morphs', have been identified. These are associated with particular localities, and may be named after them, as in the case of the San Cristobal morph. The range of coloration is such that some morphs are completely different in appearance from others. The Panamanian form, for example, has no red markings at all, being yellow with brown markings on its body.

Bright coloration in nature usually serves as a warning sign, and strawberry dart frogs have potent toxins in their skin to protect them from predators.

WHERE IN THE WORLD?

Occurs in parts of Nicaragua, Panama and Costa Rica in Central America. Also found on various offshore islands in the region.

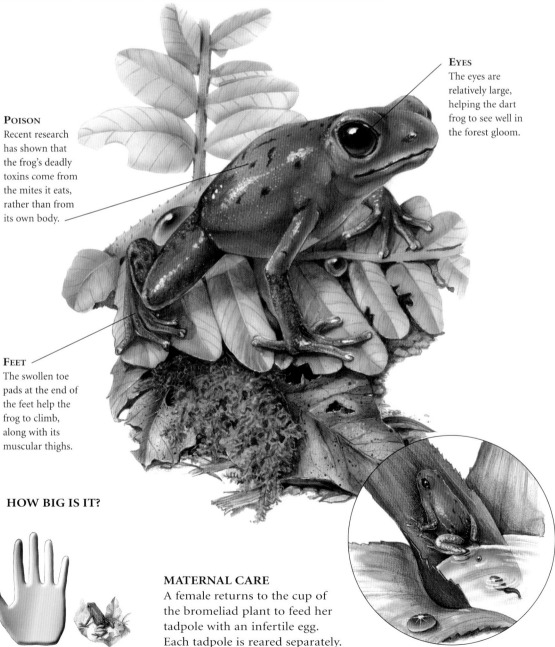

EYES
The eyes are relatively large, helping the dart frog to see well in the forest gloom.

POISON
Recent research has shown that the frog's deadly toxins come from the mites it eats, rather than from its own body.

FEET
The swollen toe pads at the end of the feet help the frog to climb, along with its muscular thighs.

Close-up of the underside of the foot

HOW BIG IS IT?

MATERNAL CARE
A female returns to the cup of the bromeliad plant to feed her tadpole with an infertile egg. Each tadpole is reared separately.

Common Midwife Toad

•ORDER• Anura •FAMILY• Discoglossidae •SPECIES• *Alytes obstetricans*

These toads are so-called because of the way males collect and carry the eggs on their backs, until the tadpoles are due to hatch.

VITAL STATISTICS

LENGTH	Up to 5.5cm (2.16in); females are generally larger than males
SEXUAL MATURITY	2 years
HATCHING PERIOD	3–6 weeks; they remain as tadpoles over the winter, not metamorph-osing until the following spring
NUMBER OF EGGS	Up to about 50 per spawning
HABITAT	Near water, from sandy areas to rocky, mountainous uplands
DIET	Feeds on a variety of invertebrates, including slugs and earthworms
LIFESPAN	7–10 years

ANIMAL FACTS

The strange egg-carrying behaviour of the male midwife toad may have evolved as a way of preventing the eggs from being destroyed by frost, which can freeze spawn in the water as it turns to ice. This also gives the females a reproductive advantage, to the extent that they may spawn more frequently during the spring and summer. These factors have helped a population survive in Britain, where they were introduced in 1904.

Mating behaviour

WHERE IN THE WORLD?

Portugal and Spain, northwards via France to Belgium and the Netherlands. Also occurs in Luxembourg, Germany and Switzerland. Has been introduced to the UK.

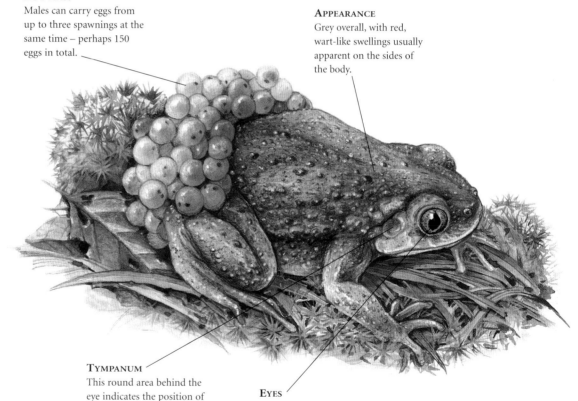

EGG MASS
Males can carry eggs from up to three spawnings at the same time – perhaps 150 eggs in total.

APPEARANCE
Grey overall, with red, wart-like swellings usually apparent on the sides of the body.

TYMPANUM
This round area behind the eye indicates the position of the toad's ear.

EYES
The eyes are quite large, with a vertical slit-like pupil.

HOW BIG IS IT?

HAZARDOUS EXISTENCE
Tadpoles face dragonfly larvae and other invertebrate predators, but they can ultimately grow up to 9cm (3.54in), giving them some protection.

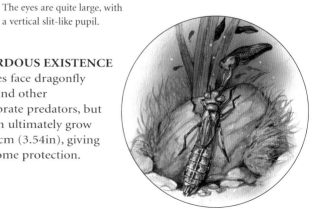

European Treefrog

• ORDER • Anura **• FAMILY •** Hylidae **• SPECIES •** *Hyla arborea*

VITAL STATISTICS

LENGTH	3–5cm (1.25–2in), with no marked difference in size between the sexes
SEXUAL MATURITY	1 year
HATCHING PERIOD	About 3 weeks; meta-morphosis complete about 3 months later
NUMBER OF EGGS	200–2000 in total, laid in smaller batches
HABITAT	Relatively open country near water
DIET	Hunts a variety of invertebrates, including flies
LIFESPAN	3–5 years on average

ANIMAL FACTS

European green treefrogs are found in wet areas rather than in dense woodland. They are quite at home on the leaves of reeds and other aquatic plants – if disturbed, they can jump down into the water below. Males call at the start of the breeding season, leading to a chorus as they compete against each other in song. Their calls are said to resemble the quacking of a duck. These treefrogs hibernate in winter.

This is the most common of Europe's two species of treefrog, although it is now considered endangered in the northern parts of its range.

WHERE IN THE WORLD?

Through mainland Europe (apart from southeastern Spain and southern France), down around the Caspian Sea, north to Denmark, but not extending to the British Isles.

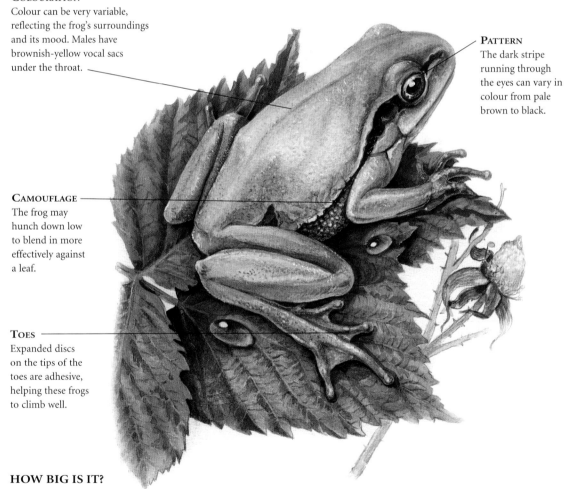

COLOURATION
Colour can be very variable, reflecting the frog's surroundings and its mood. Males have brownish-yellow vocal sacs under the throat.

PATTERN
The dark stripe running through the eyes can vary in colour from pale brown to black.

CAMOUFLAGE
The frog may hunch down low to blend in more effectively against a leaf.

TOES
Expanded discs on the tips of the toes are adhesive, helping these frogs to climb well.

HOW BIG IS IT?

The underside of the body is whitish

STAYING ALIVE
Their well-muscled hind legs allow these treefrogs to jump well, enabling them to elude predators such as herons.

Common Spadefoot Toad

• **ORDER** • Anura • **FAMILY** • Pelobatidae • **SPECIES** • *Pelobates fuscus*

VITAL STATISTICS

LENGTH	5–10cm (2–4in)
SEXUAL MATURITY	Less than a year
HATCHING PERIOD	Lasts 2–3 days, with the tadpoles metamorph-osing quickly, in less than 3 weeks; cannibalism is common if food is scarce in the temporary puddles where the eggs are deposited
NUMBER OF EGGS	10–500, with spawning occurring after heavy rainfall
HABITAT	Sandy soil in areas that flood
DIET	Invertebrates, but may also prey on small lizards
LIFESPAN	Up to 13 years

ANIMAL FACTS

One of the unusual features of these toads is their ability to produce an unpleasant-smelling secretion that resembles garlic, as a means of deterring predators. This is why they are also known as garlic toads. They can also utter a shriek, which may shock a predator into dropping the toad, enabling it to burrow to safety. Spadefoot toads can inflate their bodies in order to appear larger and more threatening if challenged.

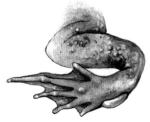

The spade on the hind leg

Living in open countryside means that this toad is vulnerable to predators, so its hind feet are specially adapted to allow it to burrow quickly to escape danger.

WHERE IN THE WORLD?

Distribution extends from eastern France, through central Europe up to southern parts of Sweden, and eastwards through western parts of Asia as far as Iran.

COLOURATION
Variable yellowish and brownish patterning helps conceal these toads in either sandy areas or heathland habitat.

FEET
The so-called 'spade' that the toad uses to dig into the ground is concealed on the inner surface of each foot.

SKIN
The skin resembles that of a frog, appearing moist, rather than dry and warty like bufonid toads.

FACE
Large, rounded jaws are used to seize prey such as earthworms.

HOW BIG IS IT?

OUT OF SIGHT
Instead of having to dig into the ground head-first, spadefoot toads burrow in backwards so they can continue watching for danger.

Moor Frog

• ORDER • Anura • FAMILY • Ranidae • SPECIES • *Rana arvalis*

VITAL STATISTICS

LENGTH	4–6.5cm (1.8–2.5in)
SEXUAL MATURITY	2–5 years; females are generally slower to mature
HATCHING PERIOD	2–3 weeks, depending on the water temperature; pH may also have an impact
NUMBER OF EGGS	1000–2000 laid between March and April; Metamorphosis lasts 2–3 months
HABITAT	Typically moorland areas, with swamps and ponds
DIET	Mainly terrestrial invertebrates; does not feed when spawning
LIFESPAN	Recorded living up to 11 years

ANIMAL FACTS

The moor frog is an adaptable species. Often encountered in open country with boggy ground, they can also be seen in meadows and gardens, and in tundra areas in the northern part of their range. During the winter, moor frogs will hibernate. In the Ural mountains, they are active between June and September, but further south their period of hibernation may only extend from November to February.

White underside to the body

The spawning grounds of this species come alive in the spring, with hundreds of frogs congregating for a brief period at this stage.

WHERE IN THE WORLD?

Occurs in northern and eastern Europe, extending from Alsace in the west, and ranging south as far as areas of Croatia and Romania, reaching Siberia.

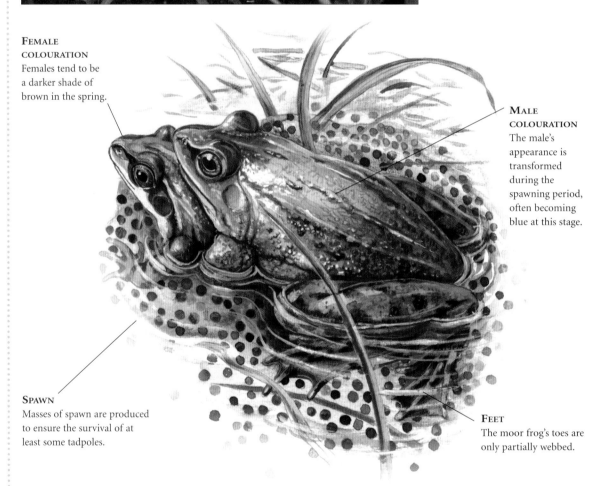

FEMALE COLOURATION
Females tend to be a darker shade of brown in the spring.

MALE COLOURATION
The male's appearance is transformed during the spawning period, often becoming blue at this stage.

SPAWN
Masses of spawn are produced to ensure the survival of at least some tadpoles.

FEET
The moor frog's toes are only partially webbed.

HOW BIG IS IT?

COMMUNITY SPIRIT

Huge numbers of these frogs may congregate in suitable spawning areas of stagnant, often shallow water, with the males chorusing together.

American Bullfrog

VITAL STATISTICS

WEIGHT	Up to 750g (26oz)
LENGTH	As much as 20cm (8in); females are larger than males
SEXUAL MATURITY	3–5 years
HATCHING PERIOD	3–5 days on average, longer in cold weather
NUMBER OF EGGS	Up to 40,000 at a single spawning
DIET	Hunts both invertebrates and small vertebrates
LIFESPAN	8–10 years in the wild; up to 16 years in captivity

ANIMAL FACTS

Males have a call resembling the bellowing of a bull, which they utter repeatedly in the spring. This is intended to intimidate rivals from entering their territories and to attract females. When spawning, the male grasps his mate in front of her forelegs with his own. The resulting tadpoles are voracious feeders, and smaller individuals are likely to be cannibalized by their companions. It can take up to three years for American bullfrog tadpoles to change into frogs.

Mating

This highly adaptable frog is the largest member of its family in North America, and is now established in other parts of the world, too.

WHERE IN THE WORLD?

Southeastern Canada, central and eastern USA. Has spread more widely across the continent, down to South America, and has been introduced into areas of Europe and Asia.

COLOURATION
Colouring is variable, depending on the individual and the temperature – colour darkens in the cold.

HIND LEGS
Hind legs are usually banded, as in this case.

TYMPANUM
This circular area is twice as big as the eye in males, but matches the size of the female's eye.

MOUTH
A wide gape allows these bullfrogs to take large prey.

POWERING AHEAD
These bullfrogs stay close to water, and will jump back into it on their powerful hind legs at any hint of danger.

HOW BIG IS IT?

Water Spider

• **ORDER** • Araneae • **FAMILY** • Agelenidae • **SPECIES** • *Argyroneta aquatica*

These air-breathing but aquatic spiders live completely under water, having evolved a way of obtaining air not unlike that used in the past by divers.

VITAL STATISTICS

LENGTH	0.9–1.5cm (0.35–0.59in); males often larger than females, which is unusual in spiders
SEXUAL MATURITY	Likely to be around 6 months
HATCHING PERIOD	Probably averages about 3 weeks
NUMBER OF EGGS	30–70, laid in the upper part of the female's bell
HABITAT	Under water, around aquatic plants
DIET	Small aquatic creatures, such as midges larvae, mayfly nymphs and water mites
LIFESPAN	Up to about 2 years

ANIMAL FACTS

Water spiders often remain hidden within their bell, using it as a retreat from where they can ambush their prey. They may sometimes come up to the water surface to obtain air to top up the oxygen supply in the bell. Generally, though, because of the osmotic pressure under water, carbon dioxide diffuses out and oxygen enters the bell from the surrounding water, making this unnecessary. These spiders live in calm water, so that their bell will not be swept away.

WHERE IN THE WORLD?

These spiders are widely distributed throughout Europe and into northern parts of Asia, including Japan. They also occur in Africa, north of the Sahara.

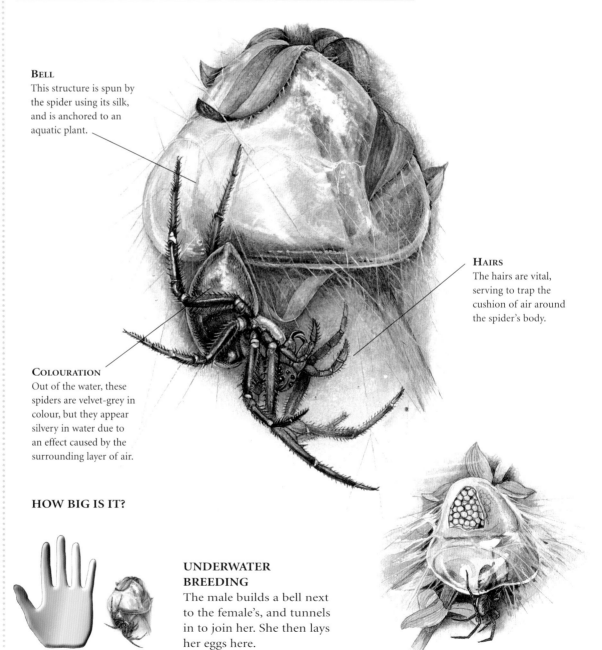

BELL
This structure is spun by the spider using its silk, and is anchored to an aquatic plant.

HAIRS
The hairs are vital, serving to trap the cushion of air around the spider's body.

COLOURATION
Out of the water, these spiders are velvet-grey in colour, but they appear silvery in water due to an effect caused by the surrounding layer of air.

Water spider's mouthparts

HOW BIG IS IT?

UNDERWATER BREEDING
The male builds a bell next to the female's, and tunnels in to join her. She then lays her eggs here.

European Garden Spider

• **ORDER** • Araneae • **FAMILY** • Araneidae • **SPECIES** • *Araneus diadematus*

This species is a member of the orb web family of spiders. Their large webs, often woven between bushes, are especially conspicuous in autumn.

VITAL STATISTICS

LENGTH	Males 0.4–0.8cm (0.15–0.31in); females 1–1.3cm (0.39–0.51in)
SEXUAL MATURITY	4 months
HATCHING PERIOD	About 9 months; laid in late summer and hatch about May in the UK
NUMBER OF EGGS	Around 500, laid in a cocoon
HABITAT	Gardens and open woodland
DIET	Medium-sized flying insects, including flies, wasps, bees and butterflies
LIFESPAN	1–2 years; the female dies soon after laying her eggs

ANIMAL FACTS

Incredibly agile, the European garden spider may lurk either in the centre of its web or on the periphery, waiting under a leaf. It will instantly react to any invertebrate that comes into contact with the web, running along its silken line to reach and overpower potential prey. The spider then injects venom and trusses up the creature in silk, giving it no opportunity for escape. The spiders themselves may in turn fall prey to birds, as well as lizards and amphibians.

When threatened, these spiders rear up

Widely distributed in Europe. Also present in North America, from Canada and the northwestern USA across to New England and southeastern areas.

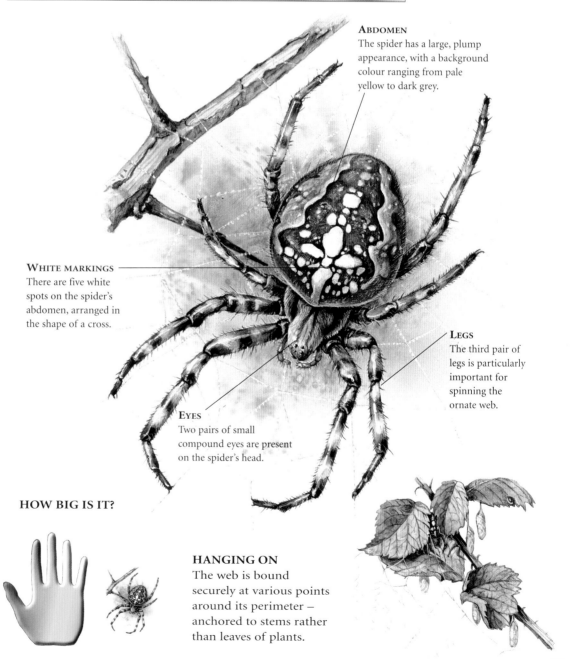

ABDOMEN
The spider has a large, plump appearance, with a background colour ranging from pale yellow to dark grey.

WHITE MARKINGS
There are five white spots on the spider's abdomen, arranged in the shape of a cross.

EYES
Two pairs of small compound eyes are present on the spider's head.

LEGS
The third pair of legs is particularly important for spinning the ornate web.

HOW BIG IS IT?

HANGING ON
The web is bound securely at various points around its perimeter – anchored to stems rather than leaves of plants.

Curved Spiny Spider

• ORDER • Araneae **• FAMILY •** Araneidae **• SPECIES •** *Gasteracantha arcuata*

VITAL STATISTICS

LENGTH	Up to 3cm (1.2in), from the tips of the spines; females larger
SEXUAL MATURITY	2–5 weeks
HATCHING PERIOD	Within 2 weeks
NUMBER OF EGGS	100–260
HABITAT	Wooded areas
DIET	Small flies and other invertebrates which enter the web
LIFESPAN	Up to 8 weeks. Females die after egg-laying, and males, soon after mating

ANIMAL FACTS

These strange-looking spiders are found in shrubs and build a typical orb-shaped web. They are protected by spines around the abdomen, and their overall body shape is flat. It may be that the long horns provide additional camouflage, breaking up the spider's outline so that it looks rather like an inanimate piece of vegetation. These arachnids are most likely to fall prey to birds, but they are also hunted and sold in mounted form as curios.

Bizarre and colourful, this arachnid is sometimes called the horned spider because of its unusual shape. It lives in wooded areas, usually occurring near water.

WHERE IN THE WORLD?

Southern parts of Asia, with its range extending from India, Sri Lanka and Myanmar eastwards to Singapore and Thailand, and through Indonesia to East Malaysia.

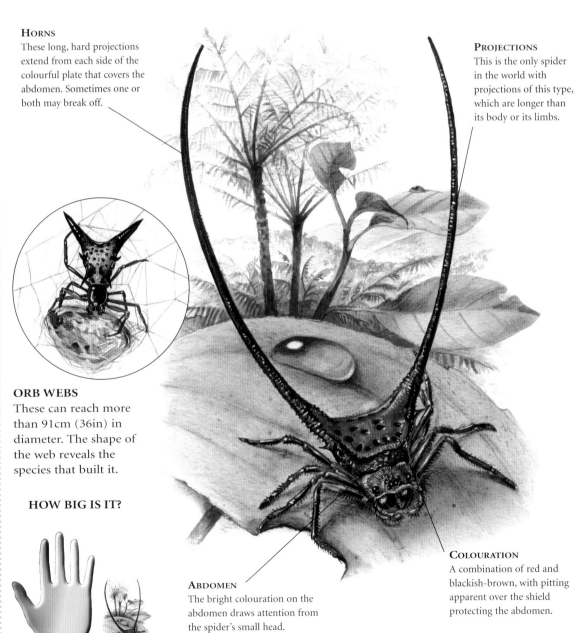

HORNS
These long, hard projections extend from each side of the colourful plate that covers the abdomen. Sometimes one or both may break off.

PROJECTIONS
This is the only spider in the world with projections of this type, which are longer than its body or its limbs.

ORB WEBS
These can reach more than 91cm (36in) in diameter. The shape of the web reveals the species that built it.

HOW BIG IS IT?

ABDOMEN
The bright colouration on the abdomen draws attention from the spider's small head.

COLOURATION
A combination of red and blackish-brown, with pitting apparent over the shield protecting the abdomen.

Trapdoor Spider

VITAL STATISTICS

LENGTH	1.6–2.3cm (0.63–0.90in); females larger
SEXUAL MATURITY	Within a year
HATCHING PERIOD	Young hatch in mother's burrow and are resident there for some time
NUMBER OF EGGS	Likely to be 50–100
HABITAT	Areas where burrows can be excavated easily
DIET	Larger invertebrates
LIFESPAN	Probably 1–3 years

ANIMAL FACTS

These spiders may incorporate an internal door into the structure of their burrow, to reduce the likelihood that they will be flooded out during periods of heavy rainfall. The burrow itself slopes backwards underground. In some cases, however, the entrance to the tunnel may simply look like a worm hole. A number of these spiders often live in close proximity to each other. They can occur in forested areas, but may also be encountered in gardens in some areas.

These spiders overcome their prey with venom

This spider family represents one of a number of different groups that do not build large webs, but rather hide away and ambush their prey.

WHERE IN THE WORLD?

Northwestern and southern parts of South America; southern Africa and Madagascar; the Iberian peninsula; Asia except the far north; Australia and New Zealand.

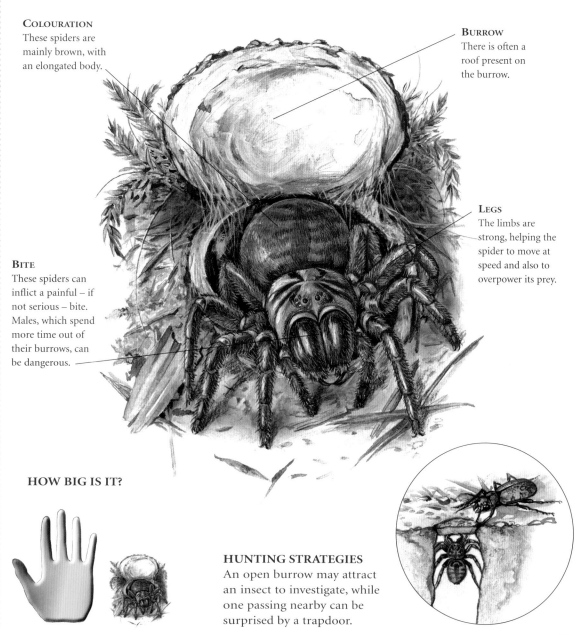

COLOURATION
These spiders are mainly brown, with an elongated body.

BURROW
There is often a roof present on the burrow.

LEGS
The limbs are strong, helping the spider to move at speed and also to overpower its prey.

BITE
These spiders can inflict a painful – if not serious – bite. Males, which spend more time out of their burrows, can be dangerous.

HOW BIG IS IT?

HUNTING STRATEGIES
An open burrow may attract an insect to investigate, while one passing nearby can be surprised by a trapdoor.

Mexican Red-Kneed Tarantula

• **ORDER** • Araneae • **FAMILY** • Theraphosidae • **SPECIES** • *Brachypelma smithi*

VITAL STATISTICS

WEIGHT	27–90g (0.06–0.2lb)
LENGTH	12.7–14.0cm (5–5.5in)
SEXUAL MATURITY	5–7 years
HATCHING PERIOD	2–8 weeks; young split up when they are 2–3 weeks old
NUMBER OF EGGS	Around 400, which are laid in an egg sac by the female
DIET	Hunts invertebrates, amphibians, rodents and small birds
LIFESPAN	Males live about 5 years, but females may have a lifespan of 25–50 years

ANIMAL FACTS

Territorial and solitary, these large spiders live underground in burrows. The relative humidity is much higher here, with dew forming each day at the entrance, providing the tarantula with fluid to avoid fatal dehydration. They emerge to hunt under cover of darkness, dragging their prey back to the burrow. The tips of their legs give them a good sensory insight into the dark world they inhabit. A female will lay her eggs in a burrow after the rainy season.

A female may kill the smaller male after mating

Although some tarantulas are arboreal by nature and live in the rainforests, the Mexican red-kneed is a terrestrial species, occurring in an arid environment.

WHERE IN THE WORLD?

Restricted to the Pacific coastal area of Mexico in central America, occurring in areas of scrubland and desert, where their habitat is being destroyed.

URTICATING HAIRS
These are shed easily and cause intense irritation, especially if they get into the eye.

MARKINGS
Exact patterning differs somewhat between individuals.

EYE CLUSTER
These tarantulas have eight eyes, looking both forwards and back, although their vision is not good.

MOUTHPARTS
These tarantulas can inflict a painful bite to overcome prey rapidly, although to humans this feels like a wasp sting.

HOW BIG IS IT?

OVERCOMING PREY

As long as the tarantula can sink its fangs into its victim, even if the creature is larger, the spider will win.

Southern Black Widow

• **ORDER** • Araneae • **FAMILY** • Theridiidae • **SPECIES** • *Latrodectus mactans*

Few spiders evoke greater fear than the black widow, because of its deadly venom. Luckily for people, it only releases a small volume.

VITAL STATISTICS

LENGTH	0.8–1.0cm (0.31–0.39in); males about half the size of females
SEXUAL MATURITY	About 3 months
HATCHING PERIOD	Young hatch in the egg case after 3 weeks, emerging 2–4 weeks later
NUMBER OF EGGS	100–300 per batch; females lay several in succession
HABITAT	May venture into homes
DIET	Assorted invertebrates, plus small vertebrates such as lizards and rodents
LIFESPAN	Males 1–2 months; females up to 3 years

ANIMAL FACTS

The black widow is found not just in grassland and woodland, but also quite commonly in urban areas. These spiders often seek shelter in outbuildings. They tend to live on their own, and the male will approach a female very cautiously when seeking to mate, tapping out a special code on the silk so he is not seen as prey. Aggression begins within the egg sac. After hatching here, less than one in 10 spiderlings survives to emerge, because of cannibalism.

WHERE IN THE WORLD?

Occurs in the southeastern parts of the USA, extending from New York down to Florida, and westwards as far as Oklahoma, Arizona and Texas.

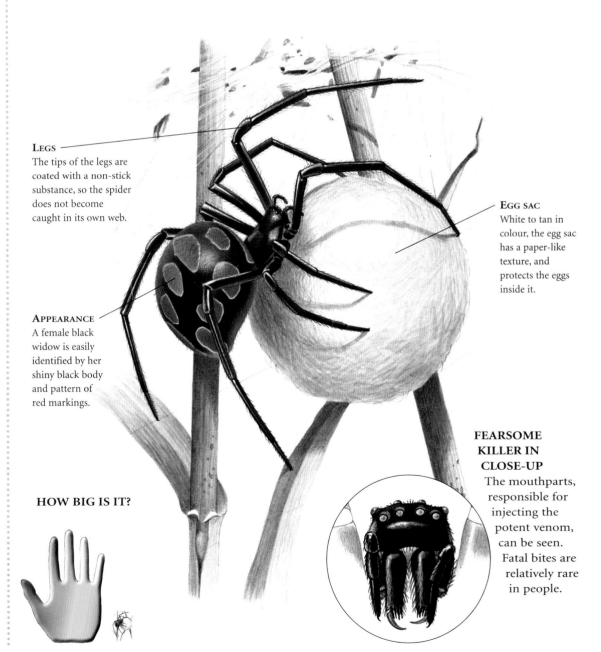

LEGS
The tips of the legs are coated with a non-stick substance, so the spider does not become caught in its own web.

EGG SAC
White to tan in colour, the egg sac has a paper-like texture, and protects the eggs inside it.

APPEARANCE
A female black widow is easily identified by her shiny black body and pattern of red markings.

FEARSOME KILLER IN CLOSE-UP
The mouthparts, responsible for injecting the potent venom, can be seen. Fatal bites are relatively rare in people.

HOW BIG IS IT?

The shape of the leg

Crab Spider

• **ORDER** • Araneae • **FAMILY** • Thomisidae

VITAL STATISTICS

LENGTH	Males 0.3–0.4cm (0.11–0.16in); females 0.9–1cm (0.35–0.39in)
SEXUAL MATURITY	6 months
HATCHING PERIOD	2 weeks for the eggs to hatch in their egg sac
NUMBER OF EGGS	Typically 45–500, depending on the species; sometimes guarded by the female
HABITAT	Variable, from desert to grassland
DIET	Insects such as bees, butterflies and hoverflies, which are attracted to flowers
LIFESPAN	1 year or less

ANIMAL FACTS

Crab spiders do not spin webs to catch their prey. Instead, they hunt by waiting on flowers to ambush unsuspecting insects. Their eyes serve as effective motion sensors, alerting them to the presence of prey. Crab spiders lack powerful jaws, but they can overcome creatures larger than themselves thanks to their potent venom. Having made a kill, these arachnids do not attempt to store their prey, but feed immediately and remain until the meal is finished.

Even stinging insects cannot escape

While the colouration of crab spiders may simply appear attractive to human eyes, it allows these spiders to trap their invertebrate prey more easily.

WHERE IN THE WORLD?

Widely distributed throughout the world, but with a restricted range in Greenland. The family overall is comprised of about 160 different genera and over 2000 species.

COLOURATION
Their colouration helps these spiders blend in amongst flowers. They can even change their colour to yellow.

BODY SHAPE
The overall appearance of these spiders is reminiscent of a crab.

EYES
The small eyes are critical in helping these spiders to locate prey.

LEGS
The first pairs are the longest, and held away from the body, enabling these spiders to walk backwards, straight ahead or sideways.

HOW BIG IS IT?

DIFFERENT STRATEGIES

A crab spider lowers itself into the pitcher of an insectivorous plant to seize an insect that has fallen in.

Pronghorn Antelope

• **ORDER** • Artiodactyla • **FAMILY** • Antilocapridae • **SPECIES** • *Antilocapra americana*

VITAL STATISTICS

WEIGHT	40–60kg (88–132lb); females lighter on average
LENGTH	130–150cm (52–60in)
SEXUAL MATURITY	About 15 months, but males do not actually breed until they are 3 years old
GESTATION PERIOD	About 235 days; mating takes place in mid-September
NUMBER OF OFFSPRING	1
DIET	Herbivorous, eating flowering plants, shrubs, grasses and even cacti
LIFESPAN	10–15 years maximum

ANIMAL FACTS

The pronghorn antelope is regarded as the fastest land mammal in the New World – able to attain a speed equivalent to some 80kph (50mph). This ability may have arisen because of its need to outpace the now-extinct American cheetah, which preyed on it. Remarkably though, these ungulates, with two toes on each foot, are unable to jump well. In the early twentieth century, their numbers had declined, but now populations have recovered thanks to protective measures.

During the Pleistocene epoch, which ended about 10,000 years ago, there were at least 12 different species in this family. Today, only the pronghorn itself survives.

WHERE IN THE WORLD?

Saskatchewan and Alberta in Canada, via southwestern Minnesota and central Texas, extending west to northeastern California and south into Mexico. Also found in Baja California.

EYES
The eyes are large and positioned high on the head, ensuring a good field of vision.

TAIL
The tail is short and relatively inconspicuous, white in colour like the rump area.

HORNS
The horns are very evident in males. The forward-pointing spur accounts for their name.

MALE MARKINGS
The black stripes running down the sides of the neck, plus the black mask on the face, are characteristic of male pronghorns.

Calves lie down to escape predators

HOW BIG IS IT?

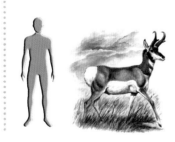

UNDER NOT OVER

Pronghorn antelopes will run under ranchers' fences at speed, instead of jumping them. They live in small groups in summer.

35

Impala

• ORDER • Artiodactyla **• FAMILY •** Bovidae **• SPECIES •** *Aepyceros melampus*

VITAL STATISTICS

WEIGHT	Around 45–80kg (100–176lb)
LENGTH	120–160cm (48–64in); males larger than females
SEXUAL MATURITY	2 years
GESTATION PERIOD	7–8 months; longer if conditions are harsh
NUMBER OF OFFSPRING	1; can be born at any time of year in equatorial Africa
DIET	Herbivorous, eating fresh grass when available, as well as leaves and shoots at other times
LIFESPAN	12–15 years maximum

The unusual name of this antelope is derived from the Zulu language, reflecting the native African name. They are generally seen in savanna areas.

WHERE IN THE WORLD?

East and southern Africa. From Kenya, Uganda and Tanzania southwards to Mozambique, northeastern South Africa and via Zimbabwe, Zambia and Botswana to Namibia and Angola.

ANIMAL FACTS

Impalas will instinctively feed both by grazing at ground level, and also by browsing on taller plants, particularly when grass is hard to find during dry spells of weather. They tend not to stray far from water. Males will establish territories with herds of females, and mating takes place at the end of the wet season. The female later breaks away from the herd, giving birth alone. Mother and fawn will then rejoin the group; weaning occurs about six months later.

HORNS
Only the male impala, known as a ram, has lyre-shaped horns. These can grow to 91cm (36in).

SENSES
Impalas have a keen sense of smell, hearing and eyesight.

COLOURATION
Reddish-brown with paler underparts and black markings.

LEGS
An impala can jump a distance of up to 9m (30ft), and leap up to 2.5m (8ft) into the air.

DANGEROUS ACQUAINTANCES
Cheetahs can outpace impalas. Lions, wild dogs and hyenas also represent a serious threat, especially if hunting in groups.

HOW BIG IS IT?

A clash of horns between males

Barbary Sheep

• ORDER • Artiodactyla **• FAMILY •** Bovidae **• SPECIES •** *Ammotragus lervia*

VITAL STATISTICS

WEIGHT	Females average 40–55kg (88–110lb); males average 100–145kg (220–320lb)
LENGTH	130–165cm (51–65in); females are smaller
SEXUAL MATURITY	2 years
GESTATION PERIOD	About 5½ months
NUMBER OF OFFSPRING	1–2 lambs, occasionally 3; ewes may produce two litters annually
DIET	Herbivorous, eats scrubby desert vegetation, including acacia shrub and lichen
LIFESPAN	About 10 years in the wild; 20 years in a zoo

ANIMAL FACTS

Originating from a part of the world where there is little natural cover, Barbary sheep rely on the colour of their coats to avoid detection. If necessary, these sheep are agile enough to jump up over 1.8m (6ft), away from danger. Males will battle each other ferociously at the start of the breeding season, although these are largely trials of strength.

Climbing a cliff face

These sheep are named after the area in which they occur, which used to be known as the Barbary coast. They are the only sheep native to Africa.

WHERE IN THE WORLD?

The mountainous area of the western Sahara, extending to Egypt and Sudan. Has also been introduced to Spain and parts of the USA, including Texas.

COLOURATION
Mainly sandy-brown, darkening with age.

HORNS
These grow away from the head, and then curve inwards, reaching up to 50cm (20in) in length.

FEET
The cloven hooves provide support when the sheep is climbing around on rocky outcrops.

BEARD
Only the male has this trailing shaggy area of hair extending down from the lower jaw on to the chest.

HOW BIG IS IT?

HEAD FOR HEIGHTS
Barbary sheep often frequent inaccessible rocky cliffs, sheltering there to avoid the heat of the desert sun at its hottest.

Springbok Antelope

• **ORDER** • Artiodactyla • **FAMILY** • Bovidae • **SPECIES** • *Antidorcas marsupialis*

VITAL STATISTICS

WEIGHT	32–45kg (70–100lb)
LENGTH	142–165cm (56–65in)
SEXUAL MATURITY	1–2 years
GESTATION PERIOD	About 171 days, with births most common between October and December at the start of the wet season, which triggers the growth of fresh vegetation
NUMBER OF OFFSPRING	1
DIET	Eats both grass and shrubs, according to the season
LIFESPAN	Maximum 7–10 years in the wild

ANIMAL FACTS

The unusual way in which springboks leap is intended to act as a distraction when there is a predator nearby. This display is described as 'pronking'. They are very social by nature, and live in herds of hundreds. Once one member of the group jumps, others will follow. They can spring up repeatedly, uttering a high-pitched alarm call at the same time. These gazelles are able to run fast from danger as well.

Evident eyelids

The name of these antelopes originates from the way they leap, springing up to 3.65m (12ft) in the air if they are frightened.

WHERE IN THE WORLD?

Restricted to southern parts of Africa, occurring in open country in Botswana, Namibia and southwestern parts of Angola, as well as South Africa.

HORNS
Both sexes have horns, but they are stouter and longer in adult males, growing up to 48cm (19in) in length.

HINDQUARTERS
This part of the springbok's body appears to be higher than the shoulders.

EARS
Long, narrow ears are a feature of these gazelles. The ears are also quite mobile, helping to detect potential danger.

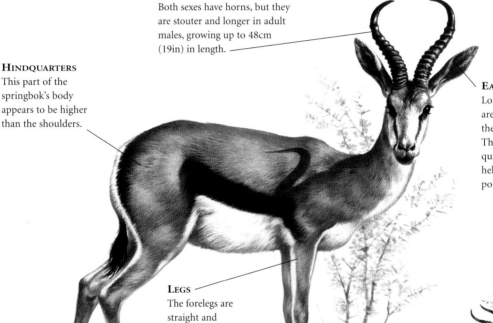

LEGS
The forelegs are straight and quite slender.

HOW BIG IS IT?

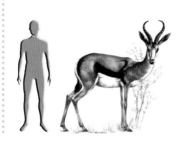

REACHING UP
By being able to support its weight on its hindquarters, the springbok is able to graze easily on branches.

American Bison

This species is now the largest North American mammal. Its ancestors crossed here from Asia about 10,000 years ago, when the continents were joined.

VITAL STATISTICS

WEIGHT	Females 318–544kg (700–1200lb); males 544–907kg (1200–2000lb)
LENGTH	Females 183–208cm (72–82in); males 274–409cm (108–161in)
SEXUAL MATURITY	4–5 years
GESTATION PERIOD	About 280 days
NUMBER OF OFFSPRING	1, although twins are recorded very occasionally
DIET	Grasses and associated plants, as well as sedges
LIFESPAN	Around 15 years in the wild; may live up to 25 in captivity

ANIMAL FACTS

Huge herds of American bison, better known in their homeland as buffalo, used to thunder across the plains, but they were wiped out by hunting during the 1800s. Part of the reason for this was an attempt by white settlers to subjugate the Native Americans by depriving them of a major food source. By the 1880s, there was a real risk of the American bison becoming extinct, but it was saved through the far-sightedness of a number of ranchers. Today, the population is around 350,000.

A young American bison calf

WHERE IN THE WORLD?

Formerly ranged from northwestern to central Canada, and southwards across most of the USA down into northern Mexico. Now largely confined to reserves.

HUMP
This raised area on the back is the result of longer spines on the thoracic vertebrate beneath.

HORNS
Horns are present on both sexes, but are usually wider, longer and less curved in bulls.

COLOURATION
The bison are usually brown or dark brown, but very rare white individuals do occur, considered sacred by the native North Americans.

BEARD
This is more profuse in the case of bulls.

HOW BIG IS IT?

TELLING THEM APART

When seen together, the male bison has a much more significant hump than the cow, which is also smaller in size.

European Bison

VITAL STATISTICS

WEIGHT	300–920kg (660–2020lb); bulls are heavier
LENGTH	240–400cm (95–158in), including tail
SEXUAL MATURITY	4–6 years; cows mature earlier
GESTATION PERIOD	Around 280 days
NUMBER OF OFFSPRING	Usually 1 calf, sometimes 2; weaned by 1 year old
DIET	Herbivorous, grazing on vegetation and also browsing on leaves and twigs
LIFESPAN	About 15 years; has lived for 28 years in captivity

ANIMAL FACTS

About 2000 years ago, the wisent – as the European bison is often known – ranged right across Europe and Asia from Britain to Siberia. However, persistent hunting pressure and forest clearance resulted in the species becoming extinct in the wild in 1927. All of today's surviving population, now numbering over 3000 individuals, traces its ancestry back to just a dozen survivors that were being kept in zoos. Reintroduction programmes started in 1951, and have proved successful.

A challenge to the existing order

40

These close relatives of the American bison differ in terms of their habitat, being forest-dwellers. They are also smaller in overall size.

WHERE IN THE WORLD?

Now present in suitable areas of habitat in northern and eastern Europe, extending to Kyrgyzstan and Ukraine, as the result of twentieth-century reintroductions.

HORNS
The horns are more fearsome than those of the American bison.

COAT
The coat is relatively short and less shaggy overall than that of the American bison.

MUSCULAR BUILD
Well-muscled forequarters help a bison to stand its ground and drive back an opponent.

TAIL
The tail acts as a switch to keep flies off the body. European bison have longer tails than their American counterparts.

HOW BIG IS IT?

SURVIVING IN SNOW
Bison must eat large amounts of vegetation. In winter, they can dig under snow, but often resort to gnawing bark.

Gaur

VITAL STATISTICS

WEIGHT	700–1000kg (1540–2200lb); cows are generally lighter
LENGTH	320–430cm (126–169in), including tail
SEXUAL MATURITY	2–3 years
GESTATION PERIOD	About 275 days; weaning occurs 7–9 months later
NUMBER OF OFFSPRING	Usually 1 calf, occasionally 2
DIET	Herbivorous, eating grass and other vegetation, as well as some fruit
LIFESPAN	Potentially up to 30 years

ANIMAL FACTS

When it comes to determining leadership of a herd, male gaurs rarely fight. Instead, the larger male is simply recognized as the dominant individual. Other adult males stay outside the herd, living on their own. These animals' great bulk also means that they can simply smash their way through the rainforest to escape danger if threatened. In areas where they have been hunted by people, gaurs have become nocturnal in their habits, making them harder to observe.

This Asiatic bovine is a giant – the largest of all the species of wild cattle. It has been domesticated in some parts of its range.

WHERE IN THE WORLD?

Throughout tropical parts of Asia, including India, Nepal, Bangladesh, Myanmar (Burma), south through Laos, Cambodia and Vietnam to peninsula Malaysia, and east to China.

HORNS
Horns are massive and curved, growing to a length of about 80cm (32in). They are located on the side, rather than the top of the head.

Horns are present in both sexes

HEIGHT
The shoulder height can exceed 200cm (79in), with those in the southeast of the range being the largest.

HOW BIG IS IT?

SOCIAL STRUCTURE
Gaurs generally live in groups, headed by a male.

DEFENSIVE POSTURE
The sheer size of the gaur proves a deterrent to most predators, but tigers will take on these huge mammals. They prefer to prey on weaker calves.

Water Buffalo

• **ORDER** • Artiodactyla • **FAMILY** • Bovidae • **SPECIES** • *Bubalus bubalis*

VITAL STATISTICS

WEIGHT	800–1200kg (1800–2600lb); females are lighter
LENGTH	240–300m (94–118in)
SEXUAL MATURITY	18 months
GESTATION PERIOD	300–340 days; weaning at 6–9 months
NUMBER OF OFFSPRING	Usually 1 calf; cows give birth every 2 years
DIET	Grass and aquatic vegetation, thus helping to prevent waterways becoming clogged
LIFESPAN	Up to 25 years in the wild, and as long as 29 in captivity

ANIMAL FACTS

Water buffalo were first domesticated thousands of years ago, probably in India. They now play a vital part in the rural economies of Southeast Asia, but unfortunately they also represent a major threat to the survival of their wild ancestor because of cross-breeding. There are currently believed to be fewer than 4000 pure water buffalo left throughout Asia. Strict segregation in reserves seems to be the only hope of ensuring the survival of this species.

Water buffalo can swim

The wild form of this species was the ancestor of the domestic water buffalo, but it is now considered to be in danger of extinction.

WHERE IN THE WORLD?

Populations survive in parts of India, Pakistan, Bangladesh, Nepal, Bhutan, Myanmar (Burma) and Thailand, plus the border region between Laos, Vietnam and Cambodia.

COLOURATION
Water buffalo are dark in colour.

HORNS
The span of the horns, from tip to tip, is wider than in any other bovid, typically measuring more than 2m (6.5ft).

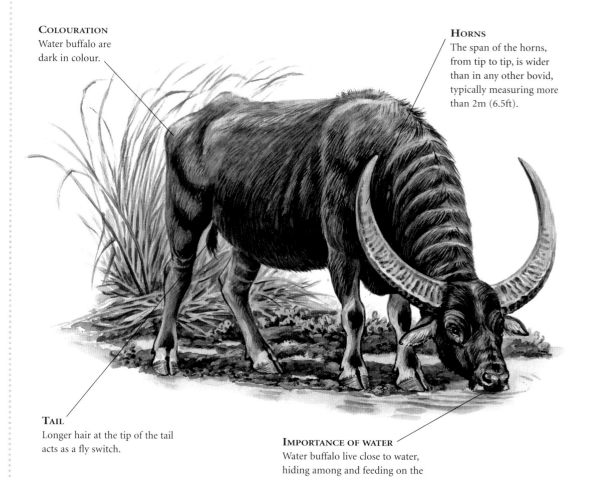

TAIL
Longer hair at the tip of the tail acts as a fly switch.

IMPORTANCE OF WATER
Water buffalo live close to water, hiding among and feeding on the lush vegetation.

HOW BIG IS IT?

HEALTHY BATHING
Wallowing in water keeps the water buffalo cool and its skin healthy. Birds will peck off larger parasites such as ticks.

Bezoar Ibex

• ORDER • Artiodactyla **• FAMILY •** Bovidae **• SPECIES •** *Capra aegagrus*

VITAL STATISTICS

WEIGHT	70–80kg (154–176lb); females are lighter
LENGTH	120–160cm (48–63in)
SEXUAL MATURITY	Females 1.5–2.5 years; males 3.5–4 years
GESTATION PERIOD	About 160 days
NUMBER OF OFFSPRING	Normally 1 kid, but occasionally 2
DIET	Herbivorous, browsing on a wide range of vegetation
LIFESPAN	Around 12 years in the wild; can be up to 22 in captivity

ANIMAL FACTS

These goats live at relatively high altitudes, on craggy cliffs and upland pastures. They may occasionally congregate in large herds numbering up to 500, although more typical groups consist of five to 20 individuals. Mating occurs from autumn through to mid-winter, and at this stage, males become far more aggressive towards each other, battling with their horns. Herds are also likely to move down to lower levels during the winter, as food may be easier to find there.

These ibexes can jump too

This species is considered to be the original ancestor of the domestic goat. Domestication began between 8000 and 9000 years ago in southwestern Asia.

WHERE IN THE WORLD?

Western Asia, occurring in the Anatolian region of Turkey as well as northeastern Iraq, Iran, western Afghanistan, the eastern Cacucasus and far south of Turkmenistan.

HORNS
Males have very long, curved horns, measuring up to 165cm (65in). Those of females are shorter.

COAT
The coat changes colour throughout the year, being more reddish-brown in the summer.

BEARD
A very distinctive long, black beard is present on the chin of mature males.

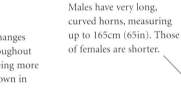

THE HIGH LIFE

Bezoar ibex will use their climbing skills to reach and browse on leaves and shoots growing well off the ground.

HOW BIG IS IT?

CALLOUSES
These hardened areas of skin form on the knees and sometimes on the chest.

Alpine Ibex

VITAL STATISTICS

WEIGHT	40–120kg (88–264lb); males can be twice as heavy as females
LENGTH	90–200cm (35–79in), including tail
SEXUAL MATURITY	Females breed from 1 year; males from 2 years
GESTATION PERIOD	Typically 165–170 days
NUMBER OF OFFSPRING	Usually 1 kid, occasionally 2
DIET	Herbivorous, eating grass, flowers, moss, leaves and twigs
LIFESPAN	10–14 years

ANIMAL FACTS

The appearance of this species is influenced by the Alpine climate. They will often seek out southern-facing slopes at lower altitudes during the winter, where food is easier to find. This is also when herds of females are joined by males. The sexes live separately for the rest of the year.

Going down safely

Climbing up

Alpine ibexes can jump well, even when they are as young as two days old. This helps to ensure their survival in the mountainous terrain they inhabit.

WHERE IN THE WORLD?

Lives in the European Alps, from the border area between France and Italy, eastwards through Switzerland to Austria, at altitudes of 1600–3200m (5100–10,200ft).

PLAYFUL FIGHTING
Males will often rear up and joust with their horns.

HORNS
The male has ridges on the horns, which can grow to 100cm (40in) long.

COAT
Males over 7 years old develop a dark chestnut-brown winter coat.

JUMPING STRENGTH
The strength of these ibexes lies in the muscular power of their hind legs.

HOW BIG IS IT?

Southern Serow

• ORDER • Artiodactyla **• FAMILY •** Bovidae **• SPECIES •** *Capricornis sumatraensis*

VITAL STATISTICS

WEIGHT	85–140kg (187–309lb)
LENGTH	165cm (65in), including tail; no marked difference between sexes
SEXUAL MATURITY	From about 2.5 years
GESTATION PERIOD	217–248 days
NUMBER OF OFFSPRING	Usually 2; young remain with their mother for about a year
DIET	Feeds on a wide range of vegetation, usually preferring to browse on leaves
LIFESPAN	10–15 years

ANIMAL FACTS

Solitary by nature, serows generally seek food in the early morning and at dusk, but rest during the day. They have been heavily hunted, because of a belief that their tissue has medicinal value. In spite of being given official protection, the illicit trade in their body parts continues. This has meant that in some areas, such as Thailand, they are now rarely observed outside protected reserves. The destruction of their habitat has contributed to their decline.

The horns are a formidable defence

One of the more unusual features of the southern serow is its swimming ability. This probably explains why it has successfully colonized various islands.

WHERE IN THE WORLD?

Ranges from India eastwards to southern China, also occurring in southeastern Asia, across Thailand and Malaysia to the island of Sumatra.

HORNS
Horns in both sexes curve backwards to sharp points. They can measure up to 28cm (11in) in males.

MANE
A long, shaggy mane of lighter hair runs down the back, extending beyond the shoulders.

GLAND
There is a large gland, called a tear pocket, which extends down the face from the corner of each eye.

LEGS
The legs are quite slender and relatively long, compared with the length of the body.

HOW BIG IS IT?

UP ABOVE
These serows frequent areas of open forest with limestone cliffs. They are adept at jumping and climbing in this terrain.

Blue Wildebeest

• **ORDER** • Artiodactyla • **FAMILY** • Bovidae • **SPECIES** • *Connochaetes taurinus*

VITAL STATISTICS

WEIGHT	140–290kg (309–638lb)
LENGTH	230–340cm (91–134in), including tail
SEXUAL MATURITY	Females 1.5–2.5 years; males 3–4 years
GESTATION PERIOD	248–262 days
NUMBER OF OFFSPRING	A single youngster, typically weaned by 4 months
DIET	Herbivorous, grazing on grass
LIFESPAN	15–20 years maximum

ANIMAL FACTS

Life for a blue wildebeest is hazardous and potentially short, as they face many predators on the open plains. The young are therefore born in an advanced state of development – up on their feet and walking within just 15 minutes of birth. Adults can sprint at about 80kph (50mph) over short distances. They can also jump well. Some herds migrate long distances, in groups of up to 1000 individuals.

Blue wildebeest

Black wildebeest

In spite of its name, the blue wildebeest's colour is variable, and can even be brownish-grey. It is also known as the brindled gnu.

WHERE IN THE WORLD?

Found in grassland and savanna regions in various parts of East Africa, from Kenya down to northern South Africa, and eastwards to Angola and eastern Namibia.

BANDING
These barred markings can be mistaken for wrinkles in the skin from a distance.

HORNS
Horns are longer in males, measuring up to 83cm (in).

TAIL
The hair in the tail is black and very long, similar to that of a horse.

A CALF
All young blue wildebeests are tawny-brown at first; their colour changes from around two months.

MASS BIRTHING
Young are born all together about two weeks before the rains arrive. This helps many elude predators and means there is fresh grass to graze on.

HOW BIG IS IT?

Topi Antelope

• ORDER • Artiodactyla **• FAMILY •** Bovidae **• SPECIES •** *Damaliscus korrigum*

VITAL STATISTICS

WEIGHT	130–170kg (287–375lb); females are lighter
LENGTH	213cm (84in), including tail
SEXUAL MATURITY	Females from 1.5 years; males from 3 years, but will not compete to breed for at least another year
GESTATION PERIOD	About 248 days
NUMBER OF OFFSPRING	A single youngster, typically weaned by 1 year old
DIET	Herbivorous, grazing exclusively on grass
LIFESPAN	12–15 years average

ANIMAL FACTS

Topis prefer flood plains to drier ground, as they are more likely to find fresh, lush grass growing there. They are very social by nature, occurring in groups averaging around 20, although herds of up to 100 individuals have been recorded when migrating. Males will fight to control groups of females. When running, topis have a bounding gait and are considered to be the fastest of all ungulates. The topi is also known as the tsessebe.

A watchful male

This antelope is unusual in several ways. Most notably, if a female detects danger when in labour, she can simply delay the birthing process and run off.

WHERE IN THE WORLD?

Ranging from Senegal to Ethiopia and down to South Africa, the species is especially numerous in southern Sudan and Tanzania, in the Serengeti National Park.

EARS
The long, flexible ears provide good hearing, to warn of potential predators such as lions and leopards.

HORNS
Horns are ringed and lyre-shaped, growing to about 53cm (21in) long.

MOUTHPARTS
The jaws are narrow, reflecting the fact that these antelopes feed only on grass.

COLOURATION
Topis are instantly recognizable by the distinctive dark markings on their bodies. Females tend to be lighter in colour.

A MUD BATH
Topis will roll in damp mud, smearing it all over their bodies, probably as a means of keeping cool.

HOW BIG IS IT?

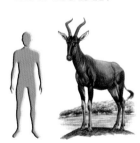

Thomson's Gazelle

• **ORDER** • Artiodactyla • **FAMILY** • Bovidae • **SPECIES** • *Eudorcas thomsonii*

VITAL STATISTICS

WEIGHT	13–30kg (29–66lb); males are heavier
LENGTH	106–142cm (42–56in), including tail; up to 90cm (35in) tall
SEXUAL MATURITY	Females 8–14 months; males 11–12 months
GESTATION PERIOD	155–186 days; weaned 4 months later
NUMBER OF OFFSPRING	1
DIET	Herbivorous, feeding on grass, but will eat other vegetation
LIFESPAN	10–15 years in the wild; up to 20 in captivity

ANIMAL FACTS

These gazelles rank amongst the fastest on the African plains, able to run at speeds of up to 80kph (50mph). Even so, they can be outpaced by cheetahs, although only over short distances. Fawns are especially vulnerable to predation, and roughly half of them die before reaching maturity. It may be due to this precarious existence that female Thomson's gazelles can give birth twice rather than once a year.

This characteristic leaping is described as 'stotting'

It is not uncommon to see these gazelles alongside other grazing animals such as zebra, and they can sometimes form a strong bond with particular individuals.

WHERE IN THE WORLD?

Occurs in East Africa, in Ethiopia, Sudan, and particularly in the serengeti grassland areas of southern and central Kenya and northern Tanzania.

HORNS
The horns spiral along their length, with the tips pointing forwards. They are much longer in males, measuring up to 30cm (12in).

EARS
Ears are long and set well back on the head; they have black insides.

COLOURATION
Light brown, with distinctive black stripes on the sides, and white underparts.

FACIAL FEATURES
The eyes are encircled with white markings, forming a stripe down the nose.

HOW BIG IS IT?

COURTSHIP

Male Thomson's gazelles begin establishing their territories from two years old. Herds of females will move through the male's territory.

Dorcas Gazelle

• **ORDER** • Artiodactyla • **FAMILY** • Bovidae • **SPECIES** • *Gazella dorcas*

Agile and fast, these gazelles are well-adapted to life in the desert. They can go their whole lives without drinking, obtaining adequate fluid from their food.

VITAL STATISTICS

WEIGHT	15–20kg (33–44lb)
LENGTH	105–130cm (41–51in), including tail
SEXUAL MATURITY	Females 9 months; males 1.5 years
GESTATION PERIOD	About 186 days; young then conceal themselves for up to 6 weeks
NUMBER OF OFFSPRING	A single youngster, occasionally 2; weaned by 3 months
DIET	Herbivorous, eating grasses, leaves and desert succulents
LIFESPAN	12 years maximum

ANIMAL FACTS

These gazelles often travel long distances in search of food in areas where there has been recent rainfall. The sexes frequently form separate herds, although males are territorial, especially during the mating period. They use their dung to mark out their range, and also rely on urine for scent-marking. When danger is detected, Dorcas gazelles utter an uncharacteristic duck-like quack through the nose, which inflates temporarily while the sound is being uttered.

The tail is used for signalling

WHERE IN THE WORLD?

Present throughout northern parts of Africa, occurring in the Sahara region, down to the horn of Africa and ranging eastwards across the Arabian peninsula.

MALE HORNS
Horns of the male are more curved and larger than in the female, growing up to 38cm (15in).

EARS
Large ears help detect sound in the still desert environment.

FEMALE HORNS
Females have narrower, straighter horns, measuring 25cm (10in).

COAT
Pale colour blends in with their sandy environment, providing camouflage. Their white underparts may reflect heat.

HOW BIG IS IT?

STAYING ALIVE
Living where there is little – if any – cover, Dorcas gazelles must rely on their agility and speed to escape predators.

Himalayan Tahr

• **ORDER** • Artiodactyla • **FAMILY** • Bovidae • **SPECIES** • *Hemitragus jemlahicus*

VITAL STATISTICS

WEIGHT	36–90kg (79–189lb)
LENGTH	99–152cm (40–60in), including tail
SEXUAL MATURITY	2–3 years; mating occurs from October to January
GESTATION PERIOD	About 217 days
NUMBER OF OFFSPRING	A single youngster, occasionally 2; weaned by 6 months
DIET	Herbivorous, eating grasses, leaves and flowers
LIFESPAN	Up to 10 years in the wild, but can be over 20 in captivity

ANIMAL FACTS

Himalayan tahrs typically live in herds of around 15 individuals, although old males can be seen on their own, probably after being driven out by younger rivals. Males will fight for dominance, wrestling with their horns in a trial of strength. Very alert, tahrs will disappear readily at any hint of danger, jumping over the rough terrain without difficulty.

Male

Female

50

Occurring in rugged countryside on the slopes of the Himalayan mountain range, this tahr is most likely to be encountered in wooded areas.

WHERE IN THE WORLD?

Found naturally in Asia, in the vicinity of the Himalayan mountains, extending from Kashmir to Sikkim. It has now also been introduced to New Zealand.

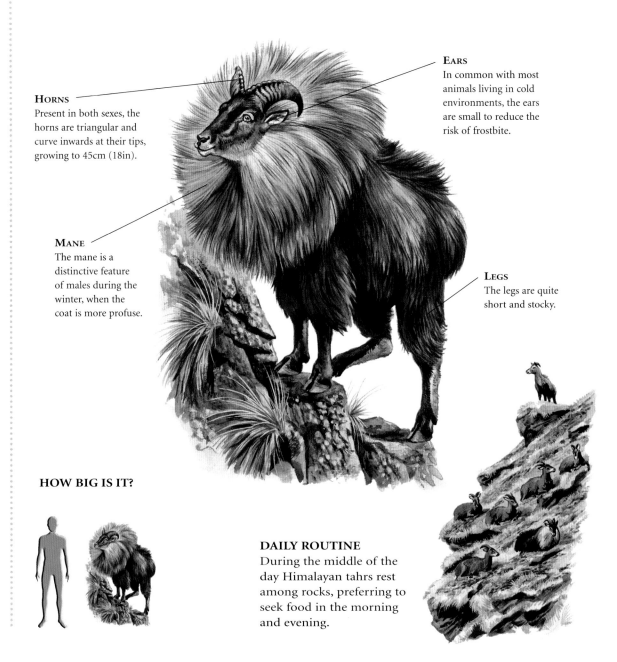

HORNS
Present in both sexes, the horns are triangular and curve inwards at their tips, growing to 45cm (18in).

MANE
The mane is a distinctive feature of males during the winter, when the coat is more profuse.

EARS
In common with most animals living in cold environments, the ears are small to reduce the risk of frostbite.

LEGS
The legs are quite short and stocky.

HOW BIG IS IT?

DAILY ROUTINE
During the middle of the day Himalayan tahrs rest among rocks, preferring to seek food in the morning and evening.

Sable Antelope

VITAL STATISTICS

WEIGHT	190–270kg (420–595lb)
LENGTH	230–330cm (91–130in), including tail
SEXUAL MATURITY	2–3 years; weaned at 8 months
GESTATION PERIOD	About 279 days; births coincide with the rainy season
NUMBER OF OFFSPRING	A single youngster; lies hidden after birth for 10 days
DIET	Herbivorous, eating grasses, leaves and flowers
LIFESPAN	Up to 17 years in the wild; may reach 20 in captivity

ANIMAL FACTS

The word 'sable' is the heraldic term for 'black', and was applied in this case to describe the predominant colour of the male. They will challenge each other for the right to lead a herd. The males will wrestle with their horns, undertaking trials of strength – with their forelegs held down on the ground – rather than seeking to inflict serious injury. If threatened by a predator such as a leopard, however, a sable antelope will aim to cripple its opponent.

Males in typical combat posture

These large antelopes can be dangerous when cornered, although they can run away quickly – at speeds of 57kph (35mph) – if chased by a predator.

WHERE IN THE WORLD?

Found in southeast Africa, from Kenya to northern South Africa, where it has been reintroduced over a wider area. There is an isolated population in Angola.

HORNS
The semi-circular horns can reach 165cm (66in) in mature males, and up to 100cm (40in) in females.

COLOURATION
Males are predominantly black, while females and young of both sexes are brown.

MANE
This thick area of hair on the neck could protect against attack by lions or leopards.

UNDERPARTS
The underparts of the body are white.

FIGHT NOT FLIGHT
When challenged, a sable antelope can prove to be quite fierce and determined, often standing its ground rather than running away.

HOW BIG IS IT?

51

Kirk's Dik-Dik

• **ORDER** • Artiodactyla • **FAMILY** • Bovidae • **SPECIES** • *Madoqua kirkii*

VITAL STATISTICS

WEIGHT	2.7–6.5kg (5.9–14.3lb)
LENGTH	59–83cm (23–32.5in), including the tail
SEXUAL MATURITY	Females from 6–8 months and males between 8–9 months
GESTATION PERIOD	From 155–186 days, with births occurring in two main periods annually
NUMBER OF OFFSPRING	1
DIET	Herbivorous, eating grasses, leaves and flowers. Actively seeks out salt, although less inclined to drink, obtaining moisture from its food
LIFESPAN	About 10 years

ANIMAL FACTS

These small antelopes face many predators – not just mammals but also reptiles such as pythons, and eagles which prey particularly on unsuspecting young. A female dik-dik will initially hide her new-born offspring to protect it from predators. Only once the youngster is at least two weeks old will it be strong enough to join its parents, and sprint if required. Dik-diks run in an unusual zig-zag pattern when being pursued, as they head towards cover.

The scent gland is located below the eye

The unusual name of these small, shy antelopes stems from the dik-dik sound of their alarm call, uttered when disturbed out in the open.

WHERE IN THE WORLD?

Mainly in East Africa, from Somalia south through Kenya and Malawi. There is also a totally separate western population occurring in Angola and Namibia.

GLANDS
Dik-diks use secretions from special glands near the eyes as a way of marking their territory.

LEGS
Narrow, athletic legs help these antelopes to be nimble on their feet.

HORNS
Only the male has horns, which measure just 11.4cm (4.5in) in length, with a forelock of longer hair between them.

STAYING TOGETHER
Dik-diks pair for life, occupying the same territory and marking the boundaries with dung. The male drives off would-be intruders.

HOW BIG IS IT?

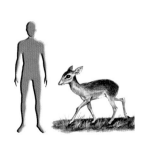

Rocky Mountain Goat

• ORDER • Artiodactyla **• FAMILY •** Bovidae **• SPECIES •** *Oreamnos americanus*

VITAL STATISTICS

WEIGHT	57–69kg (126–152lb)
LENGTH	150–165cm (59–65in), including tail
SEXUAL MATURITY	About 1.5 years
GESTATION PERIOD	175–180 days
NUMBER OF OFFSPRING	Normally 1 kid, although 2 or 3 have been recorded
DIET	Grazes on grass and lichens, and also browses on taller plants
LIFESPAN	Females up to 18 years; males 14 years maximum

ANIMAL FACTS

The lives of these goats are markedly influenced by the changing seasons. During summer they can be observed in small groups or wandering individually, but in winter they form larger herds. Mating takes place at this stage, with the young born during the early summer when conditions will be more favourable. Conflict is most likely to arise between males during the breeding season, but instead of battling head-on, they can inflict serious – if not fatal – wounds by goring their opponent's flanks.

The ancestors of this species crossed into northwestern North America from Asia about 18,000 years ago, when the Bering land bridge connected the continents.

WHERE IN THE WORLD?

Southern Alaska, and northwestern Canada, down across the US border, southwards to Utah and Colorado, through the Rocky Mountains. Introduced in some areas.

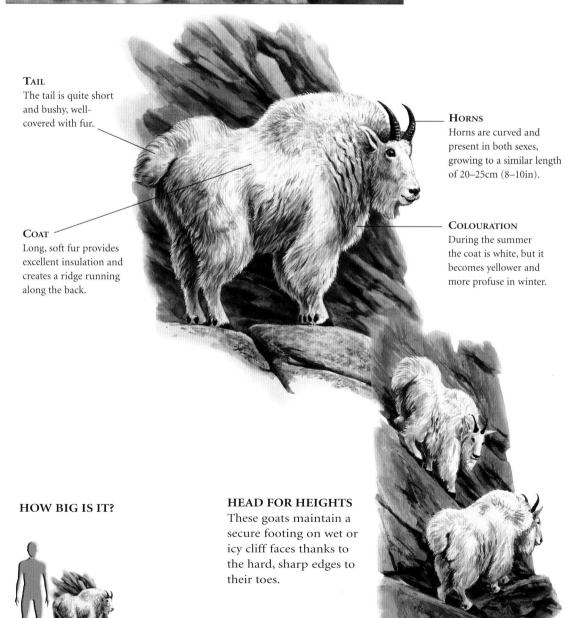

TAIL
The tail is quite short and bushy, well-covered with fur.

COAT
Long, soft fur provides excellent insulation and creates a ridge running along the back.

HORNS
Horns are curved and present in both sexes, growing to a similar length of 20–25cm (8–10in).

COLOURATION
During the summer the coat is white, but it becomes yellower and more profuse in winter.

HOW BIG IS IT?

HEAD FOR HEIGHTS
These goats maintain a secure footing on wet or icy cliff faces thanks to the hard, sharp edges to their toes.

Underside of the toes, showing stopper pads behind

Arabian Oryx

VITAL STATISTICS

WEIGHT	65–70kg (143–154lb)
LENGTH	205–220cm (81–87in), including tail
SEXUAL MATURITY	1.5–2 years
GESTATION PERIOD	255–270 days
NUMBER OF OFFSPRING	1; weaning occurs after 3.5 months
DIET	Grazes on grass and browses on leaves and shoots
LIFESPAN	Up to 20 years in captivity; shorter in the wild

ANIMAL FACTS

The case of the Arabian oryx is a heartening conservation success story. The species was hunted to extinction after World War II, finally disappearing from the wild in 1972. Luckily, there were some 500 of the animals in zoos, and captive breeding has since resulted in its reintroduction to parts of its former range, starting in 1982. This continues, with 100 Arabian oryx released in the United Arab Emirates throughout 2007, as part of a plan to return 500 to the wild there by 2012.

Drinking at a water hole

Originating from a very arid region, the ability of the Arabian oryx to detect rainfall – and thereby fresh grazing – in a particular area is truly amazing.

WHERE IN THE WORLD?

Range once extended through Syria, Iraq, Jordan, Israel and the Arabian peninsula. Now released back into the wild in several countries, including Jordan, UAE and Oman.

HORNS
Ridged horns are present in both sexes. They can reach 68cm (28in) in length.

HEAD MARKINGS
Distinctive patterning on the face, below the eyes and above the nose, identifies this species.

TAIL
The tail has a darker underside than upperside, with longer hair.

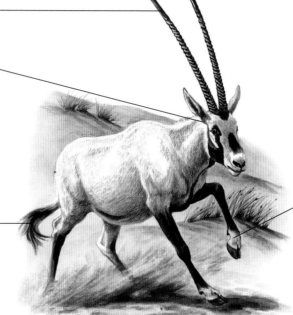

LEGS
The legs are dark in colour, apart from 'ankle bands' of white hair above the hoofs.

POSTURING
In spite of their fierce appearance, Arabian oryx are not aggressive. They communicate using the positioning of their horns.

HOW BIG IS IT?

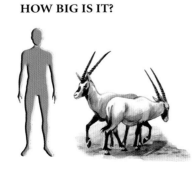

Oribi Gazelle

VITAL STATISTICS

WEIGHT	15–21kg (33–46lb)
LENGTH	92–140cm (36–55in)
SEXUAL MATURITY	Females 10 months; males 14 months
GESTATION PERIOD	200–215 days
NUMBER OF OFFSPRING	1; weaning occurs after 3.5 months
DIET	Grazes on grass and browses on leaves and shoots
LIFESPAN	Up to 14 years in captivity; shorter in the wild

ANIMAL FACTS

Oribi live in small groups all year round, either as individual pairs or a male with two or three females. Their size means that they are vulnerable to a wide range of predators, from genets to pythons. As a result, they rely on camouflage to protect themselves, freezing in position in the grass in the hope of being overlooked. When they run, they engage in an unusual behaviour called stotting, which entails jumping up into the air every few paces.

Only male oribi have horns

These graceful gazelles are denizens of grassland areas throughout Africa. They can be recognized at a glance by the white crescent over each eye.

WHERE IN THE WORLD?

Extensive distribution in suitable habitat right across Africa south of the Sahara, essentially absent only from Liberia, Equatorial Guinea and Gabon.

EYELASHES
Prominent eyelashes help prevent eye injuries when the gazelles are in tall grass.

COLOURATION
A clear division exists between the orange-brown upperparts, and the white on the underparts.

GLANDS
A distinctive large, rounded glandular patch is present below each ear; this produces scent for territorial marking.

TAIL
The tail is short and bushy, with a colour scheme matching that of the body.

ESCAPING DANGER
Unexpectedly jumping off the ground confuses a predator such as this baboon, when it is trying to catch the gazelle.

HOW BIG IS IT?

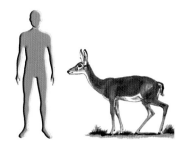

Musk Ox

VITAL STATISTICS

WEIGHT	180–380kg (396–836lb)
LENGTH	210–259cm (83–102in), including tail
SEXUAL MATURITY	Females 3–4 years; males 5–6 years
GESTATION PERIOD	About 255 days
NUMBER OF OFFSPRING	Generally 1, occasionally twins; weaning occurs at 10–18 months
DIET	Grazes on grass and sedges, and browses on shrubs
LIFESPAN	Typically 20–24 years

ANIMAL FACTS

The musk ox undertakes what is known as reverse migration, heading not to more sheltered lowland areas at the approach of the bitter Arctic winter, but out to the bleak, exposed uplands, where winds blow snow away. This allows them to find grazing. Their presence here often attracts wolves, hoping to overpower a young calf. If threatened, however, the adults form a circle, corralling the calves in the centre. This often deters any attack, as they can kill wolves with their horns.

Although it looks rather like a bison, the musk ox is actually a closer relative of sheep and goats, in spite of its huge bulk.

WHERE IN THE WORLD?

Occurs in parts of western and northern Alaska, through northern Canada west of Hudson Bay, up to Greenland, where it is more widespread in western areas.

HORNS
The horns are low-set on the central area over the top of the head, called the boss.

COAT
Individual hairs may measure up to 61cm (24in), virtually trailing down to the ground.

LEGS
The legs are free of longer hair, helping the musk ox to move through snow more easily.

STAYING SAFE
An adult charges out from the circle with its head down, directly at the wolves, while others maintain the defensive shield around the young.

HOW BIG IS IT?

Female (left) and male (right)

Argali (Mountain Sheep)

• **ORDER** • Artiodactyla • **FAMILY** • Bovidae • **SPECIES** • *Ovis ammon*

VITAL STATISTICS

WEIGHT	65–180kg (143–396lb)
LENGTH	134–214cm (53–84in), including tail
SEXUAL MATURITY	Females about 2 years; males 5 years
GESTATION PERIOD	150–160 days; weaning occurs at about 4 months
NUMBER OF OFFSPRING	Typically 1, although occasionally twins are born
DIET	Herbivorous, grazing on grass, sedges and other vegetation
LIFESPAN	10–13 years

ANIMAL FACTS

The massive horns of the rams have led to these sheep being heavily hunted in some areas, but the major threat to their survival is actually loss of habitat to their domestic relatives. Herds are targeted by wolves and snow leopards, while newborn lambs are easy targets for eagles and other birds of prey. Mating occurs in the early winter, and ewes give birth the following spring. The name 'argali' is the native Mongolian word for these sheep.

The argali is the largest species of wild sheep in the world, standing 120cm (47in) tall at the shoulder. Unfortunately, it is also endangered.

WHERE IN THE WORLD?

Occurs throughout upland areas of central Asia and northern India, at altitudes of 1300–6100m (4200–19,500ft). Present in the Himalayan region, extending east to Mongolia.

HORNS
Males have huge corkscrew horns that can measure 190cm (75in) overall. Those of females are much smaller.

COLOURATION
Colour is variable, ranging from buff to greyish-brown on the upperparts, and white on the underparts.

FACE
The face is completely white; small ears are located beneath the horns.

HOOVES
The hooves ensure these sheep do not slip when climbing in their rocky habitat.

HOW BIG IS IT?

Argali live in single-sex groups when not breeding

MATERNAL BEHAVIOUR
A ewe goes off alone to give birth, remaining with her offspring for several days before they return to the flock.

Bighorn Sheep

• ORDER • Artiodactyla **• FAMILY •** Bovidae **• SPECIES •** *Ovis canadensis*

VITAL STATISTICS

WEIGHT	45–135kg (99–297lb)
LENGTH	160–210cm (63–83in), including tail
SEXUAL MATURITY	Females about 2.5 years; males about 3 years, but often do not breed until they are older
GESTATION PERIOD	About 175 days; weaning occurs at 4–6 months
NUMBER OF OFFSPRING	1
DIET	Herbivorous, grazing mainly on grass, but also on herbs and other small plants
LIFESPAN	Up to 14 years

ANIMAL FACTS

Horn size plays a key part in the social structure of these sheep. Males with the largest horns are unchallenged, but where two males are well-matched in horn size, they will battle for their place in the social hierarchy of the herd. Living in a mountainous region, bighorn sheep are very agile, proving extremely sure-footed, and able to climb and jump without difficulty. A more unusual characteristic of this species is that they are strong swimmers.

Young bighorn sheep will lie down to avoid predators such as eagles

Occurring in suitable mountainous habitat across their extensive range, individual bighorn sheep populations tend to remain localized rather than mixing together.

WHERE IN THE WORLD?

Distribution centred on the Rocky Mountains in North America, extending from British Columbia and Alberta, western Canada, down to eastern parts of Baja California.

FEMALE HORNS
These are far less developed than those of the male, slimmer and carried above the top of the skull.

MALE HORNS
The horns of the male are massive, growing backwards and then curling forwards below the level of the top of the head.

COAT
The brownish colouration on the body varies between different populations.

HORN GROWTH
The horns grow gradually in the male, and a second curl may start to develop in individuals from about eight years old.

HOW BIG IS IT?

Mouflon

VITAL STATISTICS

WEIGHT	35–50kg (89-110lb); males are heavier
LENGTH	127–195cm (50–77in), including tail; up to 90cm (35in) tall
SEXUAL MATURITY	1 year, but may not breed for a further 2 years
GESTATION PERIOD	148–155 days
NUMBER OF OFFSPRING	1–2; weaning at around 120–150 days
DIET	Grazes on vegetation including grass and small plants in pasture
LIFESPAN	Up to 20 years

ANIMAL FACTS

These wild sheep inhabit arid, mountainous areas. Rams live on their own, but ewes will mingle in flocks with their young. It takes up to nine years for the horns of rams to reach their maximum size, by which time they can weigh up to 5kg (11lb). The skull beneath is reinforced with extra bone, giving greater protection during the winter mating season when fighting between the rams is most likely to break out. Mouflon can also hybridize with domestic sheep.

Mouflon rams in combat

This species is regarded as the original ancestor of today's domestic sheep, a process that began 7000–11,000 years ago in southwestern Asia.

WHERE IN THE WORLD?

Europe, including Cyprus and Sardinia, where it has been introduced to many areas. Found in southwest Asia, extending through parts of Iran and the Caucasus region.

SIZE
This is one of the smaller species of wild sheep.

COLOURATION
The ewe is more evenly coloured than the ram.

APPEARANCE
Rams are a rich, dark reddish-brown colour and have a short, glossy coat that thickens in the winter.

HORNS
The horns curl backwards then forwards and are only present in males.

EYES
The irises are a yellowish colour. These sheep are known for their good vision.

HOW BIG IS IT?

A FIRST CLONING SUCCESS

With a severe decline in its numbers, scientists successfully cloned the mouflon in 2001, offering hope for other endangered species.

Yak

VITAL STATISTICS

WEIGHT	305–820kg (670–1805lb)
LENGTH	Up to 385cm (152in), including tail; can measure 200cm (78in) tall at the shoulder
SEXUAL MATURITY	6 years
GESTATION PERIOD	About 258 days; calves weaned by about 1 year old
NUMBER OF OFFSPRING	1 calf every second year
DIET	Herbivorous, grazing on grass as well as other plants and tubers
LIFESPAN	Up to 23 years

ANIMAL FACTS

The domestication of the yak began over 10,000 years ago, and today this species is very important in the economies of the areas where its occurs. Domestic yaks are smaller in size, and more variable in colouration than their wild relatives. Few animals are as hardy, and yaks can be found in areas where the temperature drops far below freezing in winter. Indeed, they are uncomfortable in hot weather. Yaks mate in September, when the bulls will fight over the cows.

Wild yak (left) and domestic yak (right)

The wild yak is now scarce – the surviving population numbers no more than 15,000 individuals, in contrast to around 14 million domestic yaks.

WHERE IN THE WORLD?

Typically occurs at altitudes of 4000–6000m (12,800–19,200ft) in Tibet. Also present in China, India and possibly Nepal if it is not extinct there.

HORNS
Horns curve upwards, growing to 95cm (38in) in males, shorter in females.

HEAD AND SHOULDERS
The head is relatively low-set, and the shoulders have a distinctive humped appearance.

LEGS AND FEET
Yaks have short legs and large hooves, with dew claws to prevent them from slipping.

COAT
The coat is blackish-brown, although very rare golden-coated individuals are known.

BATTLING ON THE PLATEAU

Two bulls clash during the breeding season. This is also the time of year when they emit their distinctive grunting calls.

HOW BIG IS IT?

Mountain Reedbuck

• **ORDER** • Artiodactyla • **FAMILY** • Bovidae • **SPECIES** • *Redunca fulvorufula*

VITAL STATISTICS

WEIGHT	Around 30kg (66lb)
LENGTH	138–190cm (54–75in), including tail
SEXUAL MATURITY	9–24 months
GESTATION PERIOD	About 248 days
NUMBER OF OFFSPRING	1; the mother spends just 30 minutes daily with her youngster for the first 2 months after birth, suckling her offspring away from the herd
DIET	Herbivorous, grazing largely on grass but also browsing on leaves
LIFESPAN	Up to 10 years

ANIMAL FACTS

If disturbed, mountain reedbucks will retreat for a short distance before pausing and looking back, leaving them particularly vulnerable to hunters. They run off with their short tails raised, revealing the white underside. Occasionally, if danger is close by, an individual will drop down into the vegetation, hoping to avoid detection. Young may be born at any time of year, although there tend to be peaks that coincide with the rainy season.

Young hide from predators in the grass

This reedbuck inhabits areas of dense mountain forest. It is not especially shy, and lives in small herds comprising several females and a male.

WHERE IN THE WORLD?

Northern Cameroon, and parts of Sudan, Ethiopia, Uganda, Kenya and Tanzania, southwards to Mozambique, Botswana and South Africa, in areas of suitable habitat.

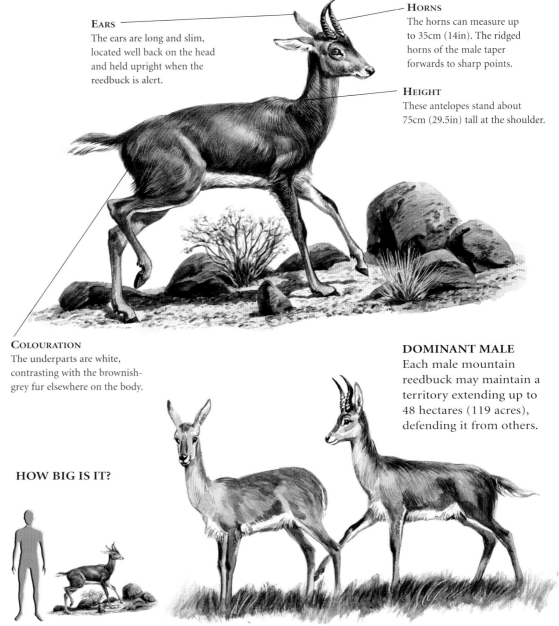

EARS
The ears are long and slim, located well back on the head and held upright when the reedbuck is alert.

HORNS
The horns can measure up to 35cm (14in). The ridged horns of the male taper forwards to sharp points.

HEIGHT
These antelopes stand about 75cm (29.5in) tall at the shoulder.

COLOURATION
The underparts are white, contrasting with the brownish-grey fur elsewhere on the body.

DOMINANT MALE
Each male mountain reedbuck may maintain a territory extending up to 48 hectares (119 acres), defending it from others.

HOW BIG IS IT?

61

Chamois (Gemse)

• **ORDER** • Artiodactyla • **FAMILY** • Bovidae • **SPECIES** • *Rupicapra rupicapra*

VITAL STATISTICS

WEIGHT	14–62kg (31–136lb)
LENGTH	120–145cm (47–57in), including tail
SEXUAL MATURITY	Females about 2.5 years; males 3.5–4 years
GESTATION PERIOD	About 170 days; young are weaned by about 6 months
NUMBER OF OFFSPRING	1, occasionally 2 or 3
DIET	Herbivorous, grazing on grass but also browsing taller plants
LIFESPAN	Typically around 14 years, but can live up to 22

ANIMAL FACTS

In the summer herds of chamois graze on the plants in alpine meadows, but in the winter food is harder to find, even at lower altitudes. They will eat shoots of pines, and have been known to survive without feeding at all for two weeks. Chamois themselves – especially the young – can fall prey to species including bears and wolves.

Summer coat colouration

Winter coat colouration

These agile mountain goats used to be extensively hunted for their hides, which were manufactured into chamois leather used for polishing cars and glass.

WHERE IN THE WORLD?

Occurs in the mountainous regions of central and southern Europe, notably in the Alps and Carpathians, extending through parts of Asia Minor to the Caucasus.

COAT
This varies in appearance throughout the year, and is shorter and lighter both in weight and colour during the summer.

HORNS
The horns measure up to 20cm (8in) and occur in both sexes. They are quite slender, curling over at their tips.

HOOVES
Chamois have slightly elastic pads on their hooves, which act as shock absorbers, helping them to maintain their balance.

HOW BIG IS IT?

BATTLE FOR SURVIVAL
If a female chamois dies, other herd members will look after any offspring. Deaths are most common during winter.

Saiga

• ORDER • Artiodactyla • FAMILY • Bovidae • SPECIES • *Saiga tatarica*

VITAL STATISTICS

WEIGHT	21–51kg (46–112lb); males are heavier
LENGTH	114–159cm (45–63in), including tail; stands up to 80cm (31in) tall
SEXUAL MATURITY	Females 8 months; males about a year later
GESTATION PERIOD	140 days
NUMBER OF OFFSPRING	1 in the first litter, then 2; weaning at 120–160 days
DIET	Grazes on vegetation including grass, small plants and lichens
LIFESPAN	6–10 years

ANIMAL FACTS

The saiga's strange-looking inflatable nostrils act largely as a filter to remove dust during the summer, while in winter, the body heat around the nostrils helps to warm the bitterly cold air before it passes into the lungs. Herds migrate north to better grazing in summer, heading back south to avoid the worst of the winter weather in their range. This is when the rutting season starts, and fights between males are often brutal – the majority actually die during this period.

The nostrils in cross-section

These unmistakable antelopes have sadly become rare in recent years because of uncontrolled hunting for their horns, which are in high demand for oriental medicine.

WHERE IN THE WORLD?

From the vicinity of the Black Sea eastwards through the arid steppes of Russia to northwestern China, with a separate population in Mongolia.

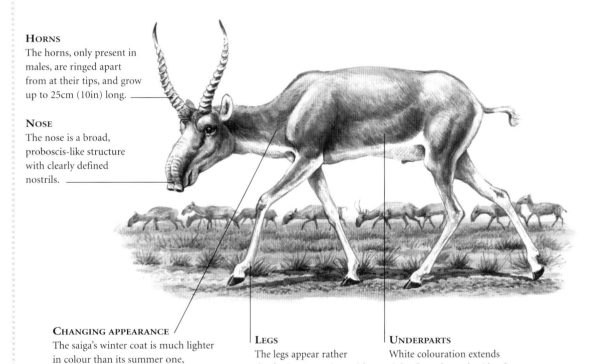

HORNS
The horns, only present in males, are ringed apart from at their tips, and grow up to 25cm (10in) long.

NOSE
The nose is a broad, proboscis-like structure with clearly defined nostrils.

CHANGING APPEARANCE
The saiga's winter coat is much lighter in colour than its summer one, providing effective camouflage in a snowy landscape.

LEGS
The legs appear rather slender in comparison with the stocky body.

UNDERPARTS
White colouration extends right along the underside of the body, contrasting with the summer coat.

HOW BIG IS IT?

SYNCHRONIZED DELIVERY
Birthing is coordinated, so all females produce their calves at the same time.

Yellow-Backed Duiker

• **ORDER** • Artiodactyla • **FAMILY** • Bovidae • **SPECIES** • *Cephalophus silvicultor*

VITAL STATISTICS

WEIGHT	45–80kg (100–175lb)
LENGTH	126–165cm (50–65in), including tail
SEXUAL MATURITY	Females 9 months–1 year; males 1–1.5 years
GESTATION PERIOD	About 217 days; young are weaned by about 5 months
NUMBER OF OFFSPRING	1, occasionally 2
DIET	Herbivorous, grazing on grass, browsing on taller plants, eating fruit, seeds and fungi
LIFESPAN	Typically 10–12 years

ANIMAL FACTS

Yellow-backed duikers inhabit dense forest. Pairs usually share a territory, and both sexes may actively fight to defend it. Nocturnal by nature, these antelopes have set places where they rest during the day, usually well-hidden in undergrowth. If frightened, they will erect their yellow crest and utter a warning whistle. They are adept at disappearing into the bush, making them difficult to pursue, although they may be ambushed by predators such as pythons.

Horns can prove effective deterrents

The name of these antelopes originates from the way they vanish into undergrowth when alarmed. Duiker, pronounced dike-er, is the Afrikaans word for 'diver'.

WHERE IN THE WORLD?

Occurs in suitable habitat in western and central parts of Africa, from Senegal to the Congo, and south to Zambia, with an isolated population in Kenya.

COLOURATION
Adults are mainly brownish-black, with a vivid whitish-orange area of hair that can be raised on the back.

HORNS
Present in both sexes, the horns are narrow and pointed, growing to about 20cm (8in) long.

LEGS
Legs are relatively slender, especially compared with the stocky body.

FACIAL GLANDS
These glands are used by both sexes to scent-mark their territory.

CHANGING APPEARANCE
Young are lighter in colour than adults, and the distinctive yellow patch does not develop until they are five months old.

HOW BIG IS IT?

African Buffalo

One of the most dangerous of all Africa's animals as far as people are concerned, these buffaloes are fearless, and equipped with fearsome horns.

VITAL STATISTICS

WEIGHT	250–900kg (551–1984lb); males are heavier, as are buffalo from plains populations compared with those living in forests
LENGTH	220–450cm (87–177in)
SEXUAL MATURITY	3.5–5 years
GESTATION PERIOD	About 340 days; weaning occurs at 6 months
NUMBER OF OFFSPRING	1, rarely 2
DIET	Herbivorous, grazing on grass, herbs and swamp vegetation
LIFESPAN	18 years in the wild; up to 29 in captivity

ANIMAL FACTS

The significant differences in appearance between plains and forest African buffaloes is related to their environment. Those living in forests have horns that are only 30cm (12in) long, as large horns here would be a handicap. The smaller size of the forest buffaloes enables them to move more easily through the vegetation and escape if danger threatens. They form smaller herds for this reason too, keeping in touch with each other by 'lowing' calls, like cattle.

The area of horn over the head is described as the boss

WHERE IN THE WORLD?

Occurs in much of Africa south of the Sahara, but sporadic distribution in Guinea and adjacent areas; largely absent now from southern parts of the continent.

HORNS
Particularly large in males, the horns can reach up to 160cm (63in) long.

COLOURATION
This can vary from black in male plains buffaloes through to red in the case of those inhabiting forests.

BODY SHAPE
A wide chest and a muscular, barrel-shaped body emphasizes the power of these buffaloes.

GETTING THE ITCH
Scratching on a tree trunk may ease irritation caused by ticks, which are often removed from the buffalo's body by birds called oxpeckers.

HOW BIG IS IT?

Eland

VITAL STATISTICS

WEIGHT	440–900kg (970–1984lb)
LENGTH	310–380cm (122–150in), including tail; up to 182cm (72in) tall
SEXUAL MATURITY	Females 15 months– 3 years; males 4–5 years
GESTATION PERIOD	About 279 days; weaning occurs at 6 months
NUMBER OF OFFSPRING	1
DIET	Herbivorous, grazing on grass and herbs, as well as browsing on taller vegetation
LIFESPAN	Up to 25 years

ANIMAL FACTS

These elands live in herds averaging 20 individuals, although larger groups comprising up to 60 individuals have been reported. Members of the groups remain together throughout the year. Males tend to be quite placid by nature. They are not easily observed, however, because they are nocturnal, hiding away during the daytime. If flushed from cover, they can run away at speeds up to about 70kph (42mph). Their range has contracted over recent years because of hunting pressures.

In spite of their bulk, these elands can jump over 150cm (60in).

The description of 'giant' for this eland refers to its horns, rather than its overall body size when compared with its relative, the common eland.

WHERE IN THE WORLD?

Mainly central Africa, from Cameroon, southern Chad and the Central African Republic to southwestern Sudan. Also occurs in a small area of West Africa.

HORNS
Straight and spiralling along their length, the horns can measure up to 120cm (48in).

PATTERNING
A series of parallel greyish-white bands runs down each side of the body from behind the shoulders.

DEWLAP
This fold of skin extends down on to the chest, and is larger in males than females.

HOW BIG IS IT?

EARLY MOMENTS
Giving birth is a dangerous time, but young are up and able to walk within minutes of being born.

Four-horned Antelope

• **ORDER** • Artiodactyla • **FAMILY** • Bovidae • **SPECIES** • *Tetracerus quadricornis*

VITAL STATISTICS

WEIGHT	15–25kg (33–55lb)
LENGTH	100–125cm (39–49in), including tail; about 61cm (24in) tall
SEXUAL MATURITY	1–2 years
GESTATION PERIOD	232–248 days; weaning occurs at 6 months
NUMBER OF OFFSPRING	1–3
DIET	Herbivorous, grazing on grass and herbs, as well as browsing on taller vegetation; also eats fruit
LIFESPAN	Up to 10 years

ANIMAL FACTS

This particular antelope, also known as the chousingha, is usually found close to water, near streams and rivers. Solitary by nature, they are not easy to spot, although they are active during the day. The breeding period coincides with the monsoons, and extends from June until September. Males become aggressive at this stage, and they have special scent-glands located below the eyes for marking their territory. They can also utter a distinctive husky call if threatened.

A young four-horned antelope, with a single pair of horns

Only the males of this species possess horns. There is usually a short set on the forehead, with a pair of longer horns behind.

WHERE IN THE WORLD?

Occurs in India, extending from the Gir forest eastwards to Orissa, and south of the Ganges down to the state of Tamil Nadu. Also found in Nepal.

HORNS
The second pair of horns emerges once the antelope is about 14 months old.

LEG STRIPE
A black line runs down the centre of the upper part of the forelegs.

COLOURATION
Yellowish-brown, with white underparts, and white at the bottom of the legs.

STANDING TALL
The slender hind legs of this species allow it to browse easily on plants.

ESCAPING DANGER
The wary nature and nimble movement of the four-horned antelope can protect it from would-be predators such as tigers.

HOW BIG IS IT?

Greater Kudu

• **ORDER** • Artiodactyla • **FAMILY** • Bovidae • **SPECIES** • *Tragelaphus strepsiceros*

VITAL STATISTICS

WEIGHT	120–315kg (265–694lb); males are heavier
LENGTH	215–300cm (85–118in); stands up to 160cm (63in) tall
SEXUAL MATURITY	Females 15–21 months; males 21–24 months
GESTATION PERIOD	Around 279 days
NUMBER OF OFFSPRING	1; weaning at around 180 days
DIET	Vegetarian, browsing leaves and shoots; seeks out fruit such as wild watermelons during droughts
LIFESPAN	7–8 years; up to 23 years in captivity

ANIMAL FACTS

Males are solitary by nature, whereas females group together in bands with their young. They lack not only horns, but also the longer hair on the throat and the white chevron. A pregnant female leaves the herd to give birth, and then conceals her offspring in the bush for up to five weeks. After this, the young kudu will start walking and follows her for periods; once the calf is about four months old, they rejoin the herd.

The horns develop with age

This is one of the largest and most impressive of all antelopes. Kudus can also swim well, in spite of their size.

WHERE IN THE WORLD?

Eastern and southern parts of Africa, especially from Angola and Namibia across to Zimbabwe and Mozambique. Found northwards up to Chad, Sudan, Eritrea and Ethiopia.

MANE
A line of longer hair extends down the back, with a beard evident on the throat.

HORNS
The male's magnificent spiralling horns can reach up to 182cm (72in) long.

CHEVRON
An area of white hair connects the eyes.

LINEAR PATTERNING
The stripes on the side of the body break up its outline, concealing its presence.

HOW BIG IS IT?

GETTING CLEAR
When sensing danger, kudus initially freeze, hoping to avoid detection, but they can also run and jump well if necessary.

Bactrian Camel

• ORDER • Artiodactyla **• FAMILY •** Camelidae **• SPECIES •** *Camelus bactrianus*

VITAL STATISTICS

WEIGHT	600–1000kg (1320–2200lb)
LENGTH	350cm (138in), including tail; stands up to 230cm (90in) tall
SEXUAL MATURITY	Females 3–4 years; males 5–6 years
GESTATION PERIOD	About 365–430 days; weaning occurs at 1–2 years
NUMBER OF OFFSPRING	1, occasionally 2
DIET	Herbivorous, grazing on grass and browsing on taller plants
LIFESPAN	Up to 40 years

ANIMAL FACTS

Living in very harsh environments, and exposed to extremes of temperature throughout the year, it is perhaps not surprising that the Bactrian camel's dense winter coat may fall off in huge chunks as the weather changes. Camels are often described as 'ships of the desert', partly because of their rolling gait. This results from their unusual way of walking, with both legs on one side of the body moving forward together, followed by the legs on the other side.

Long eyelashes keep sand out of the camel's eyes

The domestication of these camels began over 4500 years ago. Today, there are more than two million of the domestic variety, but the wild population is endangered.

WHERE IN THE WORLD?

Wild Bactrian camels – as distinct from domesticated or feral camels that have reverted to living in the wild – are found in Asia's Gobi desert.

BEARD
A long beard runs down the underside of the throat, with hairs here being 25cm (10in) long.

HUMPS
The humps are a fat store, indicating the camel's condition. A well-fed camel has upright humps, which do not slope to the side.

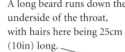

GETTING UP
To rise from the ground, camels raise their hindquarters and then push themselves up with their forelegs.

FEET
Both toes on each foot spread out as the camel walks, preventing it from sinking into sand.

HOW BIG IS IT?

VERSATILE COMPANIONS
Camels are not only valued for carrying goods in packs slung over their bodies, but they can also provide milk.

Dromedary Camel

• **ORDER** • Artiodactyla • **FAMILY** • Camelidae • **SPECIES** • *Camelus dromedarius*

VITAL STATISTICS

WEIGHT	600–1000kg (1320–2200lb)
LENGTH	350cm (138in), including tail; up to 210cm (84in) tall
SEXUAL MATURITY	Females 3–4 years; males 5–6 years
GESTATION PERIOD	About 365–400 days; weaning occurs at 1–2 years
NUMBER OF OFFSPRING	1, occasionally 2
DIET	Herbivorous, grazing on grass and browsing on taller plants
LIFESPAN	Up to 40 years

ANIMAL FACTS

Although the dromedary is thought of as having only a single hump, it does actually have a second inconspicuous hump in the shoulder region. These animals are well-adapted to desert life – able to survive for long periods without drinking, getting some of their fluid from vegetation. When they do drink, dromedaries can consume up to 571 litres (125 gallons) of water at one time.

Dromedary or Arabian camel

Bactrian camel

This species effectively died out about 2000 years ago, and all dromedaries today are the descendants of domesticated stock. Their population is estimated at about 15 million.

WHERE IN THE WORLD?

Ranges throughout northern Africa, to the Horn of Africa and through Arabia and the Middle East to northwestern India. Has been introduced to parts of central Australia.

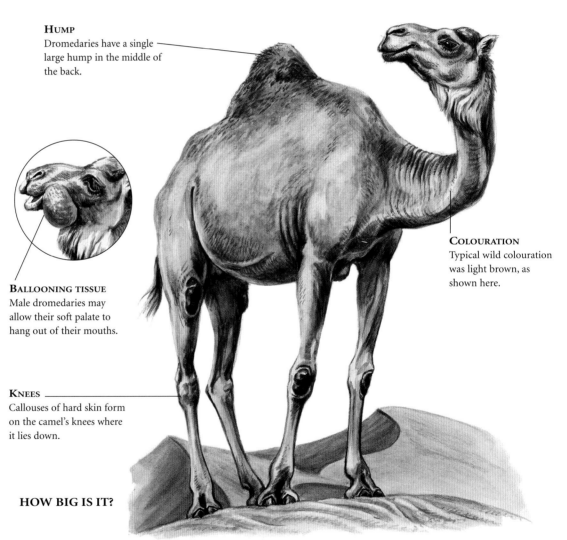

HUMP
Dromedaries have a single large hump in the middle of the back.

COLOURATION
Typical wild colouration was light brown, as shown here.

BALLOONING TISSUE
Male dromedaries may allow their soft palate to hang out of their mouths.

KNEES
Calrouses of hard skin form on the camel's knees where it lies down.

HOW BIG IS IT?

UNDERSIDE OF THE FOOT
The two toes forming the foot absorb the camel's weight as it moves. There is a claw on each toe.

Llama

• **ORDER** • Artiodactyla • **FAMILY** • Camelidae • **SPECIES** • *Auchenia glama*

VITAL STATISTICS

WEIGHT	127–204kg (280–450lb)
LENGTH	350cm (138in), including tail; stands up to 210cm (84in) tall
SEXUAL MATURITY	Females 1 year; males about 3 years
GESTATION PERIOD	331–350 days; weaning at about 6 months
NUMBER OF OFFSPRING	1, very occasionally 2
DIET	Herbivorous, grazing on grass and browsing on taller plants
LIFESPAN	15–20 years

ANIMAL FACTS

The llama's breeding cycle is unusual because the species is an induced ovulator. This means that females do not have a regular period of oestrus like most mammals, but ovulate in response to mating, greatly enhancing the likelihood of pregnancy occurring. Mating can last up to 45 minutes, and llamas mate lying down. When the youngster is born, the female cannot lick the offspring because her tongue is too short – only extending about 1.25cm (0.5in) outside the mouth.

The llama's ancestors probably originated in North America about 40 million years ago. From here, they crossed into South America three million years ago.

WHERE IN THE WORLD?

Today, llamas and their relatives are naturally confined to the Andean region of South America, but they are also kept widely throughout the world.

EARS
These are tall, narrowing along their length and often referred to as being banana-shaped.

EYELASHES
These are absent in llamas, but present in their close relative, the alpaca (*Auchenia pacos*).

TAIL
The tail is short and, like the body, is covered in a dense, soft woolly coat.

COLOURATION
Llamas are often white, brown or a mix of these colours.

A taller llama with its short cousin, the alpaca, whose wool is especially prized

HOW BIG IS IT?

FOUL TEMPER
If frightened or annoyed, llamas will react by spitting an unpleasant greenish grassy fluid at the cause of their discomfort.

Vicuña

VITAL STATISTICS

WEIGHT	45–55kg (99–121lb); males are heavier
LENGTH	161–184cm (63–72in), including tail; up to 96cm (38in) tall
SEXUAL MATURITY	About 24 months
GESTATION PERIOD	330–350 days; weaned 6–8 months later
NUMBER OF OFFSPRING	1
DIET	Herbivorous, feeding mainly on grass, which inflicts heavy wear on the teeth
LIFESPAN	20 years in the wild; up to 25 in captivity

ANIMAL FACTS

Living in family groups controlled by a dominant male, vicuñas graze during the day. They can be vulnerable to attacks by mountain lions (pumas); the young are also at risk from foxes. Vicuñas are constantly alert to danger, communicating with other members of the herd by means of a shrill whistle. They can run at speeds of up to 50kph (30mph) in the thin mountain air. Their hearts are enlarged to pump their thick blood efficiently around the body.

Young will ultimately be driven from the herd by the resident male

This is the smallest member of the Camelidae family, and it has been highly prized down the centuries for its very soft wool.

WHERE IN THE WORLD?

Occurs in western South America at altitudes of 3500–5800m (11,700–19,300ft) in the Andean mountain region of Peru, Bolivia, Chile and Argentina.

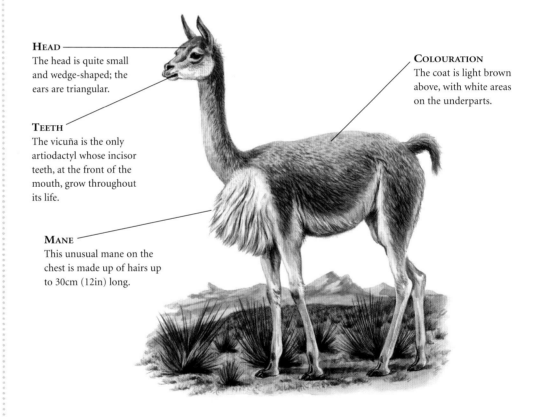

HEAD
The head is quite small and wedge-shaped; the ears are triangular.

TEETH
The vicuña is the only artiodactyl whose incisor teeth, at the front of the mouth, grow throughout its life.

MANE
This unusual mane on the chest is made up of hairs up to 30cm (12in) long.

COLOURATION
The coat is light brown above, with white areas on the underparts.

HOW BIG IS IT?

RESTING
As dusk falls, the herd members will retreat to a separate area at higher altitude, where they will sleep.

Roe Deer

• ORDER • Artiodactyla • **FAMILY** • Cervidae • **SPECIES** • *Capreolus capreolus*

VITAL STATISTICS

WEIGHT	18–29kg (40–64lb)
LENGTH	95–135cm (37–53in), including tail; up to 67cm (26in) tall
SEXUAL MATURITY	14 months old
GESTATION PERIOD	Up to 294 days; weaning occurs at 6–10 weeks, with fawns suckling intermittently through their first winter
NUMBER OF OFFSPRING	1, occasionally 2
DIET	Herbivorous, grazing on grass and browsing on leaves and bushes
LIFESPAN	10–14 years

ANIMAL FACTS

These deer are solitary, with both sexes occupying their own territories and only coming together to mate. This occurs in the summer, but the fertilized egg can remain in suspended animation within the female's reproductive tract. Up to five months later, the egg finally implants into the wall of the female's uterus, and its development begins. This means that the fawn will be born in more favourable conditions the following year.

Antler shape changes with age

Shy by nature, these deer are not easy to observe. The male's antlers are lost each autumn and then regrow up to 25cm (10in) long.

WHERE IN THE WORLD?

Occurs throughout Europe and Asia, although not present in much of England and Wales, and absent from Ireland. Their range extends eastwards all the way to Siberia.

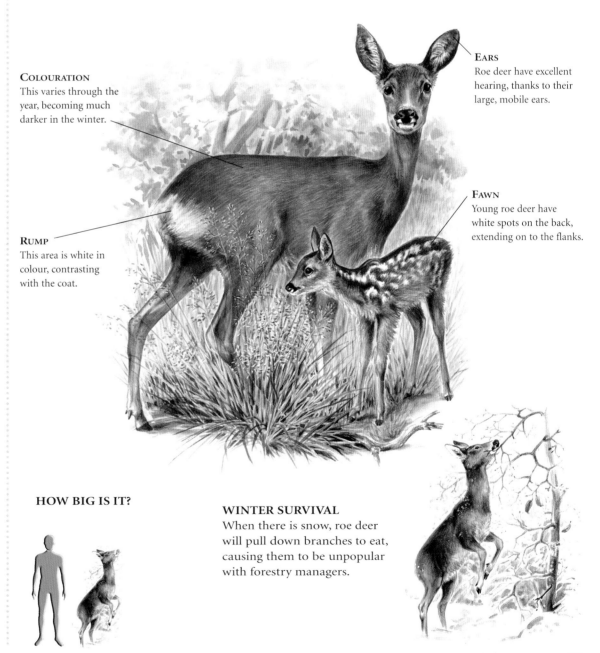

COLOURATION
This varies through the year, becoming much darker in the winter.

RUMP
This area is white in colour, contrasting with the coat.

EARS
Roe deer have excellent hearing, thanks to their large, mobile ears.

FAWN
Young roe deer have white spots on the back, extending on to the flanks.

HOW BIG IS IT?

WINTER SURVIVAL
When there is snow, roe deer will pull down branches to eat, causing them to be unpopular with forestry managers.

Chital Deer

VITAL STATISTICS

WEIGHT	75–100kg (165–220lb); males are heavier
LENGTH	130–170cm (51–67in), including tail; up to 95cm (37in) tall
SEXUAL MATURITY	1 year
GESTATION PERIOD	About 220 days; weaning occurs about 6 months later
NUMBER OF OFFSPRING	1
DIET	Herbivorous, grazing largely on grass, but also browses on taller plants
LIFESPAN	Up to 12 years in the wild; can be 20 in captivity

ANIMAL FACTS

Chital live in herds of up to 30 individuals, although they may sometimes be seen in groups of up to 100. Herds consist of females and their fawns, generally led by a single stag. In tropical areas, breeding can occur at any time of the year, with stags fighting to establish and maintain their harems. They will try to intimidate rivals by bellowing loudly when challenged. Herds are vulnerable to attacks by predators such as tigers and leopards.

Also known as the axis or spotted deer, this species is most likely to be seen in open countryside, sometimes close to agricultural land.

WHERE IN THE WORLD?

Present throughout the Indian subcontinent, and on the island of Sri Lanka. Has been introduced to other areas, including parts of Europe, Australia and the USA.

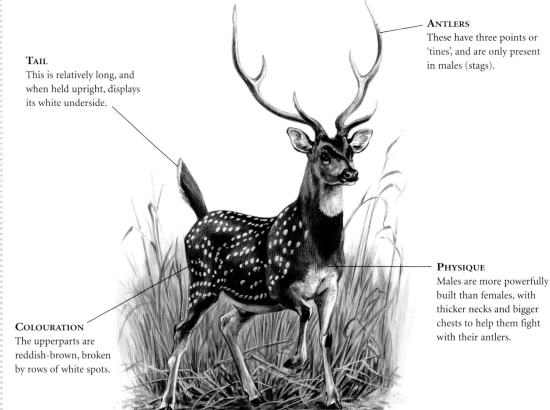

ANTLERS
These have three points or 'tines', and are only present in males (stags).

TAIL
This is relatively long, and when held upright, displays its white underside.

PHYSIQUE
Males are more powerfully built than females, with thicker necks and bigger chests to help them fight with their antlers.

COLOURATION
The upperparts are reddish-brown, broken by rows of white spots.

Changing shape of the antlers

HOW BIG IS IT?

A FREE MEAL
A herd gathers under a tree to seek fruit shaken from above by a group of monkeys. Chital deer prefer to feed on the ground.

Elk

VITAL STATISTICS

WEIGHT	Females 270–360kg (600–800lb); males 380–720kg (850–1580lb)
LENGTH	130–170cm (51–67in), including tail; up to 213cm (84in) tall
SEXUAL MATURITY	2–3 years
GESTATION PERIOD	226–246 days; weaning occurs about 6 months later
NUMBER OF OFFSPRING	1, occasionally twins and rarely triplets
DIET	Herbivorous, grazing largely on grass, but also browses on taller plants
LIFESPAN	8–12 years

ANIMAL FACTS

The male's magnificent antlers are only carried through until the end of the mating period, around October. A new pair will start to grow during the spring, attaining their full size anywhere between three and five months later. The antlers emerge covered in a protective layer of skin called felt, which is later shed. The sheer size of a mature bull elk is usually enough to deter smaller rivals and predators, although females and particularly calves are vulnerable to wolves.

An emerging set of antlers

This species is known as the elk in Europe and the moose in North America, where the elk is a completely different type of deer.

WHERE IN THE WORLD?

Occurs in northern latitudes, in parts of Europe, Asia and North America from Alaska, across Canada and down into northeastern parts of the USA and Wyoming.

ANTLERS
The male's broad antlers are described as 'palmate' (meaning they have several lobes). The span from tip to tip can be up to 180cm (72in).

SENSES
Elk rely heavily on their senses of smell and hearing, because their eyesight is poor.

COAT
Hollow hairs in the coat help insulate the elk from the cold.

VARIATIONS ON A THEME
The antlers can reveal both the age of the elk and its area of origin.

HOW BIG IS IT?

A HEALTHY APPETITE
An individual elk can eat up to 20kg (44lb) of vegetation daily. They will sometimes graze on aquatic plants.

Red Deer

• ORDER • Artiodactyla • FAMILY • Cervidae • SPECIES • *Cervus elaphus*

VITAL STATISTICS

WEIGHT	100–350kg (220–772lb)
LENGTH	177–280cm (70–110in), including tail; up to 120cm (47in) tall
SEXUAL MATURITY	Around 1.5 years
GESTATION PERIOD	About 220–240 days; weaning occurs 6–8 months later
NUMBER OF OFFSPRING	1, rarely 2
DIET	Herbivorous, grazing on grass, but may also browse on shrubs
LIFESPAN	Up to 12 years in the wild and 20 in captivity

There are a number of different types of red deer. In Britain, it is the biggest land mammal, and can be found in both wooded and open countryside.

WHERE IN THE WORLD?

Ranges across Europe and Asia and is also present in North America. It is the only deer resident in North Africa, where it is confined to the Atlas Mountains.

ANIMAL FACTS

Red deer live in groups throughout the year, although males form separate 'bachelor' herds that are more fluid in structure, with older individuals in particular becoming more solitary. Mature stags battle each other at the beginning of the rutting period, as they seek to establish harems of hinds. They bellow loudly to intimidate would-be rivals, but if this fails fighting is likely to break out. The stags clash with their antlers, sometimes with fatal consequences.

ANTLERS
There may be up to 20 points, or 'tines', on the antlers of a mature stag.

COLOURATION
The distinctive red colour of the coat is only evident during spring and summer. In the autumn it is replaced by brownish-grey fur.

EYES
Large and black, the eyes are located high up on the head to give good visibility.

Fawns have a spotted appearance

HOW BIG IS IT?

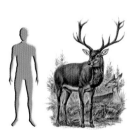

LOSING ANTLERS
After the breeding season, or 'rut', at the start of the year the stag will lose its antlers. A new set grows almost immediately.

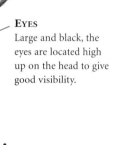

Sika Deer

VITAL STATISTICS

WEIGHT	25–110kg (55–242lb)
LENGTH	115–175cm (45-69in), including tail; up to 110cm (42in) tall
SEXUAL MATURITY	18 months–2 years
GESTATION PERIOD	About 220 days; weaning occurs 8–12 months later
NUMBER OF OFFSPRING	1, rarely 2
DIET	Herbivorous, grazing on grass and also browsing on taller plants
LIFESPAN	10 years in the wild; up to 20 in captivity

ANIMAL FACTS

While most deer are relatively quiet, the sika is an exception, having a distinctive vocabulary of 10 different sounds, including a loud scream. Hinds generally live in small groups headed by a stag. Males are highly territorial and very aggressive by nature, and will use not just their antlers but also their sharp hooves when battling with a rival. Both animals can end up being seriously injured as the result of such conflicts. Sika deer are nocturnal by nature.

The word 'sika' means 'small deer' in Japanese, and this particular species is regarded as sacred in that country. Elsewhere, however, sika populations are under threat.

WHERE IN THE WORLD?

Occurs in eastern Asia, from Siberia to China and Korea, and on islands including Taiwan and Japan. Has been introduced to the wild in the USA, Britain and New Zealand.

ANTLERS
These are only present in males, and can measure up to 81cm (32in) long.

MANE
The coat becomes thicker in winter, creating a mane around the male's neck.

SPOTTED APPEARANCE
The spots are only present in certain types, and become less evident in winter.

COLOURATION
Colour can differ quite markedly between individuals, ranging from a greyish shade through to a reddish colouration.

Some stags live solitary lives

HOW BIG IS IT?

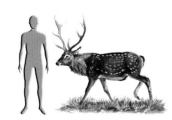

YOUNG SIKA

Fawns are born in May and June. They are particularly at risk from attacks by wolves when they are very young.

Fallow Deer

VITAL STATISTICS

WEIGHT	25–130kg (55–287lb)
LENGTH	154–215cm (60–85in), including tail; up to 110cm (42in) tall
SEXUAL MATURITY	Females 1 year; males 1.5 years
GESTATION PERIOD	About 230 days; weaning occurs 8 months later
NUMBER OF OFFSPRING	1
DIET	Herbivorous, grazing on grass and also browsing on taller plants
LIFESPAN	Up to 8 years in the wild; up to 15 years in captivity

ANIMAL FACTS

The autumn mating period, called the rut, sees these deer becoming particularly active and vocal, with females uttering barks of alarm, while stags grunt as a way of intimidating would-be rivals. After giving birth, the hind will feed her fawn every four hours for a period of about four months, then mother and offspring rejoin the herd permanently. The adaptability of the fallow deer is such that it has now become established in some 38 countries, including the USA.

Bucks battle with their antlers

These deer are not native to Europe, but have been introduced here down the centuries. They naturally live in woodland, but also thrive in parkland areas.

WHERE IN THE WORLD?

Originally native to North Africa, the Middle East, Asia Minor and the Balkans. Introduced to Britain by the Normans, this species now occurs widely throughout Europe.

ANTLERS
The antlers are described as 'palmate', because of their shape like a hand with the fingers extended. They can be over 70cm (28in) long.

SIZE
Bucks are larger than hinds in terms of their overall size.

SPOTTING
Some individuals have more pronounced spotting than normal, combined with a darker brown coat.

INCREASING MATURITY
Bucks shed their antlers in spring. By late summer they have been replaced by a more impressive set, reflecting the increasing maturity of the deer.

HOW BIG IS IT?

ON THE DEFENSIVE
A hind defends her fawn against a fox. Fawns normally stay hidden in grass until they are about three weeks old.

Père David's Deer

• **ORDER** • Artiodactyla • **FAMILY** • Cervidae • **SPECIES** • *Elaphurus davidianus*

The deer is named after the French missionary Père David, who was permitted a glimpse of the herd kept by the Chinese emperor in 1865.

VITAL STATISTICS

WEIGHT	Around 135kg (291lb)
LENGTH	230–240cm (91–95in), including tail, which can measure 50cm (20in); up to 120cm (48in) tall
SEXUAL MATURITY	14 months
GESTATION PERIOD	About 270–300 days; weaning occurs 10–11 months later
NUMBER OF OFFSPRING	1, rarely 2
DIET	Herbivorous, grazing largely on grass, but will also feed on various aquatic plants
LIFESPAN	Up to 18 years in captivity

ANIMAL FACTS

Persecution in their native habit finally resulted in Père David's deer becoming extinct in the wild in 1939. Fortunately, a number of pairs had been sent to Europe before the Chinese emperor's own herd had been wiped out completely by flood and revolution. The surviving individuals in Europe then passed into the Duke of Bedford's care, and all today's examples of the species are descended from a single stag and five hinds that were bred at Woburn Park.

WHERE IN THE WORLD?

Now extinct in the wild, its exact distribution was not recorded. It is believed to have occurred on the swampy plains of northeastern China.

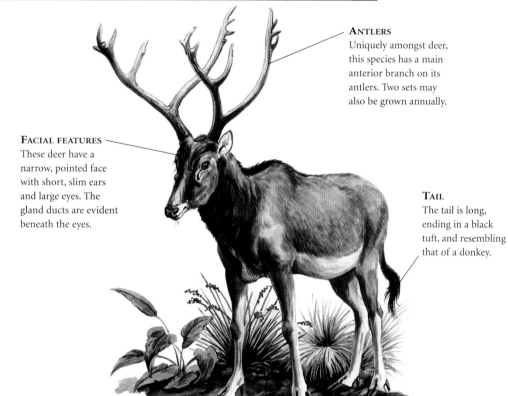

ANTLERS
Uniquely amongst deer, this species has a main anterior branch on its antlers. Two sets may also be grown annually.

FACIAL FEATURES
These deer have a narrow, pointed face with short, slim ears and large eyes. The gland ducts are evident beneath the eyes.

TAIL
The tail is long, ending in a black tuft, and resembling that of a donkey.

HOOVES
The hooves are long and slender, making it easier to walk over marshy ground.

Mother and young

HOW BIG IS IT?

AN AQUATIC LIFESTYLE
These deer will spend long periods wading, feeding and even playing in water. They are also able to swim well.

Indian Muntjac

• ORDER • Artiodactyla **• FAMILY •** Cervidae **• SPECIES •** *Muntiacus muntjak*

VITAL STATISTICS

WEIGHT	15–20kg (33–44lb)
LENGTH	122–152cm (48–60in), including tail; up to 40cm (16in) tall
SEXUAL MATURITY	12 months
GESTATION PERIOD	200–220 days; weaning occurs 2–3 months later
NUMBER OF OFFSPRING	1, rarely 2
DIET	Omnivorous, eating vegetation, fruit, fungi, as well as eggs and carrion
LIFESPAN	Probably no more than 6 years in the wild, but up to 10 years in captivity

ANIMAL FACTS

There are no less than 15 different races of Indian muntjac recognized through its wide range. These deer are not easily spotted, partly because they tend to be nocturnal by nature, but they are numerous. In some agricultural areas they are considered pests, because of the damage they cause to crops. If disturbed, they can utter a harsh barking call. The female leaves the fawn hidden in vegetation at first, returning regularly to feed her offspring until it is strong enough to accompany her throughout the day.

Although small in stature, the Indian muntjac possesses a fiery temperament, and males will fight hard to maintain their territories. They tend to be solitary by nature.

WHERE IN THE WORLD?

Occurs in India and Southeast Asia, extending north as far as southern China, south to the Indonesian islands of Java and Sumatra, and east to Borneo.

BONY RIDGES
These ridges, seen in both sexes, are the bases from which the male's antlers grow.

ANTLERS
These are only present in the male, and grow to about 15cm (6in) long. They are replaced at intervals.

GLANDS
Tear glands are evident in front of the eyes.

CANINE TEETH
The male's upper canines form small tusks, up to 2.5cm (1in) long, which can prove lethal.

ALERT AND ALIVE
The size of these muntjacs means they are vulnerable to many different predators, but their forest habitat provides some protection.

HOW BIG IS IT?

White-Tailed Deer

• ORDER • Artiodactyla **• FAMILY •** Cervidae **• SPECIES •** *Odocoileus virginianus*

These deer occur over a very wide area, and in spite of hunting pressures the species remains generally common, thanks partly to its reproductive rate.

VITAL STATISTICS

WEIGHT	50–115kg (110–254lb); northern races larger than those from the southern USA
LENGTH	195–208cm (77–82in), including tail; up to 105cm (41in) tall
SEXUAL MATURITY	2 years
GESTATION PERIOD	200–217 days; weaning occurs 4 months later
NUMBER OF OFFSPRING	2, occasionally 3 or 4
DIET	Herbivorous, eating grasses and shrubs, as well as agricultural crops
LIFESPAN	Up to 10 years in captivity

ANIMAL FACTS

White-tailed deer are very wary, and will sprint off at speeds of up to 64kph (40mph) if they feel threatened. They can also swim well, plunging readily into a river or lake to escape danger. Although occurring across a wide range of different habitats, they generally seek out lightly wooded countryside. The fawns have white spotted markings on their backs, which helps to break up their outline when they are lying still, hidden amongst vegetation.

Two bucks together

WHERE IN THE WORLD?

Occurs across most of North America, from Canada to Florida (although absent in arid western areas), extending through Central America to Bolivia in South America.

ANTLERS — These are shed between January and March, and will have started to regrow by May.

EARS — Although not very large, the ears serve to alert the deer to possible danger.

COLOURATION — White fur on the face extends down to the underside of the body.

SCENT GLANDS — There are scent glands on the legs, which are used for marking territory.

SIGNS OF ALARM

When running or alarmed, these deer raise their long tails vertically, as shown here, showing the reason for their common name.

HOW BIG IS IT?

Southern Pudu

VITAL STATISTICS

WEIGHT	9–15kg (20–33lb); young are fully grown by 3 months
LENGTH	93cm (37in), including tail; up to 38cm (15in) tall
SEXUAL MATURITY	Females 6 months; males 8–12 months
GESTATION PERIOD	200–220 days; weaning occurs 2 months later
NUMBER OF OFFSPRING	1
DIET	Herbivorous, browsing on plants, including bark, also eating fruit and seeds
LIFESPAN	8–10 years

ANIMAL FACTS

These deer can be found from close to sea-level right up almost to the snow line in their mountainous habitats. They have set paths through their territory, allowing them to move easily through dense vegetation, and these are also marked with dung. Southern pudu are most active at dawn and again in the late afternoon. They are surprisingly agile, climbing or standing upright on their hind legs to browse on vegetation that would otherwise be out of reach.

This species is the smallest deer in the world. They usually hide away in forested areas, which provide protection against predators. They live in family groups.

WHERE IN THE WORLD?

This species occurs further south than its northern relative, in the southern Andean region of Chile and Argentina, at altitudes of up to 1700m (5500ft).

ANTLERS
Present only in males, these curving spikes grow to a maximum length of just 10cm (4in).

EARS
The ears are large and rounded, set well back on the head, and are orange in colour, matching the lips.

COAT
The coat is short and reddish-brown, lighter on the legs.

PHYSIQUE
The legs are short and slender, while the body is rounded in appearance.

DANGER THREATENS
Hunters such as the cougar stalk these small deer. Smaller cats, foxes and birds of prey present dangers, too.

HOW BIG IS IT?

Clambering up

Caribou

An unusual feature of caribou is that both sexes have antlers. Their domesticated relatives, called reindeer, are heavier and shorter-legged in appearance.

VITAL STATISTICS

WEIGHT	Females 40–100kg (88–220lb); males 70–150kg (154–330lb)
LENGTH	195–235cm (77–93in), including tail; up to 120cm (47in) tall
SEXUAL MATURITY	2–3 years
GESTATION PERIOD	About 227 days; weaning occurs 4–5 months later
NUMBER OF OFFSPRING	1
DIET	Herbivorous, browsing on lichens, shrubs and similar food
LIFESPAN	Typically about 5 years, but can be up to 15

ANIMAL FACTS

Herds of caribou may undertake seasonal migrations in the far north in search of food, heading to the Arctic plains when the snow there thaws in the summer. Up to 200,000 individuals have been recorded in a single herd, but typically numbers are less than 10,000. The young are born in the summer and they can run almost at once, to escape predators such as polar bears and wolves. They lack the white spotting associated with other young deer.

Caribou hooves alter according to the season to help the animals walk easily and safely

WHERE IN THE WORLD?

Herds of wild caribou are now confined to parts of Alaska and northern Canada, as well as Scandinavia and Russia, where they are found in tundra regions.

COLOURATION
The appearance of caribou differs according to the time of year. They are brownish in summer, and become greyer in winter.

THROAT POUCHES
The male has two inflatable sacs that amplify the sound of his roaring during the breeding period.

NOSE
The sense of smell is vital to the caribou's survival, helping it locate food buried beneath the snow.

COAT
The coat is thick and is very effective in trapping air close to the skin, helping to insulate the caribou.

HOW BIG IS IT?

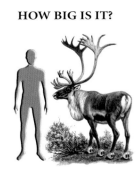

DOMESTIC COUSINS
Domestic reindeer show far more variance in colouration than their wild relatives. They were first domesticated around 3000 years ago.

Giraffe

• ORDER • Artiodactyla **• FAMILY •** Cervidae **• SPECIES •** *Giraffa camelopardalis*

The giraffe is the tallest living species on the planet, standing up to 587cm (231in) in height. It is also the heaviest ruminant.

VITAL STATISTICS

WEIGHT	Females 1100–1600kg (2425–3527lb); males 1300–2000kg (2865–4410lb)
LENGTH	457–570cm (180–224in), including tail
SEXUAL MATURITY	3–5 years
GESTATION PERIOD	434–465 days; weaning occurs 12–16 months later
NUMBER OF OFFSPRING	1, standing 180cm (72in) tall at birth
DIET	Herbivorous, browsing at high level, particularly on mimosa and acacia trees
LIFESPAN	20–25 years; up to 28 in captivity

ANIMAL FACTS

The giraffe's origins trace back to an antelope-like ancestor that lived in Europe and Asia between 30 and 50 million years ago, and grew to just 300cm (120in) tall. Modern giraffes first appeared about one million years ago. Their body shape means that their heart must produce double the blood pressure of a typical mammal, to pump blood up to the brain. As a result, the giraffe's heart can weigh up to 10kg (22lb) and measures around 61cm (2ft) in length.

WHERE IN THE WORLD?

Found in a number of different areas of Africa, south of the Sahara, particularly in eastern and southern parts. Populations are quite isolated.

HORNS
The horns are bald in male giraffes, because of the way they nuzzle females.

NECK STRUCTURE
In spite of its length, there are no more bones in the neck than there are in other mammals. The individual vertebrae are simply more elongated.

APPEARANCE
Up to nine different races are recognized, varying in size and patterning.

GUARDIANS
The keen eyesight and height of giraffes mean they can spot possible danger from afar, and alert other animals, too.

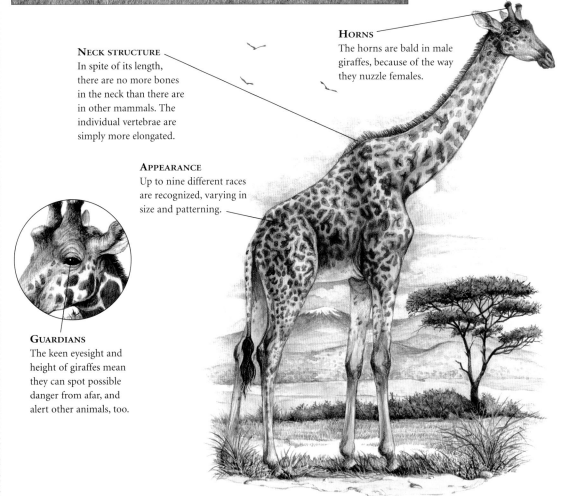

HOW BIG IS IT?

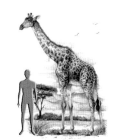

LOWER DOWN
In spite of their height, giraffes will occasionally sit down, but they can sometimes have difficulty standing up again.

Hippopotamus

VITAL STATISTICS

WEIGHT	655–3200kg (1444–7054lb)
LENGTH	335–564cm (132–222in), including tail; up to 165cm (65in) tall
SEXUAL MATURITY	Females 4–10 years; males 7–12 years
GESTATION PERIOD	About 248 days; weaning occurs 6–8 months later
NUMBER OF OFFSPRING	1
DIET	Herbivorous, grazing on grass under cover of darkness
LIFESPAN	Typically 30–40 years, but can be up to 50

ANIMAL FACTS

Hippopotamuses spend the day resting in water, with their heads raised just above the surface. They may also venture into deeper water, where they can stay submerged for up to 30 minutes, walking along the bottom. Hippopotamuses are surprisingly aggressive animals, with long, sharp lower canine teeth capable of inflicting severe injuries on others of their own kind, and even killing people. Each night, the group emerges on to land, walking up to 10km (6 miles) to their feeding grounds, before returning to water.

Hippos have a very wide gape

There is no mistaking the appearance of the hippopotamus. The broad head allows it to wallow with its eyes and nostrils above the surface of the water.

WHERE IN THE WORLD?

Occurs in Africa, south of the Sahara, usually close to watercourses such as rivers and lakes. Absent from the south of the continent.

SKIN
There are mucous glands on the surface of the skin, which secrete a reddish fluid.

BODY
The body is large and barrel-shaped, mostly free from hair.

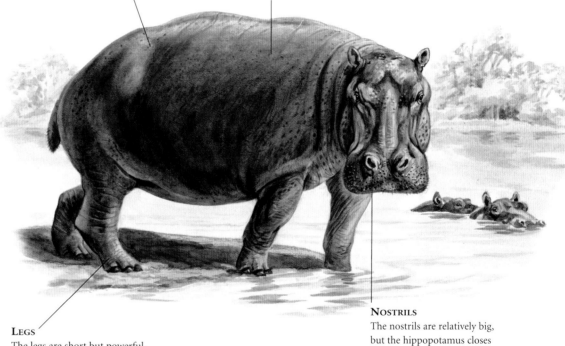

LEGS
The legs are short but powerful, allowing the hippopotamus to run quickly on land, and swim well.

NOSTRILS
The nostrils are relatively big, but the hippopotamus closes the openings with skin flaps when it is submerged.

HITCHING A RIDE
Young hippopotamuses in a group may rest on their mothers' shoulders, where the water is too deep for them to stand.

HOW BIG IS IT?

Siberian Musk Deer

• **ORDER** • Artiodactyla • **FAMILY** • Moschidae • **SPECIES** • *Moschus moschiferus*

VITAL STATISTICS

WEIGHT	11–18kg (24–40lb)
LENGTH	90–106cm (35–42in), including tail; up to 55cm (22in) tall
SEXUAL MATURITY	Females 4–10 years; males 7–12 years
GESTATION PERIOD	About 200 days; weaning occurs 3–4 months later
NUMBER OF OFFSPRING	Usually 2, sometimes 3
DIET	Herbivorous, grazing on grass and browsing on taller plants
LIFESPAN	10–14 years, but can be up to 20 in captivity

ANIMAL FACTS

Neither male nor female musk deer have antlers, but males can be distinguished by the length of their canines. They also produce a particularly potent musk, which is highly valued in perfumery and the reason these deer are widely hunted. Musk deer generally live on their own, hiding away during the day and become active at night. Females give birth in the early summer, and fawns are hidden away until they are about eight weeks old.

These deer browse on high plants, particularly when snow covers the ground

Musk deer represent the oldest ancestral line of deer. Agile by nature, they can sprint well and are capable of leaping distances of 500cm (197in).

WHERE IN THE WORLD?

Extends through central parts of the former Soviet Union to northern Mongolia and China, south to Korea, confined to the areas of mountainous forest called taiga.

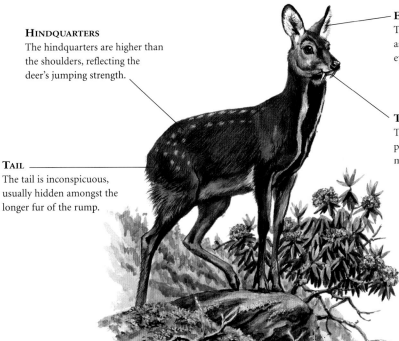

HINDQUARTERS
The hindquarters are higher than the shoulders, reflecting the deer's jumping strength.

EARS AND EYES
The ears are broad and tall, as well as mobile, and the eyes are large.

TEETH
The protruding, backward-pointing upper canines can measure up to 10cm (4in).

TAIL
The tail is inconspicuous, usually hidden amongst the longer fur of the rump.

HOW BIG IS IT?

COVERED IN SPOTS

Fawns are heavily spotted on their upperparts until they are about 18 months old. This helps conceal their presence, protecting them from predators.

Babirusa

VITAL STATISTICS

WEIGHT	60–100kg (132–220lb); some variation in size between populations on different islands
LENGTH	87–100cm (34–39in), including tail; up to 80cm (32in) tall
SEXUAL MATURITY	5–10 months
GESTATION PERIOD	155–175 days; weaning occurs 6.5–8 months later
NUMBER OF OFFSPRING	Usually 1–2
DIET	Omnivorous, eating vegetation, fruit, roots, small animals; also frequents salt licks
LIFESPAN	10–14 years

ANIMAL FACTS

While males live on their own, females associate in groups of up to five adults and their offspring. The largest female is the matriach of the group. They have set nests where the group will sleep and seek shelter from the rain. Piglets do not have stripes running down their bodies like the adults. Various predators, including pythons, will prey especially on the young, and babirusa are also hunted for food. Recent studies suggest there are fewer than 5000 left.

The babirusa's canine teeth are greatly elongated to form tusks that resemble horns. This feature is the reason for its alternative name of 'deer hog'.

WHERE IN THE WORLD?

Occurs in Indonesia, with distribution centred on the islands of Sulawesi and Buru. Also Mangole and Taliabu in the Sula archipelago, and Batudaka, Talakoh and Togian.

TEETH
The upper canines grow up and through the snout, curving round in front of the eyes.

TAIL
The tail is long and tapers significantly along its length.

SNOUT
Broad nostrils help detect scents, but the absence of a rostral bone means these pigs cannot dig well with their snouts.

HAIR
The body covering varies significantly between individuals. Some are nearly bald.

HOW BIG IS IT?

This digging is called ploughing behaviour and may be linked with scent-marking

FIGHTING
The bottom set of canines are used for fighting, but the upper set help to protect the face from injury.

Giant Forest Hog

• ORDER • Artiodactyla • FAMILY • Suidae • SPECIES • *Hylochoerus meinertzhageni*

These large, formidable members of the pig family can fight ferociously, with boars using their tusks to devastating effect if challenged.

VITAL STATISTICS

WEIGHT	100–275kg (220–606lb)
LENGTH	155–255cm (61–100in), including tail; up to 110cm (43in) tall
SEXUAL MATURITY	Females 1 year; males 3–4 years
GESTATION PERIOD	155–175 days; weaning occurs 6.5–8 months later
NUMBER OF OFFSPRING	Usually 2–6, but can be as many as 11
DIET	Omnivorous, eating vegetation, fruit, roots and carrion
LIFESPAN	Up to 12 years

ANIMAL FACTS

Giant forest hogs live in well-defined territories, tracking along the same paths each day. They will wallow in muddy areas, which keeps their skin in good condition. Members of the herd will keep in touch in the forest by grunts and other vocalizations. Piglets are born before the rainy season, with a pregnant sow creating a covered nest where she can give birth. The new family group rejoins the herd about a week later.

WHERE IN THE WORLD?

Occurs in Africa, from Guinea to Ghana, southeastern Nigeria to southwestern Sudan and Uganda, south to the Congo. Also found in Ethiopia south to Tanzania.

SKULL STRUCTURE
A clear depression, large enough to accommodate a man's fist, lies between the small ears.

SHORT TUSKS
The short tusks are modified lower canines, which rub against the longer tusks, keeping them sharp.

WARTS
These swollen areas are present beneath the eyes of boars.

LONG TUSKS
Formed from the upper canine teeth, the long tusks grow backwards and can measure up to 35cm (14in) long.

PROTECTIVE PARENTS
If a sow senses danger, she calls to her piglets, who will immediately lie down and freeze on the ground.

Male (left) and female (right)

HOW BIG IS IT?

Red River Hog

• **ORDER** • Artiodactyla • **FAMILY** • Suidae • **SPECIES** • *Potamocherus porcus*

VITAL STATISTICS

WEIGHT	45–120kg (99–265lb); boars are heavier
LENGTH	130–195cm (51–77in), including tail; up to 80cm (32in) tall
SEXUAL MATURITY	18–21 months
GESTATION PERIOD	120–127 days; weaning occurs 2–4 months later
NUMBER OF OFFSPRING	Usually 1–4, but can be as many as 6
DIET	Omnivorous, eating vegetation, fruit, roots and carrion
LIFESPAN	Can be up to 20 years

ANIMAL FACTS

These hogs are largely nocturnal, excavating burrows in woodland and swampy areas so they can rest safely during the day. Their tusks are relatively inconspicuous, although those in the lower jaw can reach 7.5cm (3in) long. Red river hogs dig using their tusks and snouts to uproot bulbs and tubers that they have located in the soil. They live in groups called 'sounders', consisting of a harem of sows and their piglets, accompanied by a boar.

These pigs are so-called because of their distinctive coat colouration, as well as their habit of wallowing in water.

WHERE IN THE WORLD?

Confined to western and central parts of Africa, from Senegal to the Central African Republic and possibly east through southern Sudan to western parts of Ethiopia.

EARS
The ears are large and taper to their tips, where there are tassels of longer hair.

TAIL
The tail is long, measuring up to 45cm (18in), and has a tuft of hair at its tip.

COLOURATION
The coat is reddish-brown with a white mane and head markings.

WARTS
Only boars have warts on their faces and a bony ridge on the forehead.

SHOVED AROUND

Fighting between boars is not especially aggressive, as the combatants generally push each other with their heads, engaging in trials of strength.

Digging for food

HOW BIG IS IT?

European Wild Boar

VITAL STATISTICS

WEIGHT	45–320kg (99–705lb); boars are heavier
LENGTH	105–240cm (41–94in), including tail; up to 110cm (43in) tall
SEXUAL MATURITY	Around 18 months
GESTATION PERIOD	112–130 days; weaning occurs 3–4 months later
NUMBER OF OFFSPRING	Usually 4–8, but can be up to 13
DIET	Omnivorous, eating vegetation, fruit, roots and carrion
LIFESPAN	Can be up to 21 years

ANIMAL FACTS

The recent growth in wild boar farming in Britain has led to this species being re-established in parts of the country, after their extinction in the 1600s. Escapees have proved adaptable, disappearing into suitable areas of countryside where there is cover available. A sow can be particularly aggressive in the spring, when she has piglets with her. Wild boar can also colonize new areas by swimming; they can travel up to 7km (4 miles) in this way.

Boar (above) and sow (below)

This species is believed to be the wild ancestor of the domestic pig, and the two will hybridize readily when they come into contact.

WHERE IN THE WORLD?

Ranges across most of Europe, including southern Scandinavia, and much of the southern half of Asia, to Japan and Indonesia. Also occurs in North Africa.

COAT
The coat is coarse, with a bristly texture, brownish in young animals, but becoming more grey with age.

LEGS
The legs are quite long and well-muscled, helping these pigs to swim.

TUSKS
Lower canines protrude beyond the lips, and are very sharp.

HOW BIG IS IT?

WALLOWING IN MUD
Wallowing is a popular activity, particularly in summer when the weather is hot, as it helps the wild boar to stay cool.

Collared Peccary

• ORDER • Artiodactyla • FAMILY • Tayassuidae • SPECIES • *Pecari tajacu*

Active during the day, these peccaries are known locally by various other names, including javelinas and forest hogs, because of their strong body odour.

VITAL STATISTICS

WEIGHT	14–31kg (31–68lb); males are heavier
LENGTH	82–110cm (32–43in), including tail; up to 50cm (20in) tall
SEXUAL MATURITY	Females 8–14 months; males 11–12 months
GESTATION PERIOD	141–151 days; weaning occurs 2–3 months later
NUMBER OF OFFSPRING	1–5
DIET	Omnivorous, eating vegetation, fruit, roots and carrion
LIFESPAN	Up to 24 years, but generally less in the wild

ANIMAL FACTS

Scent marking is very important to these peccaries, as a way of marking their territory and keeping in touch with each other. They also use their droppings for the same purpose. Any attempts by a stranger to be accepted into the herd will be vigorously repelled and the newcomer driven away. Females give birth on their own, but rejoin the herd the following day. Ultimately, some of their young will also be forced out of the area.

WHERE IN THE WORLD?

Occurs in the southern USA, through Central America (apart from north-central Mexico), and east of the Andes down to northern Argentina and Brazil in South America.

HEAD
The head is narrow, terminating in a relatively flexible snout. The ears are small.

BODY
The rounded profile is emphasized by the almost complete lack of a tail.

COAT
The coat is a greyish to grizzled black colour, with a yellow band under the neck and a bristly texture.

GLANDULAR SECRETIONS
Glands on the back release an oily fluid with a musky scent.

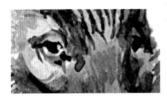

Beady eyes indicate poor eyesight

HOW BIG IS IT?

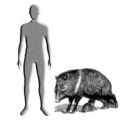

SUCKLING
Young collared peccaries are shown here suckling. They are quite different from adults in terms of colouration at this age.

Common Whelk

• **ORDER** • Caenogastropoda • **FAMILY** • Buccinidae • **SPECIES** • *Buccinum undatum*

VITAL STATISTICS

LENGTH	About 10cm (4in) tall and 6cm (2.3in) wide
SEXUAL MATURITY	1–2 years
EGGS	Laid in capsules, each containing about 1000 eggs
DEVELOPMENTAL PERIOD	Lasts several months, with miniature whelks emerging from the egg capsules
HABITAT	From shallow water right down to depths of 1200m (3937ft)
DIET	Other invertebrates, notably polychaete worms and bivalve molluscs; also eats carrion
LIFESPAN	Up to 10 years

ANIMAL FACTS

Each egg capsule produces relatively few young, because many of the eggs are not fertilized. These serve as a source of food to sustain the young whelks prior to hatching. Resembling lentils, the egg capsules can be seen attached to rocks, sometimes in clusters. Once empty, they are often called 'sea wash balls', and frequently drift on to beaches. They appear similar to sponges, and have traditionally been used for washing.

These carnivorous marine snails have a remarkable ability to smell food, thanks to their siphon. This draws in water over an organ that detect scents.

WHERE IN THE WORLD?

Common along the coasts of northwestern Europe and Britain. Most evident in rocky areas, especially rock pools, at low tide.

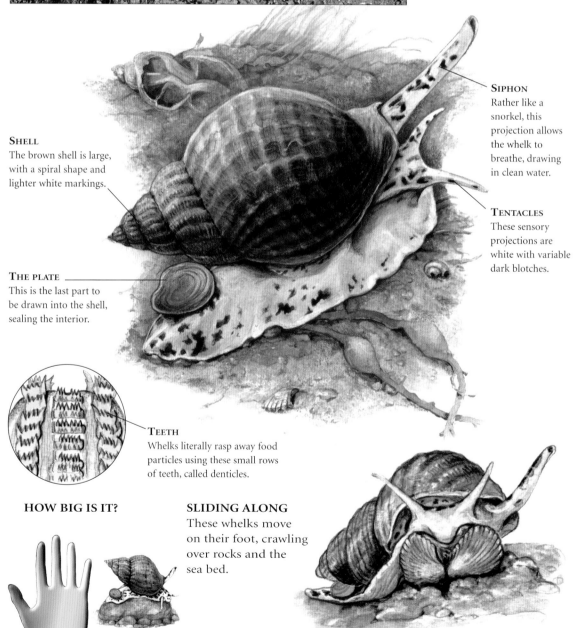

SHELL
The brown shell is large, with a spiral shape and lighter white markings.

SIPHON
Rather like a snorkel, this projection allows the whelk to breathe, drawing in clean water.

TENTACLES
These sensory projections are white with variable dark blotches.

THE PLATE
This is the last part to be drawn into the shell, sealing the interior.

TEETH
Whelks literally rasp away food particles using these small rows of teeth, called denticles.

HOW BIG IS IT?

SLIDING ALONG
These whelks move on their foot, crawling over rocks and the sea bed.

Triton

VITAL STATISTICS

LENGTH	Up to 35cm (13.7in) tall and 18cm (7in) wide
SEXUAL MATURITY	1–2 years
EGGS	Laid in capsules; may be guarded until they hatch about 2 months after laying
DEVELOPMENTAL PERIOD	Young drift in the planktonic layer of the ocean for about 3 months
HABITAT	Generally found in relatively shallow and coastal waters
DIET	Invertebrates, other molluscs and starfish
LIFESPAN	Over 10 years

ANIMAL FACTS

Tritons actively hunt their prey, and have proved especially welcome on Australia's Great Barrier Reef, as they are one of the few predators that attack the crown-of-thorns starfish, which are destroying the coral. They pursue the starfish, which have little hope of escape, as the triton can move faster. The mollusc latches on to its prey, using its rough mouthparts to break open the starfish's skin, and injects its paralyzing saliva. It then eats the soft body parts.

These large molluscs are named after the son of the Greek sea god Poisedon, who is often portrayed holding the triton's distinctive, attractively patterned shell.

WHERE IN THE WORLD?

Members of this genus are widely distributed in the world's oceans, in temperate and tropical seas. The largest species occurs in the Indo-Pacific region.

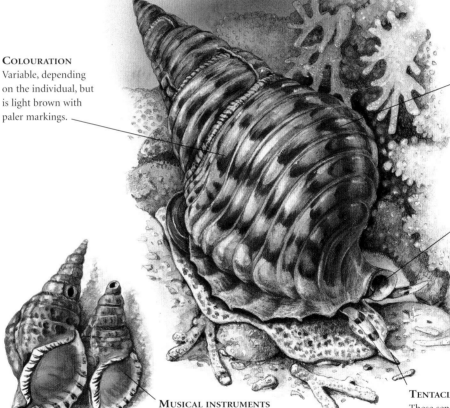

COLOURATION
Variable, depending on the individual, but is light brown with paler markings.

SHELL
The length of the shell is described as the spire, with evident ridges over it.

SHELL FOLD
This provides the breathing tube, or spiracle.

TENTACLES
These sensory projections protrude from under the shell, with the eyes at their base.

MUSICAL INSTRUMENTS
Large triton shells have traditionally been converted to musical instruments by having holes drilled through them.

HOW BIG IS IT?

INNER SHELL
The outer lip is thickened, with a distinctive fold. The inner part of the shell is orangish in colour.

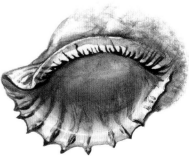

Great Hammerhead Shark

• ORDER • Carcharhiniformes • FAMILY • Sphyrnidae • SPECIES • *Sphyrna mokarran*

VITAL STATISTICS

WEIGHT	230–450kg (507–992lb); pregnant females can weigh 580kg (1278lb)
LENGTH	Females average 365cm (144in); males average 285cm (112in); can reach 610cm (240in)
SEXUAL MATURITY	Females from 210cm (83in); males from 225cm (89in)
GESTATION PERIOD	310–365 days
NUMBER OF OFFSPRING	Up to 55, measuring 70cm (28in), with faces flattened against their bodies
DIET	Rays, smaller sharks, squid and bony fish
LIFESPAN	20–30 years

ANIMAL FACTS

One of the most remarkable features of hammerhead sharks is the way that females can give birth without mating. This method of breeding, known as 'parthenogenesis', had not been recorded in cartilagenous fish, although it is quite common in invertebrates. Tests confirmed that the shark's DNA derived exclusively from its mother. The great hammerhead is not considered particularly dangerous to people.

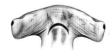

The head seen from below, with sensory pits evident

The amazing head shape of these fish is highly distinctive, and is believed to help them pick up electrical signals emitted by their prey.

WHERE IN THE WORLD?

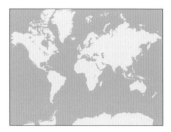

Found throughout tropical oceans worldwide, usually close to reefs, sometimes even swimming close to the coast in water just 100cm (39in) deep.

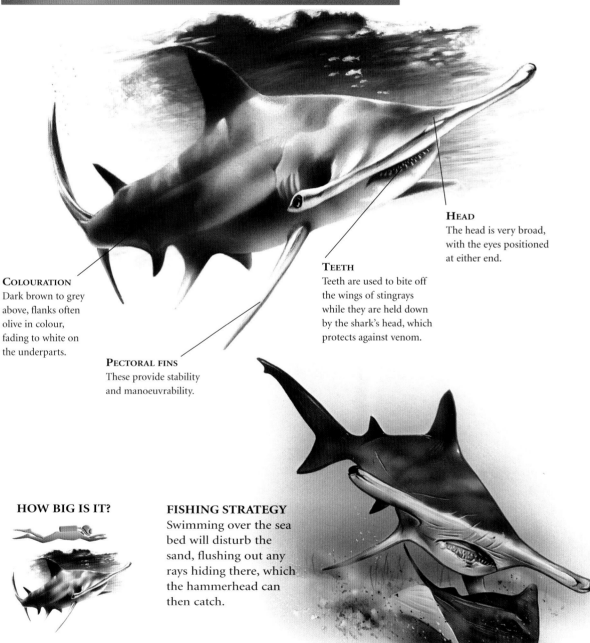

COLOURATION
Dark brown to grey above, flanks often olive in colour, fading to white on the underparts.

PECTORAL FINS
These provide stability and manoeuvrability.

TEETH
Teeth are used to bite off the wings of stingrays while they are held down by the shark's head, which protects against venom.

HEAD
The head is very broad, with the eyes positioned at either end.

HOW BIG IS IT?

FISHING STRATEGY
Swimming over the sea bed will disturb the sand, flushing out any rays hiding there, which the hammerhead can then catch.

Red Panda

This species has no close relatives, so it is now classified in its own family. It does, however, share some characteristics with the giant panda.

VITAL STATISTICS

WEIGHT	4–6kg (9–13lb)
LENGTH	Up to about 107cm (42in), including tail
SEXUAL MATURITY	About 18 months
GESTATION PERIOD	112–158 days
NUMBER OF OFFSPRING	1–5, but averaging 2; the current population is only 2500 individuals
DIET	Feeds largely on bamboo shoots, gripped with their bony wrists; also eats other vegetation, as well as birds' eggs and nestlings
LIFESPAN	12–14 years

ANIMAL FACTS

Red pandas spend most of their time off the ground, climbing in trees. Much of the day is spent asleep or foraging for food here. When resting, red pandas curl up and wrap their tails around themselves, often remaining hidden in a hollow chamber in a tree, which they line with soft material such as moss. Their diet is very specialized – based on bamboo. Clearance and fragmentation of bamboo forests in various parts of their range is adversely affecting their numbers.

The claws only partially retract

WHERE IN THE WORLD?

Mountainous forests in the Himalayan region through southern Asia, from India, Bhutan, Nepal, Myanmar (Burma) to Laos and the Chinese provinces of Yunnan and Sichuan.

COLOURATION
Rich russet fur with black legs and underparts.

STANDING TALL
These pandas can stand up on their hind legs.

EARS
The ears are broad and pointed, whitish in colour and set low on the head.

FACIAL MARKINGS
Brown stripes extend below the eyes; the muzzle is white.

TAIL
The tail is thick and well-furred, with lighter rings along its length.

HOW BIG IS IT?

GROUND LEVEL
It is usually only at night that red pandas leave the trees to roam on the ground, where they move more slowly.

Golden Jackal

VITAL STATISTICS

WEIGHT	7–15kg (15–33lb); males are heavier
LENGTH	95–130cm (38–52in), including tail; up to 50cm (20in) tall
SEXUAL MATURITY	About 11 months
GESTATION PERIOD	About 63 days; weaning occurs up to 3 months later
NUMBER OF OFFSPRING	2–4
DIET	Omnivorous, hunting birds and mammals, as well as scavenging; also eats plant matter
LIFESPAN	12–14 years

ANIMAL FACTS

These jackals are highly adaptable by nature, and are quite common throughout the areas in which they occur. In some regions, groups of up to five individuals may hunt collectively, which helps them to overpower larger and potentially faster prey. Their acute hearing means that they can locate small animals hiding in vegetation, and they can also become adept at catching fish. When hunting opportunities are reduced, they will eat invertebrates and feed on fruit in season.

Golden jackals playing

This is the largest species of jackal, but it displays considerable variation in size and appearance across its wide range, with 13 different races being recognized.

WHERE IN THE WORLD?

Found in northern and eastern parts of Africa, through Arabia and southern parts of Asia, east to Myanmar (Burma). Also occurs in parts of southeastern Europe.

COLOURATION
The fur is usually yellowish with darker tipping, but this can vary both seasonally and regionally.

DEVELOPMENT OF PUPS
Pups weigh about 200g (7oz) at birth, and their eyes open at about 10 days old.

TAIL
The bushy tail is usually held down at rest.

HELPERS
Young from a previous litter may stay with the adult pair, helping them to protect and raise their next litter.

HOW BIG IS IT?

German Shepherd Dog

• ORDER • Carnivora • FAMILY • Canidae • SPECIES • *Canis familiaris*

The ancestral appearance of the grey wolf is evident in this popular domestic dog. However, the breed was created from other dogs rather than wolves.

VITAL STATISTICS

WEIGHT	22–40kg (49–88lb)
LENGTH	Up to 76cm (30in) long; up to 65cm (26in) tall
SEXUAL MATURITY	6–12 months; bitches have two periods of heat annually
GESTATION PERIOD	63 days
NUMBER OF OFFSPRING	Typically around 8; weaning occurs at 42–56 days
DIET	Omnivorous, eating both vegetable matter and animal protein; dogs can maintain good health on vegetarian diets
LIFESPAN	11–12 years

ANIMAL FACTS

The German shepherd is one of the most intelligent dog breeds. Used originally for herding sheep, it has since been trained for a wide variety of tasks, from police work to helping handicapped people. Similar shepherd breeds have existed for centuries in Europe, but they do not enjoy the popularity of their German relative.

Body language

Confident

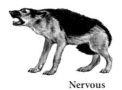

Nervous

WHERE IN THE WORLD?

This breed is also known as the Alsatian, which commemorates the area of Alsace-Lorraine on the Franco-German border where it was developed.

EARS
Upright, triangular-shaped ears help detect and localize the source of sounds.

MUZZLE
The relatively long, broad muzzle aids the dog's scenting abilities.

COAT
Short-coated examples are common, although long-haired individuals are occasionally seen.

COLOURATION
A dark area of fur extends down the back to the tail in most cases, although patterning is individual. A rare white-coated form exists.

CLAWS
Dew claws on the inside of the front legs are raised slightly off the ground – the equivalent of the human thumb.

LEGS
The forelegs are straight and powerful.

HOW BIG IS IT?

CROSS-BREEDING

The similarity between the German shepherd dog and the grey wolf encouraged a breeder to cross these two canids in the 1930s, creating what are now known as wolf-dog hybrids. The resulting puppies proved to be much more nervous than domestic dogs, as well as being significantly harder to train.

Coyote

VITAL STATISTICS

WEIGHT	7–21kg (15–46lb); males are heavier, as are those of northern races
LENGTH	105–140cm (41–55in); up to 87cm (34in) tall
SEXUAL MATURITY	12 months
GESTATION PERIOD	60–63 days
NUMBER OF OFFSPRING	1–19, average 6; weaned by 35 days
DIET	Omnivorous, opportunistic hunters, mainly of small mammals, larger insects and birds, as well as scavengers and consumers of vegetable matter
LIFESPAN	11–12 years

ANIMAL FACTS

As wolves have declined in numbers across North America, so the smaller and more adaptable coyote has become more numerous. Its range expanded markedly through the twentieth century and now coyotes can be encountered in suburban parts of New York and elsewhere, reaching the east coast only 30 years ago. These wild dogs are unpopular with farmers as they attack sheep, although they also prey more commonly on jackrabbits, which can harm the grazing.

Coyotes live on their own or in pairs

Unlike domestic dogs, female coyotes only give birth once a year, in early summer. They can hybridize, though, creating offspring called 'coydogs'.

WHERE IN THE WORLD?

Occurs throughout North America, from Alaska southwards to Mexico. Present in all US mainland states. Only absent from north-central and western Canada.

EARS
The ears are broad and, when held erect, help pinpoint sounds, allowing hunting under cover of darkness.

SNOUT
The snout is quite narrow, with black nostrils.

EYES
Watchful and alert, the eyes are green. Coyotes have excellent night vision.

COLOURATION
Coyotes from desert areas have reddish coats, while those inhabiting woodland areas are more grey.

HOW BIG IS IT?

HOWLING AT THE MOON
Coyotes regularly howl and bark at night. This is also the time of day when they are most active.

Grey Wolf

This species was one of the most widely distributed mammals in the northern hemisphere, but hunting pressures and increasing urbanization have greatly reduced its range.

VITAL STATISTICS

WEIGHT	15–80kg (33–176lb); males and northern races are heavier
LENGTH	130–200cm (51–79in); up to 87cm (34in) tall
SEXUAL MATURITY	2–3 years
GESTATION PERIOD	60–63 days
NUMBER OF OFFSPRING	1–19, average 5–6; weaned by 70 days
DIET	Primarily carnivorous, mainly hunts ungulates such as bison, deer, sheep, goat and caribou
LIFESPAN	6–9 years; may live over 12 years in captivity

ANIMAL FACTS

Wolves maintain territorial boundaries, scent-marking regularly. The size and availability of prey seems to determine pack size. There can be up to 20 or more wolves in herds in Alaska, where they face strong and dangerous prey such as moose. In desert areas though, where food is more scarce, they may live as pairs, being lighter and quicker to catch smaller and faster quarry.

Wolf

Dog

Domestic dogs are directly descended from wolves

WHERE IN THE WORLD?

Now confined to more remote areas in Canada, Michigan and Wisconsin in the USA, and Russia, as well as a few areas of Europe.

MUZZLE
Male grey wolves have broader muzzles and broader foreheads than females.

COLOURATION
In spite of its name, the grey wolf's coat colour is actually very variable.

COAT STRUCTURE
The coat is double-layered, with a weather resistant outer layer and an insulating undercoat.

PACK ORDER
There is a rigorous hierarchy in wolf packs. Usually only the dominant pair will breed, with other pack members helping to raise the cubs.

HOW BIG IS IT?

FEET
There is slight webbing between the toes, to help the wolves walk over snowy ground without sinking into it.

Dingo

VITAL STATISTICS

Weight	23–32kg (50–70lb); males are heavier
Length	157–262cm (62–103in); up to 58cm (23in) tall
Sexual Maturity	Females 2 years; males 1–3 years
Gestation Period	61–69 days; weaned at 3–6 months
Number of Offspring	5–6
Diet	Documented as preying on 170 species in Australia, ranging from invertebrates to water buffalo; may scavenge and also eats fruit
Lifespan	Up to 14 years

ANIMAL FACTS

Dingoes are feral dogs, meaning they have reverted from being domesticated to a free-living existence. This has brought them into conflict with farmers, because they will prey on sheep. Dingoes are mainly nocturnal, living on their own or in small packs. Females have just one litter each year, in common with wild canids, giving birth between May and July in temperate latitudes. They can also cross-breed successfully with domestic dogs.

Dingo (left) and Australian cattle dog (right); the dingo was used in the development of this breed

The ancestors of the dingo were brought to Australia around 4000 years ago by early Aboriginal settlers, and they now live wild on the continent.

WHERE IN THE WORLD?

The ancestral line originated in Southeast Asia, with similar dogs in New Guinea, but the dingo itself is confined to mainland states of Australia.

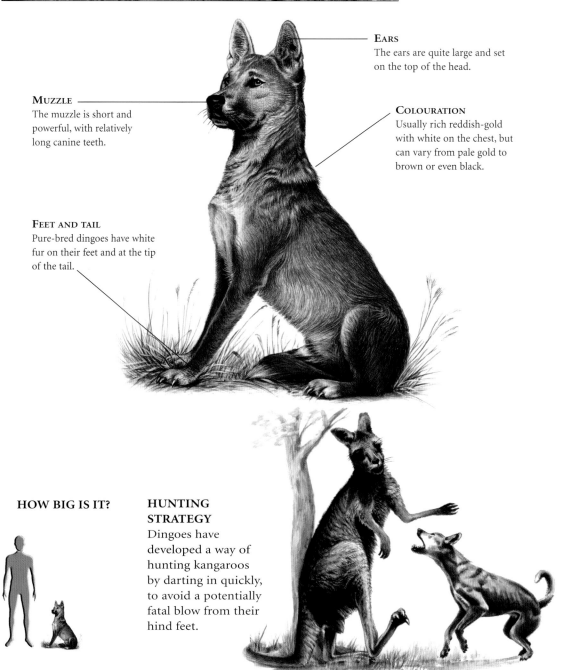

Ears
The ears are quite large and set on the top of the head.

Muzzle
The muzzle is short and powerful, with relatively long canine teeth.

Colouration
Usually rich reddish-gold with white on the chest, but can vary from pale gold to brown or even black.

Feet and tail
Pure-bred dingoes have white fur on their feet and at the tip of the tail.

HOW BIG IS IT?

HUNTING STRATEGY
Dingoes have developed a way of hunting kangaroos by darting in quickly, to avoid a potentially fatal blow from their hind feet.

Black-Backed Jackal

• **ORDER** • Carnivora • **FAMILY** • Canidae • **SPECIES** • *Canis mesomelas*

VITAL STATISTICS

WEIGHT	7–13.5kg (15–30lb); males and southern races are heavier
LENGTH	95–136cm (37–54in); up to 42cm (19in) tall
SEXUAL MATURITY	About 11 months
GESTATION PERIOD	60–65 days
NUMBER OF OFFSPRING	3–6
DIET	Omnivorous, hunting small prey like hares and rodents; also scavenges and eats fruit and berries
LIFESPAN	Up to 8 years in the wild; can be 12–14 years in captivity

ANIMAL FACTS

Female black-backed jackals tend to be paler in colour than males. Pairs form a lifelong bond, but they may sometimes join up with other black-backed jackals to take larger prey. Some of the young from the previous year may also stay with their parents, helping them to hunt and increasing the survival chances of the next set of offspring. They are opportunistic too, scavenging on whatever food might be available, including Cape fur seal carcasses.

Fossil evidence suggests this species is the oldest surviving member of its genus, existing before the grey wolf, and long before the domestic dog.

WHERE IN THE WORLD?

Two distinct populations, occurring in eastern Africa, including Somalia, Ethiopia and Kenya, and also across southern Africa, in Zimbabwe, Botswana, South Africa and Namibia.

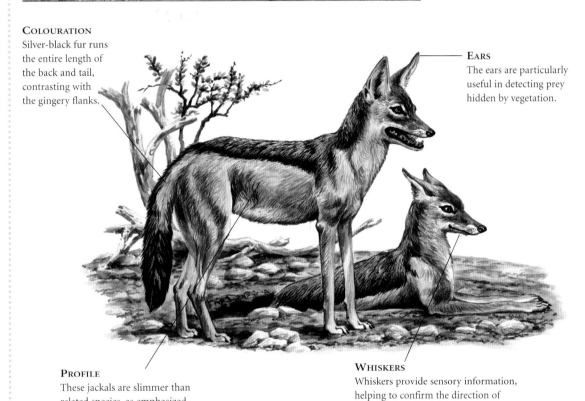

COLOURATION
Silver-black fur runs the entire length of the back and tail, contrasting with the gingery flanks.

EARS
The ears are particularly useful in detecting prey hidden by vegetation.

PROFILE
These jackals are slimmer than related species, as emphasized by their long muzzle.

WHISKERS
Whiskers provide sensory information, helping to confirm the direction of the wind when hunting.

HUNTING TOGETHER
Hunting partnerships can be very successful. Here, one jackal distracts the female gazelle, allowing the other to seize her youngster.

HOW BIG IS IT?

These jackals will dig burrows themselves

Maned Wolf

VITAL STATISTICS

WEIGHT	20–25kg (44–55lb)
LENGTH	150–160cm (59–63in); up to 91cm (36in) tall
SEXUAL MATURITY	2 years
GESTATION PERIOD	60–65 days
NUMBER OF OFFSPRING	2–6; weaning at around 105 days
DIET	Omnivorous, feeding on small animals, birds and invertebrates, but probably half of its diet consists of plant matter and fruit
LIFESPAN	7–10 years in the wild; up to 15 in captivity

ANIMAL FACTS

Maned wolves are generally nocturnal in their habits. Like other wild canids, females come into heat just once a year, between March and April. Although they live in pairs, occupying territories ranging up to 30km² (11.5 square miles), maned wolves mix only during this period. They will scent-mark their territory regularly. Their urine, used for this purpose, has a distinctive odour, resembling cannabis. This is probably the result of a pyrazine-type chemical ingested as part of their diet.

The maned wolf has a very narrow body

These distinctive wild dogs are the largest South American canid, living singly or in pairs rather than packs. They are actually not closely related to wolves.

WHERE IN THE WORLD?

Southern South America, occurring in central and southeastern parts of Brazil, plus eastern Paraguay and Bolivia. Also found in northern Argentina.

TAIL
The tail can be completely white, or have white fur just at the tip.

MANE
This ridge of fur can be raised, and extends from the neck down over the shoulders.

EARS
The ears measure up to 18cm (7in) long, and help to locate prey hidden in grass.

LEGS
Long and relatively slender, the legs emphasize the athletic nature of this canid.

CAT IN WOLF'S CLOTHING?
The way in which the maned wolf hunts rodents is similar to that of a cat, pouncing on its prey from above.

HOW BIG IS IT?

Dhole

• **ORDER** • Carnivora • **FAMILY** • Canidae • **SPECIES** • *Cuon alpinus*

VITAL STATISTICS

WEIGHT	12–20kg (26–44lb), depending on race
LENGTH	95–136cm (37–54in); up to 42cm (19in) tall
SEXUAL MATURITY	12 months
GESTATION PERIOD	60–63 days; weaned at 6–9 weeks
NUMBER OF OFFSPRING	Up to 12, but typically 5–10
DIET	Omnivorous, hunting hares and larger quarry such as deer; also scavenges
LIFESPAN	8 years; can be 12–14 years in captivity

ANIMAL FACTS

Out of all the members of the family Canidae, the dhole is the only species to have one fewer molar in each of its lower jaws. This means that it has 40 teeth in its mouth, rather than 42. Another unusual feature is that females have up to seven pairs of mammary glands rather than the typical five, which may be a reflection of their relatively large litter size. The sexes are otherwise similar in appearance, with no marked variance in size.

A family group, with the young dholes playing outside their den

At the end of the last Ice Age, about 15,000 years ago, dholes ranged right across the northern hemisphere, but now their distribution is much smaller.

WHERE IN THE WORLD?

Occurs in Southeast Asia, from India east to China, and through the Malay peninsula down to Java, but has disappeared from many areas because of forest clearance.

COLOURATION
Dholes from southern areas have shorter and redder fur than those found further north.

SKULL SHAPE
The skull is broad and domed above; dholes have large round ears and strong, powerful jaws.

TAIL
The black tail is bushy in appearance, especially towards the tip.

FEET
The front paws are partially fused – probably a legacy from the last Ice Age, when these wild dogs would have walked regularly on snow.

GROUP LIVING
Packs of dholes have the strength and determination to dispossess even a fierce predator like a tiger of food on occasion.

HOW BIG IS IT?

African Hunting Dog

VITAL STATISTICS

WEIGHT	17–36kg (37–79lb); males slightly larger
LENGTH	52–58cm (21–23in); up to 75cm (30in) tall
SEXUAL MATURITY	12–18 months
GESTATION PERIOD	65–70 days; weaning occurs at 10 weeks
NUMBER OF OFFSPRING	2–19, but an average of 10
DIET	Hunts medium-sized ungulates like impalas, and also bigger animals such as zebras and ostriches
LIFESPAN	Up to 11 years in the wild

ANIMAL FACTS

As part of the weaning process, female African wild dogs will vomit up food for their puppies. This is easier for the young dogs to eat, having been exposed to digestive juices in the stomach. The pack structure revolves around the dominant pair, and can consist of anything between six and 20 individuals. As these canids have become less common – because of hunting and disease – their pack sizes have grown smaller and they are less able to tackle traditional prey.

A female feeds her litter

The scientific name of these canids translates as 'painted wolf' and refers to their highly individual patterning, which allows individuals to be identified from some distance away.

WHERE IN THE WORLD?

Confined to Africa, especially in deciduous forests, it ranges across central and eastern parts of the continent, down to northern South Africa and northern Namibia.

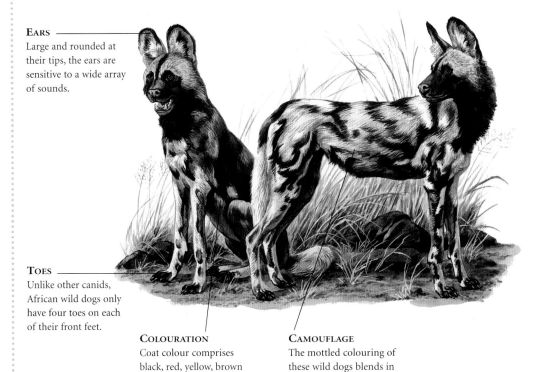

EARS
Large and rounded at their tips, the ears are sensitive to a wide array of sounds.

TOES
Unlike other canids, African wild dogs only have four toes on each of their front feet.

COLOURATION
Coat colour comprises black, red, yellow, brown and white areas. No two individuals having the same markings.

CAMOUFLAGE
The mottled colouring of these wild dogs blends in well in grassland areas.

HOLDING ON
When attacking prey, one member of the pack always holds on to the unfortunate animal's tail, allowing its companions to strike in greater safety.

HOW BIG IS IT?

Raccoon Dog

• ORDER • Carnivora • FAMILY • Canidae • SPECIES • *Nyctereutes procyonoides*

VITAL STATISTICS

WEIGHT	4–10kg (9–22lb); males are slightly larger
LENGTH	63–73cm (25–29in); up to 25cm (10in) tall
SEXUAL MATURITY	12 months
GESTATION PERIOD	About 60 days; weaning occurs at 8 weeks
NUMBER OF OFFSPRING	Large litters of up to 15 pups
DIET	Omnivorous, feeding on invertebrates, and other small animals, including frogs and lizards; also eats fruit and berries
LIFESPAN	4–5 years, but up to 11 years in captivity

ANIMAL FACTS

The fur of these canids has been highly sought-after, and there were attempts to farm these animals in the Soviet Union and in Latvia. Some raccoon dogs from these farms escaped, and have been multiplying in the wild since the late 1950s. Now established in the Baltic region, there are reports of them as far south as Italy and France. Highly adaptable by nature, they survive freezing conditions by becoming torpid during the winter months.

Raccoon dogs have a den where they can sleep over the winter

These canids are unusual, not least because, unlike virtually all other dogs, they can climb effectively using their sharp claws. They also do not bark.

WHERE IN THE WORLD?

Naturally resident in Asia, with populations in China, south to Korea, also southeastern Siberia and Japan. Has been introduced to northern Europe and is spreading further south.

FACIAL APPEARANCE
The broad face, with its distinctive black and white patterning, resembles that of the unrelated raccoon.

TAIL
The tail is used for communication, and can be raised into a U-shape by a dominant individual.

COAT
The coat is long, protecting against the elements and emphasizing the rounded outline of this species.

TEETH
The teeth are quite small compared with those of other canids.

A GROWING FAMILY

The young are born in a well-concealed den, and both adults will assist in the rearing of their offspring.

HOW BIG IS IT?

Bat-Eared Fox

• **ORDER** • Carnivora • **FAMILY** • Canidae • **SPECIES** • *Otocyon megalotis*

Unlike other canids, these small foxes are largely insectivorous in their feeding habits, hunting mainly locusts and termites, although they will also take bigger prey.

VITAL STATISTICS

WEIGHT	3–4.5kg (7–10lb); males are slightly larger
LENGTH	80–95cm (32–37in); up to 40cm (16in) tall
SEXUAL MATURITY	8–9 months
GESTATION PERIOD	About 60 days; weaning occurs at 5 weeks
NUMBER OF OFFSPRING	2–5
DIET	Largely insectivorous, the bulk of their diet consists of invertebrates; also catches small mammals, lizards and birds
LIFESPAN	4–6 years in the wild; up to 13 in captivity

ANIMAL FACTS

Living in pairs, these foxes inhabit areas of open woodland and grassland. They look rather like small jackals, and are often killed for this reason, although they pose no threat to domestic livestock such as sheep. The female gives birth at the start of the rainy season, when insect prey is likely to be most easily obtainable. The young leave the den for the first time when they are about two weeks old. Adults breed just once a year.

WHERE IN THE WORLD?

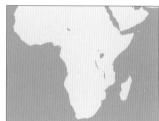

Occurs in East Africa, with populations in Ethiopia, Somalia and Tanzania, as well as further south, in Mozambique, Zimbabwe, Botswana, South Africa, Namibia and Angola.

FUR COLOUR
The fur is greyish-brown broken up with lighter yellowish areas, especially around the throat.

EARS
The remarkable ears are about 13cm (5in) long, and very broad. They help to locate underground prey.

FRONT PAWS
The front paws are often used for digging, helping to obtain prey or excavate a den.

LEGS
The legs are a dark shade of brown.

DANGEROUS LIVING

The small size of these foxes means they are vulnerable not just to ground predators such as hyenas, but also to birds of prey.

Bat-eared foxes have small teeth

HOW BIG IS IT?

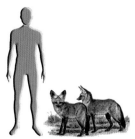

Grey Fox

• **ORDER** • Carnivora • **FAMILY** • Canidae • **SPECIES** • *Urocyon cinereoargenteus*

These attractively coloured canids differ from other species of fox in that they are adept at climbing, rather than spending all their time on the ground.

VITAL STATISTICS

WEIGHT	2.5–6.5kg (5.5–14lb); males are slightly larger
LENGTH	81–113cm (32–44in); up to 30cm (12in) tall
SEXUAL MATURITY	8–9 months
GESTATION PERIOD	51–63 days; weaning occurs at 5 weeks
NUMBER OF OFFSPRING	1–10
DIET	Omnivorous, feeding on small mammals; also eats fruit and vegetable matter
LIFESPAN	4–6 years in the wild; up to 13 in captivity

ANIMAL FACTS

Grey foxes live in pairs. They usually occupy a den in a hollow tree or under tree roots, where they will rest during the day, emerging at dusk and hunting under cover of darkness. They can be at risk from attack by coyotes, and being able to climb helps them escape their larger relatives. The young learn to hunt by accompanying their parents, and the family group remains together until the autumn.

Food is brought home for the family

WHERE IN THE WORLD?

Ranges from southern parts of Canada, across much of the USA down through Mexico and Central America, as far as Colombia and Venezuela in northern South America.

TAIL
The tail is bushy with a black tip.

STRIPE
A blackish stripe runs down the centre of the back.

COLOURATION
Grey fur predominates, particularly over the back, with white on the underparts and a noticeable chestnut-red bib.

FEET
The feet are strong, equipped with powerful claws that help the fox to maintain its grip.

HOW BIG IS IT?

HEAD FOR HEIGHTS

These foxes will climb trees in search of lizards and young birds, which they will steal from nests. They can jump well if necessary.

Bush Dog

VITAL STATISTICS

WEIGHT	5–7kg (11–15lb); males are slightly larger
LENGTH	68–88cm (27–35in); may stand only 25cm (10in) tall
SEXUAL MATURITY	1 year
GESTATION PERIOD	63 days; weaning occurs at 8 weeks
NUMBER OF OFFSPRING	Up to 6
DIET	Carnivorous, hunting rodents such as pacas in particular
LIFESPAN	Up to 10 years in captivity

ANIMAL FACTS

Bush dogs first became known from fossilized remains discovered in a Brazilian cave, rather than from a living animal. Their small size makes them hard to observe, particularly in rainforest areas, where there are numerous hiding places. They may retreat into hollow logs, or seek out the abandoned burrows of other species. Hunting in packs means that they can tackle larger quarry. Bush dogs have a distinctive whining call, which they use to keep in touch with each other.

Bush dogs have small legs

Although their range is wide, these short-legged canids are actually quite scarce. They occur in packs of up to a dozen individuals.

WHERE IN THE WORLD?

Ranges over a wide area in Central and South America, west of the Andes, from Panama down to northeastern Argentina and Amazonas state, Brazil.

FACIAL PROFILE
Bush dogs have broad nostrils, which help them pick up trails close to the forest floor. They also have powerful, compact jaws.

EARS
The ears are relatively small, set low and located well back on the skull.

COLOURATION
Adults are tan in colour but pups are dark grey at birth.

HINDQUARTERS
These are well-muscled, helping the bush dog to run or swim efficiently.

HOW BIG IS IT?

HUNTING IN WATER

The toes of bush dogs are webbed, helping them to swim more effectively, so they can pursue prey through the water.

Arctic Fox

VITAL STATISTICS

WEIGHT	3–3.5kg (6.5–7.5lb); males are heavier
LENGTH	83cm (33in)
SEXUAL MATURITY	2 years
GESTATION PERIOD	52 days
NUMBER OF OFFSPRING	6–15; weaning occurs at 35–63 days
DIET	Omnivorous, eating lemmings, birds, eggs, fish and berries; even scavenges on the carcasses of large marine mammals such as seals
LIFESPAN	5–7 years in the wild; up to 10 in captivity

ANIMAL FACTS

Arctic foxes occur where there are no trees to provide cover, so they rely on their colouration to conceal their presence and make it easier to hunt. They live in underground dens, sometimes in small groups, although there is likely to be a dominant pair. Other group members help to find food to rear their offspring. These foxes are well-insulated against the cold – even the soles of their feet are covered with fur to protect them from frostbite.

In summer, after the snow has melted, the coats are generally darker in colour

Found further north than any other member of the dog family, the Arctic fox is well-adapted to this incredibly harsh environment.

WHERE IN THE WORLD?

Occurs in the far north, extending across the circumpolar region. Present in Alaska, northern Canada and Greenland as well as in northern Europe and Asia.

MUZZLE
The short muzzle prevents heat loss. The nose is black, as are the claws.

COLOURATION
Not all Arctic foxes are white; some are greyish-brown (described as 'blue').

TAIL
The fur covering the tail, as elsewhere, is dense, giving it a bushy appearance.

HUNTING
Arctic foxes are highly adaptable in their feeding habits, scavenging on carrion and sometimes even attacking seal pups.

HOW BIG IS IT?

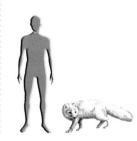

Red Fox

VITAL STATISTICS

WEIGHT	3–10kg (6.5–22lb); those from northern areas are heavier
LENGTH	90–139cm (36–55in)
SEXUAL MATURITY	1–2 years
GESTATION PERIOD	53 days
NUMBER OF OFFSPRING	Average 3–4, but up to 12 recorded; weaning occurs at around 60 days
DIET	Animals and birds up to 3kg (6.5lb); also scavenges and eats berries, fruit and vegetables
LIFESPAN	Typically 3–5 years, but can be up to 12

ANIMAL FACTS

The ghostly shrieks of these foxes, heard late at night during the courtship period, can be quite alarming. The female is known as a vixen while the male is described as a dog fox. A pair will dig an underground burrow, sometimes under a building. Their cubs will be born here in the summer. They will generally remain with their parents over the winter. Male offspring are then likely to wander off further than female offspring in search of territories.

Front paw   Hind paw

The front feet of these foxes are narrower than their hind feet

A very versatile species, the red fox is now the most widely distributed wild canid in the world and has adapted well to city life.

WHERE IN THE WORLD?

Occurs in the northern hemisphere, from above the line of latitude marking 30°N up to the Arctic. Also present in North Africa. Has been introduced to Australia.

COLOURATION
The red colouration of these foxes varies between individuals and also reflects their environment. It is generally darker in foxes living in upland areas.

TAIL
The tail of the red fox is known as the brush. It is well-covered in fur and always ends in a white tip. It can be kept low, as here, but is raised when the fox is on the move or excited.

HOW BIG IS IT?

CATCHING PREY
These foxes adapt their hunting technique to suit the environment in which they are hunting, as well as their prey.

Fennec Fox

These desert-dwelling foxes are superbly adapted to living in their particularly harsh environment. They are the smallest of all canids, with disproportionately large ears.

VITAL STATISTICS

WEIGHT	1–1.5kg (2–3lb); males slightly larger
LENGTH	43–71cm (17–28in); may stand only 20cm (8in) tall
SEXUAL MATURITY	6–11 months
GESTATION PERIOD	50–52 days; weaning occurs at 8 weeks
NUMBER OF OFFSPRING	2–5
DIET	Omnivorous, hunting rodents, rabbits, small birds and lizards, as well as invertebrates; also eats fruit
LIFESPAN	Typically 9–11 years, but up to 16 years in captivity

ANIMAL FACTS

Fennec foxes communicate using a variety of calls, including growls and barks, but they also have a distinctive purr, rather like a cat. They normally live in groups of up to 10 individuals, and are highly territorial by nature, marking their area with urine. They inhabit underground dens, where the young are born. The cubs start to emerge above ground at about a month old. Unlike other wild canids, fennec foxes can produce two litters each year.

A female will not allow a male close to her cubs

WHERE IN THE WORLD?

Restricted largely to the Sahara region of North Africa, occurring in Morocco, Algeria, Tunisia, Libya, Egypt and Sudan. Also ranges northeast of the Red Sea.

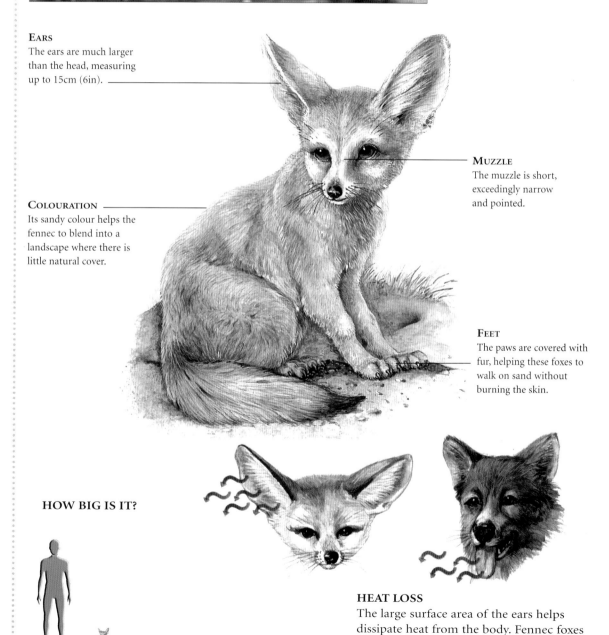

EARS
The ears are much larger than the head, measuring up to 15cm (6in).

COLOURATION
Its sandy colour helps the fennec to blend into a landscape where there is little natural cover.

MUZZLE
The muzzle is short, exceedingly narrow and pointed.

FEET
The paws are covered with fur, helping these foxes to walk on sand without burning the skin.

HOW BIG IS IT?

HEAT LOSS
The large surface area of the ears helps dissipate heat from the body. Fennec foxes also keep cool by panting.

Siberian Husky

• **ORDER** • Carnivora • **FAMILY** • Canidae • **SPECIES** • *Canis familiaris*

VITAL STATISTICS

WEIGHT	16–27.5kg (35–60lb)
LENGTH	50–60cm (20–24in) tall
SEXUAL MATURITY	6–12 months; bitches have 2 periods of heat annually
GESTATION PERIOD	63 days
NUMBER OF OFFSPRING	Typically 6; weaning occurs at 42–56 days
DIET	Omnivorous, although traditionally fed on fatty meat to meet their high energy demands; dogs can maintain good health on vegetarian diets
LIFESPAN	11–12 years

ANIMAL FACTS

Siberian huskies in Alaska saved many lives in January 1925, when appalling weather conditions cut off the town of Nome, just as the local people were facing an outbreak of diptheria. Working in relays, the sled-pulling huskies covered 1085km (674 miles) in under five days, to deliver 300,000 doses of a life-saving antitoxin to the town. This averted a catastrophy, and in commemoration of this event, the Iditarod Trail Dog Sled Race has been held annually since 1967.

Curling up to sleep retains body heat

Sled dogs have played a vital role in the lives of people in the Arctic region, probably none more so than this particular breed.

WHERE IN THE WORLD?

The Siberian husky was bred by the Chukchi tribe in Siberia, although during the late 1800s, a number of these dogs were taken to Alaska.

TAIL
A tail that curls forwards is characteristic of the spitz group of breeds, which originates from the far north.

EYE COLOUR
Bright blue rather than brown eyes are not uncommon in this breed.

HIND LEGS
The hind legs have well-developed muscles to provide power for sled-pulling.

COAT
The coat is double-layered, with long guard hairs and a thick, dense undercoat that traps warm air next to the skin.

ODD EYES
Odd-eyed individuals are not uncommon.

HOW BIG IS IT?

MUSHING
Siberian huskies have a strong pack order, and the pack leader will play a key role in pulling the sled.

Cheetah

• ORDER • Carnivora **• FAMILY** • Felidae **• SPECIES** • *Acinonyx jubatus*

VITAL STATISTICS

WEIGHT	40–65kg (88–143lb)
LENGTH	199–219cm (78–86in); about 90cm (35in) tall
SEXUAL MATURITY	Females 1–2 years; males about 1 year
GESTATION PERIOD	90–98 days
NUMBER OF OFFSPRING	Averages 3–5, but can be up to 9; weaning occurs at around 90 days
DIET	Carnivorous, often preying on gazelles; may take other herbivores occasionally
LIFESPAN	1–12 years in the wild; up to 20 in captivity

ANIMAL FACTS

The cheetah has specialized muscles that provide amazing acceleration. It can go from a standing start to a speed of 64kph (40mph) in just three strides. Its respiratory rate increases from about 60 breaths per minute up to 150, and its large heart pumps the oxygenated blood around the body. But if it has not overtaken its quarry in just 550m (600yd), the cheetah will have to slow down again.

Unlike other cats, a cheetah's claws are not retractable

The fastest land mammal on earth, the cheetah is able to sprint at speeds of up to 120kph (75mph) over short distances when pursuing prey.

WHERE IN THE WORLD?

Now mainly found in southern and eastern Africa, especially in Namibia, Botswana, Kenya and Tanzania. Rare in northern Africa. Survives in Asia, in northern Iran.

EYES
The large eyes point forwards and determine the position of prey with great accuracy.

PATTERNING
No two cheetahs have identical patterning. The spots can be up to 5cm (2in) in diameter.

COLOURATION
Colour can vary from tan to buff. The underside of the body is white.

TAIL
The spots on the tail are fused to create rings.

HOW BIG IS IT?

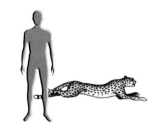

STRETCHING AHEAD
The cheetah's vertebral column is exceedingly flexible, giving these cats a stride length of 700–800cm (20–25ft).

113

Caracal (Persian Lynx)

• **ORDER** • Carnivora • **FAMILY** • Felidae • **SPECIES** • *Caracal caracal*

VITAL STATISTICS

WEIGHT	11–20kg (24–44lb); males are heavier
LENGTH	80–140cm (32–55in); about 50cm (20in) tall
SEXUAL MATURITY	About 21 months
GESTATION PERIOD	63–75 days
NUMBER OF OFFSPRING	Averages 2–3, but can be up to 6; weaning occurs at around 45 days
DIET	Carnivorous, hunting a range of small mammals, as well as birds and lizards
LIFESPAN	11–12 years in the wild; up to 17 in captivity

ANIMAL FACTS

Caracals are remarkably agile, even for cats. They can jump vertically to catch small birds, but they are also strong enough to overpower antelope more than twice their size. If threatened, they can climb to safety. The caracal's behaviour explains the remark 'putting the cat amongst the pigeons'. As they can be tamed, Indian rulers used to bet on how many pigeons could be knocked down by a caracal at a single leap.

Ear tufts help to communicate the cat's mood

The black tufts of hair on the ears of these wild cats explain their name, which is derived from the Turkish word *karakulak*, meaning 'black ears'.

WHERE IN THE WORLD?

Ranges widely in Africa, apart from the Sahara and central rainforest belt, and across the Arabian peninsula into Turkey and east through Asia, to India.

PHYSIQUE
The caracal has quite a slender body and long legs. The hind legs are longer than the front legs.

COAT
The coat is reddish-brown, short and thick.

EARS
The tufts on the ears are thought to help localize the source of a sound.

CAUGHT IN FLIGHT
The caracal's agility means it can catch birds in flight.

HOW BIG IS IT?

SLEEPING ARRANGEMENTS
A caracal resting under a rock. These cats may be active during the day or at night, and are solitary by nature.

Domestic Cat

•ORDER• Carnivora •FAMILY• Felidae •SPECIES• *Felis catus*

The domestic cat is now a popular pet around the world. Aside from companionship, cats are also valued as a means of curbing rodent populations.

VITAL STATISTICS

WEIGHT	2.5–7kg (5.5–16lb); males are heavier
LENGTH	91–114cm (36–45in), including tail, which can be 30cm (12in) long
SEXUAL MATURITY	Females about 4–10 months; males 5–7 months
GESTATION PERIOD	63–65 days
NUMBER OF OFFSPRING	Averages 3–5; weaning occurs at around 45 days
DIET	Carnivorous; will hunt rodents, small birds and invertebrates
LIFESPAN	Typically 15–17 years, exceptionally up to 36

ANIMAL FACTS

Domestication of the cat began around 9500 years ago. Until the last century, all domestic bloodlines descended from African wild cat stock. In the late twentieth century, however, breeders crossed domestic cats with their smaller wild relatives, to transfer their distinctive patterning. If abandoned, cats will revert to living wild, and this can have a serious impact on local wildlife because of the cat's predatory habits. These are known as feral cats.

Facial features indicate a cat's moods

WHERE IN THE WORLD?

Domestication began in the vicinity of Egypt, and cats were then taken to Asia, and north into Europe. They were frequently carried on ships.

EYE COLOUR
The eyes are a very variable feature, ranging from blue through shades of green to copper.

M-SHAPED MARKING
Located in the centre of the forehead, this is a distinguishing feature of tabby varieties.

MACKEREL TABBY
Distinguishable by the narrow stripes on each side of the body.

TAIL MARKINGS
All tabby cats have darker circles of fur on the tail, which ends in a dark tip.

HOW BIG IS IT?

COLOUR VARIETIES
There are many different varieties of tabby. This is a tortoiseshell tabby, often known as a torbie.

Eurasian Lynx

VITAL STATISTICS

WEIGHT	8–38kg (18–84lb)
LENGTH	91–155cm (35–61in) including tail
SEXUAL MATURITY	Females 21 months; males 33 months
GESTATION PERIOD	63–70 days
NUMBER OF OFFSPRING	1–5
DIET	Deer, wild boar and chamois, but may also hunt rabbits, rodents and birds
LIFESPAN	Average 7–9 years in the wild, but has lived more than 21 years in captivity

ANIMAL FACTS

Eurasian lynxes can be encountered in a wide range of environments, although they generally remain hidden during the day, emerging under cover of darkness. They tend to favour forested habitat where suitable hiding places are readily available, but they can also be found in treeless tundra areas. These cats are patient hunters, frequently waiting to ambush their quarry, although they can sprint over short distances to make a kill. Pairs come together in the breeding season – males are recognizable by their larger size.

The paws of the Eurasian lynx are relatively large

An adaptable species, the Eurasian lynx has one of the widest distributions of any wild cat, although it is now less common in Europe than it once was.

WHERE IN THE WORLD?

Occurs from Scandinavia to northeastern Asia, especially common in Siberia. Has been reintroduced to forested parts of Europe, including the Pyrenees and Bavaria.

EARS
The dark tufts of longer fur on the tips of the triangular ears are characteristic of this species.

NECK
The fur around the neck is longer, especially in the winter, creating the impression of a ruff.

COAT
The patterning varies. Some individuals are more striped than spotted, while others have plain coats. The underparts are paler.

TAIL
The tail is short and prominently tipped with black fur.

HOW BIG IS IT?

LYNX ATTACK
Eurasian lynxes are often blamed for attacks on farm animals, but they normally hunt wild animals such as hares and rabbits.

Sand Cat

VITAL STATISTICS

WEIGHT	2–3kg (4.5–6.5lb)
LENGTH	67–92cm (26–36in); about 25cm (10in) tall
SEXUAL MATURITY	Around 14 months
GESTATION PERIOD	59–66 days
NUMBER OF OFFSPRING	Average 4–5, but can be up to 8; weaning at around 90 days
DIET	Carnivorous, feeding mainly on desert rodents such as jerboas, as well as birds, lizards and invertebrates
LIFESPAN	6–7 years in the wild; up to 13 in captivity

ANIMAL FACTS

These small cats rely partly on their small size and colouration to hide themselves in a landscape where there is little natural cover. They are well-protected against the desert heat, with long fur covering their pads to help them to walk over the hot sand. This species is less territorial than many cats – with males actually sharing dens – and they appear to have relatively placid natures. Sand cats are solitary, and females give birth alone.

Silence and speed are vital to catching desert rodents

These small cats are hard to observe, only emerging from their burrows to hunt under cover of darkness, when the temperature is cooler in their desert habitat.

WHERE IN THE WORLD?

Sporadically distributed in sandy desert in the Sahara region of North Africa, through the Middle East and Arabian Peninsula to Turkmenistan, Kazakhstan and Pakistan.

EARS
The ears are large and low-set, able to detect the ultra-sonic calls of rodents that are inaudible to human ears.

COLOURATION
The coat is a sandy-brown colour, with both reddish and darker markings.

PROFILE
This cat has a low-set body, with a broad head and a large nose.

MARKINGS
Stripes extend back from the eyes, and there is a darker area over the back. The tail is ringed.

HOW BIG IS IT?

DANGEROUS LIVING
Various species prey on sand cats, including venomous snakes as well as birds of prey and wolves.

European Wildcat

VITAL STATISTICS

WEIGHT	3–8kg (6.5–17.5lb)
LENGTH	75–138cm (30–54in), including tail; about 40cm (16in) tall
SEXUAL MATURITY	6–12 months
GESTATION PERIOD	63–68 days
NUMBER OF OFFSPRING	Average 2–4, but can be up to 8; weaning at around 80 days
DIET	Carnivorous, hunting a variety of small prey
LIFESPAN	8–10 years, although can live up to 15

ANIMAL FACTS

These wildcats prey mainly on rodents, although they may also catch birds. The Scottish population, occurring in relatively open countryside, hunts rabbits and hares. These wildcats were heavily persecuted by gamekeepers, but the biggest threat to their survival today is the domestic cat. They will hybridize readily, and it is difficult to stop this process. Studies suggest that seven out of eight Scottish wildcats now have some domestic cat genes in their ancestry.

European wildcats can be very aggressive

The range of the European wildcat has contracted dramatically in recent years. It is a shy species and is rarely spotted by humans.

WHERE IN THE WORLD?

Confined to forested areas in the Iberian Peninsula northeastwards and along the Mediterranean, to Turkey and the Caucasus. An isolated population is present in Scotland.

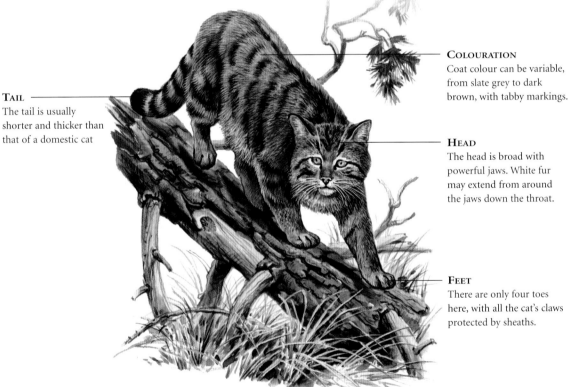

TAIL
The tail is usually shorter and thicker than that of a domestic cat

COLOURATION
Coat colour can be variable, from slate grey to dark brown, with tabby markings.

HEAD
The head is broad with powerful jaws. White fur may extend from around the jaws down the throat.

FEET
There are only four toes here, with all the cat's claws protected by sheaths.

HOW BIG IS IT?

RUNNING WILD
A domestic cat with tabby markings (top) compared with a European wildcat. The European species is descended from the African wildcat.

Ocelot

• ORDER • Carnivora **• FAMILY •** Felidae **• SPECIES •** *Leopardus pardalis*

VITAL STATISTICS

Weight	11.5–16kg (25–35lb)
Length	80–145cm (32–57in), including tail
Sexual Maturity	2 years
Gestation Period	79–85 days
Number of Offspring	2–4
Diet	Rodents and other creatures, even turtles and fish; large quarry includes peccaries and small deer
Lifespan	Probably 5–7 years in the wild, but has lived over 20 years in captivity

ANIMAL FACTS

Solitary and nocturnal by nature, ocelots are not easy to observe. In the past they were heavily hunted for their beautiful fur, but thanks to protective measures, their numbers have increased in some parts of their range. Ocelots seek cover during the day, preferring environments that offer seclusion. In daylight hours an individual will sleep in vegetation on the ground, or may dose while lying on a branch up a tree.

Ocelots haul themselves up a tree using their strong front legs

These small cats are well-adapted to tree-climbing, and may spend much of their time off the ground. They can be found in forested areas across their range.

WHERE IN THE WORLD?

Occurs over a wide area from the southern USA across Central America down to northern parts of Argentina in South America, occurring east of the Andes.

BODY PATTERN
The broader rosette-type markings tend to be concentrated on the ocelot's trunk.

LIMBS
Spotted markings tend to be confined to the legs. The paws themselves are strong, helping these wild cats to climb easily.

HOW BIG IS IT?

HUNTING HABITS
Ocelots will hunt their prey in the trees, on the ground and even in water. Rodents are their preferred quarry.

UNDERPARTS
The background colour on the underparts of the body is usually paler than the flanks.

Serval

VITAL STATISTICS

WEIGHT	8–18kg (18–40lb)
LENGTH	91–145cm (36–57in), including tail; up to 65cm (26in) tall
SEXUAL MATURITY	12–24 months
GESTATION PERIOD	66–77 days
NUMBER OF OFFSPRING	Average 1–3, but can be up to 5; weaning occurs at 120–180 days
DIET	Carnivorous, hunting a wide variety of rodents, frogs and small fish
LIFESPAN	Average 10–12 years, but can be up to 20

ANIMAL FACTS

Servals are found in grassland areas and are particularly numerous in the Ngorongoro crater in Tanzania. They are specialist hunters in such terrain, capable of achieving a kill once in every two attempts – a success rate far greater than other wild cats. This is essential for their survival, given that they mainly hunt rodents rather than larger animals. The serval's height and acute hearing allows it to detect prey, pouncing from above. Servals sometimes hunt in shallow water as well.

The ear markings are very distinctive from behind

Patience typifies the hunting behaviour of many wild cats, and servals seem to be relaxing with their eyes closed, even when they are listening intently for prey.

WHERE IN THE WORLD?

Occurs widely south of the Sahara, outside the central rainforest region and southern parts of Africa. Now almost extinct in the northwest of the continent.

HEAD
The head is relatively small; these cats have large ears and a long neck.

TAIL
The tail is quite short in relation to the legs, and ends in a dark tip.

SPOTS
The spots are black and often quite large, coalescing to form stripes over the back.

LEGS
Servals are taller than any other wild cat, in relation to their body size.

NO ESCAPE
Servals cannot only detect rodents in the grass itself, but also those hiding underground, which they will dig out.

HOW BIG IS IT?

Bobcat

• ORDER • Carnivora **• FAMILY •** Felidae **• SPECIES •** *Lynx rufus*

VITAL STATISTICS

WEIGHT	7–14kg (15–31lb); males are heavier
LENGTH	70–120cm (28–47in), including tail; about 38cm (15in) tall
SEXUAL MATURITY	1–2 years
GESTATION PERIOD	63–70 days
NUMBER OF OFFSPRING	Average 2–4, but can be up to 6; weaning occurs at around 60 days
DIET	Carnivorous, hunting a variety of prey, but especially rabbits
LIFESPAN	Up to 16 years; double this in captivity

ANIMAL FACTS

Bobcats are highly adaptable, a fact reflected by the varied terrain in which they are found. This can be arid countryside or swampland, remote areas or the fringes of cities. They are also opportunistic in their feeding habits, taking anything from insects to deer. Their appearance is equally variable, with 12 different races being recognized through their wide range. Bobcats live on their own, marking their territories with scent and by leaving scratch marks on trees.

The eyes of bobcats (left) are more yellow than those of a wildcat (right)

Unlike many wild cats the bobcat has a short tail, reflecting its preference for life on the ground rather than climbing trees.

WHERE IN THE WORLD?

Distribution extends from southern Canada down through much of the USA, apart from the central northeastern region, into Baja California and most of Mexico.

TAIL
The tail can measure just 10cm (4in) long and has a white underside.

EARS
The ears are tall and pointed, with small black tufts of hair at the tips.

COLOURATION
Background colour can vary from greyish-brown to tan; the spotted patterning is highly individual.

LEGS
The hind legs are longer than the front legs, which explains this cat's characteristic bobbing gait.

HOW BIG IS IT?

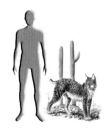

SHARP TALK
Scratching in this way sharpens the bobcat's claws and leaves a visual indicator of its presence, reinforced by its scent.

Clouded Leopard

• ORDER • Carnivora • FAMILY • Felidae • SPECIES • *Neofelis nebulosa*

VITAL STATISTICS

WEIGHT	16–23kg (35–51lb)
LENGTH	115–200cm (46–79in), including tail
SEXUAL MATURITY	2–3 years
GESTATION PERIOD	86–93 days
NUMBER OF OFFSPRING	1–5
DIET	Hunts monkeys and birds in trees, as well as deer, buffalo and even porcupines on the ground
LIFESPAN	Probably 7–10 years; has lived up to 17 in captivity

ANIMAL FACTS

These wild cats appear to have no close relatives. The canine tooth in the upper jaws is proportionately bigger than those of all other members of the family. In clouded leopards, the hyoid near the voicebox in the throat is made of bone rather than cartilage. This means that they communicate by roaring but are unable to purr like smaller cats. Young clouded leopards will have more pronounced patterning than adults until they are about six months old. Occasional melanistic individuals have also been reported – recognizable by their black fur, which obscures their markings. The status of the clouded leopard is vulnerable because of forest clearance and hunting.

This is one of the least-known of the larger cats, occurring in forested areas. In spite of its size, it is a very agile climber.

WHERE IN THE WORLD?

Occurs in Southeast Asia, from Nepal and southeastern China across the Malay Peninsula to islands including Taiwan, Hainan, Borneo and Sumatra.

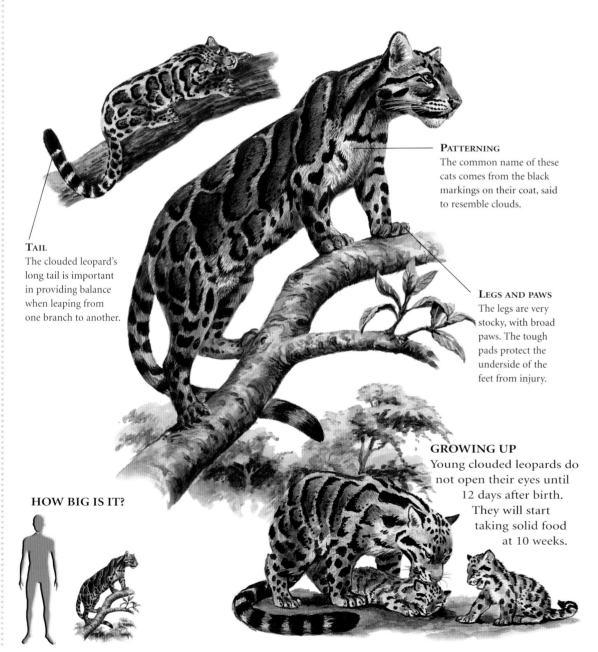

PATTERNING
The common name of these cats comes from the black markings on their coat, said to resemble clouds.

TAIL
The clouded leopard's long tail is important in providing balance when leaping from one branch to another.

LEGS AND PAWS
The legs are very stocky, with broad paws. The tough pads protect the underside of the feet from injury.

GROWING UP
Young clouded leopards do not open their eyes until 12 days after birth. They will start taking solid food at 10 weeks.

HOW BIG IS IT?

Lion

The lion is the only member of the family in which the sexes differ markedly in terms of their adult appearance. Females are known as lionesses.

VITAL STATISTICS

WEIGHT	150–250kg (330–550lb)
LENGTH	260–360cm (102–141in)
SEXUAL MATURITY	3–4 years
GESTATION PERIOD	100–119 days
NUMBER OF OFFSPRING	1–6
DIET	Typically animals weighing 50–300kg (110–660lb), especially wildebeest, buffalo and zebra
LIFESPAN	7–10 years; up to 30 in captivity

ANIMAL FACTS

Often described as the King of Beasts, lions are unusual amongst the big cats in that they are social by nature, living in groups called prides. The lionesses hunt collectively, using a combination of guile and strength to ambush and overpower creatures that can be much larger than themselves. They are usually related to each other, but young male lions will leave the pride and lead solitary lives, until they are strong enough to lead a pride themselves. The lion population in Asia is endangered, and elsewhere it is considered vulnerable, especially because of changes in land use.

Young lion cubs can be killed if a new male takes over a pride; this ensures that the lionesses will mate more quickly with the newcomer

WHERE IN THE WORLD?

Now restricted to Africa south of the Sahara, particularly on the eastern side of the continent. Also present in the Gir Forest, Gujarat state, India.

MANE
This long area of hair surrounding the face and extending on to the chest is characteristic of mature male lions.

EYES
Lions have keen eyesight to spot camouflaged prey in the grass of their habitat.

COLOURATION
The mane tends to darken with age, often ending up predominantly black in older individuals.

TAIL
The fur on a lion's body is relatively short, although the tail ends in a dark tip of longer hair.

HOW BIG IS IT?

PRIDE AT STAKE
Males fight over the right to lead a pride of lionesses. Their manes serve to protect them against serious injury.

123

Jaguar

VITAL STATISTICS

WEIGHT	36–160kg (79–350lb)
LENGTH	155–265cm (60–105in)
SEXUAL MATURITY	3–4 years
GESTATION PERIOD	93–105 days
NUMBER OF OFFSPRING	1–4
DIET	Mammals including peccaries, tapirs and capybaras; also hunts fish, turtles and crocodilians
LIFESPAN	10–12 years in the wild; up to 22 years in captivity

ANIMAL FACTS

The jaguar is the only member of the big cat clan in the New World. Fossil evidence shows that these cats once existed in southern parts of the USA, particularly in what is now Florida. Within their existing range today they come into conflict with ranchers, as they will often prey on cattle. There are also accounts of jaguars attacking people, but they are not confirmed man-eaters. Their status is vulnerable, but they are less threatened now that they are no longer hunted commercially for their fur.

Jaguars (top) can sometimes be confused with leopards (bottom), but their heads are rounder in shape

124

As with most big cats, despite the jaguar's wide range its population density is low, with just one jaguar per 25km² (9.65 square miles) on average.

WHERE IN THE WORLD?

Current range extends from Central America down across much of northern South America to the extreme north of Argentina.

COAT
The tail is barred with black markings, ending in a dark tip. A very distinctive rosette pattern with dark centres is apparent on the body.

HIND LEGS
Powerful muscles enable these cats to swim, jump and climb without difficulty, as well as run fast.

MOUTH
Strong jaws allow the jaguar to crack the shells of prey such as turtles and tortoises.

HOW BIG IS IT?

HUNTING TECHNIQUE

Jaguars often hunt near water, leaping down on their prey from an overhanging branch, catching their victims unawares.

Leopard

VITAL STATISTICS

WEIGHT	37–90kg (82–200lb)
LENGTH	150–300cm (60–118in)
SEXUAL MATURITY	3–4 years
GESTATION PERIOD	90–105 days
NUMBER OF OFFSPRING	1–6, typically 2 or 3
DIET	Hunts large mammals such as wildebeest and deer; also catches baboons and monkeys; when food is scarce it will seek smaller prey, even insects
LIFESPAN	Probably 8–10 years in the wild; has lived for more than 23 years in captivity

ANIMAL FACTS

The leopard's background colour is influenced by its habitat. Those occurring in semi-arid areas are paler yellow, while black panthers are most likely to be encountered in wooded terrain. They are solitary creatures, although a male may help a female in rearing offspring. Leopards can be dangerous to people if cornered.

Leopards can be found in a range of environments

Leopards have striking markings. The black panther is a melanistic variant; it has a black coat, but the underlying patterning can still be seen.

WHERE IN THE WORLD?

Occurs widely across Africa south of the Sahara, with an isolated population in the northwest. Also ranges through the Middle East and southern Asia.

EARS
The leopard has acute hearing so it can locate smaller prey, which may be hidden in undergrowth.

MARKINGS
The area within the leopard's rosettes is generally darker than the surrounding ground colour. Black spots are present on the lower limbs, with blotches on the underparts.

TAIL
Incomplete broad black bands are evident towards the tip of the tail, which is usually black.

HOW BIG IS IT?

CREATING A LARDER
Having made a kill, a leopard will usually seek to drag the carcass up into a nearby tree, away from scavengers.

Siberian Tiger

• ORDER • Carnivora • FAMILY • Felidae • SPECIES • *Panthera tigris altaica*

VITAL STATISTICS

WEIGHT	Females 100–180kg (220–397lb); males 167–220kg (368–485lb)
LENGTH	290–320cm (114–126in), including tail; up to 119cm (47in) tall
SEXUAL MATURITY	3 years
GESTATION PERIOD	90–105 days
NUMBER OF OFFSPRING	Average 3–4, but can be up to 6; weaning occurs at 90 days
DIET	Carnivorous, preferring larger prey
LIFESPAN	Probably 10–12 years, although can live up to 23

ANIMAL FACTS

The numbers of these tigers plummeted over the past century, largely because of hunting pressures. They died out in South Korea in 1922 and are virtually extinct in the north. There are probably no more than a dozen left in China. Thanks to strenuous conservation efforts, their numbers now stand at about 500 individuals in Russia. The strength of these tigers is such that adults can even overpower bears easily, although they more frequently hunt red deer and wild boar.

Tigers lap up water with their tongue, like a domestic cat

This is the largest of the nine races of tiger, and the biggest member of the cat family. Unfortunately, it is close to extinction.

WHERE IN THE WORLD?

Used to occur in northeastern China, parts of Mongolia and Russia and the Korean Peninsula. Now confined mainly to the Amur-Ussuri region of Russia.

STRIPES
These are less apparent in Siberian tigers, and are generally brown rather than black.

MANE
These tigers develop a substantial mane of longer fur around the neck in winter.

COLOURATION
This race has whiter colouration, alongside areas of gold rather than bright orange fur.

FUR
The fur is very dense, with around 3000 hairs per square centimetre over the body.

IDENTITY

The stripes on the face and elsewhere on the body are different in each individual, enabling them to be distinguished from one another.

HOW BIG IS IT?

Bengal Tiger

The Bengal is the most common of the surviving races of tiger, and in terms of size it rivals even the Siberian tiger.

VITAL STATISTICS

WEIGHT	Females 100–180kg (220–397lb); males 167–220kg (368–485lb)
LENGTH	275–310cm (108–122in), including tail; up to 119cm (47in) tall
SEXUAL MATURITY	3 years
GESTATION PERIOD	90–105 days
NUMBER OF OFFSPRING	Average 3–4, but can be up to 6; weaning at around 90 days
DIET	Carnivorous, preferring larger prey
LIFESPAN	Probably 10–12 years, but can be up to 23

ANIMAL FACTS

Tigers live solitary lives, hunting on their own. They are opportunistic hunters, favouring large quarry, and have been known to attack people on occasion. These man-eaters are often injured or infirm, and can develop a taste for human flesh. Tigers prefer to hunt by night, seizing their prey around the neck, and usually biting through the spinal cord to effect the kill. They can swim very well – often being found near water – and are also able to climb easily.

A tiger will ambush and then jump on its prey, bringing it down to the ground

COLOURATION
The fur is a rich shade of orange-brown, with variable black striped patterning.

TAIL
The tail helps the tiger maintain its balance when jumping, and is almost 1m (39in) long.

WHISKERS
These provide sensory input at close quarters.

TEETH
Sharp canine teeth at the corners of the mouth are slid between the vertebral bones, to sever the spinal cord of prey.

WHERE IN THE WORLD?

This southern Asian race is found mainly in areas of India and Bangladesh, as well as parts of Bhutan, Nepal, Myanmar (Burma) and Tibet.

HOW BIG IS IT?

WHITE TIGER
The rare mutant white Bengal tiger has pale stripes and bluish eyes but as in the normal Bengal Tigers, the facial patterning is still highly individual.

Puma

VITAL STATISTICS

WEIGHT	Females 34–48kg (75–105lb); males 53–72 (115–160lb)
LENGTH	152–274cm (60–108in), including tail; up to 76cm (30in) tall
SEXUAL MATURITY	18–36 months
GESTATION PERIOD	91 days
NUMBER OF OFFSPRING	Average 2–3, but can be up to 56; weaning occurs at 90 days
DIET	Carnivorous, hunting mainly medium-sized prey, including livestock
LIFESPAN	Probably 8–10 years; up to 20 in captivity

ANIMAL FACTS

These wild cats have an amazing ability to jump, thanks to their powerful hind legs. They can leap horizontally up to 12m (40ft), may spring up to 5.5m (18ft) into the air, and are adept at climbing. Their athletic prowess also includes sprinting over short distances at speeds of up to 55kph (34mph). Pumas have the biggest range of any land animal in the Americas, but in heavily populated areas, such as around Vancouver, they have been known to attack people.

Young pumas have spotted coats

The puma is known by over 40 different names (including cougar and mountain lion) – more than any other species in the animal world.

WHERE IN THE WORLD?

Ranges from western Canada down through the western USA (with a small population in Florida), right across Central America and virtually all of South America.

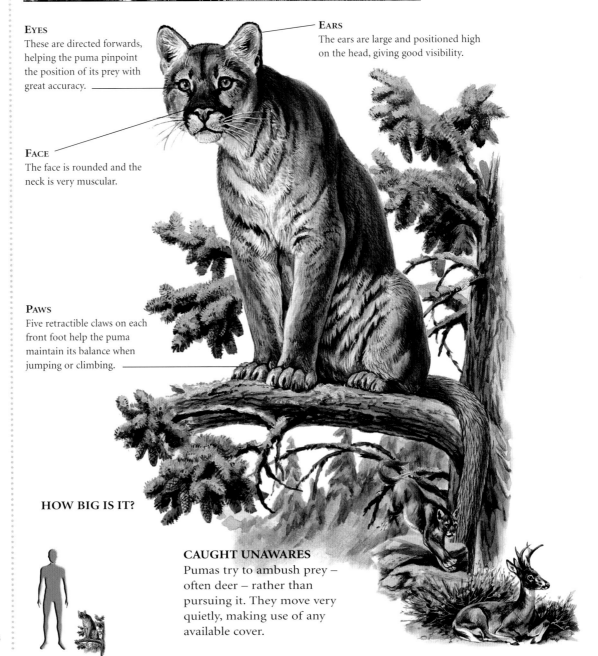

EYES
These are directed forwards, helping the puma pinpoint the position of its prey with great accuracy.

EARS
The ears are large and positioned high on the head, giving good visibility.

FACE
The face is rounded and the neck is very muscular.

PAWS
Five retractible claws on each front foot help the puma maintain its balance when jumping or climbing.

HOW BIG IS IT?

CAUGHT UNAWARES
Pumas try to ambush prey – often deer – rather than pursuing it. They move very quietly, making use of any available cover.

Jaguarundi

VITAL STATISTICS

WEIGHT	Females 4.4kg (10lb); males 5.9kg (13lb)
LENGTH	88–138cm (35–54in), including tail; up to 35cm (14in) tall
SEXUAL MATURITY	About 24 months
GESTATION PERIOD	70–75 days
NUMBER OF OFFSPRING	Average 1–4, but can be up to 5; weaning occurs at 42 days
DIET	Carnivorous, hunting rodents, birds including domestic chickens, as well as frogs and fish
LIFESPAN	Up to 15 years

ANIMAL FACTS

The confusion over the name of these cats came about because of their colouration. Originally the colour variants were thought to be separate species: the name eyra was given to all the red forms and the name jaguarundi to all the darker forms. Genetic studies have revealed the jaguarundi is closely related to the puma, in spite of differences in their appearance. This cat often spends time in the trees, becoming more active towards dusk, when it will descend to hunt on the ground.

Jaguarundis are very agile

This member of the cat family is frequently called the otter cat because of its unusual appearance. It is also known as the eyra.

WHERE IN THE WORLD?

Range extends from southern US states such as Texas and Arizona, down through Central and South America to northern Argentina. Has been introduced to Florida.

HEAD
The head is slender, with small ears, rounded at their tips.

COLOURATION
A greyish-black jaguarundi is seen here. All young of this species are spotted at birth.

LEGS
Although short, the legs are powerful and the feet are equipped with strong claws.

TAIL
The tail is very long – accounting for up to 61cm (24in) of the cat's total length.

DIFFERENT COLOURS

Two distinctive colour variants exist – greyish-black and russet red. Even so, the depth of colouration is an individual feature.

HOW BIG IS IT?

Snow Leopard

VITAL STATISTICS

WEIGHT	Females 4.4kg (10lb); males 5.9kg (13lb)
LENGTH	180–230cm (71–91in), including tail; up to 61cm (24in) tall
SEXUAL MATURITY	24 months
GESTATION PERIOD	95–100 days
NUMBER OF OFFSPRING	Average 2–3, but can be 5; weaning occurs at around 180 days
DIET	Carnivorous, hunting wild sheep, deer and boar, plus rodents and livestock
LIFESPAN	15 years; up to 20 in captivity

ANIMAL FACTS

These wild cats roam up above the snow line during the summer, coming down to lower altitudes and living in forests for the duration of the winter. They are well-protected against the cold, with fur covering their paws. They sleep curled up in a ball, with their long tail protecting their exposed nose and mouth from the bitter cold.

Tiger patterning

Snow leopard patterning

Leopard patterning

Solitary by nature, the snow leopard is an elusive species, occurring in inaccessible habitats and catching whatever prey it can.

WHERE IN THE WORLD?

Ranges across the mountainous regions of central Asia, typically between 2000–6000m (6500–20,000ft), through the Himalayas and Tibet into northwestern China.

EYES
Very keen eyesight helps pick out the movement of potential prey.

COLOURATION
A whitish-tan base colour is covered with dark brown spots and black rosettes.

TAIL
Long and strong, the tail acts as a counter-balance when jumping.

GETTING AROUND

Snow leopards are incredibly agile animals in spite of their size – they can leap easily on to rocky outcrops.

HOW BIG IS IT?

Indian Grey Mongoose

• **ORDER** • Carnivora • **FAMILY** • Herpestidae • **SPECIES** • *Herpestes edwardsii*

Famed for its ability to kill venomous snakes, this species can be encountered in many different types of terrain, from forests to agricultural land.

VITAL STATISTICS

WEIGHT	0.9–1.7kg (2–4lb); males are larger
LENGTH	80–91cm (31–36in), including tail; up to 75cm (30in) tall
SEXUAL MATURITY	6–9 months
GESTATION PERIOD	60–65 days
NUMBER OF OFFSPRING	Average 2–5; weaning occurs at around 180 days
DIET	Mainly carnivorous, hunting rodents and reptiles; sometimes attacks poultry
LIFESPAN	7–9 years in the wild; up to 11 in captivity

ANIMAL FACTS

It is not uncommon for grey mongooses to be found close to human settlements, where they are welcomed for controlling both vermin and snake numbers. They are adaptable in their feeding habits, however, and they may dig up nests of the endangered crocodilian called the gharial, hidden in a river bank, to steal the eggs. Individuals can climb well and may venture into the trees to raid birds' nests. Fruit occasionally features in their diet, and they also catch invertebrates.

WHERE IN THE WORLD?

Ranges from Saudi Arabia through Iraq, Iran, Afghanistan and Pakistan, throughout India and eastwards as far as southeastern China. Also on Sri Lanka.

HEAD
Broad jaws and very small ears; the head merges into the neck.

COAT TEXTURE
The hairs along the back are much coarser than those elsewhere on the body.

COLOURATION
In spite of their name, these mongooses range in colour from grey to tawny-red.

TAIL
The tail is very long – equivalent to the body in length.

HIDING AWAY
These mongooses live on their own or sometimes in pairs, but are rarely seen out in the open, preferring their burrows.

HOW BIG IS IT?

Meerkat

VITAL STATISTICS

WEIGHT	0.62–0.97kg (1.3–2.1lb)
LENGTH	80–91cm (31–36in), including tail; up to 30cm (12in) tall
SEXUAL MATURITY	12 months
GESTATION PERIOD	77 days
NUMBER OF OFFSPRING	1–5; weaning at 49–63 days
DIET	Mainly insectivorous, hunting caterpillars, pupae, termites, crickets and similar; also eats eggs and lizards, plus some plant matter
LIFESPAN	7–10 in the wild; up to 12 in captivity

ANIMAL FACTS

There is a rigorous social structure within a meerkat colony, to the extent that generally only the dominant pair breeds. If another female falls pregnant, her young are likely to be killed. Their burrows have more than one entrance, helping them to escape back underground if danger threatens. The members of the group each take turns to be on guard for about an hour rather than foraging for food, and they watch for predators such as jackals and wild cats.

Paws are vital for digging

Highly social by nature, these African members of the mongoose family live in warrens that may be home to as many as 30 individuals.

WHERE IN THE WORLD?

Restricted to the region of southern Africa, particularly in western parts, ranging from Angola and Namibia into Botswana and South Africa, favouring arid, open countryside.

EYES
The eyes are large and set high in the skull, giving excellent visibility.

HEAD
The skull is domed, with a pointed muzzle, while the small ears are located at the sides of the head.

UNDERPARTS
The underparts are a lighter shade of grey than the upperparts.

STANDING TALL
Meerkats stand up in this fashion when looking for possible danger.

HOW BIG IS IT?

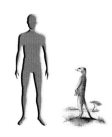

POWERFUL BITE
The sharp teeth in the meerkat's mouth can crack what is often the tough body casing of their invertebrate prey.

Spotted Hyena

• **ORDER** • Carnivora • **FAMILY** • Hyaenidae • **SPECIES** • *Crocuta crocuta*

VITAL STATISTICS

WEIGHT	45–70kg (99–154lb); females are slightly bigger
LENGTH	80–91cm (31–36in), including tail; up to 75cm (30in) tall
SEXUAL MATURITY	About 3 years
GESTATION PERIOD	77 days
NUMBER OF OFFSPRING	2; weaning occurs at 14–18 months
DIET	Carnivorous, often hunting ungulates such as wildebeest and zebra, but also scavenging
LIFESPAN	10–12 years in the wild; up to 25 in captivity

ANIMAL FACTS

Spotted hyenas can pursue prey over distances of more than 3km (1.9 miles), at speeds touching 50kph (30mph). Their reproductive organs are unique, with those of the female closely resembling those of the male, even to the extent of having pseudo-testes. If the cubs are of the same sex, one will kill the other. The protein content of spotted hyena's milk is higher than that of any other terrestrial carnivore, so the young can go days without suckling.

Hyenas are even able to bite through bone

The unusual cackling calls made by this species when it is excited or afraid explain why it is also known as the 'laughing hyena'.

WHERE IN THE WORLD?

Occurs throughout Africa, south of the Sahara, in habitats ranging from coastal areas up into the mountains; now less common than in the past.

HEAD AND JAWS
Very strong jaws are reinforced by the thick neck and a mane of longer fur.

APPEARANCE
The coat has a rough texture and individual spotted patterning; the background colour tends to fade with age.

PROFILE
Hyenas have a distinctive hunchbacked appearance, with the body sloping down to the hindquarters.

SCENT-MARKING
These hyenas produce a very distinctive yellow, oily substance from their anal glands, which is used to mark their territory.

HOW BIG IS IT?

Aardwolf

VITAL STATISTICS

WEIGHT	9–14kg (20–31lb)
LENGTH	75–110cm (30–43in), including tail; up to 50cm (20in) tall
SEXUAL MATURITY	About 2 years
GESTATION PERIOD	90–110 days
NUMBER OF OFFSPRING	1–5, averaging 2–3; weaning occurs at 4 months
DIET	Essentially insectivorous, feeding largely on termites; occasionally eats small mammals and birds
LIFESPAN	10–12 years in the wild; up to 15 in captivity

ANIMAL FACTS

The feeding habits of the aardwolf are very specific, and it only lives in the grassland and savanna areas where harvester termites occur. It will break open their mound using the sharp claws on its front feet, and then drag out the termites within, using its long, sticky tongue. A single meal can comprise up to 200,000 of these insects, but an aardwolf never destroys a colony, leaving it to recover, before returning to feed there again.

The unusual name of the aardwolf comes from an Afrikaans word, which translates as 'earth wolf', referring to the way in which they burrow.

WHERE IN THE WORLD?

Occurs in three widely spaced regions of Africa: in the east around the Horn of Africa; across southern parts; and in the central area.

EARS
The large ears help to detect prey.

MANE
The mane extends down the neck and back, and can be raised to make the aardwolf look more fearsome.

LEGS
The front legs are longer than the hind legs, which is why the bodies of hyenas slope down to the hindquarters.

APPEARANCE
Black vertical stripes run down the sides of the body.

COMMUNICATION

Although solitary by nature, aardwolves communicate with each other by leaving a musky scent in the area they inhabit.

Aardwolves display individual patterning

HOW BIG IS IT?

Striped Skunk

VITAL STATISTICS

WEIGHT	1.25–6kg (2.8–13lb)
LENGTH	51–71cm (20–28in), including tail; up to 25cm (10in) tall
SEXUAL MATURITY	About 2 years
GESTATION PERIOD	42–63 days
NUMBER OF OFFSPRING	5–6; weaning at around 42 days
DIET	Omnivorous, eating invertebrates and rodents, eggs, birds, fruit, nuts, vegetation and fish; also scavenges
LIFESPAN	6–8 years in the wild; up to 15 in captivity

ANIMAL FACTS

A skunk's short legs mean that it cannot run very fast, and as a first line of defence it will raise its tail, arching its back to appear larger and more intimidating. Should this fail, it will then spray its foul-smelling anal secretions at its opponent. This will sting painfully if it enters the eyes, allowing the skunk to escape to the safety of its burrow. Skunks are able to spray over a distance of up to 3.7m (12ft).

The unpleasant odour associated with skunks comes from their anal scent glands. A skunk will spray this foul-smelling liquid if it feels threatened.

WHERE IN THE WORLD?

Occurs widely across North America, extending from the southern half of Canada right down across the USA to Mexico; it can be found throughout this entire region.

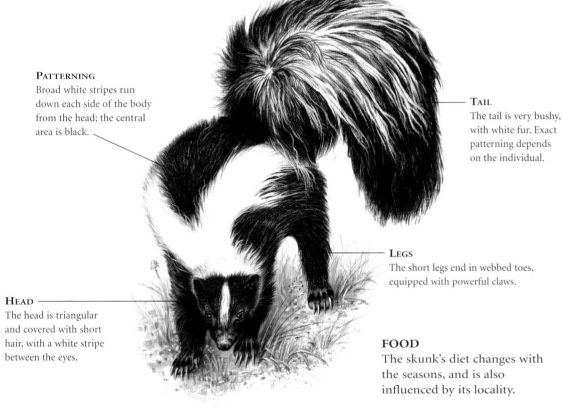

PATTERNING
Broad white stripes run down each side of the body from the head; the central area is black.

TAIL
The tail is very bushy, with white fur. Exact patterning depends on the individual.

LEGS
The short legs end in webbed toes, equipped with powerful claws.

HEAD
The head is triangular and covered with short hair, with a white stripe between the eyes.

FOOD
The skunk's diet changes with the seasons, and is also influenced by its locality.

A striped skunk spraying

HOW BIG IS IT?

Sea Otter

VITAL STATISTICS

WEIGHT	14–45kg (31–99lb); males are heavier
LENGTH	68–163cm (27–64in)
SEXUAL MATURITY	2–5 years
GESTATION PERIOD	Up to 270 days, as embryonic development may not begin straight after fertilization
NUMBER OF OFFSPRING	1, occasionally 2; weaning takes 6–12 months
DIET	Molluscs, clams, sea urchins obtained from the sea bed, and fish
LIFESPAN	10–20 years in the wild; up to 28 in captivity

ANIMAL FACTS

Sea otters live in groups known as rafts, and are well-adapted to their marine existence. Their fur is very thick, with an undercoat that traps air close to the body, aiding their buoyancy as well as keeping them warm. Sea otters can swim very well, diving down in search of food, and they use stones to smash open shellfish. Females carry their young on their chest when resting, and leave them floating on the surface while they are diving underwater.

These otters are hunted by great white sharks

These large otters live in the so-called 'kelp forests' – dense areas of seaweed – and rarely come ashore, floating on their backs when not swimming.

WHERE IN THE WORLD?

Inshore areas on both sides of the Bering Sea, and around the Aleutian Islands between Russia and Alaska, extending down as far as California in the USA.

LEGS
The legs are very short. The front legs are used for holding food, like a pair of hands.

WHISKERS
These sensory hairs are prominent around the mouth and above the eyes.

COLOURATION
Sea otters are dark brown overall, with paler fur on the head.

EARS
The ears are very small and set low down on the sides of the head.

SLEEPING SECURELY

Sea otters anchor themselves in among beds of kelp so they will not drift off in the current when sleeping.

HOW BIG IS IT?

American Mink

VITAL STATISTICS

WEIGHT	0.8–1.8kg (1.8–4lb); males are heavier
LENGTH	45–70cm (18–28in)
SEXUAL MATURITY	Females 12 months; males 18 months
GESTATION PERIOD	30 days; embryonic development may not start for a month after fertilization
NUMBER OF OFFSPRING	2–8, average 4; weaning occurs at 6 weeks
DIET	Carnivorous, hunting small mammals, fish, crayfish and frogs
LIFESPAN	2–3 years; up to 8 years in captivity

ANIMAL FACTS

Farming of American mink in Europe for their fur has led to feral populations being established in the wild. This more aggressive species has driven out its European relative, to the extent that the latter is now highly endangered and restricted to just a few areas. American mink have had an adverse impact on other species too, including water volves and waterfowl (hunting young ducklings). They face few enemies, although alligators, wolves, coyotes and great horned owls naturally prey on them.

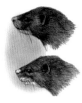

European mink (top)
American mink (bottom)

These mink are strong swimmers and thrive in an aquatic environment. They are shy by nature, preferring to hide away in dens during the daytime.

WHERE IN THE WORLD?

Occurs throughout the whole of North America, apart from the arid southwestern parts of the continent. Has been introduced to Europe and South America.

FACIAL COLOURATION
The lack of white fur on the upper lips confirms that this is an American rather than a European mink.

FUR
The water-repellant fur is dense and glossy, varying from light to dark brown.

PAWS
Partially webbed paws are equipped with sharp claws.

EYES AND EARS
The rounded eyes are small and dark; the ears are set well back on the head.

American mink can support themselves on their hindquarters

HOW BIG IS IT?

HUNTING SKILLS
Mink are adept at catching prey on land and in water, and fish feature prominently in their diet.

137

Wolverine

The powerful wolverine is the largest member of the weasel family, and its scientific name means 'glutton'. It is both a formidable hunter and scavenger.

VITAL STATISTICS

WEIGHT	22–36kg (49–79lb); males are heavier
LENGTH	82–113cm (32–44in); up to 43cm (17in) tall
SEXUAL MATURITY	1–2 years
GESTATION PERIOD	About 50 days; embryonic development does not begin straight after fertilization
NUMBER OF OFFSPRING	2–3; weaning occurs at around 70 days
DIET	Will steal from other predators such as wolves, and hunts prey up to the size of a moose
LIFESPAN	10–13 years in the wild; up to 18 in captivity

ANIMAL FACTS

The wolverine is also called the skunk bear, because of its unpleasant odour, which helps to mask its kills. Individuals roam over very large territories – that of a male can cover an area up to 620km² (240 square miles). Females have a territory of up to 260km² (100 square miles). Mating occurs in summer, but the embryos will not start developing until winter, ensuring the young are born in spring.

Wolverines are able to climb well

Circumpolar, occurring through northern latitudes in North America, extending down the west coast into the USA, and across the far north of Europe and Asia.

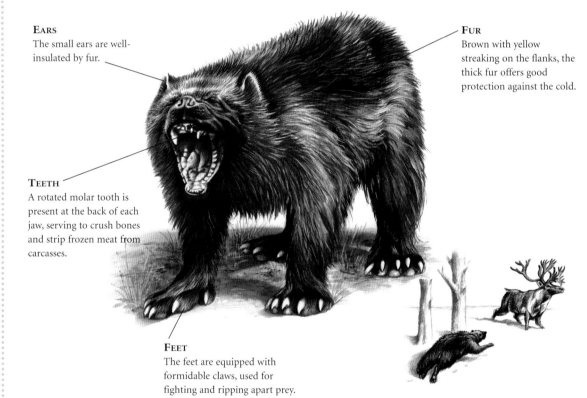

EARS
The small ears are well-insulated by fur.

FUR
Brown with yellow streaking on the flanks, the thick fur offers good protection against the cold.

TEETH
A rotated molar tooth is present at the back of each jaw, serving to crush bones and strip frozen meat from carcasses.

FEET
The feet are equipped with formidable claws, used for fighting and ripping apart prey.

HOW BIG IS IT?

POWERFUL KILLER
Old World wolverines are forced to hunt more frequently than their New World counterparts, as there are fewer opportunities to scavenge.

Otter

• ORDER • Carnivora **• FAMILY •** Mustelidae **• SPECIES •** *Lutra lutra*

VITAL STATISTICS

WEIGHT	7–10kg (15–22lb); males are heavier
LENGTH	92–165cm (36–65in); up to 30cm (12in) tall
SEXUAL MATURITY	2 years
GESTATION PERIOD	63 days; embryonic development does not begin straight after fertilization
NUMBER OF OFFSPRING	2–3; weaning occurs at around 70 days
DIET	Primarily piscivorous, feeding on a variety of fish, although will also eat frogs and water birds
LIFESPAN	5–10 years in the wild; up to 20 in captivity

ANIMAL FACTS

The otter population has suffered from pollution of its waterways, which has resulted in a loss of fish and therefore food. Toxins have also passed up the food chain, adversely affecting their health. However, environmental improvements coupled with release schemes have seen otters successfully re-established in some areas. Territorial by nature, they mark their territory with their droppings, called spraints.

An otter's paw in close-up

In spite of its wide distribution the otter population has declined, particularly in Europe, although there are now signs that it is increasing again.

WHERE IN THE WORLD?

Occurs across Europe up into Scandinavia, and in a broad band through the more temperate latitudes of Asia. Also present in northwestern North Africa.

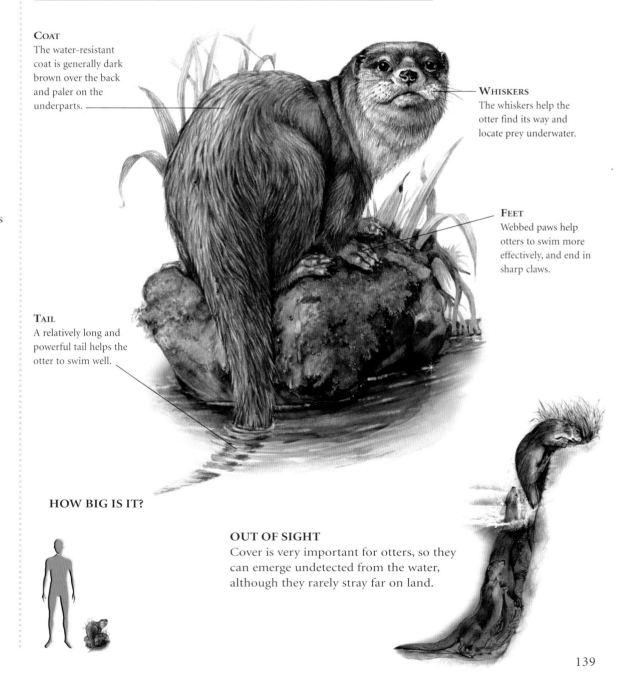

COAT
The water-resistant coat is generally dark brown over the back and paler on the underparts.

WHISKERS
The whiskers help the otter find its way and locate prey underwater.

FEET
Webbed paws help otters to swim more effectively, and end in sharp claws.

TAIL
A relatively long and powerful tail helps the otter to swim well.

HOW BIG IS IT?

OUT OF SIGHT
Cover is very important for otters, so they can emerge undetected from the water, although they rarely stray far on land.

Pine Marten

VITAL STATISTICS

WEIGHT	0.5–2.2kg (1–4.5lb); males are heavier
LENGTH	62–78cm (24–31in); up to 15cm (6in) tall
SEXUAL MATURITY	2–3 years
GESTATION PERIOD	31 days; embryonic development starts about 7 months after fertilization
NUMBER OF OFFSPRING	2–3; weaning occurs at around 49 days
DIET	Omnivorous, hunting small mammals, birds and eggs; also eats fruit
LIFESPAN	6–8 years; up to 18 in captivity

ANIMAL FACTS

The pine marten has undergone a dramatic decline in parts of its range, originally because of persecution by gamekeepers but more recently because of clearance of its forest habitat. These mustelids sleep off the ground, in a tree hollow or old bird's nest. Their agility is such that, just like a cat, they can swivel their bodies if they fall, landing on their feet to reduce the risk of any injury, from heights of up to 20m (66ft).

Pine martens sleep off the ground

Playful yet predatory by nature, pine martens are confined to areas of coniferous forests. They thrive in this environment, where they can conceal their presence easily.

WHERE IN THE WORLD?

Ranges from Ireland and Scotland eastwards across northern parts of Europe and southwards to various Mediterranean islands; also extends to Russia and the Caucasus.

HEAD
Triangular ears, prominent whiskers and a narrow pointed muzzle.

BIB
The creamy-yellow colour of the bib characterizes this species.

PAWS
The fur on the paws is a darker shade of brown than on the body.

HEADING DOWN
The pine marten's sharp claws help these mustelids maintain their grip when they are climbing trees in the forest.

HOW BIG IS IT?

FUR
The fur becomes darker and silkier in the winter, and was highly prized, being used to make royal garments.

WINTER WALKING
The undersides of the pine marten's toes are masked by fur in the winter, allowing it to walk easily over snow.

Beech Marten

VITAL STATISTICS

WEIGHT	1.1–2.3kg (2.4–5lb)
LENGTH	62–80cm (24–32in)
SEXUAL MATURITY	15–27 months
GESTATION PERIOD	Around 250 days
NUMBER OF OFFSPRING	1–4; the family splits up when the young are 1 year old
DIET	Opportunistic, hunting small mammals and birds, also taking invertebrates, fruit and berries
LIFESPAN	Up to 10 years in the wild; up to 18 in captivity

ANIMAL FACTS

Highly adaptable, these mustelids can rob birds' nests in the trees, sucking out the contents of eggs, whereas around buildings they are able to hunt rodents or simply scavenge. Beech martens are solitary by nature, with territories of males overlapping those of several females. Mating is a protracted affair, lasting perhaps an hour, with the male marten anchoring himself on top of the female's body by grasping a pad of fat at the base of her neck with his teeth.

Curious by nature, these martens will investigate all types of objects

These particular martens will inhabit areas of open beech woodland, but they are not dependent on forest and are sometimes found near human habitation.

WHERE IN THE WORLD?

Ranges through much of Europe, north to Denmark and south to Mediterranean islands such as Rhodes and Corfu. Extends into Asia as far as Mongolia.

COLOURATION
The coat is a variable shade of brown, often with a white bib extending on to the chest.

TAIL
This is long and bushy in appearance.

HEAD
The ears are broad but set quite low, with the eyes pointing forwards. The jaws are narrow but powerful.

LEGS
Powerful hindquarters allow these martens to climb well and pounce on prey.

BIB
When present, the bib on the front of the body can vary both in shape and colour.

HOW BIG IS IT?

FORAGING

Beech martens will feed on a wide variety of foods, even taking fallen fruit in gardens when available.

Sable

• ORDER • Carnivora **• FAMILY •** Mustelidae **• SPECIES •** *Martes zibellina*

VITAL STATISTICS

WEIGHT	0.7–1.8kg (1.5–4lb); males are heavier
LENGTH	44–68cm (17–27in); up to 20cm (8in) tall
SEXUAL MATURITY	2–3 years
GESTATION PERIOD	31 days; embryonic development takes 200–300 days overall
NUMBER OF OFFSPRING	Average 2, ranges from 1–4; weaning occurs at around 1 year
DIET	Carnivorous, preying on squirrels and mice, birds and fish
LIFESPAN	6–8 years; up to 18 in captivity

ANIMAL FACTS

Inhabiting areas of forest, sable are solitary by nature and live in underground dens. They are largely terrestrial in their habits, hunting during the day. Sable have keen eyesight and hearing to enable them to locate their prey. Mating takes place during the summer and, as in many mustelids, development of the embryos does not start at once. This will ensure that the young are born in the spring, when conditions for their survival will be most favourable.

Dark colouration merges into the forest background

Having been heavily hunted for its fur, which is highly prized for clothing, the sable has now disappeared from certain areas of its former range.

WHERE IN THE WORLD?

Ranges throughout northern parts of Europe, from Poland and Scandinavia eastwards across Asia via Russia and parts of China, Siberia and Mongolia to Japan.

HEAD
The narrow muzzle is equipped with sharp teeth to dispatch prey rapidly.

COLOURATION
Individuals vary in colour from shades of brown through to black, which is most highly valued in the fur industry.

FEET
There are five toes on each foot, and these bear formidably sharp claws.

TAIL
The tail is well-furred and long, about a quarter of the body length.

GROWING UP
Young sables play together, developing their agility and coordination, which will be essential for survival when they become independent.

HOW BIG IS IT?

Eurasian Badger

• **ORDER** • Carnivora • **FAMILY** • Mustelidae • **SPECIES** • *Meles meles*

These badgers are unusual because they live in groups, described as clans. They inhabit a network of underground tunnels and larger chambers known as setts.

VITAL STATISTICS

WEIGHT	8–12kg (18–26lb)
LENGTH	90cm (35in)
SEXUAL MATURITY	12–15 months
GESTATION PERIOD	42–56 days; embryonic development can be delayed for up to 10 months after fertilization
NUMBER OF OFFSPRING	Average 2–3, ranges from 1–6; weaning at 12–20 weeks
DIET	Omnivorous, feeding primarily on earthworms, insects, small creatures plus nuts, fruit and vegetable matter
LIFESPAN	3–15 years; 19 in captivity

ANIMAL FACTS

Eurasian badgers emerge above ground to seek food as darkness falls. Setts may be occupied by many generations of badgers, each of which remodels and enlarges their subterranean home, with some setts potentially dating back over a century. In spite of their placid appearance, badgers are very aggressive if cornered, capable of inflicting serious injuries with their teeth and claws. Their young are born in late winter, and will first venture out of their sett at two months old.

Badgers rely on their claws for digging for shelter and sometimes food

WHERE IN THE WORLD?

Britain and Ireland eastwards right across much of Europe, south from Scandinavia into Asia, extending as far as southern parts of China and Japan.

COLOURATION
Predominantly grey on the upperparts and black on the underparts.

STRIPING
Black and white stripes are present on the head, extending along the sides of the face to the neck.

LEGS
Like other burrowing animals, badgers have short but stocky legs.

HOW BIG IS IT?

TUNNELLING AWAY
A badger sett is an amazing piece of engineering. Bare soil is often present around the entrances, located in woodland.

Honey Badger

• ORDER • Carnivora • FAMILY • Mustelidae • SPECIES • *Mellivora capensis*

VITAL STATISTICS

WEIGHT	5.5–14kg (12–31lb); males are heavier
LENGTH	76–132cm (30–52in); up to 30cm (12in) tall
SEXUAL MATURITY	2–3 years
GESTATION PERIOD	42–56 days; embryonic development may not start straight after fertilization in northern areas
NUMBER OF OFFSPRING	Average 2, ranges from 1–4; weaning occurs at around 1 year
DIET	Primarily carnivorous, preying on insects, fish, reptiles, amphibians and mammals up to the size of antelopes
LIFESPAN	3–11 years; up to 26 in captivity

ANIMAL FACTS

Honey badgers can locate the nests of wild bees thanks to a remarkable partnership with a bird. They will follow greater honeyguides, which locate the nests for them. The honey badger will attack the nest, in search of the honeycomb. Once it has finished feeding, the honeyguide will dart in and receive its reward by eating the beeswax, as well as bee larvae. More often, though, honey badgers hunt and scavenge for food.

Claws on the front feet (left) can measure 4cm (1.6in) long

In spite of their name, honey badgers are highly opportunistic in their feeding habits, and they therefore occur in a wide range of different habitats.

WHERE IN THE WORLD?

Most of Africa, apart from the Sahara region. Extends across the Arabian Peninsula, eastwards through southern parts of Asia to Turkmenistan and the Indian subcontinent.

CLAWS
Long, sharp front claws enable a honey badger to gain access to a bees' nest easily.

EYES, NOSE AND EARS
The ears and eyes are small, while the nose is broad.

COAT AND TAIL
Thick and dense, the coat helps prevent angry bees stinging the honey badger. The tail is relatively short.

DETERMINED NATURE
The honey badger (or ratel) has been called the world's most fearless animal, often intimidating creatures much larger than itself.

HOW BIG IS IT?

Polecat

This mustelid is the original ancestor of the domestic ferret, and will hybridize with escaped ferrets, resulting in offspring that are usually paler in colour.

VITAL STATISTICS

WEIGHT	0.7–1.7kg (1.5–3.75lb); males are heavier
LENGTH	47–70cm (19–28in)
SEXUAL MATURITY	12 months
GESTATION PERIOD	40–42 days; mating occurs between February and June
NUMBER OF OFFSPRING	5–8; weaning occurs at around 4 weeks
DIET	Primarily carnivorous, hunting small mammals, particularly voles, rabbits and rats, as well as frogs and toads
LIFESPAN	3–5 years; up to 10 years in captivity

ANIMAL FACTS

The case of the polecat provides a remarkable conservation success story, and confirms its adaptability. Having been wiped out over much of its range in Britain by trapping, it has since recolonized large tracts of its former habitat, after being protected. Consequently, the area over which polecats now occur has increased by 50 per cent in just 10 years, and the population has risen more than four-fold during this period. Polecats prefer areas close to water, hunting under cover of darkness.

A polecat or fitch (above) seen with a ferret (below)

Europe (apart from Ireland), north to southern Scandinavia, and south to the Mediterranean, with a small North African population. Also present in western Asia.

COLOURATION
The outer fur is dark brown, and the undercoat is a pale shade of yellow.

FACIAL APPEARANCE
A distinctive dark mask extends across the face, covering the eyes; the background colour is whitish.

LEGS
Legs are short and usually darker than the body. The feet are powerful and equipped with sharp claws.

TAIL
The tail is quite long and dark in colour.

FOOD STORE
Polecats occupy a den, often close to water, where they may accumulate a store or so-called 'pantry' of dead frogs.

HOW BIG IS IT?

Ermine

VITAL STATISTICS

WEIGHT	0.025–0.16kg (0.05–0.35lb); males are heavier
LENGTH	22–45cm (9–18in); up to 30cm (12in) tall
SEXUAL MATURITY	Females 2 months; males 2 years
GESTATION PERIOD	42–56 days; embryonic development is delayed after fertilization
NUMBER OF OFFSPRING	Averages 2, ranges from 1–4; weaning occurs at 9 weeks
DIET	Carnivorous, preying on mammals, especially rabbits, plus other small creatures
LIFESPAN	3–11 years; up to 26 in captivity

ANIMAL FACTS

Ermine found in the far north of the range are those whose colour changes in winter, helping them to merge into a snowy landscape. Shy by nature, these mustelids rarely stray far from cover, and have a number of dens through their territory. Their ferocity means that they face few predators besides some birds of prey. Female ermine may mate at just a few weeks old, but they will not give birth until the following year.

Rabbits are often hunted by ermine

The appearance of the ermine, or stoat, may be transformed at the start of winter, when their coats become snow-white.

WHERE IN THE WORLD?

Found in northern latitudes, up to the edge of the Arctic Circle, across North America and through Europe to Asia. Has been introduced to Australia and New Zealand.

COLOURATION
Upperparts are ginger to brownish; underparts vary from white to cream.

ERMINE OR WEASEL?
The straight dividing line between the light and dark fur is characteristic of ermine.

FRONT FEET
Large and powerful, the feet have sharp claws at the end of the toes.

TAIL
Relatively short, the tail always has a black tip, even in winter.

HOW BIG IS IT?

COLOURATION THROUGH THE SEASONS

In some cases, ermine only partially change colour in the autumn, while females are always a purer shade of white.

Giant Otter

• ORDER • Carnivora **• FAMILY •** Mustelidae **• SPECIES •** *Pteronura brasiliensis*

As its name suggests, this is the biggest member of the weasel family in terms of size, but it has the shortest fur of any otter.

VITAL STATISTICS

WEIGHT	22–45kg (49–99lb); males are heavier
LENGTH	122–244cm (48–96in) overall; tail measures up to 107cm (42in)
SEXUAL MATURITY	2 years
GESTATION PERIOD	65–70 days
NUMBER OF OFFSPRING	1–5, but averages 2; weaning occurs at 36 weeks
DIET	Piscivorous, feeding on catfish, perch, cichlids and characins; also hunts crabs, snakes and young caimans
LIFESPAN	5–8 years in the wild; up to 17 in captivity

ANIMAL FACTS

Highly social by nature, giant otters live in extended family groups, with a dominant pair at the top of the social hierarchy. Much of their time is spent on land, where they maintain a series of dens, scent-marking their territory. They are active during the day and hunt mainly by sight. When tackling large and dangerous quarry such as anacondas, the group will launch a concerted attack. They keep in touch with each other by a series of calls.

Giant otters call to each other to keep in touch

WHERE IN THE WORLD?

Occurs throughout northern and central parts of South America in the major river systems, but has now declined dramatically and may even be extinct in some areas.

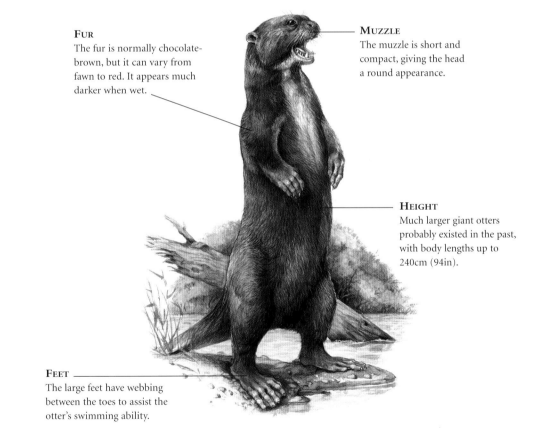

FUR
The fur is normally chocolate-brown, but it can vary from fawn to red. It appears much darker when wet.

MUZZLE
The muzzle is short and compact, giving the head a round appearance.

HEIGHT
Much larger giant otters probably existed in the past, with body lengths up to 240cm (94in).

FEET
The large feet have webbing between the toes to assist the otter's swimming ability.

HOW BIG IS IT?

HUNTING
These otters hunt at the surface, looking for shoals of fish in the water beneath, and then dive after them.

American Badger

• ORDER • Carnivora • FAMILY • Mustelidae • SPECIES • *Taxidea taxus*

VITAL STATISTICS

WEIGHT	4–12kg (9–26lb); males are heavier
LENGTH	52–88cm (20–35in)
SEXUAL MATURITY	Females 4 months; males 2 years
GESTATION PERIOD	42 days; embryonic development starts about 6 months after mating
NUMBER OF OFFSPRING	1–5, but averages 3; weaning occurs at 12 weeks
DIET	Carnivorous, hunting small animals, insects and ground-nesting birds; also eats some plant matter
LIFESPAN	4–14 years in the wild; up to 26 in captivity

ANIMAL FACTS

American badgers dig out rodent prey and build their dens using their sharp claws. Individuals usually move regularly between the different dens in their territory, although a female will stay in one den with her offspring. American badgers are able to defend themselves well, not just physically but also by releasing an unpleasant musky scent. They favour open countryside, even occurring in farmland areas.

The entrance to the badger's den may not be hidden in vegetation

Unlike its European relative, the American badger lives on its own, although the territory of a male is likely to encompass that of several females.

WHERE IN THE WORLD?

Occurs in southern Canada, through British Columbia, Manitoba, Alberta and Saskatchewan down the US coast to Indiana, Michigan, Illinois, Ohio, Missouri, Oklahoma and Texas.

FACE
The face is triangular, with a long nose that points upwards at the tip; the ears are small.

FRONT PAWS
The front paws are strong, with long, curved claws with sharp points.

TAIL
The tail is short and stocky but well-furred.

COLOURATION
Silvery-brown over much of the body, with a white stripe extending back over the shoulders from the nose.

HOW BIG IS IT?

STAYING SNUG
American badgers are able to escape the worst of the harsh winter weather by remaining below ground in their dens.

Walrus

• ORDER • Carnivora **• FAMILY •** Odobenidae **• SPECIES •** *Odobenus rosmarus*

VITAL STATISTICS

WEIGHT	555–889kg (1250–2000lb); males are heavier
LENGTH	243–350cm (96–138in); up to 152cm (60in) tall
SEXUAL MATURITY	6–7 years; males rarely mate before 15
GESTATION PERIOD	365 days; embryonic development starts 3–4 months after mating
NUMBER OF OFFSPRING	1; weaning occurs at 26 weeks
DIET	Piscivorous, hunting shellfish, fish and octopus; occasionally kills seals and scavenges on whale carcasses
LIFESPAN	40 years

ANIMAL FACTS

Male walruses, called bulls, will battle ferociously with each other on land for mating rights during the breeding period. They can inflict serious injuries with their tusks, with the largest individuals usually proving to be dominant. In the sea they can dive to depths of 75m (250ft) in search of food, relying on their whiskers to locate prey on the seabed. Walruses face few dangers, although they are at risk from killer whales. Polar bears represent a threat, too.

These massive members of the seal family are unmistakable. Their distinctive long tusks – actually modified canine teeth – are present in both sexes.

WHERE IN THE WORLD?

Occurs in the Pacific, off Alaska and in the Chukchi Sea. Atlantic population extends from northern Canada to Greenland. Both populations move south in winter.

BLUBBER
Up to 15cm (6in) of fat can be present beneath the skin, protecting against the cold.

WHISKERS
Up to 700 whiskers are arranged in 15 rows.

FLIPPERS
The flippers are smooth and free of hair on their upper surface.

TUSKS
The tusks can measure up to 90cm (36in) in males, but are shorter in females.

GAINING A HOLD
The front flippers act as initial anchorage, pulling the body up.

HAULING OUT
The walrus can then use its tusks to help haul it on to land.

SOCIAL LIFE
Walruses often rest together in groups on ice floes.

MOBILITY

Walruses need to be able to leave the sea and haul themselves on to land. Here they can actually move as fast as we can!

HOW BIG IS IT?

149

Northern Fur Seal

• ORDER • Carnivora • FAMILY • Otariidae • SPECIES • *Callorhinus ursinus*

This is the largest of the fur seal family and was once widely hunted for its coat. The males of the species are considerably larger and heavier than the females.

VITAL STATISTICS

WEIGHT	30–275kg (66–606lb); males are heavier
LENGTH	140–210cm (55–83in)
SEXUAL MATURITY	Females 3–5 years; males 5–6 years, but rarely mate before 10
GESTATION PERIOD	248 days; embryonic development starts about 4 months after mating
NUMBER OF OFFSPRING	1; weaning occurs at 26 weeks
DIET	Piscivorous, hunting a variety of fish and squid
LIFESPAN	Males up to 17 years; females up to 26 years

ANIMAL FACTS

Northern fur seals spend most of their lives in the ocean, only returning to land to breed. At this stage, the males – called bulls – will not feed for up to two months as they battle to mate with the cows, and will lose a considerable amount of body weight. Dominant bulls may establish harems numbering 40 to 50 cows. The dense underfur of this species, insulating the seals from the cold, consists of 60,000 individual hairs per square centimetre (350,000 per square inch).

Females have a significantly longer lifespan than males

WHERE IN THE WORLD?

Found in the northern Pacific Ocean, with its main breeding areas, called rookeries, on the Commander Pribilof and Tyuleni Islands in the Bering Sea.

FACE
Both sexes have a short muzzle, with the nose extending beyond the jaws in bulls.

WHISKERS
Whiskers are very long – white in adults, but black in youngsters.

MALE PHYSIQUE
Males have a thick, wide, powerful neck with a mane of longer, coarser guard hairs.

FRONT FLIPPERS
There is no fur on the upper surface, extending back up to the wrist joint.

HOW BIG IS IT?

FIGHTING
A male seeks to intimidate a rival first, but if fighting follows, they can bite using long, sharp canine teeth.

Californian Sea Lion

• ORDER • Carnivora **• FAMILY •** Otariidae **• SPECIES •** *Zalophus californianus*

VITAL STATISTICS

WEIGHT	91–340kg (201–750lb); males are heavier
LENGTH	180–250cm (71–98in)
SEXUAL MATURITY	About 5 years, but males are unlikely to mate until they are older
GESTATION PERIOD	341–365 days
NUMBER OF OFFSPRING	1; weaning occurs at 26 weeks
DIET	Piscivorous, hunting a variety of fish, including whiting, sardines and anchovies, as well as squid
LIFESPAN	10–15 years in the wild; up to 30 in captivity

ANIMAL FACTS

Males have a pronounced crest on the head with a mane of longer white hair, which explains why they are called sea lions. They are vocal animals, with a loud bark. Although often inhabiting coastal waters, Californian sea lions may spend days out at sea, and can dive down to depths of 274m (900ft). Their young grow rapidly, and are hunting with their mothers at two months old. Sea-lion milk is the only mammalian milk that does not contain lactose.

Sealions (right) have ear flaps, or pinnae, whereas these are missing in seals (left)

These pinnipeds are quite often seen in harbours and similar areas close to human activity, although now they only breed on offshore islands.

WHERE IN THE WORLD?

Occurs down the western side of North America, extending from the coast of British Columbia down to Baja California. Also found in the Sea of Cortez.

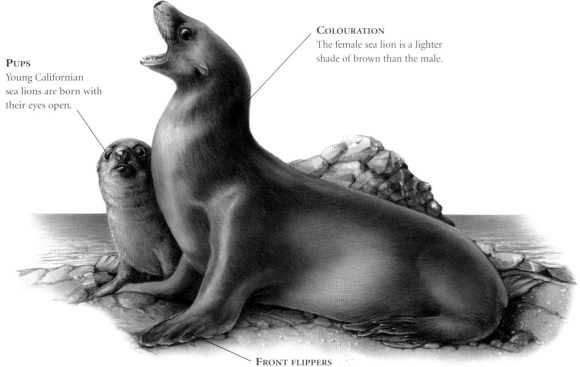

PUPS
Young Californian sea lions are born with their eyes open.

COLOURATION
The female sea lion is a lighter shade of brown than the male.

FRONT FLIPPERS
These are relatively long, and help sealions to move on land.

The ear flaps are small, and tucked close against the skull.

HOW BIG IS IT?

DIVING UNDERWATER
Californian sea lions have special flaps on their ears and nostrils, which can be closed to seal the ears and nose when underwater.

151

Hooded Seal

VITAL STATISTICS

WEIGHT	350–450kg (771–992lb); males are heavier
LENGTH	200–300cm (79–118in)
SEXUAL MATURITY	Females 3–6 years; males 5–7 years
GESTATION PERIOD	341–365 days
NUMBER OF OFFSPRING	1; weaning occurs within 4 days – the shortest period of any mammal
DIET	Piscivorous, hunting fish including herring and cod, as well as squid, starfish and shellfish, depending on their locality
LIFESPAN	30–35 years

ANIMAL FACTS

The growth of the young pups is truly phenomenal. They suckle for less than four days, doubling their weight during this period. This is achieved thanks to the richness of their mother's milk, which is of about 65 per cent fat. Their coats are bluish-grey at first and they moult at 14 months old. Males also visit the nursery grounds at this stage, and will mate with the females once their pups are weaned.

Hooded seals dive to depths of 1000m (3280ft), and can stay submerged for over 50 minutes

The pouch on the heads of mature male hooded seals explains their name. It can be expanded to about twice the size of a football.

WHERE IN THE WORLD?

North Atlantic, but makes regular migrations as far as Norway. May also travel further afield, being recorded from Alaska, Guadeloupe and the Canary Islands.

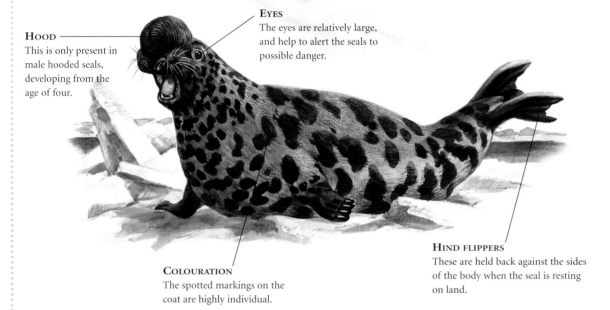

HOOD
This is only present in male hooded seals, developing from the age of four.

EYES
The eyes are relatively large, and help to alert the seals to possible danger.

HIND FLIPPERS
These are held back against the sides of the body when the seal is resting on land.

COLOURATION
The spotted markings on the coat are highly individual.

HOW BIG IS IT?

RED NOSE
This swelling results from a membrane normally kept within the nostrils, which can be inflated as a threat, like the hood.

Bearded Seal

• **ORDER** • Carnivora • **FAMILY** • Phocidae • **SPECIES** • *Erignathus barbatus*

VITAL STATISTICS

WEIGHT	200–360kg (440–794lb); females are slightly heavier
LENGTH	210–240cm (83–94in)
SEXUAL MATURITY	Females 3–8 years; males 6–7 years
GESTATION PERIOD	248–279 days; embryonic development only starts 2–3 months after fertilization
NUMBER OF OFFSPRING	1; weaning occurs by 18 days
DIET	Piscivorous, hunting fish including sculpin and cod, crustaceans such as crabs, and molluscs including clams
LIFESPAN	25–30 years

ANIMAL FACTS

These seals are solitary by nature and are most likely to be encountered amongst broken areas of ice, moving further north in summer as it melts. There are now widespread concerns for their future as the Arctic seas warm up, although they will also emerge on to land. Bearded seals favour relatively shallow waters, down to depths of about 130m (427ft), seeking their food at or near the bottom. They use their whiskers to detect shellfish and molluscs here.

Front flipper showing the digits and claws in detail

The name of this seal originates from the prominent rows of long, pale, spiralling whiskers on its snout, which create the impression of a beard.

WHERE IN THE WORLD?

Occurs in the North Atlantic, the western Laptev and Barents seas, and in the rest of the Arctic Sea. Also found in the Bering and Okhotsk seas.

BODY SHAPE
Although somewhat cumbersome on land, the seal's streamlined shape helps it to swim well.

HEAD
The head is rectangular in shape and quite small compared with the size of the body.

COAT
A dense layer of underfur and protective blubber provide insulation against the ice.

COLOURATION
Dark, typically varying from grey to brown depending on the population, with no patterning.

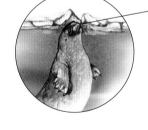

FROSTY BREATHING
As mammals, bearded seals must be able to breathe air. They can create breathing holes in areas of solid ice.

HOW BIG IS IT?

OUT OF THE WATER
Bearded seals rest on drifting ice floes, and females give birth here too.

Leopard Seal

VITAL STATISTICS

WEIGHT	200–590kg (440–1300lb); females are slightly heavier
LENGTH	240–340cm (94–134in)
SEXUAL MATURITY	Females 3–8 years; males 6–7 years
GESTATION PERIOD	248–279 days; embryonic development only starts 2–3 months after fertilization
NUMBER OF OFFSPRING	1; weaning occurs by 18 days
DIET	Carnivorous, hunting other seals, especially crabeater seals, penguins and invertebrates including squid and krill
LIFESPAN	12–15 years

ANIMAL FACTS

Solitary by nature, leopard seals wander through the Antarctic pack ice, heading further north in winter. They are opportunistic and fearsome hunters, and their prey includes the young of other seals. They will batter penguins ferociously from side to side in the water until the birds' bodies break apart. Yet the seal's molar teeth are also designed so that they act as sieves, allowing them to feed on tiny krill. Leopard seals themselves face few predators, apart from killer whales.

A leopard seal on an ice floe

It is not just its spotted coat that gives these seals their name. Like the animal after which they are named, they are fearsome hunters.

WHERE IN THE WORLD?

Found on the pack ice in Antarctic waters, and occasionally recorded as venturing further north to Australia, New Zealand, South Africa and South America.

MOUTH
This is large, giving a wide gape, and filled with an array of sharp teeth.

BODY
The body is narrow, with a distinctive spotted pattern, particularly prominent on the underparts.

FLIPPERS
These are relatively long, aiding both the swimming power and agility of these seals.

HOW BIG IS IT?

HUNTING TECHNIQUE
The seal lurks beneath an ice shelf, waiting for a penguin to dive into the water, and then ambushes it.

Southern Elephant Seal

• ORDER • Carnivora • FAMILY • Phocidae • SPECIES • *Mirounga leonina*

Males of this species are massive – the largest of all seals. Southern elephant seals can also dive deeper than other species, down to 1600m (5250ft).

VITAL STATISTICS

WEIGHT	500–3500kg (1102–7716lb); males are much bigger
LENGTH	200–690cm (79–270in)
SEXUAL MATURITY	Females 2–4 years; males 3–6 years but unlikely to breed before 10
GESTATION PERIOD	About 266 days; embryonic development only starts 3 months after fertilization
NUMBER OF OFFSPRING	1; weaning occurs by 23 days
DIET	Mainly squid, but also take fish such as deep water sharks
LIFESPAN	Up to 23 years

ANIMAL FACTS

Thanks to a highly efficient respiratory system, these seals are capable of diving for up to two hours without surfacing, nor do they suffer the 'bends' when they head back up to the surface from the depths of the ocean. Bulls stake a claim to their breeding territories first, after which the pregnant females return to the beaches, giving birth soon afterwards. Once the pups are weaned, they must fend for themselves, with the females mating again before returning to sea.

Killer whales represent the only major threat to adults

WHERE IN THE WORLD?

Circumpolar in the southern hemisphere. Major breeding grounds are the Falklands, South Georgia and southern South America; Macquarie and neighbouring islands; Kerguelen and Heard.

MOUTH
This appears very red, sometimes creating the impression of bleeding.

HEAD SHAPE
The massive, trunk-like structure on the head of males explains their common name.

COLOURATION
Both sexes are dark grey, slightly lighter in colour on the underparts.

PROTECTION
A thick layer of blubber lies under the skin. This fat provides insulation and can be metabolized as food.

HOW BIG IS IT?

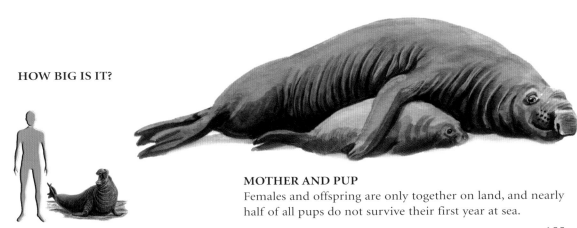

MOTHER AND PUP
Females and offspring are only together on land, and nearly half of all pups do not survive their first year at sea.

Mediterranean Monk Seal

• ORDER • Carnivora • FAMILY • Phocidae • SPECIES • *Monachus monachus*

VITAL STATISTICS

WEIGHT	250–300kg (551–661lb)
LENGTH	240–280cm (94–110in)
SEXUAL MATURITY	Females 4–6 years; males 5–6 years
GESTATION PERIOD	About 341 days; mating takes place in the water
NUMBER OF OFFSPRING	1; weaning occurs by 17 weeks
DIET	Feeds on a variety of fish, such as sardines, tuna and mullet, also lobsters and cephalopods, notably squid and octopus
LIFESPAN	20–30 years

ANIMAL FACTS

This species faces a number of major threats, particularly in developed areas of the Mediterranean where it was once common. Overfishing and persecution by fishermen – who blame the seals for declining catches – have accelerated their decline, and pollution in the Mediterranean remains a constant threat. What was thought to be an epidemic of disease also wiped out a major proportion of the surviving population on the North African coast in 1997, and relatively few reserves for them currently exist.

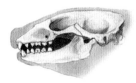

The skull of a Mediterranean monk seal

These seals are considered to be critically endangered, with fewer than 600 surviving. They used to occur throughout the Mediterranean, out into the eastern Atlantic.

WHERE IN THE WORLD?

The major surviving population is around Greece, but individuals are still present on the northwestern coast of Africa and in the northeastern Atlantic.

FLIPPERS
The flippers are quite short and end in short claws.

EARS
There are no external ear flaps on the ears.

COAT LENGTH
The fur of the Mediterranean monk seal is shorter than that of any other seal.

COLOURATION
Females are brownish with lighter underparts and blotching, while males are black, with white on the belly.

NOSTRILS
These are prominent, long and pointed upwards.

These seals occur relatively close to shore.

HOW BIG IS IT?

BIRTHING CAVES
Females now tend to give birth along very inaccessible parts of coastline, often seeking out the relative safety of caves.

Harp Seal

VITAL STATISTICS

WEIGHT	130–160kg (287–353lb)
LENGTH	160–190cm (63–75in)
SEXUAL MATURITY	Females 4–6 years; males 5–6 years
GESTATION PERIOD	About 225 days; embryonic development only starts about 4.5 months after fertilization
NUMBER OF OFFSPRING	1; weaning occurs by 12 days
DIET	Feeds on a variety of fish, including capelin, cod and herring, also crabs and cephalopods such as squid
LIFESPAN	30–35 years

ANIMAL FACTS

Harp seals spend most of the year in the ocean. They only return to the pack ice to give birth, congregating in large numbers at this stage, with up to 2000 seals per square kilometre (0.4 square miles). They are then particularly vulnerable to predation by polar bears. Young harp seals are pale yellow at birth, but by three days old their coat will have become snowy white. The pups grow very quickly, tripling their birth weight of 11kg (24lb) before they are weaned.

Females only nurse their young for about 10 minutes every four hours or so, otherwise the pups are left alone

The harp-shaped pattern on the backs of adults explains the common name of these seals. Young pups are still controversially hunted for their fur.

WHERE IN THE WORLD?

Occurs in the Arctic and northwestern Atlantic, breeding in the Gulf of St Lawrence off Newfoundland, east of Greenland and in the White Sea.

PATTERNING
Adults have black heads, in addition to the harp-shaped marking on the back. Their fur is otherwise pale grey.

HIND FLIPPERS
The seal moves these from side to side to provide propulsive power when swimming.

COLOURATION
The darker areas of fur are slightly lighter in females than in males.

FRONT FLIPPERS
These tend to look more like paws than flippers.

ON THE MOVE
Eared seals and sea lions (left) use their front flippers for swimming, whereas members of this family use their hind ones.

HOW BIG IS IT?

Common Seal

• ORDER • Carnivora • FAMILY • Phocidae • SPECIES • *Phoca vitulina*

This species is also known as the harbour seal, because it is often seen in these surroundings, not infrequently venturing up into river estuaries, too.

VITAL STATISTICS

WEIGHT	45–170kg (99–375lb); males are heavier
LENGTH	120–190cm (47–75in)
SEXUAL MATURITY	Females 4–6 years; males 5–6 years
GESTATION PERIOD	About 225 days; embryonic development only starts about 4.5 months after fertilization
NUMBER OF OFFSPRING	1; weaning occurs at around 28 days
DIET	Feeds mainly on fish, including sand eels and herring, also crustaceans and cephalopods such as squid
LIFESPAN	20–30 years; males typically have a shorter lifespan

ANIMAL FACTS

Young common seals can swim and dive soon after they are born. Females can therefore give birth in relative safety on sandbanks that are only evident during low tide. This species has the most extensive range of any pinniped, but serious outbreaks of disease have impacted its numbers locally. During 1988, over 17,000 common seals died in an epidemic caused by a new seal virus, which struck populations in the North sea. These seals are also at risk from pollution.

Common seal pup

WHERE IN THE WORLD?

Occurs in coastal areas through the northern hemisphere, present in both the North Atlantic and the North Pacific, as well as the North and Baltic seas.

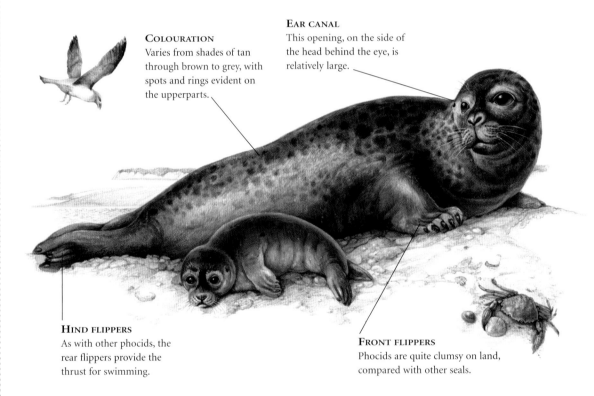

COLOURATION
Varies from shades of tan through brown to grey, with spots and rings evident on the upperparts.

EAR CANAL
This opening, on the side of the head behind the eye, is relatively large.

HIND FLIPPERS
As with other phocids, the rear flippers provide the thrust for swimming.

FRONT FLIPPERS
Phocids are quite clumsy on land, compared with other seals.

HOW BIG IS IT?

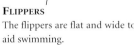

FLIPPERS
The flippers are flat and wide to aid swimming.

MOTHER AND PUP
Adopting an upright position in the water affords good all-round visibility and helps the mother to support her pup.

Northern American Ringtail

• ORDER • Carnivora • FAMILY • Procyonidae • GENUS & SPECIES • *Bassariscus astutus*

VITAL STATISTICS

WEIGHT	0.9–1.3kg (2–3lb); males are heavier
LENGTH	91–124cm (36–49in); stands up to 16cm (6in) tall
SEXUAL MATURITY	About 10 months old
GESTATION PERIOD	Between 45–50 days
NUMBER OF OFFSPRING	Averages 2–4, but can be up to 5; weaning occurs at about 42 days
DIET	Carnivorous, hunting small mammals, birds and invertebrates; also eats fruit
LIFESPAN	7–10 years, up to 19 in captivity

ANIMAL FACTS

Solitary by nature, these ringtails mark their territory using both urine and faeces. Mating occurs from spring through to early summer. At birth, the young lack the striped tail pattern, being mainly white. They are noisy, making a wide range of calls, often squeaking, hissing and growling. North American ringtails are also locally known as miner's cats. This is because their young used to be trapped and tamed, so they could keep the cabins occupied by the miners free from rodents.

They sleep in dens, usually lined with dry vegetation such as leaves

Their agile nature means that North American ringtails occur both in forests and also more arid rocky areas, where they can also move around easily.

WHERE IN THE WORLD?

South-west Oregon, California, southern Utah and Nevada, western Colorado and southern Kansas and Oklahoma, Arizona, New Mexico and Texas to Mexico and Costa Rica.

HIND FEET
These are remarkably flexible, allowing the ringtail to swivel its position by 180°, helping it to climb.

TAIL
Its appearance explains why this member of the raccoon family is known as a ringtail.

COLOURATION
Ranges from buff to greyish-brown, with the underparts being paler in colouration.

EYES
Relatively large and surrounded with white spectacles of fur.

HOW BIG IS IT?

MEETING OF TWO PREDATORS
If it finds itself under threat, the North American ringtail can escape danger by flipping backwards, pivoting on its tail.

White-Nosed Coati

• ORDER • Carnivora • FAMILY • Procyonidae • SPECIES • *Nasua narica*

VITAL STATISTICS

WEIGHT	5–9kg (11–20lb); males are heavier
LENGTH	110–120cm (43–47in); about 30cm (12in) tall
SEXUAL MATURITY	Females 2 years; males 3 years
GESTATION PERIOD	77 days
NUMBER OF OFFSPRING	3–7, averages 4; weaning occurs at 6 weeks
DIET	Omnivorous, eating small animals, carrion, eggs and fruit; may also dig up invertebrates
LIFESPAN	7–8 years in the wild; up to 15 in captivity

ANIMAL FACTS

White-nosed coatis are often encountered in family groups, although males live on their own. They are bold by nature, and it is not uncommon for them to scavenge around campsites during the day, and then retreat to the trees to sleep at night. In areas where they are hunted, however, they are much more wary, and are nocturnal in their habits. When the adult females go off foraging, the young are looked after by another member of the group.

A creche, watched over by an adult female

These members of the raccoon family are very agile when climbing, but they use their long tail for balancing rather than gripping the tree branches.

WHERE IN THE WORLD?

Southeastern Arizona and New Mexico in the USA, southwards through Central America down as far as Panama, occurring in wooded areas of various types.

NOSE
Long, very flexible and slightly turned up at its tip, the nose is used rather like another limb.

TAIL
Long and ringed along its length, the tail ends in a brown tip.

LIMBS
Limbs are strong and powerful. Long, sharp claws especially on the front legs, are useful for digging.

FACIAL MARKINGS
There are white flashes and a broader white area around the nose.

MAKING A MARK
Adult male coatis are likely to fight each other. They possess a formidable battery of teeth capable of inflicting serious bites.

HOW BIG IS IT?

Kinkajou

VITAL STATISTICS

WEIGHT	2–3kg (4–7lb); males are heavier
LENGTH	84–112cm (33–44in); about 20cm (8in) tall
SEXUAL MATURITY	Females 2.5–3 years; males 1.5–2 years
GESTATION PERIOD	98–120 days, breeding throughout the year
NUMBER OF OFFSPRING	1–2; weaning occurs at 3–5 months
DIET	Frugivorous, feeding mainly on fruit, as well as nectar
LIFESPAN	Up to 23 years; can be 40 in captivity

ANIMAL FACTS

Kinkajous have a well-developed social structure, living in family groups. They mark their territory using scent glands located on the head and throat, as well as the belly. They rely on their keen sense of smell to locate food, too. Their eyesight is poor, and they lack colour vision, living in the rainforest where the light is gloomy. They are nocturnal by nature. Kinkajous are significant in the ecology of the rainforest because they pollinate plants when taking nectar.

A Kinkajou rubs its scent on a tree branch

This species is rather confusingly called the honey bear, although it belongs to the raccoon family. Wild kinkajous have also never been observed feeding on honey.

WHERE IN THE WORLD?

Occurs widely in suitable habitat through central and northern South America. Distribution extends from southern parts of Mexico right down to southern parts of Brazil.

COLOURATION
The outer fur appears golden or burnished brown, with a grey undercoat.

HEAD
The head is rounded, with low-set, widely spaced ears and a very narrow snout.

TAIL
Covered in short hair, the tail is prehensile, allowing the kinkajou to grip branches firmly while climbing.

FEET
Sharp claws on the toes help the kinkajou to maintain its grip.

FEEDING AID
The kinkajou's long but narrow tongue measures up to 13cm (5in), helping it to lick up pollen grains from flowers.

HANGING AROUND
The kinkajou's weight can be supported just by its tail.

HOW BIG IS IT?

Raccoon

• ORDER • Carnivora • FAMILY • Procyonidae • SPECIES • *Procyon lotor*

VITAL STATISTICS

WEIGHT	4–9kg (9–20lb); males are heavier
LENGTH	109–119cm (43–47in); about 30cm (12in) tall
SEXUAL MATURITY	Females 2 years; males 3 years
GESTATION PERIOD	54–70 days; typically 65 days
NUMBER OF OFFSPRING	2–5, averages 4; weaning occurs at 16 weeks
DIET	Omnivorous, eating mainly invertebrates, plus plant matter and small animals
LIFESPAN	2–3 years; up to 16 years in captivity

ANIMAL FACTS

Raccoons have spread into urban areas, where food is readily available, tipping over rubbish bins for leftovers, and raiding gardens. They may also dig for earthworms, being able to hear them moving underground. Raccoons can also carry rabies, and a number of other serious illnesses which can be transmitted to people. Raccoons will normally seek safety by climbing trees and buildings if threatened, and they may also invade houses through roof spaces and chimneys.

The hind feet are longer and narrower than the front feet

162

Curious by nature, raccoons will examine items carefully by holding them in their paws before eating anything. They will also wash food before consuming it.

WHERE IN THE WORLD?

Extends from Canada through the USA and into Central America, as far south as Panama. Introduced to Europe and Asia, with some isolated populations established.

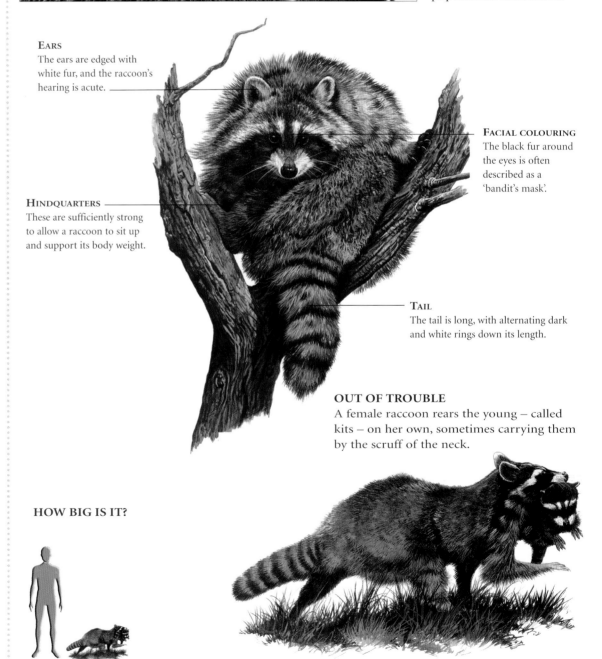

EARS
The ears are edged with white fur, and the raccoon's hearing is acute.

FACIAL COLOURING
The black fur around the eyes is often described as a 'bandit's mask'.

HINDQUARTERS
These are sufficiently strong to allow a raccoon to sit up and support its body weight.

TAIL
The tail is long, with alternating dark and white rings down its length.

OUT OF TROUBLE
A female raccoon rears the young – called kits – on her own, sometimes carrying them by the scruff of the neck.

HOW BIG IS IT?

Giant Panda

VITAL STATISTICS

WEIGHT	100–150kg (220–330lb); males are heavier
LENGTH	About 160cm (63in); about 75cm (30in) tall
SEXUAL MATURITY	4–8 years
GESTATION PERIOD	95–160 days; females come into heat just once annually
NUMBER OF OFFSPRING	1–2; weaning occurs at about 1 year
DIET	Herbivorous, feeding on 25 different types of bamboo; occasionally eats meat, even catching bamboo rats
LIFESPAN	20–30 years

ANIMAL FACTS

The giant panda is an anomaly – a bear equipped for a carnivorous diet, which has adapted to a highly specialized vegetarian diet. The problem is that the bamboos die after flowering, leaving giant pandas at risk of starvation. In the past, this was not a major issue, because they could move elsewhere, but clearance of bamboo forests is curtailing their movements. This is why the creation of reserves for this species is so critical to their survival.

Territorial marking includes spraying urine and leaving scratch marks on trees

An icon of the conservation movement, the giant panda faces an uncertain future. Its current population is thought to consist of 1000 to 3000 individuals.

WHERE IN THE WORLD?

Restricted to China, occurring in the southwest of the country, in the provinces of Sichuan, Shaanxi and Gansu, in areas of suitable temperate forest.

MATERNAL INSTINCTS

Newborn giant pandas can weigh just 90g (3.2oz), and may spend nearly seven hours a day suckling at first.

HOW BIG IS IT?

MARKINGS
The giant panda's eyes are surrounded by black fur.

FRONT PAWS
These are specially adapted to allow pandas to grasp bamboo shoots.

COAT
The coat is thick and woolly, protecting against the cold.

Sun Bear

VITAL STATISTICS

WEIGHT	60–150kg (220–330lb); males are heavier
LENGTH	120–150cm (47–59in); about 71cm (28in) tall
SEXUAL MATURITY	3–4 years
GESTATION PERIOD	About 96 days; breeding can occur throughout the year as these bears do not hibernate
NUMBER OF OFFSPRING	1–2; weaning occurs at about 18 months
DIET	Omnivorous, taking small vertebrates, insects, berries and fruit, eggs and honey
LIFESPAN	20–30 years

ANIMAL FACTS

Living in lowland areas of tropical rainforest, sun bears are solitary by nature and nocturnal in their habits. They can climb well – aided by their relatively small size and the way in which their paws curve inwards – and will even rest off the ground during the day. Relatively little is actually known about their habits, although they tend to find their food by their sense of smell as their eyesight is poor. They can occasionally cause havoc on cacao and coconut plantations.

Although the sun bear is the smallest of all bears, it is also one of the most aggressive, and is equipped with particularly fearsome canine teeth.

WHERE IN THE WORLD?

Occurs in various parts of Southeast Asia, from India eastwards to Myanmar (Burma) and China, and south through Thailand, Vietnam and Malaysia to Indonesia.

EARS
These are small and rounded, positioned well back and set quite low on the head.

BODY COLOURATION
Short, sleek blackish coat with an orange-yellow crescent area on the chest.

FACIAL APPEARANCE
There is yellowish fur on the face, which explains the bear's name.

PAWS
Paws are powerful, with no fur on the soles and sharp, sickle-shaped claws.

POWER OF THE PAWS
These bears break into insects' nests with their sharp claws and use their long tongue to scoop up honey or termites.

HOW BIG IS IT?

Spectacled Bear

• ORDER • Carnivora **• FAMILY •** Ursidae **• SPECIES •** *Tremarctos ornatus*

This is the only bear now found in South America, and the last survivor of a group that first appeared there two million years ago.

VITAL STATISTICS

WEIGHT	64–155kg (141–341lb); males are heavier
LENGTH	119–150cm (47–59in); about 71cm (28in) tall
SEXUAL MATURITY	4–7 years
GESTATION PERIOD	200–260 days
NUMBER OF OFFSPRING	2–3; weaning takes place around 18 months
DIET	Omnivorous, feeding on fruit, berries, plants, nuts, seeds, small vertebrates and carrion
LIFESPAN	Up to 25 years; as long as 36 years recorded in captivity

WHERE IN THE WORLD?

Ranges from Panama in Central America via Colombia, Venezuela, Peru and Ecuador to parts of Bolivia, Brazil and Argentina, favouring mountainous areas.

ANIMAL FACTS

What helps distinguish spectacled bears from other living members of the Ursidae family is the fact that they have just 13, rather than 14, pairs of ribs. They are small in size, however, compared with their extinct short-faced relatives, which could have weighed up to 1000kg (2205lb). Spectacled bears can be encountered in a range of different habitats, but they favour high-altitude cloud forest rather than rainforest areas. They spend much of their time off the ground in trees.

Spectacled bear swimming

FACIAL APPEARANCE
The jaws are short, and the facial markings are a combination of white and yellow fur.

COLOURATION
Fur is black or dark brown and dense, giving good protection from the elements.

PAWS
The paws are powerful and equipped with sharp claws, enabling these bears to dig effectively.

HOW BIG IS IT?

FACIAL PATTERNING
These bears can differ markedly in appearance, with only some displaying the typical paler areas of fur around the eyes that account for their name.

North American Black Bear

• **ORDER** • Carnivora • **FAMILY** • Ursidae • **SPECIES** • *Ursus americanus*

VITAL STATISTICS

WEIGHT	61–141kg (135–310lb); males are heavier
LENGTH	165–193cm (65–76in); about 95cm (37in) tall
SEXUAL MATURITY	3–4 years, but may not breed until 7
GESTATION PERIOD	Around 220 days
NUMBER OF OFFSPRING	2–3; weaning takes place around 6–8 months
DIET	Omnivorous, feeding on fruit, berries, plants, nuts, seeds, carrion, fish and deer
LIFESPAN	Up to 32 years

ANIMAL FACTS

This is the smallest of the three species of North American bear. As in all cases, the cubs are tiny at birth. They can weigh as little as 220g (8oz), but grow rapidly on their mother's rich milk in her den. By the time they emerge in the spring, they may have grown to 5kg (11lb). The family then have to be wary of encountering male bears, which will seek to kill the cubs before ultimately mating with the female.

American black bears escape danger by climbing trees

These particular bears favour thickly forested mountainous areas. They are highly territorial, with individual males occupying areas of up to 100km² (40 square miles).

WHERE IN THE WORLD?

North America, ranging from southern Alaska into southwestern Canada, extending through the western USA down to northern Mexico. Also in Florida and Georgia.

MUZZLE
This is broad, and covered in short, and quite pale hair.

HINDQUARTERS
The hindquarters are muscular, with an inconspicuous tail.

COLOURATION
Colour varies from cinnamon via darker brown to black. Occasional white individuals have been recorded.

FEET
All bears are plantigrade, walking on the soles of their feet, with the heels touching the ground.

HOW BIG IS IT?

VEGETARIAN LIVING
Plant matter accounts for over three-quarters of this bear's diet.

Brown Bear

VITAL STATISTICS

WEIGHT	97–680kg (213–1500lb); males are heavier
LENGTH	180–293cm (71–115in); about 150cm (59in) tall
SEXUAL MATURITY	5–7 years; males may not breed until 10
GESTATION PERIOD	186–248 days; embryonic development begins 5 months after fertilization
NUMBER OF OFFSPRING	1–5, averages 2; weaning occurs at 6–8 months
DIET	Omnivorous, eating fruit, vegetation, carrion and vertebrates
LIFESPAN	Up to 30 years; 40 in captivity

ANIMAL FACTS

The ancestors of today's brown bears crossed into North America over what has since become the Bering Strait, at a time when this area was land. This explains why today the distribution of this species is centred on the western side of North America. As the result of global warming, brown bears are now starting to push further northwards, expanding their range. They prefer relatively open areas of countryside, although in Europe and Asia they usually inhabit forests.

The claws are formidable

The overall range of these bears has shrunk significantly in the face of increasing urbanization, but hunting pressures have also played a part in their decline.

WHERE IN THE WORLD?

Occurs in northwestern parts of North America, and across northern Europe and Asia, from Scandinavia eastwards. Also present in some areas further south.

HUMP
This distinctive feature of this species is made of muscle.

FACIAL SHAPE
The brown bear is unique in having a concave facial profile.

COLOURATION
In spite of their name, brown bears can vary from shades of blond through brown, almost to black.

CLAWS
These are used for digging and also climbing, and measure around 15cm (6in).

ESCAPE FROM HARM
Young bears will flee up trees if they detect danger, with their mother staying at a lower level to defend them.

HOW BIG IS IT?

Grizzly Bear

• ORDER • *Carnivora* • FAMILY • *Ursidae* • GENUS & SPECIES • *Ursus arctos horribilis*

VITAL STATISTICS

WEIGHT	150–600kg (330–1322lb); males are heavier
LENGTH	180–213cm (71–84in) overall; about 150cm (59in) tall
SEXUAL MATURITY	5–7 years; males may not breed until 10
GESTATION PERIOD	186–248 days; embryonic development begins 5 months after fertilization
NUMBER OF OFFSPRING	2, ranges from 1–5; weaning occurs at 6–8 months
DIET	Omnivorous, eating fruit, vegetation, carrion and vertebrate prey
LIFESPAN	Up to 30 years; 40 in captivity

ANIMAL FACTS

Roaming over vast areas, grizzly bears are mainly vegetarian, but they will also hunt a variety of prey, particularly deer of various types. They are territorial, and most attacks on people can be explained by the bear's poor eyesight, which suggests the person is a rival bear. In spite of their weight, grizzlies can run fast, at speeds equivalent to 60kph (37mph), and they can also climb and swim well. They face few dangers, apart from being hunted by man.

Paw prints reveal the powerful claws

This particular race of the brown bear is characterised by its 'grizzled' or greyish fur, thanks to the colouration at the tips of its hairs.

WHERE IN THE WORLD?

Occurs in North America, being found mainly in Alaska and Canada, although small numbers still survive in the US, mainly in Wyoming, Montana and Idaho.

THE SENSES
Broad, wide nostrils give these bears a keen sense of smell, whereas their eyes are small.

FOREQUARTERS
These are immensely powerful, with the legs being thick and strong.

SIZE
Those grizzlies living in the far north are typically larger in size than those found further south.

COLOURATION
The bear's greyish flecking is a characteristic feature of this race.

Scratch marks made on a tree may indicate the presence of a bear.

HOW BIG IS IT?

NATURE'S BOUNTY
Grizzlies will take advantage of salmon returning to their traditional spawning grounds, wading into the water to catch these fish.

Kodiak Bear

This is the largest of the brown bears, whose range includes the Kodiak archipelago in the Gulf of Alaska, where salmon is their main prey.

VITAL STATISTICS

WEIGHT	159–680kg (350–1500lb); males are heavier
LENGTH	180–293cm (71–115in); about 150cm (59in) tall
SEXUAL MATURITY	5–7 years; males may not breed until 10
GESTATION PERIOD	186–248 days; embryonic development begins 5 months after fertilization
NUMBER OF OFFSPRING	1–5, normally 2; weaning occurs at 6–8 months
DIET	Omnivorous, eating fruit, vegetation, carrion and salmon
LIFESPAN	20–30 years; 40 in captivity

ANIMAL FACTS

The lives of Kodiak bears are closely interwoven with their environment. They start to enter dens in the autumn, and will spend the winter slumbering in them, relying on their stores of body fat to sustain them. By the following spring, the bears may have lost a third of their body weight. They mate around mid-summer but development of the young is delayed, so that the cubs – which are about the size of rats – will be born early the following year.

WHERE IN THE WORLD?

Occurs in western Alaska, on offshore islands including Kodiak, Shuyak and Afognak, and on the Alaskan mainland. The weather here is harsh, especially in winter.

COLOURATION
Individuals from southerly areas, including females, are lighter in colour.

CLAWS
The claws are black but often turn whitish in older bears. They are about 13cm (5in) long.

STANDING OUT
Kodiak bears have a distinctive profile. Genetic studies suggest they have been isolated from other races of brown bear for more than 10,000 years.

HEIGHT
These bears stand up to 4m (13ft) tall on their hind legs.

HIND PAWS
These are massive, measuring up to 41cm (16in), and support the bear's weight when it stands up.

HOW BIG IS IT?

DENNING
These bears may dig their own dens, or enlarge existing holes. Not all bears will retreat to a den over the winter.

Polar Bear

VITAL STATISTICS

WEIGHT	200–800kg (441–1764lb); males are heavier
LENGTH	190–300cm (75–118in); about 160cm (63in) tall
SEXUAL MATURITY	4–6 years; males mate after 8 years
GESTATION PERIOD	195–265 days; embryonic development begins 4 months after fertilization
NUMBER OF OFFSPRING	1–4; weaning occurs at 18–30 months
DIET	Carnivorous, feeding on seals, plus fish, reindeer, carrion and vegetation in summer
LIFESPAN	20–30 years; 45 in captivity

ANIMAL FACTS

Beneath the skin is a layer of blubber, up to 10cm (4in) thick. This protects against the cold, and provides buoyancy when the bears are swimming. The melting of the Arctic ice cap is reducing the hunting opportunities for the bears on the ice itself, forcing them to swim longer distances. Females give birth in dens dug in the snow, where the temperature will be significantly warmer than outside.

Underside of the foot, protected by hair (above) compared with that of a brown bear (below)

The biggest member of its family, the polar bear also ranks as the largest terrestrial carnivore, and can represent a real danger to people.

WHERE IN THE WORLD?

Found in the far north, right around the globe, in the circumpolar region of the Arctic. Its range extends as far south as Canada.

FUR
The bear's distinctive creamy-white colour blends into the landscape and is water-repellant.

NOSE
The nose is highly sensitive, allowing the bear to detect a seal carcass up to 32km (20 miles) away.

HIND LEGS
The hind legs are used for swimming, and are longer than the front legs.

FEET
Covered with hair, the feet act as snowshoes, helping the bear to walk on snow and ice without suffering frostbite.

HOW BIG IS IT?

HUNTING TECHNIQUE

Polar bears can locate an air hole in the ice made by a seal from over 1.6km (1 mile) away. They wait patiently for the seal to surface.

Asian Black Bear

These bears still occur in areas close to major centres of human habitation, as in Japan, but forest clearance and hunting threatens their survival.

VITAL STATISTICS

WEIGHT	50–200kg (110–440lb); males are heavier
LENGTH	130–190cm (51–75in); about 100cm (39in) tall
SEXUAL MATURITY	3–4 years
GESTATION PERIOD	186–248 days; embryonic development begins about 5 months after fertilization
NUMBER OF OFFSPRING	2–3; weaning occurs from 3.5 months; family stays together for 2 years
DIET	Omnivorous, eating small mammals, carrion, acorns, nuts and vegetable matter
LIFESPAN	15–20 years; 25 in captivity

ANIMAL FACTS

This species is known by various names, including the Tibetan black bear and the moon bear, because of its chest marking. They have been heavily hunted in recent years for their gall bladders, which are highly sought-after in Chinese medicine. These bears can be very aggressive towards people, and this hampers conservation efforts. In the autumn they feed on nuts in the forests, which help them to gain weight for the winter. They are nocturnal in their habits.

WHERE IN THE WORLD?

Ranges westwards from Iran and Iraq via the Himalayas to Malaysia. A separate population occurs further north in eastern Asia, in eastern Russia, Japan and Korea.

COLOURATION
The fur is black, with a distinctive, pale, crescent-shaped marking across the chest.

FUR LENGTH
The fur is longest over the shoulders and under the throat.

STRENGTH
It is not uncommon for bears to break branches as they climb on them.

NESTS
These bears may build nests 40m (131ft) up in a tree.

HOW BIG IS IT?

GROWING UP
Cubs are blind and completely helpless at birth. Born in a den during late winter, they emerge in the spring.

Binturong

VITAL STATISTICS

WEIGHT	13–27kg (29–60lb); females are heavier
LENGTH	115–186cm (45–73in); body and tail are of similar lengths
SEXUAL MATURITY	3 years
GESTATION PERIOD	84–91 days; sometimes embryonic development is delayed
NUMBER OF OFFSPRING	Normally 1–2, but can be up to 6; weaning occurs from 3.5 months
DIET	Omnivorous, eating mainly fruit and vegetation, rodents, birds and their eggs
LIFESPAN	15–20 years; 25 in captivity

ANIMAL FACTS

Also known as the bearcat, the binturong lives mainly off the ground in its rainforest home. Its diet ensures its significance in the ecology here, by dispersing indigestible seeds passed out in its droppings. Binturongs have a peculiar body odour, said to resemble the smell of buttered popcorn. They scent-mark their territory with a special gland beneath the tail.

The prehensile tail serves as another hand for grasping branches

The unusual-sounding name of the binturong originates from a native language that died out some time ago, and its actual meaning is unknown.

WHERE IN THE WORLD?

Occurs in India, east to China and the Philippines, and southwards via Laos, Vietnam and Thailand to Indonesia, where it is found on various islands such as Sumatra, Java and Borneo.

FEET
Binturongs grip with their claws when coming down a tree, when their ankles are directed backwards.

COAT
Long and shaggy, the coat helps protect against the rain.

TAIL
The binturong is unique in the Old World in having a prehensile tail.

HOW BIG IS IT?

EASY LIVING
Slow-moving, binturongs are largely nocturnal by nature, and will sleep in the branches during the day, often sunning themselves.

Common Genet

• **ORDER** • Carnivora • **FAMILY** • Viverridae • **SPECIES** • *Genetta genetta*

Various races of the common genet exist through its wide range, one of which is restricted to Majorca and the Balearic Islands in the Mediterranean.

VITAL STATISTICS

WEIGHT	1–3kg (2.2–7lb)
LENGTH	80–106cm (32–42in); body and tail are of similar lengths; about 15cm (6in) tall
SEXUAL MATURITY	2 years
GESTATION PERIOD	70–78 days
NUMBER OF OFFSPRING	1–3; weaning occurs at about 8 weeks
DIET	Carnivorous, feeding on invertebrates, rodents, birds and their eggs, amphibians and reptiles
LIFESPAN	10–13 years

ANIMAL FACTS

These genets are adept at climbing and hunting off the ground. Their sharp claws – which are not always evident – help them to maintain their balance and grab prey. They can fall victim to snakes such as pythons, as well as owls and leopards. Common genets become active at dusk, as reflected by their large eyes. They also have keen hearing. They look rather like cats, and have a similar vocabulary of sounds – able to miaow, purr and hiss.

WHERE IN THE WORLD?

Occurs throughout Africa in wooded areas, being the most widely distributed species of genet. Also present in mainland Western Europe and the Middle East.

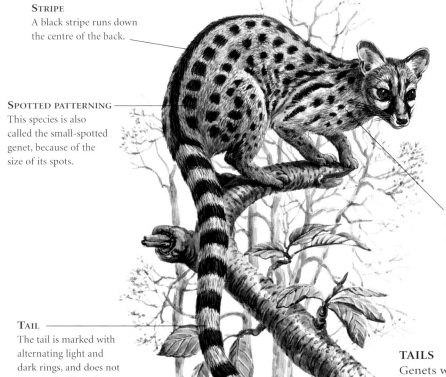

STRIPE
A black stripe runs down the centre of the back.

SPOTTED PATTERNING
This species is also called the small-spotted genet, because of the size of its spots.

BACKGROUND COLOUR
This can vary from silver to yellowish-grey, depending on the individual.

TAIL
The tail is marked with alternating light and dark rings, and does not narrow significantly along its length.

TAILS

Genets will investigate tree holes in search of possible prey, using their long tails to help them maintain their balance.

HOW BIG IS IT?

Common Mudpuppy

• ORDER • Caudata • FAMILY • Proteidae • SPECIES • *Necturus maculosus*

VITAL STATISTICS

LENGTH	30cm (12in)
SEXUAL MATURITY	5–8 years
HATCHING PERIOD	Temperature-dependent, typically 38–63 days; young are about 2.5cm (1in) at this stage
NUMBER OF EGGS	35–85 a year
HABITAT	Aquatic environment with underwater hiding places
DIET	Carnivorous, hunting small invertebrates and fish, tadpoles and small amphibians; may also eat aquatic vegetation
LIFESPAN	Up to 34 years

ANIMAL FACTS

The mudpuppy's gills look rather like ostrich feathers. They have a large surface area, which allows oxygen to be extracted from the water and carbon dioxide to be released efficiently. They are active through the year, and mating takes place in the autumn, followed by egg-laying in the spring.

The gills can be fanned out to increase their surface area

The unusual name of these primitive amphibians, which keep their gills throughout their lives, comes from the mistaken belief that they could bark like a dog!

WHERE IN THE WORLD?

Occurs in central and eastern North America, from Ontario and Manitoba to Québec, via New York and the Carolinas to Mississippi, Alabama, Georgia and Louisiana.

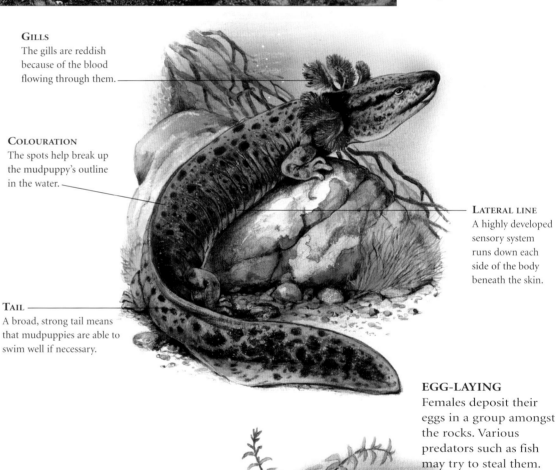

GILLS
The gills are reddish because of the blood flowing through them.

COLOURATION
The spots help break up the mudpuppy's outline in the water.

TAIL
A broad, strong tail means that mudpuppies are able to swim well if necessary.

LATERAL LINE
A highly developed sensory system runs down each side of the body beneath the skin.

EGG-LAYING
Females deposit their eggs in a group amongst the rocks. Various predators such as fish may try to steal them.

HOW BIG IS IT?

Alpine Salamander

• **ORDER** • Caudata • **FAMILY** • Salamandridae • **SPECIES** • *Salamandra atra*

Unlike most amphibians, in this species the eggs develop inside the body, and the female gives birth to live young. She produces very few offspring as a result.

VITAL STATISTICS

LENGTH	9–15cm (3.5–6in); females are slightly larger
SEXUAL MATURITY	4–5 years
HATCHING PERIOD	The young develop inside the female, carried for 2–3 years before birth
NUMBER OF OFFSPRING	2
HABITAT	Damp alpine meadows and woodland
DIET	Carnivorous, hunting small invertebrates such as worms, and feeding both in the water and on land
LIFESPAN	10–15 years

ANIMAL FACTS

Not all members of this species are black; an endangered race known as the golden Alpine salamander from northern Italy has bright yellow markings on its back. Their unusual breeding biology means that these salamanders can survive in areas where standing bodies of water are not widely available, and the climate becomes very cold in the winter. Alpine salamanders hibernate over this period. They normally hunt at night, emerging from their hiding places especially after rainfall.

Poison protects these salamanders from predators

WHERE IN THE WORLD?

Occurs in Alpine regions, in parts of Switzerland, France, Liechtenstein, Germany, Austria, Italy, Albania, Croatia, Serbia, Montenegro, Bosnia and Herzegovina, at altitudes of up to 2800m (9186ft).

COLOURATION
The glossy black appearance explains why this species is also called the black salamander.

PAROTID GLANDS
These swollen areas behind the eyes mark the start of the poison glands.

PROTECTIVE POISON
Parallel rows of protective poison glands run down the back on each side of the body.

HIND LEGS
These are often kept flattened and extended, away from the body.

WINTER SURVIVAL
Their habitat means that these salamanders may remain dormant for up to eight months of the year.

BREEDING STRATEGY
Most amphibians lay large numbers of eggs to ensure a few young will survive, but Alpine salamanders produce miniature adults.

HOW BIG IS IT?

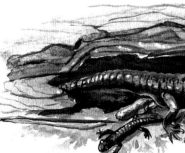

Fire Salamander

The markings of these salamanders are highly individual, while their bright colouration serves as a warning of their toxicity. Fifteen different races have been recognized.

VITAL STATISTICS

LENGTH	Typically 15–25cm (6–10in); males are smaller
SEXUAL MATURITY	4–5 years
NUMBER OF OFFSPRING	Varies according to subspecies; may be born as up to 70 larvae that develop in water, or fewer miniature adults
HABITAT	Damp areas, especially woodland
DIET	Carnivorous, hunting invertebrates such as worms, snails and slugs, especially after rainfall
LIFESPAN	Up to 50 years

ANIMAL FACTS

Changes in climate during the last Ice Age, some 15,000 years ago, may help to explain the fractioned distribution of these salamanders in Europe today. Some are now very localized, such as *S.s. alfredschmidti*, which is found only in the Tendi Valley in northern Spain. One of the most variable is *S.s. bernardezi*, which may display either colourful stripes or spotted patterning on its body. The most brightly coloured fire salamander is the Italian race (*S.s. giglioli*).

WHERE IN THE WORLD?

Occurs across much of southern and central Europe, to the western shores of the Black Sea, although many of the races are isolated in their distribution.

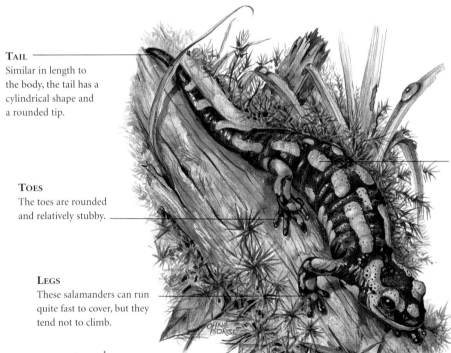

TAIL
Similar in length to the body, the tail has a cylindrical shape and a rounded tip.

TOES
The toes are rounded and relatively stubby.

LEGS
These salamanders can run quite fast to cover, but they tend not to climb.

PAROTID GLANDS
Irrespective of the individual body markings, these glands are always coloured, so they appear more prominent.

SEASONAL BEHAVIOUR
Fire salamanders often mate in the autumn, but the young will not be born until the following spring.

HOW BIG IS IT?

TYPICAL APPEARANCES
No two fire salamanders are identical in appearance. Yellow spots and lines are common, but some individuals have orange markings.

Alpine Newt

VITAL STATISTICS

LENGTH	8–12cm (3–5in)
SEXUAL MATURITY	2–3 years
NUMBER OF EGGS	75–200; development of young depends on temperature, sometimes overwintering as tadpoles in mountainous areas
HABITAT	Damp areas, especially woodland
DIET	Carnivorous, hunting small invertebrates in water and on land; may occasionally be cannibalistic
LIFESPAN	6–8 years

ANIMAL FACTS

There are 10 different races of Alpine newt, which vary in size, profile and patterning. Some are very localized, the rarest being the Yugoslavian race (*T.a. lacusnigri*). It is also one of the largest, growing to 13.5cm (5.3in), and distinguished by its dark colouration. Climatic changes at the end of the last Ice Age effectively trapped populations of these newts in isolation, and since then, they have started to develop distinctive characteristics that reflect their individual environments.

The female deposits each egg under the leaves of aquatic plants

Males of this species undergo a dramatic change in colouration each spring at the start of the breeding season, when they return to water.

WHERE IN THE WORLD?

As well as occurring in Alpine regions, these newts are also found in lowland areas from Belgium to eastern Russia and south to Greece.

BREEDING COLOURATION
Males develop a crest along their back, with brilliant blue colouring on the flanks and tail.

EYES
The eyes are brightly coloured and relatively large; newts rely partly on their eyesight to locate prey.

TAIL
The tail is broad and flat, tapering along its length to a point.

FEMALE
Females are duller in appearance, with speckling extending down to the underparts, which are paler yellow.

OUT OF THE WATER
These newts leave the water after the breeding season, and appear much drabber throughout the rest of the year.

HOW BIG IS IT?

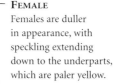

DEVELOPMENT OF TADPOLES
The gills are lost as the lungs become functional, allowing the young newts to breathe on land.

Northern Right Whale

• ORDER • Cetacea • FAMILY • Balaenidae • SPECIES • *Eubalaena glacialis*

VITAL STATISTICS

WEIGHT	Up to 63.5 tonnes (70 tons); females are heavier
LENGTH	14–17m (46–56ft)
SEXUAL MATURITY	6–10 years
GESTATION PERIOD	About 365 days; females give birth once every 3–5 years
NUMBER OF OFFSPRING	1; weaning occurs at 8–12 months
DIET	Use their baleen plates to filter zooplankton, including euphausiids and copepods out of the ocean water
LIFESPAN	Likely to be 50–100 years

ANIMAL FACTS

Despite being protected from whaling fleets since 1935, the northern right whale's population has continued to decline according to most estimates. There are now probably no more than 300 in the ocean, and relatively few calves are being reported. The underlying cause is probably their diet. They are highly specialized planktonic feeders, and a decline in the availability of these microscopic marine creatures in the areas where the whales occur means they are short of food.

The testicles of the male are the largest of any creature, weighing up to 500kg (1100lb); mating occurs in winter

Its name indicates why this species is now the most endangered whale in North Atlantic waters, having been the 'right' whale for whalers in the past.

WHERE IN THE WORLD?

Restricted to the North Atlantic Ocean, off the eastern seaboard of North America, and in European waters from the Iberian Peninsula to Scandinavia.

CALF LENGTH
Newborn calves measure up to 6m (20ft) and may double their length in a year.

CALF WEIGHT
Young of this species already weigh about 900kg (1 ton) at birth.

MOUTH
The mouth is long and arches upwards, above the eyes.

CALLOSITIES
These white swellings identify the whales, and are usually evident on the head. They are huge colonies of whale lice.

IDENTIFYING THE SPECIES
The 'blow' of water is a distinctive V-shape because of the spacing of the two blowholes.

HOW BIG IS IT?

INDIVIDUAL RECOGNITION
Breaking the surface – called breaching – allows individuals to be identified by their callosities.

Blue Whale

VITAL STATISTICS

WEIGHT	Up to 133.3 tonnes (147 tons); females are much heavier
LENGTH	At least 30m (100ft)
SEXUAL MATURITY	6–10 years
GESTATION PERIOD	About 365 days; females give birth once every 3–5 years
NUMBER OF OFFSPRING	1; weaning occurs at 8–12 months
DIET	Use their baleen plates to filter zooplankton; krill forms the major part of their food intake
LIFESPAN	Up to 110 years

ANIMAL FACTS

These cetaceans have huge appetites. An individual may consume as much as 3.6 tonnes (4 tons) of krill daily, representing some 40 million of these tiny shrimp-like creatures. Blue whales live in small groups, comprising two or three individuals, and swim at speeds of about 19kph (12mph), although they can travel up to 48kph (30mph). Whaling nearly led to the extinction of these giants, and although they have been protected since 1966, their population is still relatively small.

Blue whales are not just the largest animals on the planet today, they are also probably the biggest creatures that have ever lived.

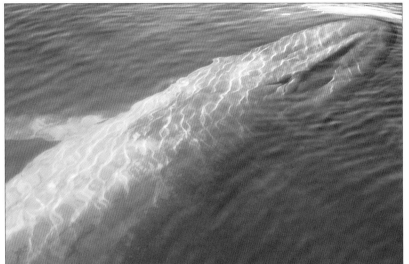

WHERE IN THE WORLD?

Ranges widely through the world's oceans, but has distinct populations in the North Atlantic, in the North Pacific and in the vicinity of Antarctica.

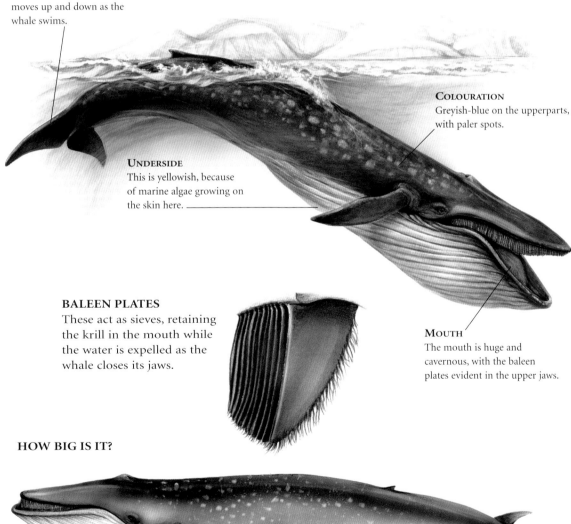

TAIL
Flat, broad and thick, the tail moves up and down as the whale swims.

UNDERSIDE
This is yellowish, because of marine algae growing on the skin here.

COLOURATION
Greyish-blue on the upperparts, with paler spots.

BALEEN PLATES
These act as sieves, retaining the krill in the mouth while the water is expelled as the whale closes its jaws.

MOUTH
The mouth is huge and cavernous, with the baleen plates evident in the upper jaws.

HOW BIG IS IT?

Humpback Whale

• ORDER • Cetacea • FAMILY • Balaenopteridae • SPECIES • *Megaptera novaeangliae*

These whales are relatively conspicuous because they often come quite close to shore, swim at the surface and jump above the waves.

VITAL STATISTICS

WEIGHT	19.9–32.6 tonnes (22–36 tons); females are much heavier
LENGTH	12–15m (40–50ft)
SEXUAL MATURITY	6–10 years
GESTATION PERIOD	About 365 days; females give birth once every 2–3 years
NUMBER OF OFFSPRING	1; weaning occurs at about 12 months
DIET	Use their baleen plates to obtain krill, which form the major part of their food intake; also eats small fish
LIFESPAN	Up to 100 years

ANIMAL FACTS

The remarkable song of the male humpback whale is uttered repeatedly for hours, each segment lasting up to 20 minutes. This probably helps them to keep in touch with one another when separated in the oceans. Their song patterns are distinctive and change over time. Humpbacks are quite often seen jumping above the water, with this behaviour described as breaching. Like singing, this may be part of their courtship ritual.

A mating embrace

WHERE IN THE WORLD?

Occurs worldwide, migrating to temperate and polar waters to feed, and then mates and calves in the tropics. A resident population occurs in the Arabian Sea.

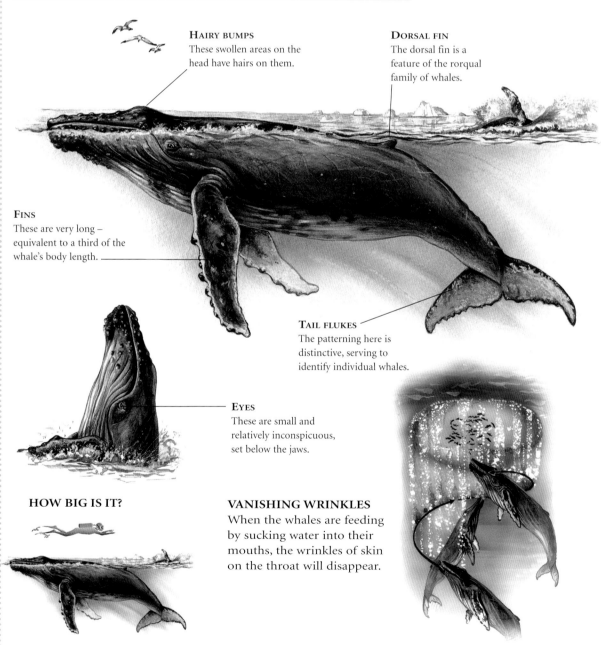

HAIRY BUMPS
These swollen areas on the head have hairs on them.

DORSAL FIN
The dorsal fin is a feature of the rorqual family of whales.

FINS
These are very long – equivalent to a third of the whale's body length.

TAIL FLUKES
The patterning here is distinctive, serving to identify individual whales.

EYES
These are small and relatively inconspicuous, set below the jaws.

HOW BIG IS IT?

VANISHING WRINKLES
When the whales are feeding by sucking water into their mouths, the wrinkles of skin on the throat will disappear.

Commerson's Dolphin

• **ORDER** • Cetacea • **FAMILY** • Delphinidae • **SPECIES** • *Cephalorhynchus commersonii*

These dolphins are the smallest of all cetaceans. It was only during the 1950s that the separate Indian Ocean population of this species was discovered.

VITAL STATISTICS

WEIGHT	35–60kg (77–132lb)
LENGTH	130–170cm (48–68in)
SEXUAL MATURITY	6–9 years
GESTATION PERIOD	About 334 days; young are large – nearly half the size of their mothers at birth
NUMBER OF OFFSPRING	1; weaning may take over a year
DIET	Feeds on a variety of fish and squid, and also crustaceans
LIFESPAN	Up to 18 years; more than 26 years in captivity

ANIMAL FACTS

These dolphins occur relatively close to the shore, often entering coastal inlets, and are very conspicuous, frequently leaping from the water. They also accompany boats, and may even be observed swimming upside down at the surface. The species is named after the French naturalist Dr Philibert Commerçon, who recorded them in the Straits of Magellan in 1766. Today, there are about 3400 of these dolphins in the region, while the genetically distinct Kerguelen population lies 8000km (5000 miles) away.

WHERE IN THE WORLD?

Two distinct populations exist. The largest is off southern South America and the Falkland Islands. Also occurs around the Kerguelen Islands in the southern Indian Ocean.

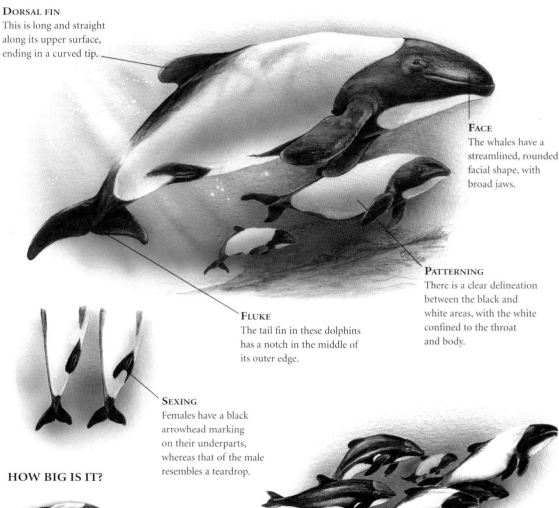

DORSAL FIN
This is long and straight along its upper surface, ending in a curved tip.

FACE
The whales have a streamlined, rounded facial shape, with broad jaws.

PATTERNING
There is a clear delineation between the black and white areas, with the white confined to the throat and body.

FLUKE
The tail fin in these dolphins has a notch in the middle of its outer edge.

SEXING
Females have a black arrowhead marking on their underparts, whereas that of the male resembles a teardrop.

HOW BIG IS IT?

COLOUR SHIFTS
Young are born grey, black and brown, and then become black and grey. The grey areas ultimately become white.

181

Common Dolphin

• ORDER • Cetacea **• FAMILY •** Delphinidae **• SPECIES •** *Delphinus delphis*

VITAL STATISTICS

WEIGHT	70–110kg (155–242lb)
LENGTH	180–240cm (71–95in)
SEXUAL MATURITY	4–5 years; males mature slightly earlier than females
GESTATION PERIOD	About 310 days
NUMBER OF OFFSPRING	1; weaning may take about a year
DIET	Feeds on a variety of small schooling fish such as sardines, as well as squid
LIFESPAN	Up to 20 years; more than 34 in captivity

ANIMAL FACTS

These dolphins congregate in schools, ranging from a few individuals up to 10,000, depending on the time of year and availability of food. They face a number of hazards, such as becoming trapped in fishing nets, but more insidious threats to their well-being stem from chemical pollution. This can affect the kidneys and other organs by accumulating there. The problem is particularly severe in the Mediterranean, and common dolphins have already disappeared from the shallow Azov Sea.

The beak is full of sharp teeth

The classification of these dolphins has been controversial, and the long-beaked form is now regarded as a separate species, known scientifically as *D. capensis.*

WHERE IN THE WORLD?

Occurs in various localities in temperate and tropical areas, in the Atlantic and Pacific oceans, as well as the Mediterranean and Black seas.

FACIAL FEATURES
Its long beak assists the dolphin in catching prey.

DORSAL FIN
This is tall and held erect, curving back on its upper surface to a point.

FLANKS
Grey predominates towards the rear, with a pale yellow or buff area further forwards, and white below.

COLOURATION
Four colours are apparent over the body, with black being prominent along the back.

HOW BIG IS IT?

SONAR
Dolphins can make a repeated clicking sound, to detect information about their environment. The sound waves reverberate back to them, as with sonar. This is known as echolocation.

GIVING BIRTH

The female gives birth tail-first, preventing her calf from trying to breath prematurely. The mother then helps the calf to the surface to obtain air.

Long-Finned Pilot Whale

• ORDER • Cetacea **• FAMILY •** Delphinidae **• SPECIES •** *Globicephala melas*

VITAL STATISTICS

WEIGHT	1.2–2.4 tonnes (1.3–2.6 tons); males are much bigger
LENGTH	4.88–6.10m (16–20ft)
SEXUAL MATURITY	Females 6–7 years; males around 12 years
GESTATION PERIOD	About 310 days
NUMBER OF OFFSPRING	1; weaning typically occurs by 2 years old
DIET	Feeds mainly on squid, as well as octopus, cuttlefish and herring
LIFESPAN	Over 50 years

ANIMAL FACTS

Pods of pilot whales can comprise up to 90 individuals. Males in the group are likely to join up for a period and then move on, fighting amongst themselves to mate with the females. They can ram each other and bite, leaving permanent scars. The long-finned species tend to be found in cooler water than its short-finned relative, but both in the north and southern parts of their range there are areas where their distributions overlap.

Rounded head shape of the pilot whale (right) compared with a true whale (left)

In spite of their name, pilot whales are actually members of the dolphin family. Highly social by nature, they live in groups called pods.

WHERE IN THE WORLD?

Circumpolar range through southern waters, from southern parts of South America, South Africa and Australia to the Antarctic. Also in the North Atlantic and Mediterranean.

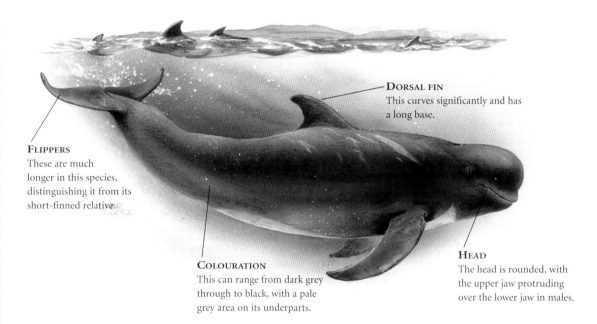

DORSAL FIN
This curves significantly and has a long base.

FLIPPERS
These are much longer in this species, distinguishing it from its short-finned relative.

COLOURATION
This can range from dark grey through to black, with a pale grey area on its underparts.

HEAD
The head is rounded, with the upper jaw protruding over the lower jaw in males.

SOFT FOOD
Feeding on squid, pilot whales only have about 40 teeth in their jaws, whereas fish-eating dolphins have over 100.

HOW BIG IS IT?

MASS STRANDINGS

Pilot whales sometimes beach themselves, possibly because of illness or interference in their navigational abilities caused by sonar from vessels.

Killer Whale

• ORDER • Cetacea • FAMILY • Delphinidae • SPECIES • *Orcinus orca*

VITAL STATISTICS

WEIGHT	3.6–8.2 tonnes (4–9 tons); males are much bigger
LENGTH	7.0–9.8m (23–32ft)
SEXUAL MATURITY	10–18 years; females tend to mature earlier
GESTATION PERIOD	400–520 days
NUMBER OF OFFSPRING	1; weaning occurs after 13–17 months
DIET	Feeds mainly on larger vertebrates, including sea lions, penguins, sharks and porpoises; also hunts squid
LIFESPAN	Can be over 80 years

ANIMAL FACTS

Like other members of the dolphin family, killer whales must surface regularly to breathe, although they can remain submerged for 15 minutes at a time. Many pods roam through the oceans, travelling up to 161km (160 miles) per day, although some are sedentary, especially in areas where fish are plentiful. The pod is led by the matriarch of the group. Pod members keep in touch with each other by echolocation, uttering high-pitched sounds that are generally inaudible to human ears.

The mouth is straight, rather than curved

Also known as the orca, this species has a fearsome reputation – with pod members hunting together – but it is not known to attack people.

WHERE IN THE WORLD?

Occurs widely throughout the world's oceans, often close to the shore, but is most common in temperate and polar regions rather than in tropical waters.

DORSAL FIN
Can be up to 1.8m (6ft) long. It is triangular in males, shorter and curved in females and young of both sexes.

PATTERNING
Markings are consistent but sufficiently individual to allow separate members of a pod to be easily recognized.

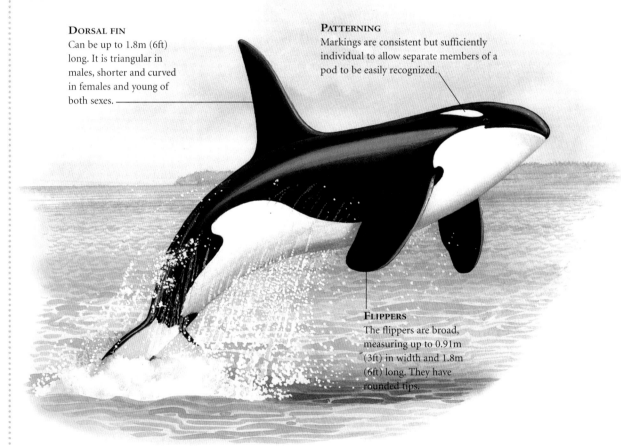

FLIPPERS
The flippers are broad, measuring up to 0.91m (3ft) in width and 1.8m (6ft) long. They have rounded tips.

GROUP HUNTING
Killer whales are called 'wolves of the sea', because of the way they hunt as a pack, surrounding their prey.

HOW BIG IS IT?

Grey Whale

VITAL STATISTICS

WEIGHT	3.6–8.2 tonnes (4–9 tons); females are slightly bigger
LENGTH	7–9.8m (23–32ft)
SEXUAL MATURITY	5–11 years
GESTATION PERIOD	365–400 days
NUMBER OF OFFSPRING	1; weaning occurs after 7–8 months
DIET	Filter-feeders, sucking up small amphipods and other crustaceans as well as worms, digging on the sea bed to obtain their food
LIFESPAN	Over 80 years

ANIMAL FACTS

These whales swim huge distances – up to 22,530km (14,000 miles) – when migrating to and from their traditional breeding grounds. They feed on small marine creatures, which they suck up into their mouths. These become trapped in the sieve-like baleen plates before being swallowed. The baleen itself, known as whalebone, used to be in great demand to make items such as corsets. Grey whale numbers have recovered significantly since protection of the species began in 1947.

The underlying grey colouration of these whales is not always obvious

Grey whales undertake one of the longest migratory journeys of any creature on earth. Their size means that their only major predators are killer whales.

WHERE IN THE WORLD?

Occurs in the eastern North Pacific Ocean, in the Bering and Chukchi seas, migrating each October, travelling for two to three months to their breeding lagoons in Baja California.

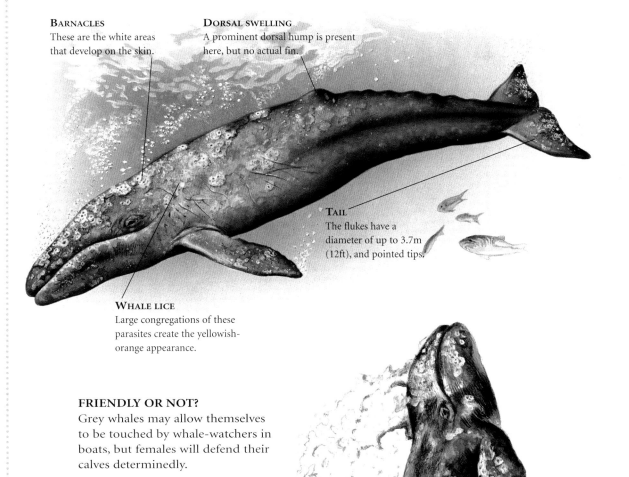

BARNACLES
These are the white areas that develop on the skin.

DORSAL SWELLING
A prominent dorsal hump is present here, but no actual fin.

TAIL
The flukes have a diameter of up to 3.7m (12ft), and pointed tips.

WHALE LICE
Large congregations of these parasites create the yellowish-orange appearance.

FRIENDLY OR NOT?
Grey whales may allow themselves to be touched by whale-watchers in boats, but females will defend their calves determinedly.

HOW BIG IS IT?

Amazon River Dolphin

This is a freshwater species, known locally by its Portuguese name *boutu vermelho*, which translates as 'red dolphin' and describes its distinctive colouration.

VITAL STATISTICS

WEIGHT	85–160kg (187–350lb); males are slightly bigger
LENGTH	1.8–2.7m (6–9ft); the largest of the 5 species of river dolphin
SEXUAL MATURITY	5–7 years
GESTATION PERIOD	Up to 365 days
NUMBER OF OFFSPRING	1; weaning probably occurs within a year
DIET	Mainly piscivorous, hunting large catfish and piranhas; also feeds on crabs and turtles
LIFESPAN	Up to 30 years

ANIMAL FACTS

This dolphin's ancestors entered the Amazon from the sea, and adapted to living in freshwater surroundings. Their neck vertebrae are not fused, so they can move their heads through 90° from side to side, using this flexibility to search for prey, aided by echolocation. Another unique feature is the sensory hairs on the beak, which detect edible items in muddy water. These river dolphins also have good eyesight and hearing, though, and are very agile by nature.

WHERE IN THE WORLD?

Widely distributed throughout the Amazon river basin in northern and central South America, occurring both in rivers and lakes. Also present in the Orinoco River.

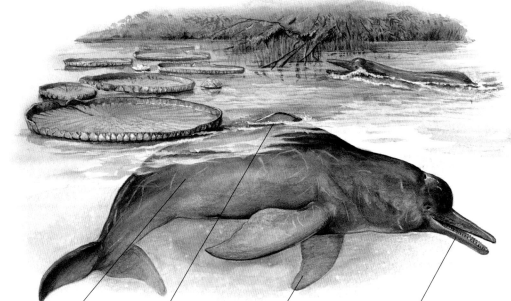

COLOURATION
Young Amazon river dolphins become increasingly pinkish in colour as they mature.

RIDGE
There is a hump rather than a dorsal fin on the back, which may break the surface of the water.

FLIPPERS
These are very large, helping the dolphin manoeuvre easily in shallow or thickly vegetated water.

BEAK
The beak is long, with sharp teeth at the front and molar teeth behind.

Crocodilians prey on these dolphins

HOW BIG IS IT?

A FORESTED WORLD

Some areas of the forest flood seasonally, and then these dolphins will expand their range temporarily, in pursuit of prey.

Beluga

VITAL STATISTICS

WEIGHT	900–1500kg (1984–3306lb); Males are bigger
LENGTH	3.5–5.5m (12–18ft)
SEXUAL MATURITY	Females 5 years; males 8 years
GESTATION PERIOD	Around 465 days
NUMBER OF OFFSPRING	1; weaning may last for 2 years
DIET	Fish such as capelin, salmon, Arctic char and cod, as well as squid, octopus and marine worms
LIFESPAN	Over 50 years

ANIMAL FACTS

Belugas are often seen in shallow coastal waters, sometimes even at the mouths of rivers, although they have been recorded diving to depths of 1000m (3280ft). They may occasionally congregate in large groups numbering several thousand, although they generally live in pods made up of a dozen or so individuals. Their lifestyle varies according to their location, with some populations being migratory, a fact revealed by satellite tracking. Five distinct and separate groups have been identified through their extensive range.

The 'melon' on the head emits sound waves

Belugas possess a remarkable ability to find open stretches of water in the Arctic pack ice, enabling them to surface and breathe in this environment.

WHERE IN THE WORLD?

Occurs in the seas of the far north, having a circumpolar distribution through the Arctic region, extending as far south as Hudson Bay in Canada.

NECK STRUCTURE
The cervical vertebrae are not fused, allowing belugas to turn their heads from side to side.

COLOURATION
Adults turn white at around seven to nine years; females change first.

BACK
There is no dorsal fin on the back. The beluga's generic name *Delphinapterus* means 'dolphin without a fin'.

YOUNG
Young belugas are greyish-cream at birth, soon becoming bluish-grey.

HUNTING
Polar bears represent a significant danger to belugas and especially to young calves, seizing them when they surface for air.

HOW BIG IS IT?

Narwhal

• ORDER • Cetacea • FAMILY • Monodontidae • SPECIES • *Monodon monoceros*

VITAL STATISTICS

WEIGHT	907–1587kg (2000–3500lb); males are much bigger
LENGTH	4–4.6m (13–15ft)
SEXUAL MATURITY	Females 4–7 years; males 8–9 years
GESTATION PERIOD	Around 465 days; calves are brown at birth
NUMBER OF OFFSPRING	1; weaning may take 2 years
DIET	Includes fish such as Arctic cod, plus squid, octopus and crustaceans
LIFESPAN	Up to 50 years

ANIMAL FACTS

The bizarre horn of the narwhal is actually derived from an elongated tooth that grows out through the skull and skin. It can reach 267cm (105in) long. Although its exact function is unclear, it is probably significant as part of the narwhal's mating ritual. These porpoises live in small groups, but may occasionally congregate in much larger groups, numbering thousands of individuals. Their unusual name literally means 'corpse whale', referring to the way in which they often swim upside down.

The male narwhal's horn helps explain the unicorn myth in medieval Europe. These porpoises sometimes fence with their horns, using them like swords.

WHERE IN THE WORLD?

Found in the far north, in eastern Canada and around much of the coast of Greenland, extending across the polar region north of Europe and Asia.

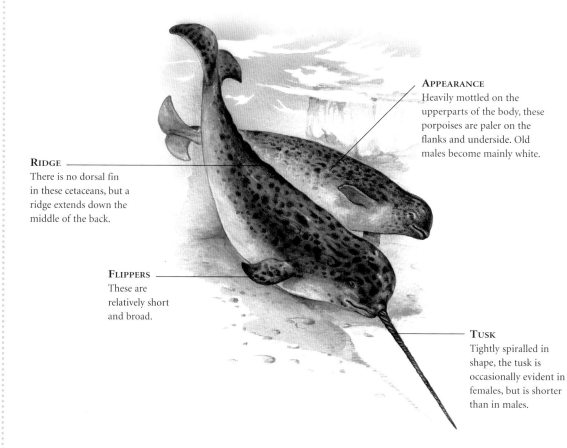

APPEARANCE
Heavily mottled on the upperparts of the body, these porpoises are paler on the flanks and underside. Old males become mainly white.

RIDGE
There is no dorsal fin in these cetaceans, but a ridge extends down the middle of the back.

FLIPPERS
These are relatively short and broad.

TUSK
Tightly spiralled in shape, the tusk is occasionally evident in females, but is shorter than in males.

HOW BIG IS IT?

DANGEROUS LIVING
Narwhals may fall victim to attacks by killer whales. They can also sometimes drown after becoming trapped under the ice.

The male's tusk grows most rapidly after sexual maturity

Harbour Porpoise

• ORDER • Cetacea • FAMILY • Phocoenidae • SPECIES • *Phocoena phocoena*

Small in size and relatively shy by nature, these porpoises live in coastal waters, often frequenting bays and sometimes swimming up the mouths of rivers.

VITAL STATISTICS

WEIGHT	60–90kg (130–200lb); females are slightly larger
LENGTH	1.5–1.8m (5–6ft)
SEXUAL MATURITY	3–4 years
GESTATION PERIOD	Around 341 days; calves are about 71cm (27in) long at birth
NUMBER OF OFFSPRING	1; weaning takes about 8 months
DIET	Piscivorous, hunting smaller fish such as whiting, herring, pollock and sardines, as well as squid
LIFESPAN	10–20 years, typically shorter than most other cetaceans

ANIMAL FACTS

Living close to the shore can be hazardous for these porpoises, as they may be caught in fishing nets, with fatal consequences. This has led to a major decline in their populations in the Baltic and Black seas. They are usually seen in small groups comprising up to 10 individuals, increasing the likelihood of finding sufficient food. Each porpoise must eat up to 10 per cent of its body weight daily. They make an unusual snuffling sound when surfacing.

WHERE IN THE WORLD?

Occurs in northern coastal areas on both sides of the Pacific and Atlantic oceans, to southern Greenland and also western Africa. Also present in the Black Sea.

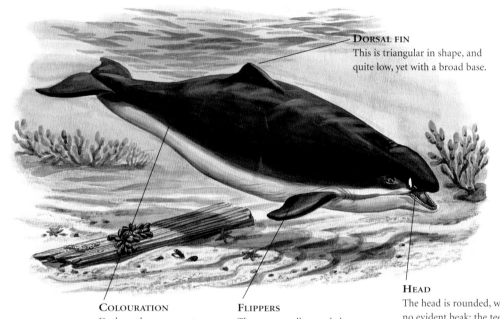

DORSAL FIN
This is triangular in shape, and quite low, yet with a broad base.

COLOURATION
Dark on the upperparts, with a whitish underside.

FLIPPERS
These are small, rounded and dark in colour, with a dark stripe extending forwards towards the eyes.

HEAD
The head is rounded, with no evident beak; the teeth are quite small in the jaws.

TAIL FIRST
The young porpoise is born tail-first, and then helped up to the surface by its mother, so that it can obtain air.

Harbour porpoises may be hunted by killer whales

HOW BIG IS IT?

Sperm Whale

• ORDER • Cetacea • FAMILY • Physeteridae • SPECIES • *Physeter catodon*

This is the largest of the toothed whales – as distinct from those that filter their food with baleen plates – and has a very characteristic profile.

VITAL STATISTICS

WEIGHT	12.7–36 tonnes (14–40 tons); males are at least a third bigger
LENGTH	11–16m (36–52ft); individuals up to 20.5m (68ft) existed until recently
SEXUAL MATURITY	Females 8–11 years; males around 10 years
GESTATION PERIOD	About 18 months
NUMBER OF OFFSPRING	1; weaning takes about 2 years
DIET	Cephalopods, notably giant squid and octopus
LIFESPAN	Can be 75 years

ANIMAL FACTS

These whales are able to dive to tremendous depths, reaching 3000m (9,840ft) below the surface, and can stay submerged for up to two hours. It is thought that this allows them to prey on giant squid, which live in the ocean abyss. In fact, scars caused by the suckers of the squid were reported on the sides of sperm whales before the existence of these cephalopods was confirmed, providing evidence of the titanic battles that must occur between them.

A sperm whale battles with a giant squid, which can itself grow to 16m (53ft) long

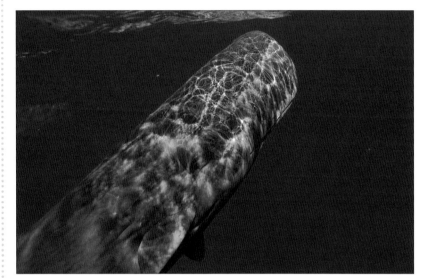

Occurs throughout the world's oceans, extending to the polar ice fields, occurring in areas of deep water. Populations tend to move towards the poles in summer.

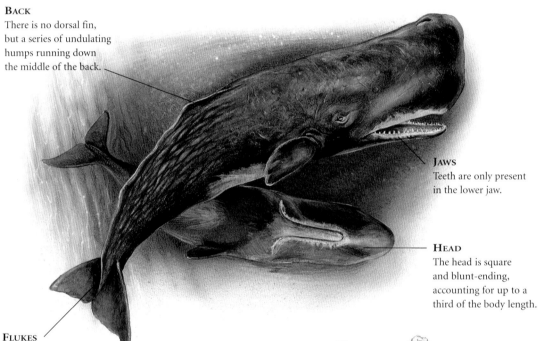

BACK
There is no dorsal fin, but a series of undulating humps running down the middle of the back.

JAWS
Teeth are only present in the lower jaw.

HEAD
The head is square and blunt-ending, accounting for up to a third of the body length.

FLUKES
These are broad and triangular in shape, and are lifted out of the water just before a dive.

HOW BIG IS IT?

BLOW HOLE
This is located to the left and close to the front of the head in a sperm whale (bottom), compared with other whales. The blow itself is directed forwards, enabling these whales to be recognized from a distance.

Herring Gull

• ORDER • Charadriiformes **• FAMILY •** Laridae **• SPECIES •** *Larus argentatus*

VITAL STATISTICS

WEIGHT	800–1250g (28–44oz); males are larger
LENGTH	56–66cm (22–26in)
SEXUAL MATURITY	3–4 years
NUMBER OF EGGS	2–3, light brown with darker blotches
INCUBATION PERIOD	28–30 days; young fledge at around 40 days, and are watched over by the adults
DIET	Feeds on fish, but also scavenges, eating carrion and human leftovers
LIFESPAN	Up to 31 years

ANIMAL FACTS

These relatively large gulls have undergone a remarkable change in their habits over the past 50 years or so, by expanding their range into towns and cities. This has been made possible by the increasing amount of food waste left on the streets. They have even learnt to rip apart bags of refuse in search of edible items. Pairs breed on the roofs of buildings, which replicate their traditional cliff nesting sites. They are exceedingly protective of their young.

Highly adaptable, these gulls can often be found inland, especially in winter, where there are large areas of water such as lakes nearby.

WHERE IN THE WORLD?

Ranges widely. Found across most of the northern hemisphere, predominantly, but not exclusively, in coastal areas across much of Europe, Asia and North America.

BACK
Light grey, contrasting with the white underparts.

BILL
The bill is stout, with the nostrils incorporated as slits in the upper bill, with a variable red spot near the tip.

FEET
The toes are webbed – helping these gulls to swim well – and equipped with sharp claws.

CHICK
Spotted down feathering ensures the young merge into their surroundings.

COMING TOGETHER
Noisy and aggressive by nature, herring gulls will call loudly as part of their courtship ritual. Pairs may mate for life.

HOW BIG IS IT?

CHANGING APPEARANCE
An adult herring gull and a newly fledged chick with its mottled brownish plumage. It will take four years for the young to obtain full adult plumage.

Ruff

VITAL STATISTICS

WEIGHT	150–170g (5–6oz)
LENGTH	Cocks 29–32cm (11–13in); hens (reeves) 22–26cm (9–10in)
SEXUAL MATURITY	By 3 years
NUMBER OF EGGS	3–4, light brown with darker blotches
INCUBATION PERIOD	28–30 days; young fledge at around 26 days
DIET	Various invertebrates; also known to eat seeds in the winter
LIFESPAN	Up to 14 years

ANIMAL FACTS

The colouring of male ruffs in breeding plumage is highly individual. There are those with chestnut or black ruffs, called resident males, which occupy their own area of the communal display ground, or lek. Another smaller group, distinguished by whitish ruffs and called satellite males, do not have their own display territory but try to mate with females attracted by the resident males. A few males adopt a different breeding strategy, by resembling hens. They are described as female mimics.

Huge flocks of these waders, comprising up to a million individuals, may be encountered on their wintering grounds. They have a complex mating ritual.

WHERE IN THE WORLD?

Breeds in the far north of Europe and Asia, and overwinters in southern Europe and Africa, but may also be sighted in North America.

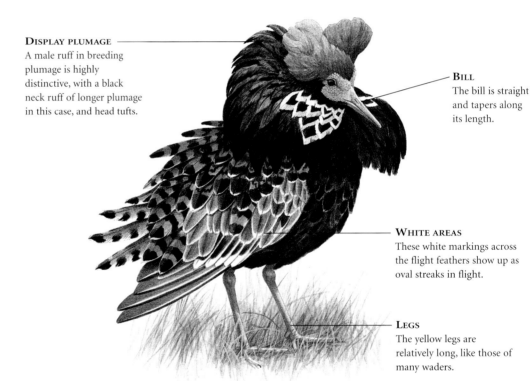

DISPLAY PLUMAGE
A male ruff in breeding plumage is highly distinctive, with a black neck ruff of longer plumage in this case, and head tufts.

BILL
The bill is straight and tapers along its length.

WHITE AREAS
These white markings across the flight feathers show up as oval streaks in flight.

LEGS
The yellow legs are relatively long, like those of many waders.

BREEDING PLUMAGE
Ruffs have the most diverse breeding plumage of any avian species. A satellite male is shown on the right here.

HOW BIG IS IT?

THE RUFF'S NAME
The longer feathers around the male's neck create the impression of a ruff during the display process, explaining the bird's name.

The plumage is kept sleek in flight, to minimize air resistance

Common Vampire Bat

• ORDER • Chiroptera • FAMILY • Phyllostomidae • SPECIES • *Desmodus rotundus*

VITAL STATISTICS

WEIGHT	Typically 57g (2oz) but can double after feeding
LENGTH	9cm (3.5in); wingspan of 18cm (7in)
SEXUAL MATURITY	9–10 months
GESTATION PERIOD	About 217 days; mothers fly with their newborn offspring, clasping them
NUMBER OF OFFSPRING	1–2; weaning occurs at 1 month
DIET	Blood, often from farm animals, but can be taken from a wide array of species, including humans
LIFESPAN	Up to 12 years

ANIMAL FACTS

Vampire bats are unique amongst mammals because they feed entirely on blood, emerging from the caves where they sleep in colonies during the day to seek their prey at night. Cattle and horses are their usual targets, and they pierce the skin with their sharp teeth, injecting an anti-coagulant as they feed. A vampire bat climbs up on to its prey from the ground, rather than flying directly on to its body.

The hook-like claws on the front legs allow these bats to haul themselves up on to their prey

Feared in legend and life, the vampire bat is dangerous not because it sucks blood, but rather because it can transmit the deadly rabies virus.

WHERE IN THE WORLD?

Ranges from Mexico southwards across much of South America to Chile and Argentina, favouring warm areas, up to altitudes of about 2400m (7800ft).

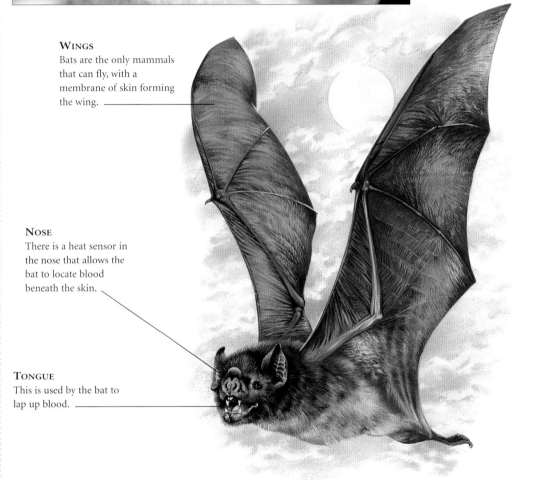

WINGS
Bats are the only mammals that can fly, with a membrane of skin forming the wing.

NOSE
There is a heat sensor in the nose that allows the bat to locate blood beneath the skin.

TONGUE
This is used by the bat to lap up blood.

HOW BIG IS IT?

ON THE MOVE
Vampire bats can walk effectively using their thumbs, while keeping their wings folded, as well as run, hop and jump.

Indian Flying Fox

• **ORDER** • Chiroptera • **FAMILY** • Pteropodidae • **SPECIES** • *Pteropus giganteus*

VITAL STATISTICS

WEIGHT	Females 454–908g (1–2lb); males 1361–1816g (3–4lb)
LENGTH	30cm (12in); wingspan up to 127cm (50in)
SEXUAL MATURITY	1–2 years
GESTATION PERIOD	About 155 days
NUMBER OF OFFSPRING	1, occasionally 2; weaning occurs at 1 month
DIET	Frugivorous, feeding on mangoes, guavas and bananas, spitting out seeds and fruit pulp; also eats pollen and nectar
LIFESPAN	Up to 15 years; can be 31 in captivity

ANIMAL FACTS

Flying foxes live in large colonies called camps, which may comprise several thousand individuals. They take over entire trees, stripping off the leaves as they clamber around on the branches. These traditional roost sites are used over many generations. Their offspring are born feet rather than head-first, and are covered with fur. Youngsters are then carried by their mother when she goes foraging for food, perhaps over 48km (30 miles) away.

The bat's wings can be used for swimming as well as flying

194

Flying foxes represent the largest members of the bat family, and they are quite harmless to people, although they are now raiding fruit farms.

WHERE IN THE WORLD?

Found in India, Bangladesh, Pakistan, Myanmar (Burma) and Sri Lanka, as well as the Maldives. Favours areas of forest and swampland, usually near the coast.

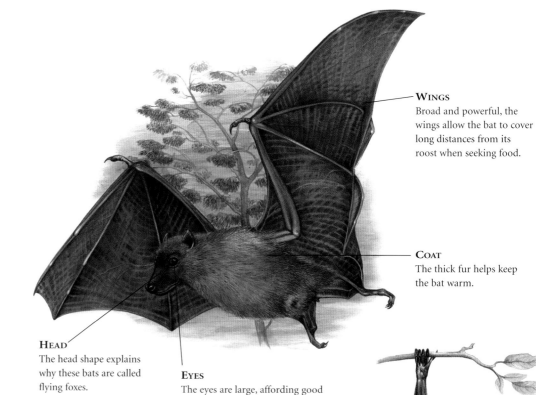

WINGS
Broad and powerful, the wings allow the bat to cover long distances from its roost when seeking food.

COAT
The thick fur helps keep the bat warm.

HEAD
The head shape explains why these bats are called flying foxes.

EYES
The eyes are large, affording good night vision; flying foxes rely on their sight to fly in darkness.

HOW BIG IS IT?

HANGING ON
The hind feet each have five digits, which are equipped with sharp claws, so they can grasp branches when roosting.

Lesser Horseshoe Bat

• ORDER • Chiroptera • FAMILY • Rhinolophidae • SPECIES • *Rhinolophus hipposideros*

VITAL STATISTICS

WEIGHT	4–9.4g (0.15–0.35oz)
LENGTH	3.5–4cm (1.4–1.6in); wingspan up to 25cm (10in)
SEXUAL MATURITY	1–2 years; males generally mature earlier
GESTATION PERIOD	About 49 days; young are born in June and July
NUMBER OF OFFSPRING	1, rarely 2; weaning at 42–49 days
DIET	Insectivorous, hunting a variety of invertebrates including spiders, beetles, gnats and moths
LIFESPAN	Up to 7 years

ANIMAL FACTS

Like other insectivorous bats, the lesser horseshoe relies on a highly sophisticated method of echolocation to find its prey. It often hunts close to the ground, uttering ultrasonic calls that reverberate back and reveal the presence of prey in the darkness of night. Besides the nose leaf, there are also two other structures, called the sella and lancet, which aid this process. From autumn until spring, when food is scarce, these bats will hibernate in caves or similar localities.

Acute hearing is very important, to interpret the sounds from echolocation

These bats are becoming increasingly scarce in many parts of their range, partly because of the use of insecticides is depriving them of their prey.

WHERE IN THE WORLD?

Has been recorded across much of Europe and in North Africa, but has declined significantly in some areas, and has recently become extinct in northern England.

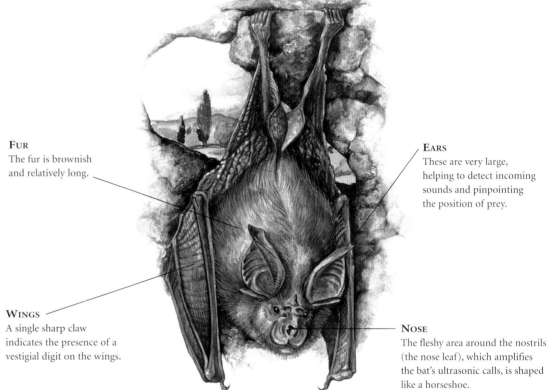

FUR
The fur is brownish and relatively long.

EARS
These are very large, helping to detect incoming sounds and pinpointing the position of prey.

WINGS
A single sharp claw indicates the presence of a vestigial digit on the wings.

NOSE
The fleshy area around the nostrils (the nose leaf), which amplifies the bat's ultrasonic calls, is shaped like a horseshoe.

HOW BIG IS IT?

ROOSTING
There can be as many as 500 lesser horseshoe bats in the largest colonies. They wrap their wings around themselves when they sleep.

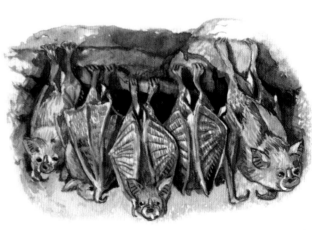

Daubenton's Bat

• ORDER • Chiroptera • FAMILY • Vespertilionidae • SPECIES • *Myotis daubentonii*

VITAL STATISTICS

WEIGHT	7–12g (0.2–0.4oz)
LENGTH	4.5–5.5cm (1.8–2.2in); wingspan up to 27cm (11in)
SEXUAL MATURITY	10 months–2 years; males mature earlier
GESTATION PERIOD	About 49 days; young are born in June and July
NUMBER OF OFFSPRING	1, rarely 2; weaning at 42 days
DIET	Insectivorous, hunting a range of invertebrates including mosquitoes, gnats and moths, as well as small fish
LIFESPAN	Up to 22 years

ANIMAL FACTS

These bats are incredibly agile, buzzing like a small hovercraft over the surface of a pond or a larger stretch of calm water. Their flight is fast, which increases their turning circle. They often take advantage of bridges – roosting beneath stone ones in particular – and they emerge once evening has settled. Prey may also be sought away from water, usually in wooded areas. When she is ready to mate in the autumn, the female Daubenton's bat will develop a black chin spot.

Head of the Daubenton's bat

These bats live near water and have evolved an unusual way of hunting – by grabbing invertebrates from the water surface with their large feet.

WHERE IN THE WORLD?

Present across much of Europe, except northern Scandinavia, and increasing in numbers in some areas. Extends through Asia as far east as Japan and Korea.

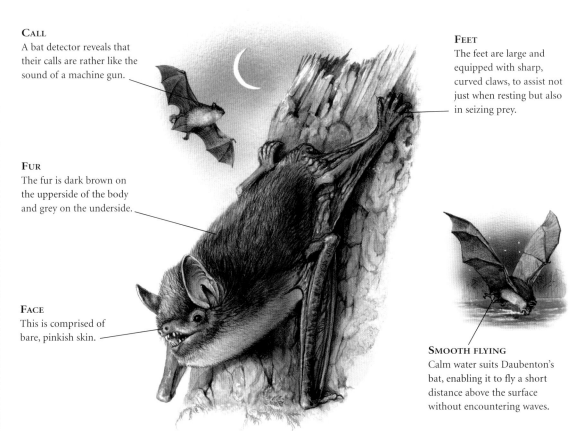

CALL
A bat detector reveals that their calls are rather like the sound of a machine gun.

FUR
The fur is dark brown on the upperside of the body and grey on the underside.

FACE
This is comprised of bare, pinkish skin.

FEET
The feet are large and equipped with sharp, curved claws, to assist not just when resting but also in seizing prey.

SMOOTH FLYING
Calm water suits Daubenton's bat, enabling it to fly a short distance above the surface without encountering waves.

ROOSTING

These bats have adapted to roosting in human structures, although they naturally adopt underground hollows for this purpose. They often hibernate in caves.

HOW BIG IS IT?

Noctule Bat

VITAL STATISTICS

WEIGHT	19–40g (0.7–1.4oz)
LENGTH	6–8cm (2.4–3.1in); wingspan up to 45cm (18in)
SEXUAL MATURITY	10 months–2 years; males mature earlier
GESTATION PERIOD	About 49 days; mating takes place in autumn but development of the eggs does not occur until spring
NUMBER OF OFFSPRING	1–2; weaning at 42–49 days
DIET	Insectivorous, hunting moths, lacewings and beetles
LIFESPAN	Up to 12 years

ANIMAL FACTS

These bats are migratory within some parts of their range across mainland Europe, but in Britain they tend to be sedentary. They have colonized North Sea oil rigs, and can be seen hunting moths drawn to street lights in cities, but their numbers have fallen because of intensive agriculture in some areas. This causes loss of suitable habitat, both for roosting and feeding. Summer roosts are usually in trees, but the bats may move to buildings over the winter.

While hibernating, noctule bats may not feed for nearly four months

These woodland bats rank among the largest European species. They emerge from their roosts in the early evening and can often be seen flying before sunset.

WHERE IN THE WORLD?

Occurs throughout much of Europe, but is absent from Ireland and northern areas, and very scarce on the Iberian Peninsula and the adjacent area of France.

WINGS
The wings are pointed and narrow; these bats tend to fly straight and fast, at speeds of up to 50kph (30mph).

COLOURATION
Golden-brown overall, but paler on the underside of the body.

EARS
These are set low on the head.

SKIN COLOUR
The nose, ears and wing membranes are dark brown.

HOW BIG IS IT?

ON THE TRAIL
Noctule bats hunt by means of ultrasound, which can be made audible to human ears using a bat detector. The difference in the returning sound waves allows the bat to localize the position of its quarry, as well as avoid obstacles in its path.

Nine-Banded Armadillo

• **ORDER** • Cingulata • **FAMILY** • Dasypodidae • **SPECIES** • *Dasypus novemcinctus*

VITAL STATISTICS

WEIGHT	4–8kg (9–18lb); males are heavier
LENGTH	36–105cm (14–41in)
SEXUAL MATURITY	6–12 months
GESTATION PERIOD	120 days; mating occurs in summer but embryos only start developing 3 months later
NUMBER OF OFFSPRING	4 of the same sex develop from one egg; weaning occurs at 4–5 months
DIET	Omnivorous, eating invertebrates, small animals, carrion, vegetation and fruit
LIFESPAN	Up to 15 years

ANIMAL FACTS

These armadillos live alone, but create a large number of dens, excavating the soil with their powerful claws. In some cases, these dens can act as food traps, luring invertebrates inside. Dens intended for breeding have an enlarged chamber at the end, lined with vegetation, which helps to keep the young warm. If they need to swim, these armadillos can swallow air. This helps maintain their buoyancy and keep them afloat.

Nine-banded armadillos use their sharp claws for digging rather than defending themselves

Unlike most mammals, armadillos have little body hair to provide insulation. In part, this explains why they are such avid burrowers – in order to avoid extremes of temperature.

WHERE IN THE WORLD?

South-central and southeastern parts of the USA, via Central America to South America, as far as Peru and Uruguay. Also present in the Caribbean.

UPPER BODY
The nine bands extend around the centre of the body, with shields across the rump and shoulders.

HIND FEET
The shorter of the five toes on each foot are the outer ones.

FRONT FEET
The middle two of the four toes on each foot are the longest.

FACIAL SHAPE
The face is long, with sensitive nostrils and a sticky tongue to catch insects.

HOW BIG IS IT?

ARMOURED BODY

The armadillo's body armour extends over the forehead. The number of bands varies between species, from three to nine.

Brazilian Three-Banded Armadillo

• **ORDER** • Cingulata • **FAMILY** • Dasypodidae • **SPECIES** • *Tolypeutes tricinctus*

VITAL STATISTICS

WEIGHT	1–1.6kg (2.2–3.5lb); males are heavier
LENGTH	28–35cm (11–14in)
SEXUAL MATURITY	9–12 months
GESTATION PERIOD	120 days; births occur in November to January
NUMBER OF OFFSPRING	1; weaning occurs at around 72 days
DIET	Largely insectivorous, feeding on ants and termites during the dry season and beetle larvae at other times; also eats carrion, vegetation and fruit
LIFESPAN	12–15 years

ANIMAL FACTS

The word 'armadillo' is of Spanish origin and means 'little armoured one'. The three-banded is particularly well-protected, as it can conceal its vulnerable underparts by rolling into a ball. Although their eyesight is poor, these armadillos have a keen sense of smell. They have a long, sticky tongue, which allows them to probe into a termite colony and collect a number of these insects at once.

Stripping off bark to reach insects is not difficult with the armadillo's sharp claws

The flexibility of three-banded armadillos is such that they can roll into a ball to protect themselves, rather than having to lie down on the ground.

WHERE IN THE WORLD?

Occurs in South America, in the northern highlands of Brazil. Found in the provinces of Pernambuco, western Bahia, Piauí, Maranhão and in northern Minas Gerais.

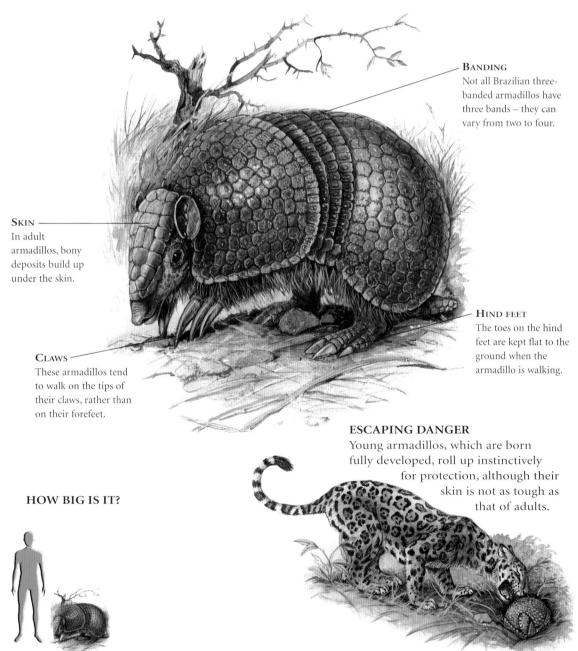

BANDING
Not all Brazilian three-banded armadillos have three bands – they can vary from two to four.

SKIN
In adult armadillos, bony deposits build up under the skin.

CLAWS
These armadillos tend to walk on the tips of their claws, rather than on their forefeet.

HIND FEET
The toes on the hind feet are kept flat to the ground when the armadillo is walking.

HOW BIG IS IT?

ESCAPING DANGER

Young armadillos, which are born fully developed, roll up instinctively for protection, although their skin is not as tough as that of adults.

199

Bombardier Beetle

• ORDER • Coleoptera **• FAMILY •** Carabidae **• SPECIES •** *Brachinus*

VITAL STATISTICS

LENGTH	0.2–3cm (0.07–1.1in), depending on species
SEXUAL MATURITY	Probably 3–6 weeks
NUMBER OF EGGS	1, laid in rotting wood or in soil
DEVELOPMENT PERIOD	Metamorph-osis takes about 3 weeks
HABITAT	Occurs in a wide range of environments, from desert through grassland to forest
DIET	Insectivorous, feeding on various other invertebrates; larvae may cannibalize related species
LIFESPAN	3–6 weeks

ANIMAL FACTS

Bombardier beetles release hydroquinone and hydrogen peroxide through tubes in their abdomen. These are mixed with a catalytic enzyme, which partially transforms the liquid into a toxic gas, with a very unpleasant smell. It literally explodes out of the body, and may well prove deadly to other invertebrates. There are usually nozzles along the side of the beetle's body, allowing it to target its output of these chemicals in the direction of its attacker.

Although the spray is often used against ants, it may protect the beetle against larger creatures

Protected by a cocktail of chemicals that are fired out of its abdomen, the bombardier beetle is well-placed to defend itself against predators.

WHERE IN THE WORLD?

Bombardier beetles occur globally, both in temperate and tropical climates, although they may not be numerous in certain areas, and populations can be very localized.

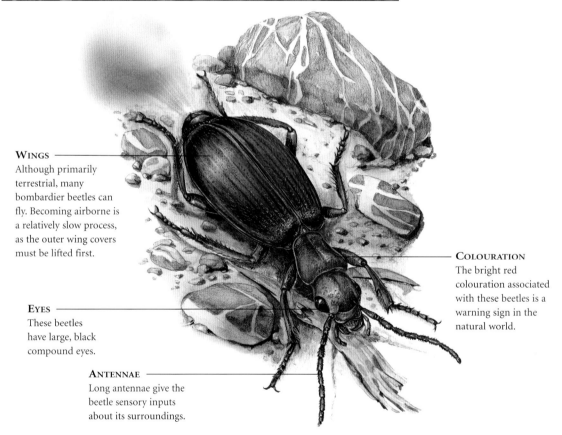

WINGS
Although primarily terrestrial, many bombardier beetles can fly. Becoming airborne is a relatively slow process, as the outer wing covers must be lifted first.

EYES
These beetles have large, black compound eyes.

ANTENNAE
Long antennae give the beetle sensory inputs about its surroundings.

COLOURATION
The bright red colouration associated with these beetles is a warning sign in the natural world.

HOW BIG IS IT?

CROSS-SECTION
This illustration shows the mixing chamber in the beetle's body. The temperature of the spray it produces is around 100°C (212°F).

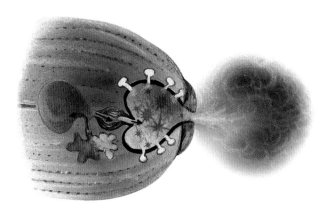

Green Tiger Beetle

• ORDER • Coleoptera **• FAMILY •** Carabidae **• SPECIES •** *Cicindela campestris*

VITAL STATISTICS

LENGTH	1.2–1.6cm (0.47–0.63in)
SEXUAL MATURITY	Within 6 weeks of the end of pupation
NUMBER OF EGGS	3–4 laid daily in burrows in the ground
DEVELOPMENT PERIOD	Lifecycle typically lasts up to 3 years
HABITAT	Open country, present in heathland and sandy areas
DIET	Insectivorous, feeding on various other invertebrates
LIFESPAN	Adults up to 6 weeks, having remained as larvae for over 2 years

ANIMAL FACTS

Green tiger beetles are most commonly seen in spring and summer. They are very agile, and will run both to pursue prey and escape danger – they are able to fly if necessary, although the thin, transparent hind wings are not normally evident. These are protected beneath the elytra, or hardened forewings that are usually kept folded over the top of the beetle's abdomen. They are called tiger beetles because of their aggressive feeding habits; they have sharp teeth in their strong mandibles.

In spite of its name, both bronze and black variants of this beetle can be seen occasionally. Green tiger beetles favour sunny areas.

WHERE IN THE WORLD?

Distribution of this species extends across Europe into Asia, and as far east as Siberia. It is the most common tiger beetle found in Britain.

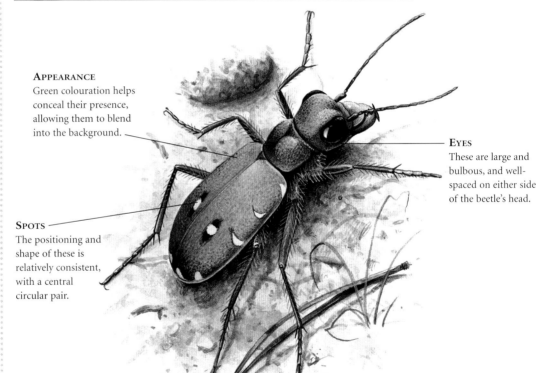

APPEARANCE
Green colouration helps conceal their presence, allowing them to blend into the background.

SPOTS
The positioning and shape of these is relatively consistent, with a central circular pair.

EYES
These are large and bulbous, and well-spaced on either side of the beetle's head.

LEGS
Long and powerful, the legs enable these beetles to pursue their prey very efficiently.

CATCHING PREY
Tiger beetle larvae lurk in holes in the ground, grabbing small invertebrates that venture within range of their powerful jaws.

HOW BIG IS IT?

A green tiger beetle takes flight

Musk Beetle

• ORDER • Coleoptera **• FAMILY •** Cerambycidae **• SPECIES •** *Aromia moschata*

VITAL STATISTICS

LENGTH	1.3–3.5cm (0.51–1.38in)
SEXUAL MATURITY	Almost as soon as the adults emerge from the pupa
NUMBER OF EGGS	3–4 laid daily in willow trees
DEVELOPMENT PERIOD	Lifecycle typically lasts up to 3 years
HABITAT	Occurs in areas where there are willow trees
DIET	Adults feed on plant sap, plus pollen and nectar from flowers
LIFESPAN	Perhaps 6 weeks, having been larvae for over 2 years

ANIMAL FACTS

This species can inflict considerable damage on willow trees, thanks to the wood-boring actions of its larvae. Musk beetles have a fairly classic invertebrate lifecycle, with females laying eggs that hatch into larvae. They are segmented, with a rounded head. The larvae pupate, becoming inactive, although dramatic changes in appearance take place at this stage. At the end of this process, an adult beetle will emerge from the pupa.

Adult beetles will feed on the sap of trees, taking advantage of any damage to the bark

The name of these beetles comes from the distinctive musky odour they emit when disturbed, which is said to resemble the smell of roses.

WHERE IN THE WORLD?

Occurs widely throughout Europe, and is also present in North Africa and Asia, extending eastwards to Japan. Adult beetles are usually only seen during the summer.

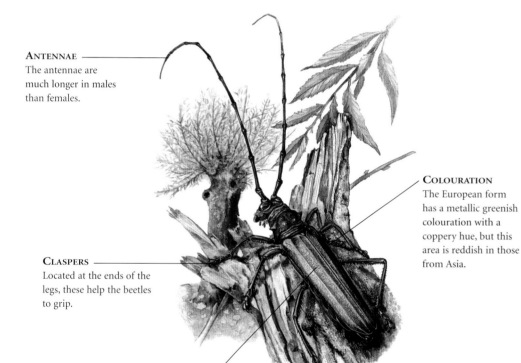

ANTENNAE
The antennae are much longer in males than females.

COLOURATION
The European form has a metallic greenish colouration with a coppery hue, but this area is reddish in those from Asia.

CLASPERS
Located at the ends of the legs, these help the beetles to grip.

SPINES
The spines are present on the thorax, which is the mid-segment of the body.

HOW BIG IS IT?

DEEP-SEATED DAMAGE

A cross-sectional view showing the damage inflicted on a tree by the boring of the larvae by opening up passageways within the trunk.

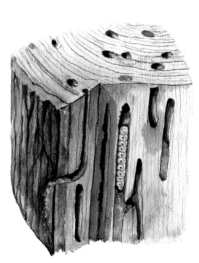

Seven-Spot Ladybird

• **ORDER** • Coleoptera • **FAMILY** • Coccinellidae • **SPECIES** • *Coccinella 7-punctata*

VITAL STATISTICS

LENGTH	0.5–0.8cm (0.2–0.3in)
SEXUAL MATURITY	As soon as the adults emerge from the pupa; lifecycle takes 4–6 weeks
NUMBER OF EGGS	Females lay around 2000 yellowish eggs; larvae are elongated and predominantly black
DEVELOPMENT PERIOD	Larval phase extends over 3 weeks; pupation lasts a week
HABITAT	Frequently seen in gardens, hedgerows and open woodland
DIET	Insectivorous, favouring soft-bodied prey such as aphids
LIFESPAN	1 year

ANIMAL FACTS

These beetles are a welcome sight in a garden, helping curb the number of insect pests here, particularly aphids that frequent roses and some vegetable crops. A single ladybird is likely to consume some 5000 aphids during its lifetime, confirming just how important they are as pest controllers. Unlike many insects, ladybirds pass the winter by hibernating together in large numbers, probably to keep each other warm. They tend to use the same sites every year.

Ladybirds produce a foul-smelling, oily fluid on their legs to deter would-be predators

The red colouration of these flying beetles matches the colour of the Virgin Mary's cloak in medieval paintings, and so they became known as ladybirds.

WHERE IN THE WORLD?

This species is widely distributed across Europe, where it is common and has occasionally (as in 1976) undergone massive population explosions.

ANTENNAE
These are quite short and widely spaced on the ladybird's head.

WINGS
These transparent membranes are hidden by the tough outer wing cases.

BODY STRUCTURE
Much of the ladybird's body is made up of its abdomen.

SPOTS
The number of spots is significant in terms of distinguishing the species.

HOW BIG IS IT?

BREEDING

Not all ladybirds hunt invertebrates. These 22-spot ladybirds eat microscopic fungi and mildews, assisting plant health.

Great Diving Beetle

• **ORDER** • Coleoptera • **FAMILY** • Dystiscidae • **SPECIES** • *Dysticus marginalis*

VITAL STATISTICS

LENGTH	Up to 3.5cm (1.4in)
SEXUAL MATURITY	At the end of pupation
NUMBER OF EGGS	20, deposited in the stems of aquatic plants
DEVELOPMENT PERIOD	Hatching in 2–3 weeks; larval stage lasts 6–8 weeks; may overwinter as pupae
HABITAT	Ponds and slow-flowing water, also seen on land
DIET	Carnivorous, eating other invertebrates, amphibians and fish
LIFESPAN	2–3 years

ANIMAL FACTS

Although this species is described as the great diving beetle, these invertebrates often leave the water under cover of darkness and take to the air. Concealed on the back is a pair of wings. They are frequently drawn to street lights at night. If handled, they may even give a painful nip. Diving beetles have become an important indicator in the monitoring of aquatic environments, as they move rapidly from areas where conditions are not favourable.

These aggressive beetles will not hesitate to prey on creatures larger than themselves and even attack aquatic vertebrates. The same applies to their larvae.

WHERE IN THE WORLD?

Found throughout much of Europe in suitable habitat, extending across northern Asia. Favours areas where there is dense aquatic vegetation, often occurring in garden ponds.

LEGS
There are three pairs of legs; the longest and most powerful are the hind pair.

WING CASES
The ridges on the wing cases indicate a female. This area of the body is smooth in males.

COLOURATION
These beetles are brownish-black, with light borders around the edge of the body.

MOUTHPARTS
These are powerful, allowing the beetle to rip apart its prey.

MATING
Mating may take place in or out of the water.

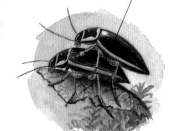

The wing covers are raised during flight

HOW BIG IS IT?

GETTING AROUND

These beetles rely on their hind limbs when swimming, using their front legs for grasping. They have a short tail too.

204

Stag Beetle

An unmistakable species, the male's prominent antlers explain its common name. If threatened, these beetles will freeze to escape detection, rather than running.

VITAL STATISTICS

LENGTH	Males up to 7cm (2.8in) from the tip of the horn to the end of the abdomen; females average 3.5cm (1.4in)
SEXUAL MATURITY	After pupation
NUMBER OF EGGS	12–24, hatching after 3 weeks
DEVELOPMENT PERIOD	Lifecycle lasts 4–7 years
HABITAT	Woodland areas where plenty of rotting tree stumps are present
DIET	Feeds on nectar and tree sap
LIFESPAN	Adults live for about 4 months

ANIMAL FACTS

The quality of the food that stag beetle larvae eat affects both the length of their metamorphosis and their ultimate size. Adults are seen over the summer period, typically from May through until August. They will take to the air during calm, warm evenings in search of mates, and are then at risk of being preyed on by large bats. Females may use rotting fence posts rather than tree stumps as sites to deposit their eggs.

WHERE IN THE WORLD?

Present across Europe, east to Greece, Turkey and Syria, but localized, requiring not just tree stumps but also ground that will not become waterlogged to survive.

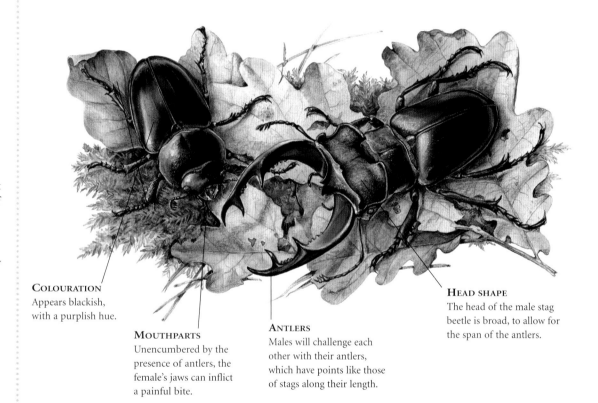

COLOURATION
Appears blackish, with a purplish hue.

MOUTHPARTS
Unencumbered by the presence of antlers, the female's jaws can inflict a painful bite.

ANTLERS
Males will challenge each other with their antlers, which have points like those of stags along their length.

HEAD SHAPE
The head of the male stag beetle is broad, to allow for the span of the antlers.

BORING TOGETHER
Up to 50 grubs may be present in a single tree stump. They have a distinctive C-shape, and are blind.

A comparison between the head of the male (left) and female (right)

HOW BIG IS IT?

Common Cockchafer

• ORDER • Coleoptera • FAMILY • Scarabaeidae • SPECIES • *Melolontha melolontha*

VITAL STATISTICS

LENGTH	2–3cm (0.79–1.2in)
SEXUAL MATURITY	After pupation
NUMBER OF EGGS	60–80, buried in the ground, hatching after 4–6 weeks
DEVELOPMENT PERIOD	Lifecycle lasts 3 years
HABITAT	Deciduous woodland, including parks and gardens
DIET	Adults feed on leaves, especially of oak trees, and also pine needles; larvae eat roots
LIFESPAN	Adults live for 5–7 weeks

ANIMAL FACTS

Although adult cockchafers only live for a short time, plagues can still denude all the trees in an area, stunting their growth. These occur every three to four years, thanks to the cockchafer's long breeding cycle, with particularly large numbers being recorded once in 30 years. Today, however, cockchafers are far less numerous than in the past, when there could be upwards of 20 million in just 18km^2 (7 square miles) of forest. Emerging from their pupae in May, they are also called maybugs.

How the cockchafer can expand its antennae (left)

The name of these beetles originates from the old English word 'cockchafer', which simply means a large beetle. When flying, they create a loud whirring sound.

Occurs widely throughout Europe, right up into Scandinavia. More common in southern England than in the north. Ranks as the most serious insect pest in Hungary.

COLOURATION
Black head and thorax, with black and white barring on the underside of the abdomen.

WING CASES
These are brown, with ridges running along their length.

ANTENNAE
These distinctive, fan-shaped structures project almost at right-angles to the side of the head.

BROAD MOUTHPARTS
These help the cockchafer to feed more easily on vegetation.

STUNTED GROWTH
The growth of plants can be stunted by cockchafer grubs eating their roots.

HOW BIG IS IT?

SURVIVAL UNDERGROUND
Cockchafer grubs make a tasty meal for a range of other creatures, especially moles.

European Rhinoceros Beetle

• **ORDER** • Coleoptera • **FAMILY** • Scarabaeidae • **SPECIES** • *Oryctes nasicornis*

The male's horn identifies this species, although in some cases both sexes have horns. These are the strongest creatures in the world for their size.

VITAL STATISTICS

LENGTH	2.7–6.4cm (1.1–2.5in)
SEXUAL MATURITY	After pupation
NUMBER OF EGGS	Females lay about 100 eggs, burying them in tree stumps
DEVELOPMENT PERIOD	Larvae hatch after 1 month and pupate after another 2 months
HABITAT	Woodland areas; some species found in tropical rainforest
DIET	Adults feed on ripe fruit and plant sap; larvae feed on rotting wood
LIFESPAN	About 4 months

ANIMAL FACTS

This beetle's strength results from its lifestyle. Although rhinoceros beetles are nocturnal – only emerging from hiding places under rocks and logs as night falls – they are still vulnerable to predators. They can bury themselves quickly underground, using their strength to lift the soil and dig themselves away safely, especially under a covering of leaves. The horns of the males are not used defensively against predators, but they will be employed in struggles with other males.

WHERE IN THE WORLD?

Absent from Britain, but widespread in mainland Europe, occurring right up into Scandinavia. Also extends into Asia, found in Iran and the Middle East.

EYES
These are well-spaced and relatively small.

HEAD STRUCTURE
Apart from the horn, the protective raised area at the back of the head distinguishes the male.

COLOURATION
Adults are a dark shade of reddish-brown.

BACK
The broad, strong back enables the beetle to carry up to 850 times its own weight.

PUPAE
A young male rhinoceros beetle breaking out of its pupae, soon to emerge above ground.

BATTLING WITH A RIVAL
Males tussle together in combat, with the horn serving as a means of overturning an opponent, rather than inflicting injury.

HOW BIG IS IT?

Adult female with antennae

Dung Beetle

VITAL STATISTICS

LENGTH	0.3–5cm (0.12–2in), depending on species
SEXUAL MATURITY	After pupation
NUMBER OF EGGS	Up to 3 per day
DEVELOPMENT PERIOD	Lifecycle takes 5–16 weeks
HABITAT	Open countryside, especially where there are herds of herbivorous mammals
DIET	Feeds on dung, even extracting water from it
LIFESPAN	Adults live 2–6 months

ANIMAL FACTS

A strong sense of smell enables dung beetles to home in on their target, although some species are carried by animals, dropping off at the appropriate time to obtain a meal. Having created a dung ball, the beetle will seek to roll it away as quickly as possible using its hind legs, so it cannot be stolen by another beetle. Once it is safe, the beetle will then bury the dung ball in soft ground.

Unpleasant though it may sound, these beetles play a vital role in breaking down animal dung, and returning the nutrients back to the soil.

WHERE IN THE WORLD?

This beetle can be found on all continents apart from Antarctica. The majority occur in Africa, alongside elephants and other large herbivores.

BODY SHAPE
The body is flat but broad over the thorax and abdomen, helping the beetle push the balls of dung.

HEAD
The head is flat, and shaped rather like a shovel.

ANTENNAE
These sensory projections are small in dung beetles, ending in tufts.

LEG STRUCTURE
The tooth-like projection on the front legs helps the beetle create the dung ball.

BREEDING BEHAVIOUR
The pair will set off together with the dung and, after mating, the female lays her eggs in the ball (A).

It is then described as a brood ball, with the young larvae feeding on the dung underground.

A so-called brood 'pear', showing a larva inside (B). Some species lay their eggs in dung that they have buried underground (C).

HOW BIG IS IT?

Rose Chafer

• **ORDER** • Coleoptera • **FAMILY** • Scarabaeidae • **SPECIES** • *Cetonia aurata*

In spite of its beauty, this beetle is a cause of annoyance to gardeners, as adults will 'chafe' or gnaw flowers, nibbling at roses especially.

VITAL STATISTICS

LENGTH	About 2cm (0.79in)
SEXUAL MATURITY	After pupation
NUMBER OF EGGS	Females lay eggs in rotting wood, compost or leaf mould
DEVELOPMENT PERIOD	Larvae overwinter, pupating the following summer, creating a 2-year lifecycle
HABITAT	Frequently found in gardens, but also in areas of light woodland
DIET	Adults eat flowers, nectar and pollen; larvae feed on rotting wood and plant matter
LIFESPAN	3–4 months

ANIMAL FACTS

Rose chafers are very quick in flight, unlike many beetles. This is a reflection of the way in which they fly, as they do not raise their wing cases high in flight. Adults emerge from pupation in spring, and are active over the summer, dying before the autumn. Meanwhile, their larvae will already have grown rapidly. They have a rather bizarre way of moving on their back, with their bodies shaped like the letter C.

WHERE IN THE WORLD?

Ranges from southern parts of Britain south across Europe, becoming widespread over southern and central parts of the continent, but less common in northern areas.

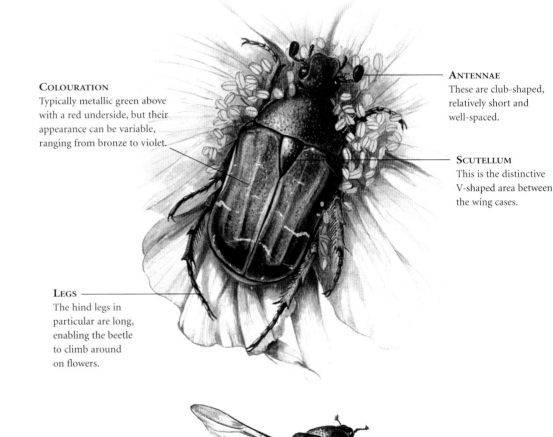

COLOURATION
Typically metallic green above with a red underside, but their appearance can be variable, ranging from bronze to violet.

ANTENNAE
These are club-shaped, relatively short and well-spaced.

SCUTELLUM
This is the distinctive V-shaped area between the wing cases.

LEGS
The hind legs in particular are long, enabling the beetle to climb around on flowers.

HOW BIG IS IT?

IDENTITY CRISIS
This particular beetle is not the same species as the rose chafer found in parts of America.

Gravedigger Beetle

• ORDER • Coleoptera • FAMILY • Silphidae • SPECIES • *Nicrophorus*

The grim habits of these beetles are reflected by their name. They feed on carrion, and will bury their food to nourish their larvae.

VITAL STATISTICS

LENGTH	2.5–4.5cm (1–1.77in)
SEXUAL MATURITY	After pupation
NUMBER OF EGGS	1–30, laid near rotting corpses
DEVELOPMENT PERIOD	Larvae mature after a week, pupating in the soil before emerging as adult beetles; lifecycle takes 45–60 days
HABITAT	Areas such as light woodland where both rodents and small birds are present
DIET	Adults eat flesh, as do the young
LIFESPAN	Up to 1 year

ANIMAL FACTS

These beetles can home in on a carcass thanks to their keen sense of smell. A number of individuals may have been drawn to the carcass, and the sexes will fight between each other, until a pair remains in the vicinity of the corpse, although occasionally, several pairs may share the body. It is then prepared for burial, with the female laying her eggs alongside the corpse. When the larvae hatch, they can feed themselves, but they are also fed by the adults.

WHERE IN THE WORLD?

Occurs in North America. Some, like the American burying beetle, have dramatically declined. The species once occurred naturally in 35 states, but is now restricted to just five.

ANTENNAE
These are equipped with special chemoreceptors, allowing the beetle to detect a corpse.

CARCASS
This beetle feeds on the carcasses of rodents or small birds.

THE BURYING PROCESS

The body must be buried to prevent it being taken by other scavengers.

As they dig the hole, the beetles spray anti-bacterial and fungal secretions over the body, to slow the rate of decay and mask its smell.

The carcass is rolled into a ball in the ground. The entire burial process takes about eight hours. Then the fur or feathers are stripped off.

The eggs are laid in what is called the crypt near the body, hatching after a few days. The larvae will then strip the flesh from the body.

If there are too many larvae for the available food, some will be killed by the adult beetles.

TIP OF THE ABDOMEN
A male can release a chemical messenger here, called a pheromone, which is carried in the air to attract a mate.

PATTERNING
Orange-red markings are set against a black background.

HOW BIG IS IT?

Kingfisher

VITAL STATISTICS

WEIGHT	35–40g (1.25–1.5oz)
LENGTH	16–18cm (6.5–7in)
SEXUAL MATURITY	Likely to breed in the year after hatching
NUMBER OF EGGS	6–7, white in colour
INCUBATION PERIOD	19–21 days; young fledge by 27 days, and the adult pair breeds up to 3 times annually
DIET	Feeds on fish, also tadpoles, adult amphibians, aquatic crustaceans such as shrimps, and molluscs
LIFESPAN	7–15 years

ANIMAL FACTS

In spite of their speed and agility, kingfishers are not always successful in obtaining food. They are most likely to be encountered on relatively slow-flowing stretches of fresh water such as lakes and canals with overhanging branches, which allow them to perch and watch the water closely. Kingfishers are especially vulnerable during spells of cold weather, when water may freeze and fish are harder to locate. Water pollution, wiping out aquatic life, will also impact adversely on their numbers.

A young kingfisher

A brief flash of colour on the riverbank indicates the presence of these kingfishers. At other times, they tend to perch quietly out of sight.

WHERE IN THE WORLD?

Occurs in much of Europe, apart from northern areas, and North Africa across the Arabian Peninsula eastwards to Southeast Asia and the Solomon Islands.

BILL
This is completely black in cocks, while hens have a reddish-orange base to the bill.

NOSTRILS
These are slit-like and positioned at the base of the bill.

EYES
The eyes are protected by a transparent membrane, which covers them when the bird dives underwater.

BACK
There is an iridescent bluish colour here, extending up on to the head.

BREEDING HABITS

Kingfishers construct a tunnel in a riverbank, which ultimately expands to form a nesting chamber where their brood is reared.

HOW BIG IS IT?

HUNTING TECHNIQUE

A kingfisher watches patiently and quietly for fish.

It then dives down, folding its wings back as necessary.

The kingfisher can see when underwater, and grabs the fish in its bill.

It then breaks the surface and flies to a convenient branch.

Here the fish is hit repeatedly against the wood, before being positioned head first, to be swallowed.

American Alligator

• **ORDER** • Crocodylia • **FAMILY** • Alligatoridae • **SPECIES** • *Alligator mississippiensis*

VITAL STATISTICS

WEIGHT	453–500kg (1000–1100lb); males are much bigger
LENGTH	3–4.6m (10–15ft)
SEXUAL MATURITY	About 10 years, at 3m (9.8ft) long
NUMBER OF EGGS	25–60 per clutch
INCUBATION PERIOD	Around 63 days; females watch over their newly hatched young, carrying them to water
DIET	Predatory, feeding on fish, turtles, snakes, amphibians, mammals; youngsters hunt amphibians, fish and invertebrates
LIFESPAN	40–60 years

ANIMAL FACTS

Alligators are surprisingly noisy creatures. They communicate by roaring and bellowing, and slap their jaws in the water. These sound waves may be detected underwater by other alligators. They impact on the landscape of their habitat, digging what are called 'gator holes', and thus creating small ponds. Their eggs are laid in spring, and covered with a mound of decomposing vegetation, which gives off heat and acts as a natural incubator.

Typical alligator habitat

The American alligator faced extinction in the last century because of hunting pressures, but now its survival seems assured.

WHERE IN THE WORLD?

Occurs in the southeastern USA, concentrated largely in the states of Florida and Louisiana, also occurring in Texas, Alabama and Georgia, in wetlands and swamps.

TAIL
The tail moves from side to side in the water when the alligator is swimming. The tail is half the body's length.

HIND FEET
The webbed toes help the alligator to swim.

SCUTES
These extend down the back, reinforcing the tough skin.

HEAD
The head is broad, with a blunt snout and nostrils located high up.

ON THE MOVE
Alligators are able to move on land, becoming a nuisance in some areas, hauling themselves out on to golf courses, for example.

HOW BIG IS IT?

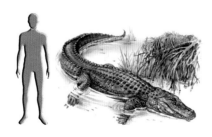

ALLIGATOR OR CROCODILE?
The lower teeth of alligators (bottom) are hidden in the mouth when the jaw is closed, but visible in crocodiles (top), which also have longer snouts.

Nile Crocodile

VITAL STATISTICS

WEIGHT	680–1000kg (1500–2205lb); males are heavier
LENGTH	3.3–5.5m (10.8–18ft)
SEXUAL MATURITY	About 10 years, at 3m (9.8ft) long
NUMBER OF EGGS	25–80 per clutch
INCUBATION PERIOD	Around 90 days; females watch over their newly hatched young, carrying them to water
DIET	Feeds on fish, but mature adults kill larger mammalian prey; youngsters hunt amphibians and larger invertebrates
LIFESPAN	70–90 years

ANIMAL FACTS

Nile crocodiles are highly efficient predators, often working collectively, as demonstrated by the so-called 'death roll', when one crocodile seizes and holds an animal, while others dismember it by gripping its limbs and spinning around their bodies. They favour rivers, but also occur in brackish water. It is very hard to spot a crocodile in the water, as these reptiles lie concealed, with just the very top of the head, including their eyes, above the waterline.

A young crocodile emerges from its egg, which is about the size of a hen's egg

These large and very dangerous crocodiles account for possibly several thousand human deaths every year, lurking at the water's edge while remaining out of sight.

WHERE IN THE WORLD?

Occurs throughout sub-Saharan Africa, extending to Egypt in the east, and also present in western Madagascar. Absent from the southwest of the continent.

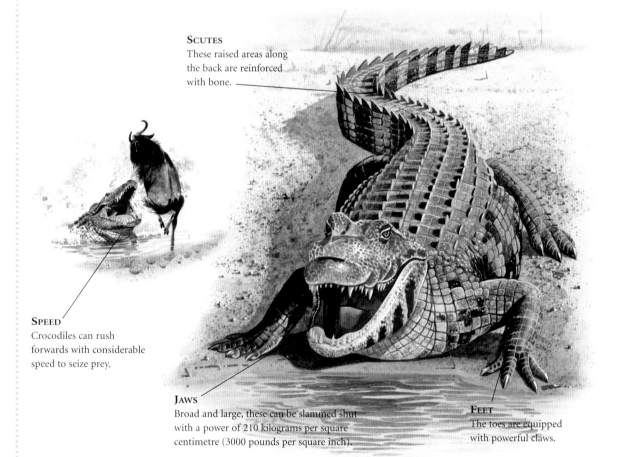

SCUTES
These raised areas along the back are reinforced with bone.

SPEED
Crocodiles can rush forwards with considerable speed to seize prey.

JAWS
Broad and large, these can be slammed shut with a power of 210 kilograms per square centimetre (3000 pounds per square inch).

FEET
The toes are equipped with powerful claws.

HOW BIG IS IT?

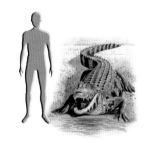

BASKING
Crocodiles haul themselves on to land, warming up their bodies under the sun's rays to raise their level of activity.

213

Gharial

• ORDER • Crocodylia **• FAMILY •** Gavialidae **• SPECIES •** *Gavialis gangeticus*

This crocodilian is the longest member of this feared family, but it is harmless to people. Its narrow snout is used to catch fish.

VITAL STATISTICS

WEIGHT	680–1000kg (1500–2205lb); males are heavier
LENGTH	5–6m (16.4–19.7ft)
SEXUAL MATURITY	About 10 years, at 3m (9.8ft) long
NUMBER OF EGGS	30–50 per clutch
INCUBATION PERIOD	Around 90 days; females watch over their newly hatched young, but do not carry them to water
DIET	Feeds on fish when adult; youngsters also prey on amphibians and larger invertebrates
LIFESPAN	40–60 years

ANIMAL FACTS

Although appearing rather clumsy on land, the gharial is streamlined and very agile in water, with its narrow snout encountering minimal resistance as it pursues its prey. There are less than 2000 alive today. Harvesting and artificial hatching of this crocodilian's eggs, followed by the release of the young, have been attempted as a way of increasing its numbers. Pollution, however, possibly combined with a shortage of food, has meant that this scheme has not been as successful as hoped.

WHERE IN THE WORLD?

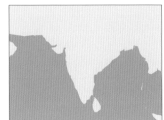

Occurs in India, but is scarce through much of its former range in Bhutan, Pakistan, Bangladesh, Myanmar (Burma) and Nepal. Numbers are increasing in India itself.

SNOUT
Males have a swelling on the tip described as a 'ghara', which derives from an Indian word for a pot of this shape.

JAWS
Over 100 sharp teeth are present in the jaws, helping to grasp fish effectively.

COLOURATION
Adults are a darker shade of olive than youngsters.

TAIL
Long and flattened, the tail aids the gharial's swimming abilities.

BREEDING STRATEGY
Nesting occurs during the dry season when the sandy river banks are exposed.

Male (above), female (below)

HOW BIG IS IT?

FISHING STRATEGY

Gharials can grab fish by moving their snouts from side to side, repositioning and then swallowing their prey head-first.

Hoatzin

VITAL STATISTICS

WEIGHT	816g (1.8lb)
LENGTH	65cm (25in) overall
SEXUAL MATURITY	Around 2 years
NUMBER OF EGGS	2–3, cream with brown, blue or pinkish spotting
INCUBATION PERIOD	28 days; young fledge around 10–14 days, before they are fully developed
DIET	Vegetarian, feeding mainly on marsh and swamp plants of the philodendron family
LIFESPAN	20 years in the wild; up to 30 in captivity

ANIMAL FACTS

Hoatzins are unusual in that they feed on vegetation, eating leaves from more than 50 different species of plant, as well as both flowers and fruit. What makes them unique amongst birds is that they rely on beneficial microbes in their digestive system to ferment and digest this plant matter, so they can obtain the nutrients from it. This creates an unpleasant odour, explaining why they are known locally as 'stinkbirds'. They live in groups and nest communally.

A cross-section of the crop, with food inside

Zoologists have long argued about the relationships of this primitive bird. DNA studies suggest it is most closely related to cuckoos, but this remains controversial.

WHERE IN THE WORLD?

Occurs throughout northern South America, in the region of the Amazon rainforest – associated with the Amazon and Orinoco river basins, and living along watercourses there.

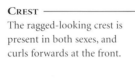

CREST
The ragged-looking crest is present in both sexes, and curls forwards at the front.

BILL
Relatively short and stocky, the bill is well-suited to plucking vegetation.

CROP
Located at the base of the neck, this storage organ can become extremely swollen with food.

WINGS
The flight feathers are all of a similar length. Hoatzins are not strong fliers.

CHICK
A young hoatzin chick with its claws soon to be shed.

HOW BIG IS IT?

CLINGING ON TO SURVIVE
Hoatzin chicks have claws on their wings, allowing them to climb out of water if they fall in.

215

Common Carp

• **ORDER** • Cypriniformes • **FAMILY** • Cyprinidae • **SPECIES** • *Cyprinus carpio*

VITAL STATISTICS

WEIGHT	0.5–4kg (1.1–8.8lb), but can reach 20kg (44lb)
LENGTH	30–60cm (12–24in)
SEXUAL MATURITY	Females 4–5 years; males 3–5 years
NUMBER OF EGGS	Around 300,000; related to the size of the female
HATCHING INTERVAL	3 days at 25°C (77°F)
DIET	Bottom-feeder, consuming invertebrates and seeds, filtering mud for this purpose
LIFESPAN	40–50 years

ANIMAL FACTS

The way that carp feed – by digging in the substrate – can have lasting effects on the water quality. They make it hard for plants to become established and stirring up the mud makes it difficult for sunlight to penetrate to the lower levels, interfering with photosynthesis and further inhibiting plant growth. Colour variants of the common carp have given rise to the popular ornamental pond fish called koi, which are indelibly linked with Japan, where they developed.

These fish eat invertebrates readily

This is a fish beloved by anglers and capable of growing to a large size. It is also one of the longest-living freshwater species.

WHERE IN THE WORLD?

Occurs naturally in Europe, but now has an almost worldwide distribution (apart from northern Asia), having been introduced to many countries for angling purposes.

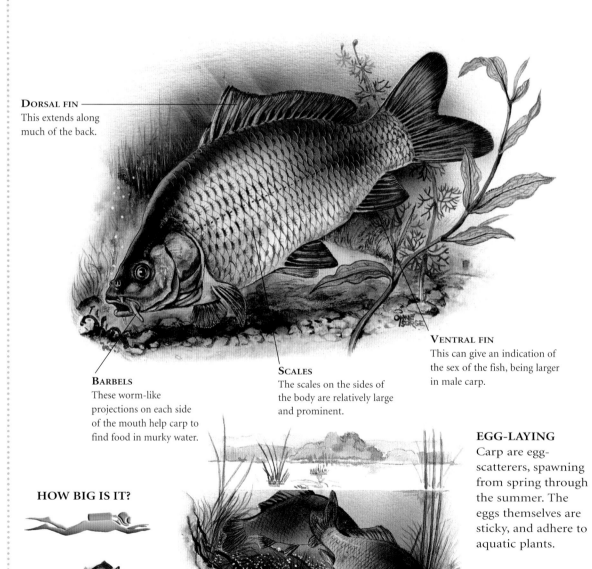

DORSAL FIN
This extends along much of the back.

BARBELS
These worm-like projections on each side of the mouth help carp to find food in murky water.

SCALES
The scales on the sides of the body are relatively large and prominent.

VENTRAL FIN
This can give an indication of the sex of the fish, being larger in male carp.

HOW BIG IS IT?

EGG-LAYING
Carp are egg-scatterers, spawning from spring through the summer. The eggs themselves are sticky, and adhere to aquatic plants.

Tasmanian Devil

• **ORDER** • Marsupialia • **FAMILY** • Dasyuridae • **SPECIES** • *Sarcophilus harrisii*

VITAL STATISTICS

WEIGHT	6–8kg (13–18lb); males are heavier
LENGTH	81–90cm (32–35in)
SEXUAL MATURITY	2 years
GESTATION PERIOD	21 days; the tiny young then move instinctively into their mother's pouch, where there are 4 nipples
NUMBER OF OFFSPRING	20–30; most die due to lack of food, survivors leave the pouch at around 100 days old
DIET	Meat-based, including carrion
LIFESPAN	Up to 8 years

ANIMAL FACTS

A deadly cancer is threatening to wipe out these unique marsupials in their last remaining stronghold. Dubbed devil facial tumour disease (DFTD), it appeared in 1995, and already entire populations have died out in some areas. More than two-thirds of their range is affected, and it is feared that the inbred nature of the population makes them vulnerable to this illness. Tumours develop around and inside the mouth, causing infected animals to starve to death.

The Tasmanian devil's bite is proportionately stronger than that of any other living mammal

This is the largest of Australia's carnivorous mammals and the biggest carnivorous marsupial in the world, although it is currently under threat of extinction.

WHERE IN THE WORLD?

Now restricted entirely to the island of Tasmania, off Australia's southeastern coast, having become extinct on the mainland in the fourteenth century, before European settlement.

TAIL
This serves as a fat store, so a thin tail may indicate ill-health.

WHISKERS
These specialist sensory hairs are prominent on the head.

FRONT LEGS
Unlike in other marsupials, the front legs are longer than the hind legs.

NOCTURNAL HUNTER
Tasmanian devils hide away during the day, and hunt at night.

HOW BIG IS IT?

FIGHTING

Fighting is common among Tasmanian devils, as their territories overlap. They often end up carrying the scars for life.

Cleaner Shrimp

• ORDER • Decapoda • FAMILY • Hippolytidae • SPECIES • include *Lysmata* and *Thor*

VITAL STATISTICS

LENGTH	3–4cm (1.25–1.5in)
SEXUAL MATURITY	1–2 months
NUMBER OF EGGS	Up to 1000, produced every 1–2 weeks, carried under the female's abdomen; some species are hermaphrodite
INCUBATION PERIOD	Larvae hatch at 12–14 days, emerging at night
HABITAT	Coral reefs in warmer waters around the world
DIET	Meat-based, scavenging on fish and amongst the tentacles of anemones
LIFESPAN	4–12 months

ANIMAL FACTS

There are special areas on a reef, described as cleaner stations, where these shrimps will congregate, and fish are also attracted to these areas. The fish have particular swimming patterns that allow the shrimps to recognize that they are not in danger. This applies even if the fish is normally a predatory species that would feed on crustaceans. Ironically, however, male cleaner shrimps may sometimes cannibalize their mates after breeding.

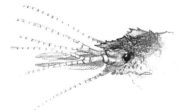

Close-up of the shrimp's head, showing the segmented feelers or antennae

These remarkable crustaceans have formed some strange alliances with fish that would normally be expected to prey on them on the tropical coral reefs.

WHERE IN THE WORLD?

Members of this family are found on the world's tropical reefs, in the Caribbean and Pacific. Some species live in association with sea anemones.

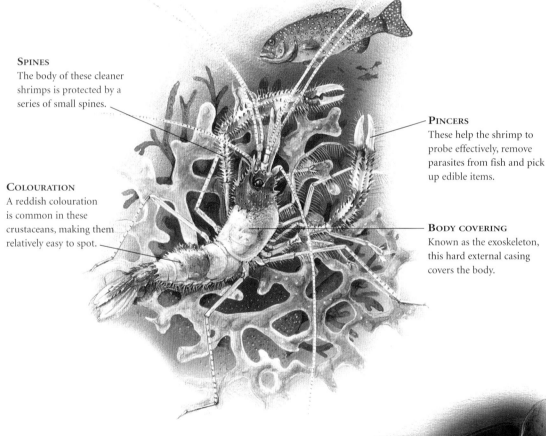

SPINES
The body of these cleaner shrimps is protected by a series of small spines.

COLOURATION
A reddish colouration is common in these crustaceans, making them relatively easy to spot.

PINCERS
These help the shrimp to probe effectively, remove parasites from fish and pick up edible items.

BODY COVERING
Known as the exoskeleton, this hard external casing covers the body.

HOW BIG IS IT?

SYMBIOSIS
The relationship between fish and shrimp is described as symbiotic. This means that both parties benefit. The shrimp helps maintain the fish's health, and obtains food in the process.

Lobster

VITAL STATISTICS

WEIGHT	Typically 0.5–4kg (1.1–8.8lb); can reach over 20kg (44lb)
LENGTH	20–60cm (8–24in) but may grow to over 1m (3.2ft)
NUMBER OF EGGS	4000–50,000 or more, depending on size
INCUBATION PERIOD	Eggs are carried by the female for 9–11 months
DIET	Fish and other marine creatures, such as starfish; young feed on zooplankton
LIFESPAN	Can live over 100 years in the wild

ANIMAL FACTS

Lobsters are remarkable crustaceans, with a life expectancy equivalent to our own. They continue growing throughout their lives, potentially attaining a very large size, although commercial lobster fisheries mean that such giants are rare. Internally, lobsters have blue blood and a green fluid often described as tomalley, which serves as a combined liver and pancreas. Living in murky surroundings, often under rocks, means that their eyesight is poor, and they rely mainly on their antennae for information about their surroundings.

Young lobsters are very vulnerable to predators

A number of different crustaceans can be described as lobsters, but it is those with broad claws that are highly valued as seafood.

WHERE IN THE WORLD?

Lobsters occur worldwide, although some are more significant in terms of the seafood industry, including those found on the eastern seaboard of North America.

HEAD
The lobster's small head, with its long antennae, forms part of the thorax.

BODY CASING
The body is protected beneath a hard, chitinous covering which forms a hard exoskeleton.

CLAWS
Both claws are of similar size and can be used to defend the lobster against predators.

ON THE MOVE
Lobsters normally walk over the seabed, but they can swim backwards from danger, using their tail to propel themselves away.

HOW BIG IS IT?

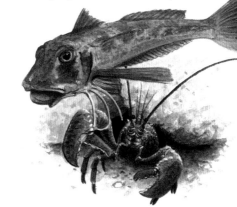

HUNTING PREY
Lobsters use their powerful claws to seize fish, ambushing their prey.

Fiddler Crab

• ORDER • Decapoda • FAMILY • Ocypodidae • SPECIES • *Uca*

VITAL STATISTICS

LENGTH	Up to 5cm (2in); the male's claw is of similar length
NUMBER OF EGGS	850–1600; the female remains in a burrow for 2 weeks while carrying the eggs, guarding against dessication
INCUBATION PERIOD	Larvae hatch after 12–14 days, and stay in this form for 2 weeks
HABITAT	Beaches, mud flats, mangroves
DIET	Digs for food such as algae, rolling mud into balls
LIFESPAN	2–3 years

ANIMAL FACTS

After these crabs have mated, the fertilized eggs develop under the female's abdomen. Egg-carrying females are often described as sponge crabs because of their appearance. They will head back to the sea, where their eggs hatch into microscopic, free-swimming larvae called zoea. These then grow through a series of moults, with the older larvae known as megalopa. The larvae finally change into miniature crabs and emerge on to land. At this stage, the sexes are indistinguishable.

When picking up food, the small claw of the male fiddler crab creates the impression of a bow plucking a fiddle, corresponding to the larger claw.

WHERE IN THE WORLD?

Occurs widely in warmer climates, being present on the Pacific and Atlantic coast of the Americas and in the Indian Ocean.

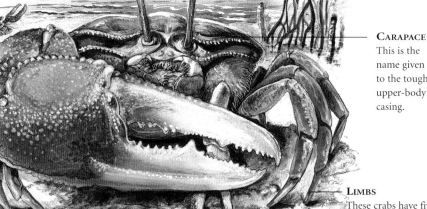

EYES
The eyes are raised on stalks, giving the crab a better view of its surroundings.

CARAPACE
This is the name given to the tough upper-body casing.

CLAW
Only the male develops this massive claw, giving the crab an asymmetric appearance.

LIMBS
These crabs have five pairs of legs. They walk on the back four pairs and use the front pair like hands.

PUTTING ON THE SQUEEZE
Male fiddler crabs use their large, powerful claws to wrestle with each other. Nearly 100 species have been identified worldwide.

CLAW WAVING

If the large claw is lost, another will develop on the opposite side of the body when the crab moults again. A small one later replaces the original large claw.

HOW BIG IS IT?

Hermit Crab

These crustaceans are best-known for carrying their homes on their backs, but some have abandoned living in shells and look more like true crabs.

VITAL STATISTICS

LENGTH	2–30cm (0.8–12in)
NUMBER OF EGGS	200–7000; females can carry viable sperm in their bodies for months
INCUBATION PERIOD	Larvae hatch after 2–3 weeks, once the female releases her eggs into the sea
HABITAT	In the sea and on land, although terrestrial species are vulnerable to dehydration
DIET	Scavenges on plant and animal-based foods
LIFESPAN	Up to 10 years; can be 20 in captivity

ANIMAL FACTS

There are over 500 species of hermit crab, the vast majority of which live in the sea, sometimes being briefly exposed in rock pools at low tide. They tend to live in colonies, and will fight over the ownership of shells. Hermit crabs need to change shells regularly when they are growing. Otherwise, once their shell is too small, this not only affects their growth but also leaves them more vulnerable to predators, as they cannot withdraw their bodies inside.

A hermit crab in its larval state

WHERE IN THE WORLD?

Occurs widely, particularly in the world's warmer oceans such as the Atlantic and Pacific, although they are also found in temperate regions, including around the British coast.

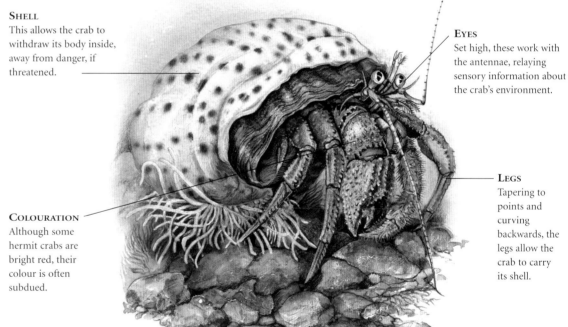

SHELL
This allows the crab to withdraw its body inside, away from danger, if threatened.

EYES
Set high, these work with the antennae, relaying sensory information about the crab's environment.

COLOURATION
Although some hermit crabs are bright red, their colour is often subdued.

LEGS
Tapering to points and curving backwards, the legs allow the crab to carry its shell.

HOLDING ON
Hermit crabs have a clasper on the abdomen, which anchors around the central supporting bar of the mollusc's shell.

HOW BIG IS IT?

PREDATORS
Marine cephalopods such as cuttlefish or octopus can use their strong arms to pull hermit crabs out of their shells.

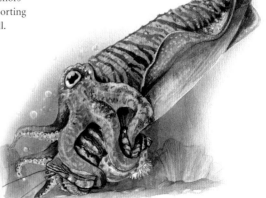

221

Common Earwig

• ORDER • Dermaptera • FAMILY • Forficulidae • SPECIES • *Forficula auricularia*

VITAL STATISTICS

LENGTH	0.8–1.8cm (0.3–0.7in)
NUMBER OF EGGS	20–80, laid in spring; eggs are often hidden under stones
INCUBATION PERIOD	About 2 weeks; the family group disperses when the nymphs are about 2 weeks old
HABITAT	Damp surroundings, in gardens and woodland, often hiding in flowers such as dahlias
DIET	Scavenges on plants and also eats other insects
LIFESPAN	Up to 1 year

ANIMAL FACTS

These insects are most commonly seen in late summer, being nocturnal by nature. The female earwig displays a remarkable degree of parental care, guarding her eggs at first. She keeps them clean so they will not be attacked by fungus, and then watches over her offspring once they hatch. Young earwigs resemble adults, only in miniature. Earwigs are adept at escaping from danger, being able to run fast, while their flattened shape allows them to squeeze into small crevices.

A female with her eggs

The earwig's name comes from an old story that describes how they crept into people's ears at night, possibly because these insects may be seen in straw bedding.

WHERE IN THE WORLD?

Can be found throughout cooler areas of Europe in particular, and have also been inadvertently introduced to many other parts of the world.

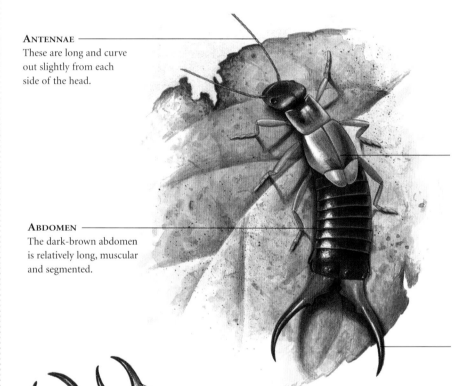

ANTENNAE
These are long and curve out slightly from each side of the head.

ABDOMEN
The dark-brown abdomen is relatively long, muscular and segmented.

WINGS
Tough, brownish forewings cover fan-shaped hind wings.

PINCERS
These can give a nip, although it will not be painful. They help the earwig to fold its wings.

SEXING EARWIGS
The pincers of the male (left) are more curved than those of the female (right).

HOW BIG IS IT?

IN FLIGHT
Earwigs can fly quite well on occasion, but their usual response to danger is to scuttle away out of sight.

Colugo

The scientific name of these arboreal mammals literally means 'dog's head', and describes their facial appearance. Colugos can glide long distances from tree to tree.

VITAL STATISTICS

WEIGHT	1–2kg (2–4lb)
LENGTH	55–65cm (22–26in)
SEXUAL MATURITY	About 3 years
GESTATION PERIOD	60 days; young are born in a very immature state
NUMBER OF OFFSPRING	1; weaning occurs from 6 months
DIET	Vegetarian, feeding mainly on leaves and flowers, as well as sap; may also eat fruit
LIFESPAN	Up to 15 years

ANIMAL FACTS

It was thought that colugos were closely related to bats because of their ability to glide, combined with their nocturnal nature. Today, however, they are considered most closely related to primates. In terms of their breeding behaviour, though, colugos are more reminiscent of marsupials, with their tiny young weighing only 35g (1.2oz) at birth. They develop very slowly, and will take two to three years to reach adult size. Females carry their offspring on the underside of their bodies for six months.

Unlike bats, the colugo's gliding membrane extends between the individual toes

WHERE IN THE WORLD?

Found in the rainforests of the Philippines, off the eastern coast of Asia, on the islands of Mindanao, Samar, Basilan, Bohol and Leyte.

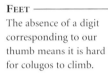

FEET
The absence of a digit corresponding to our thumb means it is hard for colugos to climb.

GLIDING MEMBRANE
This is kept folded away while the colugo is resting on the tree.

CLAWS
Colugos hop up branches, using their sharp claws to anchor themselves.

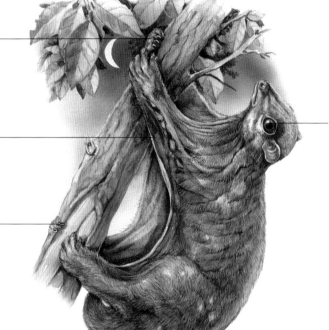

EYES
Keen eyesight is very important, helping the colugo to land safely on another tree.

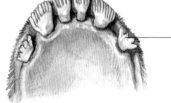

TEETH
The colugo's incisor teeth look rather like combs, with as many as 20 lines on each one.

HOW BIG IS IT?

GLIDING ABILITY
Colugos can cover up to 70m (230ft) using their extensive gliding membranes, which extend down each side of their bodies.

Virginia Opossum

• ORDER • Didelphimorphia • FAMILY • Didelphidae • SPECIES • *Didelphis virginiana*

VITAL STATISTICS

WEIGHT	1–2kg (2–4lb)
LENGTH	55–65cm (22–26in), including tail
SEXUAL MATURITY	By 1 year
GESTATION PERIOD	13 days; young stay in their mother's pouch for 1–2 months
NUMBER OF OFFSPRING	6–25, but mortality is higher in bigger litters; weaning occurs from 3 months
DIET	Omnivorous, eating rodents, eggs, carrion, invertebrates, plant matter and fruit
LIFESPAN	2–4 years

ANIMAL FACTS

Once the young opossums leave the safety of their mother's pouch, they will still be carried by her for up to eight weeks. If threatened, opossums can growl and bare their teeth menacingly, but in reality there is little that they can do to defend themselves. They may be able to deter an attack by pretending to be dead – cats in particular lose interest in dead prey. This behaviour is reflected in the phrase 'playing possum'.

A convincing impression of being dead can save an opossum's life

This is the only marsupial found in North America, and represents one of the oldest surviving mammalian groups, whose ancestry dates back 70 million years.

WHERE IN THE WORLD?

Widely distributed in North America, from British Columbia in Canada, through the USA east of the Rocky Mountains and along the west coast, into Mexico.

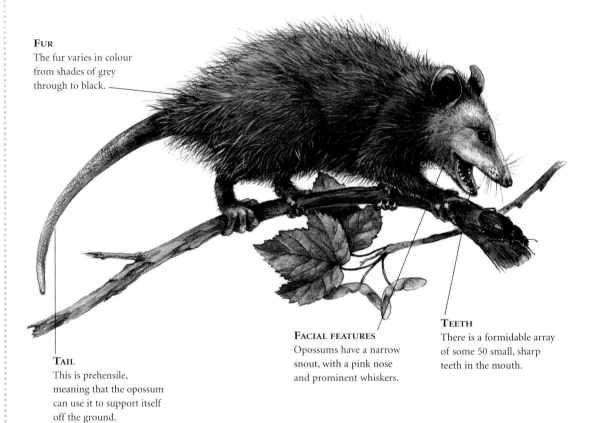

FUR
The fur varies in colour from shades of grey through to black.

TAIL
This is prehensile, meaning that the opossum can use it to support itself off the ground.

FACIAL FEATURES
Opossums have a narrow snout, with a pink nose and prominent whiskers.

TEETH
There is a formidable array of some 50 small, sharp teeth in the mouth.

HOW BIG IS IT?

POSTURE

These opossums can walk on all fours along a branch, and then sit up and support themselves on their hindquarters.

Common Mouse Opossum

• ORDER • Didelphimorphia • FAMILY • Didelphidae • SPECIES • *Marmosa murina*

In spite of being a marsupial, the female common mouse opossum lacks any pouch, so instead her young simply cling on her teats at first.

VITAL STATISTICS

WEIGHT	About 38g (1.33oz); males are slightly larger
LENGTH	25–36cm (10–14in) overall; tail is usually longer than the body
SEXUAL MATURITY	3 months
GESTATION PERIOD	13 days
NUMBER OF OFFSPRING	5–10; weaning occurs at about 62 days
DIET	Omnivorous, feeding on invertebrates and other small prey such as lizards, raids birds' nests and eats fruit
LIFESPAN	Up to 3 years

ANIMAL FACTS

Hiding away during the day, often in a hollow tree or an abandoned birds' nest, the common mouse opossum can climb well, emerging under cover of darkness. It is aided by the opposable thumb on its front paws, which helps the opossum grip branches easily when climbing. These marsupials are solitary by nature. They will use their flexible tail to carry leaves and vegetation when making a nest. The young are tiny at birth, weighing just 0.09g (0.003oz).

These marsupials can rear up on their hind legs, showing their teeth to appear more intimidating

WHERE IN THE WORLD?

Occurs in northern parts of South America, from Colombia and Venezuela east to Guyana, Surinam and French Guiana. Also present in Brazil, Peru, Ecuador and Bolivia.

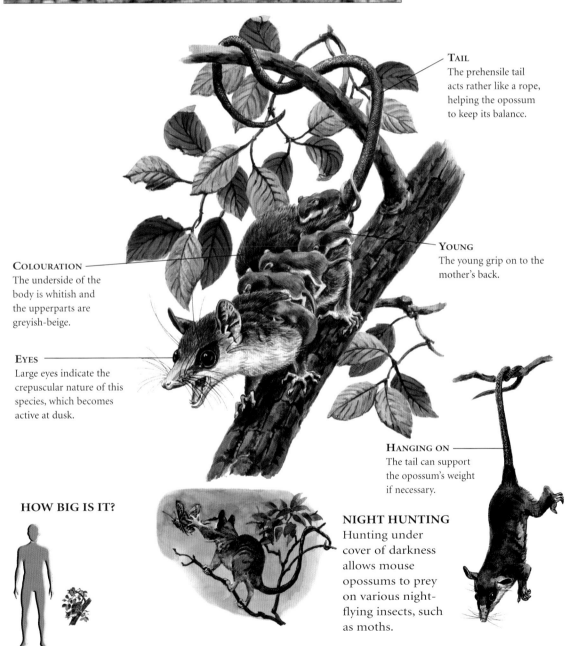

TAIL
The prehensile tail acts rather like a rope, helping the opossum to keep its balance.

YOUNG
The young grip on to the mother's back.

COLOURATION
The underside of the body is whitish and the upperparts are greyish-beige.

EYES
Large eyes indicate the crepuscular nature of this species, which becomes active at dusk.

HANGING ON
The tail can support the opossum's weight if necessary.

HOW BIG IS IT?

NIGHT HUNTING
Hunting under cover of darkness allows mouse opossums to prey on various night-flying insects, such as moths.

Matschie's Tree Kangaroo

• ORDER • Diprotodontia • FAMILY • Macropodidae • SPECIES • *Dendrolagus matschiei*

VITAL STATISTICS

WEIGHT	6–7.5kg (13–17lb); females are larger
LENGTH	93–168cm (37–66in), including tail, which is almost as long as the body
SEXUAL MATURITY	2 years
GESTATION PERIOD	39–45 days; young tree kangaroos measure 2.5cm (1in) long
NUMBER OF OFFSPRING	1
DIET	Mainly herbivorous, eating plant matter including bark; also takes invertebrates and birds' eggs
LIFESPAN	Up to 14 years

ANIMAL FACTS

Despite its size, this tree kangaroo is well-suited to its arboreal lifestyle, able to climb well and jump up to 9m (30ft) between branches. On the ground they walk rather than hop but up in the trees, they can leap to the ground from a height of 18m (60ft) without injury. These tree kangaroos live solitary lives. The young joey remains completely hidden in the female's pouch for nearly 3.5 months.

Sharp claws aid anchorage, but these tree kangaroos lack thumbs to help them grip the branches

226

This species has a longer gestation period than any other marsupial. The youngster, called a joey, uses its mother's pouch for almost a year.

WHERE IN THE WORLD?

Confined to the tropical forests of Papua New Guinea, in the vicinity of the Huon Peninsula, where hunting has rendered it endangered.

NOSE
The nose is large and pink, with prominent nostrils.

BACK
Fur grows in opposite directions on this part of the body, ensuring rainwater runs off the coat efficiently.

COLOURATION
A fairly unusual mahogany and yellow patterning distinguishes this species.

TAIL
The tail is long but is simply used for balancing, rather than for gripping tree branches.

LIMB LENGTH
An obvious feature of tree kangaroos is the fact that their forelimbs are almost as long as their hind limbs.

HOW BIG IS IT?

CLIMBING
Both the front and hind legs are important in assisting tree kangaroos to move around in their natural environment.

Pretty-Faced Wallaby

• **ORDER** • Diprotodontia • **FAMILY** • Macropodidae • **SPECIES** • *Macropus parryi*

This wallaby lives in groups, or 'mobs', comprising up to 80 individuals. It is also called the whiptail wallaby because of its long tail.

VITAL STATISTICS

WEIGHT	7–26kg (15–57lb); males are bigger
LENGTH	150–195cm (59–77in), including tail, which is almost as long as the body
SEXUAL MATURITY	Females 18 months–2 years; males 2 years
GESTATION PERIOD	34–38 days; weighs 1g (0.03oz) at birth
NUMBER OF OFFSPRING	1; the joey spends around 275 days in the pouch
DIET	Grasses, ferns, other herbaceous plants
LIFESPAN	Up to 14 years

ANIMAL FACTS

These wallabies tend to be found in a relatively specific environment, living in upland wooded areas of Australia. They are quite common through their range and face few dangers, other than attacks by dingoes, which are also widespread in this area. Pretty-faced wallabies can be seen throughout the day over the cooler winter period, but during the heat of summer they are more active in the early morning and at dusk, resting when the sun is at its hottest.

WHERE IN THE WORLD?

Common on the eastern side of the Australian continent, ranging from around Cooktown in Queensland down to Grafton in New South Wales.

COLOURATION
The white stripe below the eyes, which distinguishes this species, contrasts with the brown colouration.

HIND FEET
Three toes are present on each foot, the longest one in the middle.

TAIL
This acts as a counterbalance, preventing the wallaby from toppling over.

STAYING COOL
In hot weather, these wallabies lick their forearms to keep cool.

HOW BIG IS IT?

ON THE MOVE
Wallabies rely on their strong hind legs to propel themselves along by hopping, with both legs moving together in harmony.

Red Kangaroo

• ORDER • Diprotodontia • FAMILY • Macropodidae • SPECIES • *Macropus rufus*

VITAL STATISTICS

WEIGHT	82–412kg (37–187lb); males are bigger
LENGTH	1.3–2.9m (4.3–9.5ft)
SEXUAL MATURITY	Females 14–20 months; males about 20 months
GESTATION PERIOD	33–34 days
NUMBER OF OFFSPRING	1; the joey spends around 235 days in the pouch
DIET	Herbivorous, grazing almost entirely on grass
LIFESPAN	Up to 15 years in the wild; can be 18 in captivity

ANIMAL FACTS

Living in hot, open countryside has shaped the biology and behaviour of these kangaroos. They only become active towards dusk and their fur is short, which helps them to stay cool. Their field of vision extends almost completely around the head, making it very difficult to approach them without being seen. Males may challenge each other in boxing contests, often jabbing with their front legs and lashing out with their hind legs.

Kangaroos usually only have one youngster at a time, but females are often pregnant for most of their lives

This is the largest member of the kangaroo family, with males standing up to 1.8m (6ft) tall. They can jump 9.1m (30ft) at a bound.

WHERE IN THE WORLD?

Occurs across most of the interior of Australia, in arid countryside, but is absent from coastal areas in the north, south and east of the continent.

MUSCULAR HINDQUARTERS
These allow the kangaroo to bound along at high speed.

RUNNING POSTURE
The kangaroo runs with its head low and forelegs bent backwards.

TAIL
The heavy tail of these kangaroos measures over 1m (3ft) long in adults.

IN THE POUCH
The young joey suckles on one of its mother's teats within the pouch.

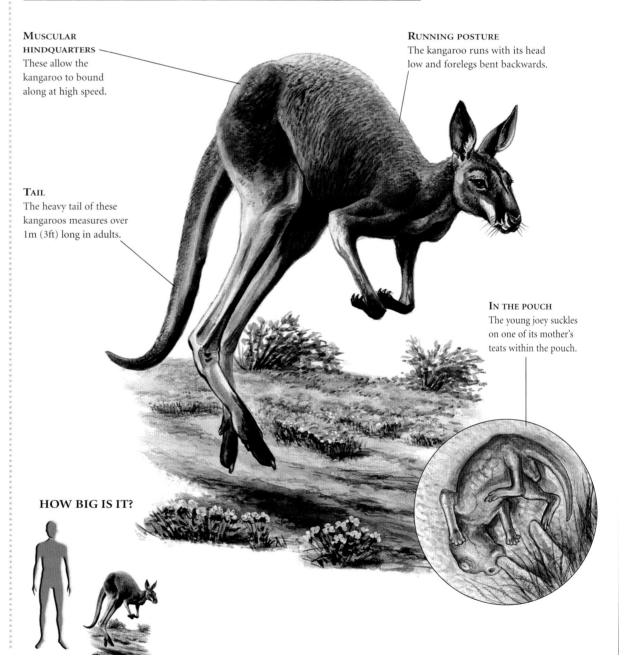

HOW BIG IS IT?

Yellow-Footed Rock Wallaby

• **ORDER** • Diprotodontia • **FAMILY** • Macropodidae • **SPECIES** • *Petrogale xanthopus*

This is one of the most brightly coloured members of the kangaroo family. Its population is declining, though, and is now among the most rare.

VITAL STATISTICS

WEIGHT	2.7–9kg (6–20lb); males are bigger
LENGTH	89–147cm (35–58in), including tail, which is almost as long as the body
SEXUAL MATURITY	Females 18–24 months; males about 20 months
GESTATION PERIOD	30–34 days
NUMBER OF OFFSPRING	1; the joey spends around 250 days in the pouch
DIET	Herbivorous, eating vegetation including plants, grass and even bark
LIFESPAN	12–18 years

ANIMAL FACTS

Living in a harsh environment means that the breeding cycle of these wallabies is strongly influenced by the availability of food. During periods of drought they can face starvation, and females may be unable to produce enough milk for their offspring. A lack of food will also delay the development of an embryo. Only once conditions improve will the pregnancy proceed. Females often have a fertilized egg in their reproductive system.

These wallabies leap across rocky outcrops with ease, holding their front legs at right angles to steady themselves

WHERE IN THE WORLD?

Occurs in eastern Australia, from southwestern Queensland down through western New South Wales to South Australia, occurring in rocky and mountainous areas.

UPPERPARTS
These are grey, with a blackish band extending from the nose and encircling the eyes.

HIND FEET
The soles are covered with thick, rough skin to stop the wallaby from slipping.

TAIL
The tail is long and does not taper significantly along its length. It is barred, with a dark tip.

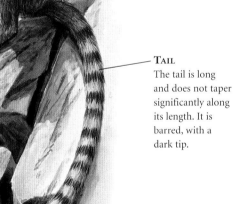

HOW BIG IS IT?

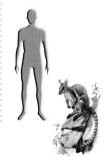

DANGER ABOVE
Although they can outrun would-be terrestrial predators by their agility, these wallabies at at risk from birds of prey.

Common Spotted Cuscus

• **ORDER** • Diprotodontia • **FAMILY** • Phalangeridae • **SPECIES** • *Spilocuscus maculatus*

VITAL STATISTICS

WEIGHT	3–6kg (3–13lb); males are bigger
LENGTH	65–85cm (26–33in), including tail, which is almost as long as the body
SEXUAL MATURITY	About 1 year
GESTATION PERIOD	13 days
NUMBER OF OFFSPRING	1, but can be up to 4; young spend up to 220 days in the pouch
DIET	Herbivorous, eating vegetation, mainly leaves, as well as fruit
LIFESPAN	Up to 11 years

ANIMAL FACTS

The colourful cuscus is a rather secretive arboreal possum. It has a prehensile tail with a scaly inner surface, free from fur. This acts like another hand, helping the cuscus to clamber around without difficulty. Mating can occur at any time of year, with the young being born after a very short gestation period, following which they transfer to the pouch, where there are four teats. Cuscuses can fall victim to snakes such as pythons, and birds of prey.

The common spotted cuscus spends its time sleeping in a nest built in the fork of a tree

This marsupial has forelimbs like hands, which help it to pick up food and climb. The inner toes are free of claws, acting as thumbs.

WHERE IN THE WORLD?

Ranges from New Guinea to the Moluccan Islands; also occurs in tropical parts of Australia, inhabiting rainforest up to an altitude of 1200m (3900ft).

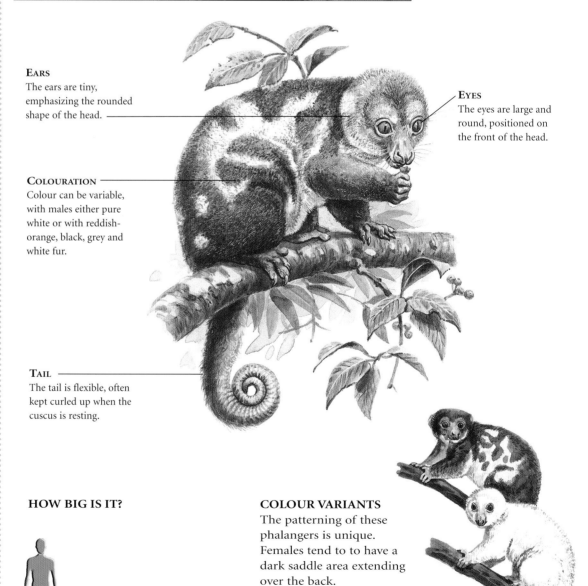

EARS
The ears are tiny, emphasizing the rounded shape of the head.

EYES
The eyes are large and round, positioned on the front of the head.

COLOURATION
Colour can be variable, with males either pure white or with reddish-orange, black, grey and white fur.

TAIL
The tail is flexible, often kept curled up when the cuscus is resting.

HOW BIG IS IT?

COLOUR VARIANTS
The patterning of these phalangers is unique. Females tend to to have a dark saddle area extending over the back.

Common Brushtail Possum

• **ORDER** • Diprotodontia • **FAMILY** • Phalangeridae • **SPECIES** • *Trichosurus vulpecula*

The largest member of the possum family, this has also proven to be one of the most adaptable, and can often be seen in city areas.

VITAL STATISTICS

WEIGHT	1.2–4.5kg (2.6–10lb); males are bigger
LENGTH	95cm (37in), including tail, which is almost as long as the body
SEXUAL MATURITY	About 1 year
GESTATION PERIOD	17 days
NUMBER OF OFFSPRING	1; young spend about 155 days in the pouch
DIET	Herbivorous, feeding mainly on leaves and flowers, especially of eucalypts, but may eat invertebrates, eggs and carrion
LIFESPAN	Up to 12 years

ANIMAL FACTS

The adaptability of these possums has been confirmed following their introduction to New Zealand during the 1830s, carried out as a means of providing fur and food. They have since decimated areas of native woodland, and frequently raid the nests of birds. These possums make a range of calls, often uttering clicking sounds. Males will indicate their territories by hissing loudly if confronted by a rival, and also by rearing up on their hind legs.

WHERE IN THE WORLD?

Found in Australia, from Northern Territory and West Australia to New South Wales, Queensland, Victoria, South Australia and Tasmania. Introduced to New Zealand.

HEAD
The head has a long, pointed snout ending in a pink nose with prominent whiskers.

EARS
Large and oval, the ears measure up to 6cm (2.4in) long.

COLOURATION
Colour is variable, with some individuals being a coppery colour, but more often greyish or black.

TAIL
The tail helps the possum to climb, with the bald area providing a good grip.

CLAWS
Arboreal by nature, these possums have strong claws on their toes, helping them to move around in the trees.

HOW BIG IS IT?

POISONED FOOD
The toxic chemicals present in eucalypt leaves offer no protection against them being eaten regularly by the common brushtail possum.

Koala

• **ORDER** • Diprotodontia • **FAMILY** • Phascolarctidae • **SPECIES** • *Phascolarctos cinereus*

VITAL STATISTICS

WEIGHT	5–14kg (11–31lb); males are bigger
LENGTH	95cm (37in)
SEXUAL MATURITY	Females 2–3 years; males 3–4 years
GESTATION PERIOD	34–36 days; newborn koalas measure 2cm (0.8in) and weigh under 1g (0.03oz)
NUMBER OF OFFSPRING	1; young spend about 215 days in the pouch
DIET	Eucalypt leaves, which create its distinctive body odour
LIFESPAN	12 years

ANIMAL FACTS

One of the most instantly recognizable animals in the world, the koala is one of only three mammals capable of eating eucalypt leaves, which are toxic to most species. Their sharp incisor teeth allow them to nip off the leaves, which are ground up by the cheek teeth behind. The reproductive system of both male and female is unusual. Males have a penis that is split into two branches, and females are the only mammal to have two vaginas.

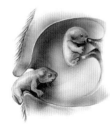

Twin births are rare, although there are two nipples in the female koala's pouch

Although often described as a bear, the koala is actually a marsupial, like a kangaroo. Its fur has an odour reminiscent of cough sweets.

WHERE IN THE WORLD?

Found in Australia, from the Atherton Tablelands in Queensland in the north down through New South Wales to Victoria and South Australia, including offshore islands.

OFFSPRING
After leaving the pouch, a young koala will be carried on its mother's back.

SIZE
Those koalas living further south, where the weather is cooler, are largest in size.

NOSE
The black nose is prominent, with downward-facing nostrils.

FOREFEET
The presence of opposable thumbs makes it easier for koalas to climb and grip on to branches.

HOLDING ON
The inverted thumbs on the hind feet help the koala to maintain its grip while it feeds using its forelegs.

HOW BIG IS IT?

SAFE IN THE TREETOPS
Although they are not active by nature, koalas are adept at moving from branch to branch without falling to the ground.

Brush-Tailed Bettong

• ORDER • Diprotodontia • FAMILY • Potoroidae • SPECIES • *Bettongia penicillata*

VITAL STATISTICS

WEIGHT	1.1–1.6kg (2.4–3.5lb)
LENGTH	48–76cm (19–30in), including tail, which is almost as long as the body
SEXUAL MATURITY	By 6 months
GESTATION PERIOD	21 days
NUMBER OF OFFSPRING	1; young spend about 90 days in the pouch
DIET	Feeds mainly on fungi but may also eat some bulbs, seeds and insects
LIFESPAN	4–6 years in the wild; can be up to 9 in captivity

ANIMAL FACTS

The diet of brush-tailed bettongs is unusual, as they feed on fungi, which can only be broken down in their digestive tract by bacteria. In the absence of regular grassland fires, these fungi may not grow as well, reducing their food supply, although grazing by sheep and predation by foxes has also contributed to their decline. After mating, the bettong's embryo is retained in the female's uterus at first, and will only start developing once the pouch is empty.

The population of this unusual marsupial has dropped dramatically for various reasons, including a decline in the number of grassland fires in its territory.

WHERE IN THE WORLD?

Occurs in Australia, in areas of scrub and grassland in South Australia; favours open eucalypt forest with a grass floor in Western Australia.

MUZZLE
The muzzle is usually quite bare.

COLOURATION
Predominantly grey above, whitish on the underparts and with a dark tip to the tail.

FORELEGS
These are very short, but the sharp claws allow the bettong to dig effectively.

NIGHT-TIME FORAGING
These marsupials are nocturnal by nature, spending the day hidden in their nests.

HOW BIG IS IT?

NEST-BUILDING
The prehensile tail of the brush-tailed bettong is used to carry the grass used for nest-building.

Long-Footed Potoroo

• ORDER • Diprotodontia • FAMILY • Potoroidae • SPECIES • *Potorous longipes*

VITAL STATISTICS

WEIGHT	1.6–2kg (3.5–4.4lb)
LENGTH	72cm (28in), including tail, which is almost as long as the body
SEXUAL MATURITY	By 2 years old
GESTATION PERIOD	21 days
NUMBER OF OFFSPRING	1; young spend about 145 days in the pouch
DIET	Feeds largely on fungi, which it digs up from the ground
LIFESPAN	Up to 13 years

ANIMAL FACTS

These small, solitary marsupials were only discovered in 1968, and they have a very localized distribution. They play a significant part in the ecosystems of the areas where they occur, because they help to spread the fungi that they eat through their droppings. Long-footed potoroos are regarded as endangered, partly because of their restricted range, and any loss of their forest homeland is significant. They are also vulnerable to attack by foxes as well as feral cats.

These marsupials are also described as rat kangaroos because of their distinctive rat-like appearance. They even hold food in their front paws like rats.

WHERE IN THE WORLD?

There are three distinct populations of this Australian species, occurring in New South Wales, in the vicinity of the Great Dividing Range and in east Gippsland.

FACIAL FEATURES
The head is triangular, with a prominent nose, whiskers and small, rounded ears. The eyes are also small.

FRONT FEET
These are equipped with powerful claws for digging for food.

COLOURATION
The body has brownish-black upperparts and a pale grey belly.

HIND FEET
The length of the peach-coloured hind feet is partly responsible for the name of this marsupial.

FIRE AND FUNGI
Forest fires may actually encourage the growth of the fungi that make up almost the entire diet of these marsupials.

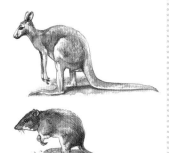

The shape of the long-footed potoroo's head, compared with that of a kangaroo (above)

HOW BIG IS IT?

PUSHED FOR SPACE
The female can only accommodate one youngster at a time in her pouch.

Honey Possum

This is the only survivor of a group of ancient marsupials that evolved about 20 million years ago, and is somewhat reminiscent of a tiny mouse.

VITAL STATISTICS

WEIGHT	7–16g (0.24–0.56oz); females are larger
LENGTH	Females 14.5–19.5cm (5.7–7.7in); males 13.5–18.5cm (5.3–7.2in); the tail is longer than the body
SEXUAL MATURITY	By 6 months old
GESTATION PERIOD	28 days
NUMBER OF OFFSPRING	2–3, occasionally 4; young spend about 60 days in the pouch
DIET	Nectivorous, feeding exclusively on nectar and pollen collected from flowers
LIFESPAN	1–2 years

ANIMAL FACTS

Honey possums are very unusual animals. Unlike many marsupials, their life is brief, and females will mate with many males. This may be why males of this species have the largest testes – relative to their body size – of all mammals. They also produce the largest spermatozoa of any mammalian species, measuring 0.36mm (0.01in). Yet their offspring rank as the smallest, weighing just 0.0005g at birth. When they finally emerge from their mother's pouch, they still weigh only 2.5g (0.09oz).

WHERE IN THE WORLD?

Southwestern parts of Australia, occurring in areas of heathland, shrubland and light woodland where flowering bushes such as banksias and dryandras are present.

STRIPE
This is blackish and extends from between the ears to the base of the tail.

COLOURATION
Greyish-brown on the upperparts, with an orange suffusion on the flanks, and cream underparts.

TAIL
The tails is long and prehensile in part, allowing the marsupial to grip stems.

FACIAL FEATURES
Facial features include a long nose, round pink ears, black eyes and prominent whiskers.

DELVING DEEP
The elongated tongue of the honey possum allows these marsupials to probe deep inside a flower to reach the nectar.

HOW BIG IS IT?

GROWING NUMBERS
A family of young honey possums. These tiny marsupials produce relatively large litters, but their lives are correspondingly short.

Common Wombat

• **ORDER** • Diprotodontia • **FAMILY** • Vombatidae • **SPECIES** • *Vombatus ursinus*

VITAL STATISTICS

WEIGHT	15–54kg (33–100lb); males are slightly larger
LENGTH	67–130cm (26–51in); the tail is 2.5cm (1in) long
SEXUAL MATURITY	Typically 2–3 years
GESTATION PERIOD	20–22 days
NUMBER OF OFFSPRING	1; young spend 248–310 days in the pouch
DIET	Herbivorous, eating grass, leaves, bark and mushrooms
LIFESPAN	5–15 years in the wild; up to 26 in captivity

ANIMAL FACTS

Common wombats spend much of their time hidden beneath ground, creating tunnels that can extend back over 30m (100ft). They are just about wide enough for the wombat to move through without becoming stuck, although the animal's agility is such that it can turn around in the tightest of spots. The shorter tunnels are only intended as retreats, while others are used for living purposes. The wombat's sleeping quarters are usually at a higher level to avoid the dangers of flooding, and are lined with vegetation.

Females produce offspring every second year at the most

A wombat's newborn joey is helpless and tiny – roughly the size of a jellybean – but it manages to clamber into its mother's pouch.

WHERE IN THE WORLD?

Coastal eastern Australia, from southeastern Queensland via New South Wales into Victoria. Also on the Victoria and South Australia border, Flinders Island and Tasmania.

EARS
The triangular ears are small and relatively inconspicuous.

HEAD
This is rounded and broad, terminating in a large black nose, surrounded by whiskers.

FUR
The texture is quite coarse to the touch, with softer insulating fur beneath.

COLOURATION
Colour is variable, ranging from black and shades of grey through brown to a sandy colour.

USEFUL TOOLS
Sharp claws aid the wombat's digging efforts.

TUNNELLING UNDERGROUND

An underground network created by a wombat. These marsupials are solitary creatures, and their burrows serve a number of purposes.

HOW BIG IS IT?

Common House Fly

• **ORDER** • Diptera • **FAMILY** • Muscidae • **SPECIES** • *Musca domestica*

VITAL STATISTICS

LENGTH	0.6–0.7cm (0.2–0.3in)
SEXUAL MATURITY	Lifecycle takes 7–41 days, depending on temperature
NUMBER OF EGGS	Up to 500 laid over 3–4 days
INCUBATION PERIOD	8–20 hours, but is temperature-dependent
HABITAT	Highly adaptable, occurring in rural and urban areas, often venturing inside buildings
DIET	Faecal matter and household waste
LIFESPAN	Adults live 25–62 days

ANIMAL FACTS

These insects have become known as house flies, because they regularly come into buildings, particularly when the weather is hot and stormy. They are active during the daytime. House flies seek out faecal matter, but are drawn to any waste containing meat, laying their eggs in these surroundings. This will sustain the larvae, known as maggots, once they hatch. They then pupate, with the adult flies cutting their way out, using a sac on their heads to literally smash open the pupal casings.

This is one of the most dangerous insects on the planet, not because it has a venomous bite but due to its disease-spreading capabilities.

WHERE IN THE WORLD?

Its origins lie on the plains of Central Asia, but this species is now distributed worldwide, and has adapted particularly well to urban living.

COLOURATION
These flies have a blackish body, with very little gloss; the wings are transparent.

ANTENNAE
These sensory projections, located between the large eyes, are small and short.

PROBOSCIS
This feeding tube helps liquefy and then suck up the fly's food. It is usually heavily contaminated with bacteria.

EYES
Very sensitive, large compound eyes detect movement around the fly's body.

EGG-LAYING
A female house fly lays her white eggs on dung. The larvae (right) are able to move when they hatch, to avoid becoming dehydrated.

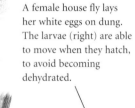

HOW BIG IS IT?

FEEDING HABITS

Flies liquefy their food using digestive enzymes, releasing this fluid from the proboscis, and then sucking up the nutrient-rich solution.

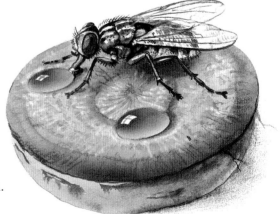

Sea Urchin

Sea urchins represent a very ancient group of creatures, with a spiny appearance, whose origins stretch back some 450 million years in the fossil record.

VITAL STATISTICS

LENGTH	3–10cm (1.2–4in), with spines measuring up to 20cm (8in)
SEXUAL MATURITY	2–5 years
NUMBER OF EGGS	Several million released at once
INCUBATION PERIOD	Eggs develop into tiny larvae, which float in zooplankton
HABITAT	Live on the sea bed, often in shallow water
DIET	Feed largely on algae, but may also prey on other invertebrates, including sponges and mussels
LIFESPAN	Up to 200 years

ANIMAL FACTS

The unusual name of these invertebrates reflects their spiny appearance, as 'urchin' is an old English word for a hedgehog. Treading on a sea urchin is very painful, as the spine often breaks off to create a splinter in the flesh, and it may be tipped with venom. If some of the spines are touched gently, the neighbouring spines alter position, directing towards the point of contact. Tiny tube feet on the lower side of the body provide mobility.

Sea urchins have penta-radial bodies, like starfish, meaning they display five-fold symmetry

WHERE IN THE WORLD?

Members of this group occur in oceans throughout the world, but are most common in tropical seas, found in association with coral reefs.

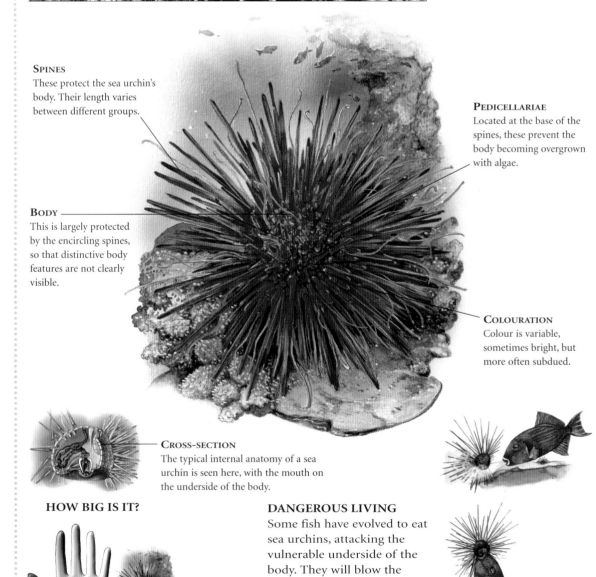

SPINES
These protect the sea urchin's body. Their length varies between different groups.

PEDICELLARIAE
Located at the base of the spines, these prevent the body becoming overgrown with algae.

BODY
This is largely protected by the encircling spines, so that distinctive body features are not clearly visible.

COLOURATION
Colour is variable, sometimes bright, but more often subdued.

CROSS-SECTION
The typical internal anatomy of a sea urchin is seen here, with the mouth on the underside of the body.

HOW BIG IS IT?

DANGEROUS LIVING

Some fish have evolved to eat sea urchins, attacking the vulnerable underside of the body. They will blow the urchin off the sea bed with a jet of water, and then seize it from below to avoid the spines

Hedgehog

• ORDER • Erinaceomorpha **• FAMILY •** Erinaceidae **• SPECIES •** *Erinaceus europaeus*

VITAL STATISTICS

WEIGHT	1.5–2kg (3.3–4.4lb)
LENGTH	15–30cm (38–76in)
SEXUAL MATURITY	1 year
GESTATION PERIOD	35 days; females may produce 2 litters a year
NUMBER OF OFFSPRING	1–9, typically 5; weaning occurs after 35 days
DIET	Mainly insectivorous, hunting slugs, snails, worms, beetles and the eggs of ground-nesting birds
LIFESPAN	Up to 8 years in the wild; 10 years in captivity

ANIMAL FACTS

Nocturnal by nature, hedgehogs are most likely to be seen out on summer's evenings after rainfall, when their invertebrate prey will also be more active. As autumn approaches, they start to put on weight for hibernation, and will remain dormant until the following spring. Although common in gardens, they face dangers here, particularly if they decide to hibernate in garden rubbish piled up for a bonfire. They can also get trapped in garden netting or be poisoned.

Rolling into a ball protects the hedgehog's vulnerable head and underparts from attack by a would-be predator

The flexible snout of this insectivore, combined with its snuffling behaviour when sniffing around for food, helps explain why it became known as the hedgehog.

WHERE IN THE WORLD?

These hedgehogs range across most of Europe, including southern Scandinavia, and eastwards into parts of Asia. They have also been introduced to New Zealand.

SPINES
There are 5000–7000 spines covering the upperparts.

SENSES
Hedgehogs have poor eyesight but keen hearing and smell.

UNDERPARTS
The underparts are covered in dark hair.

GRABBING A MEAL
The hedgehog's sharp teeth help it to grab prey, with the first incisors at the front of the mouth resembling canines.

HOW BIG IS IT?

Northern Pike

• ORDER • Esociformes • FAMILY • Esocidae • SPECIES • *Esox lucius*

VITAL STATISTICS

WEIGHT	Up to 27kg (60lb)
LENGTH	Up to 152cm (60in)
SEXUAL MATURITY	2–3 years
NUMBER OF EGGS	35,000–300,000, depending on female size; young measure 1cm (0.4in) when they hatch
INCUBATION PERIOD	5–26 days or longer, depending on water temperature
DIET	Opportunistic predators, eating other fish, sometimes smaller pike, as well as ducklings and other aquatic creatures
LIFESPAN	Up to 25 years

ANIMAL FACTS

Pike are the dominant predator in waters where they are present, and so it is often thought that taking out the few large individuals will curb fishery losses. Instead, thanks to their amazing reproductive potential, this can simply trigger an explosion in the pike population, and the level of predation on fish such as trout will actually increase. Studies have revealed that pike regulate their own numbers by cannibalism.

After a period of up to 12 days of being largely immobile, the young pike start swimming and begin to feed on plankton

One of the most feared freshwater fish, this pike has existed largely unchanged for over 62 million years, according to fossil evidence from Canada.

WHERE IN THE WORLD?

Widely distributed throughout the northern hemisphere, ranging from North America through Europe and Asia, and also present in brackish water in the Baltic.

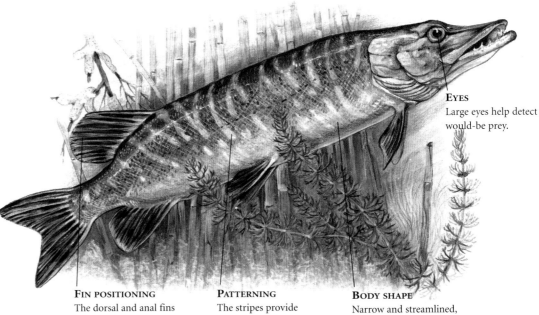

EYES
Large eyes help detect would-be prey.

FIN POSITIONING
The dorsal and anal fins are set well back near the caudal fin, giving the pike great acceleration.

PATTERNING
The stripes provide camouflage for young pike; they are replaced by spots in older individuals.

BODY SHAPE
Narrow and streamlined, the body shape allows these fish to swim easily and quickly after prey.

CHOMPING AWAY
A formidable battery of teeth, capable of inflicting a sharp bite, is present in the jaws.

HOW BIG IS IT?

HIDDEN DANGER
Large pike will not hesitate to seize young ducklings by their feet, dragging them underwater, drowning and then eating them.

Golden Eagle

• **ORDER** • Falconiformes • **FAMILY** • Accipitridae • **SPECIES** • *Aquila chrysaetos*

These magnificent eagles are a spectacular sight, able to attain speeds of 128kph (80mph) when pursuing prey. They frequent upland and often treeless areas.

VITAL STATISTICS

WEIGHT	3–6.1kg (6.6–13.4lb); hens are larger
LENGTH	70–91cm (28–36in); wingspan 1.8–2.2m (6–7.2ft)
SEXUAL MATURITY	5 years
NUMBER OF EGGS	2, white broken with variable darker markings
INCUBATION PERIOD	About 45 days; young fledge after about 50 days
DIET	Hunts birds and mammals such as rabbits; sometimes eats carrion
LIFESPAN	Up to 38 years in the wild; 50 in captivity

ANIMAL FACTS

These eagles have been heavily persecuted in the past in areas such as northern Scotland, where they will prey on young lambs. Even where food is readily available, however, they are not common. Pairs occupy large territories, which can extend up to 56km² (35 square miles). When breeding, they construct a very large, bulky nest often on a rocky crag or in a tree, and the pair will return to the same site every year, adding to the nest.

WHERE IN THE WORLD?

Occurs sporadically in Western Europe and North Africa, and from Scandinavia across Asia. Also found in North America, from Alaska to Mexico, but is less common in eastern areas.

EYES
Golden eagles can scan the open country and spot potential prey from afar.

BILL
The large, powerful bill has a hooked tip to hold on to prey and rip flesh off a carcass.

COLOURATION
Colour varies in individuals, ranging from a consistent dark to golden brown.

TAIL
The feathers here are broad and short, with slightly rounded tips.

LIFTING ABILITY
The feet of the golden eagle are equipped with powerful claws and called talons. This allows the bird to carry prey back to its nest securely in a vice-like grip.

HOW BIG IS IT?

REMAINING HIDDEN

Having spotted potential prey, a golden eagle will fly low over the landscape, using the natural terrain as cover.

Black Kite

• **ORDER** • Falconiformes • **FAMILY** • Accipitridae • **SPECIES** • *Milvus migrans*

VITAL STATISTICS

WEIGHT	0.56–1.2kg (1.2–2.6lb), varying through its wide range; hens are larger overall
LENGTH	47–55cm (19–22in); wingspan 130–155cm (51–61in)
SEXUAL MATURITY	2–3 years
NUMBER OF EGGS	1–3, white with brownish spots and blotches
INCUBATION PERIOD	About 28 days; young fledge after about 40 days
DIET	Hunts invertebrates and vertebrate prey, including fish, birds and mammals; also scavenges
LIFESPAN	15–25 years

ANIMAL FACTS

These kites are not just hunters but also scavengers, even congregating at rubbish dumps to search for either edible items or invertebrates. Their feeding habits vary through their range, with those in Asia sometimes stealing food from temples left as offerings. In Australia they congregate where there are grassland fires, seizing small creatures attempting to run from the flames. Black kites can also be sighted far from their usual range.

As with many birds of prey, black kites can carry prey in their talons

Unlike many birds of prey, black kites are observed in groups numbering up to 3000 at a single locality, having benefited from human settlement.

WHERE IN THE WORLD?

Has a very extensive range, from mainland Europe and Africa, the Middle East and India right across southern Asia, south to New Guinea and Australia.

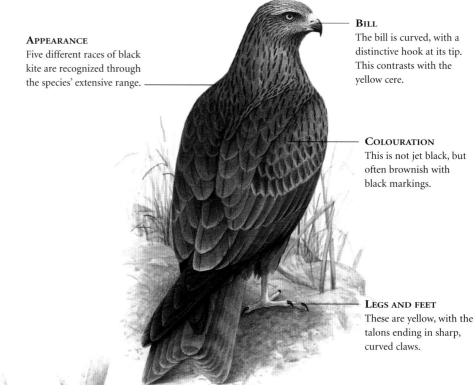

APPEARANCE
Five different races of black kite are recognized through the species' extensive range.

BILL
The bill is curved, with a distinctive hook at its tip. This contrasts with the yellow cere.

COLOURATION
This is not jet black, but often brownish with black markings.

LEGS AND FEET
These are yellow, with the talons ending in sharp, curved claws.

BREEDING BEHAVIOUR
Black kites build their nests in trees, usually preferring a forest setting where several pairs can breed in relatively close proximity.

HOW BIG IS IT?

DISTINCTIVE FLIGHT SILHOUETTE

When seen in flight, the black kite does not have a strongly forked tail, distinguishing it from its close relative, the red kite.

Andean Condor

• ORDER • Falconiformes **• FAMILY •** Cathartidae **• SPECIES •** *Vultur gryphus*

This species is one of the world's largest flying birds. Its huge wingspan helps it to glide almost effortlessly on hot air currents called thermals.

VITAL STATISTICS

WEIGHT	39–73kg (17.5–33lb); males are much heavier than females
LENGTH	109–130cm (43–51in); wingspan 3.1m (10.1ft)
SEXUAL MATURITY	6 years
NUMBER OF EGGS	1, white, measuring about 10cm (4in) long
INCUBATION PERIOD	About 59 days; young fledge after about 180 days
DIET	Mainly a carrion feeder, seeking out the carcasses of mammals, including marine mammals washed ashore
LIFESPAN	50 years

ANIMAL FACTS

The mountains are important to these gigantic birds of prey, serving as launch pads for them. The warmth of the morning sun raises the air temperature sufficiently to allow these birds to take off and stay airborne on the upcurrents of hot air. These allow the condor to maintain its altitude with very little effort, as its weight is supported by the column of air. This means that they don't have to flap their wings frequently, but can simply glide.

Andean condors will feed in groups

WHERE IN THE WORLD?

Western South America, in association with the Andean mountains, but will forage further afield over open country and coasts. It is not seen in forested areas.

HEAD
An absence of plumage on the head allows this bird to feed without feathers becoming matted by blood.

WINGS
These have an immense span when fully extended, with long flight feathers.

BILL
Powerful and quite curved at its tip, the bill enables the condor to tear strips off meat.

MARINE PREY
Condors often search beaches, looking for dead seals and similar creatures. Occasionally, they may kill prey.

FEET
Food cannot be held in the condor's toes, so feeding must occur on the ground.

HOW BIG IS IT?

SEEKING FOOD

Soaring over the open landscape allows the condor to spot a carcass on the ground with its acute eyesight. The sight of other condors in an area is an indication of the presence of food.

Peregrine Falcon

• ORDER • Falconiformes • FAMILY • Falconidae • SPECIES • *Falco peregrinus*

VITAL STATISTICS

WEIGHT	530–1600g (1–3lb); females are heavier
LENGTH	36–49cm (15–19in); wingspan 100–110cm (39–43in)
SEXUAL MATURITY	2 years
NUMBER OF EGGS	2–5, whitish to buff with reddish or darker brown blotching
INCUBATION PERIOD	30–33 days; fledging occurs around 44 days
DIET	Hunts other birds, often preying on pigeons
LIFESPAN	Up to 15 years

ANIMAL FACTS

The peregrine's hunting technique sees it soaring up to over 1km (0.62 miles) before plunging down on its prey, closing in at speeds approaching 320kph (200mph). The resulting impact usually proves fatal, knocking the unfortunate bird to the ground. The numbers of peregrines had fallen severely by the 1960s because of the pesticide DDT, which worked up through the food chain, causing these falcons to lay thin-shelled eggs. Since DDT has been banned, their numbers have risen again.

Differences in plumage are evident between the 19 recognized races

'Peregrine' means 'wanderer', and describes the huge distances that these bird may travel, flying, for example, from the Canadian tundra to overwinter in South America.

WHERE IN THE WORLD?

Ranks as one of the most widely distributed of all birds, occurring on every continent apart from Antarctica, and absent from various oceanic islands.

WINGS
Long and pointed, these aid the peregrine's aerial athleticism. They reach almost to the tip of the tail.

CERE
This yellow area above the bill encompasses the nostrils.

MARKINGS
Underparts are barred, with these markings being more pronounced in hens.

TOES
These are yellow – with the centre toe the longest – and end with curved black claws.

ON THE MOVE
Peregrines typically travel at speeds of 40–55kph (25–34mph), and may cover distances of 25,000km (15,500 miles) annually if migrating.

HOW BIG IS IT?

HUNTING STRATEGY
When diving down on prey, the peregrine folds its wings to lessen air resistance and increase its velocity.

Common Kestrel

• **ORDER** • Falconiformes • **FAMILY** • Falconidae • **SPECIES** • *Falco tinnunculus*

The name of this falcon is derived from the sound of its calls. The common kestrel is one of the smaller birds of prey, and is active during the day.

VITAL STATISTICS

WEIGHT	140–190g (5–6.7oz); females are larger
LENGTH	32–36cm (13–15in); wingspan 60–80cm (24–32in)
SEXUAL MATURITY	2 years
NUMBER OF EGGS	3–5, whitish or pale yellowish-buff with reddish-brown markings
INCUBATION PERIOD	About 30 days; fledging occurs around 35 days
DIET	Feeds mainly on small mammals such as voles but will also prey on small birds and invertebrates
LIFESPAN	Up to 10 years

ANIMAL FACTS

In many areas the common kestrel is one of the most conspicuous of all birds of prey. This is partly because it has adapted to hunt on motorway verges, and may also take up residence in larger city parks. It has acute eyesight, enabling it to recognize possible prey moving on the ground. Common kestrels can also see ultraviolet light, allowing them to home in on the urine trails around rodent burrows, watching for their occupants to emerge.

WHERE IN THE WORLD?

Northern Europe, extending up to Scandinavia and northern Russia in the summer, overwintering further south. Also occurs in North Africa and Asia, east to China.

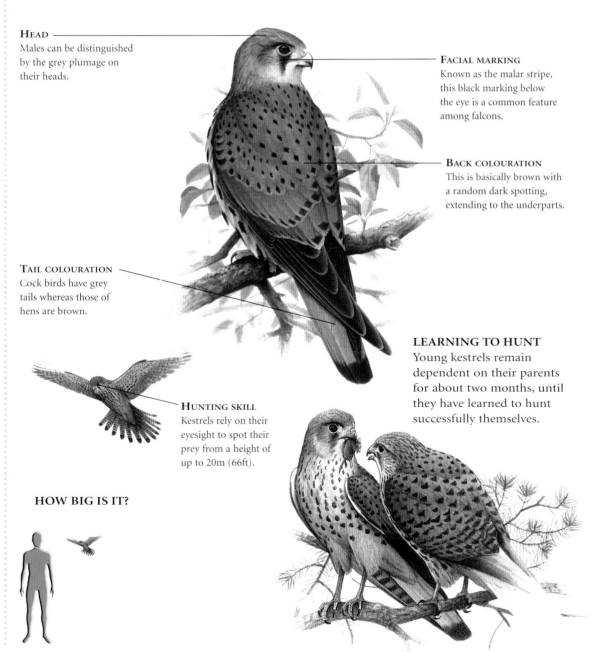

HEAD
Males can be distinguished by the grey plumage on their heads.

FACIAL MARKING
Known as the malar stripe, this black marking below the eye is a common feature among falcons.

BACK COLOURATION
This is basically brown with a random dark spotting, extending to the underparts.

TAIL COLOURATION
Cock birds have grey tails whereas those of hens are brown.

HUNTING SKILL
Kestrels rely on their eyesight to spot their prey from a height of up to 20m (66ft).

LEARNING TO HUNT
Young kestrels remain dependent on their parents for about two months, until they have learned to hunt successfully themselves.

HOW BIG IS IT?

245

Secretary Bird

This species' name may derive from the Arabic *sekareteur*, meaning 'hunter bird', but also its crest feathers resemble the old quill pens that were carried behind secretaries' ears.

VITAL STATISTICS

WEIGHT	3.3kg (7.3lb)
LENGTH	140cm (55in); wingspan over 2m (6.6ft); 130cm (51in) tall
SEXUAL MATURITY	4 years
NUMBER OF EGGS	2, occasionally 3, pale green in colour; male offspring may kill each other
INCUBATION PERIOD	About 45 days; fledging occurs at 65–80 days
DIET	Eats snakes, lizards, rodents, eggs and birds as well as locusts and other invertebrates
LIFESPAN	10–15 years; 20 in captivity

ANIMAL FACTS

Secretary birds spend most of their time on the ground. Although they share territory, members of the pair hunt independently, and are usually seen apart. Snakes are their favoured prey, and they have evolved a unique way of killing these reptiles, with little risk of being bitten by venomous species. The secretary bird grabs the snake by the neck, and throws it repeatedly into the air to stun it, before jumping up and down on the body, flapping its wings.

The crest feathers are erected as part of the display process

Restricted to Africa, south of the Sahara, found in open countryside on the plains and in savanna areas, where they can hunt easily.

CREST FEATHERS
These are usually folded backwards, extending over the nape of the neck.

TAIL
There are two long tail plumes here.

THIGHS
Covered in black plumage, these are long, adding to the secretary bird's height.

LEGS
The legs are long, allowing the bird to take large strides as it walks. Its height also gives good visibility over a wide area.

TAKING TO THE AIR
The secretary bird will fly on occasion, especially up to its nest, which is usually located in an acacia tree, and reused every year.

HOW BIG IS IT?

ON THE MOVE
Secretary birds frequently walk over 32km (20 miles) every day, looking out for any feeding opportunities. They can also run fast.

Three-Spined Stickleback

•ORDER • Gasterosteiformes • FAMILY • Gasterosteridae • SPECIES • *Gasterosteus aculeatus*

VITAL STATISTICS

WEIGHT	0.9g (0.027oz)
LENGTH	6–10cm (2–3in)
SEXUAL MATURITY	1–3 years
NUMBER OF EGGS	Each female lays 100–150 eggs
INCUBATION PERIOD	6–10 days; the male destroys the nest just prior to hatching
DIET	Feeds on plankton both at sea and at the surface of deeper lakes; otherwise eats invertebrates, eggs and fry of other fish
LIFESPAN	Up to 3 years

ANIMAL FACTS

Few fish are as diverse as these sticklebacks. The anadromous variety lives in the sea, but spawns in freshwater, being the ancestor of the freshwater three-spined sticklebacks that inhabit streams and lakes. Here the shallow-water lake populations, with long bodies and small eyes, feed on the lake bed. In deeper lakes, the limnetic form of the three-spined stickleback eats at the surface, having developed an upturned jaw, and a relatively short body, with large eyes.

These small freshwater fish vary significantly in appearance, even locally, with different populations being quite distinctive as they are frequently isolated from each other.

WHERE IN THE WORLD?

Found throughout Britain and much of northern Europe, introduced to areas further south, and ranges into Asia. Other races occur in North America.

SPINES
These projections, running down the centre of the back, are a deterrent to larger predators, making sticklebacks hard to swallow.

IRIS
The blue colouration here is another sign of a mature male.

UNDERPARTS
The reddish appearance is associated with breeding males, and is derived from carotenoid pigments in the diet.

JAW STRUCTURE
This is variable, depending on the fish's locality.

DISPLAY

The male constructs a nest, then displays to the female, hoping to lure her inside to lay her eggs.

NESTING
Several female sticklebacks may be attracted to lay in the same nest
The male fertilizes the eggs in the nest
He will then guard it, watching over the young at first as well.

HOW BIG IS IT?

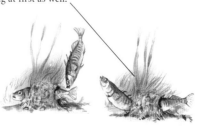

Sun Bittern

• ORDER • Gruiformes • FAMILY • Eurypygidae • SPECIES • *Eurypyga helias*

This unusual species is the only member of its family. It lives near water, staying in the shallows, but lacks any webbing between its toes.

VITAL STATISTICS

WEIGHT	210g (7.4oz)
LENGTH	46–53cm (18–21in)
SEXUAL MATURITY	2 years
NUMBER OF EGGS	2, buff with dark spotting at the larger end; adults may display to deter predators
INCUBATION PERIOD	About 27 days; fledging occurs at 17–24 days; chicks are covered in thick down
DIET	Hunts various invertebrates, as well as fish and smaller vertebrates
LIFESPAN	10 years; up to 17 years in captivity

ANIMAL FACTS

Living on their own or sometimes in pairs, sun bitterns are shy birds. At the start of the breeding period, the cock bird will display, revealing the vibrant colouration of the wings and tail. The domed nest, made from grass and mud, may be constructed either on the ground or in the branch of a tree or shrub. The young sun bitterns hatch in an advanced state of development, with their eyes open, but they do not leave the nest immediately.

Bright colours are a feature of the plumage

248

WHERE IN THE WORLD?

Ranges from southern Mexico down to Ecuador, with some reports in Chile, and also extends across northern parts of South America, east of the Andes, in Brazil.

BILL
Stout and long, the bill tapers to a sharp point, and is used to spear or grab prey. —

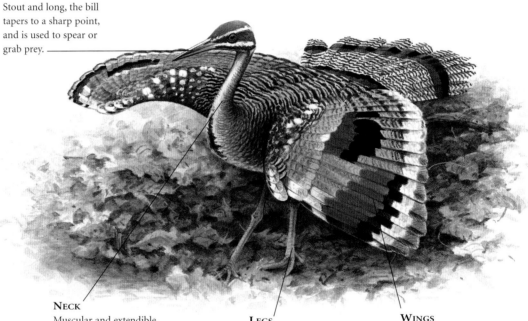

NECK
Muscular and extendible, the neck helps the bird to strike forcibly with its bill.

LEGS
These are strong, as sun bitterns prefer to walk rather than fly.

WINGS
Stunning sun-like marking on the wings give the sun bittern its name.

HUNTING STRATEGY
The sun bittern is a watchful hunter, looking for signs of movement in the water, walking slowly and striking quickly.

HOW BIG IS IT?

FISHING
The bill can be a formidable weapon.

Common European Earthworm

• **ORDER** • Haplotaxida • **FAMILY** • Lumbricidae • **SPECIES** • *Lumbricus terrestris*

These invertebrates have a series of five hearts to pump blood around the body, with two main blood vessels running the length of their bodies.

VITAL STATISTICS

WEIGHT	4–5g (0.12–0.15oz)
LENGTH	20–25cm (8–10in)
SEXUAL MATURITY	1 year
NUMBER OF EGGS	20–30 per worm per year
INCUBATION PERIOD	70–100 days; young emerge almost fully developed, with sexual organs developing within another 90 days
DIET	Feeds on organic material such as leaves and decaying plant matter; also consumes insects and faeces
LIFESPAN	4–8 years

ANIMAL FACTS

Earthworms play a vital part in maintaining the condition of the soil, by feeding on leaf matter, and taking it down into the soil. They can be seen at the surface, particularly after periods of heavy rain, and they may mate at this stage, entwining around a partner. Common earthworms are hermaphrodite, having both male and female sex organs. The egg case is produced by the clitellum, where the worm's eggs are mixed with another's sperm.

WHERE IN THE WORLD?

This earthworm is native to Europe, but has been introduced to many other parts of the world, including Canada, the USA and New Zealand.

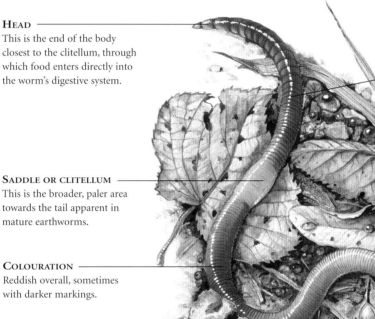

HEAD
This is the end of the body closest to the clitellum, through which food enters directly into the worm's digestive system.

BODY STRUCTURE
The body is annular or ring-like, and extendible, helping the worm to move.

SADDLE OR CLITELLUM
This is the broader, paler area towards the tail apparent in mature earthworms.

COLOURATION
Reddish overall, sometimes with darker markings.

HOW BIG IS IT?

UNDER ATTACK
Predators such as birds will try to pull worms from their burrows, but they can anchor themselves in place with tiny bristles on their bodies, called setae.

BURROWING
Worms soon become dessicated if stranded above ground, and they will burrow deeper into the soil in dry conditions.

Shield-Backed Bug

VITAL STATISTICS

LENGTH	0.6–1.5cm (0.2–0.6in)
SEXUAL MATURITY	Often 1 generation produced annually, especially in more northerly areas
NUMBER OF EGGS	30–75 eggs laid together and covered by the female's body
INCUBATION PERIOD	70–100 days; nymphs grow over 5 moults into adults
HABITAT	Open country, from fields to lightly wooded areas
DIET	Represent a danger to plants because of their diet of sap
LIFESPAN	1 year

ANIMAL FACTS

Shield-backed bugs are sometimes confused with beetles, but they can be distinguished quite easily because the scutellum over the back is not divided into two, hence it forms a shield over the insect's body. More than 450 different species have been identified, divided into some 80 genera. Some are serious pests, affecting important agricultural crops such as wheat and cotton. Females lay on the underside of leaves, and guard both their eggs and recently hatched young.

Sometimes known as jewel bugs because of their attractive colouration, these insects can protect themselves against potential predators by giving off an unpleasant scent.

WHERE IN THE WORLD?

Family members occur worldwide. In the Americas, these bugs extend from the Arctic region down to South America. Also present in Europe, Asia and Australia.

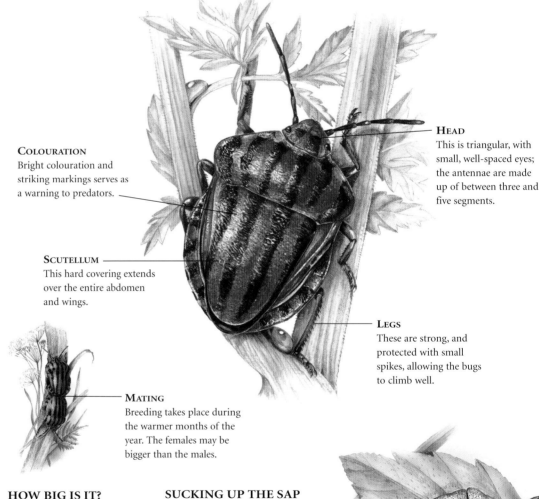

COLOURATION
Bright colouration and striking markings serves as a warning to predators.

SCUTELLUM
This hard covering extends over the entire abdomen and wings.

MATING
Breeding takes place during the warmer months of the year. The females may be bigger than the males.

HEAD
This is triangular, with small, well-spaced eyes; the antennae are made up of between three and five segments.

LEGS
These are strong, and protected with small spikes, allowing the bugs to climb well.

HOW BIG IS IT?

SUCKING UP THE SAP
Different shield-backed bugs prefer different plants, but they can puncture the stem with their proboscis to obtain the sap.

Honeybee

• ORDER • Hymenoptera **• FAMILY •** Apidae **• SPECIES •** *Apis mellifera*

VITAL STATISTICS

LENGTH	Workers 1–1.5cm (0.4–0.6in); queen 1.8–2.2cm (0.7–0.9in)
SEXUAL MATURITY	23 days
NUMBER OF EGGS	Up to 2000 daily; can be 80,000 bees in a colony
DEVELOPMENTAL PERIOD	21 days from egg to worker bee; 16 days for a queen
HABITAT	Open country with flowering plants nearby
DIET	Pollen and nectar
LIFESPAN	Queens 3–5 years; workers 4 weeks in summer, longer in winter

ANIMAL FACTS

As social insects, these bees live together in colonies and have various tasks to perform. Workers are the most versatile and numerous group, responsible for collecting honey, caring for the brood and defending the hive. The queen is the reproductive force within the colony, and her premature death can threaten its existence. Under normal circumstances, however, a young queen takes over beforehand. The short-lived drones are males, whose sole task is to mate with young queens.

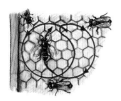

Honeycomb is built up by the worker bees returning from their foraging flights

This is the most important insect in the world, in economic terms, because these bees are kept to both pollinate crops and to provide honey.

WHERE IN THE WORLD?

Their origins lie in southern Asia, based on the distribution of wild species, but they were already present in Europe over 35 million years ago.

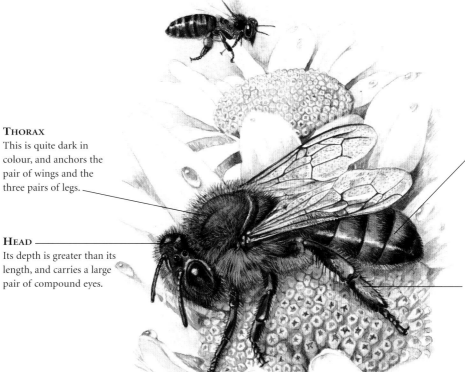

THORAX
This is quite dark in colour, and anchors the pair of wings and the three pairs of legs.

HEAD
Its depth is greater than its length, and carries a large pair of compound eyes.

ABDOMEN
Dull brown, with indistinctive yellow markings, the abdomen is longer than other body parts.

LEGS
The hind legs are stockier in appearance than the front legs.

HOW BIG IS IT?

NAVIGATION
Honeybees can find their way back to the hive without difficulty. Members of the hive use both dancing movements and scent to communicate about navigation.

Buff-Tailed Bumblebee

• **ORDER** • Hymenoptera • **FAMILY** • Apidae • **SPECIES** • *Bombus terrestris*

VITAL STATISTICS

LENGTH	Workers 1.5–2cm (0.6–0.8in); queen up to 2.7cm (1.1in)
SEXUAL MATURITY	Males within a few weeks; queens by a year old
NUMBER OF EGGS	Perhaps 1000, laid by the queen
DEVELOPMENTAL PERIOD	5 weeks from larva to worker bee
HABITAT	Open country with flowering plants nearby
DIET	Pollen and nectar from flowers
LIFESPAN	Queens 1 year; workers a few weeks

ANIMAL FACTS

Queens emerge from their hibernation early in the year, even though nectar may not be readily available. They create their own nests, laying eggs that initially produce female workers. These help to build up the colony quickly, while the queen continues to lay her eggs. Males are produced with young queens in late summer, and they leave the nest to mate. The males will die shortly afterwards. The new queens will find somewhere snug to hibernate before winter.

Bees have three pairs of legs; the difference between the more streamlined front leg (right) and a hind leg (left) is clearly evident here

The lifecycle of these bumblebees means that only the young fertilized queens survive the winter, with the previous colony having died in the colder weather.

WHERE IN THE WORLD?

Occurs throughout Europe, although not normally seen in winter. Milder winters in some areas have seen queens feeding on ivy flowers, however, rather than hibernating.

COLOURATION
Worker bees have white hairs on their abdomen, whereas those of the larger queen are orangish-yellow.

WINGS
These are transparent in appearance and veined.

ABDOMEN
The bee's buzzing sound results from air being expelled from holes here while it is flying.

POLLEN CARRIERS
Bees carry the pollen granules, which are a valuable source of protein, back to the nest in special pollen sacs on their hind legs.

HOW BIG IS IT?

BEARING FRUIT
Workers are responsible for collecting nectar and pollen, and while doing so, they are likely to fertilize the flowers too.

Foraging Ant

• **ORDER** • Hymenoptera • **FAMILY** • Formicidae • **SPECIES** • *Eciton*

VITAL STATISTICS

LENGTH	Workers 0.3–1.2cm (0.1–0.5in); queen is larger
SEXUAL MATURITY	Males mate after pupation, then die within 48 hours
NUMBER OF EGGS	Thousands are laid, with colonies comprising up to 2 million ants
DEVELOPMENTAL STAGES	Eggs hatch into larvae, and then pupate
HABITAT	Areas of tropical forest
DIET	Feeds on invertebrates, small vertebrates and carrion
LIFESPAN	Queens 3–5 years; workers several months

ANIMAL FACTS

The regimented way in which these ants move has led to them also becoming known as army ants. They stop each night, and may also create a 'bivouac', a temporary nest in a tree. The queen lays eggs in a continuous three-week cycle, and as the workers help new adults out of their pupae, the egss there are stimulated to hatch into larvae. These will pass through five distinct stages until they themselves pupate.

The mouthparts of the soldier ant (top) are broad, compared with those of a typical worker (bottom)

Huge numbers of these ants march across the floor of the forest, devouring almost anything that they can catch, overwhelming invertebrates much larger than themselves.

WHERE IN THE WORLD?

Can be encountered throughout the rainforests of Central and South America, in swarms up to 6m (20ft) long, although they also form temporary encampments.

MOUTHPARTS
In the colony's soldiers, these are long, hooked and fearsome, helping them to defend the colony.

THORAX
This is relatively long, but also narrow, especially near the abdomen.

DEFENSIVE STRATEGY
Some of the workers amongst the army ants are significantly larger. These are soldiers who defend the group.

LEGS
These are long, possibly reflecting the fact that these ants are constantly on the move, increasing their stride length.

COLOURATION
The head and abdomen are yellowish, with a black thorax.

HOW BIG IS IT?

OVERPOWERING PREY
One soldier ant grabs on to prey, then is assisted by others in overpowering the unfortunate creature. These ants are remarkably strong and possess a potent sting.

Red Wood Ant

• ORDER • Hymenoptera • FAMILY • Formicidae • SPECIES • *Formica polyctena*

VITAL STATISTICS

LENGTH	Workers 1–1.5cm (0.6–0.8in); queen is larger
SEXUAL MATURITY	Males after pupation
NUMBER OF EGGS	The queen lays thousands; some workers lay eggs too
DEVELOPMENTAL STAGES	Ants hatch into larvae, and then pupate
HABITAT	Areas of forest
DIET	Omnivorous, milking aphids for nectar, killing other invertebrates such as caterpillars, and scavenging
LIFESPAN	Queens live for 5 years, workers for a few weeks

ANIMAL FACTS

The nests of these ants can be over 1m (3.3ft) high, with a diameter of 2m (6.6ft), constructed from material such as pine needles. They are determinedly defended, and even standing close by may draw an aggressive response, as the worker ants can squirt formic acid. The nest is often built around a tree stump and equipped with ventilation passages. There is ongoing discussion about the red wood ant's classification, with very similar ants occurring in North America.

Worker ants will fight to defend their nest, battling other ants

Nests of these ants can comprise over half a million individuals, and in some areas several nests can be located in close proximity.

Occurs in Europe and Asia, with its range extending up to the coniferous forests of Scandinavia, south to the Mediterranean and eastwards into Russia.

HEAD
Quite large, the head is equipped with powerful mouthparts.

ABDOMEN
Relatively large, the abdomen is dark in colour and equipped with the ability to inflict a painful sting.

THORAX
This is the narrow part of the body, supporting the three angled pairs of legs.

THE NEST
A cross-section of a nest, showing the range of entrances plus the nursery area, where the young are raised by workers.

HOW BIG IS IT?

HOW IT WORKS
This cross-section of the ant's body reveals its digestive system, with the organs concentrated in the abdomen.

European Hornet

• ORDER • Hymenoptera • FAMILY • Vespidae • SPECIES • *Vespa crabro*

These large wasps can inflict an unpleasant sting, but they are actually not aggressive, only stinging if they or their nests are directly threatened.

VITAL STATISTICS

LENGTH	Workers 1–1.5cm (0.4–0.6in); queen around 3.5cm (1.4in)
SEXUAL MATURITY	After pupation; only young queens overwinter
NUMBER OF EGGS	Queens lay thousands of eggs in the summer
DEVELOPMENTAL PERIOD	30 days from egg to adult
HABITAT	Typically lightly wooded areas with hollow trees
DIET	Attacks plants for their sap, damaging the bark, and also eats fruit
LIFESPAN	Queens 1 year; workers up to 4 weeks

ANIMAL FACTS

European hornets appear threatening partly because of their sound, but they will avoid confrontation if possible. Problems with people often arise because the hornets may construct their nest within the roof space of a home, rather than inside a tree. Besides increasing the likelihood of hornets gaining access to living areas, the insects' droppings can create an unpleasant odour. Hornets are drawn to lights at night, causing further problems in domestic surroundings.

The queen (right) is larger than the workers

WHERE IN THE WORLD?

Southern England and Scandinavia to eastern Asia. Introduced originally to New York about 1840, and now found east of the Mississippi, continuing to spread westwards.

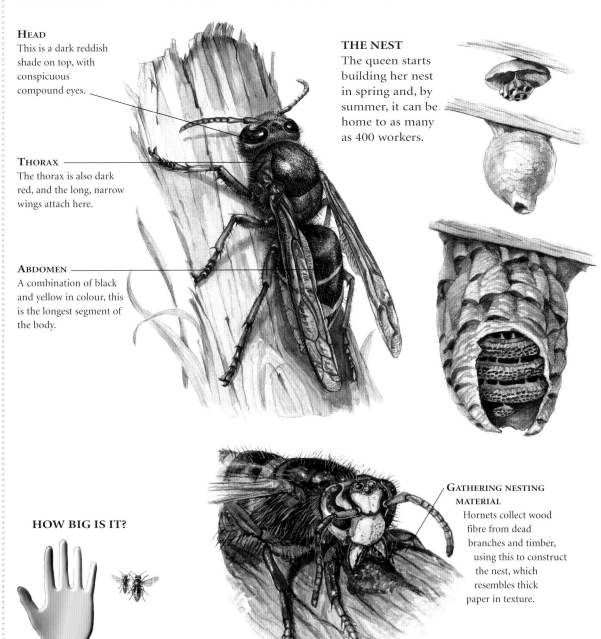

HEAD
This is a dark reddish shade on top, with conspicuous compound eyes.

THORAX
The thorax is also dark red, and the long, narrow wings attach here.

ABDOMEN
A combination of black and yellow in colour, this is the longest segment of the body.

THE NEST
The queen starts building her nest in spring and, by summer, it can be home to as many as 400 workers.

GATHERING NESTING MATERIAL
Hornets collect wood fibre from dead branches and timber, using this to construct the nest, which resembles thick paper in texture.

HOW BIG IS IT?

255

Common Wasp

• ORDER • Hymenoptera **• FAMILY •** Vespidae **• SPECIES •** *Vespula vulgaris*

These highly social wasps live in colonies of up to 10,000 individuals. They are often drawn to picnics, not being easily deterred from seeking food.

VITAL STATISTICS

LENGTH	Workers 1.9cm (0.74in); queen around 3.5cm (1.4in)
SEXUAL MATURITY	After pupation; only young queens overwinter
NUMBER OF EGGS	Queens lay thousands of eggs
DEVELOPMENTAL PERIOD	30 days from egg to adult
HABITAT	Gardens, parks and lightly wooded areas
DIET	Hunts other insects, carrying them back to the nest, raids bees' nests, eats fruit and also scavenges
LIFESPAN	Queens 1 year; workers up to 4 weeks

ANIMAL FACTS

The wasps' nest is constructed from wood pulp mixed with saliva, and the structure hardens as it dries out. Wasps are aggressive insects by nature, and will sting without hesitation. Unlike bees, they do not die after one sting, but can sting repeatedly. Their venom contains a chemical messenger called a pheromone, which is wafted on air currents. Other wasps in the area recognize this as a sign of danger, making them more likely to sting.

A queen wasp (right) with a worker (left)

WHERE IN THE WORLD?

Common throughout Europe during the warmer months of the year, but most prevalent in late summer and early autumn. Introduced to New Zealand and Australia.

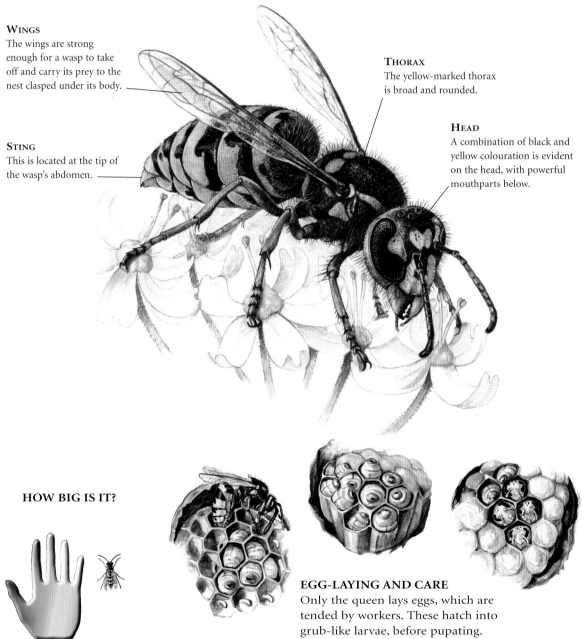

WINGS
The wings are strong enough for a wasp to take off and carry its prey to the nest clasped under its body.

STING
This is located at the tip of the wasp's abdomen.

THORAX
The yellow-marked thorax is broad and rounded.

HEAD
A combination of black and yellow colouration is evident on the head, with powerful mouthparts below.

HOW BIG IS IT?

EGG-LAYING AND CARE
Only the queen lays eggs, which are tended by workers. These hatch into grub-like larvae, before pupating.

Cape Hyrax

VITAL STATISTICS

WEIGHT	1.8–5.4kg (4–12lb)
LENGTH	44–54cm (17–21in)
SEXUAL MATURITY	After 16 months
GESTATION PERIOD	210–235 days
NUMBER OF OFFSPRING	1–4; births of the females in a group are synchronized, occurring within a period of 3 weeks; weaning occurs after 70 days
DIET	Herbivorous, grazing mainly on grass
LIFESPAN	Up to 12 years; females live longer than males

ANIMAL FACTS

These mammals live in groups of up to seven related females. They will huddle together to keep warm, because they are not able to regulate their body temperature as effectively as most mammals. Cape hyraxes will also bask in the sun as a way of raising their body temperature. Males are territorial and, in common with other members of the family, have testes that are retained inside the body.

Although it looks like a member of the rodent family, the Cape hyrax is actually more closely related to elephants, being descended from larger ancestors.

WHERE IN THE WORLD?

In rocky areas, ranging across much of Africa, particularly in the mountainous parts of the Sahara and Namib deserts, extending eastwards to the Arabian Peninsula.

FACIAL FEATURES
The rounded ears are set low and the nose is black. The eyes are dark, surrounded by pale fur.

LONG HAIRS
Distributed randomly over the body, these long hairs resemble whiskers and have a similar sensory function.

TEETH
The incisors are enlarged, being developed into small tusks, projected over the lower lips.

HIND FEET
These are equipped with a sharp inner claw.

HOW BIG IS IT?

DANGER OVERHEAD

Living in rocky areas means that these mammals must climb well. They are vulnerable to birds of prey from overhead.

Cape hyraxes have a very distinctive brown scent gland on their backs

Termite

VITAL STATISTICS

LENGTH	0.4–2cm (0.15–0.78in)
SEXUAL MATURITY	Old queens will be replaced, with some colonies being over 100 years old
NUMBER OF EGGS	Queens may lay 2000 eggs daily
DEVELOPMENT	Larvae moult 5 times, then pupate and emerge as adults
HABITAT	Areas where wood is available, including savanna
DIET	Cellulose in plant matter
LIFESPAN	Queens 10–25 years; other colony members up to a few months

ANIMAL FACTS

The exact number of termite species that exist is unknown. It may well be over 4000, with scientists having currently classified only some 2600 in total. By helping to break down dead plant matter, termites are beneficial, but they can be economically damaging too, destroying buildings and crops. In locations where they are prevalent, other building options such as steel are frequently used instead of wood. Some trees contain naturally occurring chemicals that protect them from attacks by termites.

These insects live in large colonies comprising up to several million individuals. Although sometimes called white ants, termites are actually quite distinct from ants.

WHERE IN THE WORLD?

Found in warmer areas, occurring between the latitudes of 50°N and 50°S, being most common in the Mediterranean and tropical forests.

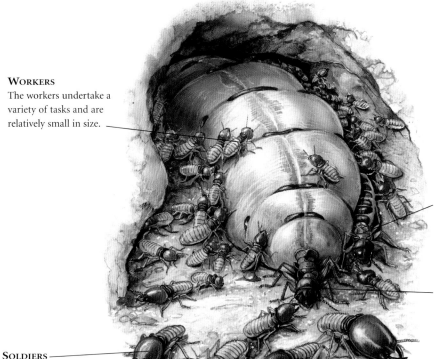

WORKERS
The workers undertake a variety of tasks and are relatively small in size.

QUEEN AND KING
The queen develops into an egg-laying machine after mating. The king is significantly smaller.

ABDOMEN
The queen's head and thorax are inconspicuous compared with her enormous white abdomen.

SOLDIERS
The fearsome mouthparts and large heads of the soldier ants help them defend the colony.

HOW BIG IS IT?

VENTILATION AND HEAT EXCHANGE

Termite mounds can measure up to 9m (30ft) high in wooded areas, but rarely exceed 3m (10ft) on the savanna.

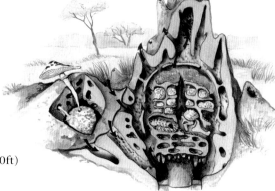

Snowshoe Hare

• ORDER • Lagomorpha • FAMILY • Leporidae • SPECIES • *Lepus americanus*

VITAL STATISTICS

WEIGHT	0.9–1.8kg (2–4lb)
LENGTH	41–51cm (16–20in)
SEXUAL MATURITY	1 year
GESTATION PERIOD	36–40 days; breeds from mid-March to August
NUMBER OF OFFSPRING	1–7, typically 3; weaning occurs by 28 days; females may have up to 4 litters per year
DIET	Herbivorous, eating grass, herbs and bark
LIFESPAN	Up to 5 years, although many die in their first year

ANIMAL FACTS

The population of these hares undergoes distinctive cyclical fluctuations. Their numbers build up over the course of a decade, as do those of their predators (such as the snowy owl), before suddenly crashing. They then start increasing again, to the point at which there are 600 hares per square kilometre (0.39 square miles). Unlike many of their relatives, their young are born fully developed, with their eyes open, and they can run almost immediately. Females may mate again the day after giving birth.

The contrast between the winter coat (left) and summer coat (right) is shown here

Their appearance helps these hares to blend into the landscape, and they can also sprint at speeds of up to 43kph (27mph) to escape predators.

WHERE IN THE WORLD?

Across northern North America (with its southerly range extending to California and New Mexico), around the Great Lakes and reaching North Carolina in the east.

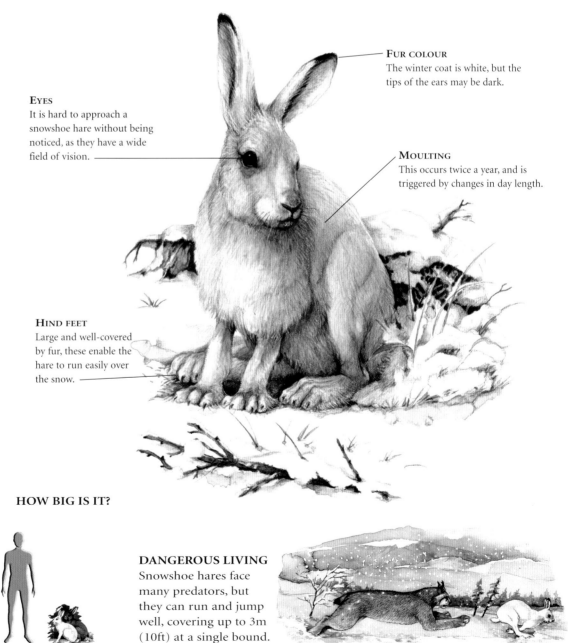

FUR COLOUR
The winter coat is white, but the tips of the ears may be dark.

EYES
It is hard to approach a snowshoe hare without being noticed, as they have a wide field of vision.

MOULTING
This occurs twice a year, and is triggered by changes in day length.

HIND FEET
Large and well-covered by fur, these enable the hare to run easily over the snow.

HOW BIG IS IT?

DANGEROUS LIVING
Snowshoe hares face many predators, but they can run and jump well, covering up to 3m (10ft) at a single bound.

Black-Tailed Jackrabbit

• ORDER • Lagomorpha • FAMILY • Leporidae • SPECIES • *Lepus californicus*

VITAL STATISTICS

WEIGHT	2.2–5.5kg (5–12lb); females are heavier
LENGTH	46–76cm (18–30in)
SEXUAL MATURITY	May be mature by 7 months, but do not breed until the following year
GESTATION PERIOD	41–47 days
NUMBER OF OFFSPRING	1–6, typically 3; weaning occurs by 28 days; females may have up to 6 litters per year
DIET	Herbivorous, eating grass, herbs and twigs
LIFESPAN	Up to 5 years, although many die in their first year

ANIMAL FACTS

Living in relatively open country poses particular dangers to a species like the black-tailed jackrabbit, making it an obvious target for a host of predators. These hares therefore tend to rest during the day, becoming active towards dusk. Although they are solitary by nature, jackrabbits tend to feed in groups. They can run at speeds of up to 72kph (45mph) and are able to jump as far as 6m (19ft) at a single bound.

The ears of the black-tailed jackrabbit are nearly 11cm (4.25in) long

This desert-dwelling species is a true hare. It is able to twist and turn at speed, and can even swim away from danger.

WHERE IN THE WORLD?

Western and central USA, east to Texas and southwards into northern Mexico as well as Baja California. Introduced to Kentucky, New Jersey and Nantucket Island.

EYES
Eyesight is important for alerting these lagomorphs to potential danger.

EARS
Sound travels over long distances in the desert, and the large ears help detect noises. They also help the hare to stay cool.

COLOURATION
Brownish-black upperparts and white underparts.

HIND LEGS
These are strong and powerful, enabling the hare to run quickly.

RECOGNITION
The distinctive feature of this species is the black stripe extending down the tail. They are very wary by nature.

HOW BIG IS IT?

FORMS
These jackrabbits do not burrow, but instead, rest in holes, known as forms, that they excavate in the ground.

Hare

VITAL STATISTICS

WEIGHT	3–5kg (6.6–11lb)
LENGTH	61–75cm (24–30in)
SEXUAL MATURITY	8 months
GESTATION PERIOD	30–40 days; breeds in late winter and mid-summer
NUMBER OF OFFSPRING	1–8, typically 4; weaning at 30 days; females may have 2–4 litters per year
DIET	Herbivorous, eating grass, herbs and twigs; can be a crop pest
LIFESPAN	Up to 10 years

ANIMAL FACTS

Hares do not live in burrows, but rest in hollows in the ground. Rather than risk having all her offspring killed by a predator, the female hare places them at different spots within an area. Called leverets, the young are born in an advanced state of development, covered in fur. The appetites of these hares are such that three are said to eat as much as a sheep, making them unpopular with farmers, especially as they can breed so fast.

Hares are always alert and they rely on speed to escape danger

These hares face many dangers, and their senses are acute. They can run at speeds of up to 60kph (35mph), changing direction frequently to escape pursuing predators.

WHERE IN THE WORLD?

Occurs across Europe, including the British Isles, the Arabian Peninsula and into Asia. Introduced elsewhere including the USA, Canada, Argentina and Australia.

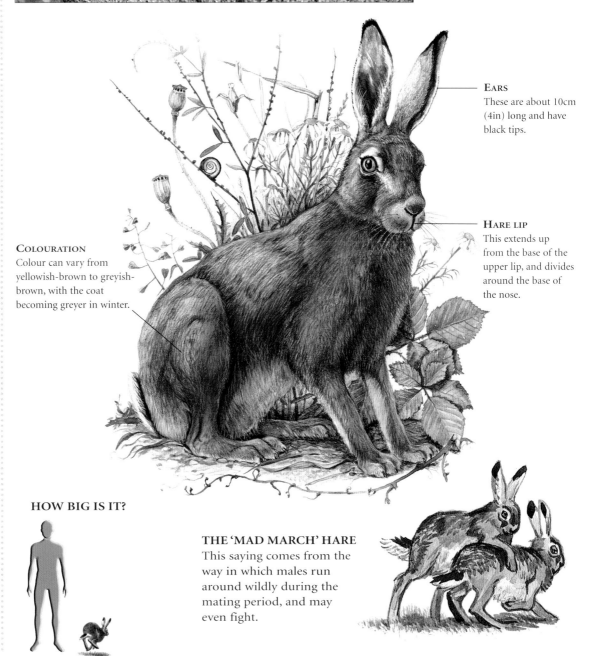

COLOURATION
Colour can vary from yellowish-brown to greyish-brown, with the coat becoming greyer in winter.

EARS
These are about 10cm (4in) long and have black tips.

HARE LIP
This extends up from the base of the upper lip, and divides around the base of the nose.

HOW BIG IS IT?

THE 'MAD MARCH' HARE
This saying comes from the way in which males run around wildly during the mating period, and may even fight.

European Rabbit

• ORDER • Lagomorpha **• FAMILY** • Leporidae **• SPECIES** • *Oryctolagus cuniculus*

VITAL STATISTICS

WEIGHT	1.5–2.5kg (3–5.5lb)
LENGTH	38–50cm (15–20in)
SEXUAL MATURITY	About 8 months
GESTATION PERIOD	30–35 days; breeds through much of the year, especially in spring
NUMBER OF OFFSPRING	1–14, typically 6; weaning at 28 days; females may have 2–3 litters per year
DIET	Herbivorous, eating grass, herbs and twigs
LIFESPAN	Up to 9 years

ANIMAL FACTS

The adaptable nature of rabbits has led to them becoming significant pests in some areas. They are often numerous in sandy localities, where they can tunnel easily into the ground to build their warrens. When they were exposed to the deadly disease myxomatosis, however – spread by rabbit fleas – the survivors tended to move out of their burrows and spend longer above ground. Social by nature, rabbits communicate with each other by banging with their feet. They also scream if they experience pain.

Rabbits are sometimes called cottontails, because their white tails look like cotton balls

Rabbits depend on microbes in their intestinal tract to digest their food, and they also eat their own droppings to absorb the nutrients.

WHERE IN THE WORLD?

Spread across Europe from the Iberian Peninsula and southern France. Introduced to the British Isles after 1066, and many other countries worldwide, including Australia.

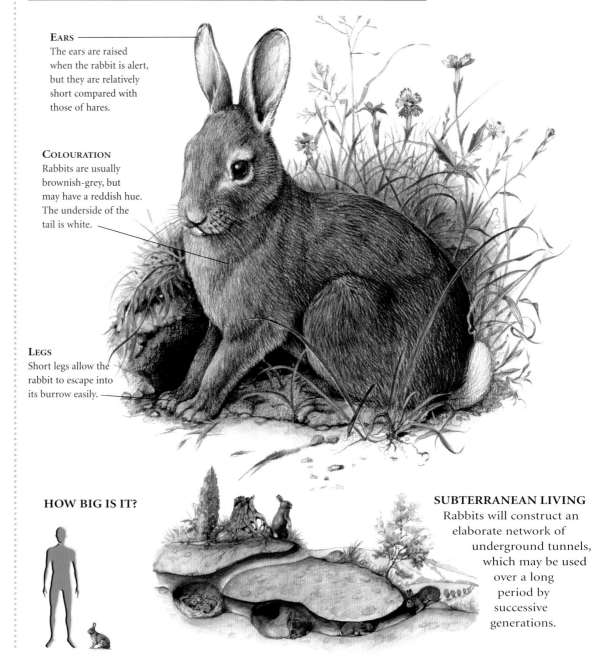

EARS
The ears are raised when the rabbit is alert, but they are relatively short compared with those of hares.

COLOURATION
Rabbits are usually brownish-grey, but may have a reddish hue. The underside of the tail is white.

LEGS
Short legs allow the rabbit to escape into its burrow easily.

HOW BIG IS IT?

SUBTERRANEAN LIVING
Rabbits will construct an elaborate network of underground tunnels, which may be used over a long period by successive generations.

262

Plateau Pika

VITAL STATISTICS

WEIGHT	0.1–0.2kg (0.2–0.4lb)
LENGTH	12–25cm (5–10in)
SEXUAL MATURITY	About 8 months
GESTATION PERIOD	21–24 days; females produce litters every 3 weeks in the summer
NUMBER OF OFFSPRING	1–8, typically 6; weaning at 21 days
DIET	Herbivorous, eating grass, herbs, flowers and seeds; may make hay
LIFESPAN	Can be up to 2.5 years, but most live no more than 3.5 months

ANIMAL FACTS

Highly social by nature, plateau pikas live in groups consisting of a pair with up to 10 offspring from several litters. They inhabit a network of inter-connecting burrows, with tunnels extending back up to 8m (26ft) and with a range of entrances. These may sometimes be shared with other animals, including snowfinches. Above ground in particular, plateau pikas are vocal – with members of the group keeping in touch with each other and warning of any possible danger.

Living and staying close to their network of tunnels affords these pikas protection from predators

Pikas are relatives of rabbits, found at high altitudes throughout northern areas. Their name comes from an Asiatic word which describes their squeaking call.

WHERE IN THE WORLD?

Plateau pikas are found at relatively high altitudes, inhabiting the meadows and steppe areas of the Tibetan Plateau, in the Chang Taung region of China.

COLOURATION
Upperparts are brown to tan in colour, and underparts are greyish-whitish.

NOSE
Dark colouration here, extending around the lips, typifies this species.

APPEARANCE
Pikas are short-legged and stocky, and do not have a tail. The sexes are indistinguishable by sight.

PAWS
These are quite broad and end in small, dark claws.

MAKING HAY
Plateau pikas collect vegetation which they leave to dry, transforming it into hay to sustain them over the bitterly cold winter.

HOW BIG IS IT?

Great White Shark

• ORDER • Lamniformes • FAMILY • Lamnidae • SPECIES • *Carcharodon carcharias*

VITAL STATISTICS

WEIGHT	2250–3180kg (5000–7000lb)
LENGTH	5.5–6.5m (18–21ft)
SEXUAL MATURITY	Females from 4m (13ft) long, typically at 12–14 years; males from 3.5m (11.5ft), 9–10 years
GESTATION PERIOD	1 year
NUMBER OF OFFSPRING	8–9, but can be up to 14
DIET	Predatory, hunting rays, smaller sharks, dolphins, seals, squid and bony fish; larger individuals prefer mammalian prey
LIFESPAN	40–60 years, possibly longer

ANIMAL FACTS

Although the great white shark is well known as the largest predatory fish alive, aspects of its life remain unclear. There are indications that its predatory nature sets in before birth, with young sharks destroying other eggs developing in their mother's body. Great whites have even been found with teeth in their stomachs that have been swallowed prior to birth. Newborn pups measure about 1.37m (54in).

Great whites have immensely powerful jaws

The most notorious of all sharks, the great white is a fearsome predator. It is usually solitary, but can be encountered in pairs or larger groups on occasion.

WHERE IN THE WORLD?

Roams throughout the world, occurring in coastal waters, especially in temperate areas. Prevalent around Australia and South Africa, as well as off the Californian coast.

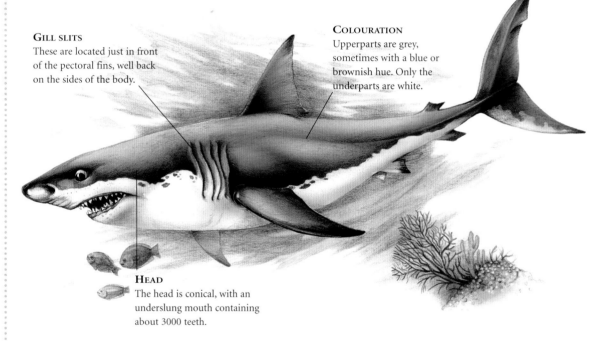

GILL SLITS
These are located just in front of the pectoral fins, well back on the sides of the body.

COLOURATION
Upperparts are grey, sometimes with a blue or brownish hue. Only the underparts are white.

HEAD
The head is conical, with an underslung mouth containing about 3000 teeth.

REPLACEMENT TEETH

These sharks have rows of sharp teeth. When a tooth breaks or is lost, another replaces it.

HOW BIG IS IT?

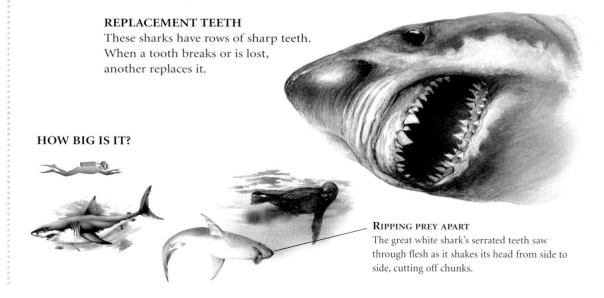

RIPPING PREY APART
The great white shark's serrated teeth saw through flesh as it shakes its head from side to side, cutting off chunks.

Common Blue Butterfly

• **ORDER** • Lepidoptera • **FAMILY** • Lycaenidae • **SPECIES** • *Polyommatus icarus*

VITAL STATISTICS

LENGTH	Caterpillars reach 1cm (0.4in) long; wingspan of butterflies averages 3.5cm (1.4in)
SEXUAL MATURITY	After pupation
EGG-LAYING	Eggs laid individually
DEVELOPMENTAL PERIOD	About 6 weeks from egg to adult; hatching takes 1 week and pupation lasts 2 weeks
HABITAT	Meadows, grassland, heaths and woodland clearings
DIET	Caterpillars feed on trefoils and white clover; butterflies drink nectar
LIFESPAN	Butterflies live for about 21 days

ANIMAL FACTS

The lifecycle of the common blue butterfly is unusual, because the slug-like caterpillar may overwinter in this state. It will produce a sweet substance called honeydew, which ants find attractive. In southern parts of its range, two generations of common blues may hatch in the summer, but in northern areas, there will only be one.

Adult butterflies uncurl their proboscis when feeding, sucking up nectar

This is the most numerous blue butterfly occurring in Europe, found as far north as Orkney and the Outer Hebrides off the Scottish mainland.

WHERE IN THE WORLD?

Throughout Europe, extending into temperate parts of Asia and across the Mediterranean Sea to North Africa.

LIFECYCLE

Like other butterflies, the female lays eggs, which hatch into larvae, described as caterpillars. They browse on vegetation, growing in size before becoming pupae, during which time they appear essentially inert. Within the chrysalis though, radical changes are taking place, as is apparent when the pupa splits open and the adult butterfly emerges.

COLOURATION
Only the males are primarily blue.

BORDER
There is a thin white stripe running right around the edges of the wings.

EGG-LAYING
Bird's foot trefoil, with its distinctive yellow flowers, is the plant favoured for egg-laying.

EGGS
These are laid individually on the plant's fresh growth.

HOW BIG IS IT?

Purple Emperor

• ORDER • Lepidoptera • FAMILY • Nymphalidae • SPECIES • *Apatura iris*

The purple emperor is hard to observe, living in the trees rather than feeding on the ground. It is the largest of Britain's woodland butterflies.

VITAL STATISTICS

LENGTH	Wingspan averages 8cm (3in)
SEXUAL MATURITY	After pupation
EGG-LAYING	Eggs are laid individually
DEVELOPMENTAL PERIOD	Hatching occurs in August, and caterpillars overwinter, completing their lifecycle in the summer
HABITAT	Woodland; males may have display areas
DIET	Caterpillars feed on sallow and willow at night; females especially feed in trees, but males may sometimes land on people to drink sweat
LIFESPAN	Butterflies live for about 28 days

ANIMAL FACTS

These butterflies are most likely to be seen between mid-June and mid-August. It seems that males have a particularly strong sense of smell, which may draw them to carrion as well as dung, on which they feed, and even melting road tar, which is likely to have fatal consequences. Purple emperors also seek out aphids in order to feed on the honeydew (a sugary secretion) that aphids produce. Their proboscises are an unusual bright shade of yellow.

WHERE IN THE WORLD?

Occurs in central Europe, extending north to central southern parts of England, Demark, southern Sweden and Estonia. South to Greece and the northern Iberian Peninsula.

WINGS
The purple iridescence is apparent only in males, on the central area of the wings.

OCELLI
These circular areas on the wings are a deterrent to would-be predators, and resemble eyes.

ANTENNAE
Attached to the top of the head, these provide sensory information.

WING MARKINGS
Stripes radiate from the abdomen, breaking up into a more random series of spots.

LESSER SPECIES
This is the lesser species (*A. ilia*), which also occurs in central Europe, but not the British Isles.

HOW BIG IS IT?

EGG-LAYING
Females seek out willows and sallows onto which they lay their eggs. Their caterpillars are predominantly green, with a pair of horns.

Monarch Butterfly

• **ORDER** • Lepidoptera • **FAMILY** • Nymphalidae • **SPECIES** • *Danaus plexippus*

VITAL STATISTICS

LENGTH	Wingspan may reach about 10cm (4in)
SEXUAL MATURITY	After pupation
EGG-LAYING	Eggs are laid individually
DEVELOPMENTAL PERIOD	Hatching takes 4 days; caterpillars then pupate after 2 weeks; butterflies emerge after a similar interval
HABITAT	Open country and woodland
DIET	Caterpillars feed on milkweed; butterflies extract nectar from flowers
LIFESPAN	Butterflies live for 2–8 weeks if emerging in the early summer

ANIMAL FACTS

Beginning in August until the first frosts of autumn, these butterflies form swarms and head south to their wintering grounds in Mexico or parts of California, travelling up to 4500km (2800 miles) in two months. Their lifespan is dramatically prolonged, up to seven months or more, allowing them to complete the journey, and then head back north again. Monarchs are great wanderers, and have even been known to cross the Atlantic and reach Europe.

Weighing less than 1g (0.03oz), this butterfly undertakes one of the most spectacular migratory journeys, made even more remarkable by the perceived frailty of this insect.

WHERE IN THE WORLD?

Occurs across much of North America, down to the Amazon region of South America. Also found in various parts of Europe, plus Australia and New Zealand.

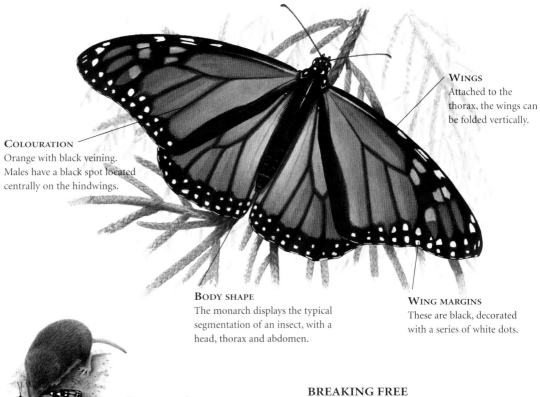

COLOURATION
Orange with black veining. Males have a black spot located centrally on the hindwings.

WINGS
Attached to the thorax, the wings can be folded vertically.

BODY SHAPE
The monarch displays the typical segmentation of an insect, with a head, thorax and abdomen.

WING MARGINS
These are black, decorated with a series of white dots.

BAD EATING!
The caterpillars feed on milkweed, and the toxins from this plant stay in the body of the adult butterflies, making them unpalatable.

BREAKING FREE
A silk pad is spun by the caterpillar to attach itself to the underside of a leaf or branch at the start of the pupation process. The butterfly must inflate its wings before being able to fly.

HOW BIG IS IT?

Morpho Butterfly

• ORDER • Lepidoptera • FAMILY • Nymphalidae • SPECIES • *Morpho*

VITAL STATISTICS

LENGTH	Wingspan 7.5cm–20cm (3in–8in), depending on species
SEXUAL MATURITY	After pupation
EGGS	Pale green in colour
DEVELOPMENTAL PERIOD	About 19.5 weeks from egg to adult
HABITAT	Tropical forests
DIET	Caterpillars eat members of the leguminous (pea) family; butterflies feed on nectar and fruit juice
LIFESPAN	Butterflies live for 4 weeks

ANIMAL FACTS

The way in which the wing scales of morpho butterflies create their unique appearance has attracted interest from those working in fields as diverse as anti-counterfeiting technology and fabric design. At least one species shows the more traditional pattern of iridescence, however, and a few are pure white. These butterflies are well-protected against predators thanks to the accumulation of toxic compounds in their bodies, which they acquire when feeding on plants as caterpillars.

Over 80 species of morpho butterfly exist, often in metallic shades of blue or green. Their colour is an effect of the light, resulting from iridescence.

WHERE IN THE WORLD?

Ranges from Mexico through Central America to South America, down to Brazil. They are butterflies of the forest, often seen fluttering in forest clearings.

APPEARANCE
The even colouration is thought to be due in part to the diamond-like arrangement of the scales covering the wings.

SHINY SURFACE
Iridescence often varies significantly according to the viewing angle, but generally not in these butterflies.

BODY
This is dark in colour, and free from iridescence.

PATTERNING
Markings of this type are not seen in all species.

HOW BIG IS IT?

CAMOUFLAGE
The brown colouration and patterning on the closed wings helps these butterflies blend into the background.

Red Admiral Butterfly

• **ORDER** • Lepidoptera • **FAMILY** • Nymphalidae • **SPECIES** • *Vanessa atalanta*

These butterflies are among the first to be seen in the spring, often appearing as early as March in Britain after their winter hibernation.

VITAL STATISTICS

LENGTH	Wingspan up to 7.5cm (3in)
SEXUAL MATURITY	After pupation
EGGS	Females can lay 100 eggs per day
DEVELOPMENTAL PERIOD	From egg to chrysalis takes about 4 weeks; butterfly emerges 2–3 weeks later
HABITAT	Open, sunny areas, including gardens
DIET	Caterpillars feed on nettles; butterflies feed on nectar from plants like sedum, asters and buddleia, and rotting fruit
LIFESPAN	Butterflies live for 4 weeks– 10 months

WHERE IN THE WORLD?

Ranges from Europe into Asia, North Africa, the Azores and Mediterranean islands. Also occurs from Canada to Guatemala, as well as Hawaii and New Zealand.

ANIMAL FACTS

The red admiral ranks among the most conspicuous garden butterflies, being both bold and territorial by nature. It is common for them to fly long distances, with the British population being boosted each year by the appearance of migrants through the warmer months. Generally two generations will be produced over the summer and in the autumn survivors will seek snug, dry localities where they can hibernate until the following spring. During warm spells, they may even emerge to feed.

FOOD PLANT
Females lay their eggs on nettles of the genus *Urtica*, as here; hop plants and pellitory are alternatives.

WING OUTLINES
The edges of the red admiral's wings are naturally indented.

BANDING
Orange edging is present on the rear of the hindwings, with similarly coloured banding across the forewings.

BODY
This is quite stout and blackish in colour.

Pupae of red admiral caterpillars are very distinctive in appearance.

BREEDING CYCLE
A magnified view of the egg, partially protected by being laid on a stinging nettle.

The caterpillar is able to eat the leaves, nibbling at the edges with its strong mouthparts. When not feeding, it ties the edges together to disguise its presence.

HOW BIG IS IT?

Queen Alexandra's Birdwing

• ORDER • Lepidoptera • FAMILY • Papilionidae • SPECIES • *Ornithoptera alexandrae*

VITAL STATISTICS

LENGTH	Body 7.5cm (3in); wingspan 28cm (11in)
SEXUAL MATURITY	After pupation
EGGS	Spherical, laid individually under vine leaves
DEVELOPMENTAL PERIOD	Egg to adult can take 4 months
HABITAT	Rainforest of Oro province, Papua New Guinea
DIET	Caterpillars feed on climbing vines; butterflies feed on nectar
LIFESPAN	Butterflies can live for 12 weeks

ANIMAL FACTS

It is not just the size of these butterflies that explains why they are called birdwings. This name also reflects their lifestyle, as they spend much of their time in the forest canopy, feeding on the flowers growing there. They are actually important pollinators of these plants. Caterpillars are largely protected from predation by feeding on poisonous vines, and retaining the deadly chemicals in their bodies. Female butterflies are far less colourful than males, usually brown with cream spots.

These spectacular, brightly coloured butterflies can be the size of small birds, making them the largest of all the world's 17,500 species.

WHERE IN THE WORLD?

Range extends from India and Southeast Asia down via Papua New Guinea and the Solomon Islands to northeastern Australia.

COLOURATION
Striking bright patterning is apparent on the wings of the male butterflies.

EYES
Large compound eyes are situated on the sides of the butterfly's head.

THE HEAD IN CLOSE-UP
The formidable mouthparts of the caterpillar, which also has red antennae and protective spines.

BODY
This is often colourful, particularly the abdomen, which is yellowish.

LEGS
Three pairs of legs are attached to the thorax. The front pair are articulated to extend in front of the body.

HOW BIG IS IT?

TRADE THREAT
These large butterflies used to be hunted for collectors, and this trade threatened their survival, but now they are being bred on butterfly farms. This has helped to safeguard their future and provides local employment, too.

Western Tiger Swallowtail Butterfly

• ORDER • Lepidoptera • FAMILY • Papilionidae • SPECIES • *Papilio rutulus*

VITAL STATISTICS

LENGTH	Wingspan can be 10cm (4in)
SEXUAL MATURITY	After pupation
EGGS	Females may lay up to 100 eggs each
DEVELOPMENTAL PERIOD	Hatching takes around 4 days; lifecycle depends on locality
HABITAT	Woodland areas, often at higher elevations
DIET	Caterpillars eat leaves of trees and shrubs; butterflies feed on nectar from a range of flowers
LIFESPAN	Adult butterflies live for 4–6 weeks

ANIMAL FACTS

Western swallowtails are seen between February and July, depending on the locality. Caterpillars develop on leaves, which they curl up to hide their bodies. They are protected by an organ called the osmeterium behind the head, which emits a foul smell to deter predators. In northern areas, there may be just one generation annually, but in the south, there can be three.

Caterpillars moult five times before pupating

Ranking as one of North America's largest butterflies, this species is also one of the most common in western parts of the continent.

WHERE IN THE WORLD?

Ranges from British Columbia and North Dakota in the USA, southwards down to Baja California in the west and Mexico to the east.

WINGS
The projections along the rear edge of the wings are said to resemble the tail feathers of a swallow.

EGGS
Eggs are laid individually on the underside of the leaves of food plants such as willow, ash, wild cherry, aspen and cottonwood.

CATERPILLAR
Caterpillars are mainly green with red markings, which helps conceal their presence.

HEAD COLOURATION
The pale yellow colour of the head extends back on to the thorax.

HOW BIG IS IT?

271

Apollo Butterfly

• **ORDER** • Lepidoptera • **FAMILY** • Papilionidae • **SPECIES** • *Parnassius apollo*

VITAL STATISTICS

LENGTH	Wingspan up to 9cm (3.5in)
SEXUAL MATURITY	After pupation; 1 brood annually
EGGS	Deposited near the food plant; female is prevented from mating again by the male's sphragus, which he attaches to her abdomen
DEVELOPMENTAL PERIOD	Overwinter as eggs; larvae hatch in spring
HABITAT	Open country between 500–2400m (1640–7875ft)
DIET	Caterpillars eat stonecrop; butterflies feed on nectar
LIFESPAN	Butterflies live for 4–6 weeks

ANIMAL FACTS

The markings and colour of these butterflies varies over their wide range, with individual populations having become quite isolated. It was thought that the decline of these butterflies in parts of Scandinavia was due to acid rain, but studies have shown this is unlikely. A disease may have been responsible, or there may be a link to stonecrop, the caterpillar's food source.

Spots appear as eyes, even when the wings are closed

Numbers of this butterfly of meadows and mountain pastures have recently plummeted in some parts of its range, for reasons that are unclear.

WHERE IN THE WORLD?

Scattered across Europe, from Scandinavia via the Alps to southern Europe, ranging from Spain to the Balkans and Greece. Also present throughout Italy to Sicily.

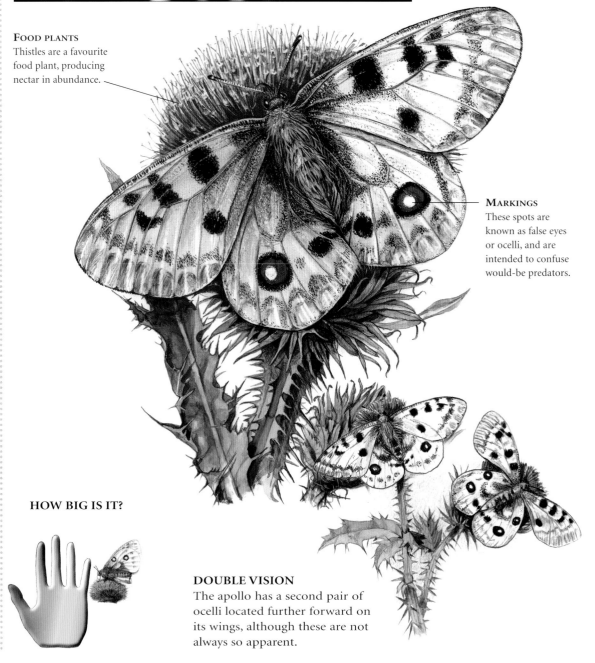

FOOD PLANTS
Thistles are a favourite food plant, producing nectar in abundance.

MARKINGS
These spots are known as false eyes or ocelli, and are intended to confuse would-be predators.

HOW BIG IS IT?

DOUBLE VISION
The apollo has a second pair of ocelli located further forward on its wings, although these are not always so apparent.

Death's Head Hawkmoth

• **ORDER** • Lepidoptera • **FAMILY** • Saturniidae • **SPECIES** • *Acherontia atropos*

This moth was a creature to be feared, not just because of its skull emblem, but also because it can make a menacing hissing sound.

VITAL STATISTICS

LENGTH	Wingspan up to 12cm (4.8in)
SEXUAL MATURITY	After pupation
EGGS	Laid individually on the underside of the food plant's leaves
DEVELOPMENTAL PERIOD	Breed throughout the year; larvae are relatively immobile, but can inflict a painful bite
HABITAT	Dry, sunny open country
DIET	Caterpillars eat solanaceaous plants such as potato; moths drink juices of ripe fruit and honey
LIFESPAN	Moths live for 2–3 weeks

ANIMAL FACTS

This moth has a remarkable ability to gain access to bees' nests undetected. They actually have a scent that bees recognize as similar to their own, and they move in a similar way to bees in these surroundings. If threatened, they utter their shrieking calls, pushing air out through their proboscis, and will generate an unpleasant odour from special glands located on the abdomen. Individuals may breed in Europe over the summer, and occasionally reach as far north as Scandinavia.

WHERE IN THE WORLD?

Occurs mainly in tropical regions of Africa, extending northwards to the Mediterranean. Sometimes seen as a summer migrant in parts of central and northern Europe.

WINGS
Dark patterning on the wings breaks up the moth's outline, providing camouflage.

ABDOMEN
Yellow and black banding is apparent on the abdomen.

HEAD
This part of the body is dark in colour, with short sensory antennae.

DEATH MASK
The skull-like pattern on the thorax accounts for the name of this moth.

AT REST
The moth keeps its wings folded by the sides of its body when resting during the day.

HOW BIG IS IT?

STEALING FOOD
These moths fly at night, seeking to invade bees' nests under cover of darkness and feed on the honey there.

Emperor Moth

• **ORDER** • Lepidoptera • **FAMILY** • Saturniidae • **SPECIES** • *Pavonia pavonia*

VITAL STATISTICS

LENGTH	Wingspan up to 6cm (2.4in)
SEXUAL MATURITY	After pupation
EGGS	Laid in clusters around the caterpillar's food plant
DEVELOPMENTAL PERIOD	Overwinter as pupae; moths hatch in the spring; lifecycle takes roughly 10 months
HABITAT	Open country, particularly moorland
DIET	Caterpillars eat heather, blackthorn and bramble; moths do not feed
LIFESPAN	Moths live for 2 weeks

ANIMAL FACTS

Protected by its eye spots, the male emperor moth spends its days flying in search of potential mates, which become active at dusk. Females are much duller in colour, being primarily grey. One of the key features that identifies these insects as moths rather than butterflies is the appearance of their antennae, which do not have a swollen club-like ending, but instead are fringed. These help males to detect the minute traces of the chemical attractant released by the female.

Unlike many moths, the male emperor is brightly coloured, more closely resembling a butterfly. This relates to its lifestyle, as it flies during the day.

WHERE IN THE WORLD?

Occurs widely, ranging from Ireland to Siberia, and from Scandinavia and northern Russia down to northern parts of Spain, the Alps, Slovakia and the Caucasus.

EYE SPOTS
The eye spots make the wings look rather like a face.

WINGS
Only males have the orange hind wings, decorated with eye spots.

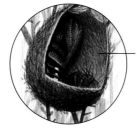

PUPA
Development of the moth takes place within a pupal case.

NEWLY-HATCHED LARVAE
Caterpillars at this stage are dark in colour, and relatively inconspicuous.

HOW BIG IS IT?

GROWING UP

Mature caterpillars before pupation are green, with black hoops and hairs covering the body. Heather is a favoured food plant.

Giant Elephant Shrew

• **ORDER** • Macroscelidea • **FAMILY** • Macroscelididae • **SPECIES** •*Rhynchocyon cirnei*

The term 'giant' is relative, given the size of this elephant shrew, although it is regarded as a distant relative of the elephant.

VITAL STATISTICS

WEIGHT	0.4–0.6kg (0.9–1.3lb)
LENGTH	41–56cm (16–22in) overall; tail is almost as long as the body
SEXUAL MATURITY	Probably around 6 months
GESTATION PERIOD	About 40 days
NUMBER OF OFFSPRING	1; weaning occurs at 28 days; females may have 4–5 litters per year, and can be pregnant and lactate simultaneously
DIET	Mainly insectivorous, feeding on invertebrates such as ants and termites
LIFESPAN	4–5 years

ANIMAL FACTS

Marking their territories is an important aspect of social communication in these elephant shrews. They have a special gland at the base of the tail for this purpose. Living in pairs or family groups, they are noisy by nature, squeaking regularly to stay in touch. At any sign of danger, an elephant shrew will slap down its tail, creating an instantly recognizable signal to other members of the group. They tend to be active during the day, rather than at night.

Scent marking

WHERE IN THE WORLD?

Occurs in central, eastern and southeastern parts of Africa, in Uganda, Tanzania, Zaire and the Democratic Republic of the Congo down to Mozambique, Zambia and Malawi.

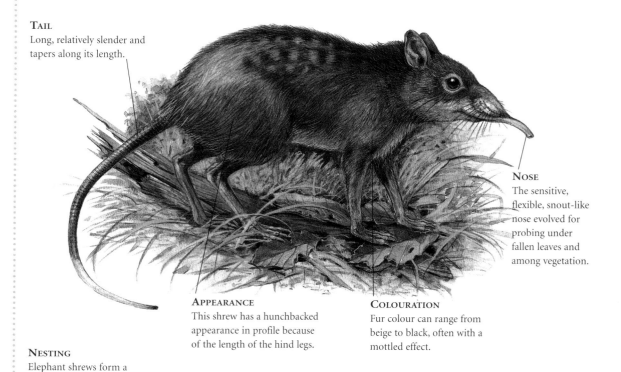

TAIL
Long, relatively slender and tapers along its length.

NOSE
The sensitive, flexible, snout-like nose evolved for probing under fallen leaves and among vegetation.

APPEARANCE
This shrew has a hunchbacked appearance in profile because of the length of the hind legs.

COLOURATION
Fur colour can range from beige to black, often with a mottled effect.

NESTING
Elephant shrews form a pile of leaves as their nest, collecting them in a hollow in the ground.

HOW BIG IS IT?

TERRITORIAL NATURE
The word 'shrew' actually means 'villain', and may be a reflection of the aggressive nature of these small mammals.

Praying Mantis

VITAL STATISTICS

LENGTH	5–7.5cm (2–3in); females are larger
SEXUAL MATURITY	Late summer, after hatching in the spring
EGGS	Females lay around 300 in an egg sac
DEVELOPMENTAL PERIOD	Egg sacs may overwinter on twigs, hatching in spring; nymphs are often dispersed on the breeze, avoiding excessive cannibalism
HABITAT	Relatively open countryside
DIET	Insectivorous, eating flies, grasshoppers, crickets, butterflies and moths
LIFESPAN	Up to 1 year

ANIMAL FACTS

The gruesome reputation of these insects comes from the way in which males are sometimes decapitated and eaten by their female partners (which are larger) after mating. Praying mantises rely on their acute sense of sight to detect possible prey, and can turn their triangular-shaped heads through an angle of 180° for this purpose. When an unfortunate invertebrate does come within reach, the praying mantis will strike with devastating speed, giving its target little opportunity to escape.

Catching prey

It is the way in which these insects rest, with their front legs held together as if they were praying, that gives them their name.

WHERE IN THE WORLD?

Occurs in southern parts of Europe, but was introduced on plants to North America in 1899, and now ranges from northeastern America to the Pacific Northwest.

EYES
Their vision is so acute that praying mantises can detect movement from 18m (60ft) away.

THORAX
The enlarged and well-armoured front legs attach to the thorax, beneath the protective shield.

COLOURATION
Green predominates in these insects, serving as camouflage.

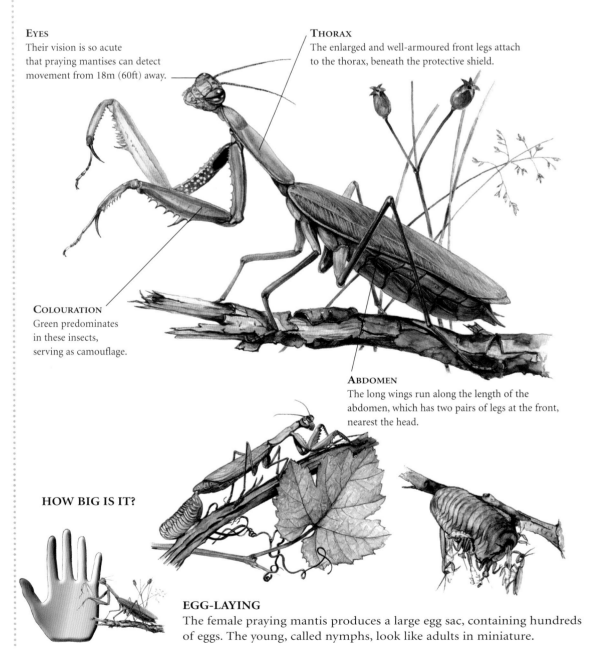

ABDOMEN
The long wings run along the length of the abdomen, which has two pairs of legs at the front, nearest the head.

HOW BIG IS IT?

EGG-LAYING
The female praying mantis produces a large egg sac, containing hundreds of eggs. The young, called nymphs, look like adults in miniature.

Duck-Billed Platypus

• **ORDER** • Monotremata • **FAMILY** • Ornithorhynchidae • **SPECIES** • *Ornithorhynchus anatinus*

VITAL STATISTICS

WEIGHT	0.7–2.4kg (1.5–5.3lb); males are larger
LENGTH	43–50cm (43–50in)
SEXUAL MATURITY	2 years
GESTATION PERIOD	Eggs develop in the body for 28 days, and are then incubated for 10 days
NUMBER OF OFFSPRING	1–3, emerging from their nesting burrow at around 4 months old
DIET	Insectivorous, typically feeding on worms, shrimps and crayfish
LIFESPAN	Up to 11 years; 17 in captivity

ANIMAL FACTS

One of the things that makes the duck-billed platypus so unusual is the fact that it is an egg-laying mammal. It was not until almost a century after its discovery that its method of reproduction was confirmed. Another oddity of this species is the way in which it locates its prey underwater by means of electroreception. It also has sensory receptors in its bill, but the electroreceptors confirm the presence of living prey.

The front claws are covered with webbing

When this species first became known Europe in 1798, its appearance was considered so bizarre it was thought to be a hoax.

Restricted to Australia, occurring along suitable watercourses in the east of the continent, ranging from eastern Queensland south to Victoria; also present on Tasmania.

BILL
Rubbery in texture, the bill is used for digging underwater to find food.

DENSE FUR
This traps air next to the body, keeping the platypus warm.

TAIL
Broad and flat, the tail helps the platypus steer itself underwater.

BREEDING BIOLOGY

The female incubates the eggs by curling around them. The young are blind and hairless when they hatch.

HOW BIG IS IT?

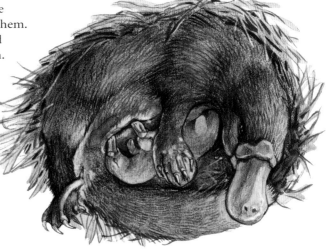

Short-Beaked Echidna

• **ORDER** • Monotremata • **FAMILY** • Tachyglossidae • **SPECIES** • *Tachyglossus aculeatus*

VITAL STATISTICS

WEIGHT	2–5kg (5–11lb)
LENGTH	30–45cm (12–18in)
SEXUAL MATURITY	Probably 5 years, although may not breed until 12 years
GESTATION PERIOD	Egg develops in the body for 21–28 days, and is incubated by the female, hatching 10 days later
NUMBER OF OFFSPRING	1; weaning occurs at at 6 months
DIET	Insectivorous, feeding on ants and termites
LIFESPAN	Up to 45 years

ANIMAL FACTS

The female echidna carries her rubbery egg in a pouch on the underside of her abdomen. The youngster, called a puggle, will then be reared in a burrow. It measures about 1.5cm (0.6in) at birth and subsequently feeds not on a nipple, but on a patch of skin that secretes a rich milk, allowing the female echidna to leave her offspring alone for up to 10 days. The milk is pink because of its high level of iron.

The echidna can defend itself with its claws or roll into a ball

These primitive mammals have difficulty regulating their body temperature, which is normally only 30°C (86°F), because they lack sweat glands and do not pant.

WHERE IN THE WORLD?

Coastal and upland areas of southwestern New Guinea and through Australia, including Tasmania. It is the most widely distributed native mammal on the continent.

SNOUT
The snout measures 7.5cm (3in), with the tiny mouth at the end only opening to 0.5cm (0.2in).

SPINAL CORD
This is shortest of any mammal, actually ending in the thoracic region.

LIMBS
Short and equipped with sharp claws, the limbs allow the echidna to bury itself rapidly.

BODY COVERING
The fur in between the sharp spines insulates the body.

GETTING TOGETHER
Solitary by nature, echidnas give off a body odour at mating time, and as many as 10 males may compete to mate with a single female.

HOW BIG IS IT?

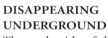

DISAPPEARING UNDERGROUND

The underside of the body is covered by fur, so echidnas dig quickly to escape danger, leaving their spines exposed.

Common Antlion

• **ORDER** • Neuroptera • **FAMILY** • Myrmeleontidae • **SPECIES** • *Myrmeleon formicarius*

The strange name of these insects comes from a mistaken translation, as they were originally called ant-ambushers in Hungarian, reflecting how the larvae trap prey.

VITAL STATISTICS

LENGTH	Wingspan of adults 2–15cm (0.8–6in)
SEXUAL MATURITY	After pupation
EGGS	About 20, laid individually in the sand
DEVELOPMENTAL PERIOD	Larvae pupate after 2–3 years; adults emerge about 1 month later
HABITAT	Favours arid, open country
DIET	Larvae are insectivorous, often preying on ants; adults generally feed on nectar
LIFESPAN	Adults 20–25 days on average, but can be up to 45 days

ANIMAL FACTS

Antlion larvae leave a distinctive trail resembling doodles across the sand, as they search for somewhere to dig their trap, and so they are known as doodlebugs in North America. The trap itself is created by the larva crawling backwards, piling up the sand with its abdomen, and moving round in circles. The trap can end up being about 7.5cm (3in) in diameter and 5cm (2in) deep, and the angle of the sides is such that it will collapse easily.

An antlion cocoon has a globular shape, and is buried in sand; the adult insect clambers out from here to the surface

WHERE IN THE WORLD?

The 65 species of antlion have a worldwide distribution. This particular species occurs in North America and mainland Europe, but not in the British Isles.

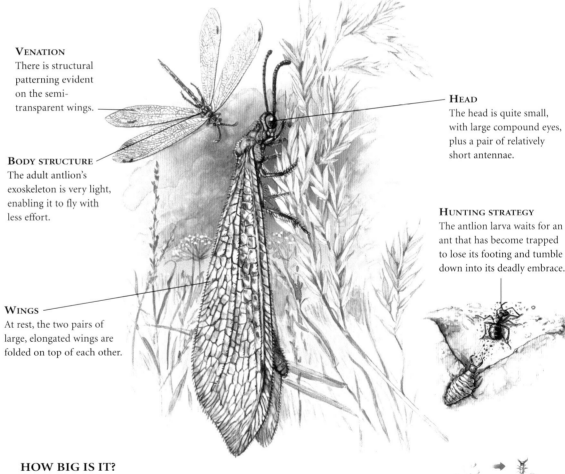

VENATION
There is structural patterning evident on the semi-transparent wings.

BODY STRUCTURE
The adult antlion's exoskeleton is very light, enabling it to fly with less effort.

WINGS
At rest, the two pairs of large, elongated wings are folded on top of each other.

HEAD
The head is quite small, with large compound eyes, plus a pair of relatively short antennae.

HUNTING STRATEGY
The antlion larva waits for an ant that has become trapped to lose its footing and tumble down into its deadly embrace.

HOW BIG IS IT?

EGG TO ADULT
The lifecycle of the antlion. The larvae are formidable predators, with strong mouthparts to dispatch and dismember their prey.

279

Common Octopus

• ORDER • Octopoda **• FAMILY •** Octopodidae **• SPECIES •** *Octopus vulgaris*

Octopuses are considered the most intelligent of all invertebrates, able to solve problems and learn from their past experiences. Their senses are also highly evolved.

VITAL STATISTICS

WEIGHT	3–6kg (6.6–15lb)
LENGTH	Mantle can be 25cm (10in); legs up to 1m (3.3ft)
SEXUAL MATURITY	1–2 years
HATCHING PERIOD	Eggs hatch after about 1 month
NUMBER OF OFFSPRING	Females lay 100,000–500,000 eggs, which they guard until hatched; they die soon afterwards
DIET	Shellfish, including lobsters, which may be stolen from traps, and fish
LIFESPAN	1–2 years

ANIMAL FACTS

Few creatures are able to camouflage their presence better than the octopus. These cephalopods, related to cuttlefish and squid, have a remarkable ability to change colour. If threatened, they are able to produce a cloud of purplish-black ink, squirted in the direction of an aggressor, which provides them with an opportunity to escape undetected. These octopuses live in dens, and will store shellfish there to ensure they have food available, opening the shells with their powerful arms.

WHERE IN THE WORLD?

Occurs from the English Channel southwards through the Mediterranean, to the coast of West Africa and west via Cape Verde and the Canary Islands to the Azores.

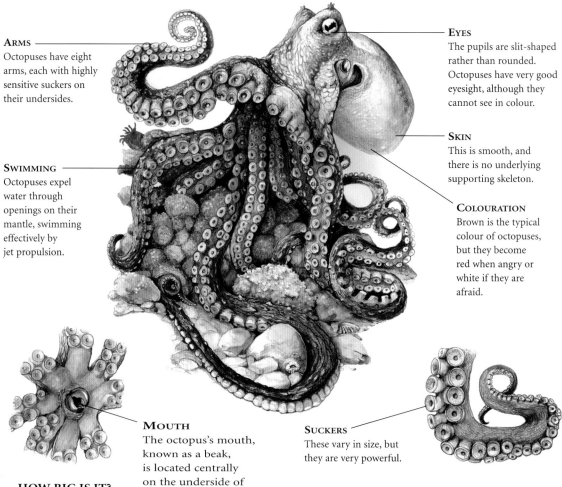

ARMS
Octopuses have eight arms, each with highly sensitive suckers on their undersides.

SWIMMING
Octopuses expel water through openings on their mantle, swimming effectively by jet propulsion.

EYES
The pupils are slit-shaped rather than rounded. Octopuses have very good eyesight, although they cannot see in colour.

SKIN
This is smooth, and there is no underlying supporting skeleton.

COLOURATION
Brown is the typical colour of octopuses, but they become red when angry or white if they are afraid.

MOUTH
The octopus's mouth, known as a beak, is located centrally on the underside of the body.

SUCKERS
These vary in size, but they are very powerful.

HOW BIG IS IT?

EGGS
The female octopus lays her eggs in crevices.

Emperor Dragonfly

• **ORDER** • Odonata • **FAMILY** • Aeshnidae • **SPECIES** • *Anax imperator*

VITAL STATISTICS

LENGTH	About 7.8cm (3.1in); wingspan up to 10.5cm (4.1in)
SEXUAL MATURITY	After the larval stage
EGGS	Up to 500
DEVELOPMENTAL PERIOD	Cream-coloured eggs hatch after 3 weeks; nymphs spend 2 years in the water before becoming adults
HABITAT	Slow-flowing rivers, canals, larger ponds and similar stretches of water
DIET	Nymphs hunt fish fry and tadpoles; adults catch flies and butterflies
LIFESPAN	Dragonflies live about 4 weeks

ANIMAL FACTS

Highly territorial, these dragonflies are very fast in flight, but they are easily identifiable by their appearance. They fly with their abdomen in a slightly down-curved position, and each pair of wings can be moved independently. At intervals, they will settle on vegetation surrounding water, particularly if they have just caught prey, which they will then eat. Females lay their eggs in weedy areas of water.

This is one of the biggest hawking dragonflies, so-called because it catches prey in flight, sometimes soaring up into the sky to do so.

WHERE IN THE WORLD?

Extends from Wales and southern parts of England through Europe via the Middle East eastwards to northwestern India. Also present in parts of Africa.

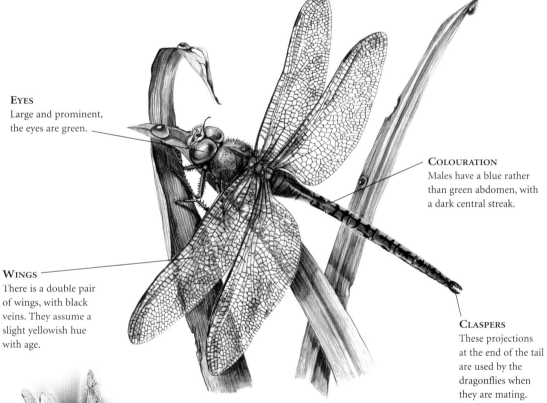

EYES
Large and prominent, the eyes are green.

WINGS
There is a double pair of wings, with black veins. They assume a slight yellowish hue with age.

COLOURATION
Males have a blue rather than green abdomen, with a dark central streak.

CLASPERS
These projections at the end of the tail are used by the dragonflies when they are mating.

MATING
This brief encounter takes places with the dragonflies usually resting on the stem of a plant, with the female looping her body under the male.

HOW BIG IS IT?

NYMPHS
The larvae, known as nymphs, are highly aggressive by nature and brown in colour. They also have very large eyes.

Broad-Bodied Chaser

• **ORDER** • Odonata • **FAMILY** • Libellulidae • **SPECIES** • *Libellula depressa*

VITAL STATISTICS

LENGTH	7.8cm (3.1in); wingspan 7cm (2.8in)
SEXUAL MATURITY	After the larval stage
EGGS	Laid singly
DEVELOPMENTAL PERIOD	Eggs hatch after 2–3 weeks; the brown nymph spends 1–3 years in the water, then climbs out on to a reed; the larval casing splits and the adult emerges
HABITAT	Lakes and ponds
DIET	Nymphs hunt small aquatic prey; adults catch winged invertebrates
LIFESPAN	Up to 4 weeks

ANIMAL FACTS

Chasers as a group can be identified by the dark areas at the base of their wings. The broad-bodied chaser can be seen from mid-May until early August, and males are particularly aggressive towards each other, chasing off rivals who venture into their territory. After mating, the female flies down to the water surface, dipping her abdomen under the water and depositing her eggs amongst aquatic vegetation. Meanwhile, the male hovers nearby, alerting her to any possible danger.

This species is often attracted to garden ponds. Its stocky appearance and flight pattern is similar to those of the wasp, so initially, the broad-bodied chaser may be confused with the wasp.

WHERE IN THE WORLD?

Found in Wales and southern England, extending across Europe north to Scandinavia, south to Italy and east into Turkey, at altitudes below 2000m (6560ft).

APPEARANCE
The stocky and relatively short body shape of these dragonflies aids identification.

COLOURATION
The male has a blue abdomen edged with yellow. Females have a brown abdomen with yellow stripes.

LEGS
Segmented and relatively thin, the legs allow the dragonfly to cling on to vegetation.

WING MARKINGS
There are short, black bars on the leading edge of the wings, near the wing tips.

MATING
Mating takes place in flight, and the dragonflies are only joined together for a brief moment.

HOW BIG IS IT?

A DEADLY CATCH
These dragonflies are equipped with strong claws that allow them to seize their prey in flight and prevent it escaping.

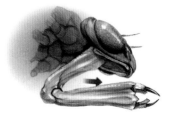

Whale Shark

• ORDER • Orectolobiformes • FAMILY • Rhincodontidae • SPECIES • *Rhincodon typus*

This is not only the biggest shark in the oceans today, but also the largest fish. Fortunately, it is not an aggressive species.

VITAL STATISTICS

WEIGHT	Up to 13.6 tonnes (13.3 tons)
LENGTH	Can measure 12.2m (40ft)
SEXUAL MATURITY	Females may not breed for the first time until they are 30 years old
GESTATION PERIOD	Eggs develop in the female's body, resulting in the birth of live young
NUMBER OF OFFSPRING	300 pups recorded in 1 female; no parental care
DIET	A filter feeder, sieving plankton from the sea
LIFESPAN	Up to 100 years

ANIMAL FACTS

The whale shark's mouth measures approximately 1.5m (4.9ft) in diameter, allowing it to sieve large volumes of water through its mouth to obtain food. The water passes over 350 rows of small teeth, but these have no function in terms of feeding. The plankton is sieved out by what are effectively filters on the gills and then swallowed directly, with water exiting the body through the gill flaps. These sharks are not fast swimmers, usually travelling at just 5kph (3mph).

WHERE IN THE WORLD?

Occurs in tropical and warmer temperate areas in the world's oceans, often near the shore. Seasonal aggregations of these sharks can be observed in some localities.

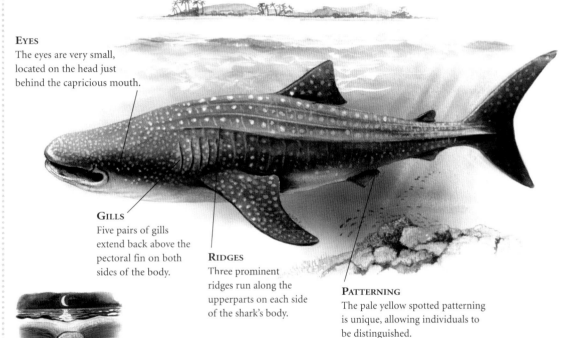

EYES
The eyes are very small, located on the head just behind the capricious mouth.

GILLS
Five pairs of gills extend back above the pectoral fin on both sides of the body.

RIDGES
Three prominent ridges run along the upperparts on each side of the shark's body.

PATTERNING
The pale yellow spotted patterning is unique, allowing individuals to be distinguished.

FEEDING MOVEMENTS
Shoals of plankton move up from the depths of the sea at night, attracting whale sharks to feed near the surface.

TRAVELLING COMPANIONS
Whale sharks are often accompanied by small cleaner fish, which will keep the bodies of these giants free from parasites.

The flattened profile of the whale shark lessens water resistance, so it can swim more easily

HOW BIG IS IT?

Blue-Winged Grasshopper

• **ORDER** • Orthoptera • **FAMILY** • Gryllidae • **SPECIES** • *Oedipoda caerulescens*

The blue colouration of these grasshoppers is only evident in flight. Otherwise, they are well-camouflaged on the ground and hard to spot unless disturbed.

VITAL STATISTICS

LENGTH	Females 2.2–2.8cm (0.9–1.1in); males 1.5–2.1cm (0.6–0.8in)
SEXUAL MATURITY	Grasshoppers overwinter in the egg, emerging as nymphs the following year
EGGS	Around 400 overall, laid in a foam-like substance
DEVELOPMENTAL PERIOD	2-year cycle
HABITAT	Dry, relatively open areas of sandy countryside
DIET	Grass, herbs and other plants, including crops such as tea
LIFESPAN	About 6 months

ANIMAL FACTS

As with other grasshoppers, the blue-winged female lays soon after mating. The young look like adults in miniature when they hatch and grow through a series of moults, defined as instars, to become adults. In contrast with many invertebrates, there is no inert pupal stage in their lifecycle. The blue-winged grasshopper is able to adapt its body colour to match that of the soil, which provides camouflage. This ability is acquired at the second instar stage.

WHERE IN THE WORLD?

Extends from the Channel Islands through much of Europe into western areas of Asia, reaching as far east as the Caucasus. It is endangered in some areas, and now reintroduced to parts of Switzerland.

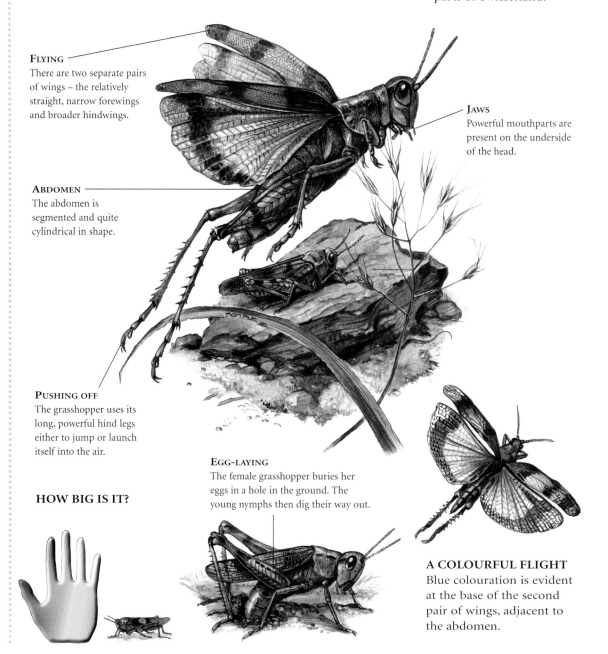

FLYING
There are two separate pairs of wings – the relatively straight, narrow forewings and broader hindwings.

JAWS
Powerful mouthparts are present on the underside of the head.

ABDOMEN
The abdomen is segmented and quite cylindrical in shape.

PUSHING OFF
The grasshopper uses its long, powerful hind legs either to jump or launch itself into the air.

EGG-LAYING
The female grasshopper buries her eggs in a hole in the ground. The young nymphs then dig their way out.

HOW BIG IS IT?

A COLOURFUL FLIGHT
Blue colouration is evident at the base of the second pair of wings, adjacent to the abdomen.

Great Green Bush Cricket

• **ORDER** • Orthoptera • **FAMILY** • Tettigoniidae • **SPECIES** • *Tettigonia viridissima*

This is the largest orthopteran found in the British Isles, and also undoubtedly the loudest – which means that it is relatively conspicuous wherever it occurs.

VITAL STATISTICS

LENGTH	Up to 5cm (2in)
SEXUAL MATURITY	Eggs hatch in the year after being laid or the year after that; nymphs pass through 6 instar stages
EGGS	Females lay several hundred eggs
DEVELOPMENTAL PERIOD	Up to 3 years, depending on when the nymphs hatch
HABITAT	Meadows, open country and edges of woodland
DIET	Largely predatory, hunting caterpillars, moths and flies, but will eat vegetation
LIFESPAN	6 months

ANIMAL FACTS

Males make their distinctive calls not by vocalizing, but by rubbing their rigid forewings together – a process known as stridulating. The resulting sound can be audible at least 50m (165ft) away, with males competing against each other to attract females. Although they sing during the day, bush crickets tend to be noisier from dusk onwards, into the evening. Females may also communicate with similar sounds during the mating period. Females are identifiable by their down-curved ovipositor.

Female laying eggs

WHERE IN THE WORLD?

Occurs throughout much of Europe, extending via Turkey into Asia, across to Siberia. Also present in North Africa. In England it is usually found in coastal areas.

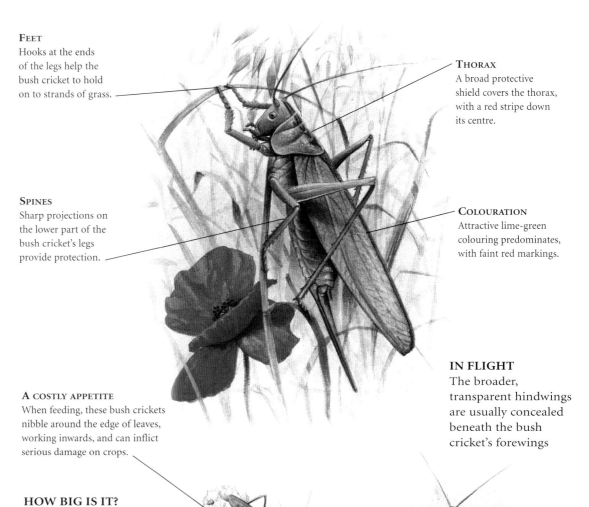

FEET
Hooks at the ends of the legs help the bush cricket to hold on to strands of grass.

SPINES
Sharp projections on the lower part of the bush cricket's legs provide protection.

THORAX
A broad protective shield covers the thorax, with a red stripe down its centre.

COLOURATION
Attractive lime-green colouring predominates, with faint red markings.

IN FLIGHT
The broader, transparent hindwings are usually concealed beneath the bush cricket's forewings

A COSTLY APPETITE
When feeding, these bush crickets nibble around the edge of leaves, working inwards, and can inflict serious damage on crops.

HOW BIG IS IT?

Field Cricket

• **ORDER** • Orthoptera • **FAMILY** • Gryllidae • **SPECIES** • *Gryllus campestris*

VITAL STATISTICS

LENGTH	1.7–2.3cm (0.6–0.9in); males slightly larger
SEXUAL MATURITY	Young crickets overwinter in burrows as nymphs, maturing the following year
EGGS	About 5 eggs daily, around 70–100 in all
DEVELOPMENTAL PERIOD	Adults start breeding in May; nymphs hatch in July and August
HABITAT	Dry, sunny localities with well-drained soil
DIET	Mainly grass, but also eats carrion
LIFESPAN	Up to 1 year

ANIMAL FACTS

Field crickets are only active over the summer, favouring sunny places where the grass and other vegetation is short. In spite of having wings, these crickets cannot fly, and this makes them vulnerable to habitat changes. London Zoo has now organized a release scheme for this endangered species in England, with the first captive-bred field crickets being set free in 1992, in an area of West Sussex. Several thousand others have followed at various protected localities.

These crickets have declined dramatically in numbers in recent years, and are now endangered, particularly in England. Work is underway to prevent their extinction.

WHERE IN THE WORLD?

Found in southern and central Europe, as far north as Germany and the Netherlands. A single surviving English population exists in West Sussex.

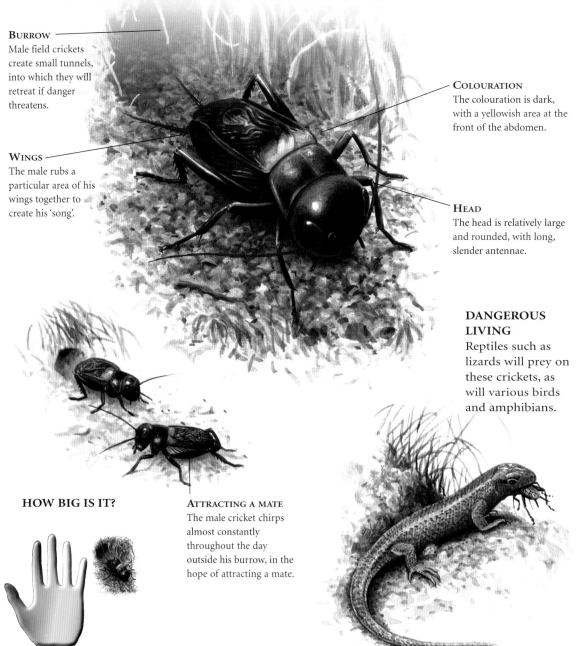

BURROW
Male field crickets create small tunnels, into which they will retreat if danger threatens.

WINGS
The male rubs a particular area of his wings together to create his 'song'.

COLOURATION
The colouration is dark, with a yellowish area at the front of the abdomen.

HEAD
The head is relatively large and rounded, with long, slender antennae.

DANGEROUS LIVING
Reptiles such as lizards will prey on these crickets, as will various birds and amphibians.

HOW BIG IS IT?

ATTRACTING A MATE
The male cricket chirps almost constantly throughout the day outside his burrow, in the hope of attracting a mate.

Oyster

PHYLUM · *mollusca* · **ORDER** · Pteriomorpha · **FAMILY** · Ostreidae ·

VITAL STATISTICS

LENGTH	25cm (10in) or more
SEXUAL MATURITY	From 7 weeks
EGGS	A female may produce 100 million eggs annually
DEVELOPMENT	There are hermaphrodite egg- and larvae-producing oysters; those that occur in deeper water brood their offspring rather than releasing eggs and sperm
HABITAT	Seas and oceans
DIET	Filter-feeder, extracting plankton from the water, consuming algae and other microscopic food particles
LIFESPAN	Up to 20 years

Members of this family are regarded as the true oysters, being separate from the pearl oysters. They are bivalves – their shells have two parts.

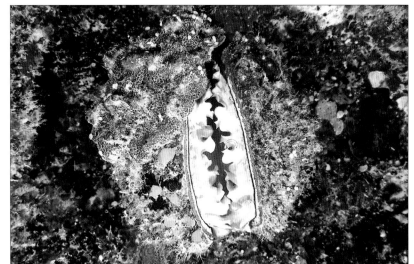

WHERE IN THE WORLD?

These oysters have a wide distribution, occurring throughout the world's oceans, including temperate areas, often in relatively shallow water.

ANIMAL FACTS

Oysters are significant in improving water quality, with each individual oyster able to filter up to 5l (1.1 gallons) per hour. Oyster colonies can be home to many marine creatures, including fish. Breeding in some colonies may be a communal event, with a concentrated release of eggs and sperm maximizing the likelihood of fertilization in the sea's currents. Young oysters may all be male, changing gender as they grow.

Oysters grow in diameter, adding concentric rings to their upper shell

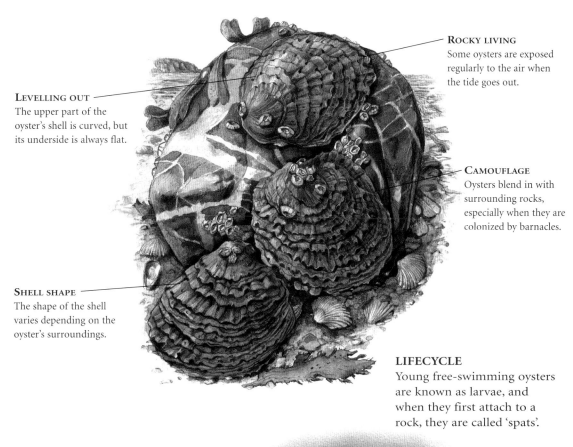

ROCKY LIVING
Some oysters are exposed regularly to the air when the tide goes out.

LEVELLING OUT
The upper part of the oyster's shell is curved, but its underside is always flat.

CAMOUFLAGE
Oysters blend in with surrounding rocks, especially when they are colonized by barnacles.

SHELL SHAPE
The shape of the shell varies depending on the oyster's surroundings.

LIFECYCLE
Young free-swimming oysters are known as larvae, and when they first attach to a rock, they are called 'spats'.

HOW BIG IS IT?

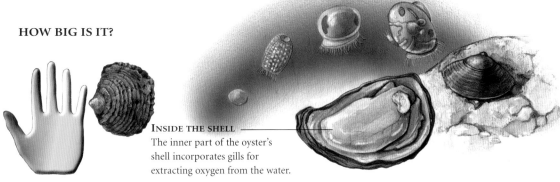

INSIDE THE SHELL
The inner part of the oyster's shell incorporates gills for extracting oxygen from the water.

Chaffinch

• **ORDER** • Passeriformes • **FAMILY** • Fringillidae • **SPECIES** • *Fringilla coelebs*

VITAL STATISTICS

WEIGHT	18–29g (0.6–1oz)
LENGTH	14–18cm (5.5–7in)
SEXUAL MATURITY	Breeds in the year after hatching
NUMBER OF EGGS	2–8, pale blue with dark purplish blotches
INCUBATION PERIOD	13–16 days; young fledge by 18 days, and the adult pair may breed twice annually
DIET	Various seeds, often foraging beneath bird tables and feeders for spilt seed; also eats invertebrates
LIFESPAN	7–15 years

ANIMAL FACTS

After the breeding season, pairs will split up and head for their wintering grounds. Banding studies have revealed a distinctive difference in the chosen localities between the sexes. Cock chaffinches are frequently observed further north, often heading to Scandinavia, whereas hens are more common in Ireland. Their natural haunts are wooded areas, but chaffinches have adapted well to living and breeding in parks and gardens, although cats can be a serious menace in such surroundings.

The hen chooses the site of the nest and collects materials such as lichens and moss

There is no mistaking the appearance of this common finch, although young of both sexes are indistinguishable, and look rather like hens.

WHERE IN THE WORLD?

Occurs throughout most of Europe, and is one of the most common British birds. Extends south to North Africa, and eastwards via Russia to the Ukraine.

FLIGHT FEATHERS
These extend along the rear edge of the wing.

BILL
The conical bill, used to crack seeds, changes from grey to pale brown in winter.

UNDERPARTS
Brighter pink feathering can be seen here after the spring moult.

FEET
Three toes grip the front of a perch or are extended forwards on the ground, with the hind toe directed backwards.

HOW BIG IS IT?

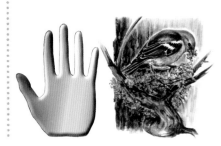

FLIGHT DISTINCTIONS

The white wing bars differ between the sexes, and are most evident when the wing is extended. Hens also have greyer plumage.

Raggi's Bird of Paradise

• **ORDER** • Passeriformes • **FAMILY** • Paradisaeidae • **SPECIES** • *Paradisaea raggiana*

Named in 1873 after the Marquis Raggi of Genoa, this bird of paradise has since been adopted as the national bird of Papua New Guinea.

VITAL STATISTICS

WEIGHT	240–295g (8.5–10.4oz)
LENGTH	34cm (13in)
SEXUAL MATURITY	Cock birds take about 5 years to acquire adult plumage
NUMBER OF EGGS	1–2, pale buff with darker markings, more prominent at the broad end
INCUBATION PERIOD	18–20 days; young fledge by 17 days, and are fed by the hen for up to 2 months
DIET	Frugivorous, eating fruit and berries, plus some invertebrates
LIFESPAN	Up to 33 years

ANIMAL FACTS

Cock birds congregate at specific display grounds in the forest, known as leks. As they go through their range of display movements, the hens are drawn there to watch, and may dart down briefly alongside a male to mate. Afterwards, the hen will build a flimsy, bowl-shaped nest in the fork of a tree, laying her eggs and caring for the offspring on her own. Breeding occurs throughout much of the year, and these birds of paradise are common.

WHERE IN THE WORLD?

Found in southern and northeastern parts of Papua New Guinea, ranging from sea level up to an altitude of 1500m (4920ft), in forested areas.

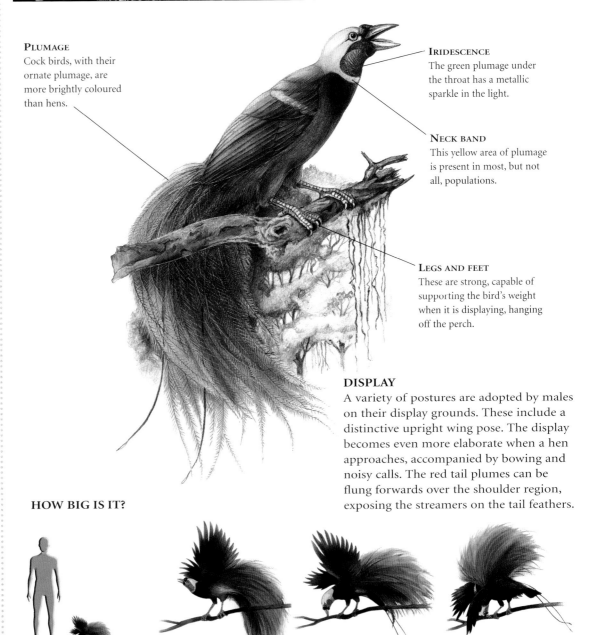

PLUMAGE
Cock birds, with their ornate plumage, are more brightly coloured than hens.

IRIDESCENCE
The green plumage under the throat has a metallic sparkle in the light.

NECK BAND
This yellow area of plumage is present in most, but not all, populations.

LEGS AND FEET
These are strong, capable of supporting the bird's weight when it is displaying, hanging off the perch.

DISPLAY
A variety of postures are adopted by males on their display grounds. These include a distinctive upright wing pose. The display becomes even more elaborate when a hen approaches, accompanied by bowing and noisy calls. The red tail plumes can be flung forwards over the shoulder region, exposing the streamers on the tail feathers.

HOW BIG IS IT?

European Nuthatch

· ORDER · Passeriformes **· FAMILY ·** Sittidae **· SPECIES ·** *Sitta europaea*

VITAL STATISTICS

WEIGHT	20–24g (0.7–0.8oz)
LENGTH	20–25cm (8–10in)
SEXUAL MATURITY	Breeds the year after hatching
NUMBER OF EGGS	4–13, white with reddish spots
INCUBATION PERIOD	16–18 days; young fledge by 25 days, and the adult pair may breed twice annually
DIET	Seeds and nuts in winter, but more insectivorous in summer; may take wild bird food
LIFESPAN	Up to 11 years

ANIMAL FACTS

These fairly dumpy birds will rest clinging on to the sides of a tree, rather than perching. They bear some similarity to woodpeckers, although they do not use their bills for boring into wood. They may drive nuts into holes in the tree bark, however, and then chip away pieces with their bill. They forage for hazelnuts and acorns in woodland, but they are also seen in city parks, and in gardens where there are mature trees.

Nuthatches are noisy by nature, with a varied repertoire of calls that reveals their presence in an area, but they can still be difficult to spot.

WHERE IN THE WORLD?

Much of Europe, including Wales and England, up to southern Scandinavia, down via the Iberian Peninsula to Morocco, and eastwards to Turkey and the Caucausus.

TAIL FEATHERS
The tail feathers are short, barely extending beyond the folded wings.

LEGS
These are strong enough to allow the nuthatch to move down a tree trunk head-first, rather than edging down backwards.

MALAR STRIPE
This runs from the base of the upper bill, passing through the eyes and down the sides of the neck.

BILL
Narrow and pointed, the bill is good for pulling invertebrates out of bark.

NESTING
Nuthatches nest in tree hollows, and may sometimes actually plaster up the entrance with mud if it is too broad.

HOW BIG IS IT?

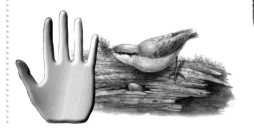

FEEDING THE YOUNG
There can be a large number of hungry mouths for the nuthatches to feed, all clammering for insects.

European Robin

• **ORDER** • Passeriformes • **FAMILY** • Turdidae • **SPECIES** • *Erithacus rubecula*

VITAL STATISTICS

WEIGHT	16–22g (0.6–0.8oz)
LENGTH	14cm (5in)
SEXUAL MATURITY	Breeds in the year after hatching
NUMBER OF EGGS	3–9, white to shades of pale blue with reddish spotting
INCUBATION PERIOD	12–15 days; young fledge by 15 days, and the adult pair may breed 2–3 times annually
DIET	Invertebrates, particularly earthworms, and eats seeds, especially in winter
LIFESPAN	Up to 8.5 years but usually less

ANIMAL FACTS

The robin has a reputation as a gardener's companion, and quickly reveals its bold nature. It will not hesitate to dart in and pick up a worm dug up in the soil. Robins are very watchful birds, and their keen eyesight helps them detect moving invertebrates. They can be encountered in woodland and parks but they are harder to spot in such surroundings. Some seasonal movements take place, with Scandinavian robins heading south in winter.

Robins are unusual in that they will venture into shallow water to catch small fish

This member of the thrush family is linked with Christmas, often featuring on greetings cards. The tradition may have arisen partly because of its cheery winter song.

WHERE IN THE WORLD?

Occurs throughout most of Europe, north to southern Scandinavia, east to Iran and the Caucasus and across the Mediterranean to western North Africa and the Azores.

BILL
Slender yet relatively long, the bill is ideal for picking up seeds, turning leaves and seizing invertebrates.

LOW DOWN
Robins spend much of their time close to the ground, often concealed in undergrowth.

RED BREAST
The red breast is present in both sexes. Members of a pair appear identical.

MOVEMENT
Robins will hop along on the ground rather than walk.

TOUCHING DOWN
The robin uses its wings as brakes to slow its descent, adopting an almost vertical position and extending its legs forwards.

HOW BIG IS IT?

Nightingale

• **ORDER** • Passeriformes • **FAMILY** • Turdidae • **SPECIES** • *Luscinia megarhynchos*

VITAL STATISTICS

WEIGHT	17–23g (0.6–0.8oz)
LENGTH	16cm (6in)
SEXUAL MATURITY	Breeds in the year after hatching
NUMBER OF EGGS	4–5, white to shades of pale blue with reddish spotting
INCUBATION PERIOD	13–15 days; young fledge by 13 days, and the adult pair may breed 1–2 times annually
DIET	Feeds largely on insects of various types, caught close to or on the ground
LIFESPAN	Up to 11 years

ANIMAL FACTS

The nightingale's song has inspired many poets and other writers over the centuries. Cock birds often sing at night when their surroundings are quiet, in the hope of finding a mate nearby. Nightingales naturally frequent wooded areas but studies have shown that in urban environments these thrushes now sing louder than used to the case, in order to be heard, thus emphasizing their crescendo song patterns. In northern areas they arrive in April and then migrate south again in September.

The song of the Nightingale is well known

Renowned for its beautiful song, the return of the nightingale to Europe each year is traditionally considered a sign that summer is coming.

WHERE IN THE WORLD?

Occurs from southern England eastwards into Asia, and south through the Mediterranean and the Middle East into northwest Africa. Overwinters further south on this continent.

EYES
The eyes are relatively large and dark in appearance.

SONG
It is actually only the cock nightingale that sings.

COLOURATION
Both sexes are dull in colour, brown on the head and wings, with buff-coloured underparts.

REDDISH SUFFUSION
This is evident on the plumage of both the rump and tail, and explains why this species is also called the rufous nightingale.

READY TO FLY
Rapid development is essential, as the young nightingales must fly 2500–5500km (1600–3400 miles) to their wintering grounds.

HOW BIG IS IT?

DISPLAY
The cock nightingale displays to a hen by raising his tail feathers vertically, and then bowing and drooping his wings.

Cormorant

• **ORDER** • Pelicaniformes • **FAMILY** • Phalacrocoracidae • **SPECIES** • *Phalacrocorax carbo*

VITAL STATISTICS

WEIGHT	17–23g (0.6–0.8oz)
LENGTH	16cm (6in)
SEXUAL MATURITY	3 years
NUMBER OF EGGS	3–4, chalky white in colour
INCUBATION PERIOD	28–31 days; young fledge by 52 days, and the adult pair breeds once annually
DIET	Mainly fish, but will also eats small cephalopods
LIFESPAN	11 years in the wild but up to 23.5 recorded

ANIMAL FACTS

Adaptable by nature, cormorants can often be seen in the vicinity of harbours, perching on groynes. They are adept at swimming underwater, diving for up to 30 seconds at a time. They also have excellent eyesight, and unlike most birds they can move their eyes to focus. Fish are brought to the surface and battered to death before being swallowed head-first. Afterwards, the cormorant rests with its wings outstretched, allowing the plumage to dry off in the sun.

Although these cormorants are regarded as sea birds, they will often frequent inland lakes, much to the annoyance of fishermen, and are even known to breed in such surroundings.

WHERE IN THE WORLD?

Around the European coastline, from Scandinavia through the Mediterranean to West Africa. Also in parts of South Africa, southern Asia, Australia, New Zealand and North America.

BILL
The bill is quite slender, with a hook at the tip to impale slippery fish.

PATCH
This area of white feathering at the top of each leg is only apparent when the birds are in breeding condition.

ON LAND AND IN THE AIR
Breeding cormorants can be fierce, driving would-be predators away from their nesting site.

COLOURATION
Black and white colouration is typical of many seabirds, including cormorants.

FEET
The feet are strong, with webbing between the toes to help the cormorant swim well.

The broad wings are apparent in flight

HOW BIG IS IT?

DIVING
The cormorant's neck is long and extendible, allowing the bird to grab fish more easily underwater. The plumage is waterproof.

293

Greater Bilby

• ORDER • Marsupialia • FAMILY • Thylacomyidae • SPECIES • *Macrotis lagotis*

This species is the largest of the group of mammals called bandicoots. In Australia it is also known as the pinkie because of its nose colour.

VITAL STATISTICS

WEIGHT	0.9–2.3kg (2–5lb); males are slightly larger
LENGTH	51–91cm (20–36in); tail is ¾ the body length
SEXUAL MATURITY	Females 6 months; males 8 months
GESTATION PERIOD	13–16 days
NUMBER OF OFFSPRING	1–2, occasionally 3; young spend 75 days in the pouch and are independent by 90 days
DIET	Invertebrates plus bulbs and seeds, particularly bush onion
LIFESPAN	5–7 years

ANIMAL FACTS

The range of the greater bilby is directly affected by the soil because of its tunnelling habits. The species is often found in grassland areas, where it can dig burrows with relative ease. These underground retreats provide shelter from the hot sun and a refuge from predators. They only provide temporary homes, however, and bilbys move on and dig a new home when food becomes scarce. They live singly or sometimes in pairs, shuffling along slowly when walking.

While the front toes (left) are of similar size, there is a large swollen toe on each hind foot (right)

WHERE IN THE WORLD?

Range has reduced over the last century, partly because of predation by cats. It is now confined to Western Australia, Northern Territory and southwestern Queensland.

EARS
Long and pointed, the ears help the greater bilby to hear well as its eyesight is poor.

TAIL
The banded tail is grey at the base, black in the middle and white at the tip.

TUNNELLING
The spiralling tunnel leads to a sleeping chamber around 1.5m (5ft) below the surface.

NOSE
The nose is pink, with prominent whiskers.

GROOMING
The claws on the hind feet are used for grooming.

HOW BIG IS IT?

SLEEPING
This bandicoot puts its muzzle between its front paws, with its ears covering the eyes, and sleeps standing up.

Jewel Fish

VITAL STATISTICS

WEIGHT	10g (0.3oz)
LENGTH	Up to 15cm (6in)
SEXUAL MATURITY	4–6 months
NUMBER OF EGGS	200–500, laid in lines by the female and then fertilized by the male
HATCHING PERIOD	At 25°C (77°F), the fry emerge after 2–3 days, resting until they have reabsorbed their yolk sacs
DIET	Feeds on aquatic invertebrates and some plant matter
LIFESPAN	2–3 years

ANIMAL FACTS

Spawning occurs on rocks, after which the male will guard the eggs, while the female may dig spawning pits in the surrounding substrate. Once the fry hatch, they are shepherded into one of these depressions and guarded by the adult fish. They will be moved repeatedly to other similar localities, helping to keep them safe from predators. The cichlids will stay with their parents for up to a month, by which time the adult fish may be spawning again.

Cichlids are a remarkably diverse group of fish, and one of their unusual characteristics is the high degree of parental care shown by many species.

WHERE IN THE WORLD?

Found in waters in West Africa, from southern Guinea to Liberia. The family is represented in the Middle East, southern Asia, the USA to South America, and in Africa.

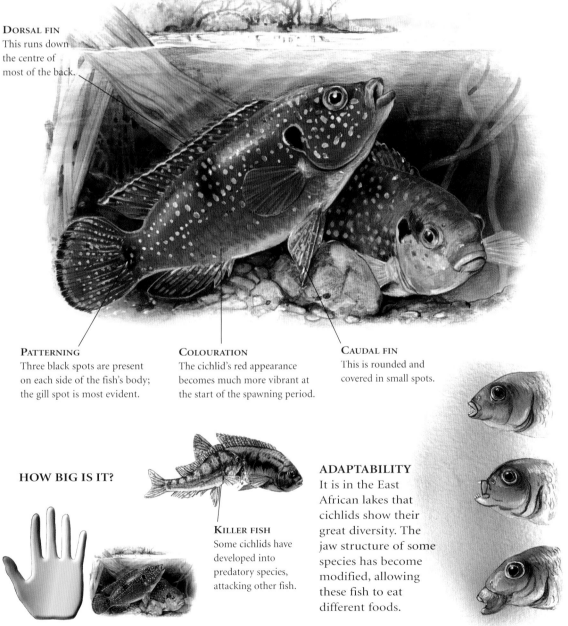

DORSAL FIN
This runs down the centre of most of the back.

PATTERNING
Three black spots are present on each side of the fish's body; the gill spot is most evident.

COLOURATION
The cichlid's red appearance becomes much more vibrant at the start of the spawning period.

CAUDAL FIN
This is rounded and covered in small spots.

HOW BIG IS IT?

KILLER FISH
Some cichlids have developed into predatory species, attacking other fish.

ADAPTABILITY
It is in the East African lakes that cichlids show their great diversity. The jaw structure of some species has become modified, allowing these fish to eat different foods.

Mudskipper

• ORDER • Perciformes • FAMILY • Gobiidae • SPECIES • *Oxudercinae*

These unusual fish can survive out of water and move on land. They occur on mudflats that are exposed each day by tidal movements.

VITAL STATISTICS

WEIGHT	12–23g (0.4–0.8oz)
LENGTH	15–25cm (6–10in)
SEXUAL MATURITY	1–2 years
NUMBER OF EGGS	60–400, laid inside walled, aerated burrows often guarded by the male
HATCHING PERIOD	5 days; tiny larvae live at first on plankton, moving back from the sea into the inter-tidal zone after 7 weeks
DIET	Generally carnivorous, catching various crustaceans and other invertebrates; some are vegetarian
LIFESPAN	5 years

ANIMAL FACTS

The pectoral fins of the mudskipper are modified, serving as a combination of primitive arms and legs, helping the fish both to climb and walk on land, as well as dig burrows in the sand. The gill chambers are very large, and are sealed when the mudskipper is out of water. This not only prevents the gills from becoming dessicated, but also means that the mudskipper can continue to extract oxygen from water when on land.

WHERE IN THE WORLD?

Mudskippers are restricted to sub-tropical and tropical areas. They occur on the western coast of Africa and the Indo-Pacific region eastwards to Japan.

COLOURATION
Generally grey, but with colourful spots and stripes on the fins and body.

SKIN
This needs to be kept moist, so the mudskipper can breathe on land like an amphibian.

EYES
Prominently located on the top of the head, the eyes alert the fish to danger.

BODY SHAPE
The body is long and quite slender, and the head is large.

LIFESTYLE
Mangrove swamps are typical mudskipper habitat. When the tide is out, these fish can breathe air through their mouths.

HOW BIG IS IT?

SUCKER DISC
A suction pad on the underside of the body, between the pectoral fins, helps to anchor the fish either in or out of water.

Siamese Fighting Fish

• ORDER • Perciformes • FAMILY • Osphronemidae • SPECIES • *Betta splendens*

These stunning fish – found in many colours – have been bred in Asia for centuries and they are now popular aquarium fish around the world.

VITAL STATISTICS

LENGTH	7.5cm (3in)
SEXUAL MATURITY	6 months
NUMBER OF EGGS	Up to 500; these are collected, deposited and guarded in the bubblenest by the male
HATCHING PERIOD	1–2 days; fry are immobile at first and start swimming about 4 days later
HABITAT	Shallow, still water with aquatic vegetation to provide anchorage for their bubblenests
DIET	Insectivorous, hunting small aquatic invertebrates of various types
LIFESPAN	2 years

ANIMAL FACTS

Although naturally aggressive, male Siamese fighting fish are also diligent in caring for their offspring, creating a bubblenest for the eggs using their own saliva. This structure floats at the surface, anchored between plants. These fish can also breathe atmospheric air directly, thanks to their labyrinth organs, located near their gills. This enables them to survive in slow-flowing water that has a low oxygen content.

Young males (right) can be distinguished from two months onwards

WHERE IN THE WORLD?

The original range is unclear because of movements of these fish though Southeast Asia, but the centre of their distribution is regarded as Thailand.

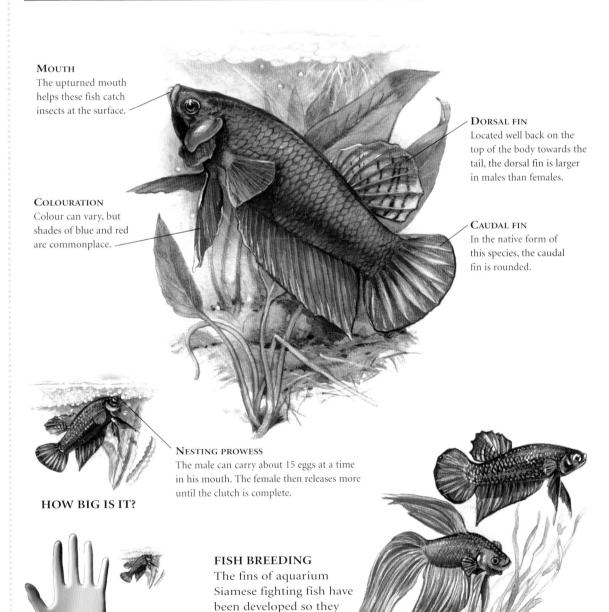

MOUTH
The upturned mouth helps these fish catch insects at the surface.

COLOURATION
Colour can vary, but shades of blue and red are commonplace.

DORSAL FIN
Located well back on the top of the body towards the tail, the dorsal fin is larger in males than females.

CAUDAL FIN
In the native form of this species, the caudal fin is rounded.

NESTING PROWESS
The male can carry about 15 eggs at a time in his mouth. The female then releases more until the clutch is complete.

HOW BIG IS IT?

FISH BREEDING
The fins of aquarium Siamese fighting fish have been developed so they are longer than those of their wild relatives.

297

Yellow-Masked Angelfish

• **ORDER** • Perciformes • **FAMILY** • Pomacanthidae • **SPECIES** • *Pomacanthus xanthometopon*

VITAL STATISTICS

WEIGHT	1.1kg (2.4lb)
LENGTH	38cm (15in)
SEXUAL MATURITY	1 year; females are protogynous hermaphrodites, which means they can transform into and breed as males
NUMBER OF EGGS	25,000–75,000, tiny and buoyant, floating in the planktonic layer
HATCHING PERIOD	1 day; young stop drifting by 4 weeks, after feeding initially on plankton
DIET	Omnivorous, feeding on sponges, tunicates and marine algae
LIFESPAN	5–12 years

ANIMAL FACTS

This species is one of the largest angelfish. It roams the reef in search of food and is often observed in gulleys and near caves. Young fish are relatively inconspicuous, hiding away in shallow caves that serve as shelters, often with marine algae that they can browse nearby. When spawning, yellow-masked angelfish form pairs, depending on the number of fish in the area, although where they are more numerous, spawning is communal. There is no visible means of distinguishing between the sexes.

Most young angelfish are blue with stripes or concentric patterning on their bodies

Marine angelfish are amongst the most colourful of creatures inhabiting the world's tropical reefs. They are solitary by nature and their appearance changes dramatically as they mature.

WHERE IN THE WORLD?

Occurs in the Indo-Pacific, from East Africa and the Maldives east to Vanuatu and north to the Yaeyama Islands. Also present around Palau and Krosae, Micronesia.

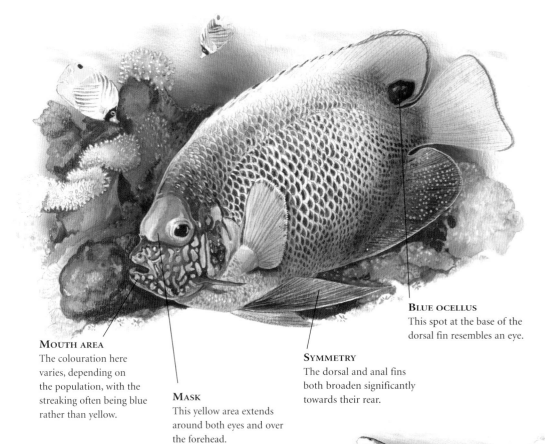

MOUTH AREA
The colouration here varies, depending on the population, with the streaking often being blue rather than yellow.

MASK
This yellow area extends around both eyes and over the forehead.

SYMMETRY
The dorsal and anal fins both broaden significantly towards their rear.

BLUE OCELLUS
This spot at the base of the dorsal fin resembles an eye.

HOW BIG IS IT?

STAYING SAFE
Angelfish use retreats on the reef where they can hide from predators like sharks. They defend these retreat areas from other fish.

Common Clownfish

• **ORDER** • Perciformes • **FAMILY** • Pomacentridae • **SPECIES** • *Amphiprion ocellaris*

The markings of these fish resemble the face paint of clowns, but they are also called anemonefish, having forged a remarkable partnership with these particular invertebrates.

VITAL STATISTICS

LENGTH	Up to 11cm (4.3in); females are larger
SEXUAL MATURITY	1–1.5 years
NUMBER OF EGGS	100–10,000, depending on female's age
HATCHING PERIOD	About 7 days, depending on water temperature; the young drift in plankton for up to 12 days
HABITAT	Shallow, calm areas of reef, with host anemones
LIFESPAN	6–10 years in the wild; 12 in an aquarium

ANIMAL FACTS

These fish live in close proximity to *Heteractis* and *Stichodactyla* sea anemones, darting in amongst their stinging tentacles if danger threatens. Clownfish are prevented from being stung themselves by a protective mucus covering their bodies. The anemones benefit because the fish brings food back to them. As with a number of marine species, all young clownfish are males, and the dominant individuals change to become females. There is, however, no obvious difference in colouration between the sexes.

The dorsal fin is divided into two parts, with protective spines at the front

WHERE IN THE WORLD?

Occurs in the eastern Indian Ocean via the Andamans, Thailand and Malaysia to northwestern Australia, and north via the Philippines, Taiwan and Japan to the Ryukyu Islands.

TAIL
The tail is short and the fins are edged in black.

FIN SHAPE
Generally rounded, with the pectoral fins in particular being quite large.

PATTERNING
Patterning is quite consistent, but sufficiently distinctive to allow individuals to be identified.

BREEDING BEHAVIOUR
Pairs will usually spawn very near to their host anemone, with the male cleaning an area for the eggs beforehand.

HOW BIG IS IT?

Queen Parrotfish

• ORDER • Perciformes • FAMILY • Scaridae • SPECIES • *Scarus vetula*

VITAL STATISTICS

LENGTH	15–30cm (6–12in); 'supermales' reach double this length
SEXUAL MATURITY	Supermales mate with females, and spawning occurs collectively; usually each supermale has 3–4 females
NUMBER OF EGGS	Several thousand
HATCHING PERIOD	1 day; larvae drift and do not feed for 3 days
HABITAT	Coastal tropical and sub-tropical waters
DIET	Marine algae on corals and rocks, plus sponges
LIFESPAN	Up to 5 years

ANIMAL FACTS

These parrotfish are found at depths of 3–25m (10–82ft). Their powerful jaws tend to crunch up limestone when they are feeding, causing them to pass sand out of their bodies. At dusk, they produce a cocoon of mucus, where they spend the night. This protects them from predators by masking their scent. Queen parrotfish are hermaphrodite at first, with all the fish being female, but some will develop into supermales. They spawn in open sea.

The shape of the parrotfish's mouthparts helps these fish to obtain their food

300

So-called because of their gaudy appearance, parrotfish are relatively large and spectacular residents of the coral reef. They are active during daylight hours.

WHERE IN THE WORLD?

This species occurs in the western Atlantic, ranging from Bermuda to Florida and the Bahamas, south to the area around northern South America.

CAUDAL FIN
This is broad, with evident extensions on the top and bottom.

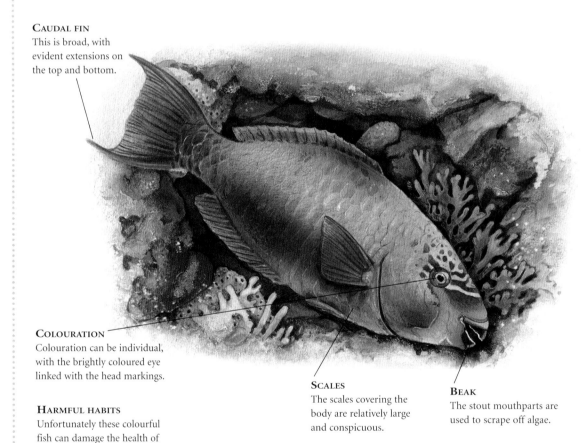

COLOURATION
Colouration can be individual, with the brightly coloured eye linked with the head markings.

HARMFUL HABITS
Unfortunately these colourful fish can damage the health of the reef, destroying coral.

SCALES
The scales covering the body are relatively large and conspicuous.

BEAK
The stout mouthparts are used to scrape off algae.

HOW BIG IS IT?

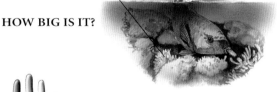

TRANSFORMATION

It is not just the parrotfish's gender that may change as it matures, but also its appearance, particularly its colouration.

Yellow-Fin Tuna

• ORDER • Perciformes • FAMILY • Scombridae • SPECIES • *Thunnus albacares*

The yellow-fin tuna is becoming more popular amongst fishermen as stocks of its relative the blue-fin are depleted through over-fishing. However, this may place the yellow-fin itself in danger.

VITAL STATISTICS

WEIGHT	Up to 200kg (440lb)
LENGTH	Up to 2.4m (7.9ft)
SEXUAL MATURITY	1.6–2 years
NUMBER OF EGGS	Up to 2–3 million annually; spawning occurs almost all year round
HATCHING PERIOD	1 day; young drift in the plankton as larvae
DIET	Zooplankton and small nektonic (free-swimming) organisms; adult fish eat 540g (1lb) daily
LIFESPAN	15–30 years

ANIMAL FACTS

The flesh of these tuna fish is reddish, due to a chemical called myoglobin that binds oxygen, ensuring that there is a supply of oxygen in their bodies which can be utilized as necessary so they can swim faster. Yellow-fin tuna are often seen near dolphins. This protects them from sharks, which are reluctant to approach dolphins, but has led to the deaths of many dolphins, which become trapped in fishing nets with the tuna.

WHERE IN THE WORLD?

Occurs in tropical and sub-tropical waters on both sides of the Equator, from approximately 40°N to 35°S. Not present in the Mediterranean Sea.

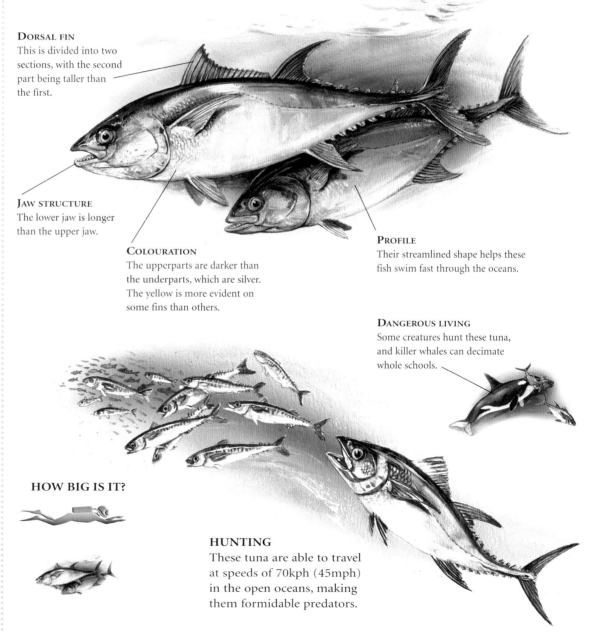

DORSAL FIN
This is divided into two sections, with the second part being taller than the first.

JAW STRUCTURE
The lower jaw is longer than the upper jaw.

COLOURATION
The upperparts are darker than the underparts, which are silver. The yellow is more evident on some fins than others.

PROFILE
Their streamlined shape helps these fish swim fast through the oceans.

DANGEROUS LIVING
Some creatures hunt these tuna, and killer whales can decimate whole schools.

HOW BIG IS IT?

HUNTING
These tuna are able to travel at speeds of 70kph (45mph) in the open oceans, making them formidable predators.

African Wild Ass

• ORDER • Perissodactyla • FAMILY • Equidae • SPECIES • *Equus africanus*

VITAL STATISTICS

WEIGHT	230–275kg (500–600lb)
LENGTH	2m (6.6ft); tail up to 50cm (20in); up to 1.45m (4.75ft) tall
SEXUAL MATURITY	2 years
GESTATION PERIOD	11–12 months
NUMBER OF OFFSPRING	1; weaning occurs at 6–8 months
DIET	Grazes on grasses and other plants, also eating bark and leaves
LIFESPAN	Up to 40 years

ANIMAL FACTS

These wild asses live in a harsh environment, resting during the heat of the day and emerging in the late afternoon to feed and drink. Herds also move in the early morning. Males use their dung as territorial markers, but will tolerate the presence of younger stallions in their territories. Hunting by people has pushed the African wild ass to the edge of extinction. There are now only just over 500 left in the wild.

This species is the wild ancestor of the donkey. Unfortunately, it has suffered a significant decline in numbers and it is currently regarded as endangered.

WHERE IN THE WORLD?

Northeastern Africa, now restricted to Eritrea, Ethiopia and Somalia. Formerly ranged more widely to the west and north, reaching Libya, Sudan and Egypt.

EARS
These are tall – helping the ass to detect sounds over long distances – and edged with black hair.

COLOURATION
Greyish with brown on the upperparts and white underparts.

STRIPING
The variable striped patterning on the neck is also apparent on the legs, allowing individuals to be distinguished.

HOOVES
The black hooves are tough but slender in appearance, corresponding to the width of the leg.

The Poitou donkey is a distinctive French breed, with a long, shaggy brown coat and no stripe on its back

HOW BIG IS IT?

MALE DOMINANCE

Males will fight each other by rearing up on their hind legs and lashing out with their hind feet. The distinctive black stripe running down from the mane can be seen here.

Mustang

VITAL STATISTICS

WEIGHT	Typically 317–362kg (700–800lb), but depends on the individual's ancestry
LENGTH	Variable; may be around 2.1m (6.9ft), with a tail of 60cm (24in); 122–173cm (48–68in) tall
SEXUAL MATURITY	2 years
GESTATION PERIOD	11–12 months
NUMBER OF OFFSPRING	1; weaning occurs at about 8 months
DIET	Grazes on grasses and other plants, also eating bark and leaves
LIFESPAN	Up to 20 years

ANIMAL FACTS

Wild horses lived in North America around 12,000 years ago, but they died out for reasons that are unclear. European explorers reintroduced horses to this continent about 600 years ago. Over time some escaped, and formed independent herds. Mustangs are therefore feral horses, that have reverted from a domesticated state back to living in the wild. By 1900, there were an estimated two million mustangs in North America, which were often caught and sold, but today there only around 33,000.

Herds of mustangs have become a symbol of the American West, but because of their ancestry they are not considered a separate species from the domestic horse.

WHERE IN THE WORLD?

Most mustangs today inhabit the state of Nevada, with others roaming in Montana, Wyoming and Oregon. Some also occur in Alberta and British Columbia, Canada.

MANE
The mane extends down the neck from the back of the head, over the shoulders.

COLOURATION
This is a variable feature in mustangs, being influenced by their origins.

HOOVES
The outer wall is worn down by the horse running over the ground.

TAIL
The long tail is used to keep flies off the body.

VIEWING ANGLE
The positioning of the horse's eyes means that it has very good visibility, alerting it to danger.

HOW BIG IS IT?

DISTINCTIVE MARKINGS
North American tribes favoured attractively coloured horses. This is an example of the Pinto, which has coloured and white patches.

Domestic Horse

• ORDER • Perissodactyla • FAMILY • Equidae • SPECIES • *Equus caballus*

One of the defining features of domestic horses is their height, which is measured in hands, with a hand being equivalent to 10cm (4in).

VITAL STATISTICS

WEIGHT	27–1520kg (700–3360lb), depending on breed
HEIGHT	43–220cm (17–87in)
SEXUAL MATURITY	2 years, but not bred until 3
GESTATION PERIOD	335–340 days
NUMBER OF OFFSPRING	1; twins are rare and not normally viable; weaned at about 8 months
DIET	Grazes on grasses and other plants, also eating bark and leaves
LIFESPAN	25–30 years, but can be up to 50

ANIMAL FACTS

Although there is only one surviving species of wild horse, DNA tests suggest four wild bloodlines contributed to the ancestry of the domestic horse, and there are now around 300 breeds. These have been developed both for their speed, as in the case of the thoroughbred, and their strength, such as the Shire horse – the tallest of all breeds.

Alert

Nervous

Cross

Uncertain

Ear posture helps to indicate the horse's mood

WHERE IN THE WORLD?

Worldwide distribution, although less common in Africa than elsewhere. Originally domesticated from wild horses that used to roam extensively in Europe and Asia.

NOSTRILS
The broad nostrils help the horse breathe quickly when running.

COLOURATION
Shades of brown and black are commonly associated with horses, often broken up with white areas.

TEETH
Incisors are well suited to nibbling plant matter, but may also inflict a painful bite.

HOOVES
Horses have just a single toe, enlarged to form a hoof.

HOW BIG IS IT?

SPEED OF MOVEMENT
Horses have a recognized series of 'paces': walk, trot, canter and gallop.

Kiang Tibetan Ass

• ORDER • Perissodactyla **• FAMILY •** Equidae **• SPECIES •** *Equus kiang*

This is the largest of the wild asses. It inhabits some of the most inaccessible terrain on earth and lives in herds of up to 400 individuals.

VITAL STATISTICS

WEIGHT	250–400kg (550–880lb)
LENGTH	2.1m (6.9ft); tail up to 50cm (20in); up to 140cm (55in) tall
SEXUAL MATURITY	1–2 years
GESTATION PERIOD	11–12 months
NUMBER OF OFFSPRING	1; weaning occurs at about 12 months
DIET	Grazes on grasses and other low-growing plants on the plains
LIFESPAN	Up to 20 years

ANIMAL FACTS

The name kiang is the native Tibetan description for these asses. They live in closely structured herds, led by an older female. Males tend to live solitary lives, although younger males do form herds over the winter. Mating occurs in the late summer, when food is at its most plentiful. Pregnant females go off on their own at this stage to give birth. The young can run soon afterwards, and the families rejoin the herd in a few weeks.

WHERE IN THE WORLD?

The Tibetan Plateau in Asia, in remote montane grassland areas at altitudes of 4000–7000m (13,123–22,966ft). Also found in northern Nepal, along the Tibetan border.

EARS
The ears are both large and mobile.

MANE
The short, dark-brown mane stands vertically.

COLOURATION
The upperparts are reddish-brown, with clearly defined white underparts and rump.

CHESTNUT
All members of the horse family have this rough area on the inside of the front legs above the knee. It is thought to be the remnant of a lost digit.

Unlike horses, these asses do not spend time grooming each other

HOW BIG IS IT?

DETERRING ATTACK
Wolves are the only major predators threatening these asses, who can defend themselves by kicking with their hind legs.

Burchell's Zebra

• **ORDER** • Perissodactyla • **FAMILY** • Equidae • **SPECIES** • *Equus quagga burchelli*

VITAL STATISTICS

WEIGHT	Around 350kg (770lb); males are larger
LENGTH	2.5m (8.2ft); up to 140cm (55in) tall at the shoulder
SEXUAL MATURITY	2–4 years
GESTATION PERIOD	12–13 months
NUMBER OF OFFSPRING	1; weaning occurs at about 12 months
DIET	Grazes on grasses and other low-growing plants on the plains
LIFESPAN	20–25 years; up to 40 in captivity

ANIMAL FACTS

Social by nature, these zebras are seen in small groups, comprising a stallion with several mares and their foals. Young males, however, live in temporary herds, splitting away as they mature to form their own harems by taking young mares from other groups. Each adult herd also has a dominant mare. It is also not uncommon for zebras to associate with other creatures of the plains, such as wildebeest and ostriches. This can help them detect predators more effectively.

Even the facial patterning of these zebras is individual

Each zebra has a distinctive individual patterning on its body. This is believed to allow herd members to recognize each other from some distance away.

WHERE IN THE WORLD?

Eastern Africa, from parts of Sudan and Ethiopia southwards via Kenya, Tanzania, Uganda, Zambia, Zimbabwe, Angola, Botswana and south as far as northern South Africa.

SHADOW STRIPING
These markings are quite distinctive. The underlying body colour is not pure white.

MANE
The mane stands upright, with the striped patterning extending through the hair.

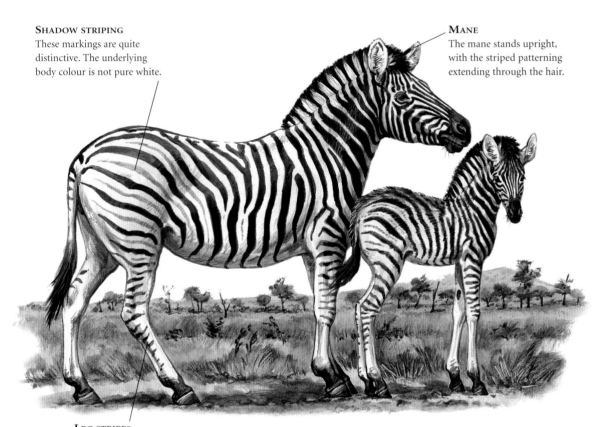

LEG STRIPES
The legs of this particular race are largely free from stripes.

HOW BIG IS IT?

DEFENDING THEMSELVES
Zebras may appear defenceless against predators such as hyenas, but a well-struck blow from their hind feet can be fatal.

White Rhinoceros

• ORDER • Perissodactyla • FAMILY • Rhinocerotidae • SPECIES • *Ceratotherium simum*

VITAL STATISTICS

WEIGHT	1800–2700kg (4000–6000lb); males are bigger
LENGTH	3.3–4.2m (10.8–13.8ft); up to 185cm (73in) tall at the shoulder
SEXUAL MATURITY	Females 6–7 years; males 10–12 years
GESTATION PERIOD	16–18 months
NUMBER OF OFFSPRING	1; weaning occurs at about 12 months
DIET	Grazes on grasses and other low-growing plants on the plains
LIFESPAN	Up to 45 years

ANIMAL FACTS

In spite of being protected, many white rhinoceroses have been slaughtered for their horns in recent years. This material is sought after in Oriental medicine, although it simply consists of keratin – the same material present in human hair. Male rhinos will use their horns for fighting, being territorial by nature, while females will defend their offspring in the same way. These large herbivores have poor eyesight, relying mainly on their sense of smell.

Rhinoceroses have very small eyes, but can swivel their ears to detect sounds well

Two distinctive populations – northern and southern – are recognized, but the northern is now feared extinct, not having been seen in the wild since 2006.

WHERE IN THE WORLD?

The northern subspecies occurred in parts of Sudan, Uganda, Chad, Central African Republic and DRC. The southern race occurs in Kenya, Uganda, Zimbabwe and South Africa.

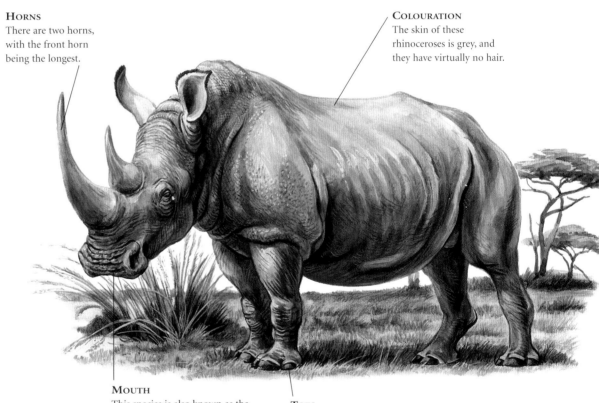

HORNS
There are two horns, with the front horn being the longest.

COLOURATION
The skin of these rhinoceroses is grey, and they have virtually no hair.

MOUTH
This species is also known as the wide-lipped rhinoceros because of its wide mouth.

TOES
These rhinos are ungulates, with three toes on each foot.

HOW BIG IS IT?

WATER BABIES

Rhinoceroses wallow regularly in mud. This keeps their skin in good condition, protecting them from insects.

Indian Rhinoceros

• **ORDER** • Perissodactyla • **FAMILY** • Rhinocerotidae • **SPECIES** • *Rhinoceros unicornis*

VITAL STATISTICS

WEIGHT	1800–2700kg (4000–6000lb); males are bigger
LENGTH	3.3–4.2m (10.8–13.8ft); up to 185cm (73in) tall at the shoulder
SEXUAL MATURITY	Females 5–6 years; males 9 years
GESTATION PERIOD	16–18 months; females give birth once every 3 years
NUMBER OF OFFSPRING	1; weaning occurs at 18 months
DIET	Grazes on grasses, leaves, branches and aquatic plants
LIFESPAN	Up to 45 years

ANIMAL FACTS

Rhinoceroses pluck vegetation using their prehensile lips. This particular species occurs in tall grasslands and open forests, which help to conceal its presence. Unfortunately, their dunging spots have been used by poachers to locate the species. Although the population had declined, it has increased once again thanks to strict protection throughout their remaining range. Indian rhinoceroses can move surprisingly fast, at speeds of up to 56kph (35mph).

A series of ridges covers the back as well as the sides of the rhinoceros's body

The Indian is the largest of Asia's three rhinoceros species, and has a very distinctive appearance. Males develop pronounced neck folds as they mature.

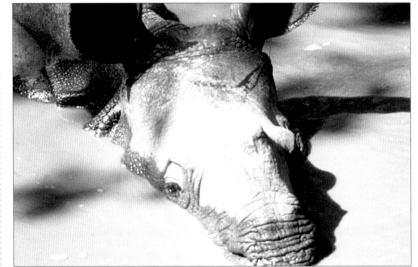

WHERE IN THE WORLD?

The range formerly extended from Pakistan eastwards, possibly as far as China, but these rhinos are now confined to Nepal and northeastern India, in the Himalayan foothills.

HORN
Just a single, relatively short horn is present on the head.

SKIN
The hairless skin is brownish-grey. It forms a series of plates that look as if they are joined by rivets.

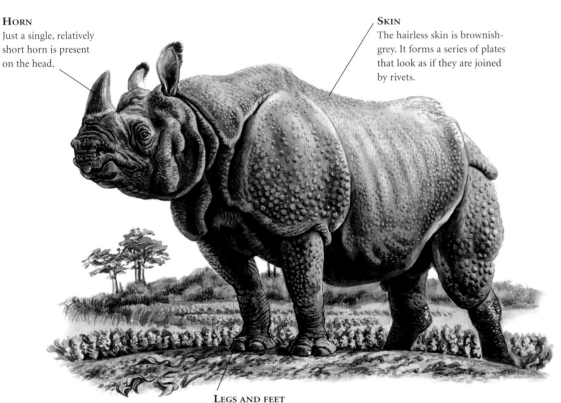

LEGS AND FEET
The legs are stumpy and there are three toes on each foot.

HOW BIG IS IT?

DEFENSIVE STRATEGY
Adult Indian rhinoceroses are unlikely to be attacked, but their calves can be vulnerable to tigers. The female will defend her calf by charging repeatedly.

Malayan Tapir

• **ORDER** • Perissodactyla • **FAMILY** • Tapiridae • **SPECIES** • *Tapirus indicus*

These tapirs are creatures of the forest, usually occurring close to water. They are hard to observe, being shy as well as nocturnal by nature.

VITAL STATISTICS

WEIGHT	250–300kg (550–660lb); males are bigger
LENGTH	1.9–2.5m (6.2–8.2ft); up to 105cm (42in) tall at the shoulder
SEXUAL MATURITY	2.5–3.5 years
GESTATION PERIOD	390–400 days; young have a mainly brown coat
NUMBER OF OFFSPRING	1; weaning occurs at 6–8 months
DIET	Grazes on grasses, aquatic plants, twigs and leaves; also eats fruit
LIFESPAN	Up to 30 years

ANIMAL FACTS

The Malayan tapir appears to follow the same paths within its territory regularly. It can negotiate steep mountain tracks without difficulty, and tends to move further into such terrain during the wet season. These tapirs can swim well, and their footprints have shown that there are particular points where they wade into a river. They frequently wallow in water and will feed on aquatic vegetation. If frightened, they can run off quickly, being vulnerable to attacks by big cats.

WHERE IN THE WORLD?

Southeast Asia, occurring in Myanmar (Burma), Cambodia, Vietnam, Laos, Thailand and Malaysia. Also present in southern and central parts of Sumatra.

NOSE
The long, prehensile nose allows the tapir to pluck its food as required.

TAIL
The tail is very short and curls round the rump.

HOOVES
Nails are present higher up the legs on either side of the hooves.

COLOURATION
The coat is a distinctive black and white pattern.

HOW BIG IS IT?

MEETING UP
Tapirs tend to be solitary by nature, but recent research has revealed they may be more social than was once thought.

BROWSING TECHNIQUE
These tapirs can use their height, combined with their primitive trunk-like nose, to browse on branches.

Leaf Insect

VITAL STATISTICS

LENGTH	6–10cm (2.3–4in)
SEXUAL MATURITY	When nymphs are fully grown
NUMBER OF EGGS	40–200, laying small numbers daily
HATCHING PERIOD	100–114 days; eggs are vulnerable to fungal attack
HABITAT	Tropical areas where there are trees and shrubs
DIET	Feeds on the plants where they take up residence, nibbling around the edge of the leaves
LIFESPAN	About 6 months

ANIMAL FACTS

A remarkable fossil of a leaf insect dating back some 47 million years has been discovered in Germany, revealing just how little members of this group have altered since then. Leaf insects undergo incomplete metamorphosis, with a nymph emerging from the egg. A series of moults through to adulthood follows, with no pupal stage in the lifecycle, unlike many insects. Young leaf insects are red when they hatch.

These phasmids have evolved to resemble leaves rather than twigs, as typified by the stick insects. They are sometimes described as walking leaves. About 30 species are recognized.

WHERE IN THE WORLD?

Occurs widely throughout most of Southern Asia, and extends from Southeast Asia across the Indonesian islands and New Guinea to parts of Australia.

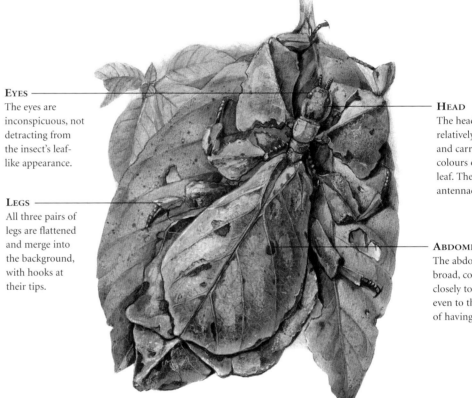

EYES
The eyes are inconspicuous, not detracting from the insect's leaf-like appearance.

LEGS
All three pairs of legs are flattened and merge into the background, with hooks at their tips.

HEAD
The head is relatively small, and carries the colours of the leaf. The paired antennae are short.

ABDOMEN
The abdomen is broad, corresponding closely to the leaf, even to the extent of having veins.

UNDER ATTACK
Leaf insects can come under attack from other invertebrates such as ants.

HOW BIG IS IT?

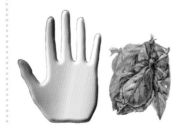

Greater Flamingo

• **ORDER** • Phoenicopteriformes • **FAMILY** • Phoenicopteridae • **SPECIES** • *Phoenicopterus roseus*

VITAL STATISTICS

WEIGHT	4kg (8.75lb)
LENGTH	91–127cm (36–50in); wingspan 152cm (60in)
SEXUAL MATURITY	3–5 years
NUMBER OF EGGS	1–2; may breed twice annually
INCUBATION PERIOD	27–30 days; young fledge at 70–75 days, and will not acquire adult plumage until they are at least 2
DIET	Sieves small invertebrates, including shrimp and molluscs, from the water
LIFESPAN	Up to 20 years

ANIMAL FACTS

These flamingos live in large colonies that can number many thousands of individuals. Much of their time is spent wading and feeding in shallow waters. They breed communally, and once the straight-billed, grey-feathered chicks are walking around, they are herded into crêches and protected by the adult birds. Flamingos are nervous creatures and do not react well to disturbances in their environment, which may explain why they are no longer commonly seen on the US mainland.

Adult flamingos have filtering plates, called lamellae, in their bills, which remove food particles from the water

The pinkish-red colouration of flamingos stems from their diet – tiny crustaceans are the source of the carotenoid pigment that is assimilated into their plumage.

WHERE IN THE WORLD?

Coastal USA, from the Carolinas to Texas. Occurs in the Bahamas and Caribbean through Mexico and northern South America. Also present on the Galapagos Islands.

NOSTRILS
These are elongated and slit-like. Flamingos, like most birds, do not have a sense of smell.

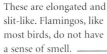

BILL
Thick in shape, with a down-curving tip, the bill reflects the flamingo's distinctive feeding habits.

NECK
Long and flexible, the neck allows the flamingo to trawl for food. It is kept extended in flight.

LEGS
The legs are long and straight, allowing these birds to wade easily through water.

NESTING
The female flamingo constructs a distinctive dome-shaped nest of mud, about 25cm (10in) high, which should not become flooded.

PAIRING
A strong pair bond exists in flamingos, even though they live in colonies. Elaborate courtship dances occur before mating.

HOW BIG IS IT?

Pangolin

• ORDER • Pholidota • FAMILY • Manidae

VITAL STATISTICS

WEIGHT	Ranges from 1.6kg (3.5lb) in the tree pangolin to 33kg (73lb) in the giant pangolin
LENGTH	63–150cm (25–60in)
SEXUAL MATURITY	2 years
GESTATION PERIOD	65–139 days; scales are soft in newborn pangolins
NUMBER OF OFFSPRING	1, but can be up to 3 in Asiatic species; weaning occurs at about 3 months
DIET	Feeds on ants and termites
LIFESPAN	Up to 20 years

ANIMAL FACTS

Many pangolins are nocturnal by nature, but the long-tailed pangolin hunts during the day. Their keen sense of smell enables them to locate ants' nests, which they will break open. They then use their long tongues, measuring up to 40cm (16in), to draw out the insects within. Pangolins have a special salivary gland that ensures their tongue remains sticky, trapping as many insects as possible. If threatened, they can also spray an acid secretion from anal glands.

The pangolin's front legs are relatively short

The name of these unusual mammals comes from the Malaysian word 'pengguling', which literally means 'something that rolls up'. Pangolins are also called spiny anteaters.

WHERE IN THE WORLD?

There are seven species, occurring in Asia, from India to Indo-China, east to China and south to Indonesia, and also across much of Africa.

SCALES
These are tough and are formed of keratin – the same material found in human hair and fingernails.

FACE
Long and narrow, with no teeth but an extendible tongue in the mouth.

FRONT FEET
Specialized in function, the front feet have long, sharp claws to break into nests of ants and termites.

TAIL
Long and flexible, the tail is well-protected by scales.

HOW BIG IS IT?

LIFESTYLE
While some pangolins live in trees, others burrow into the ground, tunnelling as far as 3.5m (11ft) below the surface.

PREHENSILE TAIL
The pangolin can use its tail as a hand to support its weight.

Pygmy Anteater

• **ORDER** • Pilosa • **FAMILY** • Cyclopedidae • **SPECIES** • *Cyclopes didactylus*

VITAL STATISTICS

WEIGHT	175–357g (6–13oz)
LENGTH	36–52cm (14–21in)
SEXUAL MATURITY	Probably about 1 year
GESTATION PERIOD	120–150 days; young are born in a tree hole lined with leaves
NUMBER OF OFFSPRING	1; weaning occurs at around 5 months
DIET	Feeds almost exclusively on arboreal ants, eating up to 8000 per day; may also prey on termites and coccinellid beetles
LIFESPAN	At least 2.5 years

ANIMAL FACTS

These anteaters inhabit areas of continuous rainforest, moving easily from one tree to another without descending to the ground. They may frequent silk cotton trees, whose seed pods are the same colour as the anteater, which offers them protective camouflage. They are at risk from harpy eagles, which will seize them out of the treetops, as well as from other birds of prey, especially spectacled owls that hunt at night, when the anteaters are also active.

Difference in the structure of the front (left) and hind claws

This is the smallest anteater in the world. It is also sometimes called the silky anteater because of the soft feel of its fur.

WHERE IN THE WORLD?

Occurs in the New World, ranging from southern Mexico down through Central America and the Amazon region in South America, reaching Brazil and possibly Paraguay.

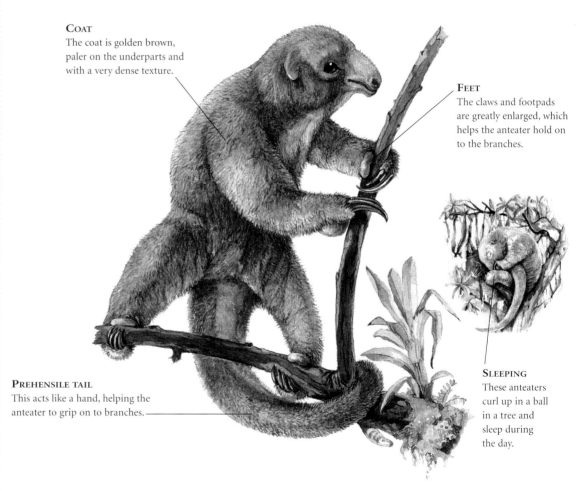

COAT
The coat is golden brown, paler on the underparts and with a very dense texture.

FEET
The claws and footpads are greatly enlarged, which helps the anteater hold on to the branches.

SLEEPING
These anteaters curl up in a ball in a tree and sleep during the day.

PREHENSILE TAIL
This acts like a hand, helping the anteater to grip on to branches.

HOW BIG IS IT?

AGGRESSIVE DISPLAY

When threatened, pygmy anteaters rear up on their hind legs, so they appear larger, and lash out with their claws.

313

Hoffman's Two-Toed Sloth

• ORDER • Pilosa • FAMILY • Megalonychidae • SPECIES • *Choloepus hoffmanni*

Slow-moving and nocturnal by nature, these sloths spend most of their lives hanging upside down from branches. Their young are born with claws to serve this purpose.

VITAL STATISTICS

WEIGHT	4–8kg (8.8–17.6lb)
LENGTH	58–70cm (23–28in)
SEXUAL MATURITY	Females 3 years; males 4–5 years
GESTATION PERIOD	Up to 365 days
NUMBER OF OFFSPRING	1; weaning occurs at 1 month; the youngster remains with its mother for 2–3 months
DIET	Feeds on vegetation, fruit, berries, bark and sometimes eggs and rodents
LIFESPAN	12 years; up to 31 in captivity

ANIMAL FACTS

There are two different species of two-toed sloth. Although they are similar in appearance, they rarely overlap in areas of forest, and tend to occur separately, like their three-toed relatives. An easy way to tell these two groups apart is that two-toed sloths climb down trees head-first, rather than backwards. They eat large quantities of vegetation, which can take up to a month to pass through their digestive systems. Unlike most mammals, they do not have the ability to shiver.

The pads behind the claws help the sloth to maintain its grip

WHERE IN THE WORLD?

Occurs in the rainforest canopy, extending from Nicaragua in Central America down to Peru, Bolivia and Brazil in South America. Probably most common in Panama.

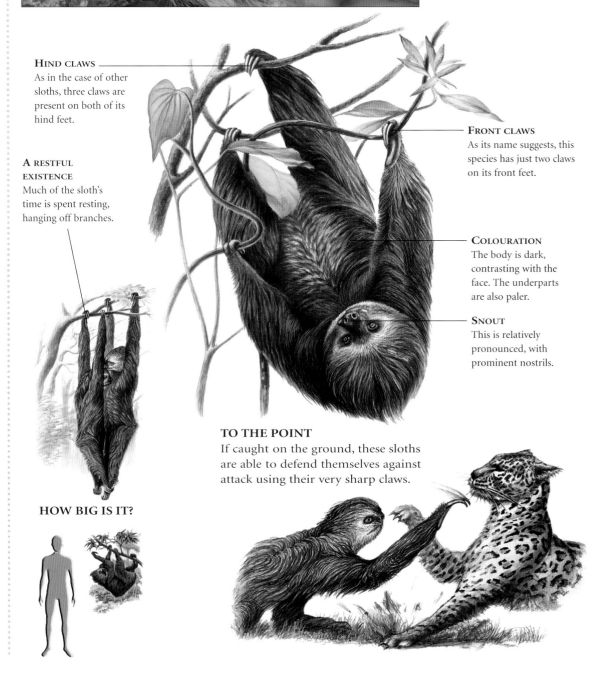

HIND CLAWS
As in the case of other sloths, three claws are present on both of its hind feet.

A RESTFUL EXISTENCE
Much of the sloth's time is spent resting, hanging off branches.

FRONT CLAWS
As its name suggests, this species has just two claws on its front feet.

COLOURATION
The body is dark, contrasting with the face. The underparts are also paler.

SNOUT
This is relatively pronounced, with prominent nostrils.

TO THE POINT
If caught on the ground, these sloths are able to defend themselves against attack using their very sharp claws.

HOW BIG IS IT?

Giant Anteater

• ORDER • Pilosa **• FAMILY •** Myrmecophagidae **• SPECIES •** *Myrmecophaga tridactyla*

VITAL STATISTICS

WEIGHT	22–40kg (49–88lb); males are bigger
LENGTH	165–220cm (65–87in)
SEXUAL MATURITY	2.5–4 years
GESTATION PERIOD	190 days; mother gives birth standing up, using her tail for support
NUMBER OF OFFSPRING	1, sometimes 2; weaning occurs at about 6 months
DIET	Feeds on ants and termites, although avoids aggressive army ants
LIFESPAN	Up to 15 years in the wild; 26 years in captivity

ANIMAL FACTS

Giant anteaters tend to be more terrestrial than their smaller relatives, although they can climb and are remarkably good swimmers. Individuals occupy large areas with sufficient nests for them to plunder. A single anteater can consume up to 30,000 ants daily. They have a very efficient feeding method, with their tongue being able to slide in and out of the nest up to 160 times a minute. The young are carried on the backs of their mothers.

The anteater's sharp front claws can rip apart the wall of ant or termite nests very easily.

The largest of the anteaters, this species lives in relatively open countryside and relies on its amazingly long tongue and powerful claws to obtain its food.

WHERE IN THE WORLD?

Ranges from Guatemala in Central America through South America to the east of the Andes, as far south as northwestern parts of Argentina and Uruguay.

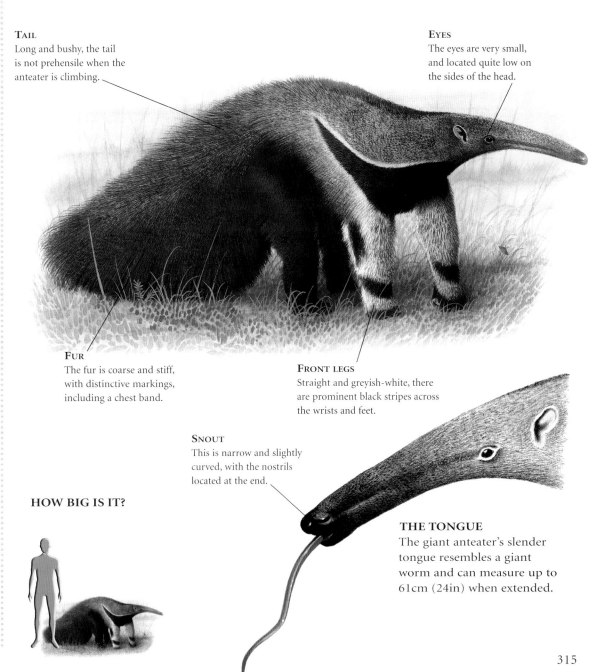

TAIL
Long and bushy, the tail is not prehensile when the anteater is climbing.

EYES
The eyes are very small, and located quite low on the sides of the head.

FUR
The fur is coarse and stiff, with distinctive markings, including a chest band.

FRONT LEGS
Straight and greyish-white, there are prominent black stripes across the wrists and feet.

SNOUT
This is narrow and slightly curved, with the nostrils located at the end.

HOW BIG IS IT?

THE TONGUE
The giant anteater's slender tongue resembles a giant worm and can measure up to 61cm (24in) when extended.

Southern Tamandua

• ORDER • Pilosa • FAMILY • Myrmecophagidae • SPECIES • *Tamandua tetradactyla*

VITAL STATISTICS

WEIGHT	3–7kg (7–16lb); males are bigger
LENGTH	93–147cm (37–58in); the tail is almost as long as the body
SEXUAL MATURITY	From 1 year
GESTATION PERIOD	130–150 days
NUMBER OF OFFSPRING	1; weaning occurs at around 3 months
DIET	Feeds largely on arboreal ants and termites, avoiding those that can defend themselves effectively, such as army ants
LIFESPAN	Up to 9.5 years

ANIMAL FACTS

These anteaters spend much of the day asleep in tree holes. They can have difficulty walking on the ground, as they are forced to use the outside of their feet to prevent injury to their palms because of their sharp claws. Southern tamandua seem to attract insects such as flies and mosquitoes. This may be linked in part to their body odour, as they can produce an unpleasant scent from their anal glands.

This species of anteater cannot run on the ground, but will lunge at a predator if cornered

This member of the anteater family is also known as the collared anteater. Colouration varies markedly, depending on the area of origin.

WHERE IN THE WORLD?

Occurs in South America, in an area ranging east of the Andes from Venezuela in the north, southwards as far as Argentina and Uruguay.

EARS
The ears are large and elongated.

FRONT PAWS
There are four claws present on the front paws, with five on each hindfoot.

COLOURATION
Those from southeastern areas have black markings from shoulder to rump. Elsewhere colours vary from solid blond to black.

TAIL
The prehensile tail supports the anteater off the ground. The underside and tip are hairless.

HOW BIG IS IT?

FLEXIBLE FEEDING

Southern tamanduas can hang off branches to reach insect nests. They also adopt this posture if threatened, so they can strike out with their powerful forelegs.

Nancy Ma's Night Monkey

• **ORDER** • Primates • **FAMILY** • Aotidae • **SPECIES** • *Aotus nancymaae*

VITAL STATISTICS

WEIGHT	Around 780g (28oz)
LENGTH	72cm (28.5in); up to 35cm (14in) tall
SEXUAL MATURITY	From 2 years
GESTATION PERIOD	133 days
NUMBER OF OFFSPRING	1; weaning occurs at 6–8 months
DIET	Omnivorous, feeding on fruit, vegetation, invertebrates, plus eggs and small birds
LIFESPAN	Up to 20 years in captivity

ANIMAL FACTS

These primates represent the only nocturnal group of monkeys, emerging from their sleeping dens shortly after nightfall, and returning before dawn. They forage in groups, seeking out fruiting trees, and have remarkable reflexes that allow them to catch night-flying insects such as moths in flight. They can also jump distances of up to 4m (13ft) safely. Night monkeys spend their time in the upper part of the forest canopy, and face few predators, other than birds of prey.

Until 1983, there was thought to be only one species of night monkey, but genetic tests have shown that eight separate species actually exist.

Found in South America, south of the Amazon, restricted to the border area between Peru and Brazil, from Marañon in the north, extending south to the Juru.

ENHANCED NIGHT-TIME VISION
This is made possible by large eyes, with a relatively spherical lens and more rod cells on the retina where the image forms.

FACE SHAPE
This monkey has a flattened face, with owl-like disc markings of white fur around the eyes.

HANDS AND FEET
This species is very agile, and can grasp branches securely.

TAIL
The long tail acts as a counter-balance to prevent falls.

FEEDING OPPORTUNITIES
A bird can be plucked off its nest more easily in the darkness than would be possible during the day.

HOW BIG IS IT?

MOVING SAFELY
Night monkeys are quadrupeds, moving along the branches on all four feet, and this helps them to maintain their balance.

Red-Faced Black Spider Monkey

• **ORDER** • Primates • **FAMILY** • Atelidae • **SPECIES** • *Ateles paniscus*

These long-limbed monkeys are not only the largest members of their genus, but also rank amongst the biggest monkeys in the New World.

VITAL STATISTICS

WEIGHT	9.7–10.8kg (21.3–21.8lb); males are slightly heavier
LENGTH	About 55cm (22in)
SEXUAL MATURITY	From 2 years
GESTATION PERIOD	133 days
NUMBER OF OFFSPRING	1; weaning occurs at 6–8 months
DIET	Feeds mainly on fruit, but also eats flowers, leaves, bark and honey
LIFESPAN	Up to 33 years

ANIMAL FACTS

Living in the upper levels of the rainforest canopy, typically at 25–30m (82–98ft) off the ground, these monkeys are adept at using their prehensile tails to anchor themselves on to branches. This then leaves their hands free to forage for food. The red-faced black spider monkey's tail actually has more vertebrae than usual, which are smaller in size, improving its flexibility. These monkeys can also move quickly through the forest thanks to their elongated arms and their hook-like hands.

WHERE IN THE WORLD?

Occurs in northern South America, from Guyana, Surinam and French Guiana south to Brazil, north of the Amazon River, and also east of the Rio Negro.

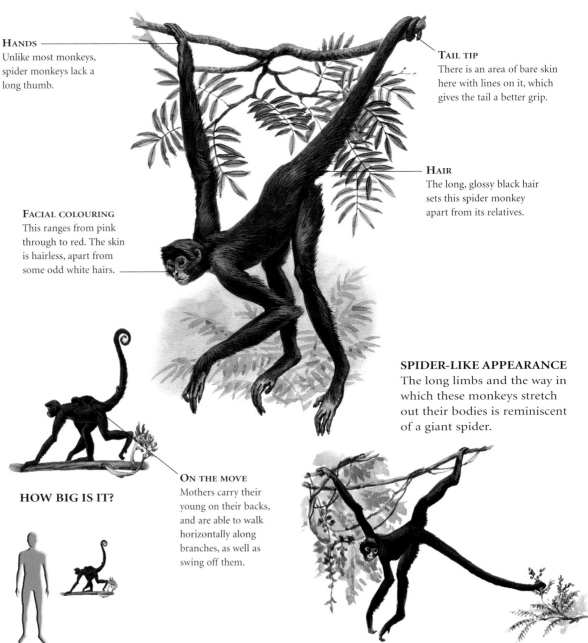

HANDS
Unlike most monkeys, spider monkeys lack a long thumb.

TAIL TIP
There is an area of bare skin here with lines on it, which gives the tail a better grip.

FACIAL COLOURING
This ranges from pink through to red. The skin is hairless, apart from some odd white hairs.

HAIR
The long, glossy black hair sets this spider monkey apart from its relatives.

SPIDER-LIKE APPEARANCE
The long limbs and the way in which these monkeys stretch out their bodies is reminiscent of a giant spider.

HOW BIG IS IT?

ON THE MOVE
Mothers carry their young on their backs, and are able to walk horizontally along branches, as well as swing off them.

Brown Howler Monkey

• **ORDER** • Primates • **FAMILY** • Atelidae • **SPECIES** • *Alouatta guariba*

The loud calls made by these monkeys indicate their presence and deter neighbouring troops from invading their feeding territory, thereby avoiding conflict.

VITAL STATISTICS

WEIGHT	4–7kg (8.8–15.4lb); females are smaller
LENGTH	93–126cm (37–50in) overall; the tail is slightly longer than the body
SEXUAL MATURITY	Females 3 years; males 3.5 years
GESTATION PERIOD	About 190 days
NUMBER OF OFFSPRING	1; weaning occurs at 12–13 months; females give birth every 1.5–2 years
DIET	Feeds on vegetation and fruit, depending on the time of year; also eats invertebrates
LIFESPAN	Up to 20 years

WHERE IN THE WORLD?

Occurs in southern parts of South America, in southeastern Brazil and northeastern Argentina. May also be found in adjacent areas of Uruguay and Bolivia.

ANIMAL FACTS

These monkeys have a very unusual way of digesting their food. As with all animals that feed on vegetation, they need beneficial microbes to break down the cellulose present in the cell walls of the plants they eat. These are concentrated in two areas of the stomach, and produce volatile fatty acids as a by-product of the breakdown process. It is these gases that are absorbed in the body and help to meet the monkey's energy needs.

FACE
This is free of fur, allowing facial gestures, indicating the monkey's mood, to be seen clearly.

HOWLING
Unlike other species, the brown howler does not regularly stage a dawn chorus.

MANE
The fur is longer around the face, creating the appearance of a beard.

HANDS
The hands have five digits, with the first finger and thumb opposing the other three.

SOUNDING OFF
There are often several males in a troop. Disputes are rare but fights between males and females do occur.

HOW BIG IS IT?

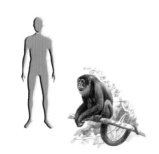

RESTING

Howler monkeys are relatively inactive, resting during the day when they are not feeding, although they are more active in winter, when food is scarcer.

Brown Woolly Monkey

• **ORDER** • Primates • **FAMILY** • Atelidae • **SPECIES** • *Lagothrix lagotricha*

These noisy primates are very playful by nature, and juvenile monkeys in particular spend a lot of time playing around with each other.

VITAL STATISTICS

WEIGHT	3.5–10kg (7.7–22lb); males are bigger
LENGTH	99–140cm (39–55in) overall; the tail is slightly longer than the body
SEXUAL MATURITY	Females 6–8 years; males 5 years
GESTATION PERIOD	About 225 days
NUMBER OF OFFSPRING	1; weaning occurs at 9–12 months; females give birth every 1.5–2 years
DIET	Frugivorous, eating fruit, as well as vegetation and invertebrates
LIFESPAN	Nearly 26 years in captivity

ANIMAL FACTS

Active during the daytime, these woolly monkeys live in groups numbering between 10 and 45 individuals, although they will split up and head off separately when foraging. Wild figs are their favoured food. Although there is a hierarchy within the troop, all males will mate with receptive females, but it is the dominant male that assumes precedence. Their territory may overlap with neighbouring groups, which can be joined by young females as they mature and leave their natal troop.

WHERE IN THE WORLD?

Found in South America, in parts of Colombia, Venezuela, Peru and Ecuador, as well as Bolivia and Brazil, favouring different areas of habitat throughout its range.

HEAD
The head is rounded, with very small ears on the side.

EYES
The frontal location of the eyes helps the monkey land safely when jumping.

TAIL IN CLOSE-UP
There is no fur on the underside of the tail, near the tip, making it easier for the monkey to grip branches.

TAIL
Long and prehensile, the tail helps the monkey hold on to branches securely.

COLOURATION
The colour varies from a relatively light to a very dark, blackish-brown shade.

HOW BIG IS IT?

DANGER FROM ABOVE
The huge harpy eagle represents a serious danger to these primates, who utter a warning call on sighting an eagle, then hide under the leaves in the hope of escaping detection.

Pygmy Marmoset

• ORDER • Primates **• FAMILY •** Cebidae **• SPECIES •** *Callithrix (Cebuella) pygmaea*

The smallest of all monkeys, the size of these primates allows them to feed off slender branches that are out of the reach of their relatives.

VITAL STATISTICS

WEIGHT	120–140g (4–5oz); females are smaller
LENGTH	29–36cm (11.4–14.1in) overall; the tail is longer than the body
SEXUAL MATURITY	1–1.5 years
GESTATION PERIOD	119–140 days
NUMBER OF OFFSPRING	2, occasionally 3; males are responsible for carrying the young for 2 months until they are largely weaned
DIET	Sap from trees, returning daily to feed on the exudate; also eats fruit and invertebrates
LIFESPAN	Up to 11 years

ANIMAL FACTS

These marmosets use their teeth in an unusual way, cutting notches in the bark of trees, which allows them to reach sap. Pygmy marmosets live in small groups comprised of an adult pair and perhaps four younger individuals. They are very vocal, uttering a series of whistles, squeaks and clicks. This enables them to communicate any hint of danger in their vicinity. At close quarters, they also communicate by means of facial gestures and body posture.

Facial gestures are used to communicate

WHERE IN THE WORLD?

Found in northern South America, restricted to the rainforest areas of southeastern Colombia, eastern parts of Ecuador and Peru, northern Bolivia and western Brazil.

FACE
The face is quite broad, with the eyes appearing close together and the ears hidden by fur.

ACROBATIC HUNTING
Their agility helps pygmy marmosets to catch invertebrates. They can jump vertically up to 5m (16ft), and bound between branches.

LEGS AND FEET
Nimble by nature, these marmosets can run up and down branches easily.

COLOURATION
Tawny patterning helps to conceal the presence of these marmosets.

TAIL
Long and slender, this is banded along its length and tapers to a tip. It is not prehensile.

HOW BIG IS IT?

PREDATORS
Larger snakes hunt pygmy marmosets, as do wild cats. They are also vulnerable to birds of prey flying over the canopy.

Golden Lion Tamarin

• ORDER • Primates • FAMILY • Cebidae • SPECIES • *Leontopithecus rosalia*

VITAL STATISTICS

WEIGHT	400–800g (14–29oz)
LENGTH	45–56cm (18–22in) overall; the tail is longer than the body
SEXUAL MATURITY	Females 24 months; males 18 months
GESTATION PERIOD	About 130 days; young are born from September to March
NUMBER OF OFFSPRING	1; weaning occurs at 3–5 months; females give birth every 1.5–2 years
DIET	Fruit, also eats invertebrates and small lizards
LIFESPAN	Up to 15 years; 28 in captivity

ANIMAL FACTS

The wild golden lion tamarin population had fallen to about 100 by the early 1980s, before a release scheme involving zoo-bred stock was established. Their numbers in the wild are now estimated at about 1500 individuals. They live in family groups, consisting of a pair and their offspring. When the female gives birth again, they help to care for the young, learning parenting skills for when they leave the group.

Strong bonds exist between members of a group

One of the most colourful of all monkeys, the golden lion tamarin has suffered from the extensive deforestation of its forest habitat, and is now considered endangered.

WHERE IN THE WORLD?

Occurs in coastal areas of Brazil, in Rio de Janeiro and Espirito Santos states. By 1981, it was restricted to just 900 square kilometres (350 square miles) in the Rio São João Basin.

HITCHING A RIDE
Young tamarins are carried on the backs of adults – usually the male.

MANE
In both sexes, a long mane of fur surrounds the dark-coloured face.

FEET
The toes are long, helping the tamarin to probe into crevices to flush out invertebrates.

CLAWS
Primates generally have nails, but the tamarin's claws are useful for grabbing invertebrates.

HOW BIG IS IT?

FEEDING POSTURE
The front feet can be used to hold food, allowing the tamarin to eat while sitting on its haunches.

Emperor Tamarin

• **ORDER** • Primates • **FAMILY** • Cebidae • **SPECIES** • *Saguinus imperator*

The distinctive moustachioed appearance of these monkeys led to them being named after Emperor Wilhelm II of Germany, following their discovery in the early 1900s.

VITAL STATISTICS

WEIGHT	350–450g (10.5–13.5oz)
LENGTH	58–67.5cm (23–27in) overall; tail is longer than the body
SEXUAL MATURITY	1–1.5 years
GESTATION PERIOD	140–145 days
NUMBER OF OFFSPRING	2; all members of the troop help raise the youngsters
DIET	Fruit during the wet season, along with sap, plus nectar in the dry season; also eats invertebrates
LIFESPAN	Up to 11 years

ANIMAL FACTS

Emperor tamarins live in groups comprised of a single female accompanied by two or three males. They spend most of their time in the trees, but can walk or run across the ground on all fours legs. Noisy by nature, they call particularly frequently when close to a neighbouring territory, as a way of deterring incursions by members of the other troop. They form mixed bands with saddleback tamarins, however, as which allows them to spot aerial predators more effectively.

There is a short, clawless inner digit on each hind foot

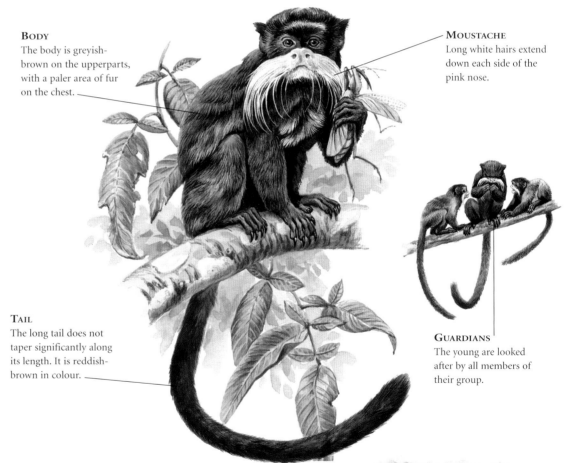

WHERE IN THE WORLD?

Occurs throughout western Amazonia in South America, in lowland tropical rainforest. Present in areas of Peru, Brazil and Bolivia, sometimes isolated by rivers.

BODY
The body is greyish-brown on the upperparts, with a paler area of fur on the chest.

MOUSTACHE
Long white hairs extend down each side of the pink nose.

TAIL
The long tail does not taper significantly along its length. It is reddish-brown in colour.

GUARDIANS
The young are looked after by all members of their group.

HOW BIG IS IT?

UP AND DOWN

These tamarins are territorial by nature, with a group occupying an area of about 0.4 square kilometres (0.15 square miles) of forest.

Cottontop Tamarin

• ORDER • Primates • FAMILY • Cebidae • SPECIES • *Saguinus oedipus*

VITAL STATISTICS

WEIGHT	400–450g (14.1–15.9oz)
LENGTH	45–50cm (18–20in) overall; tail is longer than the body
SEXUAL MATURITY	Females around 1.5 years; males 2 years
GESTATION PERIOD	125–140 days
NUMBER OF OFFSPRING	2, sometimes 1; female troop members assist in raising the youngsters
DIET	Fruit and invertebrates, plus leaves, sap and nectar
LIFESPAN	Up to 13.5 years

ANIMAL FACTS

These tamarins have a remarkable ability to communicate with each other, possessing 38 distinctive calls, ranging from bird-like whistles to much more staccato vocalizations. These help to indicate the monkey's mood and also indicate possible danger. Their body language is much more limited, but they can lower their foreheads over their eyes and erect their cotton-like crest, as a warning gesture. If threatened by another troop, cottontop tamarins will display their hindquarters as a means of intimidating them.

Viewed face-on, it is easy to see where the cottontop tamarin gets its name

These tamarins have a very limited range, and three-quarters of their forest habitat has now been destroyed. Their population consists of around 2000 individuals.

WHERE IN THE WORLD?

Found in Colombia, in northwestern South America. Their distribution lies between the Atrato River and the Magdalena River in the remaining areas of forest.

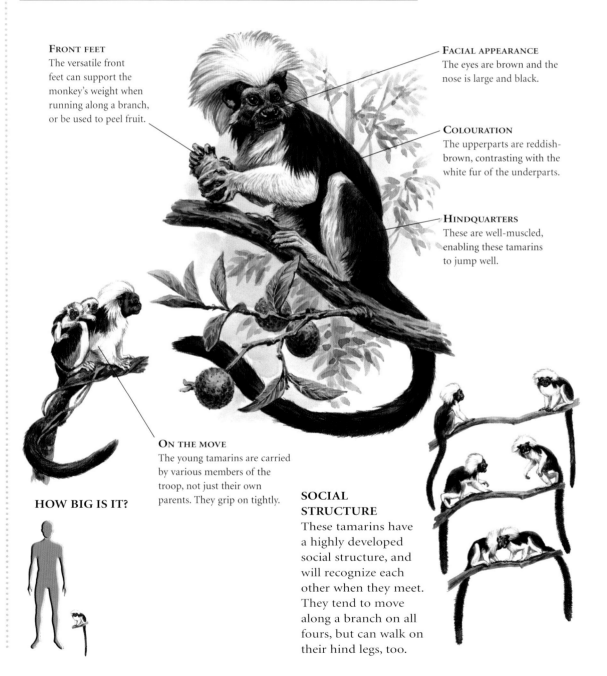

FRONT FEET
The versatile front feet can support the monkey's weight when running along a branch, or be used to peel fruit.

FACIAL APPEARANCE
The eyes are brown and the nose is large and black.

COLOURATION
The upperparts are reddish-brown, contrasting with the white fur of the underparts.

HINDQUARTERS
These are well-muscled, enabling these tamarins to jump well.

ON THE MOVE
The young tamarins are carried by various members of the troop, not just their own parents. They grip on tightly.

HOW BIG IS IT?

SOCIAL STRUCTURE
These tamarins have a highly developed social structure, and will recognize each other when they meet. They tend to move along a branch on all fours, but can walk on their hind legs, too.

Common Squirrel Monkey

• **ORDER** • Primates • **FAMILY** • Cebidae • **SPECIES** • *Saimiri sciureus*

VITAL STATISTICS

WEIGHT	560–1250g (19.5–44.1oz); males are heavier
LENGTH	64–84cm (25–33in) overall; tail is longer than the body
SEXUAL MATURITY	Females about 2 years; males 4 years
GESTATION PERIOD	160–170 days; births coincide with the wet season
NUMBER OF OFFSPRING	1; weaning occurs at 6 months
DIET	Fruit and invertebrates, plus leaves and flowers
LIFESPAN	Up to 20 years in captivity

ANIMAL FACTS

These primates practise an unusual form of scent-marking, by urinating on their hands and then depositing their scent as they walk along the branches. Squirrel monkeys spend most of their time in the treetops, and rarely descend to the ground. They tend to split up into small groups each day, heading off in different directions in the forest to search for food, with individuals keeping in touch by calling. Members of the troop roost communally at night.

The position of the monkey's eyes, at the front of the head, mean that it can pinpoint prey with great accuracy

These monkeys, so-called because they look rather like squirrels, live in large groups of up to 200 individuals, with a complex social structure.

WHERE IN THE WORLD?

Ranges across northern forested parts of South America, from Colombia and Venezuela through the Guianas into Brazil; range also extends south to Peru, Ecuador and Bolivia.

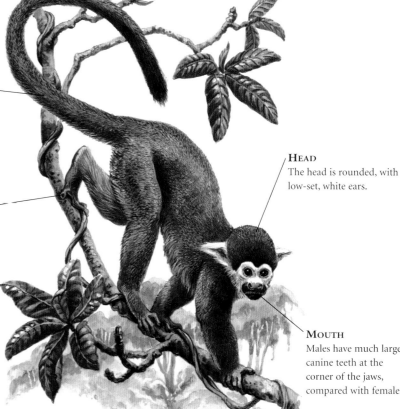

TAIL
This is long, and acts as a balancing aid rather than being prehensile.

HIND FEET
A shorter inner digit, corresponding to our big toe, is present on each foot.

HEAD
The head is rounded, with low-set, white ears.

MOUTH
Males have much larger canine teeth at the corner of the jaws, compared with females.

TAIL AND FEET
The squirrel monkey's tail is longer than its body. These primates will scent-mark by using their feet.

HOW BIG IS IT?

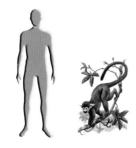

WRESTLING

Young squirrel monkeys have no apparent fear of falling, although individuals do occasionally lose their footing, with fatal consequences.

White-Faced Capuchin Monkey

• **ORDER** • Primates • **FAMILY** • Cebidae • **SPECIES** • *Simia capucinus*

VITAL STATISTICS

WEIGHT	2.6–5.5kg (5.7–12lb); males are heavier
LENGTH	74–96cm (29–38in) overall; tail is longer than the body
SEXUAL MATURITY	5–6 years
GESTATION PERIOD	About 150 days; births coincide with the wet season
NUMBER OF OFFSPRING	1; twins are rare; weaning takes place by 2 years
DIET	Fruit and invertebrates, plus leaves and flowers
LIFESPAN	Up to 44 years in captivity

ANIMAL FACTS

Living in groups that can consist of up to 30 individuals, these capuchins occupy the lower understorey of the forest. They engage in regular grooming both of themselves and other members of the troop, mainly using their hands. They have also been observed rubbing themselves with certain leaves, possibly as a way of deterring parasites. The young are cared for by various females in the group, rather than just their own mothers.

Capuchins as a group are named after the Capuchin friars; the distinctive black head of the different species resembles that of the monks' cowls

These capuchins are not only found in forests but also in coastal areas, where they live in mangroves and forage in the mud at low tide.

WHERE IN THE WORLD?

Range extends from Belize in Central America southwards into South America, where they can be found in northern and western parts of Colombia.

TAIL
The prehensile nature of the tail allows the monkey to use it rather like another hand.

FACIAL FEATURES
The skin on the face is pink and the surrounding fur is white.

FUR
This is dense and is predominantly black all over the body.

EARS
These are relatively large and flattened on the sides of the head. They are not hidden by hair.

HOW BIG IS IT?

FOOD AND DRINK

Capuchins come down to the ground to collect fruit and may drink by using their hands to scoop up water.

Vervet Monkey

These monkeys have developed what is effectively a language, with a vocabulary of different calls that can warn of different predators such as snakes and eagles.

VITAL STATISTICS

WEIGHT	2.5–4.5kg (5.5–10lb); males are heavier
LENGTH	64–93cm (25–37in) overall; tail is usually longer than the body
SEXUAL MATURITY	4–6 years
GESTATION PERIOD	About 210 days; births coincide with the start of the wet season
NUMBER OF OFFSPRING	1; weaning occurs from 6 months
DIET	Feeds mainly on fruit, plus other plant matter, invertebrates and small vertebrates
LIFESPAN	Up to 20 years

ANIMAL FACTS

Intelligent and adaptable, these monkeys inhabit relatively open country. They may forage either on the ground or in the trees. They live in troops of up to 80 individuals. Vervets are very vocal, and also communicate by facial gestures. Their curiosity can lead them into trouble, however, as in the Caribbean, where they have a reputation for stealing alcoholic drinks from holiday-makers.

WHERE IN THE WORLD?

Occurs in Africa, south of the Sahara. Also present in the Caribbean on Barbados and St Kitts, having been introduced there during the era of the slave trade.

VERVET
The slight greenish tinge to the fur explains why they are called vervets.

HANDS
The hands, like the feet, are black and similar to human hands in structure.

SCROTUM
A bright blue colouration of the skin on the scrotum shows a male of high social status.

FAMILY TIES
Females in the group are responsible for taking care of the young and will discipline them if they behave badly.

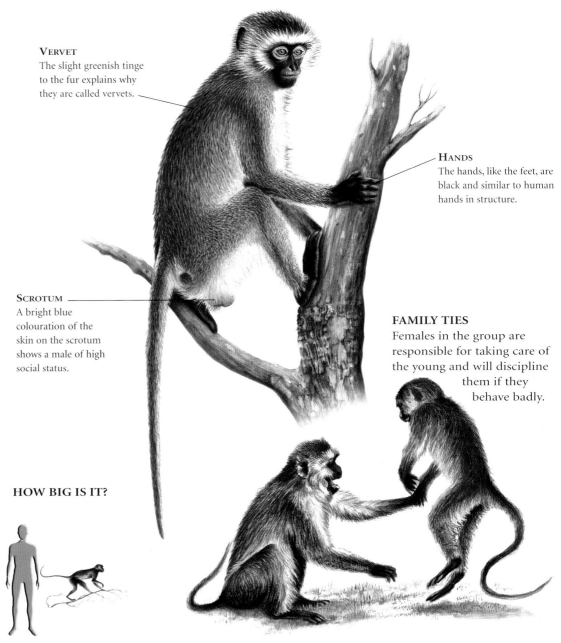

Wild cats will prey on these monkeys, but vervets are agile and can usually escape easily off the ground

HOW BIG IS IT?

Mantled Guereza

• **ORDER** • Primates • **FAMILY** • Cercopithecidae • **SPECIES** • *Colobus guereza*

VITAL STATISTICS

WEIGHT	9.2–13.5kg (20.3–29.8lb); males are heavier
LENGTH	96–129.5cm (38–51in) overall; tail is usually longer than the body
SEXUAL MATURITY	4–6 years
GESTATION PERIOD	About 150 days; births coincide with the start of the wet season
NUMBER OF OFFSPRING	1; weaning occurs by 6 months
DIET	Feeds largely on leaves, but will also eat some fruit
LIFESPAN	Up to 23 years in captivity

ANIMAL FACTS

These monkeys eat a specialist diet of leaves, which has led to their digestive system adapting to break down the cellulose so they can thrive on a high-fibre diet. In the upper part of the monkey's stomach there are bacteria and protozoa that undertake this task, buffered by saliva produced in the salivary glands. This area is separated from the other part of the stomach, whose main function is simply to store the leaves.

These strikingly patterned monkeys belong to a group that are mainly black and white. They spend most of their time in the treetops.

WHERE IN THE WORLD?

Occurs in Africa, from Nigeria, Cameroon and the Democratic Republic of Congo to Sudan and Ethiopia in the northeast, and parts of Uganda, Tanzania and Kenya.

HANDS
These monkeys have only four fingers on each hand.

TAIL
The tail is black along much of its length, but tipped with long white fur.

DANGER OVERHEAD
Mantled guerezas have to be watchful in the canopy because of the risk of being seized by birds of prey.

COAT COLOURATION
Adults are black and white, but newborn mantled guerezas are pure white.

HOW BIG IS IT?

JUMPING SAFELY
These monkeys can leap from branch to branch, supporting themselves as they land with their hands and then their feet.

Pigtail Macaque

This species of macaque occurs in the tropical zone. The porcine appearance of its short and essentially bare tail explains its common name.

VITAL STATISTICS

WEIGHT	4.7–14.5kg (10.4–32lb); males are heavier
LENGTH	56–85cm (22–33in)
SEXUAL MATURITY	Females 3–4 years; males 6–8 years
GESTATION PERIOD	About 165 days
NUMBER OF OFFSPRING	1; weaning occurs from 4 months
DIET	Mainly vegetarian, eating fruit and plant matter, including corn and cassava crops, plus invertebrates
LIFESPAN	Probably 10–15 years; up to 30 in captivity

ANIMAL FACTS

Pigtail macaques prefer undisturbed rainforest areas where there is likely to be a plentiful supply of fruit all year round. They have become adept at raiding crops, however, particularly during thunderstorms. One of the troop will stay on guard, screaming loudly if a person is spotted. Some farmers have taken advantage of this, training young macaques to pick coconuts for them

Young macaques are carried on their mother's backs, and soon learn to use this vantage point to observe the world around them.

WHERE IN THE WORLD?

Occurs in Southeast Asia, from western India and Bangladesh to China, via Laos, Cambodia, Thailand and Malaysia to parts of Indonesia, including Sumatra and Borneo.

TAIL
This is carried in a distinctive, half-erect porcine fashion, although it is not twisted in a corkscrew shape.

COAT
The coat is brown, paler around the face and white below.

FACE
The face is a pale shade of pink, not deep red as in some macaques.

HOW BIG IS IT?

GETTING ALONG WITH THE NEIGHBOURS
Members of different troops may come into close contact with each other on occasion, but they are usually quite tolerant.

Rhesus Macaque

• **ORDER** • Primates • **FAMILY** • Cercopithecidae • **SPECIES** • *Macaca mulatta*

VITAL STATISTICS

WEIGHT	5.5–12kg (12–26lb); males are heavier
LENGTH	64–96cm (25–38in)
SEXUAL MATURITY	Females 3–4 years; males around 6–8 years
GESTATION PERIOD	About 165 days
NUMBER OF OFFSPRING	1; weaning occurs from 4 months
DIET	Mainly vegetarian, eating fruit, leaves, seeds, nuts, roots and bark; will eat some invertebrates
LIFESPAN	Probably 10–15 years; can be up to 30 in captivity

ANIMAL FACTS

Although they spend much of their time on the ground, these monkeys are found in a very wide range of habitats, from tropical landscapes to temperate areas where winter snow is common. Wooded areas are often chosen, but in India they are found in open agricultural landscapes and have adapted to living alongside people. They are seen in groups, led by females, despite the larger size of males.

Body language is important in these macaques: staring at an another individual, revealing the teeth, is a threat gesture

The part played by these monkeys in the discovery of the different human blood groups in the 1940s is commemorated by the term 'rhesus antigen'.

WHERE IN THE WORLD?

Their natural range is in southern Asia, extending from Afghanistan eastwards via India to Thailand and southern China. An introduced population also exists in Florida.

TAIL
The tail is short, indicative of the relatively terrestrial lifestyle of these monkeys.

APPEARANCE
The fur is predominantly brown. This species often walks on all fours.

TEATS
Females have a pair of teats on their chest for suckling their offspring.

FACIAL PATTERNING
The fur on the faces of these monkeys is short, emphasizing their expressions. The ears are conspicuous.

SWIMMING
Rhesus monkeys swim well, so they are able to cross stretches of water in search of food.

HOW BIG IS IT?

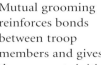

GROOMING
Mutual grooming reinforces bonds between troop members and gives them opportuinities to remove parasites such as ticks.

Barbary Ape

• ORDER • Primates **• FAMILY •** Cercopithecidae **• SPECIES •** *Macaca sylvanus*

VITAL STATISTICS

WEIGHT	5.5–13kg (12–29lb); males are heavier
LENGTH	38–76cm (15–30in)
SEXUAL MATURITY	Females 3–4 years; males 4.5–7 years
GESTATION PERIOD	190–196 days
NUMBER OF OFFSPRING	1, rarely twins; weaning occurs at around 12 months
DIET	Mainly vegetarian, eating fruit, leaves, seeds, nuts, roots and some invertebrates
LIFESPAN	Up to 22 years

ANIMAL FACTS

The Gibraltarian population consists of around 200 monkeys, which live on the steep-sided rock, although individuals occasionally roam down into the town. In North Africa, however, Barbary apes inhabit forested areas, up to an altitude of 2160m (7086ft). They live in mixed-sex troops, headed by a matriarch, and unlike other macaques, males of this species are involved in the care of the offspring.

Barbary apes can be fierce and can give a powerful bite

In spite of their name, these primates are monkeys rather than apes, and the only ones to be found in Europe, albeit in a very small area.

WHERE IN THE WORLD?

As their name suggests, these macaques originate from Africa's Barbary coast, occurring in Morocco and northern Algeria. They are also present on the Rock of Gibraltar.

UPPERPARTS
The colour of the upperparts can vary from yellowish-grey to greyish-brown. The fur around the face is darker.

FORELIMBS
They are strong and powerful, allowing these monkeys to climb well.

UNDERPARTS
Underparts are whitish. The fur tends to be longer around the face.

MOUTH POUCHES
In common with other members of their family, Barbary apes have pouches in their mouths in which they can store food.

HOW BIG IS IT?

Mandrill

VITAL STATISTICS

WEIGHT	11–27kg (24–60lb); males are heavier
LENGTH	63–88cm (25–35in), including short tail
SEXUAL MATURITY	Females 3.5 years; males 4.5–7 years
GESTATION PERIOD	About 186 days
NUMBER OF OFFSPRING	1, rarely twins; weaning occurs at around 8 months
DIET	Mainly vegetarian, eating fruit, leaves, seeds, nuts, roots and some invertebrates
LIFESPAN	Up to 46 years

ANIMAL FACTS

These monkeys live in groups, with more than 1300 recorded together in Gabon's Lopé National Park. This is the largest association of primates apart from humans ever recorded. Generally, though, mandrills occur in much smaller groups, numbering perhaps 12. They spend most of the time on the ground, where they forage for food. Females carry their young slung beneath their bodies.

Mandrills have formidable canines, measuring up to 5cm (2in) long. Exposing them like this is often a welcoming sign

The mandrill is the largest species of monkey – its name actually means 'man-ape'. Males will grow to about twice the size of females.

WHERE IN THE WORLD?

Occurs in the tropical rainforests of West Africa, from the Sanaga River southwards, in southern Nigeria, Cameroon, Gabon, Equatorial Guinea and the Congo.

CHANGE IN APPEARANCE
The skin colour becomes brighter when the monkey is excited.

FUR
This is mainly olive-brown, with a whitish underside.

COLOURATION
The colour of the mandrill's distinctive rump may help them to see each other in the forest.

HOW BIG IS IT?

CHANGING APPEARANCE
Young mandrills have predominantly dark faces at first, and will start to develop their distinctive colouration as they grow older.

Proboscis Monkey

• **ORDER** • Primates • **FAMILY** • Cercopithecidae • **SPECIES** • *Nasalis larvatus*

There is no mistaking these monkeys, mainly because of the male's protruding nose. Troops may occasionally be seen walking upright like people, along forest paths.

VITAL STATISTICS

WEIGHT	10–20kg (22–44lb); males are twice as heavy as females
LENGTH	135–147cm (53–58in) overall; tail is longer than the body
SEXUAL MATURITY	Females 4 years; males 4–7 years
GESTATION PERIOD	166 days
NUMBER OF OFFSPRING	1; weaning occurs at around 8 months
DIET	Young leaves in the first part of the year, followed by unripe fruit
LIFESPAN	Up to 23 years

ANIMAL FACTS

These leaf-eating monkeys became known locally as Monyet belandas or Dutch monkeys, caricaturing the Dutch settlers who colonized this part of Southeat Asia. Living close to water, proboscis monkeys can swim well and wade upright in the shallows. They drop off branches into water to escape predators such as clouded leopards, but are vulnerable to crocodilians. Habitat clearance has meant that the numbers of this primate have fallen in recent years.

Even when drinking, proboscis monkeys rarely descend to the ground

WHERE IN THE WORLD?

Populations are restricted to Southeast Asia, found on the island of Borneo. Here they occur at low altitude, in areas of forest, mangrove and swamp.

NOSE
Up to 18cm (7in) long, this swells with blood if the male feels threatened, and amplifies his calls.

HANDS
These monkeys use their hands to pick the young leaves from the trees.

TOES
Webbing between the toes help these monkeys to swim.

BELLY
Large and rounded, the chambered stomach houses microbes to break down vegetation.

HOW BIG IS IT?

DIFFERENT SIZES
The difference in size between the male (foreground) and female proboscis monkey is greater than in any other primate. The male's nose attracts mates.

Hamadryas Baboon

• ORDER • Primates • FAMILY • Cercopithecidae • SPECIES • *Papio hamadryas*

VITAL STATISTICS

WEIGHT	9–21.5kg (20–47lb); males are about twice as heavy as females
LENGTH	99–137cm (39–54in) overall; tail can be as long as the body
SEXUAL MATURITY	Females 4.3 years; males 4.8–7 years
GESTATION PERIOD	172 days
NUMBER OF OFFSPRING	1; weaning occurs at 6–15 months
DIET	Omnivorous, eating vegetable matter, fruit and small vertebrates and invertebrates
LIFESPAN	Up to 38 years

ANIMAL FACTS

When a female is ready to mate, the skin beneath her tail becomes engorged with an increased blood flow. Young baboons are totally dependent on their mothers at first, and are carried around by them. Males develop slowly, but are usually able to mate before they have acquired full adult colouration. These primates can converse in a variety of ways, by vocalizations and also by body language. Yawning, which exposes the canine teeth, is a threat gesture.

These adaptable primates live in a harsh area of the world, favouring rocky areas where they can climb. They will not stray far from water.

WHERE IN THE WORLD?

Occurs in parts of Africa adjacent to the southern Red Sea, in parts of Ethiopia, Somalia and Eritrea, extending to the Middle East, in Saudi Arabia and Yemen.

TAIL
This is long and curved, and its length varies between individuals.

MALES
Males are large, with a silvery mane on the head.

FEMALES
Females are olive-brown and lack any mane, although the area beneath the tail is pink, as with males.

YOUNG
These baboons have black fur at birth, which becomes olive-brown from six months onwards.

MATING
The dominant male will chase, attack and bite a female in the group who is seen showing interest in young males.

HOW BIG IS IT?

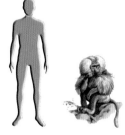

Red-Shanked Douc

• **ORDER** • Primates • **FAMILY** • Cercopithecidae • **SPECIES** • *Pygathrix nemaeus*

VITAL STATISTICS

WEIGHT	5–7kg (11–15lb); males are heavier
LENGTH	117–152cm (46–60in) overall; tail is longer than the body
SEXUAL MATURITY	Females around 4 years; males 4–5 years
GESTATION PERIOD	165–190 days
NUMBER OF OFFSPRING	1, rarely twins; weaning occurs at 11 months
DIET	Vegetarian, favouring leaves, but will also eat fruit in season, flowers and seeds
LIFESPAN	Up to 25 years

ANIMAL FACTS

These amazingly athletic monkeys can leap distances of 6m (20ft) from branch to branch in the forest canopy. They live in small groups, each one occupying a particular area of the forest where they move on what are effectively set pathways around the treetops. Young doucs cling on to their mothers from birth, and travel with the rest of the troop. It takes around 10 months for them to obtain adult colouration.

The douc's slanted eyes point forwards, helping it to judge distances accurately when jumping

WHERE IN THE WORLD?

Found in Southeast Asia, in Laos as well as northern and central parts of Vietnam, at altitudes of up to 2000m (6600ft) in forested areas.

FACIAL DISTINCTION
Males of this species have much fluffier white hair framing the face.

SHARING
Unusually, members of a troop will pick leaves and share these with each other.

HANDS
These are relatively long and strong, helping the douc to pluck vegetation easily.

TAIL
This is white along its length and is used for balancing, not for grasping.

HOW BIG IS IT?

SWIMMING
A lesser-known characteristic of this douc is its ability to swim, although it rarely descends to the ground.

Hanuman Langur

VITAL STATISTICS

WEIGHT	11.2–18.3kg (25–40lb); males are heavier
LENGTH	109–178cm (43–70in) overall; tail is longer than the body
SEXUAL MATURITY	Females around 4.3 years; males 4.8–7 years
GESTATION PERIOD	170–200 days
NUMBER OF OFFSPRING	1; weaning occurs at 13–20 months
DIET	Vegetarian, eating a range of fruit, leaves and flowers
LIFESPAN	Up to 20 years

ANIMAL FACTS

Life for the young in a troop is hazardous, because if a new male displaces the established dominant male, he will kill youngsters still being nursed by their mothers. This means that these females will mate again more quickly, helping the male exert a wider, lasting influence on the genetic make-up of the group. These monkeys spend most of their time on the ground, walking on all fours, and they can be quite common in urban areas.

There is a short thumb on the front feet, which assists the monkey's climbing abilities, and nails on each digit

Also known as the grey or common langur, this species is named after the Hindu monkey-god Hanuman, and is regarded as sacred in India.

WHERE IN THE WORLD?

Occurs in southern Asia, extending across India and Pakistan to Bangladesh and Myanmar (Burma). Also present on the island of Sri Lanka, off India's southeastern coast.

HABITAT
They favour open woodland rather than dense forest, where they can climb and walk along the branches.

COLOURATION
These langurs are mainly grey, with a black face, feet and hands.

SIZE
The largest of these langurs occur in northern parts of the species' range.

HIND FEET
These monkeys often support their bodies by sitting up on their hindquarters.

HOW BIG IS IT?

PAUSING TO DRINK
Splaying their front feet out in this fashion enables these langur monkeys to lap up water easily.

Gelada Baboon

These monkeys are not actually true baboons, as their nostrils are located further from the end of their muzzle, but they resemble baboons in appearance.

VITAL STATISTICS

WEIGHT	11–20kg (24–44lb); males about twice as heavy as females
LENGTH	82–114cm (32–45in)
SEXUAL MATURITY	Females around 4–5 years; males 5–7 years
GESTATION PERIOD	150–180 days
NUMBER OF OFFSPRING	1; weaning occurs at 12–18 months
DIET	Herbivorous, having adapted to feed on grass, although eats roots in the dry season
LIFESPAN	Up to 30 years

ANIMAL FACTS

The gelada baboon's ancestors used to range over a much wider area. It is the last survivor of a group that once extended as far as India. The red patch on the chest, which becomes more swollen in females when they are in oestrus, is similar to the skin in the genital region of baboons. It has evolved on the chest, however, because geladas spend most of their time sitting on their buttocks.

Male and female gelada baboons have a very different physique and appearance once they reach maturity

WHERE IN THE WORLD?

Restricted to the highlands of northern Africa, occurring at altitudes of 1400–4400m (4600–14,400ft) in open areas of grassland in Ethiopia.

FEMALES
Smaller than males, females also lack the longer mane of fur.

HANDS
The thumb is very flexible, helping these monkeys to pick shoots of grass easily.

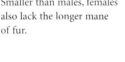

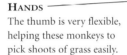

TAIL
The hair at the tip of the female's tail is much longer than in males, forming a tuft.

SKIN COLOURATION
The bright red patch of skin on the chest is another way of distinguishing this species from baboons.

PROFILE
The head profile differs between sexes, with the nose of the male (bottom) quite different to that of the female.

HOW BIG IS IT?

SOCIAL STRUCTURE
Geladas live in harems comprising a male with several females, which come together in areas where food is plentiful.

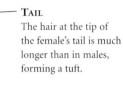

337

Aye-Aye

• ORDER • Primates • FAMILY • Daubentoniidae • SPECIES • *Daubentonia madagascariensis*

These strange creatures were originally classified as rodents, but now they are recognized as the largest of the nocturnal primates. They are solitary by nature.

VITAL STATISTICS

WEIGHT	About 2.6kg (1.1lb)
LENGTH	74–90cm (29–35in) overall; tail is longer than the body
SEXUAL MATURITY	About 2.5 years
GESTATION PERIOD	160–172 days; young remain in the nest for 2 months
NUMBER OF OFFSPRING	1; weaning occurs at 5.5–7 months
DIET	Fruit, nuts and plant matter, as well as various wood-boring insects
LIFESPAN	Up to 24 years

ANIMAL FACTS

Aye-ayes have a very distinctive method of hunting invertebrates, tapping on branches with their elongated third digits. The resulting sound reveals hollows beneath the bark where prey could be lurking. They use their powerful incisors to bite through the bark, just like a rodent, to reach any invertebrates lurking beneath, which they can then prise out with their slender finger. These adaptable digits may also be employed to scrape out the pulp of fruits.

The third digit on each hand is particularly slender and gnarled

WHERE IN THE WORLD?

Found only on the island of Madagascar, off the southeastern coast of Africa. These primates are quite widely distributed through various wooded areas there.

EARS
These are very large and have a distinctive triangular shape.

SNOUT
This is short, with a pink nose.

DIGITS
The third digits on the aye-aye's hands are enlarged, so it can extract insect larvae from bark.

TAIL
The tail is long and bushy, covered – like the body – in coarse dark hair, with odd white hairs.

THE NEST
Aye-ayes build a nest of twigs and leaves up in the treetops, where they sleep during the day.

HOW BIG IS IT?

THE SEARCH
These primates are supremely adapted to finding and accessing hidden food.

Bushbaby

VITAL STATISTICS

WEIGHT	150–250g (5.3–8.8oz)
LENGTH	27–44cm (11–17in) overall; tail is longer than the body
SEXUAL MATURITY	9–12 months
GESTATION PERIOD	About 125 days
NUMBER OF OFFSPRING	1–2; weaning occurs at 3.5 months; females produce litters at intervals of 4–8 months
DIET	Mainly invertebrates such as moths and grasshoppers; also fruit, seeds and flowers
LIFESPAN	Up to 16 years

ANIMAL FACTS

Emerging under cover of darkness, bushbabies may travel distances of up to 2km (1.2 miles) during the course of a single night. They have a number of nests throughout their territory where they can rest. Living in relatively open country, they can also hop along the ground and can walk on all fours, too. Although usually solitary, they may occasionally be observed in small family groups. Males are territorial by nature, defending an area from others of their own kind.

Scent-marking is very important to these small primates. Males will urinate on their hands, thereby depositing their scent as they climb around on branches.

WHERE IN THE WORLD?

These bushbabies occur in areas of bush in the central part of southern Africa, in savanna and semi-arid woodland areas.

EARS
These have four distinctive ridges and can be bent, helping the bushbaby locate the source of a sound.

EYES
Relatively large and directed forwards, these allow the bushbaby to jump safely.

TAIL
This helps the bushbaby to balance and is covered with long hair at its tip.

HANDS
The thumbs are not opposable but this does not disadvantage the bushbaby when climbing.

MOTHERHOOD
A young bushbaby spends the first 10–14 days of its life in its nest, then moves around with its mother, clinging on to her fur.

HOW BIG IS IT?

A bushbaby's front paw, showing the lack of a functional thumb

JUMPING
The bushbaby springs off a branch with its hind legs and grabs the branch with its hind feet on landing.

Gorilla

• **ORDER** • Primates • **FAMILY** • Hominidae • **SPECIES** • *Gorilla gorilla*

The largest of the world's primates, it is thought that the gorilla lineage split from that of the chimpanzee and humans about seven million years ago.

VITAL STATISTICS

WEIGHT	60–275kg (132–606lb); males are larger
LENGTH	140–180cm (55–71in)
SEXUAL MATURITY	Females 10 years; males 15 years
GESTATION PERIOD	251–289 days
NUMBER OF OFFSPRING	1, very rarely twins; weaning occurs at 3–4 years
DIET	Feeds mainly on leaves, also fruit, flowers, roots and invertebrates; will eat clay to detoxify plant matter
LIFESPAN	Up to 50 years

ANIMAL FACTS

In spite of their fearsome appearance, gorillas are not aggressive by nature. They live in small family groups, moving through their territory and making fresh beds (nests) of grass where they sleep each night. They will climb trees on occasion, particularly the younger, more agile members of the group, to reach fruit. There are fears that, aside from poaching, the Ebola virus may be decimating populations of these great apes.

Male gorillas appear especially formidable when they stand up on their hind legs

WHERE IN THE WORLD?

Western Africa, occurring in the forests of Gabon, Equatorial Guinea, Central African Republic, Democratic Republic of the Congo, Cameroon and south as far as Angola.

HEAD COLOURATION
The reddish area on the head is a distinctive feature of lowland gorillas.

FEET
These are very broad, facilitating walking, but the toes are relatively short and the big toe is widely spaced.

FOREARMS
These are strong, and gorillas walk on their knuckles rather than their palms.

FEMALES
Females have a rounded belly, and lack the silver fur on the back that characterizes dominant males.

HOW BIG IS IT?

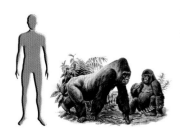

FEEDING
These gorillas may venture into wet areas, feeding on aquatic vegetation. They have also been known to use primitive tools.

Bonobo

• **ORDER** • Primates • **FAMILY** • Hominidae • **SPECIES** • *Pan paniscus*

The bonobo's alternative name of pygmy chimpanzee is thought to refer to the stature of the native people in the area in which it is found.

VITAL STATISTICS

WEIGHT	27–61kg (59.5–134lb); males are larger
LENGTH	104–124cm (41–49in)
SEXUAL MATURITY	13–15 years for both sexes
GESTATION PERIOD	About 240 days
NUMBER OF OFFSPRING	1, very rarely twins; weaning occurs at 4 years
DIET	Feeds mainly on fruit but also eats flowers, roots and some invertebrates; may catch duiker and bats
LIFESPAN	Up to 50 years

ANIMAL FACTS

Social by nature, these chimpanzees keep in touch when they are on the move with a variety of calls, some of which have been likened to words in terms of their specific meanings. Members of the group bond by grooming activities and will stare intently at another individual to attract its attention. They can be aggressive, too. In this species, it is the young males that remain in the troop, and the females leave as they mature.

The longer-legged, darker and slimmer bonobo (left) can be distinguished easily in profile from the common chimpanzee (right)

WHERE IN THE WORLD?

Occurs in forests in the Democratic Republic of the Congo, occupying an area between the Congo and Lualaba rivers, south to the Kasai River.

NOSTRILS
These are large and open at the front of the nose.

HAIR
This is black and clearly apparent on the cheeks. The skin is also dark in colour.

HIND LEGS
These are relatively long, with distinctive knees.

FRONT FEET
Bonobos can walk upright on their back feet, but generally walk on their knuckles as well.

DAILY LIFE
Finding food occupies a large amount of the bonobo's day.

HOW BIG IS IT?

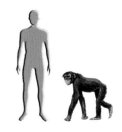

TOOL USE
These chimpanzees use basic tools, creating objects such as simple vessels for collecting and drinking water.

Chimpanzee

• **ORDER** • Primates • **FAMILY** • Hominidae • **SPECIES** • *Pan troglodytes*

VITAL STATISTICS

WEIGHT	26–70kg (57–154lb); males are larger
LENGTH	64–93cm (25–37in)
SEXUAL MATURITY	13–15 years for both sexes
GESTATION PERIOD	About 230 days
NUMBER OF OFFSPRING	1, rarely twins; weaning occurs at 3.5–4.5 years
DIET	Feeds mainly on fruit although also eats flowers, roots and some invertebrates; may also catch small mammals and reptiles
LIFESPAN	Up to 60 years

ANIMAL FACTS

Studies of chimpanzees have revealed that they consume various plants that may have medical properties in treating ailments, from parasites to tumours. These can be identified by the way in which the chimps eat them, which is different to how they eat their normal food: they may seek out specific plants when needed, and swallow their leaves without chewing them.

Young chimpanzees playing together; they are able to laugh like humans

342

Regarded as our closest surviving relatives, chimpanzees stand up to 170cm (67in) tall on their hind legs. They live in groups, largely on the ground.

WHERE IN THE WORLD?

Found in central Africa, in areas of tropical forest and ranging from the Gambia across to the Congo and eastwards to Uganda.

COLOURATION
The skin of chimpanzees darkens with age, although their hair often becomes greyish over the back.

HANDS
The long fingers can be curled into the hand when the chimpanzee is walking on the ground.

HOW BIG IS IT?

COMMUNICATION
Chimpanzees are noisy. Their calls indicate their moods and keep members of the group in touch with each other.

Bornean Orangutan

VITAL STATISTICS

WEIGHT	40–90kg (88–198lb); males are larger
LENGTH	78–97cm (31–38in)
SEXUAL MATURITY	15 years for both sexes
GESTATION PERIOD	About 260 days; the youngster may be carried by its mother for 3 years
NUMBER OF OFFSPRING	1, rarely twins; weaning occurs at 3.5–4.5 years
DIET	Feeds mainly on fruit, but will also eat leaves and seeds
LIFESPAN	Up to 60 years

ANIMAL FACTS

Orangutans are the largest of all arboreal mammals and they rarely come down to the ground. They have a very slow reproductive rate, with females giving birth only once every eight years or more. Although they are hunted, it is loss of habitat that represents the greatest threat to orangutans, combined with natural disasters such as forest fires that may sweep through their habitat. They feed on more than 400 different plants, with wild figs being a favourite.

Their feet, like their hands, support these great apes

Orangutan literally means 'person of the forest', referring to the hominoid appearance of these great apes. The Sumatran orangutan is now considered a separate species.

WHERE IN THE WORLD?

Occurs only on the island of Borneo, in rainforest up to altitudes of 800m (2620ft). Fossil evidence suggests their ancestors occurred on the Southeast Asian mainland, too.

FLANGE
Only males have the flattened area around the face, extending as a dewlap under the throat.

ARMS
These are very long and may reach up to 2m (6.6ft). The hands are largely free of fur.

COAT
The coats of these great apes are shaggy and reddish.

HOW BIG IS IT?

ON THE MOVE
Orangutans can use both their arms and legs together to grip on to branches alternately as they swing through the forest.

Lar Gibbon

• **ORDER** • Primates • **FAMILY** • Hylobatidae • **SPECIES** • *Hylobates lar*

VITAL STATISTICS

WEIGHT	Around 5.5kg (12lb); males are slightly larger
LENGTH	45–50cm (18–20in)
SEXUAL MATURITY	About 9 years for both sexes
GESTATION PERIOD	217–248 days
NUMBER OF OFFSPRING	1; weaning occurs at 1.5 years; females breed every 2–3 years
DIET	Mainly fruit, also leaves and other vegetation, plus eggs and sometimes invertebrates and small vertebrates
LIFESPAN	25–30 years

ANIMAL FACTS

Lar gibbons are incredibly agile and able to jump 15m (50ft) from tree to tree. Aside from swinging under the branches, they can also walk along them, extending their arms out to keep their balance. Their calls are very loud, and carry through the forest, amongst the cacophony of other sounds, helping to indicate their territory. The arboreal nature of these gibbons means they are particularly vulnerable to the effects of deforestation in the areas where they are still present.

The elongated palms of the hand (left) help these gibbons maintain their grip; the foot is shown on the right

These gibbons inhabit the upper canopy of the rainforest, swinging confidently between branches using their hands. They are rarely seen on the forest floor.

WHERE IN THE WORLD?

Occurs in Southeast Asia, in Myanmar (Burma), China and through Thailand and Malaysia to Indonesia, reaching south to the island of Sumatra.

HANDS
This species is also called the white-handed gibbon, because of the colour of its fur here.

BODY COLOURATION
Colour can vary from black through shades of brown to fawn, with white fur around the face.

HUNTING TECHNIQUE
A lar gibbon may surprise a nesting bird, as its reflexes are quick enough to grab it in flight.

HOW BIG IS IT?

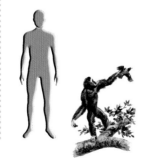

SWINGING FREE

The arms are long, allowing the gibbon to swing through trees. This method of locomotion, with the gibbon using its hands to grip the branches alternately, is called brachiation.

Siamang Gibbon

VITAL STATISTICS

WEIGHT	10–12kg (22–26lb)
LENGTH	100cm (39in)
SEXUAL MATURITY	7–9 years for both sexes
GESTATION PERIOD	About 235 days; the youngster may be carried by its mother for 3–4 months
NUMBER OF OFFSPRING	1, occasionally twins; weaning occurs at 18–24 months
DIET	Mainly fruit, especially wild figs; also eats young leaves, seeds and flowers
LIFESPAN	Up to 30 years

ANIMAL FACTS

The siamang is the largest of the gibbons, occupying the mid-upper layers in the forest. They are very territorial by nature, with the male seeking to drive out any intruders, which can include people. When moving slowly through the trees, they grab a branch with one hand before releasing the other, but when travelling at a quicker pace, they use their momentum to carry them through the air. They can cover 8–10m (26–33ft) between one grasp and the next in this fashion.

Young siamang gibbons have to cling on to the underside of their mother's body as she moves through the forest

Few primates are as noisy as the siamang gibbon, with members of a pair calling repeatedly to each other as they move through the rainforest.

WHERE IN THE WORLD?

Restricted to areas of the rainforest in Southeast Asia, ranging from the Malay Peninsula southwards to the island of Sumatra.

FACIAL HAIR
The area around the eyes and nose, reaching the lower chin, is free from hair.

ARMS
These are twice as long as the body, allowing the gibbon to swing along below branches.

THROAT SAC
This allows amplification of the duetting calls of these gibbons.

FEET
Two of the fingers on each foot are fused together, aiding their grip.

HOW BIG IS IT?

DOWN ON THE GROUND

These gibbons must walk with their hands help up, because their length means they would otherwise drag along the ground.

Indri Lemur

VITAL STATISTICS

WEIGHT	7–10kg (15.4–22lb); males are slightly larger
LENGTH	66–96cm (26–38in)
SEXUAL MATURITY	7–9 years for both sexes
GESTATION PERIOD	120–150 days
NUMBER OF OFFSPRING	1; weaning occurs at around 6 months; females typically breed every 2–3 years
DIET	Mainly fruit, but also leaves and other vegetation, including flowers
LIFESPAN	Probably up to 40 years

ANIMAL FACTS

These lemurs spend most of their time off the ground. Their feet are well-adapted for their environment as, apart from the big toe, their toes are fused together. In the trees, they jump vertically, and move in a similar way on the ground, with their long arms raised above the head. Pairs are active during the day, and mark their territory with urine. Wiping their muzzles on branches may also leave a scent behind to warn off those who might encroach into their territory.

The wailing calls of these lemurs can be heard 1.9km (1.2 miles) away; the sound is amplified in the throat

The description 'indri' simply means 'there it is', a term that was mistakenly believed to be the native name for this particular lemur!

WHERE IN THE WORLD?

Restricted to Madagascar, off the southeastern coast of Africa. Found in the northeast of the island, from sea level up to 1800m (5900ft).

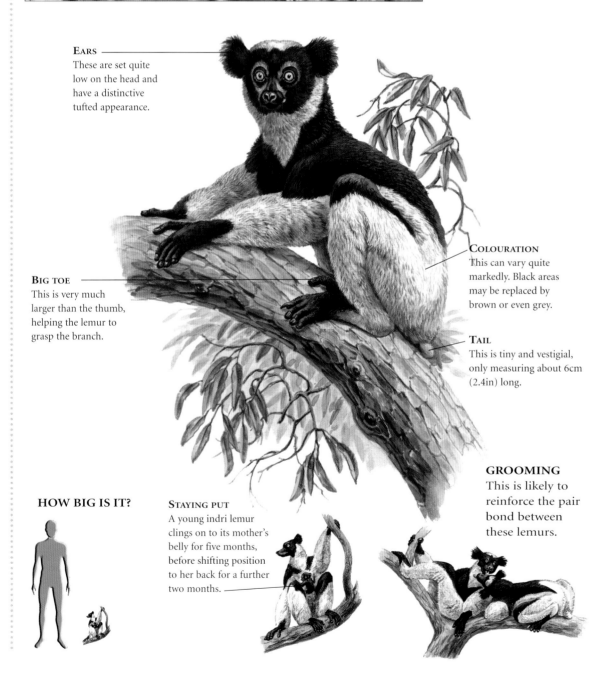

EARS
These are set quite low on the head and have a distinctive tufted appearance.

BIG TOE
This is very much larger than the thumb, helping the lemur to grasp the branch.

COLOURATION
This can vary quite markedly. Black areas may be replaced by brown or even grey.

TAIL
This is tiny and vestigial, only measuring about 6cm (2.4in) long.

GROOMING
This is likely to reinforce the pair bond between these lemurs.

HOW BIG IS IT?

STAYING PUT
A young indri lemur clings on to its mother's belly for five months, before shifting position to her back for a further two months.

Ring-Tailed Lemur

• ORDER • Primates • FAMILY • Lemuridae • SPECIES • *Lemur catta*

VITAL STATISTICS

WEIGHT	2.3–3.5kg (5.1–7.7lb)
LENGTH	103–110cm (41–43in) overall; tail is much longer than the body
SEXUAL MATURITY	2.5–3 years
GESTATION PERIOD	About 135 days
NUMBER OF OFFSPRING	1, very rarely twins; weaning occurs by 5 months
DIET	Fruit and leaves, particularly of the tamarind tree; also eats flowers, nuts, invertebrates and small vertebrates
LIFESPAN	Up to 19 years; 27 years in captivity

ANIMAL FACTS

The striped appearance of the lemur's tail, as well as its unusual purring sounds, are reminiscent of a cat, which explains its scientific name. There are a number of glands on the lemur's body, ranging from the forearms to the genital area, which it uses for scent-marking. Males scrape the spur on their front legs to leave a scent behind on trees.

These lemurs have highly specialized hands, with a sharp claw on each front foot for grooming purposes

The ancestors of today's lemurs reached their island homeland somewhere between 50 and 80 million years ago. This is the only surviving member of its family.

WHERE IN THE WORLD?

Restricted to the island of Madagascar, mainly in the southern and southwestern parts of the island, extending inland to the Andringitra mountains.

EYES
The bright yellow or orange eyes are surrounded by black spectacles of fur.

ON THE GROUND
Ring-tailed lemurs are more terrestrial than most other lemurs, and are sometimes observed travelling across the ground in groups.

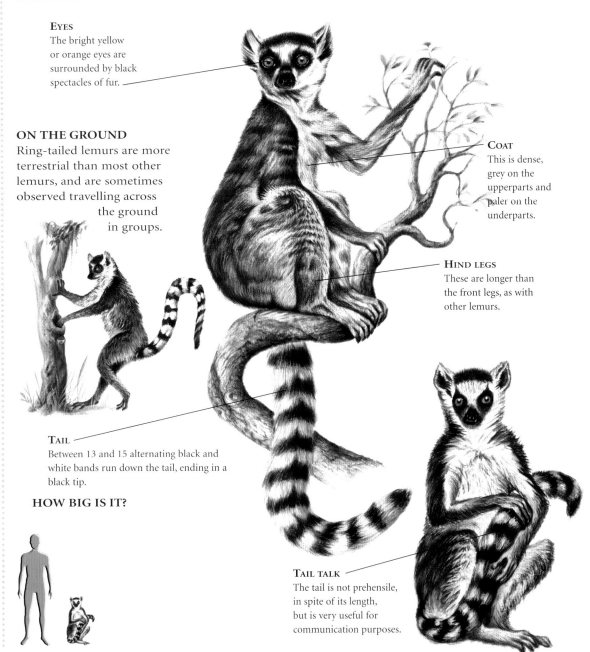

COAT
This is dense, grey on the upperparts and paler on the underparts.

HIND LEGS
These are longer than the front legs, as with other lemurs.

TAIL
Between 13 and 15 alternating black and white bands run down the tail, ending in a black tip.

HOW BIG IS IT?

TAIL TALK
The tail is not prehensile, in spite of its length, but is very useful for communication purposes.

Uakari Monkey

• ORDER • Primates • FAMILY • Pitheciidae • SPECIES • *Cacajao calvus*

The distinctive faces of these monkeys have a purpose. Females select males with the reddish faces, as they are regarded as the strongest in the troop.

VITAL STATISTICS

WEIGHT	2.3–3.5kg (5.1–7.7lb)
LENGTH	54–56cm (21–22in) overall; tail is a third of the body length
SEXUAL MATURITY	Females about 3.5 years; males 5.5 years
GESTATION PERIOD	About 135 days
NUMBER OF OFFSPRING	1; weaning occurs at 15–21 months
DIET	Strong teeth allow these monkeys to crack tough-cased fruit, nuts and invertebrates
LIFESPAN	Up to 20 years in the wild

ANIMAL FACTS

Part of the difficulty in studying these monkeys is that they occur in areas of forest that tend to be flooded for much of the year. They live high up in the canopy, where they are hard to observe due to their generally quiet nature. In fact, the existence of a new species in Brazil was confirmed in 2008. If they do descend to the ground, other members of the troop serve as look-outs, warning of approaching danger.

The nostrils in these monkeys are well separated (left), unlike those of gorillas (right)

WHERE IN THE WORLD?

Occurs in northern South America, but its precise distribution is unclear. Concentrated in the central Amazon basin, from Colombia and Venezuela down to Peru and Brazil.

FACIAL FEATURES
The face is hairless up to the top of the head and is bright red.

NOSE
Females release a chemical messenger when ready to mate so males require a good sense of smell.

FUR
This race (*C. c. calvus*) is characterized by its silver-white fur.

TAIL
These monkeys have the shortest tails of all New World monkeys.

NEWBORNS
Young bald uakaris are carried on their mother's backs at first, gripping on to the sides of her body. They have dark fur.

HOW BIG IS IT?

SUBSPECIES
Bald uakaris with this orange-red fur belong to the subspecies *C.c. rubicundus*, rather than being a separate species.

Dusky Titi

VITAL STATISTICS

WEIGHT	0.88–1.02kg (1.9–2.2lb)
LENGTH	Around 73cm (29in) overall; tail is longer than the body
SEXUAL MATURITY	Around 2.5 years
GESTATION PERIOD	Around 128 days
NUMBER OF OFFSPRING	1; weaning occurs at 15–21 months
DIET	Mainly on fruit, but also young leaves and invertebrates
LIFESPAN	Probably 20 years; up to 25 in captivity

ANIMAL FACTS

Living in relatively open areas of forests and being active during the day exposes these monkeys to birds of prey – their major predators. The monkeys freeze, and rely on their colouration to blend into the background when such birds are sighted. Other monkeys, notably capuchins (*Cebus* species) may also attack them, especially when they are feeding on fruit. When breeding, female titi monkeys will seek out more invertebrates, as a way of increasing their protein intake.

These small monkeys are active during the day, waking up at dawn. During the night, they usually huddle together in nests, holding each other's tails.

WHERE IN THE WORLD?

Occurs in South America, with this particular species confined to Brazil, in forested areas ranging across the country to the south of the Amazon River.

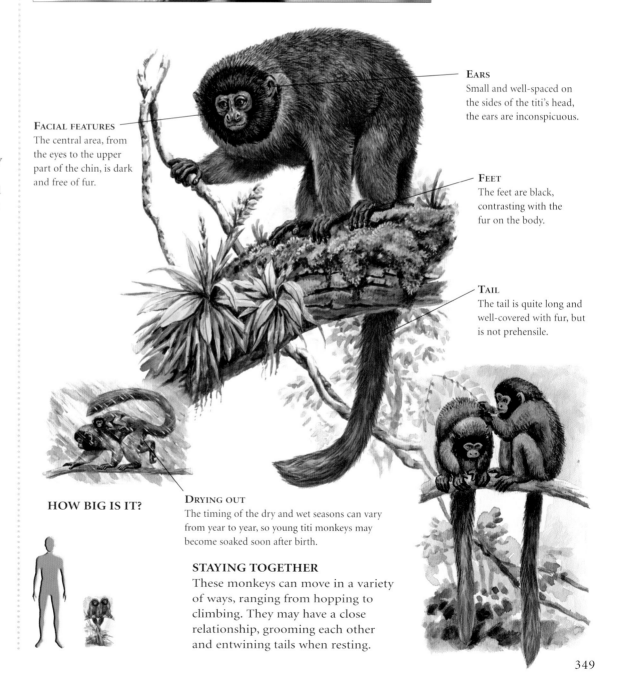

EARS
Small and well-spaced on the sides of the titi's head, the ears are inconspicuous.

FACIAL FEATURES
The central area, from the eyes to the upper part of the chin, is dark and free of fur.

FEET
The feet are black, contrasting with the fur on the body.

TAIL
The tail is quite long and well-covered with fur, but is not prehensile.

HOW BIG IS IT?

DRYING OUT
The timing of the dry and wet seasons can vary from year to year, so young titi monkeys may become soaked soon after birth.

STAYING TOGETHER
These monkeys can move in a variety of ways, ranging from hopping to climbing. They may have a close relationship, grooming each other and entwining tails when resting.

Spectral Tarsier

VITAL STATISTICS

WEIGHT	94–132g (3.3–4.7oz)
LENGTH	35–39cm (13.8–15.3in) overall; tail is longer than the body
SEXUAL MATURITY	Around 1 year
GESTATION PERIOD	184–194 days
NUMBER OF OFFSPRING	1; weaning occurs by about 69 days
DIET	Mainly insectivorous, but may also prey on small vertebrates
LIFESPAN	Probably up to 12 years

ANIMAL FACTS

The size of the spectral tarsier's eyes in relation to its body are the largest of any mammal. They are avid hunters, watching from a convenient branch for signs of prey that may come within reach. These primates are quite solitary, and rank as the smallest of the nocturnal tarsiers. Females carry their single offspring in their mouths initially, in a similar way to a cat, but will temporarily abandon their youngster when seeking food.

The heads of these remarkable small primates – related to both monkeys and lemurs – can be turned through 180 degrees.

WHERE IN THE WORLD?

Restricted to Southeast Asia, on the islands of Sulawesi (formerly Celebes), Peleng and Great Sangihe, where they inhabit both primary and secondary rainforest.

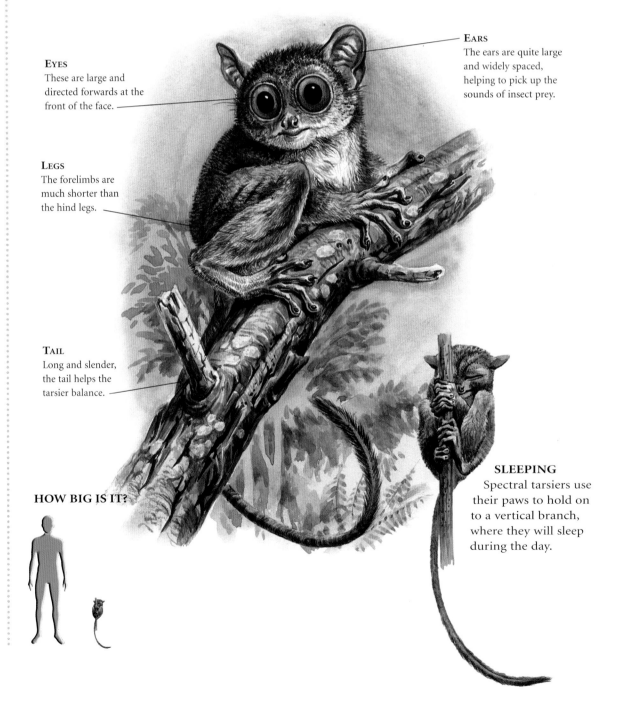

EYES
These are large and directed forwards at the front of the face.

EARS
The ears are quite large and widely spaced, helping to pick up the sounds of insect prey.

LEGS
The forelimbs are much shorter than the hind legs.

TAIL
Long and slender, the tail helps the tarsier balance.

SLEEPING
Spectral tarsiers use their paws to hold on to a vertical branch, where they will sleep during the day.

HOW BIG IS IT?

The digits are specialized, with flattened, disc-like swellings at their tips that help the tarsier maintain its grip

Asian Elephant

• ORDER • Proboscidea • FAMILY • Elephantidae • SPECIES • *Elephas maximus*

VITAL STATISTICS

WEIGHT	3000–5000kg (6600–11,000lb)
LENGTH	6.5–7.7m (21–25ft); stands up to 3m (9.8ft) tall at the shoulder
SEXUAL MATURITY	Around 14 years
GESTATION PERIOD	18–22 months
NUMBER OF OFFSPRING	1; weaning occurs by 4 years
DIET	Plant matter, eating up to 150kg (331lb) of grasses and leaves a day
LIFESPAN	Probably up to 70 years

ANIMAL FACTS

These elephants are the largest terrestrial mammals in Asia. While it has proved easier to domesticate Asian elephants than their African relatives, this has not protected them against being hunted for their ivory and as a source of meat. Clearance of large tracts of their forest environment has also had an adverse impact on the numbers of Asian elephants.

These elephants are highly significant in the cultures of many of the countries they inhabit, as well as being beasts of burden.

WHERE IN THE WORLD?

Extends across much of southern Asia, from parts of India and Sri Lanka eastwards, across to China and south to islands including Sumatra and Borneo.

SKIN
Tough and greyish-brown in colour, with a scattering of stiff dark hair.

EARS
The ears are small, helping to distinguish Asian elephants from their African relatives.

TUSKS
Only males, called bulls, may have tusks. These modified incisor teeth can grow to about 1.5m (5ft).

FEET
The feet are large and circular, with four nails on the hind feet.

Asian elephants have just a single, upper finger on their trunk (above), whereas the African species (below) has two

HOW BIG IS IT?

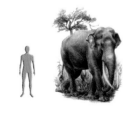

DIVING DEEPER
Asian elephants can swim well, and use their trunk rather like a snorkel to allow them to breathe underwater.

351

African Elephant

• ORDER • Proboscidea **• FAMILY •** Elephantidae **• SPECIES •** *Loxodonta africana*

The largest of all land animals, the African elephant can be distinguished from its Asian relative by its much bigger ears.

VITAL STATISTICS

WEIGHT	2270–6350kg (5000–14,000lb); males are larger
LENGTH	2.8–3.4m (9.2–11.2ft); up to 4m (13ft) tall at the shoulder
SEXUAL MATURITY	Females 10–11 years; males 10–20 years
GESTATION PERIOD	Around 22 months (the longest of any mammal)
NUMBER OF OFFSPRING	1; weaning occurs at 6.5 years; females give birth every 4 years
DIET	Herbivorous, feeding on plant matter
LIFESPAN	Up to 70 years

ANIMAL FACTS

Elephants roam over large areas, in herds led by a matriarch, who knows the territory well and can locate waterholes, for example, in times of drought. They have huge appetites, with adult elephants capable of eating 136kg (300lb) of food daily. It is thought that herd members keep in touch by ultrasound, which is too high-pitched to be audible to human ears. Herds consist of females of various ages and their young. Mature male elephants, called bulls, live alone.

WHERE IN THE WORLD?

Poaching for their tusks has seriously impacted the numbers of these elephants across Africa. Their distribution is now scattered, occuring in areas south of the Sahara.

EARS
These help the elephant to keep cool, dissipating heat from the body.

TRUNK
Controlled by 100,000 muscles, the trunk is agile enough to pick up small objects.

TUSKS
These modified incisor teeth, made of ivory, can grow to a length of 2.4m (8ft) and weigh up to 45kg (100lb).

SKIN
The rough skin has a thick, leathery texture.

THE MOTHERHOOD

Herd members are very protective towards their young, and females will challenge predators such as lions that attack young elephants.

HOW BIG IS IT?

There is a difference in foot structure between African elephants (left) and their Asian relatives (right)

Edible Snail

As their name suggests, these snails are favoured by gourmets – they are sold in France as escargots – and they are so popular that they are farmed.

VITAL STATISTICS

LENGTH	2.5cm (1in); shell diameter 5cm (2in)
SEXUAL MATURITY	2–4 years
NUMBER OF EGGS	40–60 eggs, which may take up to 30 minutes each to lay
DEVELOPMENTAL PERIOD	Young miniature snails hatch after about 25 days, remaining below ground for up to 10 days, eating their egg cases
HABITAT	Limestone countryside
DIET	Feeds on plant matter, often favouring young, succulent shoots
LIFESPAN	5–10 years

ANIMAL FACTS

An amazing duel takes place when two of these hermaphrodite snails meet to mate. They each transfer sperm to fertilize their eggs, but they also release 'love darts'. These have a harpoon-like tip that can penetrate the other snail's skin. The hormone on the dart will favour the survival of that male's sperm if it is able to land its love dart early. The darts are not actually fired, but are transferred by stabbing their partner.

Under adverse conditions, particularly when it is dry, the snail seals itself into its shell, creating a calcareous cover

WHERE IN THE WORLD?

Restricted to limestone areas of central and southeastern Europe. Introduced to Britain by the Romans, and now established in southern areas on chalk downland.

SHELL
This has a slight reddish hue and is made of calcium ingested from the snail's surroundings.

FOOT
The underside of the snail's body, which it moves on, lubricates a path with a trail of slime.

EYES
These are located at the tips of the antennae. These sensory projections can be drawn into the snail's body.

EATING
The snail can rasp vegetation with its strong mouthparts, although it has no teeth.

HOW BIG IS IT?

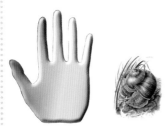

EGG-LAYING
The snail will lay its relatively large, white eggs in a damp spot, burying them in the ground.

Slug

VITAL STATISTICS

LENGTH	Up to 30cm (12in)
SEXUAL MATURITY	2 months–2 years
NUMBER OF EGGS	30–75; slugs are hermaphrodite
DEVELOPMENTAL PERIOD	About 14 days, depending on temperature and humidity
HABITAT	Damp areas with hiding places and vegetation
DIET	Plant matter, often succulent shoots; may also eat carrion and dung
LIFESPAN	Variable, but typically 3–5 years; in some temperate populations, adults die off each winter

ANIMAL FACTS

The mouthparts of slugs are equipped with a rasp-like structure, known as a radula, which enables them to obtain their food easily. They are susceptible to dehydration and will hide away in damp spots during prolonged spells of sunny weather. They are most inclined to emerge after dark, when the weather is cooler and there may be dew on the ground. Young slugs hatch as miniature adults, sometimes overwintering in their eggs and hatching in the spring.

Slugs are gastropod molluscs that lack shells, while semi-slugs have shells but they are too small to withdraw into.

WHERE IN THE WORLD?

Have a very wide distribution throughout the world, in temperate and tropical areas in particular. Require surroundings where the level of humidity is high.

FOOT FRINGE
This is the edging that runs along each side of the body.

MANTLE
The relatively smooth area incorporating the respiratory opening or pneumostome.

SENSORY TENTACLES
These short tentacles, close to the ground, are sensory and pick up pheromones released by slugs ready to mate.

EYESTALKS
These long tentacles detect light and movement, and can be retracted if danger threatens.

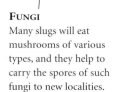

FUNGI
Many slugs will eat mushrooms of various types, and they help to carry the spores of such fungi to new localities.

HOW BIG IS IT?

RESPONSE TO DANGER
When in danger, slugs contract their bodies and draw in their tentacles. Their body slime makes them difficult to pick up.

Devil Ray

• **ORDER** • Rajiformes • **FAMILY** • Myliobatidae • **SPECIES** • *Mobula japanica*

VITAL STATISTICS

WEIGHT	Around 350kg (770lb)
LENGTH	Up to 520m (17ft)
SEXUAL MATURITY	Possibly not attained until 20–30 years
GESTATION PERIOD	Uncertain – could be up to 25 months
NUMBER OF OFFSPRING	1; weighs 35kg (77lb) at birth
DIET	Feeds largely on plankton sieved out via gill plates, crustaceans and fish
LIFESPAN	Probably 70 years or more

ANIMAL FACTS

Unlike most fish, rays have a skeleton made of cartilage rather than bone. Relatively little is known about their breeding habits, but fertilization is internal. Female devil rays produce live offspring, with the eggs developing in their bodies. The young rays are effectively rolled up during their growth here and ultimately unfurl their wings when they are born. In spite of their size, these rays do fall victim to various sharks, and they are also hunted by humans.

These rays are often accompanied by smaller fish called remoras, which cling to their bodies, helping to remove any parasites

In spite of their appearance, these fish are usually harmless to people, unless they crash on a boat accidentally when jumping out of the water.

WHERE IN THE WORLD?

Occurs widely throughout the warmer areas of the oceans, from east Africa through the Pacific to the west coast of America. Also in the Atlantic.

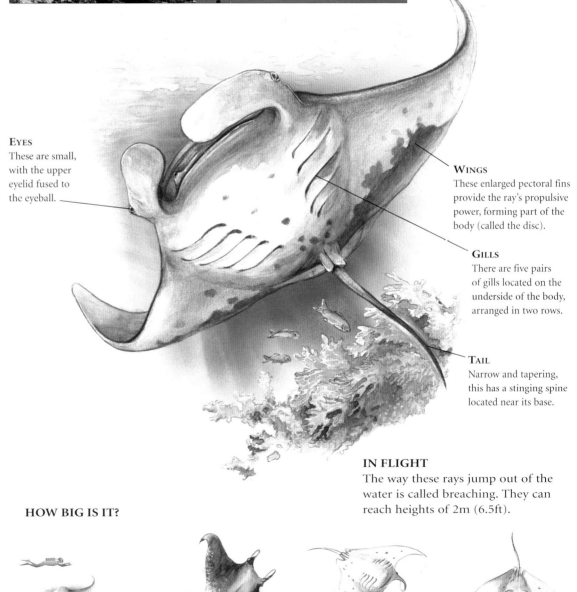

EYES
These are small, with the upper eyelid fused to the eyeball.

WINGS
These enlarged pectoral fins provide the ray's propulsive power, forming part of the body (called the disc).

GILLS
There are five pairs of gills located on the underside of the body, arranged in two rows.

TAIL
Narrow and tapering, this has a stinging spine located near its base.

IN FLIGHT
The way these rays jump out of the water is called breaching. They can reach heights of 2m (6.5ft).

HOW BIG IS IT?

Naked Mole Rat

• **ORDER** • Rodentia • **FAMILY** • Bathyergidae • **SPECIES** • *Heterocephalus glaber*

VITAL STATISTICS

WEIGHT	30–80g (1–2.8oz); queens are significantly larger than workers
LENGTH	8–10cm (3.1–3.9in)
SEXUAL MATURITY	6–12 months
GESTATION PERIOD	66–74 days
NUMBER OF OFFSPRING	3–12, but can be up to 27 pups per litter, with queens having up to 4 litters a year
DIET	Feeds on roots and vegetation
LIFESPAN	Up to 25 years in captivity, making them the longest-lived rodent

ANIMAL FACTS

There can be up to 300 mole rats in a group, but at its heart will be a dominant female, corresponding to the queen in a termite colony. She is the only female who breeds, managing to repress the reproductive cycles of the other females. If this individual dies or is killed, however, another female will soon take her place. All the other mole rats either work, or grow larger and serve to defend the colony.

The structure of the mole rat's mouth is such that the lips actually close behind, not in front of, the incisor teeth

These bizarre rodents are well-suited to their subterranean lifestyle, having narrow bodies and short legs. Their social structure is similar to that of termites.

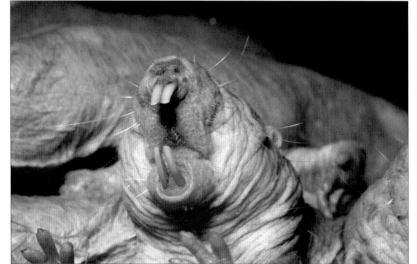

WHERE IN THE WORLD?

Occurs in grassland areas in East Africa, mainly in southern Ethiopia and Somalia, as well as Kenya.

EYES
These are tiny and almost non-functional, although they can detect light in comparison with darkness.

BODY
The skin is largely hairless, apart from some longer sensory hairs around the mouth and body.

EARS
The ear flaps are very small, almost inconspicuous.

TEETH
The large, protruding incisors in the upper and lower jaws extend out over the lips.

UNDERGROUND LIVING
Mole rats live in a series of interconnecting tunnels, where they will seek out tubers growing in the sandy soil. These may sometimes be stored in a burrow.

HOW BIG IS IT?

TUNNELLING

Mole rats literally bite into the hard soil, and then scoop it backwards with their legs, out of the burrow.

North American Beaver

• ORDER • Rodentia **• FAMILY •** Castoridae **• SPECIES •** *Castor canadensis*

One of the most recognizable of all rodents, this species has a marked impact on the landscape, altering the flow of watercourses through the area.

VITAL STATISTICS

WEIGHT	11–30kg (24–66lb)
LENGTH	105–170cm (41–67in)
SEXUAL MATURITY	1.5–2 years
GESTATION PERIOD	About 106 days
NUMBER OF OFFSPRING	2–3, but can be up to 8 kits per litter, born in late spring
DIET	Feeds on vegetation, preferring softer, non-woody plants during the warmer months, switching to bark and twigs in the winter, when other food is not available
LIFESPAN	10–15 years

ANIMAL FACTS

Beavers may occupy an area for many years if undisturbed, adding to and remodelling their dam and living quarters. The lodge can have an external diameter of up to 4m (13ft), with an entrance below the water line, allowing them to come and go without being seen. It also means they can escape underwater in winter when the surface water may be frozen. There is a raised dry area within the lodge which provides the family with a living area.

Beavers are slightly ungainly on land, but they will often sit up on their hindquarters, especially when gnawing through saplings

WHERE IN THE WORLD?

Range extends from Alaska eastwards to Labrador, and south across most of North America down to Florida and Mexico. Introduced to other localities worldwide, including Asia.

COAT
Dense and waterproof, the coat is typically reddish-brown, but may vary from yellowish to black.

FACE
The head is quite square, accommodating the sharp incisor teeth and powerful jaw muscles.

TAIL
The large, flat, scaly tail, with no fur on it, acts like a paddle and a rudder for the beaver.

HOW BIG IS IT?

THE LODGE
Beavers are great builders. They construct lodges using sticks, and will also dam rivers, increasing their security.

Guinea Pig

VITAL STATISTICS

WEIGHT	About 340g (12oz)
LENGTH	35cm (13.8in)
SEXUAL MATURITY	74–77 days; sows mature slightly earlier than boars
GESTATION PERIOD	63–68 days
NUMBER OF OFFSPRING	2–3, able to feed themselves almost immediately, but not normally weaned for 3–4 weeks
DIET	Grass and herbage, clipping this with their sharp incisor teeth
LIFESPAN	Up to 6 years

ANIMAL FACTS

Guinea pigs are often called cavies, which reflects their scientific name. These rodents have a peculiar biochemical quirk shared with humans and marmoset monkeys. They must have Vitamin C in their diet to avoid developing scurvy, as they cannot manufacture this vitamin in the body. Social by nature, they will make chattering noises when out in the open to keep in touch with each other. They will hide in undergrowth or under rocks.

Young resemble miniature adults and are born with their eyes open

These ancestors of the popular pet of today were first domesticated in their South American homeland as a source of food several thousand years ago.

WHERE IN THE WORLD?

Found in South America, east of the Andes in Colombia, Ecuador, Paraguay, Brazil, Argentina and Uruguay. This species is also misleadingly called the Brazilian guinea pig.

COLOURATION
Wild guinea pigs are grey, helping them to blend into the background when they are out grazing.

EARS
These are broad yet relatively short. Guinea pigs have good hearing.

PROFILE
The body curves down over the rump. Guinea pigs have no tail.

HINDQUARTERS
These are well-muscled, helping guinea pigs to run fast across the ground.

DANGER OVERHEAD
Guinea pigs live in areas where there is little natural cover, and they are vulnerable to birds of prey.

HOW BIG IS IT?

Mara

VITAL STATISTICS

WEIGHT	8–16kg (17.6–35.3lb)
LENGTH	73–80cm (29–32in)
SEXUAL MATURITY	Around 6 months for both sexes
GESTATION PERIOD	90–98 days
NUMBER OF OFFSPRING	1–3; weaning occurs after about 60 days
DIET	Grass and herbage, but will eat almost any greenstuff, clipping it with their sharp incisor teeth
LIFESPAN	5–7 years; up to 15 in captivity

ANIMAL FACTS

When on the move, maras may simply walk, but they can also hop. They are able to run fast to escape predators, and can reach a top speed of 45kph (28mph) over short distances. Their young are well-developed at birth and will initially live in a community den. The female will return here at intervals to suckle her offspring amongst the group. Adults live in solitary pairs, but may form larger groups where grazing is good.

Although known as the Patagonian hare because of its speed when running, this species is a rodent from the same family as guinea pigs.

WHERE IN THE WORLD?

Occurs in South America, in the pampas grasslands in central and southern parts of Argentina. Pairs move together, feeding on the vegetation.

HEAD
Keen hearing and large eyes help alert these rodents to danger.

LEGS
These are long and slender, with four sharp claws on each front foot and three behind.

COLOURATION
Upperparts of the body are grey, becoming chestnut on the sides of the face and underparts.

BODY SHAPE
Unlike most rodents, maras are athletic, and will seek to outrun would-be predators.

A COMMUNAL DEN
The offspring of up to 15 pairs of mara will share a communal den. Adults become territorial when visiting their offspring.

HOW BIG IS IT?

Pairs are constantly alert to danger, but may sit down to graze

Capybara

These particular rodents are semi-aquatic and are found close to water where they browse on vegetation. They live in groups led by a male.

VITAL STATISTICS

WEIGHT	8–16kg (17.6–35.3lb)
LENGTH	73–80cm (29–32in)
SEXUAL MATURITY	Around 22 months for both sexes
GESTATION PERIOD	130–150 days
NUMBER OF OFFSPRING	Typically 4, but can be 2–8; weaning occurs after about 16 weeks
DIET	Grass and herbage, clipping this effectively with their incisor teeth
LIFESPAN	5–7 years; up to 15 in captivity

ANIMAL FACTS

The dominant male in the group has a large scent gland on the nose, with which he marks an area as he feeds on vegetation. A typical group consists of 10 to 30 individuals, but larger aggregations of up to 100 have been observed. These rodents have big appetites, with each adult consuming up to 3.6kg (8lb) of vegetation daily. As a result of the hinging of the jaw, the capybara will grind its food back and forth, rather than side to side.

As with other rodents, the capybara's teeth continue growing throughout its life, so they do not become worn down

WHERE IN THE WORLD?

Occurs in South America, east of the Andes, from Panama and Colombia to Venezuela. Also present in Ecuador, Peru, the Guianas, Brazil, Bolivia, Paraguay, Argentina and Uruguay.

HAIR
This is coarse and quite thin, so adults roll in mud to protect against sunburn.

FEEDING
Capybaras start feeding themselves from a week old, well before they are weaned.

FRONT FEET
Webbing between the toes helps the capybara to walk on marshy ground and swim.

YOUNG
Young capybaras are born on land and follow their mother almost immediately.

HOW BIG IS IT?

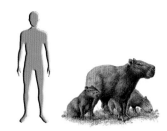

DIVE, DIVE
Capybaras can remain completely submerged for up to five minutes in order to get away from predators.

Mountain Viscacha

• ORDER • Rodentia • FAMILY • Chinchillidae • SPECIES • *Lagidium viscacia*

VITAL STATISTICS

WEIGHT	Around 1.45kg (3.2lb)
LENGTH	73cm (29in)
SEXUAL MATURITY	8–12 months for both sexes
GESTATION PERIOD	120–140 days
NUMBER OF OFFSPRING	1; weaning occurs after about 56 days
DIET	Grass and herbage, including mosses and lichens, but will eat almost any vegetation
LIFESPAN	6 years; up to 10 in captivity

ANIMAL FACTS

The viscacha's breeding season extends through the southern summer, from October to December. Females release approximately 300 eggs on each ovulation, but only one will develop into a young viscacha. As with many other South American rodents, the gestation period is lengthy, but the youngster is born in an advanced state of development and can feed itself if necessary soon after birth. Their colouration helps these rodents blend into the rocky landscape of their habitat.

Chinchillas (above), found in similar terrain, are recognizable by their shorter ears and are close relatives of viscachas

These hardy rodents are found living in groups at high altitudes. They are constantly on the lookout for birds of prey and other predators.

WHERE IN THE WORLD?

Occurs in mountainous country in western South America; present in southern Peru, western and central parts of Bolivia, northern and central Chile and western Argentina.

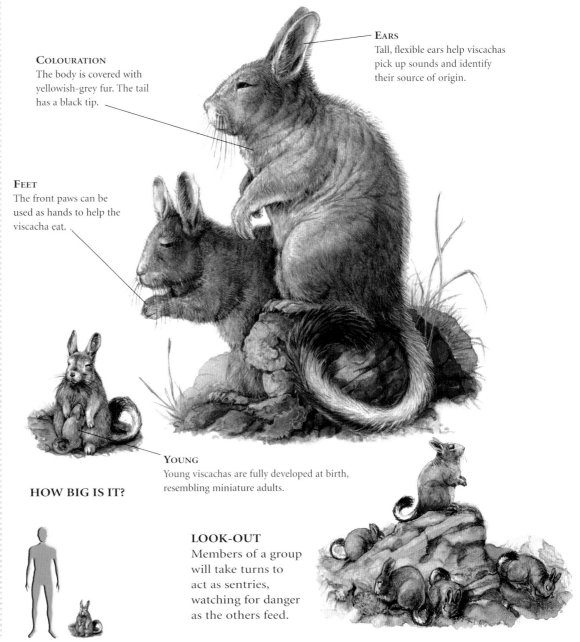

COLOURATION
The body is covered with yellowish-grey fur. The tail has a black tip.

EARS
Tall, flexible ears help viscachas pick up sounds and identify their source of origin.

FEET
The front paws can be used as hands to help the viscacha eat.

YOUNG
Young viscachas are fully developed at birth, resembling miniature adults.

HOW BIG IS IT?

LOOK-OUT
Members of a group will take turns to act as sentries, watching for danger as the others feed.

European Water Vole

•ORDER • Rodentia • FAMILY • Cricetidae • SPECIES • *Arvicola amphibius*

This is the largest of the voles occurring in Eurasia. Its size helps to explain why it is also known as the water rat.

VITAL STATISTICS

WEIGHT	160–350g (6–12oz)
LENGTH	25–35 cm (10–14in) overall; tail is slightly shorter than the body
SEXUAL MATURITY	After the first winter
GESTATION PERIOD	21 days; 2–5 litters annually
NUMBER OF OFFSPRING	Up to 8; weaning occurs after about 56 days
DIET	Grass and plants growing close to water, plus roots and bulbs
LIFESPAN	Up to 18 months, but many die prematurely

ANIMAL FACTS

The number of these small rodents has fallen dramatically in some areas. This has been linked with the escape of some American mink from fur farms – they prey heavily on water voles – and with poor management of river banks, which reduces available habitat. Luckily, the water vole's high reproductive rate means that populations can regenerate quite quickly under suitable conditions. Occasionally, their numbers can build up to plague proportions.

WHERE IN THE WORLD?

Found in the British Isles and northern Europe, extending through parts of central Europe into Russia. Sometimes seen in gardens and fields.

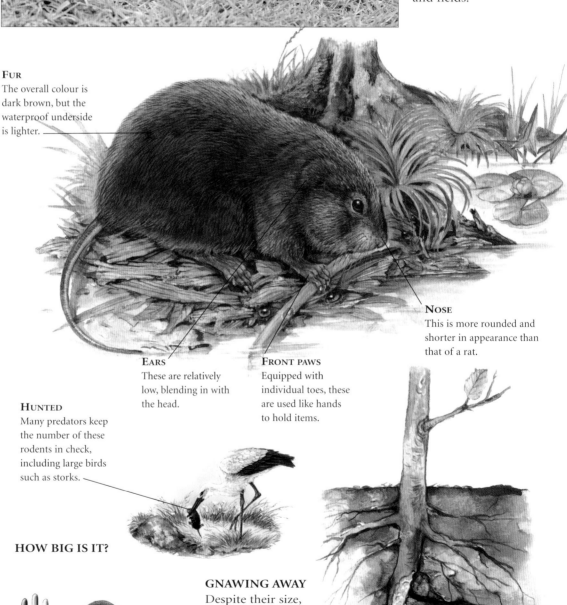

FUR
The overall colour is dark brown, but the waterproof underside is lighter.

NOSE
This is more rounded and shorter in appearance than that of a rat.

EARS
These are relatively low, blending in with the head.

FRONT PAWS
Equipped with individual toes, these are used like hands to hold items.

HUNTED
Many predators keep the number of these rodents in check, including large birds such as storks.

HOW BIG IS IT?

GNAWING AWAY
Despite their size, water volves can have a marked impact on the landscape, killing young trees and shrubs.

European Hamster

• ORDER • Rodentia **• FAMILY •** Cricetidae **• SPECIES •** *Cricetus cricetus*

VITAL STATISTICS

WEIGHT	160–350g (6–12oz); males are bigger
LENGTH	22–32cm (10–14in) overall; tail is significantly shorter than the body
SEXUAL MATURITY	Females 2–3 months; males 2 months
GESTATION PERIOD	18–21 days; 2–5 litters annually
NUMBER OF OFFSPRING	4–12; weaning occurs at around 3 weeks
DIET	Seeds, roots, bulbs, plants, plus small animals, including vertebrates
LIFESPAN	Up to 8 years

ANIMAL FACTS

These nocturnal mammals live solitary lives and are usually seen only above ground during the spring and summer. Once the air temperature drops below 10°C (50°F), they start hibernating. Their body temperature drops dramatically and they may retreat as far as 2m (6.5ft) underground into their burrow. When foraging for food, hamsters stuff their cheek pouches with edible items, bringing these back to their burrow, often entering by a separate entrance to the exit point.

This is easily the largest of the world's 15 hamster species. Its common name reflects the fact that it often occurs in agricultural areas.

WHERE IN THE WORLD?

Now largely confined to central and eastern parts of Europe to Russia. It was once numerous further west, but populations have been badly affected by habitat change.

MATERNAL CARE
Females may move their young by carrying them individually by the scruff of the neck.

PAWS
These can be used for a wide variety of tasks, including grooming, digging and holding food.

EARS
Cup-shaped and set well back on the head, the ears trap sound waves effectively.

NOSTRILS
Scent is important to hamsters and indicates when a female is ready to mate.

HOW BIG IS IT?

SUBTERRANEAN LIVING
A hamster creates a range of tunnels and chambers, where it can store food and sleep, relatively safe from predators.

Norwegian Lemming

• **ORDER** • Rodentia • **FAMILY** • Cricetidae • **SPECIES** • *Lemmus lemmus*

VITAL STATISTICS

WEIGHT	20–130g (0.5–4.5oz)
LENGTH	10–15cm (4–6in)
SEXUAL MATURITY	From around 14 days
GESTATION PERIOD	Typically 16 days; 3–6 litters annually
NUMBER OF OFFSPRING	4–12; weaning occurs at around 12 days
DIET	Grass, herbage, moss, lichens, leaves, berries and bark
LIFESPAN	Typically up to 2 years

ANIMAL FACTS

The reproductive abilities of these lemmings mean their numbers can build up rapidly in an area, but their food supply is limited and often scarce. Their energy needs mean that, on average, lemmings must eat every two hours. As a result, large groups will ultimately be driven out of an area by starvation, seeking food elsewhere. It is these massive, uncontrolled exoduses that can lead to disasters, causing lemmings to plummet into water and drown. After a population crash, their numbers then build up again, and the cycle repeats itself.

Most people have heard stories of lemmings leaping over cliffs and committing suicide, but the reality is different – they are driven out of their harsh environment in search of food.

WHERE IN THE WORLD?

Occurs throughout Scandinavia, but not just in Norway. Also present in Sweden and Denmark, extending into adjacent areas of Russia. Often seen near water.

HARE LIP
The upper lip is split and, behind here, at the front of the mouth, are the sharp incisor teeth.

COLOURATION
The colour provides camouflage, helping the lemmings merge into the landscape.

FUR
This is waterproof and offers good insulation against the cold.

LEGS
These enable lemmings to burrow under the snow in search of food, creating underground tunnels.

HOW BIG IS IT?

A VITAL FOOD SOURCE
Lemmings provide food for predators such as snowy owls, whose population is directly linked to that of lemmings in some areas.

Meadow Vole

• ORDER • Rodentia **• FAMILY •** Cricetidae **• SPECIES •** *Microtus pennsylvanicus*

VITAL STATISTICS

WEIGHT	33–65g (1.2–2.3oz)
LENGTH	18–27cm (7–11in) overall; tail is less than half body length
SEXUAL MATURITY	Females from 25 days; males from 45 days
GESTATION PERIOD	21 days; up to 17 litters a year recorded
NUMBER OF OFFSPRING	6–7, but can range from 2–9; weaning at 14 days
DIET	Grasses, herbs, seeds, fruit, even bark and animal matter
LIFESPAN	1 year

ANIMAL FACTS

Meadow voles are exceptionally prolific, with females producing litters constantly for most of the year. Their lives are short and hazardous, as they face many predators, including coyotes, foxes wild and domestic cats, as well as birds of prey. If it detects a predator, a vole may try to reach its burrow or just freeze in vegetation, hoping it will not be spotted. They have large appetites, eating up to 60 per cent of their body weight each day.

These small voles can kill trees by stripping off the bark close to the ground, which provides them with food in the winter

The meadow vole is a very adaptable and common species and ranks as the most widely distributed member of its group in North America.

WHERE IN THE WORLD?

Range extends from Alaska eastwards across Canada, south to New Mexico and Georgia and to the west of the Rocky Mountains.

EARS
These may be small and relatively inconspicuous, but these voles have keen hearing.

COLOURATION
Blackish-brown upperparts, often with a reddish hue, and paler underparts.

FEET
The toes on each foot have sharp, pointed claws.

HOW BIG IS IT?

TUNNELLING
Meadow voles construct underground burrows with various entrances that expand into chambers, where they will rear their young and hide.

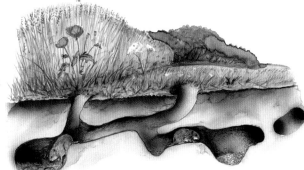

Bank Vole

• ORDER • Rodentia • FAMILY • Cricetidae • SPECIES • *Myodes glareolus*

These voles can be encountered in various localities – not just banks but hedgerows, woodland, parks and even gardens, where they can fall victim to cats.

VITAL STATISTICS

WEIGHT	15–40g (0.5–1.4oz)
LENGTH	10–20cm (4–8in)
SEXUAL MATURITY	4–5 weeks
GESTATION PERIOD	18–20 days; 3–6 litters annually
NUMBER OF OFFSPRING	3–5; weaning occurs at around 3 weeks
DIET	Leaves, buds, flowers, fungi, nuts and invertebrates
LIFESPAN	Up to 18 months

ANIMAL FACTS

Like many of the world's more prolific rodents, female bank voles can mate just after they have given birth, with their new litter being produced just as the previous litter becomes independent. This allows them to breed quickly under favourable conditions. The young are usually born in an underground nest. Many species prey on these voles, including foxes, birds of prey and snakes, and a significant proportion die over the winter, when food is harder to find.

WHERE IN THE WORLD?

Occurs in Europe, apart from the far north and south, extending east to Asia. Absent from various islands, but introduced to southwest Ireland in the 1950s.

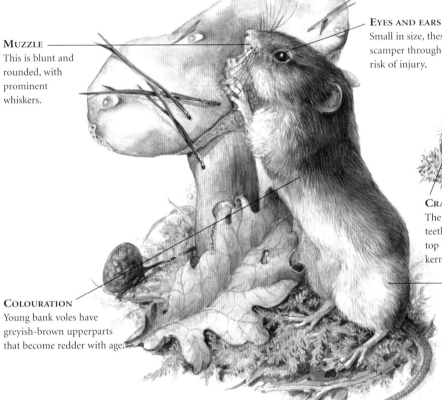

MUZZLE
This is blunt and rounded, with prominent whiskers.

EYES AND EARS
Small in size, these allow the vole to scamper through vegetation with less risk of injury.

COLOURATION
Young bank voles have greyish-brown upperparts that become redder with age.

CRACKING IT
The bank vole's sharp incisor teeth mean that it can gnaw the top off hazelnuts to reach the kernel inside.

POSTURE
The bank vole can stand up on its hind legs if necessary, and will also sit on its haunches.

HOW BIG IS IT?

PREPARING FOR WINTER
Bank voles often collect and store food during the autumn, which they can eat when snow is blanketing the ground.

Muskrat

• ORDER • Rodentia **• FAMILY •** Cricetidae **• SPECIES •** *Ondatra zibethicus*

VITAL STATISTICS

WEIGHT	0.7–1.8kg (1.5–4lb)
LENGTH	40–60cm (16–24in) overall; tail is almost as long as the body
SEXUAL MATURITY	By 4 months
GESTATION PERIOD	25–30 days; 1–5 litters annually
NUMBER OF OFFSPRING	4–7, but can be up to 11; weaning occurs at 3–4 weeks
DIET	Aquatic vegetation and creatures such as turtles; also plunders agricultural crops
LIFESPAN	3–4 years, but can be up to 10

ANIMAL FACTS

Muskrats are so-called because of a pair of scent glands located close to the tail. They produce a musky scent which serves as a territorial marker. These semi-aquatic rodents are very adaptable by nature, even surviving in relatively polluted stretches of water. They were highly valued for their fur, and this led to them being farmed in parts of Europe and Asia, where some escaped. These became the ancestors of today's muskrats in these parts of the world.

In cross-section, the height of the tail is greater than its width, helping their swimming ability

In spite of their name, these are not true rats, but belong to the same family as voles and lemmings, although they are significantly larger.

WHERE IN THE WORLD?

Occurs across North America, from Alaska to the east coast, but absent from southeastern areas. Has been introduced right across northern mainland Europe and Asia.

FUR
Fur is thick, double-layered, water-resistant and brown in colour. The underparts are slightly paler.

EARS
Small and inconspicuous, these are sealed when the muskrat is underwater.

FRONT PAWS
Equipped with sharp claws, these act like hands, allowing the muskrat to hold its food.

TAIL
This is covered with scales not hair, and helps the muskrat to swim effectively.

HOW BIG IS IT?

LODGES
These homes are made of mud and vegetation. In winter, the entrance may be closed to keep the inside warmer.

Gundi

· **ORDER** · Rodentia · **FAMILY** · Ctenodactylidae · **SPECIES** · *Ctenodactylus, Felovia*

VITAL STATISTICS

WEIGHT	170–190g (6–7oz); females are slightly heavier
LENGTH	19–28cm (7.5–11in)
SEXUAL MATURITY	8–12 months
GESTATION PERIOD	25–30 days; births occur in the summer
NUMBER OF OFFSPRING	2; weaning by 4 weeks
DIET	Herbivorous, eating most plants in its native habitat
LIFESPAN	Up to 6 years; 10 in captivity

ANIMAL FACTS

When members of this family were first recorded in 1774, they were called gundi mice. Recent DNA investigations into their origins confirm they are unrelated to true mice, however, and form a completely separate family. Gundis live in colonies that may consist of as many as 100 individuals. They forage for food from daybreak, pausing around midday when the sun is at its hottest, and hide away in rocks at night. Individuals protect themselves by appearing dead to distract a predator, running off after several minutes.

The bristles above the feet are used like a brush for grooming

The kidneys of these rodents are so efficient at conserving water that they obtain sufficient fluid from their food and do not have to drink regularly.

WHERE IN THE WORLD?

Gundis inhabit the rocky deserts that extend across northern parts of North Africa, from Algeria and Morocco southwards to countries including Niger, Chad and Ethiopia.

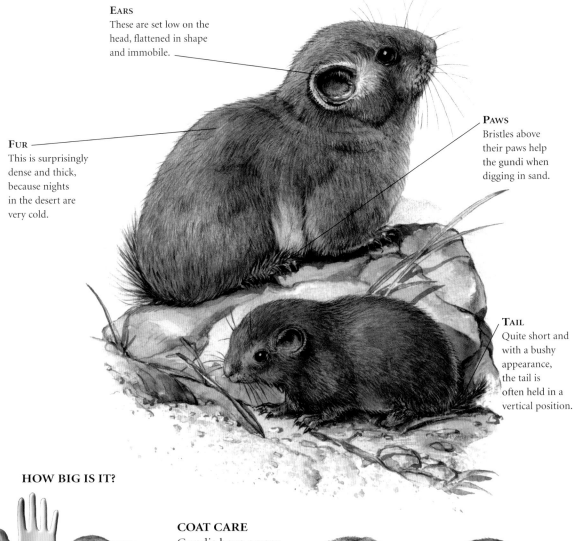

EARS
These are set low on the head, flattened in shape and immobile.

FUR
This is surprisingly dense and thick, because nights in the desert are very cold.

PAWS
Bristles above their paws help the gundi when digging in sand.

TAIL
Quite short and with a bushy appearance, the tail is often held in a vertical position.

HOW BIG IS IT?

COAT CARE
Gundis have a very distinctive grooming posture, using a hind leg for this purpose while balancing on their other legs.

Lesser Egyptian Jerboa

• **ORDER** • Rodentia • **FAMILY** • Dipodidea • **SPECIES** • *Jaculus jaculus*

Living in one of the harshest environments on the planet, lesser Egyptian jerboas are well-equipped to survive in the searing heat of the desert.

VITAL STATISTICS

WEIGHT	33–65g (1.2–2.3oz)
LENGTH	18–27cm (7–11in); tail is less than half the body length
SEXUAL MATURITY	Females from 25 days; males from 45 days
GESTATION PERIOD	21 days; up to 17 litters a year recorded
NUMBER OF OFFSPRING	6–7, but can range from 2–9; weaning at 14 days
DIET	Eats grasses, herbs, seeds, fruit, even bark; also animal matter
LIFESPAN	1 year

ANIMAL FACTS

These rodents are well-adapted to moving around on the desert sand without becoming an easy target for predators. Jerboas have very long hind legs and these improve the animal's view, as it must sit or stand up, rather than crawling along on all fours. When chased, jerboas can hop along quickly, covering distances of 3m (10ft) at a single bound. They build a variety of burrows, some of which are simply resting sites. The entrances will be obscured with sand.

WHERE IN THE WORLD?

Occurs in desert areas throughout parts of North Africa, across the Arabian Peninsula and into Iran. It has a wide distribution but is not easily seen.

EYES
Prominent and large, the eyes detect possible danger.

FRONT LEGS
These are very short and not used for locomotory purposes, just for holding food and grooming.

TAIL
The long tail acts as a counterbalance when the jerboa jumps. It has a dark tip.

HIND FEET
Jerboas originating in Africa have three toes on each foot, whereas Asian species have five toes on each foot.

HOW BIG IS IT?

BREEDING

Young jerboas are raised in underground nests by their mother. They are helpless at birth, with their eyes closed.

369

North American Porcupine

• ORDER • Rodentia • FAMILY • Erethizontidae • SPECIES • *Erethizon dorsatum*

VITAL STATISTICS

WEIGHT	4.5–18kg (10–40lb)
LENGTH	84–122cm (33–48in); quills 7.5cm (3in) long
SEXUAL MATURITY	Females 25 months; males 29 months
GESTATION PERIOD	205–217 days; quills harden after birth
NUMBER OF OFFSPRING	1–2; weaning occurs at 4–5 months
DIET	Leaves, twigs and shoots in summer; gnaws through bark to reach inner layers of trees in winter
LIFESPAN	5–6 years; 18 in captivity

ANIMAL FACTS

The quills can injure the porcupine itself, as well as predators. Porcupines often try to clamber to the tips of branches to reach buds and thinner twigs, but they are quite bulky animals and may lose their grip, tumbling to the ground below. Their skin contains anti-bacterial compounds, which protect against infections caused by a quill perforating it. These modified hollow hairs detach easily and have sharp points. Predators are often impaled in the face.

The porcupine's feet, with five toes on each hindfoot, help them maintain their grip when climbing

370

These particular porcupines live in woodland areas where they climb around in the branches in search of food. They are protected by 30,000 quills on their bodies.

WHERE IN THE WORLD?

Widely distributed across North America, extending from Alaska and Canada to Mexico. Found in areas of suitable habitat including coniferous woodland and mixed forests.

QUILLS
When the porcupine is resting, these are kept flat against the body.

TEETH
There is a broad muzzle with powerful incisor teeth at the front of the mouth.

LEGS
These are short but equipped with powerful claws to help the porcupine climb and rest safely off the ground.

TAIL
Unlike many arboreal mammals, porcupines have relatively short tails covered in quills.

HOW BIG IS IT?

DEFENSIVE STRATEGY
These porcupines pose a considerable danger to potential predators, who will face a mass of raised quills pointing at them.

Botta's Pocket Gopher

• **ORDER** • Rodentia • **FAMILY** • Geomyidae • **SPECIES** •*Thomomys bottae*

These rodents live mainly underground in a network of tunnels. They are named after Paul-Émile Botta, who studied mammals in California during the 1800s.

VITAL STATISTICS

WEIGHT	120–250g (4.2–8.8oz); males are slightly larger
LENGTH	22–26cm (8.7–10.2in)
SEXUAL MATURITY	9–10 months
GESTATION PERIOD	Around 19 days
NUMBER OF OFFSPRING	3–7, typically 6; weaning occurs at 36–40 days, and the young disperse at 2 months
DIET	Herbivorous, eating roots and pulling plants down through the soil; may cause damage to crops
LIFESPAN	Around 2.5 years

ANIMAL FACTS

The subterranean lifestyle of these rodents means there are many localized populations, and zoologists have named more than 185 different subspecies. Botta's pocket gophers are found in a wide range of localities, ranging from meadowland to desert, and are able to burrow in virtually all types of soil, including heavy clay. They usually only come up to the surface when the ground is covered with snow, expanding their tunnels through the surface material and creating trails that are described as gopher eskers.

WHERE IN THE WORLD?

Western North America, ranging from southern Oregon and California eastwards into Texas. Also present in southern Utah and Colorado, extending to central Mexico.

TEETH
The incisor teeth at the front of the mouth are sharp and can inflict a painful bite.

CHEEK POUCHES
Resembling fur-lined pockets, these extend from the sides of the mouth to beyond the shoulders.

COLOURATION
Variable, but reflects the soil where the gophers live.

FRONT FEET
These are short, yet powerful, equipped with sharp claws for digging.

DANGERS OUTSIDE THE BURROW
Individuals are territorial by nature and live alone. Out in the open, they are vulnerable to many predators, including birds of prey.

HOW BIG IS IT?

NETWORK OF BURROWS

A complicated series of interconnecting burrows and tunnels are dug by these rodents. These may extend over 150m (492ft).

Edible Dormouse

• ORDER • Rodentia • **FAMILY** • Gliridae • **SPECIES** • *Glis glis*

This species is also called the fat dormouse, because it gains weight in autumn and was fattened by the ancient Romans as a gastronomic delicacy.

VITAL STATISTICS

WEIGHT	50–250g (1.8–8.8oz); males slightly larger
LENGTH	9–15cm (3.5–6in)
SEXUAL MATURITY	10–12 months
GESTATION PERIOD	Around 25 days; females produce 1 litter per year
NUMBER OF OFFSPRING	1–11, average 4–6; weaning occurs at 30 days
DIET	Mainly vegetarian, feeding on bark, fruit and nuts, but also eats invertebrates, birds' eggs and nestlings
LIFESPAN	Up to 4.5 years

ANIMAL FACTS

This is the largest of the dormouse species. Its weight typically doubles between autumn and the start of winter, ready for hibernation. Edible dormice occur in various habitats, from forested areas to orchards. They are equally adaptable in terms of their nesting needs, using tree holes created by woodpeckers, choosing a site amongst rocks or venturing into buildings such as barns. These dormice are very agile, too, capable of leaping over 7m (23ft).

Sleeping curled up in this way conserves the dormouse's body heat, and also means that a smaller nest is required

WHERE IN THE WORLD?

Ranges across much of continental Europe, Sicily and Crete into Asia. Introduced to the UK in 1902, when some escaped from Lord Rothschild's Hertfordshire estate.

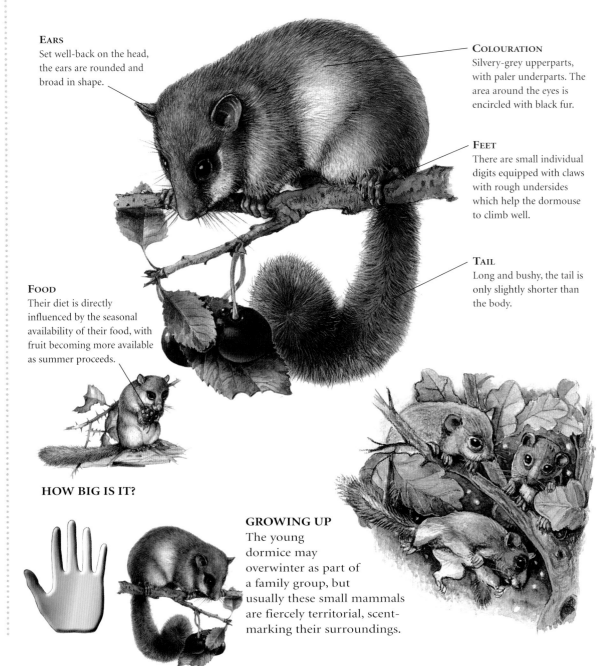

EARS
Set well-back on the head, the ears are rounded and broad in shape.

COLOURATION
Silvery-grey upperparts, with paler underparts. The area around the eyes is encircled with black fur.

FEET
There are small individual digits equipped with claws with rough undersides which help the dormouse to climb well.

TAIL
Long and bushy, the tail is only slightly shorter than the body.

FOOD
Their diet is directly influenced by the seasonal availability of their food, with fruit becoming more available as summer proceeds.

HOW BIG IS IT?

GROWING UP
The young dormice may overwinter as part of a family group, but usually these small mammals are fiercely territorial, scent-marking their surroundings.

Common Dormouse

• **ORDER** • Rodentia • **FAMILY** • Gliridae • **SPECIES** • *Muscardinus avellanarius*

The dormouse's name comes from the French verb *dormir*, meaning 'to sleep', a reflection of the fact that they may hibernate for seven months each year.

VITAL STATISTICS

WEIGHT	120–250g (4.2–8.8oz); males slightly bigger
LENGTH	22–26cm (8.7–10.2in)
SEXUAL MATURITY	Around 12 months
GESTATION PERIOD	Around 19 days
NUMBER OF OFFSPRING	2–7, typically 6; weaning occurs at 36–40 days; young disperse at 10 weeks
DIET	Flowers and pollen in spring, then increasingly fruit and nuts over the summer
LIFESPAN	Around 2.5 years

ANIMAL FACTS

From late summer through the autumn, these dormice lay down fat stores in their bodies to sustain them over the winter. They choose a site for their winter nest close to the ground. Their body temperature falls dramatically when they are hibernating, and they can even appear dead. Woodland clearance has reduced the numbers of dormice, partly because they prefer large tracts of established forest, but also because they are reluctant to move across open ground to new areas.

These dormice will grip the underside of a branch with their toes as they walk along, keeping the body low

WHERE IN THE WORLD?

Extends across Europe to the Mediterranean, and east into the Ural mountains. Found largely in southern England and Wales in the British Isles.

EYES
These are relatively large, as is typical of crepuscular species (which starts to become active at dusk).

FEET
These are agile, allowing the dormouse to walk along narrow branches.

TAIL
The long tail is covered with fur, right to the tip.

COLOURATION
Golden-brown fur over the back and sides of the body, and pale cream underparts.

HAZELNUTS
These are used by zoologists as an indicator of the presence of these dormice. Squirrels split the nuts to obtain the kernel, but dormice create a small hole and remove it in pieces.

HOW BIG IS IT?

BREEDING
Common dormice often make nests of dry grass for their young, but they may use nestboxes and hollow trees, too.

South African Porcupine

• **ORDER** • Rodentia • **FAMILY** • Hystricidae • **SPECIES** • *Hystrix africaeaustralis*

VITAL STATISTICS

WEIGHT	18–30kg (40–66lb); females slightly heavier
LENGTH	74–87cm (29–34in); tail is 2.5cm (1in)
SEXUAL MATURITY	Females 9–16 months; males 8–18 months
GESTATION PERIOD	About 135 days; 2 litters a year
NUMBER OF OFFSPRING	1–4; weaning occurs at 100 days
DIET	Mainly fruit and plant matter; also scavenges on carrion; may eat bones for phosphorus content
LIFESPAN	12–15 years

ANIMAL FACTS

These porcupines spend the day resting in underground dens, which may extend 20m (66ft) underground, opening into a large chamber. This species is solitary by nature, although pairs with young may be spotted out and about. Young are born with their eyes open, but it will take up to two weeks for their protective spines and quills to harden. These are modified over the short tail, allowing the porcupine to make an intimidating rattling sound with them as a warning if threatened.

The largest porcupine on the continent, and also the biggest rodent, this species is relatively common, although it is not especially conspicuous due to its nocturnal nature.

WHERE IN THE WORLD?

Widely distributed across Africa south of the Sahara, but absent from the Namib desert in the southwest. Occurs at altitudes of up to 3500m (11,500ft).

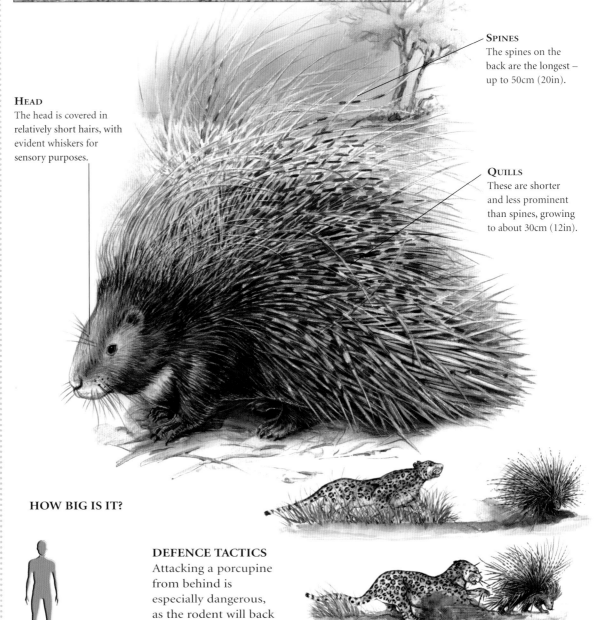

SPINES
The spines on the back are the longest – up to 50cm (20in).

HEAD
The head is covered in relatively short hairs, with evident whiskers for sensory purposes.

QUILLS
These are shorter and less prominent than spines, growing to about 30cm (12in).

Broken quills and spines grow back again quickly

HOW BIG IS IT?

DEFENCE TACTICS

Attacking a porcupine from behind is especially dangerous, as the rodent will back towards the predator and effectively impale it.

Libyan Jird

VITAL STATISTICS

WEIGHT	100g (3.5oz)
LENGTH	30cm (12in) overall; tail is the same length as the body
SEXUAL MATURITY	About 3 months
GESTATION PERIOD	Around 26 days; 2 litters a year
NUMBER OF OFFSPRING	3–5; weaning occurs at 4 weeks
DIET	Plant matter, bulbs such as wild tulips, pods containing seeds; can cause crop damage
LIFESPAN	Up to 5 years

ANIMAL FACTS

The behaviour of these rodents varies across their range, differing depending on their locality. In some places they may be active above ground during the day, whereas elsewhere they are strictly nocturnal. This may be influenced by the behaviour of predators, with hawks likely to encourage the jirds to be more active after dark. Libyan jirds are usually found in colonies, and in certain areas they may spend periods of the winter sleeping in their burrows during harsh weather.

Jirds eat using their paws as hands to hold food

Closely related to gerbils, Libyan jirds communicate in a similar way – by drumming their hind legs on the ground as a warning of danger.

WHERE IN THE WORLD?

Occurs throughout Libya and Egypt's western desert, through the Middle East, via Israel, Jordan, Syria and Saudi Arabia to Iran, Iraq, Afghanistan, Pakistan and Azerbaijan.

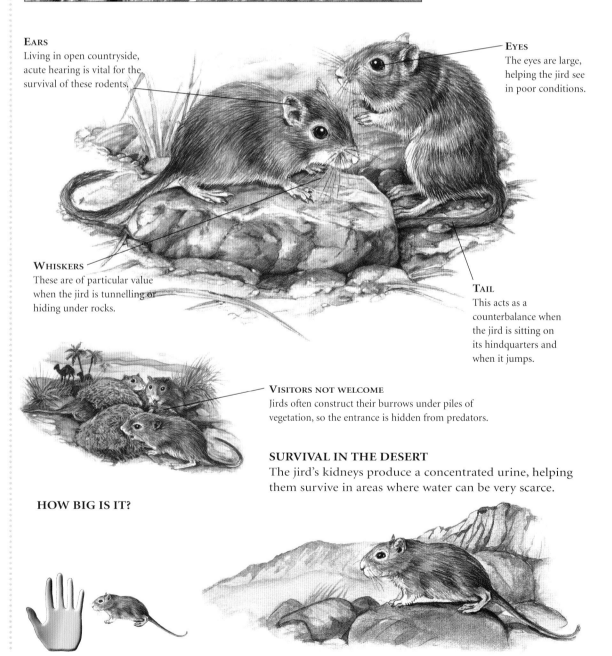

EARS
Living in open countryside, acute hearing is vital for the survival of these rodents.

EYES
The eyes are large, helping the jird see in poor conditions.

WHISKERS
These are of particular value when the jird is tunnelling or hiding under rocks.

TAIL
This acts as a counterbalance when the jird is sitting on its hindquarters and when it jumps.

VISITORS NOT WELCOME
Jirds often construct their burrows under piles of vegetation, so the entrance is hidden from predators.

SURVIVAL IN THE DESERT
The jird's kidneys produce a concentrated urine, helping them survive in areas where water can be very scarce.

HOW BIG IS IT?

Harvest Mouse

• ORDER • Rodentia **• FAMILY •** Muridae **• SPECIES •** *Micromys minutus*

Changes in agricultural practices, especially increasing mechanization, have led to a decline in the numbers of this species – one of the smallest rodents.

VITAL STATISTICS

WEIGHT	5–11g (0.12–0.39oz)
LENGTH	10–14cm (4–5.5in) overall; tail is similar length to the body
SEXUAL MATURITY	6 weeks
GESTATION PERIOD	17–19 days; 3 litters a year
NUMBER OF OFFSPRING	1–7; weaning occurs around 16 days
DIET	Seeds, bulbs and fruit, but invertebrates may be eaten in summer, along with fungi and even moss
LIFESPAN	12–18 months

ANIMAL FACTS

Harvest mice are most active around dusk, as reflected by their relatively large eyes. They are most conspicuous in the summer, when they sleep above ground in their distinctive nests. During winter they prefer to tunnel away and keep a store of food in their burrows, but they do not actually hibernate. Their habit of nesting in fields of ripening corn has led to a fall in their numbers, with their nests often being destroyed during the harvesting process.

Mothers may carry their young in their mouths

WHERE IN THE WORLD?

Occurs in Europe, south of Scandinavia, and only in southern parts of the British Isles. Extends into Asia from Russia, across to China and Korea.

A HELPING HAND
The harvest mouse is the only European rodent with a prehensile tail.

EYES
Black and quite prominent, these are located relatively close to the muzzle.

COLOURATION
Yellowish-brown on the upperparts with white underparts.

FEET
These are very important in allowing the mouse to climb easily.

TAIL
The pink tail is largely free from hair. The tip is prehensile, allowing the mouse to hold on to stems.

HOW BIG IS IT?

ALTERNATIVE LIFESTYLES

Harvest mice weave elaborate spherical nests. Conservationists have recycled tennis balls from Wimbledon to create artifical nests for these mice. They have mounted them on posts, away from the dangers of combine harvesters, with an access hole cut in the side of each ball.

House Mouse

• ORDER • Rodentia • FAMILY • Muridae • SPECIES • *Mus musculus*

One of only a few species that have benefited from the spread of human settlement, these mice have adapted to live in close association with people.

VITAL STATISTICS

WEIGHT	10–25g (0.35–0.88oz)
LENGTH	12.5–20cm (5–8in) overall; tail is similar length to the body
SEXUAL MATURITY	Females 6 weeks; males 8 weeks
GESTATION PERIOD	19–21 days; 5–10 litters a year
NUMBER OF OFFSPRING	3–14, average 6–8; weaning occurs at 17 days
DIET	Vegetable matter, such as seeds, bulbs, fruit; will also eat meat-based food
LIFESPAN	9–12 months

ANIMAL FACTS

These rodents are remarkably athletic, capable of jumping distances of 45cm (18in). They can climb well, and even swim. Scent-marking is very important, and males in particular have a very distinctive odour. Cautious by nature, house mice prefer dark surroundings. Cats are probably their major predator, but they are also frequently killed by rats. House mice are also the ancestors of today's pet and laboratory mice, which exist in a very wide range of colours.

House mice are grey, but piebald individuals with white areas of fur can also be found

WHERE IN THE WORLD?

Worldwide distribution. Originated in northern India, and spread through the Mediterranean as agriculture developed. Inadvertently taken to Australia and other areas.

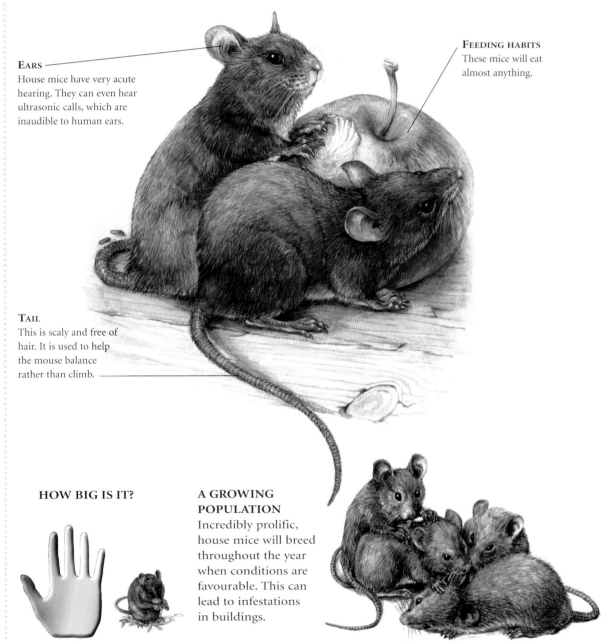

EARS
House mice have very acute hearing. They can even hear ultrasonic calls, which are inaudible to human ears.

FEEDING HABITS
These mice will eat almost anything.

TAIL
This is scaly and free of hair. It is used to help the mouse balance rather than climb.

HOW BIG IS IT?

A GROWING POPULATION
Incredibly prolific, house mice will breed throughout the year when conditions are favourable. This can lead to infestations in buildings.

Brown Rat

• **ORDER** • Rodentia • **FAMILY** • Muridae • **SPECIES** • *Rattus norvegicus*

VITAL STATISTICS

WEIGHT	200–400g (11–14oz)
LENGTH	35–45cm (13.7–17.7in) overall
SEXUAL MATURITY	8–12 weeks
GESTATION PERIOD	22–24 days; 5 litters a year; often mates again immediately after giving birth
NUMBER OF OFFSPRING	6–8; weaning occurs at 21–28 days
DIET	Omnivorous, eating crops such as wheat, vegetables, eggs and invertebrates
LIFESPAN	18–36 months

ANIMAL FACTS

The spread of brown rats began as a result of increasing trade in the 1700s, which enabled rats to get on board ships, often hiding in the supplies being carried. The rats would then be taken to other ports, escaping ashore and sometimes carrying diseases such as plague with them. Once on land, their prolific nature meant their numbers would grow rapidly. A number of ground-nesting species have become extinct because of the introduction of these rodents.

Rats have teeth strong enough to gnaw through concrete

These rats have found a niche living alongside people, and they have displaced the black rat from this role thanks to their more adaptable natures.

WHERE IN THE WORLD?

Originally found in Japan and eastern Asia, but has since spread across most of the world, even occurring on remote islands in the Pacific.

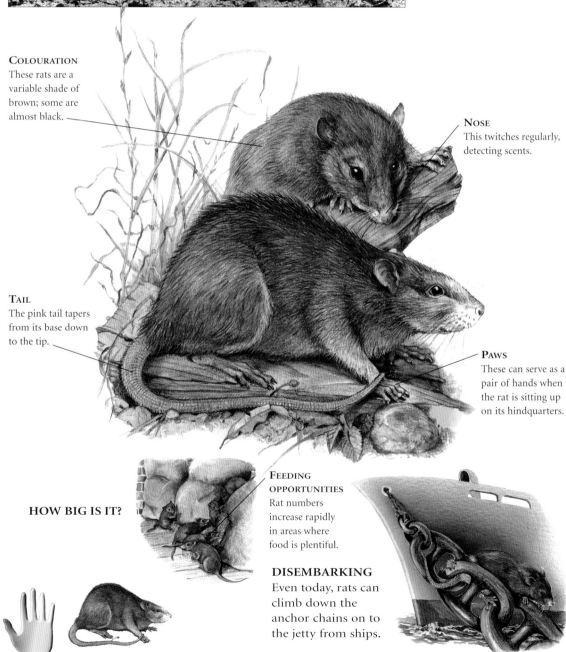

COLOURATION
These rats are a variable shade of brown; some are almost black.

NOSE
This twitches regularly, detecting scents.

TAIL
The pink tail tapers from its base down to the tip.

PAWS
These can serve as a pair of hands when the rat is sitting up on its hindquarters.

HOW BIG IS IT?

FEEDING OPPORTUNITIES
Rat numbers increase rapidly in areas where food is plentiful.

DISEMBARKING
Even today, rats can climb down the anchor chains on to the jetty from ships.

Coypu

This relatively large rodent is better known in North America as the nutria, which is the name given to its fur elsewhere in the world.

VITAL STATISTICS

WEIGHT	200–400g (11–14oz); males slightly larger
LENGTH	61cm (24in) overall
SEXUAL MATURITY	Females 3–9 months; males 4–9 months
GESTATION PERIOD	About 130 days; 2 litters a year; often mates again immediately after giving birth
NUMBER OF OFFSPRING	Average 4–5, but ranges from 1–13; weaning occurs at 56–63 days
DIET	Vegetarian, eating a variety of wetland plants, tubers and roots
LIFESPAN	2–3 years

ANIMAL FACTS

The demand for the coypu's fur saw these rodents being taken to fur farms outside their usual range. Some escaped and started to breed, which had a serious impact on the whole ecosystem as their numbers increased. Not only do coypus feed heavily on aquatic plants, taking away root systems that hold together the mud base, but they will also deepen channels elsewhere, thanks to their swimming action.

Young coypus are born fully developed, and can eat solid food within hours of birth, although they also suckle

WHERE IN THE WORLD?

Occurs in southern South America. Introduced to some 22 states in the USA. Present in England from 1929–89, and still occurs on the European mainland into Asia.

PROFILE
The coypu has a hunched body shape because the hindlegs are longer than the forelegs.

TAIL
This has a relatively thick covering of hair, is rounded in shape and tapers to its tip.

EYES
These are positioned relatively high on the head, giving good visibility when the coypu is partly submerged.

HIND FEET
Four webbed toes are equipped with sharp claws, alongside a single smaller toe.

HOW BIG IS IT?

COYPU BURROWS
These represent a serious danger if they undermine water defences such as dykes, causing potentially serious flooding of the neighbouring land.

Springhare

VITAL STATISTICS

WEIGHT	3–4kg (6.6–8.8lb)
LENGTH	71–94cm (28–37in) overall; tail is the same length as the body
SEXUAL MATURITY	About 2¾ years
GESTATION PERIOD	About 80 days; up to 3 litters a year
NUMBER OF OFFSPRING	1; weaning occurs at 49 days
DIET	Herbivorous, eating crops such as wheat, oats and barley, plus invertebrates such as grasshoppers and beetles
LIFESPAN	8–14 years

ANIMAL FACTS

The only member of its family, the springhare has suffered from loss of habitat. Living in relatively open country, these rodents rely on their ability to jump in order to evade predators. They live below ground in their burrows during the day and emerge at dusk, as reflected by their large eyes. They also have keen hearing, although their ears are protected by a tuft of external hair, to prevent sand getting into the ear canal, particularly when they are digging.

Springhares jump on their hind legs, like kangaroos

Despite its name, this species is a rodent not a hare – or indeed a member of the kangaroo family as its appearance might suggest.

WHERE IN THE WORLD?

Occurs in grassland areas in southeastern and southern parts of Africa, in Kenya, Tanzania, Congo, Botswana, Mozambique, Zambia, Zimbabwe, Angola, Namibia and South Africa.

NECK
Short and muscular, the neck supports the weight of the head.

MATERNAL BOND
Springhares are not prolific rodents, and they raise their offspring with care.

TAIL
The long tail helps the springhare maintain its balance.

COLOURATION
This can be variable, ranging from reddish-brown to a dull grey. The underparts are white.

HIND FEET
These are much longer than the front feet, each having four toes with strong claws.

HOW BIG IS IT?

HIDING AWAY
If they detect possible danger, springhares retreat to their burrows and seal themselves inside by creating a soil barrier.

Black-Tailed Prairie Dog

• **ORDER** • Rodentia • **FAMILY** • Sciuridae • **SPECIES** • *Cynomys ludovicianus*

VITAL STATISTICS

WEIGHT	0.9–1.4kg (2–3lb); males generally bigger
LENGTH	43–53cm (17–21in)
SEXUAL MATURITY	1–2 years
GESTATION PERIOD	28–35 days; 1 litter a year
NUMBER OF OFFSPRING	3–5, but can be up to 8; weaning by 49 days
DIET	Mainly grass, as well as herbage; may eat invertebrates such as grasshoppers
LIFESPAN	3–5 years

ANIMAL FACTS

These ground squirrels live in large groups, creating a network of underground burrows described as 'prairie-dog towns'. They are very important as a key species in maintaining the ecosystem. Studies suggest that up to 170 other species benefit from their presence, including the endangered black-footed ferret. Unfortunately, it is not just habitat change that has affected the population of these prairie dogs. More recently, colonies have been wiped out by a disease spread by fleas.

In the early 1800s, some five billion of these rodents lived across the North American prairies. Today there are fewer than two million individuals.

WHERE IN THE WORLD?

South-central Canada to northeastern Mexico. West of the Rockies in Colorado, Kansas, Montana, Nebraska, New Mexico, North Dakota, Oklahoma, South Dakota, Texas and Wyoming.

COLOURATION
This is a variable feature, and individuals range from shades of grey through to brown and even black.

SITTING
This upright posture gives prairie dogs a good opportunity to spot potential predators in their vicinity.

SOUND AND SIGHT
Although their earflaps are small, prairie dogs have very keen hearing. They also have good eyesight.

Prairie dogs rarely stray far from the protection of their tunnels

HOW BIG IS IT?

GREETING
Touching the front teeth in this way is described as 'kissing', and serves as a greeting between family members.

Southern Flying Squirrel

• ORDER • Rodentia • FAMILY • Sciuridae • SPECIES • *Glaucomys volans*

VITAL STATISTICS

WEIGHT	51–71g (1.8–2.5oz)
LENGTH	20–25cm (8–10in) overall
SEXUAL MATURITY	By 1 year
GESTATION PERIOD	40 days; 2 litters a year, born in tree cavities
NUMBER OF OFFSPRING	2–7; weaning by 120 days
DIET	Fruit, nuts and acorns; may also eat invertebrates, raids birds' nests and feeds on carrion
LIFESPAN	Up to 5 years; 10–12 in captivity

ANIMAL FACTS

Southern flying squirrels are unusual in being active at night, gliding distances of up to 46m (150ft) from high vantage points. They are capable of navigating back to their territory from a distance of 1km (0.62 miles). The development of young is very slow. They are completely helpless at birth. Their fur starts to grow from about a week old, but it may be nearly a month before their eyes open.

Fungi growing on the bark of trees feature in the diet of these squirrels

In spite of their name, these squirrels glide rather than fly, using wing membranes. They are vulnerable on the ground, however, and scramble to safety.

WHERE IN THE WORLD?

Occurs in eastern North America, from southeastern parts of Canada across the USA to Florida. Also present in Central America, in parts of Mexico, Guatemala and Honduras.

PATAGIUM
The membrane that connects the front and back legs allows these squirrels to glide with their limbs outstretched.

TAIL
Long and bushy, the tail helps the squirrel to steer through the air, and can act as a brake.

HIND LIMBS
These squirrels can run up branches, with their hind feet also providing support when they land.

HOW BIG IS IT?

LANDING STRATEGY
When landing, the squirrel touches down with its front feet, folding down its membrane and braking with its tail held vertically.

ON THE MOVE
The squirrels can run up and down tree trunks unhindered by the membrane.

Alpine Marmot

VITAL STATISTICS

WEIGHT	4–8kg (8.8–17.6lb); largest of all squirrels
LENGTH	66–89cm (26–35in)
SEXUAL MATURITY	1 year
GESTATION PERIOD	34 days; litters born every 2 years
NUMBER OF OFFSPRING	2–7, typically 3; weaning occurs at 40 days
DIET	Grasses and herbage, seeds and bulbs; also invertebrates, birds' egg and carrion
LIFESPAN	Up to 5 years; 14 in captivity

ANIMAL FACTS

Originating from a bitterly cold winter environment, Alpine marmots have a peculiar metabolism. They put on weight in the summer and then enter an extended period of hibernation over the winter, which can last for up to six months. The adults curl up with their offspring, keeping them warm throughout this period. The entrances to the burrows are plugged by the adults using dry grass and soil, helping to keep the interior warm.

These ground squirrels occur in grassland areas at high altitudes, inhabiting underground burrows in which they can escape the worst of the winter weather.

WHERE IN THE WORLD?

Occurs in the Swiss, Italian and French Alps. Also southern Germany and western Austria. Extends east to the Carpathian and Tatra mountains. Has been introduced to the Pyrenees.

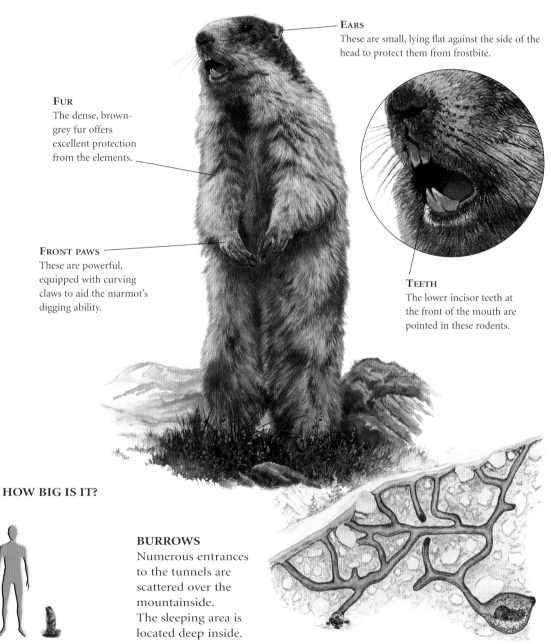

EARS
These are small, lying flat against the side of the head to protect them from frostbite.

FUR
The dense, brown-grey fur offers excellent protection from the elements.

FRONT PAWS
These are powerful, equipped with curving claws to aid the marmot's digging ability.

TEETH
The lower incisor teeth at the front of the mouth are pointed in these rodents.

HOW BIG IS IT?

BURROWS
Numerous entrances to the tunnels are scattered over the mountainside. The sleeping area is located deep inside.

Red Squirrel

• **ORDER** • Rodentia • **FAMILY** • Sciuridae • **SPECIES** • *Sciurus vulgaris*

VITAL STATISTICS

WEIGHT	250–340g (8.8–12oz)
LENGTH	34–43cm (13–17in)
SEXUAL MATURITY	11 months
GESTATION PERIOD	38 days; 2 litters annually
NUMBER OF OFFSPRING	3–6; young eat solid food from 40 days, but may suckle for 10 weeks
DIET	Seeds of trees, invertebrates, berries, shoots and birds' eggs
LIFESPAN	Up to 7 years

ANIMAL FACTS

In some areas, the red squirrel has been pushed out of its former haunts by its larger, more aggressive cousin, the eastern grey squirrel (*S. carolinensis*) from North America. Only in a few localities, such as the Isle of Wight and parts of Scotland, do red squirrels remain unchallenged. They live in broadleaf and coniferous forests, occupying nests of sticks called dreys. Red squirrels do not hibernate over the winter, but they may prepare food in the autumn.

Summer coat (top) and darker winter coat (bottom)

Although one of the most beautifully coloured of all squirrels, there can be considerable variation in their appearance, and some are brown or even blackish.

WHERE IN THE WORLD?

Ranges throughout northern parts of Europe, to the Pacific coast of Asia, but has undergone local declines in some areas, including the British Isles.

COLOURATION
Vibrant red coats are most common in the population found in the British Isles.

EAR TUFTS
These are much more prominent over the winter period, following the autumn moult.

TEETH
Their sharp incisor teeth allow these squirrels to extract seeds easily from pine cones.

HOW BIG IS IT?

JUMPING
The powerful hind legs of these squirrels allow them to jump from one branch to another.

European Ground Squirrel

• ORDER • Rodentia • FAMILY • Sciuridae • SPECIES • *Spermophilus citellus*

This species, which is also known as the European souslik, lives in open, relatively arid areas of countryside. These are burrowing rather than arboreal squirrels.

VITAL STATISTICS

WEIGHT	200–400g (7–14oz); builds up fat reserves in autumn
LENGTH	24–30cm (9.5–12in)
SEXUAL MATURITY	11 months
GESTATION PERIOD	27 days; 1 litter annually
NUMBER OF OFFSPRING	5–8, average 6; weaning occurs at 30–34 days
DIET	Nuts, seeds and plant matter including herbs; also invertebrates, small vertebrates and birds' eggs
LIFESPAN	Up to 7 years

ANIMAL FACTS

These ground squirrels live in close proximity to each other, but individuals have their own burrows. They may occupy short-term dens, where they retreat on occasion during the day, as well as deeper burrows that are used for hibernation over the winter period. The entrance to the den will be blocked off, with a side tunnel connecting to the surface through which the squirrels can emerge in the spring. Their young are also born underground, and are completely helpless at first.

WHERE IN THE WORLD?

Found in southeastern Germany and Austria to the Czech Republic and Slovakia, north to south-western Poland. Via Turkey, Romania and Greece eastwards to the Ukraine.

FACIAL FEATURES
The forehead is long and relatively flat. The dark eyes are large but the ears are small.

FORELEGS
These can act as paws to hold food and are used to dig burrows.

COLOURATION
Yellowish-grey along the back, with much paler underparts.

TAIL
This is about one-third of the body length, and is covered in hair.

STOCKING UP
Although these ground squirrels may take hay and food underground, they do not store anything to eat over the winter.

HOW BIG IS IT?

HIBERNATION
Males will start to hibernate before females, as early as August, and will not be seen above ground until March.

Siberian Chipmunk

• ORDER • Rodentia • FAMILY • Sciuridae • SPECIES • *Tamias sibiricus*

This chipmunk's generic name, Tamias, comes from the Greek word for 'storer', and describes how they create food stores to use during the harsh winter.

VITAL STATISTICS

WEIGHT	0.5–1.5kg (1.1–3.3lb), depending on the time of year
LENGTH	18–25cm (7–10in) overall; tail is about one-third of the body length
SEXUAL MATURITY	10 months
GESTATION PERIOD	28–35 days; 1 litter a year
NUMBER OF OFFSPRING	3–5, but can be up to 8; weaning occurs by 49 days
DIET	Mainly vegetarian, eating seeds, nuts, fungi, fruit and some invertebrates
LIFESPAN	Up to 8 years

ANIMAL FACTS

These lively members of the squirrel family are active during the day and very agile, leaping from branch to branch. They also construct a network of tunnels, broadening out into chambers, where they store food to eat over the winter (carried back in their cheek pouches). There will also be a sleeping chamber lined with dry grass. Although they do not hibernate, Siberian chipmunks remain below ground for long periods when the weather is unfavourable, and they may become torpid.

Mating may take place on the ground

WHERE IN THE WORLD?

Occurs in northern Asia, from central parts of Russia to China, Korea and the northern Japanese island of Hokkaidu. Small populations exist in Europe from escaped pets.

STRIPES
The white stripes are quite distinctive, explaining why these chipmunks are also called 'striped squirrels'.

FRONT PAWS
These are used for holding food as well as for digging, and as support when climbing.

UNDERSIDE
The underparts of the body are paler than the upperparts.

TAIL
Long and bushy, this has no stripes. It is often held in an S-shaped curve.

HOW BIG IS IT?

LIFE UNDERGROUND
The entrance to the chipmunk's burrow is carefully concealed, often under a tree root, and may be 9.1m (30ft) long.

Eastern Chipmunk

• **ORDER** • Rodentia • **FAMILY** • Sciuridae • **SPECIES** • *Tamias striatus*

These members of the squirrel family are named because of the 'chip-chip' sound of their calls. Groups often start calling at the same time.

VITAL STATISTICS

WEIGHT	80–150g (2.8–5.3oz), depending partly on the time of year
LENGTH	21.5–28.5cm (8.4–11.2in) overall; tail is about one-third of the body length
SEXUAL MATURITY	By 1 year
GESTATION PERIOD	31 days; 2 litters a year
NUMBER OF OFFSPRING	Typically 4–5, but can be up to 9; weaning occurs at 42 days
DIET	Seeds, nuts, fungi, corn, fruit, eggs and some invertebrates
LIFESPAN	Up to 3 years

ANIMAL FACTS

Digging underground burrows is a laborious task for these chipmunks, as they will carry all the soil away in their cheek pouches, depositing it well away from the entrance so as not to alert predators to their presence. Some chipmunks are particularly dedicated tunnellers, creating a network of burrows over 9m (30ft) long. There is usually more than one entry point. Chipmunks do not hibernate, but simply carry on feeding on food stored in their burrows over the winter.

WHERE IN THE WORLD?

Occurs throughout most of eastern North America, from southeastern Canada, Minnesota, Wisconsin to Illinois, Michigan and Iowa, and down to the Gulf Coast. Absent from Florida.

PATTERNING
Five black stripes extend down the body, separated by intervening brown, grey and white bands.

CHEEKS
These often appear swollen, because of internal cheek pouches in the mouth, used to carry food.

TOES
There are four toes on each front paw, and five on each back paw.

TAIL
The tail is well-furred, but not bushy.

A VARIED DIET
Chipmunks are opportunistic in their feeding habits. They often raid birds' nests, stealing the eggs.

BURROWS
Chipmunks will defend their burrow. It is usually well-concealed, often at the root of a tree.

HOW BIG IS IT?

Rainbow Trout

• **ORDER** • Salmoniformes • **FAMILY** • Salmonidae • **SPECIES** • *Oncorhynchus mykiss*

VITAL STATISTICS

WEIGHT	Typically 2.5–10kg (5.5–22lb)
LENGTH	Up to nearly 1.2m (4ft) but usually much smaller
SEXUAL MATURITY	Steelheads may spend 1–4 years at sea
NUMBER OF EGGS	Around 4000, influenced by the female's size
HATCHING PERIOD	About 1 month, depending on the water temperature
DIET	Young feed on invertebrates; older individuals are largely piscivorous
LIFESPAN	Typically 4–6 years, but can be up to 11

ANIMAL FACTS

The characteristic rainbow colouring of these trout is usually only maintained in a fresh-water environment. They become a steely shade of grey during their marine phase, when they are known as steelheads. They will migrate long distances down river to reach the sea. Here they will grow, and return again to spawn in fresh water. Nevertheless, it is quite possible for these salmonids to spend their entire lives in a fresh-water environment.

The jaw line lengthens beyond the eyes in older specimens (top)

The rainbow trout gets its name from the vivid colours on its flanks. It is a very adaptable species and now has a worldwide distribution.

Occurs naturally along North America's Pacific coast, extending from Alaska down to Mexico. Has been introduced to more than 80 other countries globally.

SPOTS
The spotted patterning on the fins and body is a highly individual feature.

PROFILE
Sleek body shape, with a gentle curve from the upper jaw to the dorsal fin.

PECTORAL FINS
These are located just behind and below the gill covers .

JAWS
These are powerful, with a good-sized gape and an array of teeth.

AMBUSHING PREDATORS
Larger rainbow trout will prey on other fish, including their own kind.

HOW BIG IS IT?

AGILITY
These trout have good eyesight and are capable of catching flying insects that venture close to the water's surface.

Atlantic Salmon

• ORDER • Salmoniformes **• FAMILY •** Salmonidae **• SPECIES •** *Salmo salar*

These salmon start their lives in fresh water, then enter the sea before returning again to the river where they hatched in order to spawn.

VITAL STATISTICS

WEIGHT	Typically 2.3–9kg (5–20lb), but up to 35.89kg (78.96lb) has been recorded; landlocked salmon are smaller
LENGTH	Up to 1.5m (4.9ft) but usually much smaller
SEXUAL MATURITY	After 1–2 years at sea
NUMBER OF EGGS	700–800 per 0.454kg (1lb) body weight
HATCHING PERIOD	Spawns in October–November; eggs hatch in April
DIET	Young feed on invertebrates; older individuals are largely piscivorous
LIFESPAN	4–10 years

ANIMAL FACTS

These fish have a remarkable lifecycle. The young, which live in shoals, are called alevins, then known as parr as they disperse in the river. When they head down river at about 15cm (6in) long, they are known as smolts. These salmon possess a remarkable sense of smell, which helps them locate their spawning grounds after a year or two in the sea. In spite of the arduous journey, Atlantic salmon often spawn more than once in their lives.

The top of the jaw appears twisted in salmon returning to spawn

WHERE IN THE WORLD?

Occurs in the North Atlantic, as well as in the rivers feeding into it, from the Arctic Circle south to North America's Connecticut River, and to Portugal in Europe.

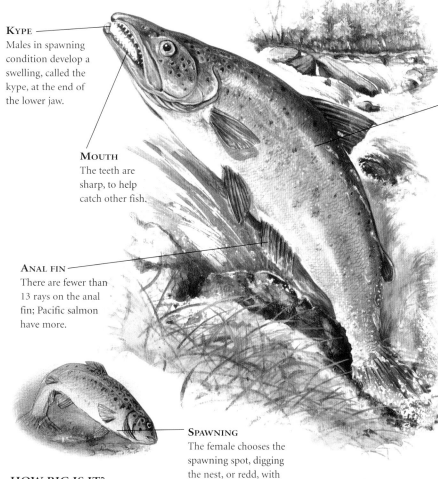

KYPE
Males in spawning condition develop a swelling, called the kype, at the end of the lower jaw.

MOUTH
The teeth are sharp, to help catch other fish.

ANAL FIN
There are fewer than 13 rays on the anal fin; Pacific salmon have more.

COLOURATION
This varies according to the age of the salmon. Reddish spots become apparent at this stage.

SPAWNING
The female chooses the spawning spot, digging the nest, or redd, with her fins, lying on her side. She covers the eggs in the same way afterwards. They may be buried up to 25cm (10in) deep.

HOW BIG IS IT?

JUMPING THE RAPIDS
Salmon can face a host of barriers – both natural and man-made – when heading back to their traditional spawning grounds.

Devil Lionfish

• **ORDER** • Scorpaeniformes • **FAMILY** • Scorpaenidae • **SPECIES** • *Pterois miles*

VITAL STATISTICS

WEIGHT	1.1kg (2.5lb)
LENGTH	Up to 38cm (15in)
SEXUAL MATURITY	2 years
NUMBER OF EGGS	2000–15,000 laid in balls, which are fertilized externally
HATCHING PERIOD	Larvae spend 25–40 days drifting and feeding in the planktonic column before descending to the reef
DIET	Predatory, hunting small crustaceans such as shrimps, and small fish; may also be cannibalistic
LIFESPAN	10–15 years

ANIMAL FACTS

These lionfish occupy relatively shallow coastal waters, to a maximum depth of about 60m (196ft), blending in against the background of the reef. Their colouration and fin patterning provide remarkable camouflage. They swim slowly – well-protected against predators by their venom – and can sometimes look rather like drifting seaweed. Being stung by a lionfish is immensely painful. Placing the affected part of the body in very hot water as an emergency treatment can help, however, by coagulating the venom.

Bright colouration often serves as a warning sign in nature, and this is certainly true of these slow-swimming lionfish, whose spines are tipped with a deadly venom.

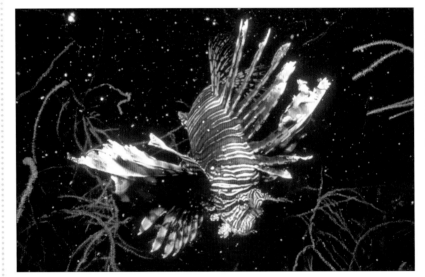

WHERE IN THE WORLD?

Occurs in the Red Sea southwards to the vicinity of Port Alfred, South Africa, and eastwards across the Indian Ocean to Sumatra. Also recorded from the eastern Mediterranean.

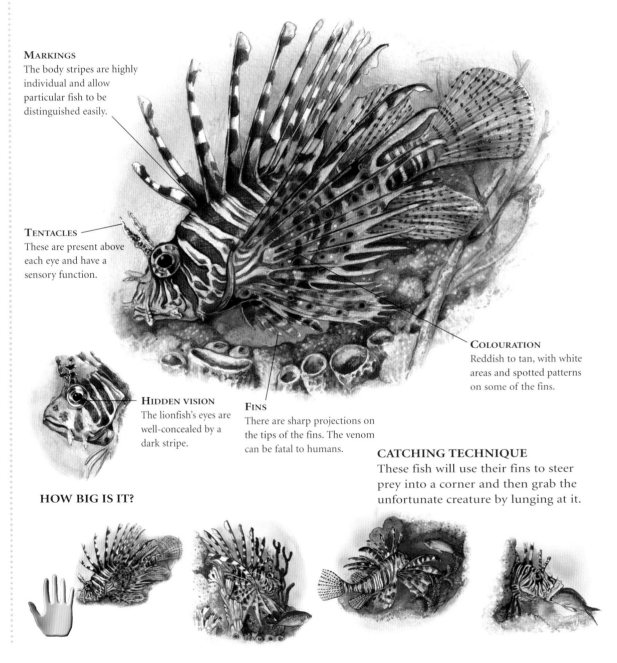

MARKINGS
The body stripes are highly individual and allow particular fish to be distinguished easily.

TENTACLES
These are present above each eye and have a sensory function.

HIDDEN VISION
The lionfish's eyes are well-concealed by a dark stripe.

FINS
There are sharp projections on the tips of the fins. The venom can be fatal to humans.

COLOURATION
Reddish to tan, with white areas and spotted patterns on some of the fins.

CATCHING TECHNIQUE
These fish will use their fins to steer prey into a corner and then grab the unfortunate creature by lunging at it.

HOW BIG IS IT?

Mediterranean Scorpion

• ORDER • Scorpiones **• FAMILY •** Buthidae **• SPECIES •** *Buthus occitanus*

Although originating in a relatively warm part of the world, these scorpions are sometimes found above the winter snow-line, at altitudes of over 1000m (3280ft).

VITAL STATISTICS

LENGTH	6–8cm (2.4–3.1in)
SEXUAL MATURITY	1–2 years
NUMBER OF EGGS	20–35, fertilized internally by the male's sperm packet or spermatophore
DEVELOPMENTAL PERIOD	Up to 8 months; young develop in the female's body, with nutrients supplied via a primitive type of placental connection
HABITAT	Arid rural areas, hiding under rocks; sometimes found in forests
DIET	Other invertebrates
LIFESPAN	5–7 years

ANIMAL FACTS

The potency of this scorpion's venom varies according to its locality. Mediterranean scorpions from North Africa are much more dangerous to humans than those from Europe. Males travel more widely than females, seeking mates. Newborn scorpions are white at birth, and are helpless at first. They are carried on their mother's body, moulting after a week, so that they then resemble miniature scorpions. The young start to roam further afield, but they are still fed by her.

WHERE IN THE WORLD?

Occurs throughout southwestern Europe, in France, Spain and Portugal. Also occurs on the opposite side of the Mediterranean, in North Africa.

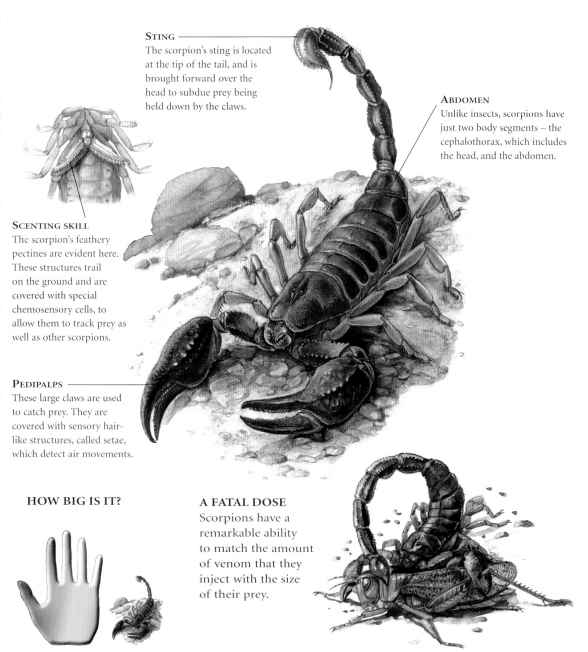

STING
The scorpion's sting is located at the tip of the tail, and is brought forward over the head to subdue prey being held down by the claws.

ABDOMEN
Unlike insects, scorpions have just two body segments – the cephalothorax, which includes the head, and the abdomen.

SCENTING SKILL
The scorpion's feathery pectines are evident here. These structures trail on the ground and are covered with special chemosensory cells, to allow them to track prey as well as other scorpions.

PEDIPALPS
These large claws are used to catch prey. They are covered with sensory hair-like structures, called setae, which detect air movements.

HOW BIG IS IT?

A FATAL DOSE
Scorpions have a remarkable ability to match the amount of venom that they inject with the size of their prey.

Common Cuttlefish

This is one of the largest species of cuttlefish, and favours relatively shallow sandy areas of sea. These invertebrates are related to octopuses and squid.

VITAL STATISTICS

WEIGHT	Up to 4kg (8.8lb)
LENGTH	Mantle 49cm (19in)
SEXUAL MATURITY	1–2 years
NUMBER OF EGGS	20–35, fertilized internally, by the male's sperm packet; both sexes die after spawning
HATCHING PERIOD	About 2 months, depending on the sea temperature
DIET	Crustaceans such as shrimps and crabs, plus molluscs including clams; sometimes eats fish and may be cannibalistic
LIFESPAN	1–2 years

ANIMAL FACTS

Cuttlefish have a remarkable way of defending themselves, squirting a cloud of ink in the direction of predators. They will then swim away quickly from danger using their own method of jet propulsion. Cuttlefish can also change colour, especially when resting on the sea bed. The young resemble miniature adults and develop set feeding preferences early in life, favouring prey in adulthood that they ate when young.

A cuttlefish makes a getaway from this predatory eel by utilizing its ink, called sepia

WHERE IN THE WORLD?

Occurs throughout the Baltic and North seas, south via the Iberian Peninsula to the Mediterranean, and along the west African coast to the southern tip of the continent.

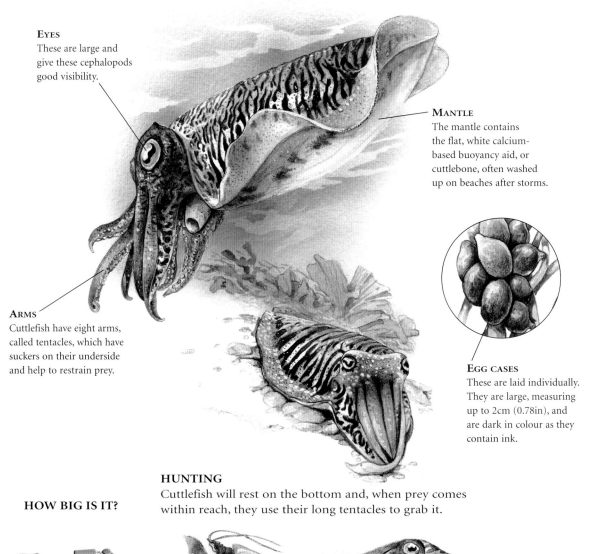

EYES
These are large and give these cephalopods good visibility.

MANTLE
The mantle contains the flat, white calcium-based buoyancy aid, or cuttlebone, often washed up on beaches after storms.

ARMS
Cuttlefish have eight arms, called tentacles, which have suckers on their underside and help to restrain prey.

EGG CASES
These are laid individually. They are large, measuring up to 2cm (0.78in), and are dark in colour as they contain ink.

HOW BIG IS IT?

HUNTING
Cuttlefish will rest on the bottom and, when prey comes within reach, they use their long tentacles to grab it.

Wels Catfish

VITAL STATISTICS

WEIGHT	Average 20kg, but giants can weigh over 150kg (330lb)
LENGTH	About 1.5m (5ft), but can reach double this size
SEXUAL MATURITY	3–5 years
NUMBER OF EGGS	30,000 per kilo (2.2lb) of body weight
HATCHING PERIOD	3–10 days, depending on water temperature
DIET	Smaller fish eat worms, crustaceans and other fish, eating amphibians, rodents and ducks as they grow
LIFESPAN	30 years or more

ANIMAL FACTS

These formidable predators can simply suck their prey into their throats. They live in relatively still waters, in areas where there is a lot of submerged debris, such as tree roots, that allows them to hide away. Although their eyes are quite small, their hearing is acute which, along with their barbels, helps them to find prey easily even in muddy waters. Warm surroundings and plentiful food supplies help to ensure their continued growth.

One of the world's largest freshwater fish, the Wels catfish can be a true monster, although it is not usually a danger to humans.

WHERE IN THE WORLD?

Occurs around the Baltic down through central, southern and eastern Europe, extending to the Caspian Sea. Has been introduced in some areas.

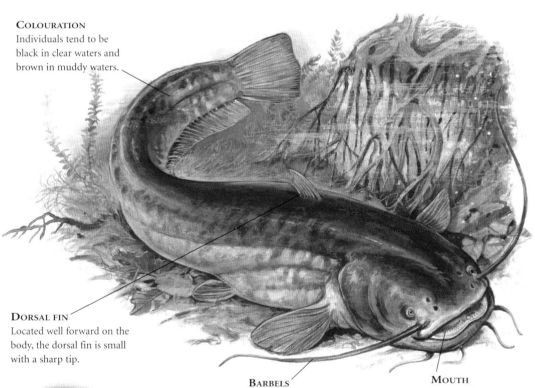

COLOURATION
Individuals tend to be black in clear waters and brown in muddy waters.

DORSAL FIN
Located well forward on the body, the dorsal fin is small with a sharp tip.

NIGHT ACTIVITY
Wels catfish tends to become more active after dark.

HOW BIG IS IT?

BARBELS
These sensory projections help locate prey. There are two long barbels on the upper jaw and four below.

MOUTH
The mouth is broad, with a wide gape and lines of teeth.

BREEDING
The male will stay with the eggs after spawning, fanning them with his tail and guarding them until they hatch.

Portuguese Man o'War

• ORDER • Siphonophora • FAMILY • Physaliidae • SPECIES • *Physalia physalis*

VITAL STATISTICS

LENGTH	The sail – an individual creature – can measure 15cm (6in)
BREEDING	The gonozooids, polyps responsible for reproduction, have male and female parts; they release fertilized eggs that drift in the plankton; larvae develop asexually into further Portuguese man o'war
HABITAT	Open ocean
DIET	Planktonic creatures, as well as larger crustaceans and small fish
LIFESPAN	1 year

ANIMAL FACTS

Portuguese man o'war cannot swim, so they drift, and they can end up being blown on to beaches. They can create a hazard even after they are dead, because of the stinging nematocyst cells attached to their tentacles, used for paralyzing prey. The effects of a sting can be very painful. There are creatures – including the loggerhead turtle – whose skin is too thick to be affected by the sting of a Portuguese man o'war, and these animals prey extensively on them.

Its appearance may resemble a single creature, but in fact the Portuguese man o'war actually represents a colony of organisms.

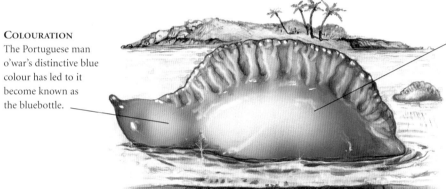

WHERE IN THE WORLD?

Distributed widely throughout the world's warmer seas, especially common in the Indian and Pacific oceans, as well as the Gulf Stream of the North Atlantic.

COLOURATION
The Portuguese man o'war's distinctive blue colour has led to it become known as the bluebottle.

AIR BLADDER
This inflated sac, measuring up to 15cm (6in) high, provides buoyancy and is called the sail.

TENTACLES
Equipped with stinging cells, these can easily measure as much as 10m (33ft) long.

POLYPS
These shorter projections help digest the man o'war's prey.

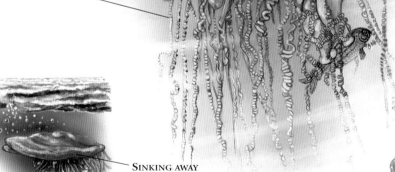

SINKING AWAY
The Portuguese man o'war can deflate its sail and then slip below the waves to escape danger.

HOW BIG IS IT?

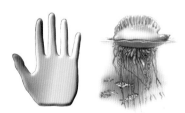

SAFETY AT SEA
Certain fish have adapted to live safely in association with Portuguese man o'war, having developed an immunity to their stings.

Dugong

VITAL STATISTICS

WEIGHT	230–500kg (507–1100lb)
LENGTH	2.4–3m (8–10ft)
SEXUAL MATURITY	8–18 years
GESTATION PERIOD	About 13 months; young are cream-coloured at birth
NUMBER OF OFFSPRING	1; young suckle upside down beneath their mother's body; weaning takes around 24 months
DIET	Aquatic vegetation, browsing on underwater grasses; may eat some invertebrates
LIFESPAN	Up to 70 years

ANIMAL FACTS

The grazing habits of these marine mammals have led to them also being called sea cows, as they feed on seagrasses growing in the shallows. They never emerge on to land, however. Dugongs live in herds or small family groups. Their similarity to elephants is reflected in the fact that male dugongs have short tusks of ivory, which they may use to settle disputes. Adults face few dangers, apart from sharks, killer whales and larger crocodilians.

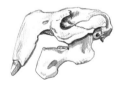

The dugong's snout turns downwards, and the overhang allows it to dig furrows, uprooting the sea grass

The way that dugongs rest, with their heads above the waves, may have been the inspiration for the myth of the mermaid.

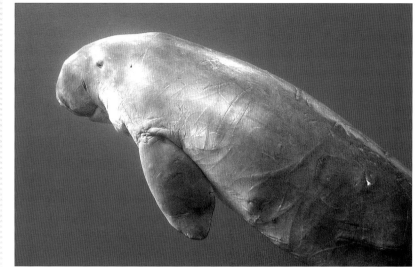

WHERE IN THE WORLD?

Occurs throughout coastal areas in the tropical seas, from East Africa and the Red Sea, across the Indian Ocean and the Pacific, south to Australia.

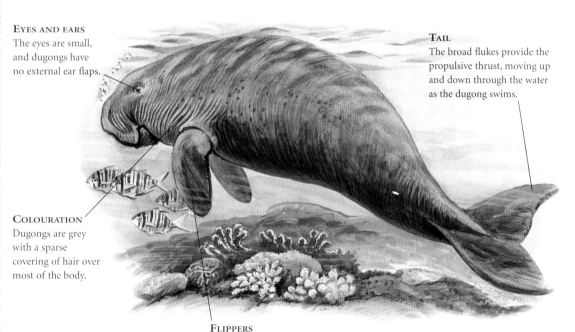

EYES AND EARS
The eyes are small, and dugongs have no external ear flaps.

TAIL
The broad flukes provide the propulsive thrust, moving up and down through the water as the dugong swims.

COLOURATION
Dugongs are grey with a sparse covering of hair over most of the body.

FLIPPERS
These measure up to 45cm (17in) long, and are used for steering.

BREATHING
Dugongs can remain submerged for up to six minutes, and may only put their nostrils above the surface when breathing.

HOW BIG IS IT?

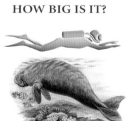

BREACHING THE SURFACE
Sometimes dugongs will be observed 'standing', even seeming to embrace each other.

395

Manatee

• ORDER • Sirenia **• FAMILY •** Trichedidae **• SPECIES •** *Trichechus*

VITAL STATISTICS

WEIGHT	400–550kg (900–1200lb); females are usually larger
LENGTH	2.8–3.6m (9–11.8ft)
SEXUAL MATURITY	8–18 years
GESTATION PERIOD	About 12 months
NUMBER OF OFFSPRING	1; young suckle upside down beneath their mother's body; weaning occurs at 12–18 months
DIET	Herbivorous, grazing on a wide variety of vegetation; has been documented feeding on over 60 different aquatic plants
LIFESPAN	Up to 60 years

ANIMAL FACTS

Many manatees in the Caribbean region bear scars on their backs from being run over by powerboats, the wounds inflicted by the propellors. They swim quite slowly in general, at speeds of around 8kph (5mph), although they can accelerate to 30kph (20mph) over short distances. Manatees have an enlarged organ called a caecum at the junction between the large and small intestines, which helps digest the plant matter that forms the basis of their diet.

Manatees can be found either exclusively in freshwater, or they may move between fresh and salt water, depending on the species.

WHERE IN THE WORLD?

West Indian manatees range from Florida through the Caribbean. The freshwater Amazonian manatee occurs in the Amazon region, and there is a West African species.

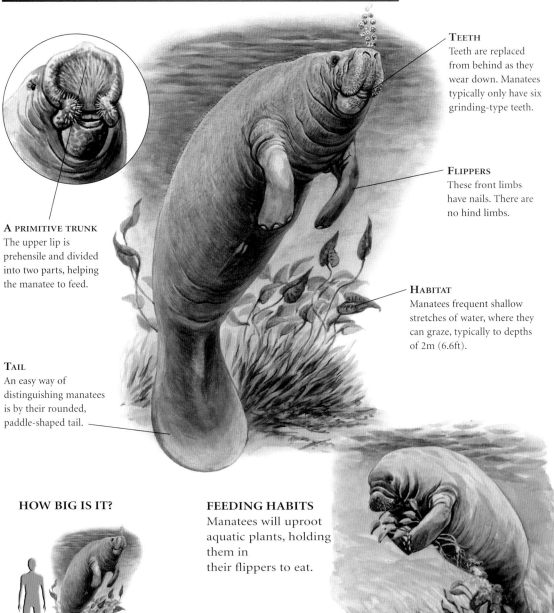

TEETH
Teeth are replaced from behind as they wear down. Manatees typically only have six grinding-type teeth.

FLIPPERS
These front limbs have nails. There are no hind limbs.

HABITAT
Manatees frequent shallow stretches of water, where they can graze, typically to depths of 2m (6.6ft).

A PRIMITIVE TRUNK
The upper lip is prehensile and divided into two parts, helping the manatee to feed.

TAIL
An easy way of distinguishing manatees is by their rounded, paddle-shaped tail.

HOW BIG IS IT?

FEEDING HABITS
Manatees will uproot aquatic plants, holding them in their flippers to eat.

Eurasian Water Shrew

• ORDER • Soricomorpha **• FAMILY •** Soricidae **• SPECIES •** *Neomys fodiens*

VITAL STATISTICS

WEIGHT	About 15g (0.53oz)
LENGTH	17.5cm (7in) overall; the tail is about three-quarters of the body length
SEXUAL MATURITY	By 3.5 months
GESTATION PERIOD	20 days; 2–3 litters a year, born in a nest of grass
NUMBER OF OFFSPRING	Average 5–6, range 3–12; weaning occurs at 42 days
DIET	Invertebrates caught in water and on land; may also hunt small fish
LIFESPAN	Up to 18 months

ANIMAL FACTS

An unusual feature of these shrews is the red appearance of their teeth. This is the result of iron deposits, which help strengthen the teeth. Eurasian water shrews live in burrows and occupy distinct territories. They hide away during the day, emerging under cover of darkness. They have prodigious appetites, thanks to their high metabolic rate, and they must eat about half their body weight every day. They are vulnerable to many predators, including birds of prey.

These small mammals are highly unusual, possessing a venomous saliva used to overcome prey, although they present no danger to people.

WHERE IN THE WORLD?

Ranges across most of northern Europe into Asia, reaching the Pacific coast, and south into north Korea. Found in close proximity to fresh water.

COLOURATION
Very dark upperparts and white underparts.

FUR
Air is trapped in the fur, which gives the shrew buoyancy, but makes it harder to dive.

EYES AND EARS
The eyes are very small, as are the ears, which are largely hidden by fur.

HEAD
The snout is very long with a pink tip on the nose.

HOW BIG IS IT?

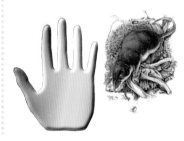

SWIMMING
Bristles are present on the underside of the tail and on the paws, helping the shrew to swim more easily.

Eurasian Shrew

This is the most common European shrew. It can be found almost anywhere with low-growing vegetation to provide cover, even alongside motorways.

VITAL STATISTICS

WEIGHT	5–14g (0.18–0.49oz)
LENGTH	7.2–12.4cm (2.8–4.9in) overall; tail is about half the body length
SEXUAL MATURITY	By 3.5 months; early-born young may breed in the year of their birth
GESTATION PERIOD	24 days; 1–4 litters a year
NUMBER OF OFFSPRING	6–7; weaning at around 23 days
DIET	Various terrestrial invertebrates, including earthworms and slugs
LIFESPAN	Up to 19 months

ANIMAL FACTS

These shrews are very active creatures, almost constantly engaged in searching for food. They need to eat about every two hours, and must consume almost their body weight in food daily in order to stay alive. This becomes even harder during the winter, but they cannot hibernate because they are too small to store sufficient body fat. When they first leave the nest, the young form a so-called 'caravan', each holding the tail of the shrew in front.

WHERE IN THE WORLD?

Occurs across much of northern Europe, down to the Pyrenees, but is absent from Ireland. Extends eastwards into Asia to the vicinity of Lake Baikal in Siberia.

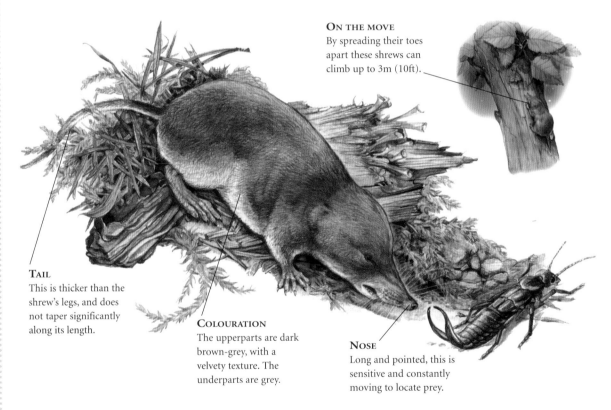

ON THE MOVE
By spreading their toes apart these shrews can climb up to 3m (10ft).

TAIL
This is thicker than the shrew's legs, and does not taper significantly along its length.

COLOURATION
The upperparts are dark brown-grey, with a velvety texture. The underparts are grey.

NOSE
Long and pointed, this is sensitive and constantly moving to locate prey.

SWIMMING
This ability has helped these shrews to spread over a wide area and to colonize various offshore islands throughout their range.

There are 32 teeth in the jaws, but only 12 are in the lower jaw

HOW BIG IS IT?

European Mole

VITAL STATISTICS

WEIGHT	72–128g (0.53oz); males slightly bigger
LENGTH	14–20cm (5.5–7.8in) overall; tail is about a quarter of the body length
SEXUAL MATURITY	About 1 year
GESTATION PERIOD	33 days;. 1 litter a year; breeds March–May
NUMBER OF OFFSPRING	2–7, average 3; weaning occurs at 30 days
DIET	Invertebrates, but may occasionally eat mice
LIFESPAN	Up to 5 years

ANIMAL FACTS

Moles are found in a range of environments where they can burrow easily through the soil. In certain areas, such as farmland and gardens, however, they may be hunted because of their digging activities, which create piles of molehills as soil is deposited at the surface. Moles often construct shallow tunnels but rarely emerge above the ground. In the spring, however, males may leave their tunnel system at night and head overland in search of potential mates.

These moles are rarely seen, but their presence in an area is evident by the piles of soil that they create across a landscape.

WHERE IN THE WORLD?

Occurs in temperate parts of Europe, but is absent from Ireland and southern areas such as Italy. Extends eastwards into Russia, as far as the Ob and Irtysh rivers.

COAT
The fur is short and black with a velvet texture. Only the nose is free of hair, although there are sensory whiskers here.

BODY
the body is cylindrical, to assist movement through tunnels.

EYES
Small and inconspicuous, as befits a species living in underground burrows.

FORELEGS
Large and shovel-like, these are turned outwards and equipped with five claws.

MOLE HILLS
Moles will tunnel when searching for worms, pushing up the soil at intervals.

TUNNEL SYSTEMS

The mole's underground burrows are extensive, with females creating snug nests within their tunnel systems, where the young are born.

HOW BIG IS IT?

Emperor Penguin

• ORDER • Sphenisciformes **• FAMILY •** Spheniscidae **• SPECIES •** *Aptenodytes forsteri*

These are the largest members of the penguin family today, but in the past there were giants that stood taller than a man.

VITAL STATISTICS

WEIGHT	30–40kg (66–88lb)
HEIGHT	Up to 1.2m (4ft)
SEXUAL MATURITY	Hens 5 years; cocks 5–6 years
NUMBER OF EGGS	1
INCUBATION PERIOD	63 days; exposure to the freezing air can be fatal; young form creches, and head to sea at about 3 months old, when the pack ice breaks up in spring
DIET	Fish, crustaceans and squid
LIFESPAN	15–20 years

ANIMAL FACTS

Emperor penguins face winds blowing at 180kph (112mph), and temperatures as low as -62°C (-80°F). Remarkably, they not only survive, but also breed during the winter period, when weather conditions are at their worst. The hen lays a single egg, which she passes to her mate. He carries it on his feet, insulated by a roll of skin serving as a brood pouch. Males then huddle together, not feeding for nine weeks, until their partners return.

WHERE IN THE WORLD?

Occurs within the Antarctic region, in the vicinity of the Weddell and Ross seas, as well as Dronning Maud land, Enderby and Princess Elizabeth lands.

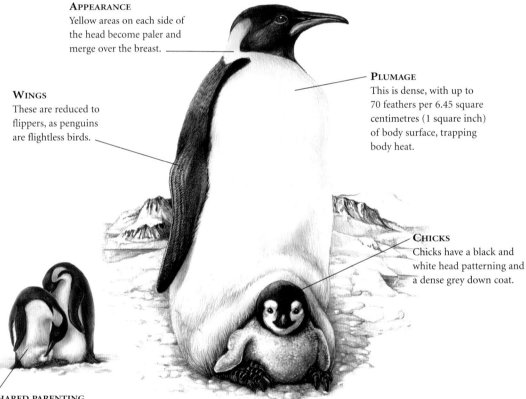

APPEARANCE
Yellow areas on each side of the head become paler and merge over the breast.

WINGS
These are reduced to flippers, as penguins are flightless birds.

PLUMAGE
This is dense, with up to 70 feathers per 6.45 square centimetres (1 square inch) of body surface, trapping body heat.

CHICKS
Chicks have a black and white head patterning and a dense grey down coat.

SHARED PARENTING
After transferring the egg, the hen goes off to feed. When the male later hands back the chick, he may have to trek 96km (60 miles) back to the ocean, after losing a third of his body weight.

HOW BIG IS IT?

DIVING DEEP

Emperor penguins dive deeper than any other bird – down to 565m (1850ft). They can stay underwater for nearly 20 minutes.

Frilled Lizard

VITAL STATISTICS

WEIGHT	567–708g (20–25oz)
LENGTH	70–95cm (27.5–37.4in) overall; tail is almost double the body length
SEXUAL MATURITY	2–2.5 years
NUMBER OF EGGS	8–23, with some females laying twice per season
INCUBATION PERIOD	2–3 months; young weigh 3–5g (0.1–0.18oz)
DIET	Insectivorous, hunting cicadas in the trees, and catching ants on the ground; also eats smaller lizards
LIFESPAN	12–15 years

ANIMAL FACTS

These lizards are sometimes called bicycle lizards, because they start running on all four legs, and then, as they speed up, they switch to sprinting on their hind legs. The frill is not only used for defensive purposes, as these lizards have few predators. It also forms part of the courtship display, and helps thermoregulation, allowing heat to escape from the lizard's body. The environment determines the sex of the hatchlings, with females developing at higher temperatures.

The frilled lizard's front foot in close-up, showing the sharp claws

These distinctive lizards have established an iconic status, and even appear on Australia's old two-cent coin. They are one of the bluffers of the natural world.

WHERE IN THE WORLD?

Occurs in southern New Guinea and Australia, ranging from Northern Territory east to northern Queensland, including the Cape York Peninsula. It favours wooded areas.

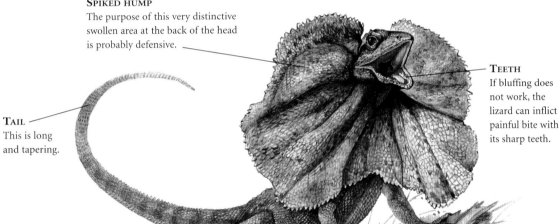

SPIKED HUMP
The purpose of this very distinctive swollen area at the back of the head is probably defensive.

TAIL
This is long and tapering.

TEETH
If bluffing does not work, the lizard can inflict a painful bite with its sharp teeth.

HIND LEGS
Longer than the front legs, these allow the reptile to run very quickly, and help it to climb.

UNDER WRAPS
Under normal circumstances, the frill is folded back.

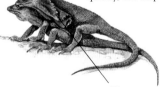

STANDING TALL

Opening the lower jaw is enough to unfurl the crest. By rearing up on its hind legs, the lizard looks even more threatening.

HOW BIG IS IT?

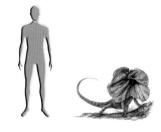

Thorny Devil

• **ORDER** • Squamata • **FAMILY** • Agamidae • **SPECIES** • *Moloch horridus*

VITAL STATISTICS

WEIGHT	33–57g (12oz); males are smaller
LENGTH	Up to 20cm (8in)
SEXUAL MATURITY	From about 3 years, before they have finished growing
NUMBER OF EGGS	3–10 per clutch; young eat their eggshells
INCUBATION PERIOD	Typically 13–18 weeks, depending on temperature
DIET	Highly specialized, feeding almost entirely on ants – up to 1000 in a single meal
LIFESPAN	20 years

ANIMAL FACTS

The colouration of the thorny devil varies according to its surroundings. Like many lizards, it becomes brighter in sunshine. At night, the desert temperature will fall rapidly, causing the lizard's level of activity to decline too. Thorny devils therefore seek out roads after sunrise, basking so they can warm up quickly on the surface, although this habit makes them vulnerable to being run over. The channels on the belly and legs help these lizards obtain dew to drink.

These lizards are well-protected against predators by the array of sharp projections covering their bodies. They look fearsome, but in fact they are not aggressive.

WHERE IN THE WORLD?

Occurs throughout much of Australia. Distribution is closely linked to sandy soils, and so it is particularly common in the interior, in areas of spinifex grass and desert.

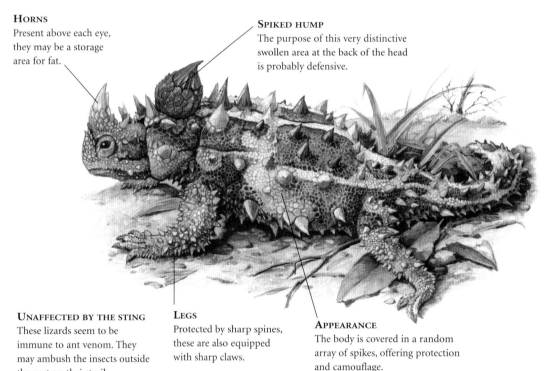

HORNS
Present above each eye, they may be a storage area for fat.

SPIKED HUMP
The purpose of this very distinctive swollen area at the back of the head is probably defensive.

UNAFFECTED BY THE STING
These lizards seem to be immune to ant venom. They may ambush the insects outside the nest on their trails.

LEGS
Protected by sharp spines, these are also equipped with sharp claws.

APPEARANCE
The body is covered in a random array of spikes, offering protection and camouflage.

DEFENSIVE POSTURE
The thorny devil uses the hump on its head to intimidate potential predators like this dingo.

HOW BIG IS IT?

Slow Worm

VITAL STATISTICS

WEIGHT	13–28g (0.45–1oz); males are smaller
LENGTH	30–50cm (12–20in)
SEXUAL MATURITY	3 years, based on growth rate; maturity is related to body size, rather than age
GESTATION PERIOD	3–5 months
NUMBER OF OFFSPRING	6–12 live young; can be up to 26
DIET	Invertebrates caught after dark, including earthworms, slugs, snails and spiders
LIFESPAN	20 years

ANIMAL FACTS

The young slow worms develop in eggs retained within their mother's bodies, with no placental connection being formed. They are born in a membrane, which they break through almost immediately. Their colouration is quite variable. Some are silvery-grey, with prominent black markings down the flanks, whereas others are golden-brown. Slow worms occur in a range of habitats. They are frequently attracted to gardens and allotments, where their prey is present. Sometimes, they burrow into compost heaps.

Slow worms hibernate over the winter, emerging in March

It may look like a snake, but the slow worm is a lizard, as reflected by the fact that it can blink, thanks to its moveable eyelids.

WHERE IN THE WORLD?

Widely distributed throughout Europe, but absent from the far north and Spain. Extends into northwestern Asia and recently introduced to Ireland's East Burren region.

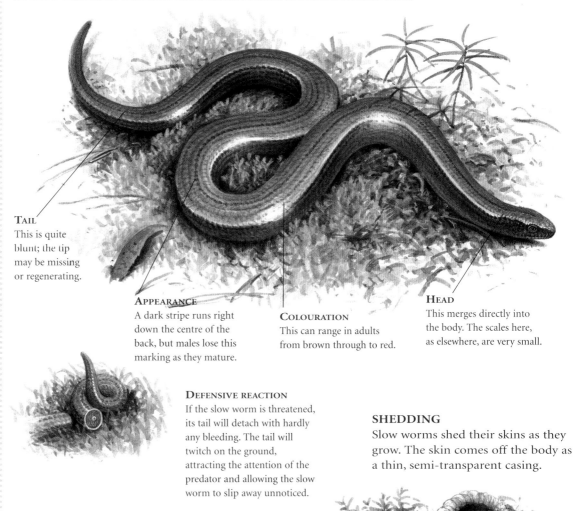

TAIL
This is quite blunt; the tip may be missing or regenerating.

APPEARANCE
A dark stripe runs right down the centre of the back, but males lose this marking as they mature.

COLOURATION
This can range in adults from brown through to red.

HEAD
This merges directly into the body. The scales here, as elsewhere, are very small.

DEFENSIVE REACTION
If the slow worm is threatened, its tail will detach with hardly any bleeding. The tail will twitch on the ground, attracting the attention of the predator and allowing the slow worm to slip away unnoticed.

SHEDDING
Slow worms shed their skins as they grow. The skin comes off the body as a thin, semi-transparent casing.

HOW BIG IS IT?

Boa Constrictor

• ORDER • Squamata • FAMILY • Boidae • SPECIES • *Boa constrictor*

These snakes will mainly hunt up in the trees. Like other constrictors, boas kill prey by suffocation, grasping it so tightly that it cannot breathe.

VITAL STATISTICS

WEIGHT	Up to 45kg (100lb)
LENGTH	2–3m (6.5–10ft) on average, but even bigger individuals have been recorded
SEXUAL MATURITY	2–4 years
GESTATION PERIOD	100–150 days; young hatch at birth
NUMBER OF OFFSPRING	20–50; they measure about 50cm (20in) initially
DIET	Lizards, small mammals including bats, rats and squirrels, plus various birds
LIFESPAN	10–30 years

ANIMAL FACTS

This is a rare case in the natural world of both the common and scientific names of a species corresponding. These boids are very adaptable, and are found in environments ranging from semi-desert landscapes through to dense rainforest. They are equally flexible in their hunting behaviour. Younger boa constrictors tend to hunt in the trees, but older, heavier individuals are more likely to ambush their prey on the ground. Prey is swallowed whole and then slowly digested.

These snakes are nocturnal hunters by nature, with bats being their favoured prey

WHERE IN THE WORLD?

Found over a wide area, from northern Mexico and various offshore islands, via parts of the Caribbean through South America down to Argentina.

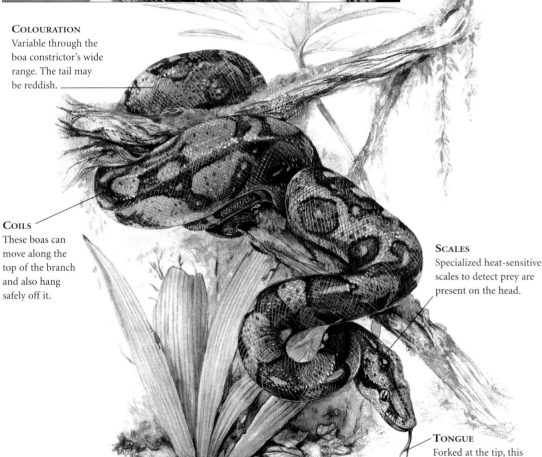

COLOURATION
Variable through the boa constrictor's wide range. The tail may be reddish.

COILS
These boas can move along the top of the branch and also hang safely off it.

SCALES
Specialized heat-sensitive scales to detect prey are present on the head.

TONGUE
Forked at the tip, this detects scent molecules of prey as well as potential mates.

HOW BIG IS IT?

MATING
This may occur on the ground, with the female emitting a scent from her cloaca when she is ready to mate.

Green Anaconda

• ORDER • Squamata • FAMILY • Boidae • SPECIES • *Eunectes murinus*

This is believed to be the largest species of snake in the world, although it is difficult to gauge the length of gigantic snakes.

VITAL STATISTICS

WEIGHT	107–250kg (235–550lb); females are much larger
LENGTH	Average 6m (20ft), but much bigger individuals have been recorded
SEXUAL MATURITY	Females 3 years; males 18 months
GESTATION PERIOD	6–7 months
NUMBER OF OFFSPRING	20–100
DIET	Large fish, crocodilians, deer, monkeys, occasionally humans
LIFESPAN	10–30 years

ANIMAL FACTS

The scientific name of these snakes, *Eunectes*, means 'good swimmer' and reflects their aquatic lifestyle. Besides capturing prey in the water, they will also grab animals that come to drink in the forest water holes, which they will kill by constriction. Anacondas can hunt in total darkness, thanks to heat-seeking pits along their lips, allowing them to detect the presence of warm-blooded prey. They can also pick up the sound of movement, even in water.

These snakes have 100 backward-pointing teeth in their jaws, with more running across the roof of the mouth

WHERE IN THE WORLD?

South America, east of the Andes, occurring throughout the Amazon and Orinoco river basins, extending into the Guianas, usually encountered close to areas of water.

COLOURATION
The anaconda's appearance helps conceal its presence. The underparts are yellowish.

SKULL
The bones in the skull are relatively flexible. This helps the snake to swallow large prey.

PATTERNING
The black blotches on these snakes are variable, enabling individuals to be distinguished.

SPURS
Present near the tail, these aid mating. They are actually the vestigial remains of the hind limbs.

HOW BIG IS IT?

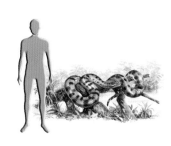

GIVING BIRTH
Female anacondas will not feed while carrying their eggs, although they may have killed and eaten the male after mating.

European Chameleon

· ORDER · Squamata **· FAMILY ·** Chamaeleonidae **· SPECIES ·** *Chamaeleo chamaeleon*

These arboreal lizards display remarkable coordination, firing their long, sticky-tipped tongue at prey, and pulling it back into their mouth in milliseconds.

VITAL STATISTICS

WEIGHT	38–58g (1.3–2oz)
LENGTH	20–38cm (8–15in), depending on locality; females slightly larger
SEXUAL MATURITY	1 year
INCUBATION PERIOD	6–11 months, depending partly on temperature
NUMBER OF EGGS	Up to 60, laid about 2 months after mating
DIET	Hunts mainly invertebrates, but also eats small vertebrates, including other reptiles and birds; may eat some plant matter
LIFESPAN	Up to 6 years

ANIMAL FACTS

These lizards occur in a wide range of habitats, from scrubland to forest, up to altitudes of 2590m (8500ft). Mating occurs in the spring. The female indicates her readiness to mate by her body colour. If she is black with yellow spotting, then she will refuse. In some areas, the winter temperature becomes very cold, to the extent that the chameleon will become dormant. This also prolongs the hatching period, with the young overwintering in their eggs.

WHERE IN THE WORLD?

Found in southern Europe, from southern parts of Spain and Portugal, to North Africa and islands in the Mediterranean, extending to Jordan, Israel, Saudi Arabia and Yemen.

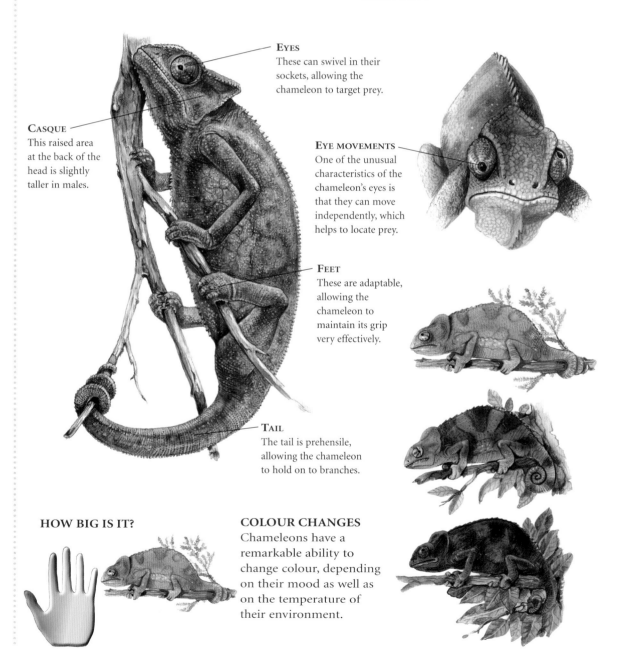

EYES
These can swivel in their sockets, allowing the chameleon to target prey.

CASQUE
This raised area at the back of the head is slightly taller in males.

EYE MOVEMENTS
One of the unusual characteristics of the chameleon's eyes is that they can move independently, which helps to locate prey.

FEET
These are adaptable, allowing the chameleon to maintain its grip very effectively.

TAIL
The tail is prehensile, allowing the chameleon to hold on to branches.

HOW BIG IS IT?

COLOUR CHANGES
Chameleons have a remarkable ability to change colour, depending on their mood as well as on the temperature of their environment.

Plumed Basilisk

• **ORDER** • Squamata • **FAMILY** • Colubridae • **SPECIES** • *Basiliscus plumifrons*

These lizards are well-known for their ability to run over stretches of water. If necessary, however, they can also swim and dive well.

VITAL STATISTICS

WEIGHT	Up to 200g (7oz)
LENGTH	61–76cm (24–30in)
SEXUAL MATURITY	1 year
NUMBER OF EGGS	5–15, laid about 2 months after mating
INCUBATION PERIOD	About 10 weeks, depending on environmental temperature; young can run, climb, swim and dive and remain submerged for up to 30 minutes
DIET	Omnivorous, eating invertebrates, smaller vertebrates, plus fruit and vegetable matter
LIFESPAN	7–10 years

ANIMAL FACTS

Visual communication is important for these lizards. Their crests enable observers to tell males from females, with movement of the head, called head-bobbing, serving as a warning of potential conflict. Males can be very aggressive. These basilisks occur in rainforest areas, typically close to water. Eggs are buried in the ground and abandoned. The young lizards head off in different directions after hatching.

Even on land, plumed basilisks can stand upright, which helps them to climb up branches

WHERE IN THE WORLD?

Occurs in Central and South America, with a range extending from Mexico southwards as far as Ecuador. An introduced US population reputedly exists in Dade County, Florida.

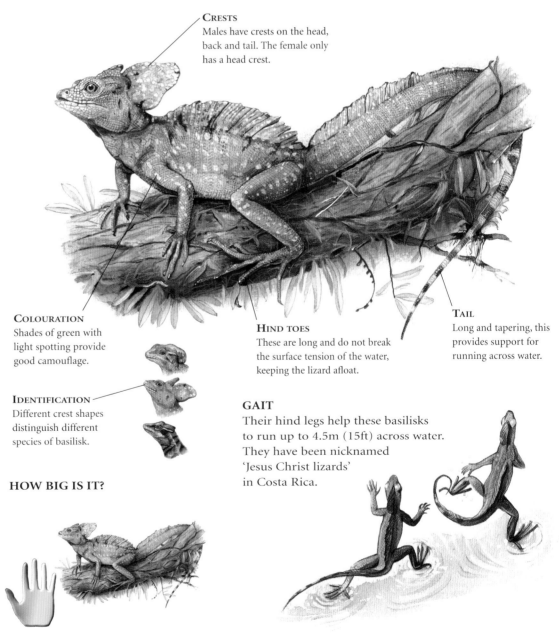

CRESTS
Males have crests on the head, back and tail. The female only has a head crest.

COLOURATION
Shades of green with light spotting provide good camouflage.

IDENTIFICATION
Different crest shapes distinguish different species of basilisk.

HOW BIG IS IT?

HIND TOES
These are long and do not break the surface tension of the water, keeping the lizard afloat.

TAIL
Long and tapering, this provides support for running across water.

GAIT
Their hind legs help these basilisks to run up to 4.5m (15ft) across water. They have been nicknamed 'Jesus Christ lizards' in Costa Rica.

Grass Snake

These snakes swim well, but spend much of their time out of water. They are also called ring snakes, because of their distinctive head markings.

VITAL STATISTICS

WEIGHT	100–300g (3.5–10.5oz)
LENGTH	100–130cm (39–51in); females can be up to 30cm (12in) longer
SEXUAL MATURITY	1 year
INCUBATION PERIOD	About 70 days, depending on environmental temperature
NUMBER OF EGGS	8–40; leathery rather than hard shells
DIET	Mainly amphibians, especially frogs and toads, but may also catch fish and small mammals
LIFESPAN	Up to 10 years

ANIMAL FACTS

Grass snakes are not venomous and so are largely unable to defend themselves from predators, which can include birds of prey, members of the crow family and foxes.

They are able to secrete a foul-smelling liquid from their anal glands, however, which offers them some protection. Females seek out warm spots for their eggs, often laying in heaps of rotting vegetation, including compost heaps. These snakes will hibernate in underground burrows.

WHERE IN THE WORLD?

Occurs across Europe, from Scandinavia down to southern Italy. Also present in northwestern Africa, but is not found in Ireland and is largely absent from Scotland.

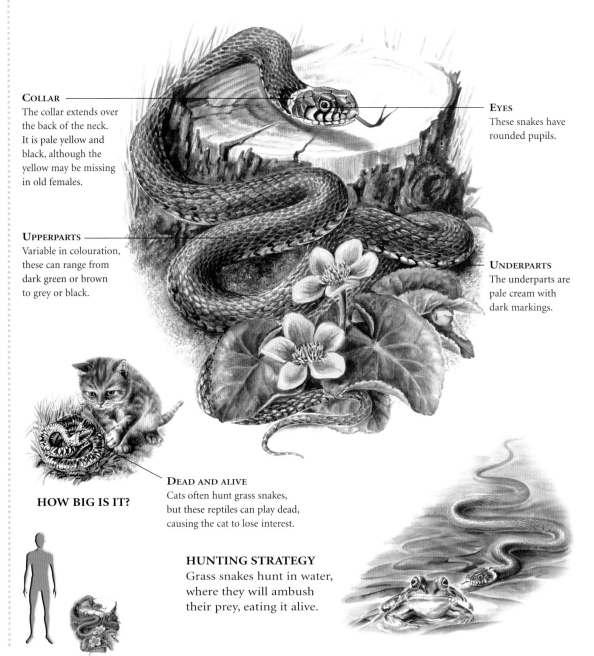

COLLAR
The collar extends over the back of the neck. It is pale yellow and black, although the yellow may be missing in old females.

UPPERPARTS
Variable in colouration, these can range from dark green or brown to grey or black.

EYES
These snakes have rounded pupils.

UNDERPARTS
The underparts are pale cream with dark markings.

DEAD AND ALIVE
Cats often hunt grass snakes, but these reptiles can play dead, causing the cat to lose interest.

HOW BIG IS IT?

HUNTING STRATEGY
Grass snakes hunt in water, where they will ambush their prey, eating it alive.

Black Mamba

• **ORDER** • Squamata • **FAMILY** • Elaphidae • **SPECIES** • *Dendroaspis polylepis*

VITAL STATISTICS

WEIGHT	Up to 1.6kg (3.5lb)
LENGTH	Typically 2.4–3m (8–10ft), but has been known to reach 4.5m (14.7ft)
SEXUAL MATURITY	2 years
NUMBER OF EGGS	10–25, laid nearly 2 months after mating
INCUBATION PERIOD	2–3 months, depending on environmental temperature; young are dangerous virtually from hatching
DIET	Mainly small mammals such as ground squirrels and hyraxes
LIFESPAN	Up to 12 years

ANIMAL FACTS

The name of these snakes derives not from their body colour, but from the black area in their mouths. They are active during the day, sunning themselves in particular localities within their range, and may sometimes climb trees. Black mambas rank amongst the fastest of all snakes, capable of moving at speeds up to 20kph (12mph), which allows them to pursue quarry. Their potent venom causes systemic paralysis – prey die from suffocation because of respiratory failure.

Jacobson's organ, in the roof of the mouth, helps to detect scents and quarry

This species is one of Africa's most feared snakes, because of its powerful venom and the speed at which it can move over the ground.

WHERE IN THE WORLD?

Widely distributed across eastern and southern parts of Africa, extending from the vicinity of Somalia in the northeast, southwards down to South Africa.

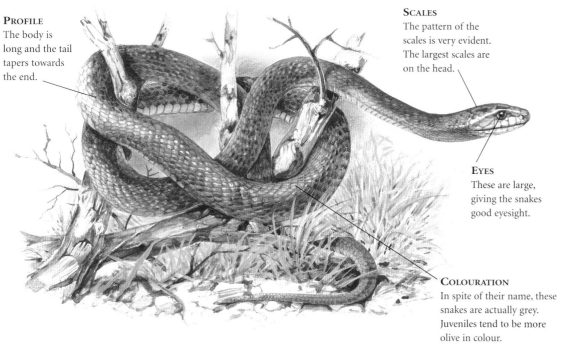

PROFILE
The body is long and the tail tapers towards the end.

SCALES
The pattern of the scales is very evident. The largest scales are on the head.

EYES
These are large, giving the snakes good eyesight.

COLOURATION
In spite of their name, these snakes are actually grey. Juveniles tend to be more olive in colour.

HUNTING STRATEGY
After biting its prey, the snake waits for the venom to take effect, although birds are generally not released after being caught.

HOW BIG IS IT?

READY TO STRIKE
A black mamba's bite can kill a person, although fatalities are rare. Their venom differs throughout their range.

Eastern Coral Snake

•ORDER• Squamata •FAMILY• Elaphidae •SPECIES• *Micrurus fulvius*

VITAL STATISTICS

WEIGHT	Up to 34g (1.2oz)
LENGTH	Typically 80cm (32in), but can reach nearly 130cm (51in)
SEXUAL MATURITY	2 years
NUMBER OF EGGS	3–12, laid underground or often in hollow logs in summer
INCUBATION PERIOD	About 3 months, depending on environmental temperature; young are dangerous virtually from hatching
DIET	Hunts other reptiles, mainly small snakes and lizards
LIFESPAN	Up to 7 years

ANIMAL FACTS

Despite their bright colouration, these snakes are shy and rarely seen. They are not especially aggressive, but their venom can be sufficiently potent to kill a person within an hour or two, so rapid hospital treatment is essential if bitten. If the snake is threatened, it raises its tail to disguise which end of the body is its head. This gives it an opportunity to strike and escape.

These snakes have a very wide gape, which allows them to sink their long fangs into their prey to inject venom

This snake is venomous, and its appearance has been mimicked by harmless species such as the scarlet kingsnake in an effort to deter predators.

WHERE IN THE WORLD?

Occurs in southeastern parts of the USA, ranging from southeastern North Carolina via South Carolina to Florida, and west through Georgia, Alabama, Mississippi and Louisiana.

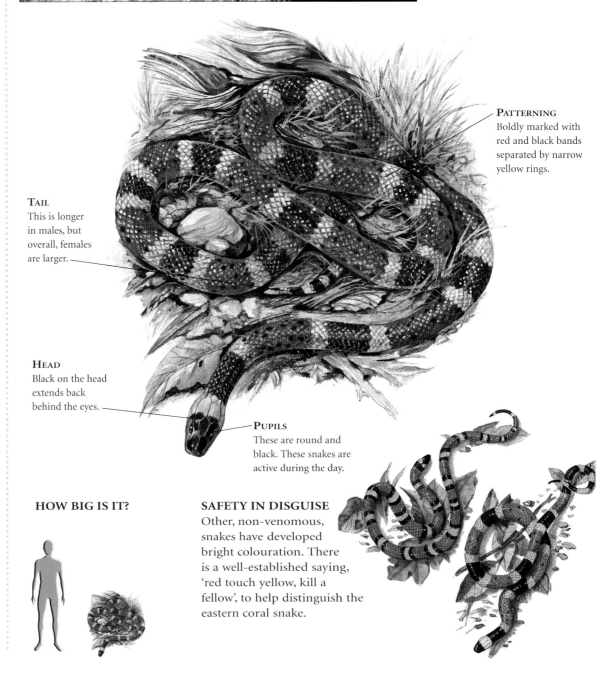

PATTERNING
Boldly marked with red and black bands separated by narrow yellow rings.

TAIL
This is longer in males, but overall, females are larger.

HEAD
Black on the head extends back behind the eyes.

PUPILS
These are round and black. These snakes are active during the day.

HOW BIG IS IT?

SAFETY IN DISGUISE
Other, non-venomous, snakes have developed bright colouration. There is a well-established saying, 'red touch yellow, kill a fellow', to help distinguish the eastern coral snake.

King Cobra

VITAL STATISTICS

WEIGHT	Up to 6kg (13.2lb)
LENGTH	Typically 3.6–4m (12–13ft), but can reach 5.7m (18.8ft)
SEXUAL MATURITY	2 years
NUMBER OF EGGS	3–12, laid underground or in hollow logs in summer
INCUBATION PERIOD	About 3 months, depending on environmental temperature; young can bite effectively virtually from hatching
DIET	Hunts other snakes, including venomous species; may also prey on vertebrates such as lizards
LIFESPAN	Up to 20 years

ANIMAL FACTS

The snake's venom is again produced by specialized upper salivary glands. It is so deadly that it can kill an adult Asian elephant in a few hours following a bite to the trunk, for example. This is a reflection of the snake's size, which enables it to produce and inject more venom at a single bite than other snakes, increasing its deadly effect. Sometimes, when feeding, king cobras have been observed to constrict small prey such as birds, rather than biting them.

This snake is the largest of all the world's venomous species. Its generic name, *Ophiophagus*, means 'snake-eater', and these cobras are very dangerous.

WHERE IN THE WORLD?

Extends from western India and Pakistan throughout Southeast Asia, including the islands of Java, Sumatra and Borneo. It is found mainly in highland forest.

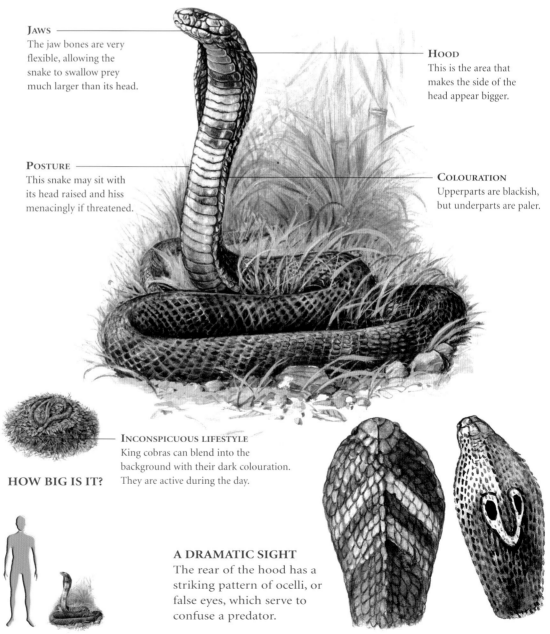

JAWS
The jaw bones are very flexible, allowing the snake to swallow prey much larger than its head.

HOOD
This is the area that makes the side of the head appear bigger.

POSTURE
This snake may sit with its head raised and hiss menacingly if threatened.

COLOURATION
Upperparts are blackish, but underparts are paler.

INCONSPICUOUS LIFESTYLE
King cobras can blend into the background with their dark colouration. They are active during the day.

HOW BIG IS IT?

A DRAMATIC SIGHT
The rear of the hood has a striking pattern of ocelli, or false eyes, which serve to confuse a predator.

Tokay Gecko

• **ORDER** • Squamata • **FAMILY** • Gekkonidae • **SPECIES** • *Gekko gecko*

VITAL STATISTICS

WEIGHT	150–300g (5–10oz)
LENGTH	20–40cm (8–15in); males are much larger
SEXUAL MATURITY	2 years
NUMBER OF EGGS	1–2, guarded by the female
INCUBATION PERIOD	Temperature-dependent, from 60–200 days; typical range 90–100 days
DIET	Hunts a wide range of invertebrates, being able to catch flies and other insects wandering over walls
LIFESPAN	7–10 years; up to 18 in captivity

ANIMAL FACTS

The name of these particular geckos comes from the sound of their calls. They often live in houses, hiding away during the day and emerging at night, running across the walls without difficulty. This is made possible by the unique structure of their toes. They will also glue their eggs together in inaccessible sites. The incubation temperature determines the gender of the hatchlings. Higher temperatures encourage male offspring.

An underside view of the gecko's foot, showing the lamellae that allow it to climb up vertical surfaces

This is the second biggest species of gecko, which, like most other members of the family, shows remarkable agility when climbing. They are solitary lizards.

WHERE IN THE WORLD?

Found in northeastern India and Bangladesh, throughout Southeast Asia and across Indonesia as far as western New Guinea. Introduced to various US localities, including Florida.

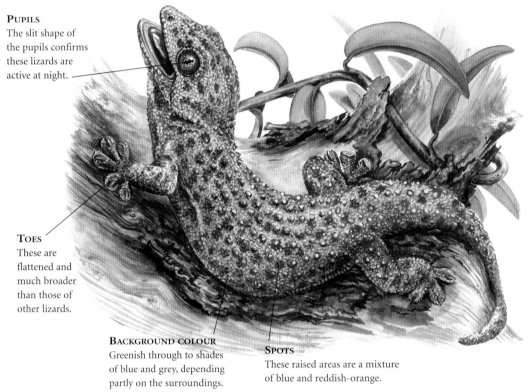

PUPILS
The slit shape of the pupils confirms these lizards are active at night.

TOES
These are flattened and much broader than those of other lizards.

BACKGROUND COLOUR
Greenish through to shades of blue and grey, depending partly on the surroundings.

SPOTS
These raised areas are a mixture of blue and reddish-orange.

HOW BIG IS IT?

STAYING ALIVE
Tokay geckos can shed their tail easily, so they can escape if attacked by predators.

Gila Monster

One of only two venomous lizards in the world, the name of this species is pronounced 'hee-la'. Its venom is not fatal to adults.

VITAL STATISTICS

WEIGHT	1.30–2.25kg (2.9–5lb); the heaviest are found in the USA
LENGTH	30–60cm (12–24in); males are much larger
SEXUAL MATURITY	3–5 years, depending on growth rate
NUMBER OF EGGS	2–12, average 5
INCUBATION PERIOD	Around 9 months
DIET	Mainly the eggs of birds and reptiles, but will also eat small vertebrates
LIFESPAN	20 years; up to 30 in captivity

ANIMAL FACTS

Unlike snakes, the venom glands of these lizards are linked to salivary glands in the lower jaw. The venom is brought up by the chewing, and is quite unique. One component, called helodermin, can inhibit the growth of lung cancer. Another constituent of its saliva has been developed into a treatment for diabetes, and may also prove useful for treating obesity. These lizards spend most of their time underground, hibernating over the winter, but they can climb well if necessary.

WHERE IN THE WORLD?

Found in the southwestern USA and into Mexico. Occurs in California, Nevada, Utah, Arizona, New Mexico and south to Sonora and Sinaloa. Not found in open farmland.

TAIL
This is used as a fat store, allowing the lizard to go long periods without eating.

FRONT FEET
These are strong and tipped with powerful claws to help the lizard dig.

SCALES
These resemble beads of different colours, including black, pink, orange and yellow.

A DEADLY BITE
The teeth are only loosely attached in the lower jaw, releasing venom when they break away.

ON THE SCENT

Gila monsters have an acute sense of smell, enabling them to find hidden prey.

HOW BIG IS IT?

Marine Iguana

• ORDER • Squamata **• FAMILY •** Iguanidae **• SPECIES •** *Amblyrhynchus cristatus*

VITAL STATISTICS

WEIGHT	0.5–1.5kg (1–3.3lb); males can be up to 10kg (22lb)
LENGTH	60–130cm (24–51in); males about twice the size of females
SEXUAL MATURITY	Females 3–5 years; males 6–8 years
NUMBER OF EGGS	2–4 annually
INCUBATION PERIOD	90–120 days
DIET	Red and green marine algae; periodic die-off of the algae adversely affects the population
LIFESPAN	15–20 years

ANIMAL FACTS

It is generally believed that the ancestors of these lizards came from northern South America, drifting to the islands, and then spreading from one to another. There is a considerable difference in size between populations, with those found on Isabela and Fernandina islands being the largest, while the smallest marine iguanas occur on Genovesa. They can swim for up to 30 minutes in the cold water before returning to land to warm up again in the sun.

These are the only marine lizards, whose ancestors colonized the Galápagos Islands thousands of years ago. They helped inspire Charles Darwin's theory of evolution.

WHERE IN THE WORLD?

Confined to the Galápagos Islands, located in the Pacific Ocean off the northwestern coast of South America. They can be found on all the islands.

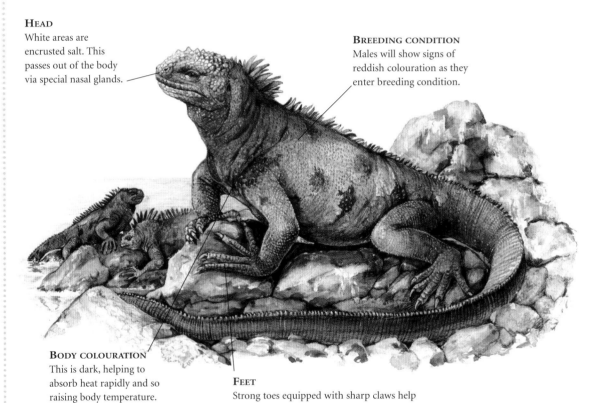

HEAD
White areas are encrusted salt. This passes out of the body via special nasal glands.

BREEDING CONDITION
Males will show signs of reddish colouration as they enter breeding condition.

BODY COLOURATION
This is dark, helping to absorb heat rapidly and so raising body temperature.

FEET
Strong toes equipped with sharp claws help these iguanas climb up slippery rocks.

These lizards can dive to depths of 15m (49ft) to browse on marine algae

HOW BIG IS IT?

DANGER!
Sharks represent a threat to these iguanas when they are in the sea.

Green Iguana

• **ORDER** • Squamata • **FAMILY** • Iguanidae • **SPECIES** • *Iguana iguana*

These herbivorous lizards are equipped with fearsome teeth, although they are not very obvious, located on the inner side of the jaws.

VITAL STATISTICS

WEIGHT	5–9kg (11–20lb)
LENGTH	150–200cm (59–79in) overall; tail same length as the body
SEXUAL MATURITY	2.5–5 years
NUMBER OF EGGS	20–70; 1 clutch per year
INCUBATION PERIOD	90–120 days; eggs laid 65 days after mating
DIET	Older iguanas feed on plant matter and fruit; young are more omnivorous, eating eggs, invertebrates and small vertebrates
LIFESPAN	20 years

ANIMAL FACTS

The skin of these lizards is remarkably robust, and they are very agile, able to survive falls from 15m (50ft) without sustaining injury. This is achieved partly by the iguana using its hind legs to grab at vegetation as it falls, slowing its descent. The tail can also detach, saving the iguana from a would-be predator. Green iguanas are active at night and, when swimming, they use their tails to propel themselves instead of their legs.

WHERE IN THE WORLD?

Found from Mexico into South America, southwards to southern Brazil and Paraguay. Also occurs on various islands in the Caribbean. Has been introduced to Florida.

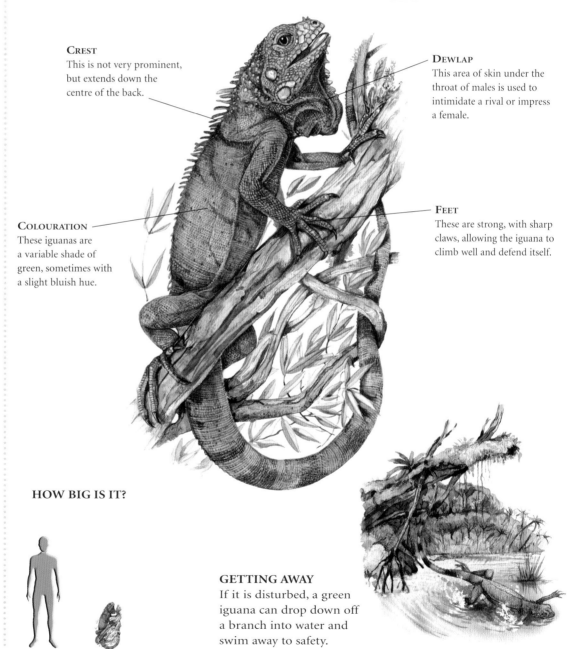

CREST
This is not very prominent, but extends down the centre of the back.

DEWLAP
This area of skin under the throat of males is used to intimidate a rival or impress a female.

COLOURATION
These iguanas are a variable shade of green, sometimes with a slight bluish hue.

FEET
These are strong, with sharp claws, allowing the iguana to climb well and defend itself.

HOW BIG IS IT?

GETTING AWAY
If it is disturbed, a green iguana can drop down off a branch into water and swim away to safety.

415

Balkan Green Lizard

• ORDER • Squamata • FAMILY • Lacertidae • SPECIES • *Lacerta trilineata*

VITAL STATISTICS

WEIGHT	Around 50g (1.76oz)
LENGTH	33–60cm (13–24in)
SEXUAL MATURITY	2 years; males may develop blue colouring on the sides of the head
NUMBER OF EGGS	7–18 per clutch; females may lay twice a year
INCUBATION PERIOD	40–90 days; young are brown, with 3 or 5 stripes
DIET	Invertebrates, but may take eggs, nestlings, young rodents and fruit
LIFESPAN	10 years

ANIMAL FACTS

Active during the day, these lizards will emerge from their hiding places in the morning and find a sunny spot, often resting on a stone. This raises the lizard's body temperature rapidly, and its colouration becomes more vivid. It will then start to hunt, using its eyesight to locate prey. Balkan green lizards are fast and agile, in spite of their size, and can seize their prey using their rapid reflexes. If danger threatens, they can scamper off to cover.

These colourful lizards are commonly seen in areas with shrubby vegetation, typically at a relatively low altitude. They may occasionally be observed swimming in ditches.

WHERE IN THE WORLD?

Occurs from northwest Croatia through the Balkan Peninsula to Greece, the Aegean Islands and Turkey. Also present in Romania and Bulgaria, extending to the Caucasus.

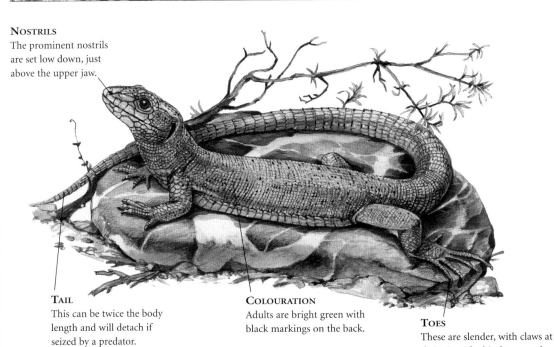

NOSTRILS
The prominent nostrils are set low down, just above the upper jaw.

TAIL
This can be twice the body length and will detach if seized by a predator.

COLOURATION
Adults are bright green with black markings on the back.

TOES
These are slender, with claws at their tips. The hind toes are longer.

STRENGTHENING EGGS
Eating snails in their shells provides female Balkan green lizards with a source of calcium for their eggshells.

The appearance of the Balkan green lizard is quite variable, with some displaying larger areas of darker speckling

HOW BIG IS IT?

OPPORTUNISTIC FEEDERS
These lizards may raid the nests of small mammals.

Common Wall Lizard

• **ORDER** • Squamata • **FAMILY** • Lacertidae • **SPECIES** • *Podarcis muralis*

These lizards are incredibly agile, able to run up walls and along ledges without difficulty. They are even capable of swimming well if necessary.

VITAL STATISTICS

WEIGHT	Up to 8g (0.3oz)
LENGTH	10–20cm (4–8in) overall
SEXUAL MATURITY	2 years
NUMBER OF EGGS	2–10; may lay up to 3 clutches per year
INCUBATION PERIOD	42–77 days; eggs typically hatch around July
DIET	Insectivorous, taking small flies through to crickets and large grasshoppers; hibernates over winter
LIFESPAN	7 years

ANIMAL FACTS

Unlike most lizards, this species lives in loose colonies consisting of a male and several females, as well as juveniles. They are active during the day and often bask in the sun, although they are nervous, and will retreat to cover at any hint of danger. They are common in urban settings, both in gardens and in the vicinity of buildings, and are highly adaptable by nature. In North America, they are now established in localities from British Columbia to Ohio.

Wall lizards often lay their eggs under rocks, and the heat given off by the stone aids incubation

WHERE IN THE WORLD?

Occurs throughout much of southern Europe, from the Netherlands and Belgium to Croatia and Italy. Has been introduced to southern England and North America.

PROFILE
Their relatively thin body shape helps these lizards to slip easily into narrow spaces.

HEAD
This is covered in much larger scales than those along the back.

TOES
The toes on the hind feet are long and slender, ending in sharp claws.

PATTERNING
This is highly individual, and colouration can vary from brown to grey.

BRUSH WITH DANGER
It is not uncommon for these lizards to lose their tails to predators. Although the tail will regrow, it may be deformed and will not often grow back to its full size.

HOW BIG IS IT?

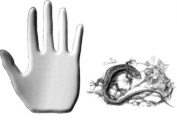

Indian Python

VITAL STATISTICS

WEIGHT	32–55kg (70–120lb), but can be as much as 91kg (200lb)
LENGTH	Average 3.7m (12ft), but has reached 6.4m (21ft)
SEXUAL MATURITY	3 years
NUMBER OF EGGS	20–60, can be up to 100, laid about 3.5 months after mating
INCUBATION PERIOD	2–3 months; young measure up to 60cm (24in)
DIET	Will prey on a variety of mammals and birds
LIFESPAN	20–30 years

ANIMAL FACTS

Indian pythons tend to ambush their prey, rather than being active hunters. They are equipped with heat-sensitive pits in the scales on the upper lip, enabling them to detect potential quarry even in total darkness. As a constrictor, the Indian python wraps itself around the animal, preventing it from breathing. The victim will be swallowed head first. These snakes eat relatively infrequently, sometimes going several weeks without food. They are often found close to water, and can swim well.

Indian pythons grow rapidly, tripling their length in their first year; they moult for the first time a week after hatching

These snakes grow to a large size. They do not represent a serious danger to people, but they are frequently killed out of fear.

WHERE IN THE WORLD?

Occurs throughout Asia, in India, Sri Lanka, Pakistan and Nepal. Replaced by the dark Burmese race to the east, in southeastern China and Indonesia.

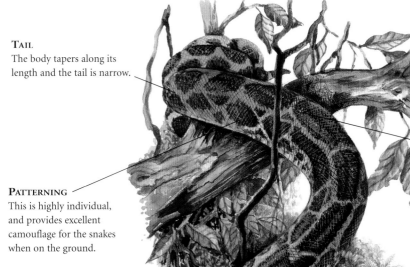

TAIL
The body tapers along its length and the tail is narrow.

CLIMBING
Young Indian pythons often climb trees, but heavier individuals tend to be more terrestrial.

PATTERNING
This is highly individual, and provides excellent camouflage for the snakes when on the ground.

TONGUE
Forked at its tip, this picks up scents through the Jacobson's organ in the roof of the mouth.

ON THEIR OWN
Young pythons will separate as soon as they hatch, and the female plays no further part in their care.

HOW BIG IS IT?

MATERNAL INSTINCTS

The female python curls around her eggs, keeping them warm by contractions of her body. She may not eat until after they have hatched.

Shingleback Skink

• **ORDER** • Squamata • **FAMILY** • Scincidae • **SPECIES** • *Tiliqua rugosa*

VITAL STATISTICS

WEIGHT	32–55kg (70–120lb), but can be as much as 91kg (200lb)
LENGTH	30–45cm (12–18in)
SEXUAL MATURITY	3 years
GESTATION PERIOD	About 5 months; young measure up to 60cm (24in)
NUMBER OF OFFSPRING	1–2, occasionally 3, measuring about 15cm (6in) at birth
DIET	Omnivorous, eating flowers, fruit and vegetation, as well as invertebrates and carrion
LIFESPAN	20–30 years

ANIMAL FACTS

These skinks often frequent highways, basking on the tarmac in the morning to raise their body temperature quickly in a landscape where the temperature drops dramatically at night. They do not run from danger, but instead curve their body round to form a distinctive C-shape, and hiss with their mouth open. Pairs tend to stay together, with mating occurring from November to April. A male relies on his sense of smell to detect when the female will be receptive.

Although they live in an arid environment, shinglebacks can swim well if necessary, using their legs to paddle along

These lizards have an unusual appearance, with their pattern of scales arranged like the overlapping shingles used on the roofs of some buildings.

WHERE IN THE WORLD?

Restricted to Australia, occurring in southern and western parts of the continent, inhabiting sandy and grassland areas to the west of the Great Dividing Range mountains.

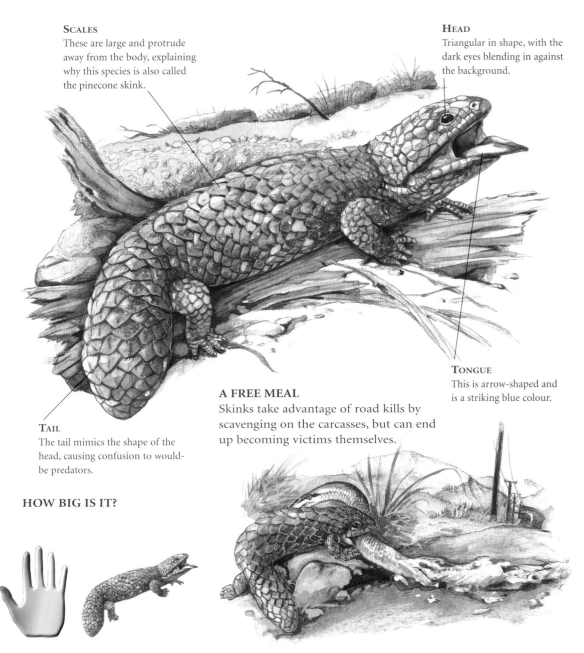

SCALES
These are large and protrude away from the body, explaining why this species is also called the pinecone skink.

HEAD
Triangular in shape, with the dark eyes blending in against the background.

TONGUE
This is arrow-shaped and is a striking blue colour.

TAIL
The tail mimics the shape of the head, causing confusion to would-be predators.

A FREE MEAL
Skinks take advantage of road kills by scavenging on the carcasses, but can end up becoming victims themselves.

HOW BIG IS IT?

419

Komodo Dragon

• ORDER • Squamata **• FAMILY** • Varanidae **• SPECIES** • *Varanus komodoensis*

The largest lizard in the world, the Komodo dragon is a formidable predator. It has the ability to detect scents from over 4km (2.5 miles) away.

VITAL STATISTICS

WEIGHT	Up to 166kg (366lb)
LENGTH	Up to 3.1m (10.3ft)
SEXUAL MATURITY	Females 6–9 years; males 7–10 years
NUMBER OF EGGS	15–30; young measure about 15cm (6in) at birth
INCUBATION PERIOD	8–9 months; young measure 40cm (16in) long
DIET	Hunts deer and wild boar, also preys on goats, digs up turtle nests and eats carrion
LIFESPAN	30–50 years

ANIMAL FACTS

Komodo dragons have been known to attack and eat people, although such occurrences are rare. A bite from one of these lizards can be equally deadly, though, as their saliva contains about 50 different types of bacteria, and these can easily lead to fatal septicaemia developing from an untreated wound. The teeth are large and serrated, allowing the lizard to gulp down large chunks of flesh at a single bite. There are only about 3000 Komodo dragons surviving today.

The curved claws of the Komodo dragon can inflict serious injury

WHERE IN THE WORLD?

Only on the Komodo Islands in southeastern Asia, and the neighbouring larger islands of Flores, Indonesia. May formerly have ranged east to Timor.

TONGUE
This collects scent molecules in the air, which are interpreted by Jacobson's organ.

TAIL
This is very powerful, and a blow can disable prey. It is also helps the lizard to swim.

LEGS
Powerful hind legs are equipped with claws to assist in climbing.

FIGHTING
These monitor lizards may fight amongst themselves, but they generally do not develop infections if they are bitten in such encounters.

HOW BIG IS IT?

BALANCE
The tail supports the body when standing.

Texan Rattlesnake

• **ORDER** • Squamata • **FAMILY** • Viperidae • **SPECIES** • *Crotalus atrox*

These venomous snakes – so-called because of the rattling sound they give as a warning before striking – remain numerous despite widespread persecution.

VITAL STATISTICS

WEIGHT	Average 6.8kg (15lb), but can be up to 10.4kg (23lb); males larger
LENGTH	Average 1.2m (4ft), but has reached 2.13m (7ft)
SEXUAL MATURITY	2–3 years
GESTATION PERIOD	6–7 months
NUMBER OF OFFSPRING	About 12; they disperse shortly after birth, already venomous
DIET	Mainly small mammals, especially rodents and rabbits, plus some birds and lizards
LIFESPAN	Up to 22 years

ANIMAL FACTS

This particular species is one of the boldest and most aggressive of all rattlesnakes. They hunt at night during the summer and hibernate throughout the winter, although they sometimes emerge on warmer winter days. These snakes retreat into caves or share the burrows of other creatures at this time of year. Although adaptable in terms of their prey, Texan rattlesnakes are able to survive for up to two years without eating if necessary, thanks to their stores of body fat.

The modified scales in the tail, called beads, vibrate against each other to create the rattle

WHERE IN THE WORLD?

Extends from California, offshore islands and central Arkansas in the USA, southwards into Mexico, to northern parts of Sinaloa and Veracruz, as well as Hidalgo.

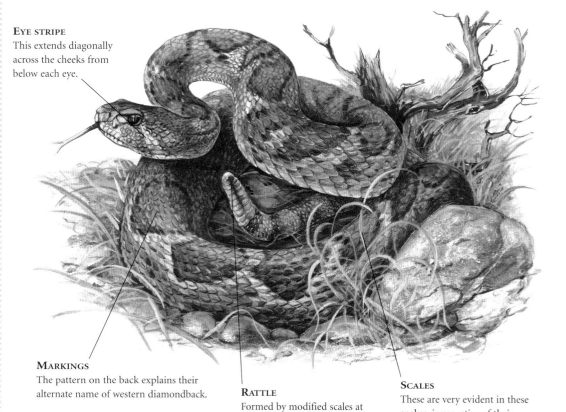

EYE STRIPE
This extends diagonally across the cheeks from below each eye.

MARKINGS
The pattern on the back explains their alternate name of western diamondback.

RATTLE
Formed by modified scales at the tip of the tail, the rattle gets larger as the snake ages.

SCALES
These are very evident in these snakes, irrespective of their underlying colouration.

HOW BIG IS IT?

BE ALARMED!
A rattlesnake may rest curled up in the open, but, if disturbed, it adopts a much more menacing posture, with its head raised to strike.

MATING
Mating occurs in spring, and as with other snakes, the male's copulatory organ is divided into two parts, called hemipenes.

European Adder

• **ORDER** • Squamata • **FAMILY** • Viperidae • **SPECIES** • *Vipera berus*

VITAL STATISTICS

WEIGHT	50–100g (1.75-3.5oz); females larger
LENGTH	60–75cm (24–30in) on average, but up to 104cm (41in) has been recorded
SEXUAL MATURITY	Females 3 years; males 5 years
GESTATION PERIOD	3-4 months; females only breed in alternate years
NUMBER OF OFFSPRING	3–20, but typically 8
DIET	Small mammals, especially mice and shrews; also birds, amphibians and lizards
LIFESPAN	10–25 years

ANIMAL FACTS

These snakes are most dangerous when they first emerge from hibernation, although they may be less active, as the weather can still be relatively cold. Animals are most at risk, and their bite is not usually fatal to humans. Recovery is slow, however, and can take up to a year. Adders often frequent heathland, but also occur in areas such as forest clearings. Mating is usually observed in late spring, with the young born towards the end of summer.

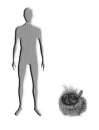

Eye shape differs between the adder (top) and the grass snake (bottom)

It may be the only venomous snake throughout much of its range, including England, but the adder is not an aggressive species and avoids conflict.

WHERE IN THE WORLD?

Occurs throughout much of western Europe, although absent from Ireland, extending north to Sweden and eastwards across most of Asia.

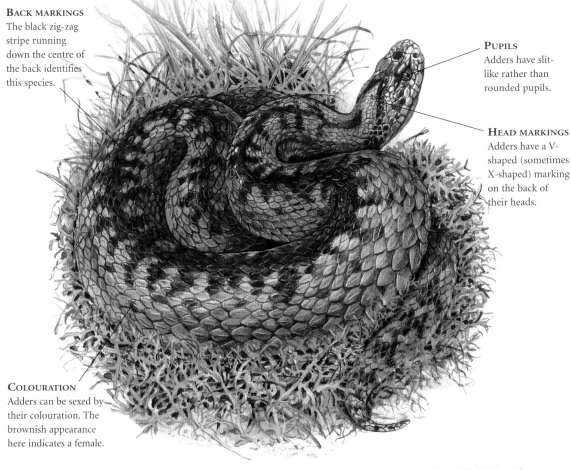

BACK MARKINGS
The black zig-zag stripe running down the centre of the back identifies this species.

PUPILS
Adders have slit-like rather than rounded pupils.

HEAD MARKINGS
Adders have a V-shaped (sometimes X-shaped) marking on the back of their heads.

COLOURATION
Adders can be sexed by their colouration. The brownish appearance here indicates a female.

HOW BIG IS IT?

HIBERNATION
These snakes seek out suitable retreats, often under tree roots. Scandinavian adders hibernate for up to nine months of the year.

Tawny Owl

This is the most common and widely distributed European owl, often found in urban areas, particularly in parks where there are trees for roosting and breeding.

VITAL STATISTICS

WEIGHT	420–590g (14.7–20.7oz); females larger
LENGTH	38cm (15in); wingspan 95–105cm (37–41in)
SEXUAL MATURITY	1 year
NUMBER OF EGGS	2–4, white in colour and rounded
INCUBATION PERIOD	About 30 days; fledging occurs at 35–39 days
DIET	Often small mammals but also preys on small birds, frogs and invertebrates
LIFESPAN	Typically 5 years in the wild, but has lived over 21 years

ANIMAL FACTS

The hooting of these owls reflects the typical 'tuwit-tuwoo' sound associated with this group of birds. But what is less widely known is that it is the hen of the pair that utters 'tuwit', with the male responding 'tuwoo', as a duet. The pair bonds in this species last for life. Tawny owls usually nest in a tree hole, and pellets containing the remains of their meals are often found scattered on the ground below.

WHERE IN THE WORLD?

These owls occur from Scandinavia southwards to the British Isles to the west and down into North Africa. Their range also extends to western Asia.

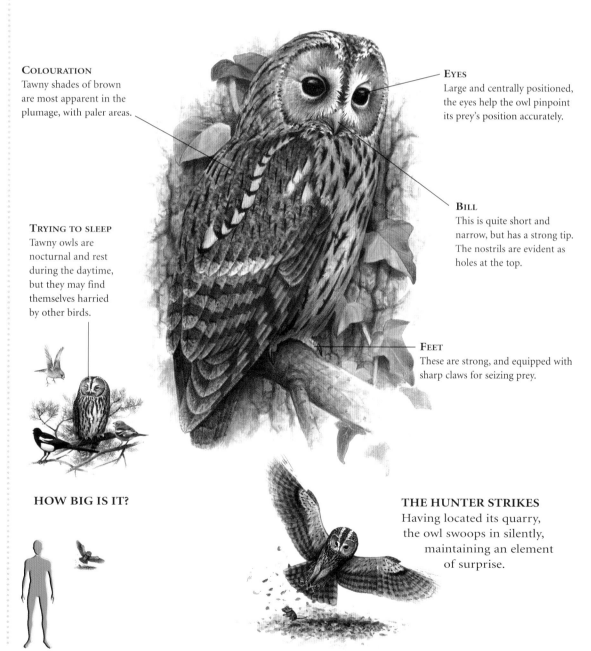

COLOURATION
Tawny shades of brown are most apparent in the plumage, with paler areas.

EYES
Large and centrally positioned, the eyes help the owl pinpoint its prey's position accurately.

BILL
This is quite short and narrow, but has a strong tip. The nostrils are evident as holes at the top.

TRYING TO SLEEP
Tawny owls are nocturnal and rest during the daytime, but they may find themselves harried by other birds.

FEET
These are strong, and equipped with sharp claws for seizing prey.

HOW BIG IS IT?

THE HUNTER STRIKES
Having located its quarry, the owl swoops in silently, maintaining an element of surprise.

North Island Kiwi

• ORDER • Struthioniformes • FAMILY • Apterygidae • SPECIES • *Apteryx mantelli*

The name of these flightless birds comes from the Maori language, and describes the sounds of their calls. Kiwis are found only in New Zealand.

VITAL STATISTICS

WEIGHT	2.2–2.8kg (4.9–6.2lb); females larger
HEIGHT	Up to 40cm (16in) high
SEXUAL MATURITY	2–4 years
NUMBER OF EGGS	2, laid 3–4 weeks apart; may weigh up to 15 per cent of the hen's body weight
INCUBATION PERIOD	75–90 day; fledging occurs at 4–6 weeks
DIET	Invertebrates and seeds; catches eels, small crayfish and amphibians in water
LIFESPAN	20 years; up to 40 in captivity

ANIMAL FACTS

This particular kiwi is the most common species today, with an estimated population of some 35,000 individuals. It has proved adaptable, in the face of clearance of its forest habitat, and may even be seen occasionally in areas of farmland. Largely nocturnal by nature, these kiwis hunt for food by scent, a characteristic that sets them apart from most other birds. Having smelt a worm in the ground, the kiwi can dig it out with its feet.

WHERE IN THE WORLD?

Found on North Island, in the far north, north-central, central-northeastern and central-western parts. Absent from the south.

FEATHERING
The brown plumage is rough and shaggy in appearance, resembling bristly hairs.

LEGS
The legs are stocky, allowing the kiwi to walk easily. They have no wings.

TOES
Three of the toes are directed forwards, splayed out at a broad angle.

NEST
Kiwis have a nesting burrow, where a pair will meet every three days or so. They mate for life.

NOSTRILS
Unlike other birds, kiwis have their nostrils at the tip of the long bill.

The North Island kiwi's ivory bill in close-up, showing how it curves down at the tip

HOW BIG IS IT?

EGG SIZE
The female kiwi lays the biggest eggs of any bird, proportionate to its size. These are incubated by the male.

Seahorses

VITAL STATISTICS

LENGTH	1.6–25cm (0.6–10in)
SEXUAL MATURITY	4 months– 1 year
NUMBER OF EGGS	5–1500, but average 100–200
INCUBATION PERIOD	14–28 days; within a day of the young leaving the pouch, the adult pair will have mated again
HABITAT	Areas of seagrass and other inshore localities where there is plenty of cover, plus coral reefs
DIET	Small marine organisms
LIFESPAN	1–5 years

ANIMAL FACTS

The colouration of seahorses can vary dramatically, and is influenced partly by their environment. They live in areas where there is plenty of marine algae, and the projections on their bony bodies resemble seaweed. They have a tail instead of a caudal fin. Although they are often associated with tropical reefs, it is not uncommon for seahorses to be found in temperate coastal waters. Pairs bond together and interact with each other.

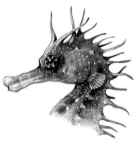

Seahorses swim by means of the small, fan-shaped dorsal fin on the back

The unmistakable equine appearance of these fish explains their common name. Despite being marine creatures, they are not strong swimmers.

WHERE IN THE WORLD?

Occurs in relatively warm coastal waters and mangroves. Most prevalent in the western Atlantic Ocean and the Indo-Pacific region, from 50°N to 50°S.

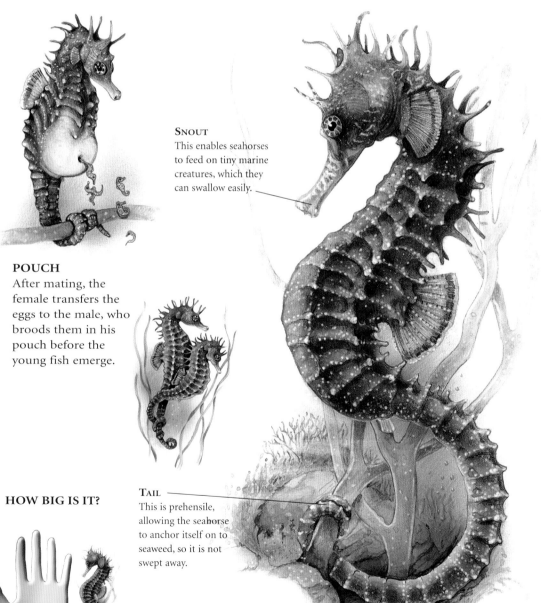

SNOUT
This enables seahorses to feed on tiny marine creatures, which they can swallow easily.

POUCH
After mating, the female transfers the eggs to the male, who broods them in his pouch before the young fish emerge.

TAIL
This is prehensile, allowing the seahorse to anchor itself on to seaweed, so it is not swept away.

HOW BIG IS IT?

Green Turtle

VITAL STATISTICS

WEIGHT	Up to 205g (451lb); males are larger
LENGTH	71–150cm (29–60in) across the centre of the shell
SEXUAL MATURITY	10–24 years
NUMBER OF EGGS	100–200, white and round
INCUBATION PERIOD	40–72 days, depending on locality
DIET	Adults feed on marine algae and seagrass growing inshore; young are omnivorous, eating crabs, jellyfish and other invertebrates
LIFESPAN	Up to 80 years

ANIMAL FACTS

How female green turtles find their way back to the beach where they hatched when they are ready to breed is still not fully understood. It is likely that the earth's magnetic field affects this process. Having mated, the turtle comes ashore under cover of darkness, digging her nest with her hind flippers. The eggs are then laboriously covered and left. The young dig themselves out of the sand in due course, and rush down to the sea.

Turtles (top) are adapted for swimming, while tortoises (bottom) walk on their toes

426

These marine reptiles spend their lives at sea, although females will return to nest on the beaches where they hatched over a decade previously.

WHERE IN THE WORLD?

The Atlantic population roams from eastern America to Europe, while the separate Pacific population extends right down the west coast from Alaska to Chile.

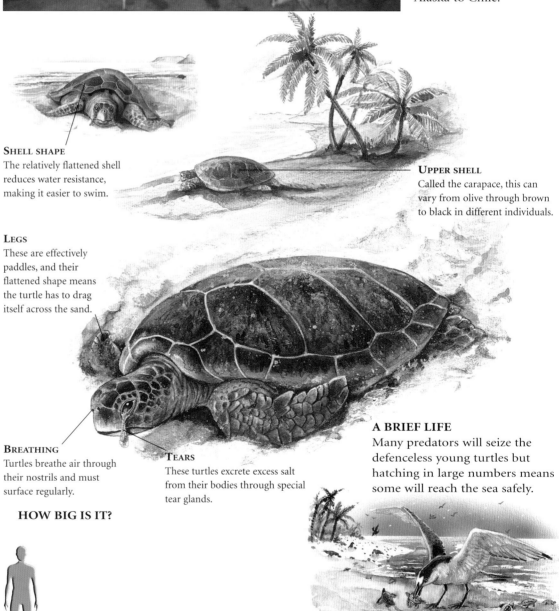

SHELL SHAPE
The relatively flattened shell reduces water resistance, making it easier to swim.

UPPER SHELL
Called the carapace, this can vary from olive through brown to black in different individuals.

LEGS
These are effectively paddles, and their flattened shape means the turtle has to drag itself across the sand.

BREATHING
Turtles breathe air through their nostrils and must surface regularly.

TEARS
These turtles excrete excess salt from their bodies through special tear glands.

A BRIEF LIFE
Many predators will seize the defenceless young turtles but hatching in large numbers means some will reach the sea safely.

HOW BIG IS IT?

Common Snapping Turtle

• **ORDER** • Testudines • **FAMILY** • Chelydridae • **SPECIES** • *Chelydra serpentina*

VITAL STATISTICS

WEIGHT	4–16kg (8.8–35.2lb)
LENGTH	20–47cm (8–18.5in) across the centre of the shell; tail is almost as long again
SEXUAL MATURITY	7–9 years
NUMBER OF EGGS	20–80, round and white
INCUBATION PERIOD	9–18 weeks; young may overwinter in the nest
DIET	Small mammals, birds, other reptiles, amphibians and fish; also eats carrion and aquatic vegetation
LIFESPAN	30–50 years

ANIMAL FACTS

The head and legs of the common snapping turtle are so large that they cannot be drawn back into the shell. There is a distinctive hook at the front of the upper mandible, which assists in grabbing prey that could otherwise slip from the turtle's grasp. These are aggressive reptiles, and even mating can be violent. Following a single encounter with a male, however, the female can remain fertile for several years, which is advantageous for a solitary species.

The claws on the feet can be useful for digging as well as feeding purposes.

One of the largest freshwater turtles, this species thrives in fresh and brackish water. It is a formidable predator, capable of killing its own kind.

WHERE IN THE WORLD?

Occurs in North America, from southern Alberta across to Nova Scotia and southwards across the USA, down to the Gulf of Mexico and west to central Texas.

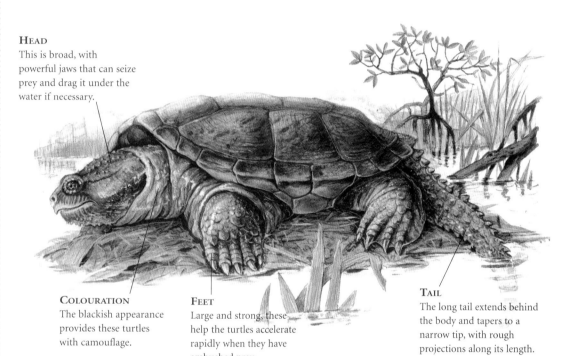

HEAD
This is broad, with powerful jaws that can seize prey and drag it under the water if necessary.

COLOURATION
The blackish appearance provides these turtles with camouflage.

FEET
Large and strong, these help the turtles accelerate rapidly when they have ambushed prey.

TAIL
The long tail extends behind the body and tapers to a narrow tip, with rough projections along its length.

MOUTHPARTS
Although turtles do not have teeth in their mouths, their hooked and sharp-edged jawlines can slice through skin easily.

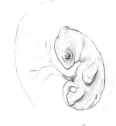

DEVELOPMENT
The youngster will initially be vulnerable to predators ranging from raccoons and herons to large fish and crocodilians.

HOW BIG IS IT?

427

Leatherback Turtle

• ORDER • Testudines **• FAMILY •** Dermochelyidae **• SPECIES •** *Dermochelys coriacea*

VITAL STATISTICS

WEIGHT	250–900kg (550–1980lb)
LENGTH	145–160cm (57–63in) over the shell; distance between the flippers can be 270cm (106in)
SEXUAL MATURITY	5–15 years
NUMBER OF EGGS	50–170, laid every 10 days, up to 7 times a year; only half will hatch
INCUBATION PERIOD	55–75 days
DIET	Primarily jellyfish, but will also eat crustaceans, cephalopods and some fish
LIFESPAN	Perhaps 50 years

ANIMAL FACTS

Leatherbacks are suffering from pollution of the oceans, ingesting plastic bags that they mistake for jellyfish, with fatal consequences. They are also adversely affected by developments alongside their nesting beaches. Leatherbacks do, however, range into cooler waters than other marine turtles. This is partly a reflection of their size, which helps maintain their core body temperature. They have an insulating layer of fat under the skin, but their circulation is also geared to retain body heat.

As with other marine turtles, the leatherback has no teeth, just sharp-edged jaws

The leatherback is one of the largest living turtles, although fossil evidence has shown that even bigger species once inhabited the oceans.

WHERE IN THE WORLD?

Occurs throughout the world's oceans up to the Arctic. Nesting beaches occur in the tropics, from French Guiana to West Africa and Papua New Guinea.

HIND FLIPPERS
These are quite short but broad, extending behind the shell when the turtle is swimming.

FRONT FLIPPERS
The massive front flippers form right angles when folded, and are longer than the hind flippers.

HOOK
The rough edges of the jaws help to grab jellyfish, which can otherwise slip away.

SHELL STRUCTURE

There are seven well-defined ridges along the length of the turtle's shell, with another five on the underside.

HOW BIG IS IT?

UNMISTAKABLE APPEARANCE
The leatherback has a very different appearance from other turtles, with bones concealed beneath its skin.

Red-Eared Terrapin

• ORDER • Testudines **• FAMILY •** Emydidae **• SPECIES •** *Trachemys scripta elegans*

This turtle belongs to the slider group, distinguished by a readiness to bask in sunshine and slip back immediately into the water if danger threatens.

VITAL STATISTICS

WEIGHT	About 907g (32oz)
LENGTH	12.7–27.9cm (5–11in)
SEXUAL MATURITY	Females 5–7 years; males 3–5 years
NUMBER OF EGGS	4–23; 1–3 clutches laid over the summer
INCUBATION PERIOD	60–75 days; breeds from March to July
DIET	Adults are largely herbivorous, grazing on aquatic plants; youngsters are mainly carnivorous, hunting invertebrates and small fish
LIFESPAN	Up to 30 years

ANIMAL FACTS

When the temperature drops to freezing, red-eared terrapins may hibernate at the bottom of their pond or stream, although sometimes they can be observed swimming beneath the ice. In the summer, adult females will excavate nesting chambers close to the water, where they lay their eggs, covering them over carefully to conceal their presence. The young turtles will face a range of predators once they hatch, which may include various birds, mammals, other reptiles and even fish.

The shell darkens in colour with age, as shown by the hatchling (left) and the adult (right)

WHERE IN THE WORLD?

This subspecies is restricted to the Mississippi River valley, extending from Illinois down to the Gulf of Mexico and west into to Kansas and Oklahoma.

HIDING AWAY
These terrapins often hang near the surface of the water, taking advantage of plant cover.

SHELL
As the turtle grows, the scutes covering the different sections of the shell peel off.

HIND FEET
These provide the main propulsive thrust when the turtle is swimming.

RED STRIPE
The characteristic red stripe of these turtles is a consistent shape.

FRONT FEET
Mature male red-eared terrapins (as here) have much longer front claws than females.

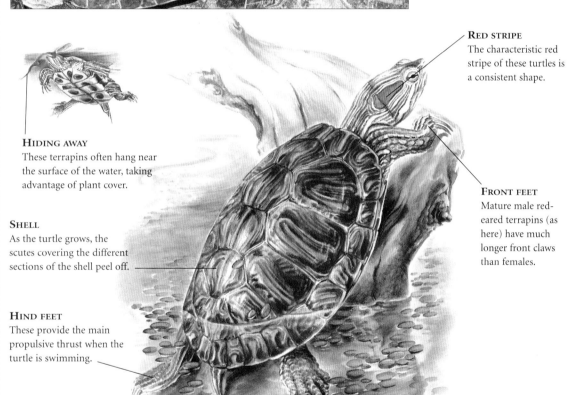

HOW BIG IS IT?

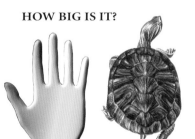

COURTSHIP

The male terrapin his long claws to fan water over the face his intended mate and caress her.

Galápagos Tortoise

VITAL STATISTICS

WEIGHT	215–250kg (475–550lb); some races are bigger than others
LENGTH	1.2–1.5m (4–5ft) across the shell
SEXUAL MATURITY	20–25 years
NUMBER OF EGGS	2–19, white in colour; 2–3 clutches a year
INCUBATION PERIOD	85–130 days
DIET	Herbivorous, grazing and browsing; even eats the prickly pear cactus
LIFESPAN	Up to 152 years – the longest-lived of all vertebrates

ANIMAL FACTS

This archipelago of islands is named after these giant reptiles – *galápago* is the Spanish word for tortoise. After their discovery, however, the tortoise population declined dramatically during the 1800s, when visiting ships took large numbers on board for food. Today, the population stands at about 15,000 individuals spread across the various islands. How the tortoises reached these remote volcanic islands is unclear, but their ancestors are thought to have been carried here on ocean currents from the American mainland.

Powerful legs support the weight of these gigantic tortoises

This is the world's largest tortoise, having grown huge on the islands where it occurs. Giant tortoises also live on the Aldabran Islands, off Africa.

WHERE IN THE WORLD?

Restricted to the Galápagos Islands, off South America's northwestern coast. Fifteen distinctive races have been recognized, three of which are now regarded as extinct.

SHELL
The raised carapace indicates a saddleback Galápagos tortoise. Others have domed shells.

RINGS
These are not annual growth rings and in fact they largely disappear with age.

NECK
The long neck permits browsing on taller plants.

TONGUE
A pink, fleshy tongue sits on the floor of the mouth.

HOW BIG IS IT?

GROOMING
Specialized finches, also developed from a common ancestor, live on the islands and may help to keep the tortoises free of parasites.

HATCHING

A tortoise will use the egg-tooth, a small temporary projection on its nose, to crack open the shell. It absorbs the remains of its yolk sac before feeding.

Gopher Tortoise

• **ORDER** • Testudines • **FAMILY** • Testudinidae • **SPECIES** • *Gopherus polyphemus*

VITAL STATISTICS

WEIGHT	4.1kg (9lb)
LENGTH	About 25cm (10in) over the central part of the shell
SEXUAL MATURITY	10–15 years
NUMBER OF EGGS	3–15; young resemble miniature adults
INCUBATION PERIOD	70–100 days, depending on temperature
DIET	Vegetarian, feeding mainly on plants such as wiregrass; also eats fruit and berries, occasionally carrion
LIFESPAN	40–60 years

ANIMAL FACTS

The ancestor of today's gopher tortoise have been present in the USA for over 60 million years, and there are three other surviving species in the region. Their remarkable burrows can be up to 40ft (12m) long. They may extend approximately 3m (10ft) in sandy soil. There is just a single entrance, with the tunnel dug so the tortoise can turn round easily within it.

Loss of habitat is a particular threat to these tortoises, because of the way that they construct long burrows in the soil.

WHERE IN THE WORLD?

Occurs in southeastern parts of the USA, ranging from southeastern South Carolina to Florida and along the Gulf of Mexico in Mississippi, Georgia and Alabama.

SHELL
This is flat rather than domed, and often becomes smooth through moving in the tunnel.

COLOURATION
The shell is brownish-black, but the body colour is often darker.

COURTSHIP AND MATING
The male sniffs at the female, and may nip at her legs. If she is ready to mate, she will stay still, allowing him to climb up on to her shell.

FEET
These are strong and used for digging the burrows, as well as shovelling soil.

SEXING
The underside of the shell, called the plastron, is slightly concave in adult males.

HOW BIG IS IT?

BURROWS
The importance of the burrows made by these tortoises to the natural world is such that over 360 other species have been found living alongside them.

Spiny Porcupinefish

• ORDER • Tetraodontiformes **• FAMILY •** Diodontidae **• SPECIES •** *Diodon holocanthus*

VITAL STATISTICS

HABITAT	Coral reefs, at depths of 2–100m (6.6–328ft)
LENGTH	20–36cm (8–15in), occasionally reaching 50cm (20in)
SEXUAL MATURITY	Around 9 months
HATCHING PERIOD	About 4 days; larvae then drift in the planktonic layer, and metamorphose after 3 weeks
SPAWNING	Occurs at the water surface, where the round eggs float
DIET	Sea urchins and hermit crabs, as well as molluscs
LIFESPAN	5–7 years

ANIMAL FACTS

The elongated but broad body shape of these fish is transformed when they are threatened, as they inflate their bodies with water. This increase in size makes them much harder to swallow, especially as their spines are also raised. The powerful teeth provide a second line of defence, capable of inflicting a painful bite, while the flesh may be toxic, too. Adults are solitary, but young specimens will often associate together in groups.

Breathing in air rather than water will inflate the body, but usually proves fatal

This bizarre fish are recognized under many different names, reflecting not just their spines but also the way that they can inflate their bodies.

WHERE IN THE WORLD?

Ranges from Florida to Brazil and around the South African coast in the Atlantic. Right across the Pacific, and also between California and the Galápagos Islands.

BODY
The body can inflate, clearl showing the protective spines.

SPOTTING
Variable, with highly individual markings concentrated on the upperparts.

EYES
These are large, and help the fish to spot danger, which is important as they are not strong swimmers.

MOUTHPARTS
These are powerful, allowing the fish to crush hard-shelled invertebrates.

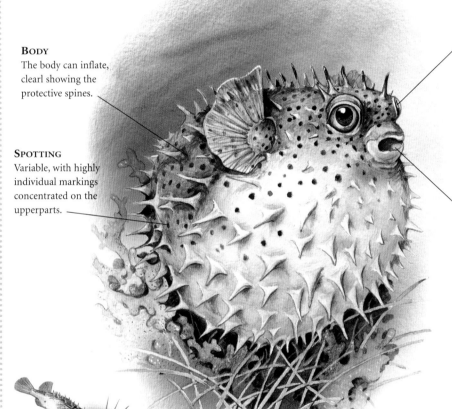

FEEDING POWER
The powerful mouthparts allow these fish to break apart tough-shelled invertebrates. They tend to hunt for food at night.

HOW BIG IS IT?

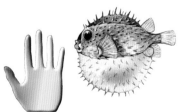

DIFFERENT PERSPECTIVE
Spiny porcupinefish may not be able to outswim predators, but their ability to change their appearance keeps them safe.

Longfin Inshore Squid

• **ORDER** • Theuthida • **FAMILY** • Loliginidae • **SPECIES** • *Loligo pealeii*

VITAL STATISTICS

WEIGHT	140–190g (5–6.7oz); males larger
LENGTH	Mantle measures 40–50cm (15.7–19.6in)
SEXUAL MATURITY	14–20 months
INCUBATION PERIOD	About 27 days, with the larvae drifting in the plankton
NUMBER OF EGGS	200, deposited in packets on the sea bed in inshore waters
DIET	Carnivorous, eating a variety of invertebrates, including worms, crustaceans and other squid, as well as fish
LIFESPAN	2–3 years

ANIMAL FACTS

Living in groups gives these squid some protection against predators, but if threatened directly they can release a cloud of ink through their funnel. This clouds the water, helping the squid escape safely. They are also able to swim fast, propelling themselves forward by water movement through the funnel, and by movement of their fins. They have three hearts to distribute oxygen efficiently, and their well-developed nervous system has been widely used in biomedical research.

These squid live in schools and are caught commercially in parts of their range. They may be attracted to night lights, which will draw them to the surface.

WHERE IN THE WORLD?

Found in the North Atlantic, ranging from the coast of Newfoundland right down through the Caribbean Sea to the gulf of Venezuela, South America.

COLOURATION
These squid can change their appearance if threatened or as part of their display.

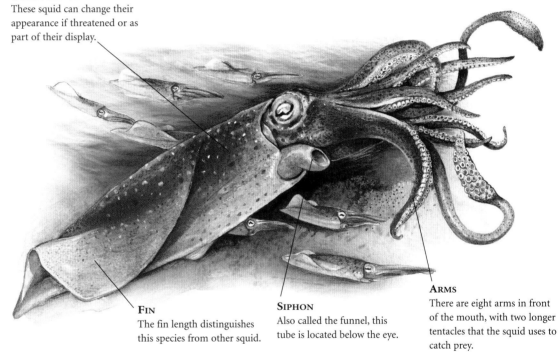

FIN
The fin length distinguishes this species from other squid.

SIPHON
Also called the funnel, this tube is located below the eye.

ARMS
There are eight arms in front of the mouth, with two longer tentacles that the squid uses to catch prey.

MATING
The male will transfer sperm to the female in a packet known as a spermatophore, following a period of courtship.

HOW BIG IS IT?

ESCAPE FROM DANGER

Sharks do prey on these squid, but their amazing manoeuvrability means that they may be able to elude their pursuer.

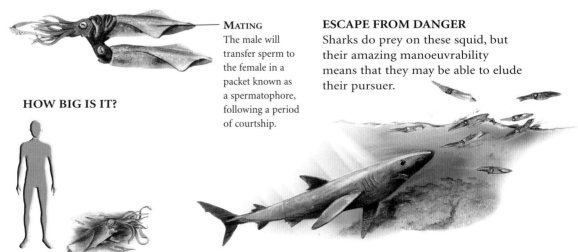

433

Aardvark

VITAL STATISTICS

WEIGHT	40–65kg (88–143lb)
LENGTH	1.7–2.2m (5.6–7.2ft)
SEXUAL MATURITY	Around 2 years
GESTATION PERIOD	About 7 months
NUMBER OF OFFSPRING	1; weaning occurs after about 4 months
DIET	Termites and ants, using its tongue measuring up to 30cm (12in); also eats aardvark cucumbers, to provide fluid
LIFESPAN	Around 10 years; up to 23 in captivity

ANIMAL FACTS

The aardvark's appetite is huge, and it can consume up to 50,000 ants in a single night. With its powerful front claws, the aardvark rips the nest apart, probing inside with its long, sticky tongue and drawing the insects into its mouth. Aardvarks also use their claws to create underground burrows, digging tunnels up to 13m (43ft) long. Once abandoned, these may be colonized by a host of other creatures, but the aardvark keeps the entrance closed when living there.

The name of these unusual mammals comes from the Afrikaans words meaning 'earth pig', but aardvarks are not related to pigs, in spite of their appearance.

WHERE IN THE WORLD?

Occurs across much of Africa below the Sahara, but not in west-central parts or the Horn of Africa. Prefers lightly wooded areas.

EARS
Tall yet quite slender, the ears can be moved independently to help detect possible predators, especially when the aardvark is feeding.

FOOT FALL
Differences in structure between the front (above) and hind feet (below).

TAIL
This is largely hairless and hangs down, very broad at its base and tapering to the tip.

SNOUT
The snout has a disc-like structure at the tip, where the nostrils are located. The mouth is small.

DEFENSIVE STRATEGY
If cornered, the aardvark rolls over so it can lash out with the claws on its front and hind feet.

HOW BIG IS IT?

Red-Knobbed Starfish

• **ORDER** • Valvatida • **FAMILY** • Ophidiasteridae • **SPECIES** • *Protoreaster linckii*

VITAL STATISTICS

HABITAT	Tropical reefs, to depths of about 30m (100ft)
LENGTH	Maximum span from the tip of one arm to another is 30cm (12in)
SEXUAL MATURITY	1 year
HATCHING	Planktonic larvae emerge, which stay in this form for several months
EGGS	A male externally fertilizes perhaps millions of eggs released by a single female
DIET	Molluscs, pulled apart with its arms
LIFESPAN	3–5 years

ANIMAL FACTS

The starfish's body is reinforced by the calcium skeleton beneath the skin. If one of the arms is lost, it may regenerate over time. It is even possible, following a serious injury, for two starfish to regenerate successfully from a single individual. This is partly assisted by the fact that starfish have no brain to control their nervous system, which is present in their individual arms. They also have no blood.

The appearance of starfish can be variable in terms of size, shape and colouration, but many are recognizable by their five arms.

WHERE IN THE WORLD?

Extends from the Red Sea, right across the Indo-Pacific Ocean and around the islands comprising Indonesia, eastwards into the Pacific tropics.

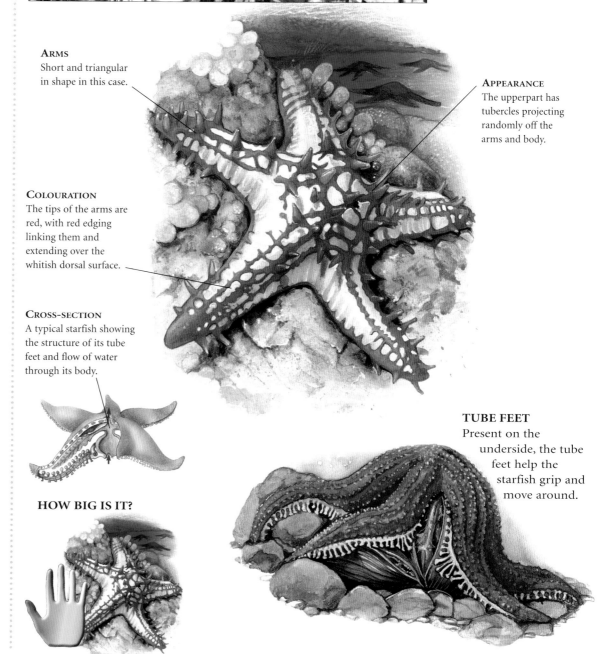

ARMS
Short and triangular in shape in this case.

APPEARANCE
The upperpart has tubercles projecting randomly off the arms and body.

COLOURATION
The tips of the arms are red, with red edging linking them and extending over the whitish dorsal surface.

CROSS-SECTION
A typical starfish showing the structure of its tube feet and flow of water through its body.

TUBE FEET
Present on the underside, the tube feet help the starfish grip and move around.

HOW BIG IS IT?

Giant Clam

VITAL STATISTICS

HABITAT	Tropical reefs, down to 15m (50ft)
LENGTH	Up to 1.2m (4ft)
SEXUAL MATURITY	About 7 years
HATCHING	Within 24–48 hours; live in the plankton for about a week; young retain a foot for movement up until they are 2.5cm (1in) long
EGGS	500 million may be released by a clam at a single spawning
DIET	Symbiotic relationship with algae; also eats plankton
LIFESPAN	Over 100 years

ANIMAL FACTS

When a young clam settles permanently on the sea bed, anchoring itself in place, it must find a relatively shallow place where sufficient sunlight can penetrate to sustain the algae in its tissues. It rests during the day with its shell open. There are also special vesicles that allow light to penetrate into the clam's tissue, supporting algae growing at a deeper level. These microscopic plants photosynthesize, producing nutrients for growth.

A giant clam, showing how the interior changes when it is partially closed

This is the largest of all molluscs, but contrary to popular myth, a giant clam cannot suddenly clamp an unsuspecting diver's leg in its shell.

WHERE IN THE WORLD?

Restricted to warmer waters, extending through the Indian Ocean and eastwards to southern parts of the Pacific and also northwards as far as the Philippines.

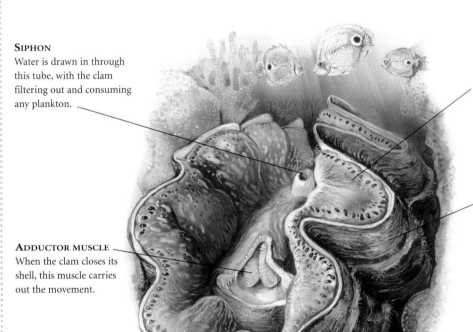

SIPHON
Water is drawn in through this tube, with the clam filtering out and consuming any plankton.

ADDUCTOR MUSCLE
When the clam closes its shell, this muscle carries out the movement.

CHANGE IN APPEARANCE
If a clam topples over, this may stop the light reaching the mantle, with the algae dying off and the clam then starving, but it may be able to readjust its position adequately.

MANTLE
There is a vivid blue lining tissue that accommodates algae. No two individuals have exactly the same colouring.

SHELL
Fluted, undulated halves are drawn together when the shell closes.

BREEDING

All giant clams start off as males, then at around eight years old, they are hermaphrodite, before becoming female.

HOW BIG IS IT?

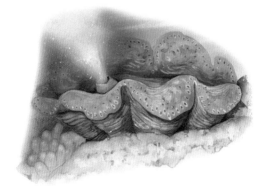

Glossary

ARBOREAL
Any animal that lives in trees.

BLUBBER
Fatty deposits found under an animal's skin that act as insulation.

CANID
A member of the family Canidae, embracing wolves, foxes and dogs.

CANINE
The long, pointed tooth often located at each corner of the mouth, especially in carnivores.

CARAPACE
The name given to the upper part of the shell of a tortoise, terrapin or turtle.

CARNIVORE
An animal which has a diet of meat.

CARRION
Dead animals, whose carcasses may be scavenged rather than being left to decompose.

CETACEAN
A member of the order Cetacea, which covers whales, dolphins and porpoises.

COLD-BLOODED
Lower invertebrates such as reptiles and amphibians that are unable to regulate their body temperature effectively, independent of their environment.

COLONY
A community of animals.

CREPUSCULAR
Animal active between the hours of dawn and dusk.

DORSAL FIN
A fin located on the backs of fish and aquatic mammals, used mainly to control direction.

ECHOLOCATION
The use of sound-wave emissions to detect objects and shapes, used by certain species of animals including bats and dolphins.

EVOLUTION
A change in the physical characteristics of animals that is believed to happen over time.

FAMILY
In the system of animal classification (taxonomy) animals are split into groups based on biological similarities. For every animal there are seven distinct groupings: Kingdom, Phylum, Class, Order, Family, Genus and Species.

FRUGIVORE
An animal that lives on fruit.

GENUS
A biological grouping between species and family, denoting animals with common characteristics. The plural is genera.

GESTATION
The development of an animal within its mother from conception to birth.

HABITAT
The natural home environment of an animal or plant.

HERBIVORE
A plant-eating animal.

INDIGENOUS
Originating and living or occurring naturally in an area or environment.

INDICATOR SPECIES
A particular plant or animal species used as a general measure of the health of an ecosystem.

INSECTIVOROUS
An animal that feeds on invertebrates.

INVERTEBRATE
An animal without a backbone.

KERATIN
A fibrous protein material occurring in the formation of structures such as hair, nails, horns, hooves, feathers and claws.

MANDIBLE
The upper or lower jaw of a vertebrate animal.

METAMORPHOSIS
A change in the form and often habits of an animal during normal development after the embryonic stage. For example, the transformation of a maggot into an adult fly, a caterpillar into a butterfly and a tadpole into a frog.

NOCTURNAL
Active at night, under cover of darkness.

OMNIVORE
An animal that eats both meat and plant material.

ORDER
A biological classification of animals between class and family.

PARASITE
An animal that obtains food or other such benefits by living off the body of another animal.

PRIMATE
A general term for any species within the order Primates, which includes lemurs, monkeys, apes and ourselves.

SOLITARY
A species which lives alone, only coming together with its own kind for mating.

TERRITORIAL
In the animal kingdom, groups or individuals will often fight to defend their territory from intruders.

THORAX
In insects, the second body region, between the head and thorax. It is the area where the legs and wings are attached.

TROOP
A name often given to a group of primates.

VERTEBRATE
An animal with a backbone.

WARM-BLOODED
Animals that produce their body heat through metabolic processes and maintain a core temperature within a constant, narrow range. All mammals are warm-blooded.

WEANING
The stage at which a young mammal no longer depends on its parents to suckle it, or, more generally, when a young animal is able to live independently.

Climate Zones

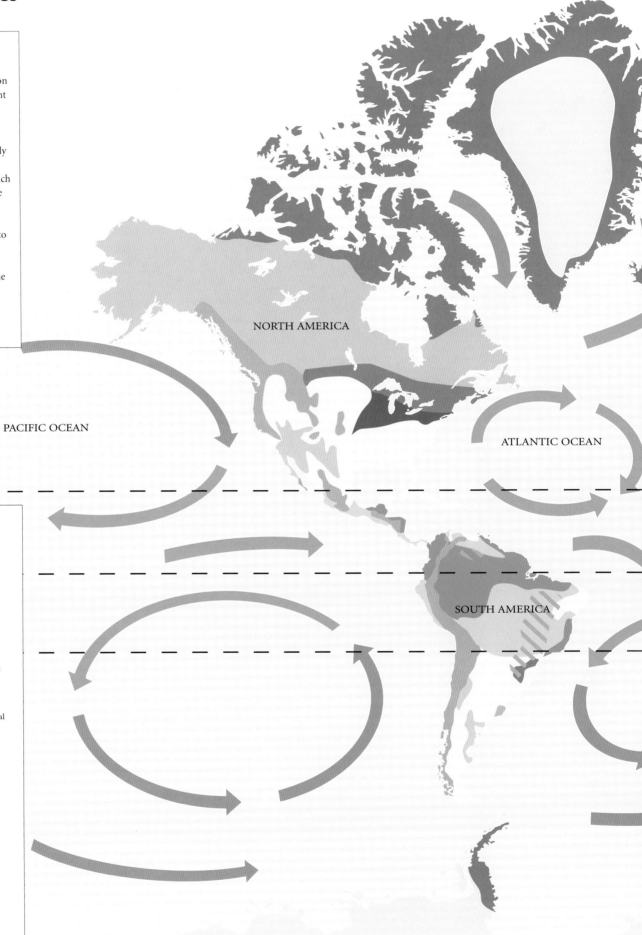

NORTH AMERICA

PACIFIC OCEAN

ATLANTIC OCEAN

SOUTH AMERICA

KEY

TROPICAL

Tropical wet

Tropical dry

DRY

Semiarid

Arid

MILD

Marine west coast

Mediterranean

Humid subtropical

SEA CURRENTS

Warm currents

Cold currents

CONTINENTAL

Warm summer

Cool summer

Subarctic

POLAR

Tundra

Ice

HIGH ELEVATION

Highlands

Uplands

ARCTIC OCEAN

EUROPE

ASIA

PACIFIC OCEAN

TROPIC OF CANCER

AFRICA

EQUATOR

INDIAN OCEAN

AUSTRALIA

TROPIC OF CAPRICORN

ANTARCTICA

439

COMMON BLUE
BUTTERFLY

Name Index

Scientific bird names are
italicised.

A

Aardvark 434
Aardwolf 134
Acherontia atropos 273
Acinonyx jubatus 113
Aepyceros melampus 36
African Buffalo 65
African Elephant 352
African Hunting Dog 104
African Wild Ass 302
Ailuropoda melanole 163
Ailurus fulgens 95
Alcedo atthis 211
Alces alces 75
Alligator mississippiensis 212
Alouatta guariba 319
Alpine Ibex 44
Alpine Marmot 383
Alpine Newt 177
Alpine Salamander 175
Alytes obstetricans 23
Amazon River Dolphin 186
Amblyrhynchus cristatus 414
American Alligator 212
American Badger 148
American Bison 39
American Bullfrog 27
American Mink 137
Ammotragus lervia 37
Amphiprion ocellaris 299
Anas platyrhynchos 17
Anax imperator 281

Andean Condor 243
Anguilla anguilla 15
Anguis fragilis 403
Antidorcas marsupialis 38
Antilocapra americana 35
Aotus nancymaae 317
Apatura iris 266
Apis mellifera 251
Apollo Butterfly 272
Aptenodytes forsteri 400
Apteryx mantelli 424
Aquila chrysaetos 241
Arabian Oryx 54
Araneus diadematus 29
Arctic Fox 109
Arctictis binturong 172
Argali (Mountain Sheep) 57
Argyroneta aquatica 28
Aromia moschata 202
Arvicola amphibius 362
Asian Black Bear 171
Asian Elephant 351
Ateles paniscus 318
Atelopus spumarius 19
Atlantic Salmon 389
Auchenia glama 71
Axis axis 74
Aye-Aye 338

B

Babyrousa babyrussa 87
Bactrian Camel 69
Balaenoptera musculus 179
Balkan Green Lizard 416
Bank Vole 366
Barbary Ape 331
Barbary Sheep 37
Basiliscus plumifrons 407
Bassariscus astutus 159
Bat-Eared Fox 106
Bearded Seal 153
Beech Marten 141
Beluga 187
Bengal Tiger 127
Bermuda Petrel 9
Betta splendens 297
Bettongia penicillata 233
Bezoar Ibex 43
Bighorn Sheep 58

Binturong 172
Bison bison 39
Bison bonasus 40
Black-Backed Jackal 101
Black Kite 242
Black Mamba 409
Black-Tailed Jackrabbit 260
Black-Tailed Prairie Dog 381
Blue Whale 179
Blue Wildebeest 46
Blue-Winged Grasshopper 284
Boa Constrictor 404
Bobcat 121
Bombadier Beetle 200
Bombus terrestris 252
Bonobo 341
Bornean Orangutan 343
Bos gaurus 41
Bos grunniens 60
Botta's Pocket Gopher 371
Brachinus 200
Brachypelma smithi 32
Brazilian Three-Banded
  Armadillo 199
Brindled Gnu 46
Broad-Bodied Chaser 282
Brown Bear 167
Brown Howler Monkey 319
Brown Rat 378
Brown Woolly Monkey 320
Brush-Tailed Bettong 233
Bubalus bubalis 42
Buccinum undatum 92
Buff-Tailed Bumblebee 252
Bufo bufo 20
Burchell's Zebra 306
Bush Dog 108
Bushbaby 339
Buthus occitanus 391

C

Cacajao calvus 348
California Sea Lion 151
Callicebus moloch 349
*Callithrix (Cebuella)
  pygmaea* 321
Callorhinus ursinus 150
Camelus bactrianus 69
Camelus dromedarius 70
Canis aureus 96
Canis familiaris 97, 112
Canis latrans 98
Canis lupus 99

Canis lupus dingo 100
Canis mesomelas 101
Cape Hyrax 257
Capra aegagrus 43
Capra aegragus 42
Capra ibex 44
Capreolus capreolus 73
Capricornis sumatraensis 45
Capybara 360
Caracal caracal 114
Carcharodon carcharias 264
Caribou 83
Castor canadensis 357
Cavia aperea 358
Cebuella pygmaea 321
*Cephalohynchus
  commersonii* 181
Cephalophus silvicultor 64
Ceratotherium simum 307
Cervus elaphus 76
Cervus nippon 77
Cetonia aurata 209
Chaffinch 288
Chamaeleo chamaeleon 406
Chamois (Gemse) 62
Charonia 93
Cheetah 113
Chelonia mydas 426
Chelydra serpentina 427
Chimpanzee 342
Chital Deer 74
Chlamydosaurus kingii 401
Chlorocebus pygerythrus 327
Choloepus hoffmanni 314
Chrysocyon brachyurus 102
Cicindela campestris 201
Cleaner Shrimp 218
Clouded Leopard 122
Coccinella 7-punctata 203
Collared Anteater 316
Collared Peccary 91
Colobus guereza 328
Colugo 223
Commerson's Dolphin 181
Common Antlion 279
Common Blue Butterfly 265
Common Brushtail Possum 231
Common Carp 216
Common Clownfish 299
Common Cockchafer 206
Common Cuttlefish 392
Common Dolphin 182
Common Dormouse 373

Common Earwig 222
Common Eel 15
Common European
  Earthworm 249
Common Genet 173
Common House Fly 237
Common Kestrel 245
Common Midwife Toad 23
Common Mouse Opossum 225
Common Mudpuppy 174
Common Octopus 280
Common Seal 158
Common Snapping Turtle 427
Common Spadefoot Toad 25
Common Spotted Cuscus 230
Common Squirrel Monkey 325
Common Tenrec 14
Common Vampire Bat 193
Common Wall Lizard 417
Common Wasp 256
Common Whelk 92
Common Wombat 236
Connochaetes taurinus 46
Cormorant 293
Cottontop Tamarin 324
Coyote 98
Coypu 379
Crab Spider 34
Cricetus cricetus 363
Crocodylus niloticus 213
Crocuta crocuta 133
Crotalus atrox 421
Ctenodactylus felovia 368
Cuon alpinus 103
Curved Spiny Spider 30
Cyclopes didactylus 313
Cynocephalus volans 223
Cynomys ludovicianus 381
Cyprinus carpio 216
Cystophora cristata 152

D

Dama dama 78
Damaliscus korrigum 47
Danaus plexippus 267
Dasypus novemcinctus 198
Daubentonia
  madagascariensis 338
Daubenton's Bat 196
Death's Head Hawkmoth 273
Deer Hog 87
Delphinapterus leucas 187
Dendroaspis polylepis 409

Dendrolagus matschiei 226
Dermochelys coriacea 428
Desmodus rotundus 190
Devil Lionfish 390
Devil Ray 355
Dhole 103
Didelphis virginiana 224
Dingo 98
Diodon holocanthus 432
Dolphinus delphis 182
Domestic Cat 115
Domestic Horse 304
Dorcas Gazelle 49
Dromedary Camel 70
Duck-Billed Platypus 277
Dugong 395
Dung Beetle 208
Dusky Titi 349
Dysticus marginalis 204

E

Eastern Chipmunk 387
Eastern Coral Snake 410
Echinoidea 238
Eciton 253
Edible Dormouse 372
Edible Snail 353
Eland 66
Elaphurus davidianus 79
Elephas maximus 351
Elk 75
Emperor Dragonfly 281
Emperor Moth 274
Emperor Penguin 400
Emperor Tamarin 323
Enhydra Lutris 136
Epidalea calamita 21
Equus africanus 302
Equus caballus 303, 304
Equus kiang 305
Equus quagga burchelli 306
Erethizon dorsatum 370
Erignathus barbatus 153
Erinaceus europaeus 239
Erithacus rubecula 291
Ermine 146
Eschrichtius robustus 185
Esox lucius 240
Eubalaena glacialis 178
Eudorcas thomsonii 48
Eunectes murinus 405
Eurasian Badger 143
Eurasian Lynx 114

Eurasian Shrew 398
Eurasian Water Shrew 397
European Adder 422
European Bison 40
European Chameleon 406
European Garden Spider 29
European Ground Squirrel 385
European Hamster 363
European Hornet 255
European Mole 399
European Nuthatch 290
European Rabbit 262
European Rhinoceros Beetle 207
European Robin 291
European Toad 20
European Treefrog 12, 24
European Water Vole 360
European Wild Boar 90
European Wildcat 118
Eurypyga helias 248

F

Falco peregrinus 244
Falco tinnunculus 245
Fallow Deer 78
Fat Dormouse
372
Felis catus 115
Felis lynx 116
Felis margarita 117
Felis silvestris 118
Fennec Fox 111
Fiddler Crab 220
Field Cricket 286
Fire Salamander 176
Flamingo 311
Foraging Ant 253
Forficula auricularia 219
Formica polyctena 254
Four-Horned Antelope 67

Frilled Lizard 401
Fringilla coelebs 288

G

Galago moholi 339
Galápagos Tortoise 430
Gasteracantha arcuata 30
Gasterosteus aculeatus 247
Gastropoda 354
Gastrotheca griswoldi 18
Gaur 41
Gavialis gangeticus 214
Gazella dorcas 49
Gekko gecko 412
Gelada Baboon 337
Gemse 62
Genetta genetta 173
Geochelone nigra 430
German Shepherd Dog 95
Gharial 214
Giant Anteater 315
Giant Clam 436
Giant Elephant Shrew 275
Giant Forest Hog 88
Giant Otter 147
Giant Panda 163

DROMEDARY CAMEL

Gila Monster 413
Giraffe 84
Glaucomys volans 382
Glis glis 372
Globicephala melas 183
Golden Eagle 241
Golden Jackal 94
Golden Lion Tamarin 322
Goldenpalace.com Monkey 8–9
Gopher Tortoise 431
Gorilla 340
Grass Snake 408
Gravedigger Beetle 210
Great Diving Beetle 204
Great Green Bush Cricket 285
Great Hammerhead Shark 92
Great White Shark 264
Greater Bilby 294
Greater Flamingo 311
Greater Kudu 68
Green Anaconda 405
Green Iguana 415
Green Tiger Beetle 201
Green Turtle 426
Grey Fox 105
Grey Parrot 10, 11
Grey Whale 185
Grey Wolf 99
Griswold's Marsupial Frog 18
Grizzly Bear 168
Gryllus campestris 286
Guinea Pig 358
Gulo gulo 138
Gundi 368

H
Hamadryas Baboon 334
Hanuman Langur 336
Harbour Porpoise 189
Harbour Seal 158
Hare 261
Harp Seal 157

Harvest Mouse 376
Hedgehog 236
Helarctos malayanus 164
Helix pomatia 353
Heloderma suspectum 413
Hemichromis bimaculatus 295
Hemitragus jemlahicus 50
Hermit Crab 221
Herpestes edwardsii 131
Herring Gull 191
Heterocephalus glaber 356
Himalayan Tahr 50
Hippocampus 425
Hippopotamus 85
Hippopotamus amphibius 85
Hippotragus niger 51
Hoatzin 215
Hoffman's Two-Toed Sloth 314
Homarus americanus 219
Honey Badger 144
Honey Possum 235
Honeybee 251
Hooded Seal 152
Horned Spider 30
House Mouse 377
Humpback Whale 180
Hydrochoerus hydrochaeris 360
Hydrurga leptonyx 154
Hyla arborea 24
Hylobates lar 344
Hylochoerus meinerzhageni 88
Hystrix africaeaustralis 374

I
Iguana iguana 415
Impala 36
Indian Flying Fox 194
Indian Grey Mongoose 131
Indian Muntjac 80
Indian Python 418
Indian Rhinoceros 308

Indri indri 346
Indri Lemur 346
Inia geoffrensis 186

J
Jaculus jaculus 369
Jaguar 124
Jaguarundi 129
Jewel Fish 295

K
Kiang Tibetan Ass 305
Killer Whale 184
King Cobra 411
Kingfisher 211
Kinkajou 161
Kirk's Dik-Dik 52
Koala 232
Kodiak Bear 169
Komodo Dragon 420

L
Lacerta trilineata 416
Lagidium viscacia 361
Lagothrix lagotricha 320
Lar Gibbon 344
Larus argentatus 191
Latimeria chalumnae 9–10
Latrodectus mactans 33
Laughing Hyena 133
Leaf Insect 310
Leatherback Turtle 428
Lemmus lemmus 364
Lemur catta 347
Leontopithecus rosalia 322
Leopard 125
Leopard Seal 154
Leopardus pardalis 119
Leptailurus serval 120
Lepus americanus 259
Lepus californicus 260
Lepus europaeus 261
Lesser Egyptian Jerboa 369
Lesser Horseshoe Bat 195
Libellula depressa 282
Libyan Jird 375
Lion 123
Llama 71
Lobster 219
Loligo pealeii 433
Long-Finned Pilot Whale 183
Long-Footed Potoroo 234
Longfin Inshore Squid 433

Loxodonta africana 352
Lucanus cervus 205
Lumbricus terrestris 249
Luscinia megarhynchos 292
Lutra lutra 139
Lycaon pictus 104
Lynx rufus 121

M
Macaca leonina 329
Macaca mulatta 330
Macaca sylvanus 331
Macropus parryi 227
Macropus rufus 228
Macrotis lagotis 294
Madoqua kirkii 52
Malayan Tapir 309
Mallard 17
Manatee 396
Mandrill 332
Maned Wolf 102
Manidae 312
Mantis religiosa 276
Mantled Guereza 328
Mara 359
Marine Iguana 414
Marmosa murina 225
Marmota marmota 383
Martes foina 141
Martes martes 140
Martes zibellina 142
Matschie's Tree Kangaroo 226
Meadow Vole 365
Mediterranean Monk Seal 156
Mediterranean Moray Eel 16
Mediterranean Scorpion 391
Meerkat 132
Megaptera novaeangliae 180
Meles meles 143
Mellivora capensis 144
Melolontha melolontha 206
Mephitis mephitis 135
Meriones libycus 375
Mesoplodon traversii 9
Mexican Red-Kneed
  Tarantula 32
Micromys minutus 376
Microtus pennsylvanicus 365
Micrurus fulvius 410
Milvus migrans 242
Mirounga leonina 155
Mobula japonica 355
Moloch horridus 402

Komodo Dragon

Monachus monachus 156
Monarch Butterfly 8, 267
Monodon monoceros 188
Moor Frog 26
Moose 75
Morpho Butterfly 268
Moschus moschiferus 86
Mouflon 59
Mountain Reedbuck 61
Mountain Sheep 57
Mountain Viscacha 361
Mudskipper 296
Muntiacus muntjak 80
Muraena helena 16
Mus musculus 377
Musca domestica 237
Muscardinus avellanarius 373
Musk Beetle 202
Musk Ox 56
Muskrat 367
Mustang 303
Mustela erminea 146
Mustela putorius 145
Mustela vison 137
Mygalomorphae 31
Myocastor coypus 379
Myodes glareolus 366
Myotis daubentonii 196
Myrmecophaga tridactyla 315
Myrmeleon formicarius 280

N
Naked Mole Rat 356
Nancy Ma's Night Monkey 317
Narwhal 188
Nasalis larvatus 333
Nasua narica 160
Natrix natrix 408
Natterjack Toad 21
Necturus maculosus 174
Neofelis nebulosa 122
Neomys fodiens 397
Nicrophorus 210
Nightingale 292
Nile Crocodile 213
Nine-Banded Armadillo 198
Noctule Bat 197
North American Beaver 357
North American Black Bear 166
North American Porcupine 368
North Island Kiwi 424
Northern American Ringtail 159
Northern Fur Seal 150

Northern Pike 240
Northern Right Whale 175
Norwegian Lemming 364
Nutria 379
Nyctalus noctula 197
Nyctereutes procyonoides 103

O
Ocelot 117
Ochotona curzoniae 263
Octopus vulgaris 280
Odobenus rosmarus 149
Odocoileus virginianus 81
Oedipoda caerulescens 284
Oncorhynchus mykiss 388
Ondatra zibethicus 367
Oophaga pumilio 22
Ophiophagus hannah 411
Opisthocomus hoazin 215
Orcinus orca 184
Oreamnos americanus 53
Oribi Gazelle 55
Ornithoptera alexandrae 270
Ornithorhynchus anatinus 277
Orycteropus afer 434
Oryctes nasicornis 207
Orycytolagus cuniculus 262
Oryx leucoryx 54
Ostrich 12, 13
Otocyon megalotis 106
Otter 139
Otter Cat 129
Ourebia ourebi 55
Ovibos moschatus 56
Ovis ammon 57
Ovis canadensis 58
Ovis orientalis 59
Oxudercinae 296
Oyster 287

P
Paguroidea 221
Pan paniscus 341
Pan troglodytes 343
Pangolin 312
Panthera leo 123
Panthera onca 124
Panthera pardus 125
Panthera tigris altaica 126
Panthera tigris tigris 127
Papilio rutulus 271
Papio hamadryas 334
Paradisaea raggiana 289

Parnassius apollo 272
Patagonian Hare 359
Pavonia pavonia 274
Pebas Stubfoot Toad 19
Pecari tajacu 91
Pedetes capensis 379
Pelobates fuscus 25
Père David's Deer 79
Peregrine Falcon 244
Persian Lynx 114
Petrogale Xanthopus 226
Phalacrocorax carbo 293
Phasolarctos cinereus 232
Philomachus pugnax 192
Phoca groenlandica 157
Phoca vitulina 158
Phocoena phocoena 189
Phoenicopterus roseus 311
Phyllidae 310
Physalis physalis 394
Physeter catodon 190
Pigtail Macaque 329
Pine Marten 140
Plateau Pika 263
Plumed Basilisk 407
Podarcis muralis 417
Polar Bear 170
Polecat 145
Polyommatus icarus 265
*Pomacanthus
  xanthometopon* 298
Pongo pygmaeus 343
Portuguese Man o'War 394
Potamocherus porcus 89
Potorous longipes 234
Potos flavus 161
Praying Mantis 276
Pretty-Faced Wallaby 227
Proboscis Monkey 333
Procavia capensis 257
Procyon lotor 162
Pronghorn Antelope 35
Proteles cristatus 134
Protoreaster linckii 435
Psittacus erithacus 10, 11
Pterodroma cahow 9
Pterois miles 390
Pteronura brasiliensis 147
Pteropus giganteus 194
Pudu pudu 82
Puma 128
Puma yagouaroundi 129
Purple Emperor 266

SEAHORSE

Pygathrix nemaeus 335
Pygmy Anteater 313
Pygmy Chimpanzee 341
Pygmy Marmoset 321
Python molurus 418

Q
Queen Alexandra's
  Birdwing 270
Queen Parrotfish 300

R
Raccoon 162
Raccoon dog 105
Raggi's Bird of Paradise 289
Rainbow Trout 388
Rana arvalis 26
Rana catesbeiana 27
Rangifer tarandus 83
Rat Kangaroo 234
Rattus norvegicus 378
Red Admiral Butterfly 266
Red Deer 76
Red-Eared Terrapin 429
Red-Faced Black Spider
  Monkey 317
Red Fox 108
Red Kangaroo 228
Red-Knobbed Starfish 435
Red Panda 93
Red River Hog 89
Red-Shanked Douc 335
Red Squirrel 13, 384
Red Wood Ant 254
Redunca fulvorufula 61
Rhesus Macaque 330
Rhincodon typus 11, 283

WHITE RHINOCEROS

Rhinoceros unicornis 308
Rhinolophus hipposideros 195
Ring Snake 408
Ring-Tailed Lemur 347
Rocky Mountain Goat 53
Roe Deer 73
Rose Chafer 209
Ruff 192
Rupicapra rupicapra 62
Rynchocyon cirnei 275

S
Sable 142
Sable Antelope 51
Sagittarius serpentarius 246
Saguinus imperator 323
Saguinus oedipus 324
Saiga 63
Saimiri sciureus 325
Salamandra atra 175
Salamandra salamandra 176
Salmo salar 389
Sand Cat 117
Sarcophilus harrisii 217
Scarabeus 208
Scarus vetula 300
Sciurus vulgaris 13, 384
Sea Otter 136
Sea Urchin 238
Seahorses 425
Secretary Bird 246
Semnopithecus entellus 336
Sepia officinalis 392
Serval 120
Seven-Spot Ladybird 203
Shield-Backed Bug 250
Shingleback Skink 419
Short-Beaked Echidna 278
Siamang Gibbon 345

Siamese Fighting Fish 297
Siberian Chipmunk 386
Siberian Husky 112
Siberian Musk Deer 86
Siberian Tiger 126
Sika Deer 77
Silurus glanis 393
Simia capucinus 326
Sitta europaea 290
Skunk Bear 138
Slow Worm 403
Slug 354
Small Strawberry Dart Frog 22
Snow Leopard 130
Snowshoe Hare 259
Sorex araneus 398
South African Porcupine 374
Southern Black Widow 33
Southern Elephant Seal 155
Southern Flying Squirrel 382
Southern Pudu 82
Southern Serow 45
Southern Tamandua 316
Spade-Toothed Whale 9
Spectacled Bear 165
Spectral Tarsier 350
Speothos venaticus 108
Sperm Whale 190
Spermophilus citellus 385
Sphyma mokarran 92
Spilocuscus maculatus 230
Spiny Anteater 312
Spiny Porcupinefish 432
Spotted Hyena 133
Springbok Antelope 38
Springhare 380
Stag Beetle 205
Stoat 146
Striped Skunk 135
Strix aluco 423
Struthio camelus 12, 13

Sun Bear 164
Sun Bittern 248
Suricata suricata 132
Sus scrofa 90
Symphalangus syndactylus 344
Syncerus caffer 65

T
Tachyglossus aculeatus 278
Talpa europaea 399
Tamandua tetradactyla 316
Tamias striatus 386, 387
Tapirus indicus 309
Tarsipes rostratus 235
Tarsius tarsier 350
Tasmanian Devil 217
Taurotragus 66
Tawny Owl 423
Taxidea taxus 148
Tenrec ecaudatus 14
Termite 258
Tetracerus quadricornis 67
Tettigonia viridissima 285
Texan Rattlesnake 421
Theropithecus gelada 337
Thomisidae 34
Thomomys bottae 371
Thomson's Gazelle 48
Thorny Devil 402
Three-Spined Stickleback 247
Thunnus albacares 301
Tiliqua rugosa 419
Tokay Gecko 412
Tolypeutes Tricinctus 199
Topi Antelope 47
Trachemys scripta elegans 429
Tradacna gigas 436
Tragelaphus strepsiceros 68
Trapdoor Spider 31
Tremarctos ornatus 165
Trichechus 396
Trichosurus vulpecula 231
Triton 93
Triturus alpestris 177

U
Uakari Monkey 348
Uca 220
Uncia uncia 130
Urocyon cinereoargenteus 107
Ursus americanus 166
Ursus arctos 167
Ursus arctos horribilis 168

Ursus arctos middendorffi 169
Ursus maritimus 170
Ursus thibetanus 171

V
Vanessa atalanta 269
Varanus komodoensis 420
Vervet Monkey 327
Vespa crabro 255
Vespula vulgaris 256
Vicugna vicugna 72
Vicuña 72
Vipera berus 422
Virginia Opossum 224
Vombatus ursinus 236
Vulpes lagopus 109
Vulpes vulpes 110
Vulpes zerda 111
Vultur gryphus 243

W
Walrus 149
Water Buffalo 42
Water Spider 28
Wels Catfish 393
Western Tiger Swallowtail
  Butterfly 271
Whale Shark 11, 283
Whiptail Wallaby 227
White-Faced Capuchin
  Monkey 326
White-Nosed Coati 160
White Rhinoceros 307
White-Tailed Deer 81
Wolverine 138

Y
Yak 60
Yello-Backed Duiker 64
Yellow-Fin Tuna 301
Yellow-Footed Rock Wallaby
229
Yellow-Masked Angelfish 298

Z
Zalophus californianus 151

General Index

A

Africa
carnivores 104, 114, 144, 173
horse family 307
lepidoptera 273
lizards 409
see also Central Africa; East
Africa; North Africa;
Sahara desert; South
Africa; sub-Saharan
Africa; West Africa
Alaska 169
Aleutian Islands 136
Alps mountains 44, 62, 175,
177, 383
Alsace-Lorraine 97
Amazon basin 19, 215, 323,
348–9, 405
America
armadilloes 198–9
artiodactyls 91
carnivores 107, 119, 128–9
lepidoptera 267
rodents 379
see also Alaska; Central
America; North America; South
America
amphibians 12, 18–27
Andes mountains 18, 71, 72, 82,
243
Antarctic circle 155, 400
anteaters 312–13, 315–16
antelopes 35–6, 38, 47–9, 51–2,
55, 61, 63–4, 66–8
ants 253–4
Arctic circle
artiodactyls 56
carnivores 109, 149–50,
152–53, 157, 170
cetaceans 187–8
armadilloes 198–9
artiodactyls see antelopes;
bison; buffaloes; camels;
deer; gazelles; goats; hogs;
sheep
Asia

artiodactyls 41, 42, 43, 45,
50, 57, 60, 69
carnivores 105, 130, 171
horse family 305
lizards 418
rodents 386
see also China; Eurasia;
Himalayan
mountains; India;
Middle East;
Southeast Asia
asses 302, 306
Atlantic Ocean 15, 152–53,
157–8, 178–9, 300, 389,
425–6, 428, 432–3
Australia 277–8, 294
carnivores 98
lizards 401–2, 419
marsupials 227–33

B

baboons 334, 337
badgers 143–4, 145
Baltic Sea 392–3
bats 193–7
bears 163–171
beavers 357
bees 251–2
beetles 200–210
Bering Sea 136, 150, 182
binomial method 11
birds 13, 191–2, 211, 248,
288–93, 311, 423–4
birds of prey 241–46
bison 39–40
Borneo 8, 343
buffaloes 65
butterflies 268–72

C

camels 69–72
Caribbean 396, 404, 415
carnivores see badgers; bears;
cat family; dog family;
otters; raccoons; seals
Caspian Sea 393

cat family 113–130
caudates 174–7
Central Africa 64, 66, 89, 341–2
see also Africa; sub-Saharan
Africa
Central America 22, 108, 124
carnivores 159-62, 165
lepidoptera 268
lizards 407
primates 326
see also America; Caribbean;
Mexico
cetaceans 9, 178-90
chimpanzees 341–2
China 79, 163, 263
chipmunks 386–7
Chukchi Sea 185
cichlids 295
coelacanths 9–10
coral reefs 16, 94, 218, 238
crabs 220–21
crickets 285, 286
crocodiles 212–214
crustaceans 92–3, 218–19, 287,
436

D

deer 73–83, 86
DNA analysis 9, 11
dog family 96–112
dolphins 181–2, 186
dormice 372–3
dragonflies 281
ducks 17

E

East Africa 306
artiodactyls 46, 48, 51, 52,
68
carnivores 96, 101, 106, 113
rodents 356
see also Africa; sub-Saharan
Africa
eels 15–16
elephants 351–2
Eurasia

amphibians 20, 25
artiodactyls 62, 63, 73,
75, 76
bats 196
beetles 201–2, 204
birds 288, 292
carnivores 116, 139, 142–43
hymenoptera 251, 254–5
insects 281, 284–5
lepidoptera 265
rodents 366, 372, 376, 384
spiders 28
see also Asia; Europe
Europe 15, 17, 353
amphibians 23, 24, 26
artiodactyls 40, 44, 59,
78, 90
bats 195, 199
beetles 203, 205–7, 209

CHEETAH

Gopher Tortoise

birds 211, 290 91
carnivores 140, 145
caudates 176–7
fish 216
hymenoptera 252, 256
insects 222, 282, 286
lepidoptera 266, 272, 274
lizards 403, 406, 408,
    416–17, 422
owls 423
rodents 362–3, 373, 383, 385
spiders 29
see also Alps mountains;
    Eurasia;
    Mediterranean Sea;
    North Europe
extinction, species 9–10

F
falcons 241–46
family 10, 11
ferrets 145
    fish 295–301, 355, 388–90,
        392–3, 432
    freshwater fish 216, 239, 247,
        389
    number of species 8
    sharks 12, 94, 264, 283
flies 237
foxes 104–5, 109–11
freshwater fish 216, 240, 247,
    389
frogs 18, 22, 24, 26–7

G
Galápagos Islands 414, 430
gazelles 48–9, 55
genus 10
gibbons 344–5
goats 43–5, 53, 62
Gobi desert 69
grasshoppers 284
Greece 156
gulls 191

H
hares 259–61
Himalayan mountains 50, 57,
    60, 95, 132, 305
hogs 87–91
horse family 302–3
hymenoptera 251–56

I
ibexes 43–4
iguanas 414–15
India 67, 74, 80, 214, 308
Indo-Pacific region
    93, 296, 298–9,
    394–5, 425,
    435, 436
Indonesia 87
insects 222, 237, 251–56, 258,
    265–74, 276, 279, 281–2,
    284–6, 310
invertebrates 11–12
    see also insects; spiders

K
kangaroos 225–9
kingdom 10
    Komodo Islands 420

L
lemurs 346–7
leopards 119, 122, 125,
    130
lepidoptera 265–74
Linnaeus, Carl 10, 11
lizards 401–22
lynx 114, 116, 121

M
macaques 329–30
Madagascar 14, 338, 346–7
mammals 13
marsupials 221, 226–36
Mediterranean Sea 15, 156,
    391–92, 406
Mexico 32, 121, 193, 404, 413,
    415, 421
mice 225, 372–3, 376–7
Middle East 54, 94, 114, 117,
    125, 131, 144, 334, 369, 375
Mississippi river 429
monkeys 317–33, 348–9
moths 273–4

N
New Zealand 424
newts 177
nomenclature 9, 10–11
North Africa 20, 28, 195
    artiodactyls 37, 49, 70, 76
    birds 287, 292
    carnivores 96, 111, 117
    horse family 302
    lizards 406
    primates 331, 334, 337
    rodents 368–9, 375
    see also Africa;
        Mediterranean Sea; Sahara
        desert
North America 27
    artiodactyls 35, 39, 53, 58,
        75, 76, 81, 83

beetles 210
birds 311
carnivores 98–9, 121, 135,
    137, 148, 151, 159–60,
    162, 166, 168
caudates 174
crocodiles 212
ducks 17
horse family 303
lepidoptera 271
lizards 410, 413, 421
marsupials 224
rabbits 259–60
rodents 357, 365, 367,
    370–1, 380–1, 387
spiders 29, 33
turtles 427, 431
    see also America
North Europe 21, 83, 92, 142,
    246–7, 384, 397–8
    see also Europe
North Sea 392
northern hemisphere
    birds 191–2, 241
    carnivores 110, 138, 146,
    158, 167
    cetaceans 189
    fish 240
    see also individual
        continents and oceans

O
oceans see Atlantic Ocean;
    Indo-Pacific region; Pacific
    Ocean; tropical oceans
opossums 224–5
order 10, 11
otters 136, 139, 147
owls 423

P
Pacific Ocean 149–50, 158, 179,
    185, 388, 426, 428, 432
    see also Indo-Pacific region
Papua New Guinea 226, 230,
    278, 289, 401
phylum 10
porcupines 370, 374

porpoises 188–9

possums 231, 235

primates 317–50

    new discoveries 8

R

rabbits 256–60

raccoons 159–62

rats 356, 367, 378

Red Sea 390, 435

reindeer 83

reptiles 12–13, 401–22

rhinoceroses 307–8

Rocky mountains 53, 58

rodents 13, 356–87

S

Sahara desert 111, 117, 257, 368–9, 375

salamanders 175–6

Scandinavia 364

scorpions 12, 391

sea birds 192, 293, 311

seals 150–58

sharks 12, 94, 264, 283

sheep 37, 57–9

shrews 275, 397–8

Siberia 112

snails 92, 353

snakes 404–5, 408–11, 421–2

South Africa 131

    artiodactyls 38, 51, 68

    carnivores 101, 106, 113

    primates 339

    rodents 380

    see also Africa; sub-Saharan Africa

South America

    amphibians 18–19

    anteaters 313–16

    artiodactyls 71, 72, 82

    bats 193

    birds 215, 243, 248

    carnivores 102, 108, 124, 147, 161, 165

    hymenoptera 253

    lepidoptera 268

    lizards 404–5, 407, 415

primates 317–26, 348–9

rodents 358–61

see also Amazon basin; America; Andes mountains

Southeast Asia 30, 77, 80, 95, 103, 122, 125, 351

    bats 194

    carnivores 127, 131, 164, 172

    fish 297

    horse family 309

    insects 310

    islands 223, 350, 411–12, 420, 435

    lepidoptera 270

    lizards 411–12

    primates 329–30, 333, 335–6, 344–5

    see also Asia; China; India; Indo-Pacific region

Soviet Union 86, 99, 126

species 10, 11

    categories of 11–13

    extinction of 9–10

    new discoveries 8–9

spiders 28–34

squirrels 13, 382, 384, 385

Sri Lanka 74

sub-Saharan Africa 434

    artiodactyls 36, 47, 55, 61, 64, 65, 84, 85, 88–9

    birds 246

    carnivores 120, 123, 125, 133, 134

    crocodiles 213

    primates 327–8

    rodents 374

    see also Africa; Central Africa; East Africa; South Africa; West Africa

sub-species 10, 11

Systema Naturae (Linnaeus) 10, 11

T

tamarins 322–4

Tasmania 8, 217, 277–8

taxonomy 10–11

temperature-dependent sex determination 12–13

tigers 126–7

toads 19–21, 23, 25

tortoises 430–1

Travers, Henry 9

tropical oceans 93–4, 283, 296, 298–301, 355, 394–5, 425, 436

turtles 426–9

type specimen 11

V

voles 362, 365–6

W

waders 191–2, 311

wallabies 227, 229

wasps 255–6

West Africa 64, 89, 295, 332, 340

whales 9, 178–9, 183–90

wolves 99, 102, 134

worldwide

    beetles 200, 208

    birds 242, 244, 293

carnivores 115

cetaceans 180, 182–4, 189

crustaceans 287

fish 264

horse family 304

insects 237, 279

lepidoptera 269

rabbits 261–2

rodents 377–8

spiders 31, 34

see also northern hemisphere; *individual continents and oceans*

worms 249, 403

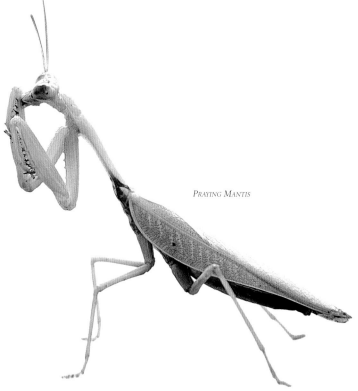

Praying Mantis

Picture Credits

Illustrations
All Illustrations © Art-Tech

Photographs:
Abdul Rahman Al-Sirhan: 375 (www.alsirhan.com) **Alamy:** 318 (M. Lane) Alexandre Buisse: 360 Corbis: 35 (A. Carey), 84 & 85 (M. Burgess), 99 (A. Carey), 110, 113 & 121 (A. Carey), 123 (J. Woodhouse), 167 (S. Lackie), 241 (A. Carey), 352 (M. Burgess), 379 (P. Burian) Dreamstime: 10br (Photomyeye), 13 (K. Broz), 21, 25, 37 (S. Dunn), 39 (E. Isselée), 41 (K. Niecieki), 46 (J.G. Swanepoel), 49 (D. Gilbey), 50 (M. Blajenov), 52 (S. Foerster), 54 (S. Ekernas), 61 (R. Argiriou), 69, 72 (U. Ravbar), 76 (J. Gough), 77, 82 (J. Haviv), 87 (R. Rondario), 90 (J.F. Costa), 105, 112, 144 (E. Chesser), 151 (P. Mitov), 153 (A. Hathaway), 156 (Z. Kizilkaya), 164, 165, 171 (C. Lips), 172 (P. Dubbeldam-Wezel), 176 (A. Huszti), 177 (H. Leyrer), 183 (D. Vander Linden), 184 (L. Christensen), 191, 192 (N. Smit), 201 (M. Hlavko), 202 (L. Nagy), 204 (H. Leyrer), 205 (V. Kirsanov), 206 (M. Hlavko), 211 (Z. Camernik), 212 (S. Pettitt), 214 (S. Siloto), 217 (C. Venus), 218 (M. Blajenov), 219 (Dark Side Photos), 221 (N. Smit), 222 (L. Hejtman), 232 (C. Wei Ong), 237, 240 (T. Haynes), 246 (J.G. Swanepoel), 249 (M. Pitkänen), 255 (H. Leyrer), 256, 257 (S. Noakes), 262 (A. Lee), 264 (J. Steidl), 265 (Sahua), 268 (D. Hewitt), 274 (C. Manci), 276 (A.T. Komorowski), 282 (M. Ushakov), 288 (L. Krivoshieva), 290 (M. Perkowski), 291 (E. Gevaert), 293 (Godrick), 296 (A. Hall), 316 (A. Hathaway), 325 (S. Foerster), 327 (H. Karius), 328, 330 (S. Ekernas), 331 (S. Gurney), 354 (C. Pithart), 355 (Nanisub), 359 (V. Alexandrova), 376 (W. Overman), 387 (B. MacQueen), 399 (M. Pwainski), 402 (J. Schulz), 404 (C. Testi), 411, 417 (M. Lachance), 423, 427 (B. MacQueen), 428 (F. Mun Kwan), 431 (P. Watson), 432 (J. Anderson), 440 (Sahua), 446 (P. Watson) **FLPA:** 14 (D. Hosking), 15, 18 (P. Oxford/Minden Pictures), 20 (J. De Cuveland/Imagebroker), 22 (M.B. Withers), 23 (D. Usher/Foto Natura), 26 (W. Wisniewski), 28 (H.&H.J. Koch/Minden Pictures), 30 (C. Ruoso/JH Editorial), 31 (M. Imamori/Minden Pictures), 34 (M. Moffett/Minden Pictures), 43 (D. Hosking), 45 (A. Forsyth), 55 (R. Du Toit/Minden Pictures), 57 (C.&T. Stuart), 63 (F.W. Lane), 64 (ZSSD/Minden Pictures), 67 (J.&C. Sohns), 79 (D. Hosking), 80 (H. Lansdown), 86, 129 (T. Whittaker), 134 (G. Lacz), 136 (T. Sbampato/Imagebroker), 142 (M. Zhilin), 145 (M. Krabs/Imagebroker), 146 (D. Middleton), 152 (S. Jonasson), 159 (M. Durham/Minden Pictures), 160 (J.&C. Sohns), 161 (M.&P. Fogden/Minden Pictures), 174 (Silvestris Fotoservice), 175 (S. Huwiler/Imagebroker), 178, 181 (D. Duckett), 185 (F. Nicklin/Minden Pictures), 186 (N. Wu/Minden Pictures), 188 (F. Nicklin/Minden Pictures), 189 (T. Bomford/Foto Natura), 190 (F. Nicklin/Minden Pictures), 193 (M.&P. Fogden/Minden Pictures), 194 (H. Lansdown), 195 (D. Hosking), 196 (H. Willcox/Foto Natura), 197 (D. Middleton), 196 (P. Oxford/Minden Pictures), 197, 207 (N. Cattlin), 223, 224 (S.D.K. Maslowski), 141 (A.D. Van Roosendaal/Foto Natura), 226 (J.&C. Sohns), 227 (T. Whittaker), 230 & 233 (G. Ellis/Minden Pictures), 235 (M.B. Withers), 242 (M. Siebert/Imagebroker), 243 (R. Tidman), 247 (W. Meinderts/Foto Natura), 250, 251 (A. Skonieczny/Imagebroker), 252 (F. Merlet), 253 (M. Moffett/Minden Pictures), 254 (M. König/Imagebroker), 266 (P. Entwistle), 274 (D. Usher/Minden Pictures), 275 (F.W. Lane), 277 (Foto Natura Stock), 283 (F. Nicklin), 286 (Panda Photo), 284 (R. Bosma/Minden Pictures), 289 (J.&C. Sohns), 292 (R. Tidman), 294 (E. Woods), 305 (K. Wothe/Minden Pictures), 313 & 314 (M.&P. Fogden), 315 (F. Lanting), 329 (I. Schulz/Imagebroker), 332 (G. Ellis), 335 (J.&C. Sohns), 336 (C. Ruoso), 338 (F. Lanting), 349 (J.&C. Sohns), 356 (R. Austing), 358 (Foto Natura Stock), 362 (M.B. Withers), 363 (R. Krekels), 364 (M. Durham), 365 (S.D.K. Maslowski), 369 (D. Hosking), 371, 372 (A. Van Roosendaal), 373 (D. Middleton), 374 (J.&C. Sohns), 377 (D. Middleton), 380 (F. Lanting), 385 (D. Hosking), 386 (M. Iwago/Minden Pictures), 389 (F.W. Lane), 391 (B. Borrell Casals), 393 (G. Lacz), 392 (Panda Photo), 92 (D.P. Wilson), 939 (C. Newbert), 397 (P. Oakenfull), 398 (H. Willcox/Minden Pictures), 401 (M.&P. Fogden/Minden Pictures), 405 (C. Mattison), 406 (M. Gore), 410, 412 (D. Hosking), 416 (R. Chittenden), 418 (M.&P. Fogden/Minden Pictures), 422 (P. Hobson), 424 (T. De Roy), 429 (N. Cattlin), 433 (N. Wu/Minden Pictures), 434 (ZSSD/Minden Pictures), 435 (F. Lanting) **Mary Forshaw:** 97 **Fotolia:** 143 (V. Zharoff), 147 (M. Lopez), 209 (R. Stiglitz), 216 (M. Wear), 229, 238 (Iofoto), 245 (G. Taylor), 279 (Errni), 337 (D. Demeyere), 339 (Eco View), 350 (H. Kratky), 353 (Tomashko), 378 (T. Mounsey), 395 (F. Steinberg), 421 (R. Dodson) **Ryan Harvey:** 444 **iStockphoto:** 11 (K. Lingbeek Van Kranen), 60 (S. Foerster), 94 (D. Sabo), 215 (M. Bruce), 220 (C. Lukhaup), 231 (G. Unwin), 236 (K. Hiki), 244 (A. Howe), 278 (E. Ferrari), 295 (S. Yagci), 297 (S. Stewart), 324 (T. De Bruyne), 341 (R. Van Der Beek), 403 (M. Divis), 409 (M. Kostich), 425 & 443 (A. Koen) **David M. Jensen:** 325 **Kevin Johnson:** 19 (Amphibian Ark) **Evgenia Kononova:** 348 **Karl Larsaeus:** 408 **Christoph Leeb:** 12tl **Paul McGuire:** 10tl **NHPA:** 270 (B. Beehler) **NOAA Photo Library:** 149 (Cpt. B. Christman), 150, 153 (Cpt. B. Christman) **John O'Neill:** 441 **Dave Pape:** 407 **Photos.com:** 8, 12br, 16, 17, 24, 27, 36, 38, 40, 42, 47, 51, 53, 56, 58, 65, 66, 68, 70, 71, 74, 75, 81, 83, 95, 98, 100, 101, 104, 107, 109, 114-116, 120, 122, 124-127, 130, 132, 133, 135, 137-139, 148, 155, 157, 158, 162, 163, 166, 168-170, 173, 179, 180, 182, 187, 203, 207, 208, 213, 228, 239, 258-261, 267, 269, 271, 272, 287, 280, 281, 285, 298, 299, 302-304, 306-308, 310, 312, 317, 332, 334, 340, 342-344, 351, 357, 367, 370, 384, 390, 392, 400, 413-415, 426, 430, 436, 445 **Photolibrary:** 300 (G. Holland/Age Fotostock), 301 (R. Herrmann/Oxford Scientific) **Photoshot:** 9 (Woodfall), 32 (E. Janes/NHPA), 131 (K. Ghani/NHPA), 234 (NHPA), 225 (H. Palo Jr./NHPA) **Public Domain:** 117, 345, 368 **Dario Sanches:** 319 **Science Photo Library:** 263 (W.K. Fletcher) **Shiva Shankar:** 447 **Trisha M. Shears:** 419 **Stock.xchng:** 33 (J. Collingwood), 44 (R.J. Leonard), 48 (N. Benjamin), 73 (A. Cerin), 78 (K. Silburn), 106 (C. Hitchcock), 111 (H. Berkovich), 347 (A. Biggs), 360 (Q. Kuiken), 366 (J. Soininen), 383 (J. Cheever), 420 & 442 (N. Hinks) **Stockxpert:** 311 (D. Thyberg) **Eti Swinford:** 108 **Ken Thomas:** 382 **U.S. Fish & Wildlife Service:** 119 (T. Smylie), 198 (J.&K. Hollingsworth), 379 (J.&K. Hollingsworth), 388 (E. Engbretson), 396 (J.P. Reid) **Luc Viatour:** 29 **Webshots:** 59, 62 (T. Kogler), 88 (A.T. Whittaker), 89, 91 (B. Brooker), 96 (S. Tautkus), 102 (B. Chloe), 103, 128, 248, 309, 320, 321, 322, 323, 346 **Peter Whitcomb:** 118 (Cat Survival Trust)